CU00658801

'Per Mare, Per Terram'

The Bands and Drums of the Royal Marines since 1664.

(Volume Two of the story of the Royal Marines Band Service)

by

John Ambler

Foreword written by HRH The Duke of Edinburgh,

Captain General Royal Marines

RMHS Special Publication Number 37

Published by: 'The Blue Band Magazine', in conjunction with
The Royal Marines Historical Society.

ISBN 978-0-9536163-9-8 (Hardback)
ISBN 978-1-908123-00-8 (Softback)

Dedicated to the memory of

Lieutenant Colonel Richard A Waterer
OBE, MVO, HonDMus, HonFLCM, LRAM, Royal Marines.
Principal Director of Music, Royal Marines, 1994 – 2002.

Highly respected, much-loved and missed by all who knew him – an officer, a gentleman and valued friend.

First published in the UK by: 'The Blue Band'.

Book layout and graphic design by SgtBug Mark Snell RM of The Blue Band Magazine, Supply Officer Music's Department, Royal Marines Band Service.

Printed and bound in Great Britain by CPI Anthony Rowe Ltd, Chippenham and Eastbourne.

ISBN 978-0-9536163-9-8 (Hardback). ISBN 978-1-908123-00-8 (Softback).

Contents

Part 6: Appendices

The Royal Marines Historical Society is open to anybody, civilian or military, interested in Royal Marines history. Requests for more details and/or applications to join should be forwarded to the RMHS at the Royal Marines Museum, Eastney, Southsea, Hants, PO4 9PX, United Kingdom.

Acknowledgements

My thanks go to two people who directly contributed to my first book, 'The Royal Marines Band Service'. SgtBug Mark Snell enthusiastically grasped the suggestion to change the layout and produced an imaginative design that enabled me to include a wider range of illustrations and captioning. Secondly, Dr Liz Le Grove, Academic Professor at the Higher Training Department of the Royal Marines School of Music and enthusiastic proof-reader! Liz brings knowledge and expertise to the task and, like Mark, enthusiasm. My thanks go to both of you. The person who deserves the most thanks is my wife Margaret who, when I suggested another book, responded with raised eyebrows. After careful planning we agreed that I should propose the idea since my Museum duties were unlikely to impact on my spare time - how wrong I was! However, Margaret supported me and also put up with the solitude, the piles of research material strewn around the study – and the extensions to the anticipated completion date. I have now promised that I will not start a third volume – until I have retired!

From the Royal Marines Historical Society I particularly thank, for reading and correcting my manuscript and his encouragement, assistance, and considered opinions, the Hon Editor, Colonel Brian Carter. Other members of this robust Society who have helped include John Rawlinson (Hon Secretary) and Major Mark Bentinck. Major Alastair Donald and Captain Derek Oakley have always been available to provide encouragement, wisdom and good humour. Thank you all.

From the Royal Marines Museum I thank the Chairman, Trustees and Director for allowing me to use images from the Museum Collections. My thanks go to the Archivist, Matthew Little, for his expert subject knowledge and for the use of his Library and Archive. Without the Collections held by this Museum much of this book, and many others, could not have been written. Matthew also kindly administered my use of Museum images.

Images were also obtained from elsewhere. I thank Les Scriver, specialist photographer of ceremonial events and concerts. He responded to my request for assistance with great generosity. Thanks also to Colin Dean for the use of his images and to John Rawlinson for allowing me to photograph a painting from his own collection. I am particularly grateful to all members of the Band Service who contributed their own personal photographs. Also, a special thank you to Ian Ellis in Malta for allowing me to use images from his family Collection.

This book could not have been written without the assistance of the men and women of the Royal Marines Band Service, both serving and retired. I would especially like to thank all of those who stood ready to recount their experiences, but were never called. Regrettably, time, space and the need to avoid duplication required me to be selective. Special thanks to Major Thornhill and Liz Le Grove for leading me through the complexities of music training, to consecutive 'Supply Officers, Music' Captains Gregory and Burns, to the 'The Blue Band' team and to WO2 Hunt for volunteering to assist.

Finally, I wish to thank Lt Col Nick Grace RM, for his personal support, encouragement and cooperation throughout this project. 'Colonel Nick' has taken command of the Royal Marines Band Service at a time of review, potential change and increasing military deployment. He kindly agreed to write the final chapter in order to give his appreciation of current, and continuing developments, a task well beyond my capability.

BUCKINGHAM PALACE.

The history of military music in Europe is a fascinating subject. The general facts are well known, but this book is specifically concerned with the details of the origins and development of the Bands of the Corps of Royal Marines. This volume is the companion to a previous work by the author 'The Royal Marines Band Service'. It traces the evolution of military music in the Royal Navy from the purely utilitarian use of drums, whistles and fifes to convey orders, to the contemporary highly trained and infinitely versatile Royal Marine marching and concert bands.

It is an absorbing account of the evolution of military music and of the 'characters' who shaped that development for what eventually became the Royal Marines Band Service. The original purpose of beating the time to help bodies of marching men to keep step remains the same, but military bands have also joined their civilian colleagues in symphony, and other, orchestras as public entertainers. With the decline in numbers in the armed services, and their heavy commitment to peace-keeping duties, military bands are probably now more frequently in the public eye than the fighting units themselves.

Bands figure prominently in military parades and displays, but they are also capable of entertaining the public on their own. In this they have become an indispensable link between the services and the general public. It is not only the quality of their music that impresses their audiences, it is also their turn-out, bearing and drill on parade that sets them apart from their civilian colleagues.

Completing this book has involved a great deal of research, and, it would seem, just in time. Records, which appear to be of little interest at the time, are only too frequently lost or destroyed. The author has dug out what remains and turned it into a most valuable, and evocative, history of one of the great band services anywhere in the world.

Author's General Introduction

When I decided to write a second book about the Royal Marines Band Service I knew that it would have to be of interest to those who had already read my first book, 'The Royal Marines Band Service' published in 2003 and now long out of print. It also needed to be written in such a way that those who had not read the first book could understand the second. To achieve this I decided to reverse the balance of the new book in comparison to the first. Areas and topics that were given less attention in the first book are now given detailed coverage. Whichever book is read or used, the reader will get the whole story but the balance will be different. How successful this technique is can only be judged by the reader.

As a result this book contains much additional information, both in the form of text and images, relating to the iconic Buglers and Drummers, as well as to the Divisional Bands.

Anticipating a profusion of appendices, I arranged for this book to have a greater number of pages than the first. Almost a decade has passed between the two publication dates and, during that period, much change and development has taken place. Having been given the opportunity to research and learn of these changes, their cause and their effect, they are fully recorded here. They particularly relate to recruitment and training at the Royal Marines School of Music and also to the recent military deployments. The transformation of the military role of Buglers and Musicians from as recent an event as the Falklands War could not go untold. Recent history it may be but it must be recorded. This is, of course, difficult to do in the current environment. Security restraints prevent access to some material, and rightly so. Access to images and to the men and women of the Armed Services is also difficult, expensive and often both. However, change is taking place as those in authority come to terms with the fact that a space must be available for the genuine historian and writer. Thankfully common sense seems to be replacing the dogma of recent years.

Writing about military deployments in a properly detailed manner (and for readers interested only in matters musical, never fear, bands take their instruments with them and there is usually music and ceremonial aplenty) has been assisted by the calibre of the men and women of the Royal Marines Band Service. Intelligent, extremely fit and highly trained both musically and militarily, they are confident, comfortable and very capable when factually describing incidents, situations and events. Whilst my own experience lies in wresting information from files, books and documents rather than through personal contact, the conversations with those who served in places such as Iraq and Afghanistan, will be the memories that will remain with me the longest. Listening to their modest accounts of tasks, well outside their normal comfort zone, accomplished successfully and well, was a humbling experience. Catching the emotion in the voices of Buglers, and Musicians, recently returned from Ramp Ceremonies and anxious to make their account as perfect as their actions, will remain with me. I hope that, within this book, I have done them full justice.

Development of the Royal Marines Band Service of 2011

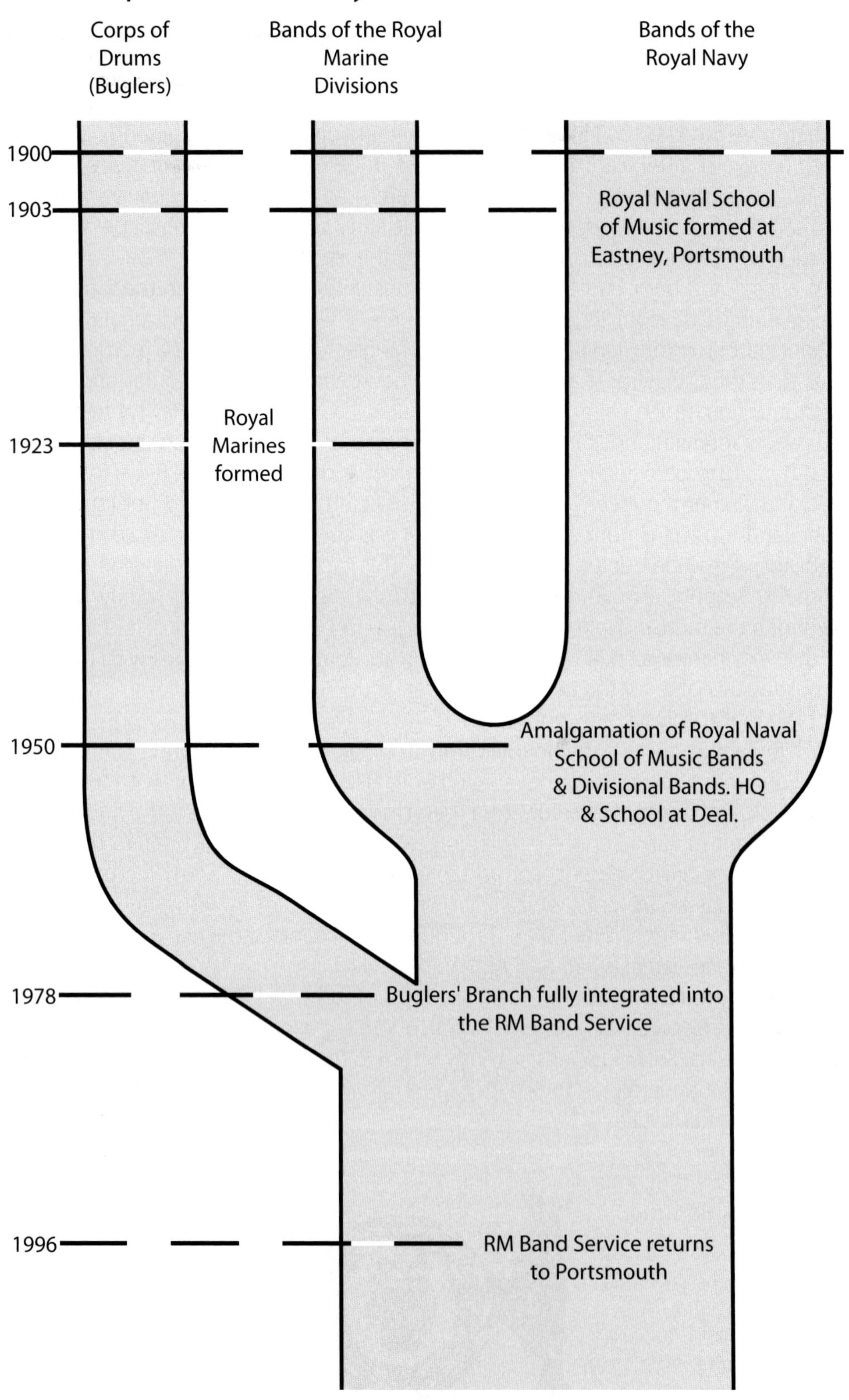

Introduction

Units of the Royal Navy, the British Army and, more recently, the Royal Air Force have had military bands for many years. In some cases these bands were part of a ship's company, in others they would be part of a Corps, Division, Regiment, Command, Squadron or other operational unit. They could also be attached to a Headquarters, or an administrative or training establishment. The early bands, mid 18th century, generally consisted of hautbois, curtalls, horns and clarinets – now known, in their developed form, as oboe, bassoon, trumpet and clarinet. This was the instrumentation for which composers such as Bach, Haydn and Mozart wrote. The purpose of these bands was two-fold: to provide entertainment for the officers and to provide a means of moving bodies of men from place to place at a regular pace through the playing of martial music.

Prior to this, military units had drums and fifes. These dated from the 16th century, possibly earlier, and, even before this, 'music' had been provided through the simple means of the drum – an instrument primarily used for passing messages by beatings but also able, like the bands that followed, to move bodies of men 'by beat of drum'. When the fifes were added to the drums the result was more musical and more entertaining.

In 1664, when the first regiment specifically recruited for sea service was formed, each company had a Drummer who was responsible for signalling. The modern Buglers are the direct descendant of these Drummers and therefore hold the distinction of being the oldest specialist branch in the Royal Marines. The Drummers could be 'massed' to form a Corps of Drums. Later, with the addition of fifes and the bugles, they could form Fife and Drum or Drum and Bugle bands. These men were responsible for the provision of signals, beatings and music on land and on sea from 1664.

The first of the 'Divisional Bands' was formed at Portsmouth in 1765, just over a hundred years after the Drummers, and later the Drums and Fifes, had begun carrying out their duties. This was followed by bands being formed at Plymouth (1767) and Chatham (1773). The Royal Marine Artillery Band and the Depot, Deal, Band came much later.

During the 18th and 19th centuries trained Musicians were recruited into the Divisional Bands, either from civilian life or from other bands, including those of the Army. At the same time Drummers, later Buglers, would usually join as boys and their military and musical training would be carried out by the Drum Major, the Bugle Major and also their peers. By 1850 the bugle had, because of the battlefield noise, become the main means of signalling. Each Division had about three hundred Drummers on complement with almost half of them serving at sea.

In 1902 Lt George Miller, Bandmaster of the Portsmouth Division, massed all of his Drummers at the head of his band as it marched to Church Parade. The effect was remarkable and the Royal Marine Bands are now renowned for the sight and the sound of the Corps of Drums at the front of the Band.

At the beginning of the 20th Century it was decided that the Royal Marines should take responsibility for training and providing bands for the Royal Navy and a school was opened at Eastney Barracks, Portsmouth. Prior to this the Royal Navy had recruited and formed its own ships' bands but the bandsmen were resented by the Officers and standards were not high. Formalised training schemes were introduced to standardise the performance of ships' bands. These bands also assumed a specialist military role when they became a part of the ships' communication and, later, gunnery control systems.

During the two World Wars many Royal Marine Buglers and Musicians were killed or died as a result of the military role which required them to work in the bowels of the ships. Sixty-two of these men were killed at the Battle of Jutland alone.

The five Divisional Bands (the bands of the Chatham, Portsmouth and Plymouth Divisions of the Royal Marines Light Infantry, the band of the Royal Marine Artillery Division at Eastney and the Depot, Deal, Band) continued in their primary role of providing musical entertainment – at which they were extremely good. These bands were amongst the premier bands of the day.

In 1950 the Divisional Bands were amalgamated with the Royal Marine Bands of the Royal Naval School of Music to form the Royal Marines Band Service and the Royal Marines School of Music. Whilst the size of the Band Service has reduced in proportion to the size and requirements of the Royal Navy, its standards have not declined. In 1978 the Buglers' Branch was completely integrated into the Royal Marines Band Service, although Buglers still retain a strong pride in their own Branch. The School of Music, now in Portsmouth, produces Musicians and Buglers of ever higher standards. Strong links with Portsmouth University and training from instructors and professors of the highest calibre ensure that the men and women who join the five Royal Marine Bands are amongst the finest in the world.

The Musicians of the current Band Service are also trained in all aspects of military ceremonial and embark upon a level of military training far higher than ever before - very necessary for their military role. This has included service in the Falklands Campaign of 1982 and the first Gulf War, as casualty handlers on hospital ships; deployment to Kosovo in support of 3 Cdo Bde and also as fire-fighters during the strikes of 1977 and 2002. In 2003 they provided casualty handlers with the Primary Casualty Receiving Facility on RFA *Argus* as well as decontamination teams/ambulance drivers on mainland Iraq. As part of Op *Herrick 9* in Afghanistan, they provided men and women for the UK Joint Force Medical Group and, based in Camp Bastion, they formed Motor Transport, Command Post and Ambulance Troops taking part in Combat Logistic Patrols to Forward Observation Bases – as well as providing musical entertainment and carrying out ceremonial duties. All of these military duties took place whilst maintaining high standards of musical and ceremonial performance.

PART 1 - THE STORY TO THE FIRST WATERSHED YEAR - 1950.

Chapter 1: Drummers, Fifers, Buglers and Corps of Drums.

> *"Twelve hundred men are to be put into one Regiment under one Colonel, one Lieutenant Colonel and one Sergeant Major and to be divided into six Companies, each Company to consist of two hundred soldiers and to have one Captain, one Lieutenant, one Ensign, one Drummer, four Sergeants and four Corporals"*[1]

Not only did these words represent the birth of the Corps but also the birth of the first specialisation within the Corps - the Drummer. These six Drummers were later increased to twelve and, by 1688, numbered fifteen since there were now thirteen Companies plus a Grenadier Company that required two. Further increases in the size of the Regiment meant reorganisation into two Battalions of fifteen Companies each, with each Company having two Drummers.[2] A few years later a Ralph Smith wrote that "All Captains must have drummes and ffifes and men to use the same who should be faithful, secrete and engenious, of able performance to use their instruments and office, and of sundrie languages, for often they be sent to parley and to summon the enemy's fforts or townes, or divers other messages, which, of necessitie, requireth languages".[3]

The side drums of that time were very different from the modern ones. They were twice as long, without snares and made of wood, all of which combined to produce a very dull sound.[4] In 1693 the Drum Major General issued a Warrant to raise a band for each Regiment. This applied to the entire Army, not just the Marines. Recruiters were expressly forbidden to recruit the listed drums (those on the Company strength). As the Marines had no wind bands in the 17th century we can therefore contend that the Corps of Drums were the earliest form of band. The only Staff-Sergeants known to be appointed to the Divisions about 1750 were a Sergeant-Major and the Drum Major, an indication of the importance and standing of the Drummers.[5]

During the Siege of Martinique, January 1761, orders were given that the drums were not to be beaten for fear of rousing the enemy; orders were to be transmitted by fife.[6]

A Standing Order of the Portsmouth Division, issued in November 1764, stated, "The Officers' servants to mount with their Masters, and to do Centinal Duty at the Guard Room door. The Quarter Master to provide cases, and carriages, for the Fifes, and to get the Drums cleaned and repaired".[7]

Marine Drummers accompanied Captain Cook on all three of his voyages to Australia and New Zealand. Firstly HMS *Endeavour* left England in 1768 carrying a Detachment of 13 Marines and one Drummer, Thomas Rossiter. He distinguished himself by being punished for stealing rum on the outward passage, and by being flogged for drunkenness and assault on the return in January 1771. He also had the distinction of being the first British 'Musician' to set foot on New Zealand and Australia. The Admiralty wanted Cook to take a Drummer who could also play violin plus two bagpipers on his next voyage. Cook resisted and a compromise resulted; two Drummers (Philip Brotherson and John

1 *Order-in-Council of 28 October 1664, also RMRO 144/77.*
2 *Article in RMM archive.*
3 *Britain's Sea Soldiers Vol 1, p32.*
4 *Military Music by Jacob Kappey.*
5 *Random Notes General Sir H E Blumberg RM.*
6 *Order Book of Robert Lloyd Richard Brooks.*
7 *Royal Marines Museum Archive.*

Drummer 1688

Fifer, Col Thomas Saunderson's Marines, 1702

Drum known to have been used by Drummer Edward Forbes in Chesterfield in 1808 whilst recruiting with Lt Richard Rouse RM. Forbes became a Marine Drummer in 1800, aged nine

Lane) and one bagpiper (Archibald McVicar) left with Cook on HMS *Resolution* and HMS *Adventure* in 1772. Accounts of the time indicate that the Maoris were impressed by the drums but did not care for fifes or bagpipes. Cook and his men returned in 1776 and left again in 1779, this time with fifes, drums and some form of wind instrument. It is known that Drummers Hooloway and Michael Portsmouth were amongst Cook's Drummers but it is not known how many were taken nor, on this voyage during which Cook was killed and the Marine Detachment had seven casualties, how many returned.

An Order of Plymouth Division, 4th February 1756, stated that Drummers were only to be paid three shillings a week from their subsistence until such time as they "are perfect in their beating". The Drum Major was to receive £1-1-0 from the subsistence of each Drummer that "he makes perfect in their beating". This payment was abolished by an Order-in-Council as late as 5th July 1918.[8]

In 1770 HMS *Swift*, a three-masted sloop, was based at Port Egmont in the Falkland Islands, sent there to conduct geographical surveys in the area. Other ships based at Port Egmont were the frigate *Tamar*, another sloop, the *Favourite* and the transport *Florida*. Captain George Farmer of the *Swift* took his ship, and crew of 91 men including two Marine Drummers, towards the shores of South America, 300 nautical miles away. Bad weather was encountered and, after several days of strong gales, they sighted land and took shelter in the Puerto Deseado estuary. Soon after entering the estuary the ship hit a submerged rock but managed to extricate herself using anchors and good seamanship. Later, as they attempted to anchor, the ship hit another rock and grounded. Unable to get the ship off and with the tide ebbing, the crew caulked up the ports and took as much of the stores ashore as they could. These efforts were thwarted when, at low tide, the ship slid back, tilted and sank. These circumstances allowed most of the crew to survive. The ship's cutter was provisioned and the ship's master and six volunteer seamen managed to sail the cutter back to Port Egmont - a five-day journey. As a result the survivors were rescued by HMS *Favourite*, although almost a month after the accident. In March 1982 the remains of the *Swift* were located by local divers. Approximately 60% of the ship was buried in the mud with a further 10% visible above that. The excavation began at the stern of the ship. During excavations in 2006 a drum was found lying on the main deck, its shell deformed from the regular, round, shape. Close alongside, human remains were found; in fact the legs were lying across the drum shell.

The human remains were recovered before any attempt was made to recover the drum, which was completely full of sediment. Other parts of the drum that were excavated and removed from the area included parts of the top and bottom hoops, the flesh hoops and the reinforcing hoop. Only the upper hoop still bears the original red paint. The tack pattern on the drum shell is currently being compared with the 1780s - 1790s drum, known as the 'Forbes recruiting drum', which is held by the Royal Marines Museum. One drumstick was found and this is also being compared with the sticks associated with the 'Forbes Drum'. Also found was what appears to be the Drummer's drum sling which is in two pieces. Both pieces were found folded. Two Marine Drummers appear on the ship's complement, as do the ship's Marine Detachment consisting of a Lieutenant, a Sergeant, a Corporal and twenty-two Privates. The two Drummers

---

8 *Random Notes General Sir H E Blumberg RM.*

were Thomas Smith, aged 25, from Bawn Grove, Worcestershire and John Bradley, aged 14, from Liverpool.

Up to about 1770 all Marine regiments were virtually considered as Fusiliers in everything but name; *The British Grenadiers* being the Regimental March of the Marines for many years.[9]

Major Tupper, Adjutant Fielding, three Captains, six Subalterns, six Sergeants, six Corporals, six Drummers and one hundred and eighty Privates of Portsmouth Division were to proceed to North America in 1775. In addition, all available Fifers were to be added to the contingent. What was to become the American War of Independence was about to begin and a reinforcing draft from Portsmouth and Plymouth Divisions was required. Very few men appear to have been available from the Portsmouth garrison as one hundred and thirty men and one Drummer had to be taken from the ships in harbour. During early 1772 Company strength had been reduced from one hundred Privates to eighty; then, at the end of the same year, the complement was further reduced to fifty Privates with one Sergeant, one Corporal and one Drummer per Company. In addition, the Portsmouth, and Plymouth, Divisional Colours were to be sent to America and to be replaced with new ones. This reinforcing draft reached Boston in May 1775 and therefore it can be assumed that some, if not all, of the Drummers were part of Major Pitcairn's force and took part in the Battle of Bunkers Hill, 17th June 1775.[10]

Drummer of Colonel, The Earl of Donegal's Regiment of Foot, 1704

In 1776 the Commissioner of the Portsmouth Dockyard objected to the sound of the Drummers beating detachments to embark upon their ships - not that his protest carried any weight with the Admiralty, the practice evidently continuing.[11] This would have been at a time when the raising of fifteen new Companies brought the Marines' strength to eighty-five Companies[12] each now having four Drummers to a Company. Fifteen more Companies were raised in March 1778, ten more in June and in December and another ten in 1779. By 1780 the Marines' strength was one hundred and forty-six Companies each having one hundred and eighteen Privates and four Drummers. The Corps reached a maximum strength in 1783 with one hundred and fifty-seven Companies which required six hundred and twenty-eight Drummers. During that year Orders for Demobilisation and a return to peace conditions resulted in a reduction to seventy Companies with one hundred and forty Drummers, two to each Company.[13]

Drummer, Colonel Henry Holt's Marines, 1707

An 'Order of Plymouth Division' dated 1784 directs the Field Adjutant to take "Band, Drums and Fifes under his entire care as to dress and interior economy and the beating of the Drummers". Drummers, because of their specialist role as signallers both on land and at sea, were paid as Corporals. There were two Adjutants, each having separate duties, one supervising administration whilst the second was the Field Adjutant. The latter's duties were further amplified on the 27th March 1785: "The Field Adjutant to attend the drill and exercise of NCOs and men, attend all parades and duties of them. Take Band and Drums and Fifes

Drummer of a Marine Regiment 1739-1748

9 *G&L 1922 p36.*
10 *General Sir H E Blumberg's précis of letters from the Admiralty to the Portsmouth Division, Royal Marines Museum Archive and 'The Story of Colours in the Royal Marines' by Major Alastair J Donald, RM, published by the Royal Marines Historical Society, 2001.*
11 *History of the Royal Marine Divisions 1931.*
12 *19 at Chatham, and 33 each at Portsmouth and Plymouth.*
13 *General Sir H E Blumberg's précis of letters from the Admiralty to the Portsmouth Division, Royal Marines Museum Archive.*

under his entire care as to dress, interior, economy, and beating of Drummers". The Master of the Band was to instruct the fifers in martial music only.[14]

On the 26th August of the same year Major General Collins of Plymouth Division was directed by the Admiralty to embark a fifty-seven strong Captain's Detachment of Marines to Spithead to board HMS *Trusty*, a third rate ship of the line. The detachment was to include a Drummer.[15] On the 21st July 1786 the Admiralty acknowledged Maj Gen Collins' letter of the 17th advising them that "a Detachment of Marines consisting of two Sergeants, two Drummers and 89 Privates joined [Head] Quarters from the ships lately returned from the East Indies which, as this Detachment belonged to the Old Establishment, on their arrival you carefully examined the whole and fixed upon two Sergeants, one Drummer and 48 Privates as proper men for future service, the remaining one Drummer and 41 Privates being old and infirm and undersize you have let remain on the Old Establishment as for objects to be discharged."[16]

A rather curious comment appeared amongst the Portsmouth Orders of October 1784: "The Drummers who are in debt are to be put on Privates pay until their debts are cleared".

In April 1786 the Commissioners of the Office of the Lord High Admiral established 'General Orders and Regulations to be observed by His Majesty's Marine Forces while in Barracks'. Regulation 4 states "The Retreat to beat at eight o'clock in the Summer and at Sunset in the Winter; at the Retreat Beating, every soldier to repair to the Barracks, the Barracks Gates to be shut, and no soldier to be suffered to go out without a written Pass from the officer of the company he belongs to. And to prevent any bad use being made of such papers, a Sergeant or Corporal of the Company to vouch for the man's being the Person intended by the Pass. The Roll to be called immediately after shutting the Gates, and the absent being reported to the Commanding Officer".[17] In the same month the Commissioners also sent to Maj Gen Collins the regulations for the allowances of coals and candles. These covered the Chatham, Portsmouth and Plymouth Barracks and the Marine Infirmary at Portsmouth. Included within the listing of allowances is an entry for the coal allowance for the "Music and Fifers Practice Room".[18]

Fifer of 1787, Australia

The Commissioners also issued a scheme of complements for various rates of ship. Guard ships of 74 and 64 guns would have a total Marine complement of 43 and 37 respectively. Ships of the Line ranging from 20 to 50 guns would have complements of between 22 and 49 whilst ships of fewer than 16 guns or carrying fewer than 100 men would have 19 Marines. All would have a single Drummer.[19]

Increases in Company strength during 1790 were countered by decreases in 1791 and 1792 and then there were further increases in 1793.[20] The strength of a Marine Company in 1793 was one Captain, two 1st Lieutenants and two 2nd Lieutenants, five Sergeants and five Corporals, four Drummers

14 *Random Notes General Sir H E Blumberg RM.*
15 *Plymouth Letterbook 1785-1786 Royal Marines Museum.*
16 *Plymouth Letterbook 1785-1786 Royal Marines Museum.*
17 *Plymouth Letterbook 1785-1786 Royal Marines Museum.*
18 *Plymouth Letterbook 1785-1786 Royal Marines Museum.*
19 *Plymouth Letterbook 1785-1786 Royal Marines Museum.*
20 *General Sir H E Blumberg's précis of letters from the Admiralty to the Portsmouth Division, Royal Marines Museum Archive.*

and sixty Privates.[21] A 1799 'General Weekly Return' indicates that the Portsmouth Division was complemented for three hundred Drummers of whom one hundred and thirty were at sea.[22]

In 1804 the Royal Marine Artillery was established with a Company at each of the Divisional headquarters. The Company complement was to be one Captain, three First Lieutenants, five Second Lieutenants, five Sergeants, five Corporals, eight Bombardiers, three Drummers and sixty-two Gunners.[23] The Drum Major, together with Drummers, Fife Major[24] and Bandmaster would be responsible to either the Field Adjutant or the Band and Drums Company Officer.

An Admiralty Order-in-Council of 1805 refers to a transfer of Sergeants, Corporals and Privates, "who are qualified and recommended for promotion", from Portsmouth Division to Woolwich. Also to be part of this transfer were "Six disciplined Drummers and eight undisciplined Drummers" - unfortunately no explanation is given.[25]

Section 14 of the Woolwich Division Standing Orders, 1809, defines the duties of the Drum Major thus: "Article 1. The Drum Major is to have the care and superintendence of all the Drummers, to be answerable for their appearance, discipline, and good order, and to make his report through the adjutant. Article 2. When boys under his care, are complete in their duty, he is to report them to the adjutant, who will, after hearing them perform all their beatings on the drum, in presence of the field officer of the week, give a certificate that the Drum Major may be paid for instruction, and that they may receive their full pay". The Orders also describe how the duty subalterns are to inspect arms and dress and call the roll of the men after they have assembled on the parade "at the beating of the Drummers call". It also describes how "A serjeant of each company is to visit the quarters of the men of their respective districts every evening at tattoo beating, and report if any of the men are out of their quarters, that the speediest method may be taken to find what has become of them". Details of guard changing and guardroom routine include: "7. The Drummer is to take charge of the furniture and necessaries in the officer's guard room. Any deficiency, or breakage, must be reported when the guard is relieved, or else be made good by the officer on guard, at the time the deficiency is discovered". This reinforces the fact that the Drummer was regarded as more than a private marine.

Documents from the Quartermaster's Office at Plymouth Division (c.1820) were described in G&L 1921, pages 3 and 4. References to band uniform were included, comments including, "The strength of the band was the Sergeant, one Corporal and twenty Drummers but this apparently does not include either the Drum or Fife Majors". Referring to the uniform of the Band the Quartermaster demands to be sent "immediately by coach 26 horse-hair plumes for the band generally, one pair of epaulettes for the Master of the Band, 16 yards 29 inches of gold lace for his coat and five yards of gold lace for his trousers, one pair of gold coloured silk epaulettes for the Corporal of the Band, 16 yards 29 inches of gold coloured silk for his trousers...". The Drummer's uniforms, by today's standards, verged upon the comic opera. The head-dress was a combination of a Lancer's cap in scarlet and gold with a white turban mounted above which had a further ornate, scarlet plumed decoration mounted upon it. The jacket was of an embroidered Zouave pattern.

---

21 *History of the Royal Marine Divisions 1931.*

22 *Records of the Portsmouth Division of Marines 1764-1800.*

23 *Britain's Sea-Soldiers. Col C Field RMLI.*

24 *Globe & Laurel p4, 1921 (Referring to 1816).*

25 *General Sir H E Blumberg's précis of letters from the Admiralty to the Portsmouth Division, Royal Marines Museum Archive.*

"The Drum Major of the Woolwich Division is in future to have but one dress coat in two years instead of annually, as the cost (30 guineas) is defrayed out of the Divisional Fund" - this order was issued in 1835.[26]

The Woolwich Punishment Book of 1821-1831[27] provides an interesting insight into the behaviour, and resultant punishments, of certain Drummers. David Nightingale of Number 20 Company was sentenced, on the 25th April 1821 at a Divisional Trial, "For absenting himself on the 23rd till the morning of the 25th" to one hundred and fifty lashes. He was given one hundred and forgiven fifty. On the 17th December 1821 Drummer Archibald Kennedy of Number 16 Company was "For irregular unsoldierly like conduct in being absent from tattoo on the night of the 15th instant and for disobeying orders and going out of barracks when confined thereto and making a practice of so doing; and for disobeying orders and insolence to Sergeant Major Kelly" sentenced, also at a Divisional Trial, to six months and 'Discharged in Disgrace'. Drummer Joseph Gaffrey of Number 8 Company had two charges against him at his Divisional Trial of the 10th June 1826. Firstly, "Unsoldierly like conduct and neglect of duty in absenting himself from his guard on the night of the 8th or morning of the 9th instant". Secondly, "Disobedience of orders in going out of Barracks when confined thereto". He received one hundred lashes. Drummer Henry Lyon, 48 Company, was tried on the 6th July 1830 for "Irregular and unsoldierly like conduct in behaving in a violent and disorderly manner when ordered to the Guard Room by Sergeant Major Harvey on the evening of the 4th". His trial did have a rather unusual twist. Having been sentenced to one hundred and fifty lashes and thirty days hard labour in the House of Correction at Brixton, he was then forgiven by the Commanding Officer "in consequence of an informality in the proceedings".

Drummer William Logie, 12 Company, appears to be the archetypal incorrigible, but not necessarily loveable, rogue. On the 30th June 1826 he, together with Private William Carpenter of Number 4 Company and Private Job Roberts, 32 Company, "made use of violent and insulting language to CSgt Samuel Smith and Cpl John Godwin of the Chatham Division". As a result the two Privates were punished with fourteen days knapsack drill whilst Logie was sentenced to one hundred lashes, of which seventy-five were given. Just over a year later Logie was with 26 Company, Portsmouth Division[28] and in trouble again. "For irregular and unsoldierly conduct in absenting himself without leave from the Band whilst on duty on the afternoon of the 8th September until the morning of the 10th of the same month he being at the time under confinement to Barracks by order of the Commandant". The punishment of twenty-eight days hard labour was given. Six months later Logie was in trouble again. "For irregular and unsoldierly like conduct in absenting himself from his quarters without leave on the morning of the 14th March 1832 and not returning until the morning of the 16th of the same month. The said William Logie having been repeatedly guilty of similar offences". Notes on his record state that he had also been absent for nine days and seventeen nights and missed eight tattoos from 3rd July 1830 to 1831, been ordered various punishments and had been tried by a Divisional Court Martial on the 15th September 1831 at which he had been forgiven for being absent for one night and missing one tattoo. However this latest in a long line of absences was to be the last. He was sentenced to two hundred lashes and was drummed out of the Corps. Other examples of the punishment of Drummers exist and many relate to being absent without leave.

---

26 *Globe & Laurel 1906 p16.*

27 *Royal Marines Museum Archive.*

28 *Portsmouth Division Punishment Book 1831-1834, Royal Marines Museum Archive.*

On the 7th June 1832 orders were given that all Drummers were to be instructed in the Fife and none embarked until competent and, in 1835, it was ordered that Drummers were to be designated Fifers when embarked; however, this idea did not last long.[29] RMLI 'Fifer' John Edwards was in the Sergeant's Detachment of eight men on board the sloop HMS *Racehorse* that took part in the 1845 New Zealand war. 'Drummer' John Partridge was on board HMS *North Star* at the same time and place.

The bugle was adopted as the signalling instrument of the Royal Marine Artillery (RMA) and the Royal Marine Light Infantry (RMLI) in the mid-19th century. In 1850 the RMA appointment of Trumpet Major had been dropped and Bugle Major took its place. Sgt G Coney was Fife Major of the Chatham Division RMLI until his retirement in 1856 but it is not known when this appointment ceased. In 1855, the Drummers became known by the clumsy title of 'Drummers and Buglers' but this was changed to 'Buglers' after twelve years. During its developmental period the RMA Division was influenced, through training and tradition, by the Royal Artillery. The Bugle Major, unlike the Drum Major, wore the Buglers' plain tunic. Whilst the principal role of the Bugle Major and Drum Major was to teach and train the Buglers, they, like the 'Fife-Major', the 'Trumpet-Major' and the 'Drum-Major' of the Royal Artillery sometimes played in the concert band or, when appropriate, in the marching band. The Royal Marine Artillery Bugle Major and Drum Major also inherited certain parts of their uniform and duties from the Royal Artillery, as did the Trumpet Major – the only Royal Marine Division to have such an appointment. The RMA was also unique, amongst the RM Divisions, in having both a Divisional bugle-call and a Divisional trumpet-call.

The guns of the Royal Marine Artillery in action at Hernani during the Spanish Carlist war of 1836. Note the Drummer in the foreground.

The military role of the Drummers, or Buglers, meant they served alongside the men of the Division at sea and on land. These men, and boys, collectively known as either Drums and Bugles Company or the Corps of Drums, and trained in drum, bugle and fife could either remain Buglers or, after the age of seventeen, could 'change over to the ranks' and become 'General Duties' Marines. Buglers were, through the calls of the day, responsible for timekeeping, for signalling and for marching troops. They were also responsible for military ceremonial and provided entertainment. The Buglers were, by comparison to

29 *RM Records 1793-1836. RMHS Special Pub No 4.*

today, a larger proportion of the Division. RMA and RMLI Buglers served on board ships and on land, accompanying Marines on exercise, during training and into battle.

Whilst the first RMA Band was formed in 1823 at Chatham, the Corps of Drums can, like the Division itself, trace their RMA inheritance back to 1804, when an RMA Company was formed at each of the Divisions. In 1861 when Colonel John Fraser, RMA, applied for, and was granted, permission to form a second Divisional Band of the same strength as those at the Royal Marine Light Infantry Divisions (the previous one having been disestablished in 1832) he had twenty Drummers on the strength.[30]

Regulations for Marines at sea were issued in 1858.[31] Some of these regulations make particular reference to the duties, and the life, of the Fifer and Drummer. "The Marine arms, fifes and drums are to be under the charge of the Commanding Officer of the Marines on board". "The Sergeants, Corporals, Bombardiers, Fifers and Drummers, Gunners and Privates of the Marine Divisional and Artillery Companies are to be allowed an uniform new clothing (sic) once a year". Welfare issues relating to this same group of men included the sale of a dead man's effects. Uniform clothing less than eight months old had to be sold and accounted for on the Ship's books. Similarly, the Officer Commanding was responsible for ensuring that any man who was sick and put ashore in England had all of his "bedding, clothes, arms and accoutrements packed and labelled, to be placed in charge of the proper Officer at such hospital". On completion of twenty-one years' service these men could apply to be sent home "provided they can be spared without inconvenience from the Ships in which they might be serving, and opportunities offer for sending them to England".

It is known that in 1867 the Chatham Division had "a particularly fine drum and fife band that was second to none, Guards not excepted, under that splendid Drum Major Charles Duncan, a handsome fellow, six feet two inch in height".[32]

Drummers, being on the Company strength and not a separate entity in the same way as the band, found themselves being used for various other tasks including, up to 1868 when the practices ceased, that of flogging and 'drumming out'. They were also very involved in recruiting 'by beat of drum'. The Bugle Major and the Bandmaster at the Divisions trained all Buglers but since not all had the same method of tuition, standardisation of training was introduced so that Band and Drums could be massed. This standardisation did not need to apply to the bugle calls themselves, since the manner of their sounding was explicit across the entire Corps.

B Company Royal Marine Light Infantry in action on the railway embankment near Kafd-Ed-Dawr, prior to the Battle of Tel-el-Kebir. This sketch, made by Colonel Field RMLI who took part in the action, shows a Bugler keeping close to his Officer during the action

It is interesting to note that in 1875 the newly promoted BdSgt Edwin Binding of Plymouth Division's band received his Royal Naval Long Service and Good Conduct Medal and was promoted to Bugle Major, Plymouth Division. He held this appointment until 1880 when he received the appointment of Bandmaster of the Band of the RN Commander-in-Chief at Devonport, transferring from the Royal Marines to the Royal Navy.[33]

A Memorial in the 1904 RMA Church (St Andrews) was inscribed, "In Memory of

30 *The Royal Marine Artillery Fraser & Carr-Laughton.*
31 *Regulations and Instructions relating to The Royal Marines serving on board Her Majesty's Ships. 1858. (Royal Marines Museum).*
32 *Random Records of the RM. Blumberg & Field.*
33 *From an article in Blue Band Lt Terry Freestone LRAM RM.*

the Officers, the NC Officers and Men of the Royal Marine Artillery killed in action, died of wounds or from the effects of climate during the Egyptian Campaign 1882,3,4". Twenty-nine names are listed by rank and, sandwiched between the Sergeants and the Gunners, is the name of Bugler Freeland Lovett. He joined the RMA in April 1876 as a Bugler in No 1 Company. Serving with the RMA Battalion he fought at Kassassin where he received a gunshot wound to the stomach and died two days later. Lovett had joined the Hants Militia as a Private in 1874 at the age of only twelve. He enlisted in the RMA two years later and his subsequent indifferent conduct resulted in twenty-six entries in the Company Defaulters Book. At the time of his death at the age of only twenty he was entitled to the Egypt Medal and the Khedives Star.

An exercise on Portsdown Hill, in 1883 or 1884. The Bugler in the forefront of this sketch gives an indication of his role in exercise or action

Following the death of General Gordon at Khartoum in 1885, a force of about thirteen thousand men prepared to recover the situation in the Sudan. This force included a Naval Brigade and a Royal Marine Battalion of five hundred RMLI and one hundred RMA. There were two major actions: Hasheen Wells where eighteen Buglers were involved; eleven of these men were then involved in the second action at Tofrek.

In 1888 regulations regarding NCOs and men being detached for duty at the Depot, Deal were issued. They had to be 'old soldiers' recently returned from embarkation but with all of their revision training complete. The regulations included "Buglers must be unmarried, of good character, and thoroughly qualified to perform on the drum, fife and bugle".[34]

Since at least 1888 problems in maintaining the flow of trained Buglers to the Divisions were evident. Colonels Commandant were instructed, via a specially issued General Order, to keep the Office Commanding London Recruiting Party advised of shortages.[35]

The following year orders regulating the training and standards were re-issued. All boys had to be instructed in bugle, drum and fife and were examined by a Board consisting of a Lieutenant Colonel, as President, a Senior Major, an Instructor of Naval Gunnery (for ships' calls), a Field Adjutant and, if required, the Divisional Bandmaster. Proficiency in all instruments was recorded and kept by the Adjutant and no Bugler could be embarked unless he was classified as 'Very Good' on the bugle. If this could not be attained within a reasonable time after enlistment the boy would be considered for transfer to the ranks. The level of proficiency on drum and fife, to qualify for service afloat, could never be less than 'Good'. Upon disembarking from service afloat, Buglers were tested, undertook revision if required and then faced the same Board to ensure that their performance was of the required standard, again recorded by the Adjutant on each occasion, before being allowed to re-embark.[36] Further regulations were issued in the same year. These stipulated that boys were not to be enlisted under the age of fourteen, they had to be able to read and write and also had to be "of sound constitution, not subject to fits, be free

34 General Orders, Royal Marines 1888 (GO1).
35 General Orders, Royal Marines 1888 (GO64 of the 24 May 1888).
36 General Orders, Royal Marines 1888 (GO92).

from any physical defects, or malformation, and offer from their appearance the promise of becoming eligible soldiers". Boys from reformatories, prisons or who had been committed by a Magistrate were not considered. A table of minimum height and chest measurement against ages from fourteen to seventeen was used. Boys had to sign up for twelve years from when they attained the age of eighteen. When recruited the boys had to provide either a birth certificate or a declaration signed by parents or a Magistrate stating that he was of the proper age. He also had to have the consent of parents or family and a certificate of character from his last schoolmaster. The Drum Major and the Bugle Major would then assess the boys to form an opinion upon their ability to learn. Boys under eighteen had to attend the Divisional School until they were eighteen or until excused by the Commanding Officer. "As it is necessary to check misconduct on the part of the Drummers, boys under the age of 16 years may be punished on the hand with the cane, but the number of stripes is not to exceed six. This punishment may be awarded by the Field Officer on duty, and is to be inflicted by the Drum Major in the presence of the Adjutant, and of the other Drummers who from their age are amenable to that punishment". The final two parts of this set of regulations stated, "The practice of Drum and Bugle Majors, RM, receiving money from the parents, or friends, of Buglers, under any pretext whatever, is forbidden and should any instance of this description come to the knowledge of the Commanding Officers it is to be severely dealt with." and "The ill-treatment of Bugler Boys at the hands of the NCOs under whose charge they are placed, is to be carefully guarded against, and the Field Adjutant is to exercise great vigilance to prevent it."[37]

Buglers who elected to transfer to the ranks had to be sent to the Depot for training and could not be considered for promotion until they had passed all drills.[38]

Further detail was added to GO46 of 1889 when, a year later, it became necessary for the attendance of the Bandmaster at the Boards of Examination to be noted. It was also stipulated that three months after being recruited for instruction the Adjutant had to record whether, in his view and that of the Bandmaster, the boys under instruction would be likely to qualify.[39] Yet more refinement to GO46 of 1889 took place at the end of 1890. All Buglers reaching the age of seventeen, and of the required physical standards, were to be informed that they would be eligible to join the ranks. If this was their intention, then drafting to distant stations with the subsequent need to relieve them and bring them home could be eliminated.[40]

Gymnastics, an important part of the development of all recruits, was re-evaluated and the course for trainee Buglers was deferred until after the trainee had passed for duty on the bugle. This hints that the number not passing for duty might have been quite high.[41]

Early in 1892 the Deputy Adjutant General fixed the complements of the Divisional and Depot Bands. Each band was allowed a number of supernumeraries: ten in the case of the Divisions and five for the Depot. These men were allowed for training to replace Musicians leaving the bands. Six of the ten and three of the five supernumeraries were to be Buglers although the proportions could be varied at the discretion of the Commanding Officer.[42]

In 1893 it was decided to create a supply of trained Buglers by enlisting twenty-six boys to be borne on the Company strength as Privates. These boys were recruited from the areas around the four Divisions and Walmer as well as through enlistment at Recruiting

37 *General Orders, Royal Marines 1889 (GO46).*
38 *General Orders, Royal Marines 1889 (GO89).*
39 *General Orders, Royal Marines 1890 (GO18).*
40 *General Orders, Royal Marines 1890 (GO80).*
41 *General Orders, Royal Marines 1891 (GO61).*
42 *General Orders, Royal Marines 1892 (GO3).*

Stations. They would be trained at the five locations and, on completion of training, would be sent to the four Divisions. As a vacancy for a Bugler arose so a Private would take his place as a Bugler and another boy enlisted to maintain the flow of trained Buglers to the Corps. Whilst a Private, the trainee Buglers wore a Bugler's uniform, except for the cloth tunic which was only issued when they became one of the authorised establishment of Buglers.[43]

The Royal Marine garrison on the island of Bermuda maintained a small band and drafting officers were told to try to ensure that men who could play musical instruments were sent to the island in order to maintain the viability of the band. However, they were also instructed that "Boy Buglers are not to be sent to Bermuda".[44] This instruction was repeated in 1895.

Naval manoeuvres, 1892. A Bugler stands with the RM guns crew. (See enlarged detail right)

Whilst recruitment of boys for service as Buglers had traditionally been from the areas surrounding each of the Divisions, an instruction was issued in 1895 that said that if a vacancy occurred and there were no applicants on the books then the other Divisions should be notified. This was an attempt to ensure that as many as possible of the sons of NCOs and other ranks obtained these appointments.[45] The practice of detaching Buglers for two year spells of duty at the Depot continued with two Buglers from each of the Royal Marine Light Infantry Divisions and one from the Royal Marine Artillery being at Deal at any one time.[46]

All these regulations, designed to organise and re-organise bands and Buglers, show that detail was not overlooked. According to General Order 96 of September 1898 drum-sticks were to be counted singly and not in pairs!

Stockpiles of side drums and drum cases were set up and maintained from 1899. These stocks were held as replacements in the Naval Ordnance Depots at Bermuda, Bombay, Esquimalt, Gibraltar, Hong Kong, Malta, Simon's Town and Sydney. Three drums and three cases were held at each establishment except Malta (4) and Simon's Town (2).[47]

A Naval Brigade was landed at Simon's Town to assist with the Relief of Kimberley during the South Africa War of 1899. Four RMLI Buglers were amongst the force that fought its way onto the Graspan Heights. Plymouth Bugler W J O'Brian of HMS *Doris* was wounded on the 25th November 1899 during the assault but recovered to take part in the battle of Paardeburg where he was again wounded. The other three were Portsmouth Buglers A Duffield, HMS *Monarch*, and W J Lader and L G Ranner of HMS *Powerful*.

43 *General Orders, Royal Marines 1893 (GO1).*
44 *General Orders, Royal Marines 1894 (6 Sept 1894).*
45 *General Orders, Royal Marines 1895 (GO58).*
46 *General Orders, Royal Marines 1897 (GO16).*
47 *General Orders, Royal Marines 1900 (GO31).*

At this time transfer of men between Services took place without a great deal of restriction. Examples are "To Royal Navy as Cook's Mate - No Po4364, Bugler T C Goddard"[48]; "To Royal Navy, Po6553 Bugler W Driver RMLI as Stoker 2nd Class", "Ply5490 Bugler T W Kennedy RMLI as Cook's Mate 2nd Class" and "From Army, No 9116 Drummer C Holdway, Depot Scots Guards, to serve with elder brother"[49]; "To Army, No Po3697, Lance-Corporal (Bugler) H Gearey, RMLI to 4th Battalion Lancashire Fusiliers as Sergeant Drummer"[50] and "To Army, No Po4292, Bugler J Rowlett, RMLI to 4th Battalion Manchester Regiment for promotion to Sergeant Drummer"[51] So, at the end of the nineteenth century the Royal Marines had Divisional Corps of Drums capable of not only carrying out their primary task of signalling by beat of drum or by bugle call but also performing in whatever combination of bugle, drum and fife instrumentation might be required.

During the Third China War (1900) thirty-one Buglers from all three RMLI Divisions and the RMA were present in either the Peking Legation Guard detachment, at the Naval Base at Wei-Hai-Wei or with the Naval Brigade which captured the Taku Forts, took the city of Tientsin and ended the 55 day siege of Peking. Bugler Webb (Portsmouth Division) was a member of the Legation Guard and would have been aware of, and possibly involved in, the incident for which Captain Lewis Halliday earned the Victoria Cross. During the same campaign Chatham Bugler E F Polkinghorne was wounded at Tientsin.[52]

A Royal Marine Light Infantry Bugler, James Thompson, aged about 14. Note the drum badge on the right arm and the Glengarry cap with RMLI badge

Boys under training as Buglers continued to attend Divisional Schools until they were eighteen and it is recorded that, during 1900, a total of ninety-seven Certificates of Education were issued.[53]

On the 24th January 1901 Orders were issued relating to the death of Queen Victoria. Mourning would be for six months from the date of the Order. All drums were to be covered and black crepe was to be hung from the top of the Colour staff of the RMLI until after the funeral.[54]

It was found necessary to issue an Order regarding Buglers aged forty-five or forty-six who, having been pensioned or discharged, applied to rejoin as privates. In these instances their applications, with length of service as a Bugler noted, had to be submitted to the Deputy Adjutant-General for approval. In special cases applications from men over the

48 *General Orders, Royal Marines 1899 (GO67).*
49 *General Orders, Royal Marines 1900 (GO54).*
50 *General Orders, Royal Marines 1900 (GO84).*
51 *General Orders, Royal Marines 1901 (GO83).*
52 *Appendix B to GO 95 Sept 1900.*
53 *General Orders, Royal Marines 1901 Appendix A.*
54 *General Orders, Royal Marines 1901 (GO24).*

The Peking Legation Guard of Royal Marines after the lifting of the siege. Sir Caude Macdonald is in the centre wearing civilian clothes. To the left of him, in the white tunic, stands Captain Halliday whose action a few days earlier was to win him the Victoria Cross. Sitting cross-legged to the right of the man at the end of the pathway is Bugler Webb

age of forty-six could also be submitted.[55] At the same time the Admiralty let it be known that any 'desirable' ex-Buglers could enrol in the Royal Fleet Reserve.[56]

Military Tattoos had been very popular entertainment during the 1890s, and later, for those living close to Barracks. A Torchlight Tattoo took place in August 1901 at the Depot, Deal and the Drum and Fife Band was featured playing alternately with the band during the various displays. Following the sounding of First Post the drums and fifes then played Tattoo and, after *Last Post*, band and bugles played a bugle march prior to the march-off. Another was held a month later at Forton Barracks when the Drum and Fife Band led by Drum Major Keen was considerably augmented. This was repeated the following year when sixty Buglers led by the same Drum Major sounded an opening fanfare before the Drum and Fife Band marched out from the colonnades. Drum Major Keen left the Corps in 1903 after twenty-five years' service, fifteen as Drum Major, having instructed a total of four hundred and fifty-six boys at Forton Barracks. Of the two hundred and seventy-eight who transferred to the ranks when eligible almost two hundred became NCOs. Some of the Drum Majors of The Manchester Regt, The Northumberland Fusiliers, and The Lancashire Fusiliers, as well as his successor, Drum Major Burns[57], were trained by him. Keen arranged many of the displays at Forton and he was at the head of the RM Massed Bands at the 1902 Coronation, for which he was awarded the Bronze Coronation Medal.[58] The following year Drum Major Burns not only led the Drum and Fife Band but also the Drum and Fife Band of the Divisional boys' school. The Torchlight Tattoos and Pageants continued, with occasional breaks, at the Divisions and at the Depot until the Second World War.

55 *General Orders, Royal Marines 190 (GO88).*
56 *General Orders, Royal Marines 1901 (GO94).*
57 *Marcher article Blue Band Spring 1998.*
58 *General Orders, Royal Marines 1902 (GO105).*

1902 exercises at Mount Batten, Plymouth. Men are from the Royal Marine Detachment of HMS Empress of India commanded by Major Halliday VC. Note the ship's Bugler standing on the left. Major Halliday's head can be seen bottom right

Since 1880 the strength of the Corps had been steadily increasing. Commitments in Egypt, the Sudan, South Africa and China were the main reasons for this. As the Corps grew so did the requirement for Buglers. In 1881 the Royal Marine Artillery had forty Buglers on their strength whilst each of the three Divisions of Royal Marine Light Infantry had seventy-two, a total of two hundred and sixty-two. By 1895 the RMA had forty-two but the RMLI had one hundred and forty-eight per Division, an overall total of four hundred and eighty-six Buglers. The balance had altered by 1900 when the RMA had eighty-two Buglers and each of the RMLI Divisions had one hundred and thirty-six. The previous year the Depot had been allowed a complement of seven Buglers so the total for 1900 was four hundred and ninety-seven. In 1896 the Depot was allowed its own Bugle Major; prior to this the Drum Major fulfilled a dual role.[59]

Bugler Ernest Frederick Doughty of the Royal Marine Artillery. Note the crossed trumpets, only worn by the RMA, on the sleeve. Doughty changed to the ranks and was promoted to CSgt

The situation at Fort Cumberland and Eastney Barracks was complex, particularly after 1903 when the Royal Naval School of Music was opened. With RMA Buglers attached to the RMA Band, Buglers in the Drum and Fife Band, duty Buglers and Buglers continuously coming and going on draft or for training, the Barracks must have been a hive of activity. In addition, all Buglers had to be tested before being drafted and again on return to see if any remedial teaching or practice was required. All Buglers also received gunnery training and, just to complicate the situation even further some Buglers would transfer to General Duties requiring replacements to be found. Unfortunately, little solid evidence exists for the day-to-day running of this part of the RMA Division. The Buglers were always heavily committed as Drummers with the Band and Drums or the Drum and Fife Band, as well as Buglers. A long tradition came to an end when swords, scabbards and frogs were withdrawn from the equipment of Royal Marine Buglers in 1904.[60]

Whilst Recruiting Instructions had always included minimum heights and chest measurements for recruits, no updates to the specific limits for Buglers had been given since 1889. In 1907 a table specifically for Buglers was added. This separation was probably due to the fact that boys could be recruited for Bugler training from the age of fourteen whereas recruits would generally be aged seventeen or more. The minimum size for a fourteen year old enlisting for Bugler training

59 *Admiralty Orders-in-Council 1873-1903. Royal Marines Museum Archive.*
60 *General Orders, Royal Marines 1904 (GO75).*

was four feet ten inches tall (1.47M) and with a chest measurement of twenty-nine and a half inches (0.75M).[61]

This is H J W Bunting, c.1894 a Chatham Division RMLI Bugler, who joined direct from Greenwich School aged fourteen years and one month. He transferred to the ranks in 1900 having served three years on HMS Rodney and at Chatham and Portsmouth Divisions. He was promoted Corporal in 1901, transferred to 'Musician', probably as a supernumerary, in 1902 and returned to Corporal in 1904. In the same year he was promoted to Sergeant and appointed Bugle Major, an appointment that he held until he retired in 1919 as a Colour Sergeant. His son of the same name joined up as a Chatham Bugler in 1916, served as Bugler on HMS Euralyus and HMS Venus and then transferred to the ranks in 1919. He served until December 1945, retiring as a Colour Sergeant after twenty-nine years' service.

The constitution of the Board for examination of Buglers, originally set in 1888, was adjusted in 1906. The president was now to be the Field Officer of the Week and the board members were to be a Gunnery Instructor, an Adjutant and the Bandmaster. No longer was the Bandmaster's attendance optional.[62] Buglers transferring to the ranks had to pass all necessary instructions at Divisional Headquarters before they could change. However, it was noted that all Buglers were to be passed through these instructions "as quickly as possible".[63] This may have been because the Buglers would have been experienced, and relatively knowledgeable about many of the subjects, allowing the Buglers to be 'fast-tracked' in many cases. In May 1911 this was changed. All Buglers transferring to the ranks would be sent to the Depot, Deal, for training. This training consisted of twenty-four working days undertaking Physical and Infantry Training; eighteen days each on the Recruits Course of Musketry and the Recruits Course of Tactical Training. This was followed by twelve days revision and the pass for duty. Total length of the course was twelve weeks of five days.[64] Two years later this was changed by adding eighteen days to the Physical and Infantry Training part of the course as well as six days to the Tactical Training Course, all of which extended the overall course length from twelve to sixteen weeks.[65]

The 1898 Order regulating the number and use of Bugler and private supernumeraries was modified in 1908 to allow men and boys with a musical ability and aptitude to be included in the list even though it might alter the set proportions. However the set number of supernumeraries could not be exceeded.[66]

In 1909 Bugle Major Bunting, Chatham Division, made a special arrangement of *Sunset* for their Tattoo. This was also played in 1911 when the report states, "Then came the sounding of *Sunset* by the drums, to music arranged by Bugle Major Bunting".

Kit issued to a Chatham Bugler about this time, 1908-1910, was his bugle with green cord, a fife, side drum with linen cover, a pair of sticks, carrier and knot.[67] Dents in the brass shells of Buglers' drums were not to result in the shells being condemned. The Armourer

61 *General Orders, Royal Marines 1905 (GO36).*
62 *General Orders, Royal Marines 1906 (GO75).*
63 *General Orders, Royal Marines 1908. Errata to General Standing Order 338.*
64 *General Orders, Royal Marines 1911. Errata to GOs 69 and 70.*
65 *General Orders, Royal Marines 1913 (GO63).*
66 *General Orders, Royal Marines 1908. Errata to General Standing Order para 858.*
67 *Globe & Laurel 1973 p28.*

Sergeant was made responsible for the removal of the dents and their return to service.[68] In 1909 an Order was promulgated stating that NCOs who had held appointments as Drum Major or Bugle Major, or a Corporal in charge of Buglers, who wished to join the Royal Fleet Reserve and retain their substantive rank at discharge had to be given the opportunity to gain the necessary qualifications in Naval Gunnery and in Musketry before they completed their Royal Marine service. Colonels Commandant were to ensure that the necessary arrangements were made.[69] In 1913 this was extended to other appointments and ranks including Buglers who, if successful in passing the course, would join as Privates.[70]

In about 1904 Bugler G E Whitwell, RMA 5380, transferred to the Royal Navy as a probationary Sick Berth Attendant.[71] However, in 1909 the Admiralty approved a general rule that no ex-soldier with more than four years' service was to be enlisted into the Royal Navy or the Royal Marines, although consideration would be given to men in this category who may be required to fill a special rank or to fill vacancies in a Royal Marine Band.[72]

The 'Pay and Wage Table' of 1908 offers an interesting insight into the comparative rates of pay between the Royal Marine Artillery and the Royal Marine Light Infantry Divisions. The Drum and Bugle Majors plus Provost Sergeant, Sergeant Cook, Hospital Sergeant, Master tailor and Officers' Messman, who were all on the same pay, would earn 23% more in the RMA than in the RMLI. Irrespective of rank they would be paid as Sergeants unless they were Colour Sergeants in which case they would be paid at that rank. An amendment was later issued which stated that, under the 'Appointments' system a Drum Major would be paid at the rank of a Colour Sergeant, if he was a Sergeant, whilst a Bugle Major was paid as a Colour Sergeant only if he held that rank. Under these circumstances they were usually both paid the same but neither received any additional pay for carrying out the duties of the appointment.[73] An RMA Bugler was paid 10% more than a RMLI Bugler. Under King's Regulations and Admiralty Instructions (Appendix XVa, Part 3) a Musical Proficiency Allowance of 1d per day was allowed to Buglers.[74]

It was in 1910 that the Admiralty decided that a Bugler should be made available to sound the *Last Post* at funerals of officers on the retired list, and of pensioners who possessed a War Medal or a Good Conduct Medal. The privilege of using a gun-carriage, together with a bearer-party and men to drag the gun-carriage, was also extended provided that no interference to training occurred, no cost to the public was entailed and that the men taking part did so on a voluntary basis.[75] The Admiralty also approved the rank of those Privates and Buglers who had at least five years' service on the establishment of the Divisional Bands, or the Depot Band, being upgraded to Corporal for pension purposes.[76]

The first edition of Stores Instructions ratified the provision of Drum Majors' dress belts and staffs. One staff, with leather bag or case, and one embroidered dress belt, with tin case, had been provided to each Division and the Depot. It was expected that the belt would last for fifteen years.[77] Another regulation stated the need for each Division, and the Depot, to retain its own instruments for its Buglers.

---

68 Stores Instructions, Royal Marines. 1st Edition, 1910. (Royal Marines Museum) When the second edition was published in 1922 it included a regulation that 'blocking' a bugle, which was a means of removing dents from the inside - a difficult and time-consuming task - was not to be done unless the bugle was worth the effort and, subsequently, would have a long period of service.

69 General Orders, Royal Marines 1909 (GO58).

70 General Orders, Royal Marines 1913 (GO91).

71 General Orders, Royal Marines 1904 (GO36).

72 General Orders, Royal Marines 1909 (GO70).

73 General Orders, Royal Marines 1910. Errata to 1908 Instructions.

74 Instructions, RM Divisions 1908.

75 General Orders, Royal Marines 1910 (GO74).

76 General Orders, Royal Marines 1914 (GO53) and Admiralty Orders-in-Council 18th June 1914.

77 Stores Instructions, Royal Marines. 1st Edition, 1910, Regulation 279. (Royal Marines Museum) When the second edition was published in 1922 it included a similar provision for the RN School of Music.

Alfred March, a Portsmouth Bugler who became Bugle Major at the Depot, Deal. c.1912

In 1915 Bugler S C Reed drowned when HMS *Formidable* was torpedoed and sunk by *U-24* in the English Channel. Politicians in the House of Commons were told that when Reed was advised to use his drum to keep him afloat he replied that he had thought of that and had given it to a blue-jacket boy who could not swim. Others who died in WW1 include Bugler A E Flory, HMS *Castor*, a member of a well-known Corps family who died at Jutland, and Bugler Timmins, age fourteen, who was killed on the bridge of HMS *Cardiff* shortly after sounding *To Quarters* at Heligoland. Bugler A Morgan was, at the age of fourteen, the youngest combatant at the defence of Antwerp where he was wounded in the leg. He also saw action, aged eighteen, at Zeebrugge. He died of anaemia in 1927 aged only twenty-seven. Bugler Wheaton was the last Musician or Bugler to die in the First World War. He was killed whilst fighting in the Caspian Sea on the 21st May 1919. A Memorial shield bearing the words "Remember the Buglers of the Royal Marine Artillery" and bearing the names of Buglers killed in the "Great War 1914-18" was hung in the RMA Church, St Andrews, at Eastney.

The Royal Naval Division was engaged in the fighting to strengthen the British and Australian positions at the head of the Monash Valley, in the Achi Baba area during the Gallipoli Campaign. "On May 4th [1915] Bugler Ernest Sillence of the Chatham Battalion gained the Conspicuous Gallantry Medal for throwing back enemy bombs into their lines at great personal risk, thereby saving the lives of many of his comrades". Bugler Sillence was also Mentioned in Despatches.[78]

Rates of pay for Drum Majors of the Divisional, and Depot, Bands were increased in October 1917 when it was decided to end the practice of them receiving the sum of one guinea for each of the Buglers that they trained to a standard suitable for sea service. This money was deducted from the individual Buglers' pay. The Drum Major's daily rate was increased by four and a half pence from four shillings and two pence (RMA) and by three and a half pence from three shillings and sixpence (RMLI). The pay of a Bugler was, on entry, one shilling and two pence a day, the same as a recruit, RM. After six months this was increased by two pence per day and on final completion of training, when ready for embarkation, the RMA Bugler received one shilling and seven pence per day and the RMLI Bugler received one shilling and five pence per day.[79]

Bugler F H Daniel, Plymouth Division. The armoured cruiser HMS Defence was pressing home an attack on the German ship Wiesbaden during the Battle of Jutland when she came under fire from four German battleships and blew up taking her entire crew, including Buglers Daniel and Rush to their deaths

78 *Britain's Sea Soldiers 1914-1919 by General Sir H E Blumberg RM and General Orders, Royal Marines 1915 (GO44).*
79 *General Orders, Royal Marines 1917 (GO210).*

Men of the Royal Marine Artillery at Fort Cumberland, Southsea. Note the Bugler

This was confirmed in an Admiralty Order-in-Council of the 5th July 1918 which referred to the Order-In-Council of the 31st December 1883 allowing the Drum Major's fee, which was now to be stopped. The new Order-in-Council went on to recommend a general increase in the rates of pay for Drum Majors, Bugle Majors and Buglers serving with both the RMA and the RMLI.

The training of Buglers at the Divisions could not keep pace with demand and so, in 1918, it was decided that twelve boys would be enlisted at the Depot and, when fully trained, four would be sent to each of the RMLI Divisions. Others would then be enlisted in their place.[80] This suggests that the Royal Marine Artillery were able to recruit and train sufficient Buglers for their needs.

Bugler Richard Gunton Ashby, RMLI, aged 13 years, 7 months

The 4th Battalion Royal Marines was raised for the operation to block the port of Zeebrugge and deny its use to the German submarines based there. It was a composite Battalion and included six officers, one Warrant Officer and one hundred and sixty five NCOs and men from Chatham Division, formed as 'A' Company of the 4th Battalion. This Company was to land on the Mole from one of the troop carrying ships but conditions were such that this was not possible. The ship had only just manoeuvred alongside when the signal was given to withdraw. The ship came under heavy and direct fire from the shore batteries during this manouvre. Many casualties were sustained and a fire started on the upper deck. Lance-Corporal Bugler Charles Heffernan bravely began moving the ammunition from the area of the fire, a task that he continued to carry out until he was killed. He was Mentioned in Despatches. As a result of the same action Portsmouth Bugler Leonard Francis Gutteridge was also Mentioned in Despatches. He was part of 'B' Company which made the journey across the Channel in HMS *Vindictive*, an old battleship especially prepared to land troops onto the Mole to attack the defences and the dock installations.[81] In September of that year it was announced that Bugler Gutteridge had been awarded the Distinguished Service Medal.[82] Earlier, in 1917, Chatham Bugler Valentine James Haines was also Mentioned in Despatches.[83]

On the 7th March 1918 HM The King decreed that in future the senior squad of Royal Marine Recruits was to be known as The King's Squad'. This led to a new badge, 'The King's Badge' being awarded to the best recruit as selected by the Commandant at Deal. A set of criteria for the award was drafted and published. This included a statement that, should no man in a Squad be considered worthy then it would not be awarded. This set of criteria was published as General Order 197 in September 1918. By this time seventeen King Squads had been selected and sixteen 'King's Badgemen' had been chosen. Since there were a large number of Squads passing out of the Depot, Deal, two or three King's Squads

80 *General Orders, Royal Marines 1918 (GO129).*
81 *General Orders, Royal Marines 1918 (GO171).*
82 *General Orders, Royal Marines 1918 (GO221) and London Gazette 13th September 1918.*
83 *General Orders, Royal Marines 1917 (GO165).*

a month were selected and, because of the system of training, the sequence of King's Badgemen was Portsmouth, Plymouth, Chatham, Portsmouth, Plymouth etc. Quite a few of these early King's Badgemen were Buglers who had changed over to the ranks; their success was not really surprising since they had served long enough to know how to act, how to behave and how the Corps worked. They were fit, they were institutionalised and they knew the routines. They were the natural leaders amongst a group of young men gaining their first taste of military life.

Private C A Smith, aged 18, who joined as a Portsmouth Bugler in 1914 and transferred to the ranks probably during 1917. He and Bugler J Kennedy, a Chatham Bugler, were taking passage on the armed boarding steamer SS Louvain heading for the Fleet anchorage in Mudros in the Aegean Sea when she was hit by a torpedo from the German submarine U-22. Both died during the incident

Although Buglers could 'change over' at any time the King's Badge criteria stated that, in order to be considered for the award, the age of ex-Buglers had to be between seventeen and twenty-three. An alteration to this took place in July 1920 when it was stated that Buglers transferring to the ranks had to be posted to a squad suitable to their standard of efficiency. When transferring, Buglers RMA had to undergo their preliminary training at RMA Headquarters whilst RMLI Buglers were trained at the Depot.[84] As a result of the young age at which boys enlisted as Buglers it was not easy to judge whether he was capable of attaining the required height and chest measurements when he reached the age for transfer to the ranks. It was decided that those Buglers unlikely to qualify would be considered for a free discharge.[85]

Seven Buglers under Bugler E Neve supported the King's Squad at the 1919 Royal Naval, Military and Air Force Tournament, their first appearance at what was to become a regular feature of the programmes before World War Two. Eight Buglers under Bugle Major C E Lidiard[86] (Plymouth Division) were used the following year.

An amendment to General Standing Orders - Duration of Appointments at RM Divisions, Depot, RM, and RN School of Music, was issued in April 1920. Appointments were arranged in four Classes, each of a different duration. Class 1 appointments were those that the appointee could hold for the length of his remaining service and included Drum Majors, Bugle Majors and Bugle Corporals.[87] In September of that year it was decided that the highest rank holding the appointments of Drum Major and Bugle Major would be that of Colour Sergeant.[88] At this time each of the Divisional Bands and also the Depot had a Drum and a Bugle Major.

Bugler L V G Cassey joined the RMA in 1916. First draft, in 1917, was to HMS Marlborough which, in 1919, received orders to proceed to Yalta in the Crimea to evacuate the Russian Royal family from the Levatia Palace. This was successfully achieved. Cassey then went to Turkey with the 11th Bn in 1922. Following a deployment on HMS Queen Elizabeth he went to China as part of 12th Bn. He changed over to the ranks at some point in his career and served until 1945

In 1920 thirty-two Silver Bugles were purchased by the officers of the Royal Marines through private subscription as a Memorial to RMLI officers who were killed during the First World War. The bugles were the standard Service pattern but in sterling silver with the Corps crest embossed upon them and an engraved inscription. They were issued, in groups of eight, to the RMLI Divisions at Chatham, Portsmouth and Plymouth as well as to the Depot, Deal. It was intended that they would be particularly used to sound a fanfare on sixteen anniversaries. They were: 14th February (St Vincent, 1797), 3rd April (Copenhagen 1801), 23rd April (Zeebrugge, 1918), 25th April (Gallipoli, 1915), 29th April (the award of 'Royal', 1802), 31st May (Jutland, 1916), 1st June ('Glorious First of June' 1794), 7th June (Belle Isle, 1761), 17th June (Bunkers Hill, 1775), 24th July

84 General Orders, Royal Marines 1918 (RM 12967/1920).
85 General Orders, Royal Marines 1920 (RM 13207/20).
86 Sgt Maj C E Lidiard was the cousin of Major H E Lidiard. He served at Gallipoli and was the Bugle Major at the unveiling of the London Cenotaph.
87 General Orders, Royal Marines 1920 (GO65).
88 General Orders, Royal Marines 1920, (RM 9094/20).

(Gibraltar, 1704), 1st August (The Nile 1798), 26th September (Grant of the Globe, 1827), 11th October (Camperdown, 1797), 21st October (Trafalgar, 1805), 28th October (Birth of the Corps, 1664) and the 11th November (Armistice Day). After the Second World War, consideration was given to adding further dates but it was decided to reduce the dates to those for Zeebrugge, Belle Isle, Gibraltar, Trafalgar and the Birth of the Corps but also to add 1st November (Assault on Walcheren, 1944). The Memorial Silver Bugles were not played together until the first massed bands Beat Retreat on Horse Guards Parade in 1950, and then were only played together at two more Beating Retreat ceremonies.[89] Although not a Band Service Memorial they are an inherent part of Band Service history. On the 23rd February 1969 RMRO 43/68 recorded that the Silver Memorial Bugles were to be withdrawn from service and issued to the Officers' Messes at Plymouth and Commando Training Centre, RM, as well as to the RMBS and the Royal Marines Museum.

The composition of the Board for the Examination of Buglers in 1921was confirmed as a Lieutenant Colonel, a Gunnery Officer, the adjutant and either the Director of Music or Bandmaster, depending upon which was serving with the appropriate Divisional Band.[90] It was also in 1921 that one of the occasional lists of 'Estimated Duration of Arms, Accoutrements and Musical Instruments' appeared as an appendix to the General Orders. Bugles were expected to remain in service for five years whilst drums, drum cases and drum sticks should last for ten years. Drum cords, drum heads and bugle strings should last for nine, twelve and thirty months respectively. At this particular time the fife was referred to as a 'Flute' and was expected to serve for six years.

Bandmasters of the Royal Marine Bands of the Royal Naval School of Music would usually assume the Drum Majors' role but, in 1922, Bandmaster (2nd Class) Frederick George Stagg was appointed the first official Drum Major of the School itself. He held this appointment until June 1924 when, as a Bandmaster (1st Class) he joined HMS *Barham*.

Amendments, 1922, to Books of Regulation included a specimen organisation for a ship's RM Detachment, the example given being for a Flagship Light Cruiser. The Detachment would comprise two Officers, three Colour Sergeants or Sergeants, eight Corporals and approximately sixty Marines with two Buglers and a Royal Marine Band. As a Flagship the RM Company Headquarters for the Cruiser Squadron would also be aboard. As well as a Commanding Officer, Company Sergeant Major and a Company Quartermaster Sergeant, there would be seventeen ranks[91] and an additional Bugler.[92]

General Standing Orders, Royal Marines, were issued in 1922, shortly before the amalgamation of the RMA and the RMLI, and replacing the much amended 1910 edition. The Drum Major now had the additional duties of Company Sergeant-Major and Company Quartermaster-Sergeant for the Band and Buglers, the Bugle Major being given an instruction to give further assistance to the Drum Major whilst retaining responsibility for instruction in fife and bugle.

The regulations relating to Buglers, some of which had been in use for many years, can be summarised as follows: the Admiralty Recruiting Department would keep a Register of candidates and when a Divisional Colonel Commandant notified them of a vacancy the first candidate in order of application would be sent for examination. However, priority was always given to the sons of Royal Marines, ex-Royal Marines and men of the Royal Navy. This prioritisation was especially strong in relation to sons of men of the RMA. Each Divisional

89 *In 1969 a RMRO stated that they should not be used again. They are now held at the Officers' Mess, Plymouth (8), CTC (6) and 42 Cdo (2). The HQ RMBS and the RM Museum hold eight each. All 32 were gathered together for only the fourth time at the Special RMBS Exhibition at the RMM 2003-2004.*

90 *General Orders, Royal Marines 1921.*

91 *One each of Batman(Runner), cook, butcher, storeman, Officers' messman/cook with six runners, four scouts and a two-man sanitary party.*

92 *General Orders, 1922 Amendment to General Standing Orders.*

Headquarters would maintain a register indicating the character and ability, later altered to efficiency, of each boy upon enlistment. The maximum age of enlistment was fifteen to ensure full value in terms of length of service as a trained Bugler prior to any transfer to the ranks - which could take place when the Bugler reached the age of seventeen, provided that he had served at least one year afloat, had gained a Third Class Certificate of Education and met the physical requirements. The recruits would be instructed in the bugle, drum and fife and, after three months, the Adjutant would record whether it was felt that the recruits would qualify as 'Efficient'. Before being passed fit for duty they would be tested in each instrument before a Board as laid down in 'Instructions for Royal Marine Divisions'. This test would be repeated each time the Bugler disembarked and before embarkation and the Adjutant would maintain a record of all examinations, including the composition of the Board, especially whether the Bandmaster or (later) the Director of Music attended, and the standard attained by each Bugler. No Bugler would be embarked unless his standard on bugle was 'Very Good' and his standard on drum and fife was never less than 'Good'.

The Adjutant was also responsible for ensuring that the "Bugler Boys" were not ill-treated by the NCOs and that they did not get into debt. The latter was particularly important for those deemed unlikely to reach the required standard and, that being the case, subject to discharge. 'Instructions for RM Divisions 1922' make it clear that the Adjutant had the powers of a Company Commander as regards the Band and Buglers. The Divisional Chaplains were responsible for personally giving Religious Instruction to the Buglers as directed by the Colonel Commandant. They were also to prepare for Confirmation any men and boys who wished it. Buglers who did elect to transfer to the ranks had to undergo the same syllabus of training as for recruits but they had to be posted to a Recruit Squad suitable to their standard of efficiency. Although these men were originally trained at the Divisions they were all later trained at the Depot, Deal. Buglers serving at the Depot had to be of good character, unlikely to transfer to the ranks for at least a year, thoroughly qualified to perform on all three Instruments and, preferably, unmarried. Young Buglers were not to be sent to the Depot if that could be avoided. Although a Bugler who transferred to the ranks would be placed at the bottom of the Recruits Roster, his service afloat would count towards his promotion to Corporal. By 1930 this benefit had been removed.[93]

Sea Service Rosters for 'Buglers (Trained Soldiers)' and 'Buglers (Recruits)' were held and maintained by the Drafting Officer. At this time, 1922, transfers to and from the Army and Royal Air Force were still allowable provided that they complied with King's Regulations for the Army.[94]

Drum Major and Bugle Major appointments were confirmed as being of Colour-Sergeant rank with one of each at Chatham, Portsmouth and Plymouth Divisions and the Depot, Deal. They would be supported by two Bugle Corporals at each of the Divisions but only one at the Depot.[95] The Royal Naval School of Music was allowed one Drum Major who was appointed for a three-year period but he was a specially trained Bandmaster Class II.[96]

Inspections of Buglers' musical instruments were made by a Board on a weekly basis. Any unserviceable instruments, or parts, were, if condemned, sent to the Naval Armament Depot. Charges against individual Buglers were made if it was felt that loss or unserviceability was due to neglect. The charge was based upon the proportionate value of the unexpired period of use but no charge would be less than a quarter of the full value – even if the instrument or part had lasted its full period of service. In addition,

93 *General Standing Orders for the Royal Marine Forces 1930.*
94 *General Standing Orders for the Royal Marine Forces (Fifth Ed) 1922.*
95 *General Standing Orders for the Royal Marine Forces (Fifth Ed) 1922, Appendix IX.*
96 *General Standing Orders for the Royal Marine Forces (Fifth Ed) 1922.*

the unexpired period was always calculated in half-years with the charge period always being rounded up.[97] The responsibility of the Armourer-Sergeant in respect of repairs to Buglers' instruments was changed by the same Instructions. From 1922 his responsibilities were to mark the "bugles, flutes and drums" and to repair iron and metal-work. He was not to "perform any special work such as the repairs of bugles and drums, except such trifling repairs as are plainly within his capability. In the event of these articles requiring more extensive repairs, the work is to be executed by local tradesmen. No repairs are to be effected by the Armourer-Sergeant as a private charge against the men". At this time the estimated duration of Buglers' instruments was still as set out in the 1921 Orders.

When the amalgamation of the RMA and the RMLI took place, Portsmouth RMLI relocated from Forton Barracks to Eastney Barracks to join with the RMA. Led by Drum Major Wilson the men of the Division, with their Band and Colours, marched down to the floating bridge. From Portsmouth Point, where they stepped ashore, they were preceded, firstly, by the Band of The Prince of Wales Volunteers (South Lancashire Regt) and then an RNSM Band under Lt S Fairfield which, led by Drum Major F G Stagg, marched them into Eastney. As a result of this amalgamation the RMA bugle call passed into history and the Portsmouth Division Royal Marine Light Infantry call was adopted as the call of the new Portsmouth Division Royal Marines.[98]

Following the end of the First World War, with its appalling numbers of casualties, Remembrance became much more formalised with the Tomb of the Unknown Warrior and the Cenotaph becoming its centrepieces and the focus of national mourning. The Cenotaph had been unveiled at 1100hrs on the 11th November 1920, a Tuesday, by King George V. Only the Guards Bands, with the Pipes of the Scots Guards, were present. A year later Buglers from the Chatham Division sounded *Reveille* after the playing and singing of *O God, Our Help in Ages Past* which immediately followed the two-minute silence. This was repeated in 1922, but in 1923 there was a reduced service. In 1924 sixteen Buglers from Chatham Division sounded *Reveille* and Trumpeters from the Royal Air Force, involved in this way for the first time, played *Last Post*. This was the first year that the Service of Remembrance took the form that we know so well today.

In 1925 the Adjutant General standardised the design of the Drum Majors' dress belt. This was as a result of the amalgamation of the Royal Marine Artillery and the Royal Marine Light Infantry. On the front face of the belt the upper scroll carrying the name "GIBRALTAR" was to be gold on a blue background. Below this, the Imperial crown and then the foul anchor on the GRIV Cipher were positioned. The globe surrounded by a laurel wreath was positioned below the anchor with a scroll beneath it bearing the words "PER MARE PER TERRAM" in gold on a blue background. Below this was the Royal Cipher "GRV". On the demise of the King this was to be changed to the cipher of the reigning Sovereign. The design of the buckle on the rear of the belt was slightly changed. The buckles of the RMLI had a crown at each side and a bugle at the bottom. These were replaced with roses as featured in each corner of the buckle. It is presumed that the RMA buckle had a bursting grenade. The buckle also featured the crowned lion over the crown upon a globe and a scroll bearing the motto "PER MARE PER TERRAM" with laurel wreaths linking the components. All gold lace was to be wire.[99]

At some time a lyre superimposed upon an anchor replaced the foul anchor on the GRIV Cypher.

---

97 *Instructions for RM Divisions, 1922.*

98 *By Corps Historian 16 Nov 1972. (RMM Archive).*

99 *File ADM1/8808 in PRO.*

In 1926 it was decided by the Royal Naval School of Music that a standard staff should be acquired for the School and for the bands of the Commanders-in-Chief at Portsmouth, Plymouth, the Atlantic Fleet, the Mediterranean Fleet and the China Fleet. The design consisted of a Malacca cane with a tapered silver ferrule, a silver grip and a silver two-part head. The upper part of the head was a dome upon which was mounted a silver Imperial crown and a crowned lion. The lower part carried the Corps crest with lyre surmounted and, around the circumference, the wording "ROYAL NAVAL SCHOOL OF MUSIC". At the junctions of the various parts were silver rings with laurels engraved upon them. The Malacca cane was embellished with silver chains. These staffs were made by Hawkes and Co.[100]

By 1934 a further staff had been added for use by the Recruits Band for Recruits and Trained Soldiers Church Parades.[101]

It was decided to standardise the style of staff being used at the Royal Marine Divisions and so, during early March 1929, the Adjutant General called for sketches of the staff in use at each of the Divisions for selection of a standard. A drawing of the staffs supplied to the Depot and to the RMA[102] in 1899 was submitted. This showed a silver crowned lion on a Victorian crown mounted on a silver globe with continents of gilt.[103] On the silver grip was a scroll carrying the name "Gibraltar" and the words "Per Mare Per Terram" over which was an anchor superimposed upon the Royal Cypher of George IV.[104] Above this, on the Depot version, was a bugle horn whilst the Royal Marine Artillery model carried a bursting grenade. The Chatham Division was of a completely different style. It had a golden lion and crown mounted on a silver globe engraved with the continents, oceans and meridians. This was mounted on a golden dome engraved with a row of oak leaves and acorns then, in silver letters, the words "FIRST DIVISION - ROYAL MARINES". Below this was a further row of oak leaves and acorns and then, below a narrow space, a floral design consisting of roses, thistles, shamrocks and their leaves over a scroll with the words "Per Mare Per Terram" and a series of Prince of Wales' Plumes. The Malacca cane was fitted with cords instead of chain and these terminated in two tassels above the long tapering brass ferrule.[105] The Plymouth Division staff was much plainer and consisted of a gilded brass lion, crown, globe and shank. The latter was partly covered by a buff grip. The Malacca cane was fitted with cords and tassels at both the grip and ferrule ends. The ferrule itself was of gilded brass.

A decision was taken to adopt the style of the Portsmouth Division, Plymouth Division and the Depot, all of which were very similar, but with certain alterations to bring them into line. These were that all crowns were to be Imperial crown; chains were to be used, not cord, and these would be of sterling silver and not gold; the bugle on the shank was to be deleted above the anchor and ciphers were to be removed and the Royal cipher was to be standardised as George IV. It was also intended that the continents were to be shown on the globe. The Depot responded by stating that they would not alter their staff since it was originally the Woolwich Division staff and therefore of historical importance. However, the Adjutant General was able to show that this staff was originally purchased for the Depot in 1892 or 1894. The Brigadier commanding Plymouth Division wrote to urge that the Portsmouth staff should be used as the pattern since its dimensions and weight

---

100 Information taken from the PRO File ADM1/8808 and from example presented to the Royal Marines Museum by the Royal Marines Band Service 26th June 2003.

101 Letter from the Depot Commandant, 3rd December 1934. PRO File ADM1.8808.

102 Being used by the Portsmouth Division.

103 The silver parts of these staffs could not be hallmarked because of the use of gilt. An item has to be completely silver to be hall-marked.

104 This was in deference to the King who had conferred the battle honour of the Globe on the Royal Marines in 1827.

105 This staff is in the Royal Marines Museum but, prior to its donation, the silver globe had been lost.

gave it a better balance. A new staff based upon the Portsmouth design was subsequently ordered and supplied by H Potter & Co of Charing Cross Road and so the original RMA and Depot design of 1899 became the basis for the current Royal Marine Drum Major's staff.

The syllabus for the training of Buglers was laid down in 1925. During the first three months scales and short calls on the bugle were taught whilst, on the fife, elementary theory and the scales of D, G, A, C and F were taught. First month drum training consisted of the open to close rolls. This was continued through months two and three with the addition of the commencement of stroke rolls seven and eleven. The fourth to seventh months were for scales, short calls, Infantry calls and Naval calls on the bugle; scales and short calls from the tutor on the fife and, for the drum, open to close rolls, flam, drag, stroke rolls three, five, seven, nine, and eleven plus two, four, six and eight beatings. The final month, the eighth, was for revision, examination and the Pass for Duty. During this period regular instruction in infantry training, swimming, Company and Religious Instruction was given and they also attended school.[106]

Buglers were very busy at sea. A report in a 1927 issue of Globe & Laurel describes a fairly typical scene on board ships of the Royal Navy, in this case, HMS *Nelson*: "The band, augmented by ex-Buglers from the Detachment with Cpl Heaton as Drum Major complete with staff and gauntlets, were very conspicuous. On Sunday mornings at 0900 there is a voluntary 'clear lower deck' to witness 'the troop'. The band presents a fine spectacle marching the length of the top deck to the strains of *Sambre et Meuse* and the Buglers, who have been organised by Cpl Desmond render a good account of themselves." Buglers were an important link between the band and the detachment on the ship as well as between the marines and the ship's company. Having joined the Corps as Boy Buglers they later had the choice of whether to remain a Bugler or transfer to General Service. If they chose the latter they would invariably find themselves as part of a ship's detachment. Many would take the opportunity of using their musical skills on drum, fife and bugle by working with the band or, if in existence, the drum and fife, drum and bugle or any other volunteer group that could make use of them. Their experience also made many of them very able, and willing, Drum Majors. According to a report in Globe & Laurel in 1928 the Bugle Band of HMS *Queen Elizabeth* was 'the envy of the Fleet' which was formed and trained by Bugler Elliott. The band comprised twelve men on bugle, four on side drum and a bass Drummer. Most of these men would have been from the ship's RM Detachment.

Bugler's Drill, to be used at all establishments, was adopted in 1929.[107] It consisted of the method of raising and lowering the bugle for playing, marching with the bugle held (not carrying a drum) and the flourish.

In 1929 Drum Major Wilson of the Portsmouth Division retired after eleven and a half years in the appointment. On 14th April, on parade after Church, he formally handed his staff to his successor BdCpl J Dacombe who would in turn hold the appointment until 1941.[108]

In 1935 a Drum and Fife band consisting of forty Buglers and ex-Buglers was formed for London Duties. Dress Cords Royal were issued to Buglers for the first time on this occasion and they have been worn by them ever since.[109] This tended to give the front rank of a ship's band an unbalanced look since the difference between the Buglers and the percussionist Drummers was immediately obvious.

---

106 General Orders, Royal Marines, 1925.

107 General Orders, Royal Marines, 1929. No: 128.

108 Jack returned to the Band Service in 1964 as Professor of Trombone, a position he held for twelve years until 1976 when he retired at the age of 74.

109 General Orders, Royal Marines, 1936/79; AFO 1539/35; Dress Regulations 749/3/35Q; Navy List post 1936.

HMS *Caledonia*, the Training Establishment at Rosyth, was able to produce a display by massed bands consisting of a Boys' Bugle and Pipe Band and an Artificers' Fife and Drum Band for the Rear-Admiral's Inspection.

The Second World War claimed its first casualties in the Buglers' Branch when HMS *Royal Oak* was torpedoed at Scapa Flow with the loss of Bugler Mountford and Boy Bugler Priestley. The next occurred when Bugler Owens was killed on HMS *Ajax* and Boy Bugler Hill was killed on HMS *Exeter* at the Battle of the River Plate. *Exeter*'s second Bugler, LCplBug Kent, was presented to the Duke of Kent when he visited Divisions at Plymouth. A further eighteen Buglers, eleven of them Boy Buglers, were killed at sea or in Shore Establishments during the Second World War.

In 1941 Drum Major J Dacombe of the Portsmouth Division retired, his place being taken by Drum Major L Beer who had enlisted as a Boy Bugler, transferred to the ranks and served on various ships including HMS *Hood* where he became Drum Major of the Home Fleet. He later became Drum Major Mediterranean Fleet and then a Drill Instructor at RM Depot, Deal before being appointed as Drum Major, Portsmouth Division.

Also in 1941, the city of Plymouth was blitzed and Stonehouse Barracks was hit. The room where the unit bagpipes were stored was hit.[110] The bagpipes were destroyed, but in 1944 it was announced that they would be replaced and that they would carry the tartan of the Argyll and Sutherland Highlanders to commemorate the association between the two Regiments.

Another Plymouth Division Drum Major had a particularly interesting, possibly unique, career. Ron Woodruff joined the Corps in 1939 and, on completion of training at Plymouth in May 1940, he was awarded the King's Badge. He served on board HMS *Rodney* and following a period as an Acting Corporal he was made substantive in 1943. Soon after returning to Stonehouse in 1946 he was appointed Drum Major with the rank of Colour Sergeant. As the Divisions were re-titled as 'Groups' in 1947 he could claim to be the last Plymouth Division Drum Major. He remained with the Band until 1952, taking part in much of the immediate post-war ceremonial, plus a visit to Paris when the Band was featured in the film '*Innocents in Paris*' starring Ronald Shiner and Claire Bloom. Most unusually for a Drum Major, he passed for RSM in 1949 and following promotion to Quartermaster Sergeant he applied to return to general duties in 1952. He passed the Commando Course and then served in Malta and the Canal Zone before returning to the UK where he was commissioned.[111]

8th RM Battalion, later to become 41 Cdo, was being formed during 1942 and one of the Unit Buglers, LCplBug Rayfield, was very much involved in running the 8th Bn Band that consisted of eight bugles, six drums and three bagpipes and which practised three times a day. They later paraded with the Guard when the Adjutant-General visited the Battalion.

The youngest member of the Corps afloat, Boy Bugler Wills, had his 15th birthday on 7th July 1943 on board HMS *Kent*. Another Boy Bugler, Patrick Robinson, was the youngest Bugler to take part in London's Victory Parade. At the age of seventeen he transferred to the ranks and won the King's Badge and Silver Whistle. He was a Corporal by the age of nineteen.

In 1945 the ancient ceremony of Drumming the Vicar to Church was revived when the Rector of Chatham arrived at his church to conduct the annual parade service of the Chatham Division escorted by two Marines and preceded by Boy Bugler D Hawdon. This custom began in the late 17th Century when the Clergy, carrying the sacramental silver

110 *The Plymouth Division was unique in having bagpipes, from time to time. The story behind this is not known.*
111 *From Maj A J Donald and Capt D A Oakley.*

to Church, were often set upon by hooligans, and it had continued into the 18th Century before lapsing.

Some Drum Majors had got into the habit of using their staff to put on a bit of a show whilst on the march or on parade but an RMRO in 1946 stated, "throwing their maces [sic] in the air will only be carried out at the discretion of the Major-General, RM, on the parade ground of a RM Establishment".[112] As from 1945, any Bugler who qualified as a Marksman would wear his Marksman badge as well as his Buglers' Branch badge.

In 1946 an extension to the training of Boy Buglers was introduced; lasting a week it covered Basic Naval Training, Royal Marine Duties and General Seamanship. Shortly after this, in December 1947, an RMRO[113] was issued that stated that training in the fife was no longer a requirement of Boy Buglers unless they specifically wanted to learn in which case, at the discretion of the relevant Commander, it might be possible for those Buglers who had completed their first commission at sea.

In 1948 it was decided that Buglers should be trained at the Royal Naval School of Music at Burford, Oxfordshire. At the time Buglers were trained as part of Band and Drums Company which, for example, at Eastney was located in B Block under Drum Major Louis Beer and Bugle Major 'Wilky' Wilkinson. On the 15th December 1948 Boy Buglers under training at Portsmouth, Chatham and Plymouth reported to Burford where their training would begin again. Three NCO Buglers were sent as the Training Team: SgtBug Crosby from Portsmouth, CplBug Rickard from Plymouth and, it is believed, CplBug Bowles from Chatham. A Drill Instructor completed the Training Team which was commanded by Bandmaster Pottle and CSgt Yardley. The Boy Buglers were not integrated with the Boy Musicians but had their own barrack room, their own table in the dining hall etc. As training progressed the routine of Duty Bugler was begun and a Corps of Drums was formed to lead the Royal Naval School of Music Boys' Band. Whilst tradition had been broken in the way that Buglers were trained, the major advantage was the additional musical training that was given.[114]

At about this time the three Commando Units that had survived the post-war cuts were using their parent Group's bugle calls; 40 Cdo used the Plymouth call, 42 Cdo were Chatham and 45 Cdo were Portsmouth. When 41 Cdo was, once again, raised in the 1970s it was suggested that it should use the old Royal Marine Artillery call. It is not known if this suggestion was taken up.[115]

The Lacadaemonians moved slowly and to the music of many flute-players, who were stationed in their ranks, and played, not as an act of religion, but in order that the army might march evenly and in true measure, and that the line might not break, as often happens in great armies when they go into battle.

Thucydides: History of the Peloponnesian Wars (of the battle of Mantinea 418 BC)

112 *RMRO1457/1946.*
113 *RMRO576/1947.*
114 *Article by D J Palmer, Blue Band Autumn 1989 p53.*
115 *By Corps Historian 16 Nov 1972 (RMM Archive).*

Chapter 2: Royal Marine Divisional and Group Bands - Introduction

A General Order, Royal Marines[1] (GORM) of 1892 fixed the numbers for the Divisional Bands as one Bandmaster, two Sergeants, two Corporals, twenty-five Musicians and ten supernumeraries.[2]

The band at the Depot, Deal comprised one Sergeant for duty as Bandmaster, one Sergeant, one Corporal, seventeen Musicians and five supernumeraries.[3] This Order left the bandmaster with the option of either training members of the Corps or recruiting from outside the Corps. Another GORM[4] states: Bandmasters will, invariably, be in uniform when leading their bands. This was to end the practice of the time of Bandmasters leading and conducting their bands wearing civilian clothes.

Standardisation of the percentage to be taken from the private engagement fees charged by the Bandmasters, on behalf the Divisional Bands, had been arranged in 1888.[5] Five per cent was to be deducted and credited to the Divisional Funds to cover the wear and tear on the instruments, which were the property of the Division, and were used for these private engagements. In 1890 officers' subscriptions to the Mess and the Library were revised as were the contributions to the Band Funds. A staggered rate was calculated in order to take account of the fact that officers served afloat or abroad. Officers based at HQ or the Depot would contribute 1½ days' pay per annum, officers on the HQ establishment but detached (other than to the Depot) would pay 1 days pay per annum and officers serving afloat would contribute ½ days' pay per annum. Each Divisional Band Fund, except the RMA, would then contribute £12 to the Depot Band Fund.[6] 1896 saw the introduction of further Band administration. Each Divisonal Band, and the Depot Band, was to maintain a Band Book and this was to be held by the President of the Band Committee and the band's accounts were to be audited by the senior Lieutenant Colonel appointed to audit the Divisional Fund Account. Annual subscriptions from officers would be paid into this account and disbursements made to meet the expenses of the bands when requested by the President of the Band Committee and approved by the Colonel Commandant.[7]

The War Office instructed Colonels Commandant to issue orders that no bands were to accept engagements to play on a Sunday without ensuring that the General, or other officer commanding the district, had no objection to the Terms of the engagement and the prices charged for entry etc.[8]

A number of official decisions and documents influenced the development of the Corps, its bands and its Bandmasters during this period. Recruitment to the Divisional and Depot Bands was tightened in 1910 when a General Order was issued which stated that all future vacancies for Musicians must be filled by the absorption of the Gunner, Private or Bugler who had been attached to the Band as a Supernumerary for the longest period.

For some reason it was found necessary, in 1911, to issue a reminder about the correct playing of the National Anthem. "The authorised arrangement for the National Anthem is invariably to be used. The correct time is MM = 84, and this is always to be adhered to. There should be no repeats. The whole is to be played 'Fortissimo' and for greater effect there should be a crescendo roll with the drums leading up to the second part".[9]

---

1 *General Orders, Royal Marines 1892 (GO3).*
2 *Six Buglers and four Gunners or Privates.*
3 *Three Buglers and two Gunners or Privates.*
4 *General Orders, Royal Marines 1895 GO46.*
5 *General Orders, Royal Marines 1888 GO43.*
6 *General Orders, Royal Marines 1890 GO56.*
7 *General Standing Orders, Royal Marines 1896 GSO4.*
8 *General Orders, Royal Marines 1904 GO43.*
9 *Errata as GO of October 1911.*

In 1914 an Order-in-Council (OIC) allowed two Musical Directors, and the two senior Bandmasters were to receive the appointments automatically. They were Honorary[10] Major G J Miller of the Portsmouth Division RMLI and Honorary Lieutenant B S Green of the RMA. From this date Musical Directors were to be eligible for promotion to Captain after ten years' commissioned service and to Major after fifteen years' commissioned service. Retirement at sixty-five years of age was compulsory. The word "Honorary" was removed by a further OIC of 1918.[11] This was followed by a General Order which also stated that the number of Directors of Music would be set at two; that the title of Commissioned Bandmaster, Royal Marines, no longer existed; Directors of Music would be compulsorily retired at the age of sixty-five and that pay, allowances and other benefits would be on the same scale as Regimental Quartermasters.[12] Directors of Music were also eligible for promotion to Lieutenant Colonel for Distinguished Service in the Field or for Meritorious or Distinguished Service other than in the Field.[13]

In January 1920 a change was made to the Warrant rank structure. Firstly, Warrant rank was assigned to a number of appointments including Bandmasters. Warrant Officers could be promoted to Commissioned Officers under the same conditions as RN Warrant Officers with the exception of the conditions relating to sea-time. Warrant Officer Bandmasters would, on promotion, become Commissioned Bandmasters.[14]

In 1921 another OIC allowed five Directors of Music to the Corps, one at each HQ of the RMLI Divisions (Lt C J Hoby at Chatham, Lt B W O'Donnell at Portsmouth and Lt P S G O'Donnell at Plymouth), one for the RMA (Lt R P O'Donnell) and one for the Depot, Deal (Lt S J Nicholson). This OIC also indicated that they were to be known as Directors of Music and not Musical Directors. It is to be noted that at this time three of the five RM Directors of Music were brothers. Pay and allowances for these Directors of Music would be the same as for Quartermasters. Retirement age, sixty-three at the time, would be reduced to sixty by 1923.

King's Regulations and Orders for the Army stated that the Lords Commissioners of the Admiralty had approved that a Guard of Honour comprising one hundred rank and file with a Captain in command, two Subaltern Officers - one carrying the Regimental Colour - and with a proportion of Sergeants and the Divisional Band, should be available at official landings of the Board of Admiralty at Port Inspections, if required.[15] A similar instruction was issued in 1921 which said that "At the RMLI Divisions the Regimental Colour will be carried when receiving The Lords Commissioners of the Admiralty, and the Commander-in-Chief on his first assuming command, and at his annual visit to the Gun Drill Batteries".[16]

1923 saw the amalgamation of the RMA and the RMLI to form, once again, the Royal Marines. This obviously had an effect on some of the bands.

A composite band was formed in 1935 to support the London Duties Battalion that, similarly, was drawn from all three Divisions as well as from the Depot.[17] With effect from 1st January 1947 instructions were issued that covered the subscriptions for the band payable by both permanent and temporary officers of the Corps together with those officers on detachment plus additional charges for those at Divisional Headquarters.[18]

---

10 Miller reverted to Honorary Rank when promoted Major and Green reverted to Honorary Rank when promoted Lieutenant in 1914 - from Navy Lists of the time.

11 The Warrant rank, similar to that in the RN, had been introduced into the Corps by an Order-in-Council in 1881 and the four Bandmasters became Warrant Officers. This was followed in 1898 by G Miller's promotion to Honorary 2nd Lt and then, in 1899, he was made 2nd Lt - the first RM Bandmaster to be commissioned.

12 General Orders, Royal Marines 1914 GO59.

13 General Orders, Royal Marines 1918.

14 General Orders, Royal Marines 1920 GO184.

15 General Orders, Royal Marines 1910 GO65.

16 General Orders, Royal Marines 1921 GO130.

17 A description of this Tour of Duty is in the Chatham Division section of this book since the band was under the direction of Capt PSG O'Donnell, DoM Chatham Division.

18 RMRO 1372/1946.

Chapter 3: The Chatham Band

The first actual mention of any Marine Band occurs in 1693 in a Royal Warrant "To presse or cause to be impressed from time to time such number of Drums and Fifes and Hautboys as shall be necessary for His Majesty's Service, either by sea, or land..." Eighty years later, in 1773, the band of the First Grand Division, Chatham, under Acting Sgt Maj Clements was ordered to go aboard HMS *Orpheus* at Sheerness to be carried to Spithead, there being occasion for it when the King reviews His Fleet there".[1]

The Chatham Division Order Book for the 8th October 1781 sets out the working arrangements of the band in no uncertain manner. "In order that the Marine Musical Band may not hereafter be looked upon in the light of common Fidlers (sic), and permitted at the desire of indifferent persons to play in that capacity at ordinary and common Balls and Concerts, it is directed that in future, the Band or any part of them, shall not have liberty to play anywhere out of Barracks, but where the Divisions Business calls upon them, or where Government may take any concern".[2]

A Mr Radigar was the Music Master at Chatham in 1796 and on the 7th February the order, "Musicians to assemble every evening at 7 o'clock to practice and receive Instruction" was given. In 1797 the six Drummers and the band of the Division marched a Captain's Guard of one hundred and forty other ranks from Chatham to London to accompany the King to St Paul's Cathedral. The band at this time probably numbered eight. The following year, and as a result of the great mutinies, Earl St Vincent issued orders for the parading of Guards and Bands in the Fleet, and for the playing of *God Save the King* every morning.[3]

In 1802 an order was issued that increased the size of the band to fourteen. However, with the introduction of 'Turkish music' and new instruments such as clarinets, bassoon, flutes, horn, trumpets, key bugles, trombones and serpents, the size of the band again increased; indeed the size and shape of the present military band can be seen starting to appear at this time.

The Chatham Royal Marine Band of 1825 by Col C Field RMLI (after O Scharf)

In 1826 the Chatham Band accompanied the British Ambassador to Russia for the Coronation of Tsar Nicholas I - the first occasion a British band had left Great Britain to attend a foreign ceremony.

By 1830 the band numbered about sixty. Chatham's first known Bandmaster, W Rogers, served between 1836 and 1857[4] and was a civilian conductor who drew his income from the Band Fund and from private sources. He laid the foundation for what became a very fine band and being asked to take the band to London for Queen Victoria's Coronation and other State ceremonial rewarded his efficiency and thoroughness. His successor was Herr J A Kappey, a German who had been serving as civilian bandmaster to the 89th Regiment of Foot, later 2nd Bn The Royal Irish Fusiliers. In the early 1860s Herr Kappey established a

1 *Tanner unpublished papers.*
2 *Random Records of the Royal Marines p52 - Order Book for the Chatham Division.*
3 *Tanner unpublished papers.*
4 *Trendell's dates. Tanner says 1845 - 1857.*

Bandmaster W Rogers of the Chatham Division. Note the sword, a gift from the Tsar of Russia that was later presented to Bandmaster Kappey as a retirement present from the officers (caricatures by Lt Col W G Masters, Barrack Master of the Chatham Division)

first-class string band and, whilst he composed many pieces of music, he will be mainly remembered as the arranger of *A Life on the Ocean Wave*. In 1874 the War Office ended the practice of employing civilian bandmasters and then, in 1881, instructed that all Kneller Hall qualified Bandmasters were to be given the rank of Warrant Officer.

Between 1889 and his retirement in 1892 when he was succeeded by John Wright, Kappey also filled the post of official examiner of Student Bandmasters at Kneller Hall. At some point in his career Jacob Adam Kappey sat for the portrait painter Constant de Bruyes. The resulting portrait, oil on canvas, now hangs in the Royal College of Music, London.

Two more caricatures by Lt Col W G Masters. He produced many paintings, sketches and caricatures of life, incidents and people within the barracks

A sketch showing the Chatham Division Drum Major

Within the first year of his appointment Mr Wright had taken his Musicians, as a string band, to play at such events as an important reception at the Foreign Office and, as a military band, to the opening of the Imperial Institute by Queen Victoria and to the opening ceremony of Tower Bridge. Also in 1893 "Ten of the most accomplished performers of the band under Bandmaster Wright made several visits to the establishment of Mr Edison in London in order to make phonographic recordings of martial airs".[5] If this did happen, and even though no recordings are known to have survived there is no reason to doubt the report, then this would be the first instance of a military band making a recording, other than those made in the United States.

Once again a contrast to the RN Bands is apparent as the dawn of the twentieth century takes place for, like the RMA, the year 1900 saw the Chatham Band with a very high reputation both as a military band and as an orchestra and, also like the RMA, with a very good Bandmaster appointed.

In January 1901 the Chatham Divisional Band was on parade in London for the funeral of Queen Victoria.[6] 1901 also saw the Band accompany the Duke and Duchess of York on board the *Ophir*, an Orient Line ship, for a tour of the colonies (the Duke was the Colonel-in-Chief of the Royal Marines at the time). The Royal Party arrived in Portsmouth to the sounds of the bands of the Royal Artillery and

Members of the Chatham Divisional Band, 1873

5 *Globe & Laurel 1893.*
6 *General Orders, Royal Marines 1901 GO34.*

This excellent photograph of 1890 shows Chatham Division on Parade. In the right foreground can be seen the Divisional Band whilst, in front of them, can be seen the Bugle Major with the Buglers, who appear to be carrying bugles and fifes. The Drum Major is standing between the Band and the Buglers.

the Royal Marine Artillery playing at the Harbour Station and the old viaduct whilst the *Ophir*'s Guard and Band from Chatham Division was on deck. As a result of the band's performance during this 45,000 miles tour, Mr Wright was commissioned, in November 1901[7], and the badge of the White Rose of York was conferred upon the thirty-four strong band in March 1902.[8] This was to become part of their cap badge and helmet plate. In the same year 2nd Lt Wright was awarded a Coronation Medal by the King.[9]

2nd Lt John Wright

A highly qualified and skilled Musician, WO Bandmaster C J Hoby, who had served as Bandmaster of one of the Punjaub Frontier Force Infantry regiments, aged 20, and later with the Natal Royal Rifles Band before joining the Musical Department of the London School Board, took Lt J Wright's place upon his death in 1907. He was appointed Warrant Office bandmaster and led the Chatham Band for twenty-one years.

In 1910 a Torchlight Tattoo and Pageant took place at Chatham Barracks. From the programme it is apparent that the Bugle Major was heavily involved since he wrote a bugle march, arranged the *Sunset* call and also arranged the marches *Along with the Soldiers* and *Red Wing*. All of these were for the drums of the Division. Hoby wrote *Echo Fanfare* and the march *Colonel Commandant* as well as arranging a chorale for trumpet and trombones.

CSgt C Y Brown, Drum Major of the Chatham Division, Royal Marine Light Infantry, c.1900

During the First World War the band raised money for War Funds and, in 1917, they went to France and were attached to 63rd (RN) Division on the Arras Front, relieving the Portsmouth RMLI Divisional Band. After the war, in 1919, they played a significant part in the RN Memorial Service held at St Paul's Cathedral. Several members of the Royal Family attended this Service.

On the 14th November 1917 Bandmaster John Charles James Hoby was appointed Director of Music and granted the honorary rank of Lieutenant.[10]

---

7 General Orders, Royal Marines 1902 GO8.
8 General Orders, Royal Marines 1902 GO31.
9 General Orders, Royal Marines 1902 GO124.
10 General Orders, Royal Marines 1917.

Lt (later Capt) J C J Hoby, Director of Music, Chatham Division, Royal Marines. 1907 – 1928

Drum Major William Day MBE, BEM, was the Chatham Division Drum Major from 1932-1945. During this period he had responsibility for leading the composite band during the 1935 Public Duties

The Chatham Divisional Band played at the Funeral Service for Admiral of the Fleet, the Marquess of Milford Haven, at Westminster in 1921.[11] In 1924 the bands of the Royal Marines (Chatham, Portsmouth, Plymouth and the Depot) were massed with the Band of the RNSM under Captain Hoby for the second week of the first Wembley Torchlight and Searchlight Tattoo.[12] In 1925 Hoby again conducted the Wembley Tattoo and, on this occasion, the bands of the RNSM and Plymouth Division also played a major part.[13] This was the first occasion that the Chatham Band had worn its new, blue, RM tunics instead of their traditional RMLI scarlet. On the 14th November 1925 Hoby was promoted Captain (Director of Music).[14] Three years later Major Hoby retired after an illustrious career spanning twenty-one years with the Royal Marines at Chatham. In 1920 he had been appointed Professor of Military Music at the Royal College of Music, a post he held until his death in 1938. Lt P S G O'Donnell, who transferred to Chatham from the position of Director of Music, Plymouth Division, succeeded him.

One of the high points of O'Donnell's leadership of the Chatham Band came when a composite band of sixty-five was responsible, with the RM composite Battalion, for Public Duties in London during 1935, the Jubilee Year of the reign of King George V. The Drums of the Battalion numbered forty and the Colours for the Battalion were furnished by Portsmouth Division. Every third day they mounted guard on the two Palaces, the Magazine in Hyde Park, the Bank of England and the Central London Recruiting Depot. At that time the ceremony of changing the guard took place daily at St James's instead of Buckingham Palace owing to the absence of Their Majesties from London. The band shared the playing of music in the forecourt with the Coldstream Guards whilst the ceremony took place. The band played standing in the traditional circular formation. Normally the Guards Band plays throughout the ceremony but this arrangement was ordered in view of the special circumstances of the visit of a RM Battalion. During this tour of duty the Royal Marines exercised their ancient right to march through the City of London with drums beating, Colours flying and bayonets fixed, this being the first time that it had occurred for over two centuries.[15] A new Slow Troop was required for these Public Duties.[16]

Other major events during Maj[17] O'Donnell's period included a visit to Brussels in 1934 for the funeral of King Albert of the Belgians; being present at the Jubilee of King George V; the musical part of the celebrated Greenwich Pageant and playing in the procession of the Coronation of King George VI and Queen Elizabeth. O'Donnell was also responsible for the music at the funeral of Admiral of the Fleet Earl Jellicoe at St Paul's Cathedral in 1935. On the 2nd August 1936 Captain P S G O'Donnell was promoted to Major (Director of Music); then a year later, he retired from the Royal Marines to become the conductor of the BBC Wireless Military Band but not without a very busy period beforehand. The Chatham and Portsmouth Bands had to combine for the Coronation[18] and O'Donnell had to organise this. He told Lt Dunn of the Portsmouth Band that a

11 *The Daily Graphic 20th September 1921 (This was the father of Earl Mountbatten. The Marquess had played an important part in reforming Royal Navy music).*

12 *From official programme.*

13 *Tattoo programmes.*

14 *General Orders, Royal Marines 1925 GO152.*

15 *Globe & Laurel Supplement 1935/Household Brigade Magazine/ The Royal Marines - A Record of the Tour of Duty in London/Brigade Orders.*

16 *See Appendix 2 p248.*

17 *Recently promoted.*

18 *'Coronation Orders for RN and RM in London' RMM Archive.*

band of sixty would be required and that the front rank of eight would be Drummers. He also told Dunn that he wanted his best players - no seconds! O'Donnell was balancing this duty with that of organising the musical display in support of the King's Squad for the Royal Tournament at Olympia. Dunn's itinerary for the period was checked by O'Donnell to ensure that all commitments, including a Portsmouth Band requirement on board the Royal Yacht, could be met.

Although it was not realised at the time Capt T Francis, by succeeding Maj O'Donnell, was to become the last Director of Music of the Chatham Band. He had previously served with various Army bands before this.

During the Second World War the Band raised money through 'War Savings Week' concerts throughout the United Kingdom, including London and Windsor - where they played for Their Majesties at Windsor Castle. As from 1st January 1944 the Divisional Bands were ordered to make quarterly visits to a number of RM Establishments, formations and units in the United Kingdom. These visits would be at public expense and would last about three days. The Chatham Band was given Combined Operations bases at Southend, Brightlingsea and Burnham-on-Crouch and the 4th Special Service Brigade.

The band went on morale boosting tours and made numerous broadcasts at home and abroad. They played at Antwerp, in the Scheldt defences, Walcheren, Brussels, Nijmegen and Paris. This band was flown to Berlin to lead the Victory Parades. On the 21st July the band led the RN Guard at the head of the official march past of British troops before Winston Churchill. They were the only band in the procession.

1947 brought the restart of the Royal Tournament; the Chatham Group Band appeared with Musicians from Plymouth and Portsmouth Groups and the RNSM. In 1948 the band, together with the Portsmouth Group Band and the St Paul's Cathedral Choir played at the unveiling of the Franklin D Roosevelt statue in Grosvenor Square. 1949 saw what was to be the last involvement of the Chatham Group Band during the Remembrance weekend. They were massed with the Portsmouth Band for the Festival at the Royal Albert Hall where their Director of Music Capt T Francis conducted both the Royal Marines and the Brigade of Guards playing Handel's *Largo*. The Silver Memorial Fanfare Trumpeters of the RNSM were used to great effect during this piece of music.

On the 8th December 1949 the Royal Marines received the Freedom of the Borough of Chatham in the RM Barracks.

The Final Parade of the Colours of the Old Chatham Division, which took place on the 27th June 1950, was a poignant, but proud, affair. Next day, Whit Sunday, the Colours were laid up in Rochester Cathedral. On the 14th August 1950, the RM Barracks at Chatham closed and the First Grand Division, Chatham, ceased to exist.

The White Rose of York

Chapter 4: The Portsmouth Band up to 1923

It is believed that this is the oldest of the full Divisional bands, as opposed to a drum and fife band, being formed in 1765. The oldest documentary evidence of a band is dated 1776 when the Colonel Commandant wrote to the Admiralty asking for funds to "buy a pair of French Horns, ours being worn out". It could be that the instruments that needed replacing were the original instruments and this, allowing a serviceable life of ten years, would corroborate the suggested date of origin as 1765.[1]

On the 10th March 1767 an agreement was signed with Mr Antonio Rocca to be enrolled as a 'Private Marine on 2nd April 1767, but to be given his discharge when obligations cease'. He was to be allowed to play at balls and concerts for his own advantage with the Commanding Officer's permission, but the service to come first. In the following year there is an order of 11th June for the band to wear white breeches and stockings with black-buckled garters at Guard Mounting.[2]

On Tuesday 23rd June 1773 the King came to Portsmouth to review the Fleet and Establishments. Prior to his arrival the Plymouth Band was ordered to Portsmouth to assist in covering the number of dinners, salutes and Guards and Bands that would be required.[3]

Although no explanation is given, Lt Gen Smith "orders that the band of music of this Division do not play anywhere but on duty on the parade without the permission of the Commanding Officer of the Division".[4] In December 1797 the Portsmouth Division Band and a Captain's Guard marched from Portsmouth to London to accompany the King to St Paul's Cathedral to attend a service with Officers who had taken part in the actions of the 1st June 1794, (Lord Howe's victory at the battle of Ushant), the 14th February 1797 (Battle of Cape St Vincent) and the 11th October 1797 (Battle of Camperdown). Originally the Divisional Colours were to be taken but this order was cancelled as the Colours captured from the enemy were to be carried instead.[5]

A Divisional letter-book contains the following letter written in 1802 from the Royal Marine Barracks Portsmouth, which at that time was Clarence Barracks in Old Portsmouth, to Mr Cramer of No 2 Pall Mall, London: "I am to request you will immediately transmit hither the undermentioned Musical Instruments and Articles for the Royal Marine Band at this Head Quarters' and for which on forwarding your bill to me, payment will be made. Seven C-Clarionetts; a sett of blank books.[6] I am Sir etc, etc George Elliot Maj-Genr." Another letter, dated the 4th October 1802, allows the Commanding Officer of the Division "to enlist a good Musician for the Royal Marine Band without bounty".[7] In the same letterbook are references to instruments being bought for the band, 3rd October 1802. In 1805 Maj Gen George Elliot ordered from Mr Thaw, Musical Instrument Maker, Red Lion Street, Holborn "an F Slide Trumpet with crooks and shanks complete".

At the beginning of 1815 the Master and principal performers of the Band of the Oxfordshire Militia (presumably being disestablished) volunteered for, and were accepted by, the Portsmouth Band.[8] In August of 1821 the band under John Smalley became the first band to sail on a Royal cruise, embarking in HMS *Action* to accompany the Royal

1 *Records of Portsmouth Division of Marines 1764-1800.*
2 *'History of the Royal Marine Divisions' 1931.*
3 *RM Records 1755-1792 (RMHS Special Pub No 2).*
4 *Standing Orders of the Portsmouth Division of Marines 1764-1793, Royal Marines Museum Archive.*
5 *Blumberg's précis of the Portsmouth Letterbooks, Royal Marines Museum Archive.*
6 *Manuscript paper.*
7 *Blumberg's précis of the Portsmouth Letterbooks, Royal Marines Museum Archive.*
8 *RM Records 1793-1836 (RMHS Special Pub No 4).*

Squadron to Ireland. The band was constantly in attendance when The Queen was on board the Royal Yacht. In 1824 Mr Arroll, who served as bandmaster until 1847, replaced Smalley. During this period the band began presenting regular concerts at the Portsmouth Assembly Rooms.

James Gunnis, bassoon player with the Royal Marine Artillery until he transferred to the Portsmouth Division, Royal Marine Light Infantry

The next Bandmaster was James Gunnis who had been the bassoon player in the original Royal Marine Artillery Band under ' Master of the Band' Thompson.

In 1848, soon after Gunnis had taken over, the Division moved from Clarence Barracks, Portsmouth to Forton Barracks at Gosport on the other side of Portsmouth Harbour and, the following year, Mr A Earle arrived as bandmaster and stayed for the next sixteen years. He formed the Division's orchestra in 1853 and, as a result of a number of successful visits to Osborne House to perform for Queen Victoria and the Prince Consort, the band accompanied the Royal couple on board the Royal Yacht for a visit to Cherbourg in 1858. The Divisional Officers appointed a German to replace Mr Earle. German civilian bandmasters were very much in vogue, possibly because of the closeness of the Royal Families at that period, and, as a result, Mr W Kreyer served with the band for nearly twenty years. He took the band of thirty on board HMS *Serapis* to accompany HRH The Prince of Wales on his 1875/1876 visit to India and Ceylon. As a result of this the band was awarded the Prince of Wales Plumes as an addition to the cap badge and helmet plate.

In January 1885 George Miller, bandmaster of the Royal Military College,[9] Sandhurst, Band was one of one hundred and fifteen applicants for the post vacated by Kreyer. He was the only Englishman on the short-list of six bandmasters for interview. As a result of his training, experience and immaculate references he was appointed to lead the Portsmouth Division Band, which he did for the next thirty-two years. He was the son of George Miller who had been Bandmaster of the 63rd Foot, later the 1st Bn. The Manchester Regt, before his retirement, and the father of another George Miller who eventually became Director of Music, Grenadier Guards. Miller continued to develop the special relationship that existed between the band and the Royal Family, the band crossing the Solent to play at Osborne House sixty-six times between 1890 and 1897.

At this time the orchestra consisted of five first violins; four second violins; three violas; two violoncellos; two double basses; two flutes; one oboe; two clarionets; two bassoons; two horns; one euphonium; two cornets; one trombone; one kettle Drummer and one bass drum. The 'double-handed' Musicians would convert to the following military band instrumentation: one piccolo; one flute, one oboe; two E*b* clarinets; nine B*b* cornets; one tenor clarinet; one bass clarinet; two bassoons; four horns; one baritone; one euphonium; five basses; four cornets; two trumpets; three trombones and two drums. It is interesting to note that amongst the list of soloists appears "Piccolo: Drum Major Shadwick".[10]

In 1887 Queen Victoria commissioned Dan Godfrey of the Grenadier Guards. He was the only bandmaster to be commissioned[11] until, in 1898, The Queen conferred the

9 Royal Military Academy was at Woolwich, Royal Military College was at Sandhurst. Amalgamated in 1947.

10 'Music and Musicians at the Edinburgh International Exhibition 1886' by R A Marr.

11 S Griffiths was commissioned on the 24/12/1890 and E C Stretton on the 25/03/1896, both as Director of Music at Kneller Hall where they held teaching posts. Zavertal, Charles Godfrey and Miller were the first Musicians in command of working bands to be commissioned since Dan Godfrey. Miller was also the first military Musician to become a Bachelor of Music (1892).

Mr (later Major) George Miller. Bandmaster of the Portsmouth Division, RMLI 1885 – 1917

same honour upon George Miller of the Portsmouth Division, RMLI, Ladislao Zavertal of the Royal Artillery and Charles Godfrey of the Royal Horse Guards. These commissions were honorary. In 1893 The Queen presented Miller with a specially inscribed baton which is now held by the Royal Marines Museum. On the 15th November 1899 the honorary rank bestowed upon George Miller was made substantive.[12] After a fine record of service to Queen Victoria one of the first Royal Duties of the 20th century for Honorary Second Lieutenant G Miller and his Portsmouth RMLI Band was, massed with the Band of the RMA, her funeral. They played the procession from Osborne House to Trinity Pier, East Cowes, being relieved by their own drums massed with those of the RMA. The Band played the Beethoven and Chopin *funeral marches* and the massed drums, without bugles or fifes, played Miller's *Solemn March*. This had been selected by Queen Victoria to be played at the funeral of Prince Henry.[13] The band also played as the Royal Family and others boarded the Royal Yacht, *Victoria and Albert*; the body being conveyed on the Royal Yacht *Alberta*. A Guard of Honour with the Band and King's Colour of the Portsmouth Division RMLI was mounted at Clarence Yard during the disembarkation of the King and the Royal Family and the remains of the late Queen. The Band of the RMLI was then in attendance the next day when, at Gosport Station, the coffin was transferred to the train for London.

At the Coronation Review, Aldershot, in 1902 an event took place that was to have a far-reaching effect for RM Bands. The massed bands of the four RM Divisions, under the Senior Bandmaster Second Lieutenant Miller, were to accompany the RM Brigade. Knowing the importance of drums in playing a march past on a large scale, Miller had ordered the bands to bring as many Drummers from the Divisional Corps of Drums as they could manage. Three of the Bands ignored this and brought only one or two percussionist side Drummers. Portsmouth Band had brought a Corps of Drums that numbered between thirty and forty and so George Miller decided to prove a point. At the church parade before the review he massed all of his drums and the sound of them with the massed bands as they played the hymns, particularly *Onward Christian Soldiers* was said to have equalled the effect of any cathedral organ. It would appear that it is with this event that the tradition of the bands of the Royal Marines always marching with a large Corps of Drums to the front of their bands began. Miller's point, and therefore the basis of the tradition, was not just that Royal Marines Bands march with drums leading, but that Royal Marines Bands have a large Corps of Drums leading, in order to provide a very effective rhythm section, essential for a marching band.

Medals were awarded to selected individuals for their participation in the 1902 Coronation celebrations by the King. Second Lieutenant Bandmaster George Miller received a Silver Coronation Medal whilst a Bronze Medal was awarded to Colour Sergeant E S Keen, the RMLI Portsmouth Drum Major.[14]

This band often went to Glasgow to take part in the Glasgow Trades Exhibition and 1903 was no exception. Permission was given for the band to remain for an additional week after completion of their engagement and this allowed the band to earn enough money to pay for a cor anglais and another violin. These instruments could not have been afforded any other way.

12 *General Orders, Royal Marines 1900 GO16.*
13 *Blumberg's Random Records – Vol 3'.*
14 *General Orders, Royal Marines 1902 GO103.*

Forton Barracks Gosport, home of the Portsmouth Division, Royal Marine Light Infantry until the amalgamation of 1923. At that time the bronze cannon was taken to Eastney Barracks where it is now held as part of the Collections of the Royal Marines Museum. (From an original by Frank Woods)

During 1903 Lt Miller raised the subject of manpower losses as a direct result of Royal Yacht service. This service prevented Yacht Musicians from supplementing their earnings through private band and orchestral engagements and through tuition. Also, whilst on the Royal Yacht, Musicians' families were not able to make reduced rate purchases from the NAAFI. None of the Musicians had enlisted to go to sea so Royal Yacht duty was regarded as a drain on their income and an inconvenience rather than a pleasure or an honour. The Band President, through the Adjutant, added that Army bandsmen would be entitled to separation allowance under such circumstances and forwarded the report on the matter. The situation was reported to the King by his Extra Equerry, Commodore Sir A Berkeley Milne. Whilst Milne had suggested that the two bands (the RMA and the Portsmouth RMLI) should each be increased by ten men, the Admiralty disagreed and said that the RMA Band should be increased by ten men to raise it to a complement of fifty and, whenever the King required a band for the Royal Yacht, a band of twenty including a Bandmaster would be provided by them. Each man would receive an additional shilling per day, whilst embarked, to cover expenses.[15] The King would meet this expense and also the cost of instruments for the additional ten men. The cost to the King was actually reduced since the initial cost of the instruments was £160 with an estimated annual cost of £45 for the additional Musicians which he would set against the annual gratuities, in excess of £300, that he had been giving to the band and which, under the formalised arrangements, he deemed to be no longer necessary.[16]

It is interesting to note that in 1905 Sir Berkeley Milne, by then a Rear-Admiral, and whilst on the '*Victoria and Albert*' at Cowes, wrote the following: "Up to the end of 1903, the Bands of the RMLI (Po) and RMA embarked alternately, whether for a long or short cruise, but the cruise to Copenhagen in September and October 1903 was the last time the RMLI Band came".[17] This dispels the story that the RMLI band fell from grace as a result of a social blunder by Lt Miller in offering the King a cigar - the reason was simply a business decision prompted by unsound judgement on the part of the RMLI Officers involved. At some point Milne also proposed that the King might confer a special badge upon the Royal Yacht Band to mark the distinguished nature of their employment.

In 1905 Lt Miller wrote to Colonel Commandant, Portsmouth Division RMLI, regarding the age of retirement of Musicians, which was 40. Miller reasoned that, since Musicians were at their peak at this age, other Services were benefitting by hiring highly trained and competent, retiring Royal Marine Musicians, whilst other specialists such as tailors and shoemakers were retained because of their expertise. Miller suggested that Musicians should be pensioned at forty and then re-enlisted, thereby saving training costs.[18] It is not known what response this letter received.

15 *General Orders, Royal Marines 1904 GO64.*
16 *'Scheme for Band for HM Yacht' - RMM Archive.*
17 *'Band for HM Yacht' - RMM Archive.*
18 *Original hand written draft in RMM Archive.*

Second Lieutenant Bandmaster George Miller was appointed a Director of Music and given the Honorary rank of Major on the 14th May 1914.[19] The Portsmouth Band was the first of the Divisional bands to be sent to France during World War I. They went there in 1916, playing not only for the RMLI Battalions of the 63rd (RN) Division but also for the RMA howitzers in that sector. They met the 2nd Bn at Abbeville and played them to rest billets at Rue, after the battle of the Ancre. Major Miller was taken ill and had to return to England a few weeks in advance of his band, which returned in January 1917. As a result of his illness Major Miller was invalided from the Royal Marines after thirty-two years' service.[20] During the period that he led this band it was honoured with more commissions from Royalty than any other band. It has been said that no Bandmaster in any service has received so many Royal acknowledgements for duty done, for pleasure given, or for the band's worth.[21]

Lt B W O'Donnell succeeded Major Miller. During an interview[22] and in response to criticism that Service bands were too quick to perform programmes made up of musical comedy selections and other 'trivial' music, he described the types of musical programme that his military band and the orchestra were performing. Typical orchestral and military concert programmes, recently performed on south coast piers, included Smetana's overture *The Bartered Bride*, *Scotch Rhapsody No 1* (Mackenzie), *Capriccio Italien* (Tchaikovsky) and Svendsen's *Norwegian Rhapsody* played by the orchestra and Wagner's *Entry of the Gods into Valhalla*, Grieg's *Solveig's Song*, the suite *Pantomime* by Lacombe and Liszt's R*hapsody Number 1* played by the military band.

In 1922 the bands of the RMA and of the Portsmouth and Plymouth Divisions RMLI gave a massed concert in Glasgow - the Musical Directors being the three brothers, Lieutenants Percival Sylvester George, Bertram Walton and Rudolph Peter O'Donnell respectively.

When the RMA and the RMLI were amalgamated in 1923 the members of the Portsmouth RMLI band became the Band of the Depot RM, still led by Lt B W O'Donnell, and retaining the famous Prince of Wales Plumes in addition to its cap badge. This had been awarded to the band in 1876 for its service to the Prince of Wales during the voyage to India on HMS *Serapis*.

Prince of Wales' Plumes

19 *General Orders, Royal Marines 1914 GO58.*
20 *Major George John Miller was placed on the retired list as from the 3rd March 1917 owing to medical unfitness. (GO 1917).*
21 *Tanner's unpublished encyclopaedia.*
22 *The Musical Times 1st Aug 1919.*

Chapter 5: The Plymouth Band

Bugler William John Phillips, Plymouth Division RMLI, c.1875

John Greenfield, Drum Major of the Plymouth Division 1875-1886

The Officers of the Division decided to form a band in 1766 and, in the following year, eight Musicians were engaged as the 'Band of Musick'. The first mention of them occurs in Plymouth Orders 12th January 1767 and refers to the payment of subscriptions by the Officers to purchase instruments. Amongst the Musicians was Antonio Rocca who was paid 2/6d a week to teach the others. Four years later the newly-formed Royal Artillery Band at Woolwich enticed Rocca from Plymouth by offering him 1/6d a day. In 1768, at roll call and at guard mounting, the band wore white stockings and breeches with black buckled gaiters. William Gilbourn succeeded Rocca but he was sacked for "being incapable of teaching a martial band and not able to teach the softer musick".[1] He was replaced in 1783, the same year as the band moved into the newly erected Stonehouse Barracks, by 'Master of the Band' James Parsons who was promoted from within the band. Parsons was told to instruct the fifers in martial music whilst Lieutenants Gibson and Gordon had volunteered to make the band 'capable of the softer musick'. Parsons was succeeded by Mr Ashweek in 1796 and then Thomas Stockham from 1822 until 1845. It is not known who succeeded Stockham but, in 1851, Thomas Winterbottom, a civilian, was appointed as 'Master of the Band'.[2] During this period the 'Master of the Band' continued to play his own instrument and did not conduct in the manner of today. Thomas died whilst serving (1869) and was succeeded by his younger brother William, who was the first to be referred to as Band Master. At about this time the bandsmen's uniform was white tunics with scarlet collars and cuffs, and scarlet trousers with white braided stripes.[3] William had already served with the RMLI Woolwich Division Band as had another family member, Henry. Four years later William exchanged positions with the Bandmaster of the 2nd Life Guards, Carl F H Froehnert - a native of Saxony who had been sponsored by the Prince Consort. Froehnert served with the band until his death in 1890. Neither he nor his fellow countryman Jacob Kappey of the Chatham Division wore uniform until 1883 when their bands were massed for a special occasion. Froehnert would return from visits to Germany with new band music including *Turkish Patrol* which the Plymouth Band claim to be the first band to play in this country. He became a naturalised British subject, was made a Corps Warrant Officer in 1881 (when the Warrant rank was first introduced into the Royal Marines) and, in 1875, became Inspecting Bandmaster of HM Training Ships in Devonport. Since the practice of Royal Marines inspecting the Bands of the Training Ships only began in 1874 Froehnert must have been one of the first to perform this duty.

In 1880 when playing at the ceremony for the laying of the foundation stone of Truro Cathedral the band attracted the attention of the Prince and Princess of Wales who asked them to play, as an orchestra, for various social functions. A new Troop, composed by Edwin Binding, a Musician, was played

1 *'As only the idle and dissipated soldier can have a wish to be out of his quarters after the close of the day, neither Serjeant, Corporal, Drummer, Musick or Private Marine are to have leave to be absent, except two married men from each parade company' – Plymouth Division Daily Order-Books 1782 – 1791, entry for 25 Nov 1787 quoted in 'Records of the Portsmouth Division of Royal Marines 1764-1800 – Portsmouth Record Series', City of Portsmouth publication.*

2 *Maj G Turner (History of British Military Bands Volume I) states Thomas Winterbottom was appointed in 1845.*

3 *Tanner's encyclopaedia.*

The Band of the Plymouth Division, Royal Marine Light Infantry, c.1880. Their Bandmaster Carl Froehnert is on the right of the picture wearing civilian clothes

on this occasion. In 1875 Binding, who had served as a Musician throughout his career, received his Naval Long Service and Good Conduct Medal, was promoted Sergeant "and was appointed Bugle Major".[4] A few years later the band returned to play at the Dedication of Truro Cathedral. On this occasion they performed as a military brass band but, for an unknown reason, wore choristers' surplices over their full dress uniform!

Upon Froehnert's death in 1890 another Winterbottom, Frank, the nephew of William, succeeded him. Frank was the first to join as a Warrant Officer Bandmaster. William had taught Frank the techniques of military band scoring and Frank was able to develop this skill to such a high degree that many of his military band arrangements of the classics remain in use. When the Division received new Colours in 1896 Winterbottom directed both the Divisional Band and the Drum and Fife Band.

Yet again, at the beginning of the twentieth century a RM Divisional Band, in this case the Plymouth Division, was held in high regard and had a very fine Musician leading it.

Mr F Winterbottom continued to lead the Plymouth Band until 1910. In 1902 the band had the honour of playing on board the HM Yacht *Victoria and Albert* for the King who then ordered them to return to play during the following evening, the 9th March 1902. On this occasion he presented Bandmaster Frank Winterbottom with the medal of the Royal Victorian Order.[5]

One of his greatest achievements was the success of his fortnightly symphony concerts that were held during the winter. They began in the Royal Hotel, Plymouth, but were soon moved to the Town Hall at Stonehouse because of the huge demand for seats. Even then the concerts soon became season-ticket holders only - such was the demand. His final concert proved to be a surprise to Mr Winterbottom because the Chairman of the Stonehouse District Council presented him with the proceeds! It was a joint orchestral concert featuring the Plymouth Division RMLI Band and the Band of the Royal Garrison Artillery.[6]

CSgt J J Moyse and son Ernest 1905. JJ Moyse joined as a 14 year old Bugler at Plymouth in 1883. He served on HMS Superb and then joined HMS Euryalus as part of the RM Brigade bound for Egypt in 1884. He was invalided home with fever and transferred to the ranks in 1887. He had five sons, all of whom served with Plymouth Division during WW1. His son Ernest, seen here, joined in 1909 and was invalided out in 1919. He and his father served together during the Defence of Ostend

4 *Blue Band July 1974 p91.*
5 *General Orders, Royal Marines 1902 GO44 and G & L 1902 Editorial and pages 40/41.*
6 *'Western Weekly Mercury' 24th Sept 1910.*

In 1910 Mr J Newton became Bandmaster. In 1894 he had been Trumpet Major, Prince of Wales' Own Norfolk Artillery. Newton was well respected by his band and received the congratulations of many including King George V. He may well have carved out an excellent career but, sadly, he was taken ill and died in June 1916.

Bandmaster P S G O'Donnell, Director of Music – Plymouth Divisional Band

The band then passed into the very capable hands of Mr Percy O'Donnell. He served with the Plymouth Band from 1916 to 1928, being commissioned in 1921. The band embarked upon a concert tour of the Western Front in 1917 winning great acclaim from the Staff Officers and from the troops, particularly for the impromptu performances that the band provided anywhere and at any time. The following year the band returned to France for a further extensive tour of the front line areas. Because of its high standard of playing it was selected to be resident band at the first post-war 'Royal Naval, Military and Air Force Tournament' - later the Royal Tournament and then, as a tribute to its dedication to duty during the war years, it was invited to accompany the Prince of Wales (later King Edward VIII) on a post World War I morale-raising tour to Canada in the battle-cruiser HMS *Renown*. For the duration of this tour he was temporarily appointed Director of Music with the rank of Lieutenant.[7] They returned to the UK four months later and the Prince was so impressed with the band that he asked them to accompany him to Australia, once again in HMS *Renown* and with O'Donnell as a Lieutenant, Director of Music. The two successful tours, and in particular the band's part in them, were acknowledged by the presentation, in 1920, of the Prince of Wales plumes to be worn as part of the cap-badge.[8] In the same year Bandmaster (Acting Director of Music) P S G O'Donnell was appointed a Member of the Fifth Class of the Royal Victorian Order.

Musician W Rawlings of Plymouth Division wearing Divisional tunic with medals in 1921

The 1923 amalgamation of the RMLI and the RMA had little effect upon this band apart from the change of title and the change to a blue uniform.

In 1928 Lt O'Donnell transferred to the Chatham Division where he became Senior Director of Music of the Corps. Lt G W E Grayson replaced O'Donnell at Plymouth but he retired two years later on the 1st May 1931.[9]

Probably the best known of all British military Musicians, Lt F J Ricketts, who was equally well known as the composer Kenneth Alford, joined from the Depot, RM in September 1930. He took the Plymouth Band to Kelvin Hall, Glasgow for almost two weeks in September and October. Lt F J Ricketts was promoted Captain (Director of Music) on the 4th July 1935.

For the Coronation of HM King George VI in 1937 the band, with a Royal Guard of Honour found by the Corps, was positioned outside Westminster Abbey.[10] Ricketts took the Plymouth Band to Paris for the 150th Anniversary of the fall of the Bastille in 1939 before boarding the RMS *Empress of Australia* to visit the Canadian National Exhibition at Toronto. He was a great believer in the necessity of rehearsal and he used the journey to full effect. Glowing press notices regarding the tour performances were received by the band. 1939 was an exceptionally busy year as Major Ricketts also found time to make ten records for HMV. In 1940 Maj Ricketts went back to the recording studio to make a further five recordings.

---

7 *General Orders, Royal Marines 1918.*

8 *General Orders, Royal Marines 1920 GO206. - helmet plates not mentioned.*

9 *General Orders, Royal Marines 1931GO20.*

10 *Coronation Orders for RN and RM in London - RMM Archive.*

As has been described earlier, from 1st January 1944 the Divisional Bands were ordered to make quarterly visits to a number of RM Establishments, formations and Units in the United Kingdom. Plymouth Band was given the School of Signalling RM, the Signal Holding Company, the Royal Marines Military School, the Home Based Ledger Office and the RM Support Craft Regiment[11] at Wimborne. Maj Ricketts was due to retire in 1940 but, in view of the war situation, his Service was extended. However, in 1944 he was forced to retire due to ill health. During the period 1940-1944 Ricketts and his band toured extensively and broadcast on many occasions.

Candidates for the Plymouth Band vacancy had to have experience as a Director of Music, or Conductor of Military Bands or Orchestra of standing. Eighty-one applications were received and ten were selected for interview. Of the seventy-one applications that were rejected fifty-one were from the Army, seven were civilians, six were from the RNSM, one each from the RN and the RM. One application came from New Zealand and two from Canada. The Board unanimously decided that the best candidate and the most suitable for the appointment was Bandmaster C Nalden of the Royal Artillery (Portsmouth) Band. Second choice was Commissioned Bandmaster R H Stoner the Port Bandmaster, Staff of C-in-C Portsmouth. The GOCRM, Maj Gen T L Hunton, decided that Lt Stoner should be appointed and wrote to the First Sea Lord to seek final approval. The recommendation was approved.[12]

During the remaining war years the band, as part of a large composite band, under their new Director of Music, toured Holland and Normandy and led British troops through Paris from the Arc de Triomphe immediately following the liberation of that city. On the previous evening the band had played in the Champs Elysees until dusk. An extensive tour of Ceylon, India, Burma and Siam took place in 1946 during which they participated in the Peace Celebrations in Bangkok, the Victory Parade in Delhi and many important functions for His Excellency the Viceroy of India and the Supreme Commander, South East Asia. On the 9th January 1946 the band, comprising elements of the three Divisional bands at Chatham, Portsmouth and Plymouth and the RNSM (and bearing the name HM RM Far East Band), performed a Ceremonial Beat Retreat on the Padang, Singapore. It is interesting to note that the musical programme contains five of Kenneth Alford's marches - perhaps Capt Stoner used it as a tribute to his predecessor who had died eight months earlier.[13]

Plymouth Division Band and Drums, 27th April 1944. In the second row, commencing from left are: Adjt, Major R J Buckley then Bugle Major T Baker, Cpl L Negus and Sgt Banning (two often featured soloists), BdSgt Redmore and Capt Ricketts. On the extreme right of this row is Drum Major T Cooke

Tragically Major Ricketts' death occurred only a year after his enforced retirement at the age of sixty-five, but he left a legacy of recorded and written music the quality of which will probably never be equalled. He had contributed a total of fifty years' service to military music in the Army and the Royal Marines.

In 1947 the title of the band was changed to the Band of HM Royal Marines (Plymouth Group).

---

11 *Later RM Armoured Support Group.*

12 *All documents relating to this - RMM Archive.*

13 *Globe & Laurel 1944 and 1946.*

Chapter 6: The Woolwich Band 1805 to 1869

Woolwich Division (the 'Fourth Division') was established on the 15th August 1805. However, the earliest known image of a band at the Woolwich Division is in the caption to a sketch by J Scharf which says "At the Marine Officers Mess Room at Woolwich, during dinner, 1826". A note in the right hand margin adds "Mr Bean, the leader of the band, took me there".[1]

Another drawing shows Bands of the Royal Marines, with a six hundred strong Royal Marines Detachment marching with arms reversed, at the funeral of the Duke of Wellington on the 18th November 1851. It is reported that the bands of the Chatham and Woolwich Divisions were massed for this occasion. Little other information exists since the Woolwich Division and its band had a short existence, being stood down in 1869.

However, a story relating to the Woolwich Band was recorded even earlier, in July 1820, when a dispute occurred between the Officer of the Barrack Guard and the Master of the Band, Serjeant Tully, regarding the playing of *God Save the King*. During the dispute, it was later claimed, some of the Band muttered that they would sooner play *God Save The Queen* - which was tantamount to treason. Following a series of charges and counter charges, upon which Gilbert and Sullivan could have constructed an excellent light opera, the whole affair, which had involved Lt Col 'Fighting' Nicholls, regarded as a legend in his own time, was resolved.[2]

It is known that during the 1850s the daily guard mounting at Woolwich was an impressive sight with music being played by the Royal Marine Divisional Band and also the Royal Artillery Band. On completion the Royal Artillery Band marched its Guard to the Royal Arsenal and the Royal Marines Guard and Band marched into the Royal Dockyard.

The original captions, including mistakes, are: "Mr Bean, the leader of the band took me there. J Scharfdel at the Marine Officers Mess Room at Woolwhich , during Dinner, 1826"

1 Used in the manuscript version of 'Britain's Sea Soldiers' by Col C Field RMLI. Photographic copy held in the Royal Marines Museum.
2 'Woolwich Crisis of 1820' – Archive of the Royal Marines Museum.

Chapter 7: The Royal Marine Artillery Band to 1923, then the Portsmouth Band

It was Admiral Lord Nelson himself who suggested that a force of artillery should be created and maintained under Admiralty control. In 1804 an Order-in-Council established the Royal Marine Artillery as an alternative to "the inconveniences attending the embarking detachments of Royal Artillery on board Your Majesty's Bomb-Vessels". A Company from the RMA was to be quartered at each of the Divisional Headquarters. In 1816 all of the companies were transferred to Chatham. The Band of the Royal Marine Artillery (RMA) was established at Chatham in 1823. A year previously the Division's Major Commandant[1], Lt Col Sir Richard Williams, asked the Admiralty for a similar band allowance to that which was available to the RMLI Divisions, the Royal Artillery and other Regiments. The Colonel Commandant, Royal Marines, at Chatham was authorised to enlist fourteen boys as private marines, to be transferred to the RMA and formed into a band. Mr Thompson, a clarinettist, was appointed Master of the Band and James Gunnis is believed to have been the band's bassoonist. During 1832 the RMA were reduced in strength and the band was disestablished. Whilst most of the Musicians joined the Royal Navy, Gunnis and two others joined the RMLI Band, Portsmouth Division.

In 1861 Colonel John Fraser, RMA, applied for, and was granted, permission to form a Divisional Band of the same strength as those at the Royal Marine Light Infantry Divisions: forty-six Musicians and eight Boy Musicians. The band was formed at the isolated Fort Cumberland, the large star-fort standing at the south-east tip of Portsmouth and guarding the approaches to Langstone Harbour. It was only in 1859 that the sixteen separate Companies of the Royal Marines Artillery had been formed into a new, composite, Division.

Upon the formation of the band in 1861 the RMA march past was chosen as Gounod's 'The Soldiers Chorus' from *Faust*; and so it remained until 1882 when *A Life on the Ocean Wave* was adopted. Thomas Smyth, who had previously served as the Bandmaster of the Royal Marines Woolwich Division during 1856 and 1857, was appointed its first Bandmaster. The band remained at the fort until 1868 when Eastney Barracks was built and occupied. Eastney Village stood midway between the Fort and the site of the barracks; the village comprised some seven cottages, two ponds, musketry ranges, huts... and a bandstand. This must have been where Thomas Smyth conducted the Royal Marine Artillery Band and entertained civilians and military men alike. Sadly nothing now remains of the bandstand or the cottages. All were overtaken by the increasing size of the military estate.

Similarly, nothing now seems to remain to give an indication of what the band's founding bandmaster, Thomas Smyth looked like. However, in May 1868, at a time when the band could have moved into the new barracks, or might still have been at Fort Cumberland, the Division was inspected by General Travis on Southsea Common. They were drawn up in marching order at Eastney Barracks, alongside what became known as Gunner's Walk, before marching from the barracks to the common.

The Drum Major is wearing a bearskin whilst the Musicians wear the busby, but why? Quite probably this was due to the fact that the RMA did tend to model its uniform upon that of the Royal Artillery and, in 1855, the Royal Artillery Band had changed from wearing the shako to wearing a busby as part of their 'Engagement Dress'. Of special interest is the figure standing to the left. He is slightly isolated and appears to be carrying a

1 *Royal Marine Artillery Vol. I p313.*

One of the first photographs taken at Eastney showing the Division drawn up with the band at the head. The band is shown in detail below

euphonium or a similar instrument. He wears a pouche-belt and a plain tunic without the famous 'lion-tamers' cording and lace. He also has a rank badge on his sleeve and has medals. Could this be Thomas Smyth? Alternatively, at the opposite end stands another slightly isolated figure but this chap is wearing both a pouche-belt and the RMA Band tunic. However he does not appear to be carrying a musical instrument. Could this fellow be Thomas Smyth? Perhaps we do now have an image

of the original RMA Bandmaster – but which is he? It is believed that Thomas Smyth is the figure on the right of the front rank because it is likely that the figure on the left in the plain tunic is the Bugle Major since the Buglers, to the rear of the band, are also in plain tunics – possibly a practice also copied from the Royal Artillery. Other points of commonality with the Royal Artillery are that the RA Bandmaster also wore a pouche-belt, whilst Musicians did not, and the Drum Major retained the bearskin.

Two years later Smyth left the band and was succeeded by John Winterbottom, one of the large family of Royal Marine Bandmasters. An Order-in-Council of 1881 introduced the Warrant rank into the Corps and John Winterbottom, like Kappey, Kreyer and Froehnert at Chatham, Portsmouth and Plymouth respectively, was given a seniority as a Warrant Officer of that date.

In 1892 John Winterbottom left to take charge of the Band of the Artists Rifles and was replaced by Albert Williams who was to remain at Eastney until 1897. He became the Bandmaster of the Grenadier Guards and, later, the Senior Director of Music of the Brigade of Guards. By this time approximately thirty years had elapsed since Smyth's band had made the move from Fort Cumberland to Eastney Barracks. So, apart from entertaining officers in the Mess and civilians at concerts and on the bandstand, what else did the band do during that period?

Military Bands have been likened to 'the first military transport department' since their primary role was to move groups of men around at a constant, standard pace with rousing, heartening, music. With the very large area occupied by the RMA, with the amount of varied training that was conducted in that area and also the number of men, the band

Lt John Winterbottom, Bandmaster of the Royal Marine Artillery, 1870 – 1892

Mr Albert Williams, Bandmaster from 1892-1897

would have been kept very busy, with training and rehearsals. On Sundays there was Church parade and there would also have been a great number of inspections and VIP visitors to entertain and/or to impress. It was little wonder that the Buglers shared these tasks.

In 1897 Bernard Steven Green, Bandmaster of the Duke of York's Royal Military School for Boy's joined the Royal Marine Artillery as Albert Williams' replacement. The policy of transferring Musicians between the services continued at this time, Bandsman W Bunnell of the 14th Hussars joining the RMA Divisional Band.[2] Later in the year Musician John Burns went in the opposite direction, moving from the RMA to join the Band of the Grenadier Guards.[3] Another Hussar, Cpl G T Tristam of the 10th, joined for service in the RMA band[4] and, in November, Musician John Box left the RMA for the Irish Guards Band.[5] In 1902 Musician R Burke left the RMA band to join the Royal Navy as a Bandmaster.[6] It is to be wondered if he found himself being offered the choice of leaving the Royal Navy or transferring to the new Royal Naval School of Music in 1903. Musician J Stamborough then joined from the Army.

Musician Alfred Bushell, RMA, with family at Eastney. Bushell joined the RMA from an Army band, possibly the Staffordshire Regiment, in 1884. He married Miss Amy Barnes who lived in Eastney Barracks and was employed by the Barracks Canteen Committee to work as a barmaid. Shortly after their marriage, Musician Bushell was given permission, as a married man, to live outside the Barracks. They lived at 16 St George's Road, Eastney. The Colonel Commandant, wrote on Bushell's application, "I certify that this residence is within the prescribed limits. It is a healthy locality". Bushell wears the distinctive Khedive's Bronze Medal for service during the Egyptian campaign of 1882-5. He must have been awarded this as a result of his earlier Army service

The beginning of the new century brought, under Bandmaster B S Green, a continuation of the Band's service to the Monarchy. Numerous visits to Osborne House as well as aboard the Royal Yacht *Victoria and Albert* included attendance upon the new King, Edward VII, in 1902 when he took a trip in the Royal Yacht to help restore his health. In early November 1903 the King gazetted the RMA Band as the permanent Royal Yacht Band but, in 1904, the Lords of the Admiralty made it clear that Bandsmen embarked in HM Yacht were not necessarily to be members of the RMA Band.[7] In 1902 Musician S G Mortlock left the RMA Band to join the Royal Artillery for service on the Permanent Staff of the Edinburgh Artillery Militia.[8] During the same year Bandmaster B S Green was awarded a Bronze Coronation Medal and Band Sergeant Thomas Holding the Royal Victorian

2 *General Orders, Royal Marines 1901 GO58.*
3 *General Orders, Royal Marines 1901 GO104.*
4 *General Orders, Royal Marines 1901 GO127.*
5 *General Orders, Royal Marines 1901 GO138.*
6 *General Orders, Royal Marines 1902 GO27.*
7 *General Orders, Royal Marines 1904 GORM GO64.*
8 *General Orders, Royal Marines 1902 GO61.*

Captain B S Green MVO RM, Director of Music, Royal Marine Artillery 1897 to 1919. He wears a black crepe armband, possibly because of the death of Queen Victoria

Medal in Bronze.[9] Transfers continued as Musician R Portelli left to join the Band of the Irish Guards.[10] whilst Musician F A Armitage and Musician A Howe left to join the Coldstream Guards and the Royal Garrison Artillery respectively.[11]

During 1911 King George V and Queen Mary travelled to India for the Delhi Durbar on board the P&O liner *Medina* with the RMA Band in attendance. The Durbar itself was a magnificent occasion. The Massed Bands of the RMA and the RM Bands of HMS *Defence*, HMS *Cochrane* and HMS *Argyll* played the first four bars of the National Anthem. After the completion of the one hundred and one gun salute the Massed Bands played the first verse of the National Anthem and then *A Life on the Ocean Wave* and the Naval Brigade led the massive march past. As the battalions of infantry marched past, the bands played the appropriate regimental marches.[12] As a result of this service to the Monarch, the band was awarded a special forage cap badge consisting of a gilt grenade on which was mounted the Royal Cypher 'GvR' and crown in silver, all surrounded by a gilt laurel wreath. This was to be worn by all NCOs and men of the RMA Band at all times instead of the current grenade.[13] It was in this year that Bandmaster Warrant Officer B S Green was commissioned as 2nd Lieutenant, 13th September 1911.[14]

The RMA Drum Major of about 1915. Although not positively identified this might be Drum Major Zwasnieski

During 1910 and 1911 Green and the RMA Band made a series of musical recordings for the Pathe Company; the music played included *Queen Alexandra* by Green, *Voices of the Past*, *Musical Inexactitude* and *The Jolly Coppersmith*. The following year 2nd Lieutenant (Bandmaster) B S Green was made a Member of the 5th Class of the Royal Victorian Order.[15] This was followed, on the 14th May 1914, by his appointment as Director of Music with the honorary rank of Lieutenant.[16] During the First World War, in 1917, Green took the Band of the RMA to France to entertain the troops. On the 14th November it was announced[17] that Lieutenant Benjamin S Green, Director of Music, had been placed on the supernumerary list where he would remain until the end of the war, or shortly after, when he would retire. He was due to retire on the 31st October 1919 but this was post-dated until the arrival of his successor, Lieutenant R P O'Donnell.[18] The hand-over and retirement actually took place on the 17th December 1919[19] although Green's final retirement date was ante-dated to 14th May 1916.[20]

Corporal (Band) Thomas Herring was awarded the Royal Victorian Silver Medal in 1922. Two years later the same honour was bestowed upon CSgt (Band) William Henry Heighway.

During 1922 AFO 2522 for the wearing of a badge by the Royal Yacht Band had been issued. Due to the amalgamation of the RMLI and the RMA in 1923 this could not be progressed. The Portsmouth Division RMLI ceased to exist and the Band of the RMA became the Band of the Portsmouth Division, RM, with Lt R P O'Donnell as its first Director of Music. In 1925 the Commanding Officer, Royal Yachts (CORY) wrote, on behalf of the King, to the Adjutant General stating that the King wished the Portsmouth Division Royal Yacht Band to wear the words

9 *General Orders, Royal Marines 1902 GO105.*
10 *General Orders, Royal Marines 1902 GO121.*
11 *General Orders, Royal Marines 1903 GO91.*
12 *From "To India With the King and Queen".*
13 *General Orders, Royal Marines 1912 GO44.*
14 *General Orders, Royal Marines 1911 GO74.*
15 *General Orders, Royal Marines 1912 GO29.*
16 *General Orders, Royal Marines 1914 GO58.*
17 *General Orders, Royal Marines 1917 GO162.*
18 *General Orders, Royal Marines 1919 GO194.*
19 *General Orders, Royal Marines 1920.*
20 *General Orders, Royal Marines 1920.*

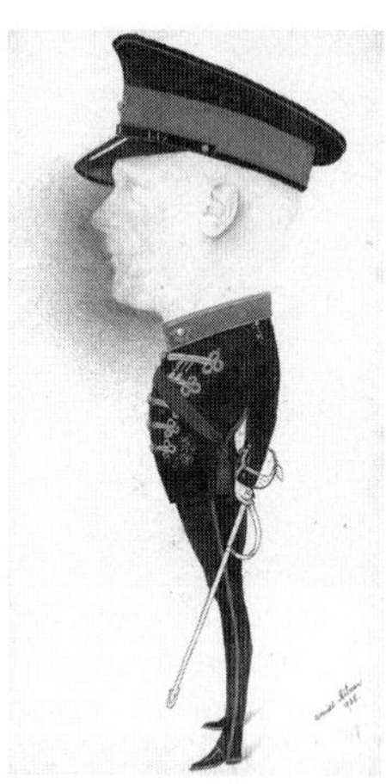

Jack Dacombe the Drum Major, Portsmouth Division from 1929-1941

Lt. (Later Lt Col) F Vivian Dunn, Director of Music, Portsmouth Division Royal Marines

'Royal Yacht' surmounted by a crown, in recognition of their service, and that of the RMA, to the King. The Rear Admiral also pointed out that the King would no doubt be aware that the special cap badge worn by the band had been specifically awarded for the 1911 trip to India in the *Medina* and therefore had no bearing on the current proposals that were designed to signify the association of the Band with the Royal Yacht. He also made it clear to the Adjutant General that the award to the Detachment was as a result of the award to the Band and not the other way around. On the bottom of the letter Rear Admiral Buller added a hand-written note dated 20th October 1925.[21] He stated that "No further correspondence took place, but the badge was issued to the whole band and to the Marine Detachment and was worn for the first time at Cowes - 1925. It is worn on the right sleeve only. On the cloth tunic it is worked in gold. On the serge tunic it is worked in red worsted. In the case of the band it is worn by all members and always".

In 1931 Capt R P O'Donnell left the Royal Marines to become Director of Music, and Officer in charge of the Royal Air Force Band and was succeeded by F Vivian Dunn, the last civilian to be appointed to lead a Royal Marines Band. He was granted the rank of Lieutenant.[22] Within four months of first wearing a RM uniform Lt Dunn found himself directing the Portsmouth Division Band when the Division was presented with new Colours by HRH Prince George, with the King watching, on Eastney Parade.

On the 25th November 1935 the Band joined with the Chatham Band and played at the funeral of the late Admiral of the Fleet, Earl Jellicoe. In 1935 the band was in attendance for the funeral of King George V and also the Jubilee Fleet Review and, in 1937, the Coronation Fleet Review. In the same year the Band accompanied King George VI and Queen Elizabeth to Ireland. A further Fleet Review took place in Weymouth in 1938. War was now on the horizon and, to quote Captain Derek Oakley, the author of 'Fiddler on the March',"...the Divisional bands... travelled the length and breadth of the country, playing concerts... broadcasting and performing on many ceremonial occasions. They helped to give the people of Great Britain a much-needed boost to their morale and in many ways it was a busier time than ever".

During 1940 Capt F V Dunn made a number of recordings for Columbia but, unlike Ricketts three years earlier, he elected to use the orchestra of Portsmouth Division rather than the military band. Further recordings were made by the orchestra in 1941. Capt Dunn always maintained that the recording studio was the ultimate expression of music and it seems as if he was smitten with the medium almost as soon as he became familiar with it. A year later he returned to make three more recordings.

Between 1942 and 1948 the Overseas Recorded Broadcasting Service (ORBS) made many variety programme style recordings that were distributed overseas for the entertainment of troops anywhere in the world. Capt Dunn and the Orchestra of the Portsmouth Division featured in a great many of these programme recordings, as did many RM dance bands, military bands and choirs.

In December 1943 the Portsmouth Band was also told to visit specific RM units and was given HQ Special Service Group, the Special Service Group Holding Commando, HQ RM Engineers and HMS *Northney*, previously the Sunshine

21 *All correspondence in the RMM Archive.*
22 *Refer to 'Fiddler on the March' by D Oakley.*

Holiday Camp on Hayling Island that was being used as a Landing Craft base. In 1945 the band went to Holland to play for the RM Commandos and the Royal Netherlands Navy. The band was also on parade for, and presented to, Prince Bernhard.

The first post-war Eastney Tattoo took place in 1947 featuring the recently re-named Portsmouth Group Band.

HMS *Vanguard* took the Royal Family on a tour to South Africa in 1947 and this provided the Band of the RM Portsmouth with a unique opportunity to show the world what a RM Group Band was capable of. A band of forty, plus fourteen Buglers, provided the capability of a full orchestra of forty, a military band of forty or a marching band of fifty-four. It also gave the facility of splitting into smaller groups to enable the large number of rehearsals and performances to be covered. Concerts were given twice daily, at lunch and at dinner, and in addition to these there would often be a need for music for ballroom and for Highland dancing, the latter requiring a special ensemble. Smaller combinations would play on the forecastle from 1000 - 1030, the upper deck or cinema from 1230 - 1315 as well as from 1730 - 1830 for the ship's company. A small band was used for occasional concerts in the Officers' Wardroom, or the Gunroom for the Midshipmen as well as elsewhere for the Warrant Officers and ship's company. Concert Party rehearsals were also necessary. Whilst in South Africa the Band played for Receptions, Royal Garden Parties, State Banquets, Beat Retreats and other ceremonial. In addition the Band undertook tours of the mining areas and visited and played in many of the country's cities and towns. After rejoining the ship they continued their work as the ship visited various ports. This included many radio broadcasts.

In 1948 the band, augmented from the Plymouth Band, visited France with a Guard of Honour and the Regimental Colour of RMB Eastney.[23] They also took part in the unveiling of the Roosevelt Memorial in London on the 12th April[24], a few days earlier.

1948 was the first year that the 23rd April, St George's Day, was commemorated as 'Corps Remembrance Day'. The band took part in a ceremonial parade at Eastney that included a march past and a Drumhead Service. Later they gave a concert and then, with the Buglers, played during the interval of the evening's ball. A week later the band were on parade in London for the 25th Wedding Anniversary of the King and Queen and the State Drive to St Paul's Cathedral. Later that day, augmented by members of the Chatham Band, they gave a concert at the foot of Nelson's Column to raise funds for King George's Fund for Sailors.

Grenade and Cypher Cap Badge

23 *'The Story of Colours in the Royal Marines'.*
24 *'Marcher' article Blue Band Spring 1998.*

Chapter 8: The Depot Band of the Royal Marines 1900 - 1930

On the 21st May 1890[1] the Admiralty supported the Depot request to replace seventeen Privates with Musicians so that a Band could be formed to promote discipline and good health amongst the recruits. This Band was increased in size in April 1900 when Sergeant[2] J S Nicholson was promoted to Warrant Officer on being appointed Bandmaster on the 1st April 1900.[3] A total of 15 men were added to bring this band up to the size of a standard band.[4] Although it was never a Divisional Band it had, from 1900, a similar structure. Inter-Service transfers were not limited to the Divisions; in March 1902 Bandsman A Templin, 4th Battalion Lancashire Fusiliers transferred for service at the Depot.

During 1901 it officially stood in for the Chatham Band which was on Royal duties. In 1902, at the Coronation of King Edward VII whilst the four Divisional bands had static positions lining the route, the Depot Band had the distinction of marching with the RMLI in the procession. By 1905 Bandmaster Nicholson had brought the orchestra to such a standard that it played at the Trafalgar Centenary Banquet. During the First World War the band was kept busy marching drafts of marines from the Depot to the railway station, en route to various parts of the world, including those who embarked upon the Zeebrugge raid.

On the 3rd March 1917 Bandmaster (WO1) James Sanderson Nicholson was appointed Director of Music and granted the Honorary rank of Lieutenant.[5] The band also visited the Western Front on at least one occasion. When the King of the Belgians made a State visit to England the band played at Dover for his arrival and departure. Massed with the Band of the Portsmouth RMLI they took part in the funeral of the Marquess of Milford Haven, father of Earl Mountbatten of Burma and, at one time, First Sea Lord. Lt Nicholson was promoted Captain on the 16th January 1924 and retired, leaving a band of a very high standard to be inherited by Lt B Walton O'Donnell who moved from Portsmouth Division RMLI to Deal upon the amalgamation of the RMLI and the RMA. A year later O'Donnell was given an extraneous appointment as Professor of Military Music at the Royal Academy of Music. In the same year he and his band were selected to accompany the Prince of Wales to the West African colonies, South Africa and South America on board HMS *Repulse*. The new, post amalgamation, blue divisional band pattern uniform was worn on this tour for the first time.

When B Walton O'Donnell accepted the position of Director of Music to the BBC Wireless Military Band in 1928 he was replaced by Lt F J Ricketts. Ricketts remained in post until 25th August 1930 when he was moved to the Plymouth Band; the Depot Band was to be disbanded as a result of the move of the RNSM to Deal. To mark the event Ricketts and his men played seven consecutive military band concerts in the mornings during the week leading up to the closure and seven orchestral concerts in the evenings. Fifty pieces of music were played by the band and fifty-seven pieces by the orchestra. Not one item of music was repeated and the last piece to be played was *A Life on the Ocean Wave*.

1 *Order-in-Council No 68, dated 21st March 1890.*
2 *Officially called 'Bandmaster-Sergeant', General Orders, Royal Marines 1895, 137 page 9.*
3 *General Orders, Royal Marines 1900 GO63.*
4 *Order-in-Council No 92, dated 3rd March 1900.*
5 *General Orders, Royal Marines 1917.*

Chapter 9: The Royal Naval School of Music 1903-1950

During the Napoleonic Wars most flagships and many battleships had bands; but it was not until the middle of the nineteenth century that the Admiralty showed an official interest in them. The rating of Bandsman was introduced in 1847 and in 1856 HM Ships had eighteen Bandsmen for First and Second Rate ships and fifteen Bandsmen for Third and Fourth Rates.

The first step towards training of Naval Bands was taken when, in 1863, Boys' Training Ships were introduced. In 1867 the Admiralty paid for musical instruments and in 1868 established Petty Officer Bandmasters. Three years later Band Boy and Bandsman 2nd Class ratings were introduced. Chief Bandmasters were introduced into the Training Ships in May 1874.[1] In the same year the Adjutant General Royal Marines (AGRM) was directed that Bandmasters of the Royal Marines Divisions should inspect Training Ship bands twice a year and to issue Certificates of Competence to Royal Navy Chief Bandmasters.[2] Also in the same year, 1874, uniform for Naval Bandsmen was introduced. A dark blue tunic with white cord braiding and a white collar was worn with similarly coloured trousers with two narrow white braids down the leg seams. Headwear consisted of a flat, peakless, cap with a black braid band, edged with white. Bandmasters wore a similar uniform but the tunic was trimmed with black braid and did not have a white collar. Silver lace was worn on the cuffs and trousers.[3]

In 1884 Vice Admiral HRH Prince Alfred, Duke of Edinburgh, suggested that bandsmen awaiting draft should be attached to the band of the Commander-in-Chief (C-in-C) at one of the Home Ports so that they could practise instead of just being held in Depot ships. He also suggested that all men took their turn at sea service. The latter suggestion did not endear the Duke to the Cs-in-C at the Home Ports since they were cultivating their own bands on the pattern of the Guards, the Royal Artillery and the Royal Marine Divisions - stable bands that offered inducements and privileges to the finest players, such as teaching or performing in leisure hours. His third suggestion was for a training school for music for the training and qualification of Bandmasters.[4]

Sketch of a Royal Naval band playing on the deck of HMS Nelson and below an engraving showing a Royal Naval band playing on the quayside for a formal occasion

Charles Sanderson[5] was orphaned in 1893 and placed in the Training Ship Exmouth at Grays, Essex, in 1900, as a Band Boy. Practice took place in the covered sand lockers in the ship's bilges. Light was provided by candle and practice was from 9am until 11am and from 1pm until 3pm each day. A Training Ship Band was the responsibility of the Chief Bandmaster (Ch BM) who was assisted by a 1st Class Bandmaster (1st Cl BM) and a Band Corporal (BdCpl) who, by courtesy, was called Band Sergeant (BdSgt) and allowed to wear three stripes.

1 *Mariners Mirror 1926.*
2 *Papers of Capt A C Green and C Sanderson interview.*
3 *'British Naval Dress' by Dudley Jarrett.*
4 *Mariners Mirror 1926.*
5 *Interviewed by Lt A C Finney 1970.*

Charles Sanderson, bombardon and double bass, as a Royal Naval Bandsman photographed on board ship in Plymouth and also, post-1903, as a Royal Marines Musician. In 1911 he purchased his release and joined the Metropolitan Police but re-enlisted for service as a Musician during World War 1. He returned to the Metropolitan Police after the war where he also played in the Police Band

Naval Musicians were not held in great esteem being regarded as 'idlers' and often given other work to do on board ship - such as Midshipmen's servants.[6] RN Officers were responsible for the financial upkeep of the bands, and in some cases the Bandmaster as well, except for pay and part of the cost of musical instruments. Many of the foreign Bandmasters and Musicians were volatile characters and disinclined to accept RN custom, tradition and discipline.

The normal complement of 1889 was eleven players who would provide a band and an orchestra, the instruments being (for a band) one piccolo and flute, three clarinets, two cornets, two saxhorns, one baritone, one euphonium and one bombardon. Orchestral instrumentation would be four violins, one viola, one violoncello, one double bass, one flute, one cornet and one euphonium. Some of the Bandsmen obviously had to be double handed.[7]

By 1897 the numbers borne were twenty Chief Bandmasters and Bandmasters, eighty-four Band Corporals and Musicians, four hundred and ninety-six Bandsmen and two hundred and twenty Boys. 'Musicians' were very often violinists and usually very few of these would be on board ship. Very often the 'Musicians' were "... so inferior and objectionable a class as to be entirely unfit to hold the rating of Petty Officer".[8] Small ships were not allowed a band but were allowed to carry "a Musician".

At the end of the nineteenth century the Royal Navy had an organisation with a basic method of training young Musicians: the support of the Royal Marines through inspections of Musicians and Bandmasters; a nucleus of good Bandmasters or those who, in the case of the foreign contingent, had alienated the Officers. Changes were needed.

The Royal Naval Band of HMS Dreadnought (ex-Fury), Malta 1891. © Richard Ellis Archive, Malta

The bands of the Royal Marine Divisions were, at the turn of the twentieth century, well trained, well led and very skilled and so the Royal Navy looked to the Corps as a means of improving the calibre of ships' bands. A Memorial from the Right Honourable the Lords Commissioners of the Admiralty was presented to the King at Buckingham Palace on the 20th of May 1903. The King approved the Memorial, which included:

6 *Unpublished papers of Capt A C Green.*
7 *Mariners Mirror 1926.*
8 *Mariners Mirror 1926.*

HMS Melita's Drum and Fife Band consists of sailors and men of the Royal Marine Light Infantry, including a Marksman and a Bugler (1892). The bass Drummer wears an apron carrying the ship's name and edged with Bugler's lace. HMS Melita, a sloop of 970 tons was laid down at Malta Dockyard. She was built there to give employment at times when work was short. Princess Melita, who launched her, was the daughter of the Duke of Edinburgh, C-in-C Mediterranean Fleet at that time. © Richard Ellis Archive, Malta

"....it is desirable to improve the efficiency of Naval Bands and to reduce the expense, which at present falls upon the officers of Your Majesty's Naval Service. We beg leave humbly to recommend that Your Majesty may be graciously pleased by Your Order-in-Council to sanction the following scheme for the entry, training and pay of Bandsmen in Your Majesty's Fleet:

In future Band ratings to be entered as Royal Marines and form part of Your Majesty's Royal Marine Force, the total number of that force being correspondingly increased.

So far as possible Naval Band ratings now serving to be gradually transferred to the Royal Marines or otherwise disposed of under such arrangements as the Admiralty may direct".[9]

Band ratings would be Chief Bandmaster (Warrant Officer); 1st Class Bandmaster with over three years' experience; 1st Class Bandmaster with less than three years' experience; 2nd Class Bandmaster; Band Corporal; Musician and Band Boy.

The Admiralty acted swiftly. On the 25th May 1903, a Naval Band was paid off from HMS *Impregnable* and on the 22nd of July 1903 Bandmaster H Lidiard led the ship's thirty-four strong band, which included a few of the older boys from HMS *St Vincent* - a Training Ship moored in Portsmouth harbour[10] - into Eastney Barracks. The band became the first Royal Marine Band (RMB) of the Royal Naval School of Music (RNSM). On the 10th July, the ship's band of HMS *Leviathan*, at Plymouth, became the first to transfer from the Royal Navy to the Royal Marines. The first man to sign his papers was Arthur William Shepard who became the Royal Marine Musician with the number 'RMB1'.[11] From this time all ships' bands, upon being paid off, would be discharged to the RNSM. Bandmaster Lidiard, after twenty-six years' service in the Royal Navy, was promoted Warrant Officer, Royal Marines (WO RM) and appointed Chief BM RM.[12] '*Second Fiddle*' wrote that "July 22 1903 saw the birth of what is now known as the Royal Marines Band Service at RMA Barracks Eastney"[13] in the 'Globe and Laurel'.

A course of training at the School of Music would be taken by all Bandsmen and the School itself would be staffed by a Commandant - Major Herbert Slessor RMA; a Musical Director (RNSM) of WO rank - Mr E C Stretton (Bandmaster, 1st Battalion The York and Lancaster Regiment was brought from India and promoted WO RM); a Superintending Clerk - Mr J M Mitchell RMLI who was promoted Quartermaster and Acting Adjutant RNSM with rank of Honorary Lieutenant[14] (Hon Lt); two Bandmaster-Instructors of 1st Cl BM rank and a Schoolmaster who would be a Sergeant, RM[15] (Sgt RM). Whilst the Commandant reported directly to the Deputy Adjutant-General RM (DAG RM) regarding the administration of the

9 *Copy of Order-in-Council.*
10 *Letter from BM Hammond to A C Green.*
11 *Service Papers of Arthur William Shepard.*
12 *In 1910 Lidiard signed a declaration to say that his name was Henry Ernest Lidiard, not Harry Lidiard.*
13 *A C Green believed this to be H Lidiard.*
14 *Navy List 1903.*
15 *Globe & Laurel 1903 p91.*

The first Commandant of the Royal Naval School of Music, Major Herbert Slessor, RMA

School, all matters of discipline were to be referred to the Colonel Commandant (Col Comdt) RMA.

The "raison d'être" of the RNSM was to form and train bands for service in His Majesty's Fleets and Naval Shore Establishments and the bands, known as Royal Marine Bands (RMBs) were not to be confused with the Divisional Bands of the Royal Marines. The object of the School was to provide efficient small military bands, orchestras and dance combinations. So the Admiralty had recognised the shortcomings of ships' bands, examined the Royal Marine model, prepared a scheme that addressed the deficiencies in musical training, discipline and leadership and then made the Royal Marines responsible for raising the standards to that of their own bands. From this time the Royal Marines were to be totally responsible for, and representative of, Royal Navy music in all its forms.

Over the next few months many discussions took place between the infant school and its hosts, the RMA, particularly with regard to uniform detail.

A letter[16] dated August 1903 was sent by the Admiralty to all 'Commanders-in-Chief, Captains, Commanders, and Commanding Officers of HM Ships and Vessels at Home and Abroad' outlining the structure of the school but including, for the first time, "and a limited number of visiting professors with a knowledge of the requisite instruments". The Admiralty undertook to supply, free of charge, a ceremonial band, instruments, music stands, accessories and music to all those ships and RN establishments that were allowed a band. If the Officers of a ship or shore establishment also required a string band then the Officers were expected to contribute towards the supply, on loan, of the required instruments. New entries to the School would be recruited under the supervision of the Royal Marines. It was anticipated that a higher standard of musical knowledge and ability would be required of recruits. Formalised training at the School of Music (SoM) was to include physical training, elementary infantry and rifle drill and swimming, all concurrent with the musical training. Courses for first aid and stretcher drill were carried out on board ship and eligibility for promotion was dependent upon certificates being awarded for these courses. The foundation of the modern Royal Marines Band Service (RMBS) can be seen emerging through these arrangements. However, the practice of Musicians and Band Corporals serving as personal servants to Officers whilst afloat or in Depots was to continue but, from now on, Officers were obliged to pay gratuities as set out by the Admiralty.

The standard composition of bands was also set out. Senior Flagship bands of the Home, Channel, Mediterranean and China Fleets would have a 1st Cl BM, a BdCpl and twenty-two Musicians.[17] Other Flagships, Schools and Depots would have a 1st Cl BM, a BdCpl and fifteen Musicians. The existing bands of the Port Admirals would be reduced to a 1st Cl BM, a BdCpl and eleven Musicians.[18] Battleships and 1st Class Cruisers would have a 2nd Cl BM, a Bd Cpl and thirteen Musicians whereas other ships allowed bands also had a 2nd Cl BM and a BdCpl but only nine Musicians. A limited number of Chief Petty Officers (CPO) holding the rating of Chief Bandmaster (Ch BM) were to be selected for promotion to the new rank of Chief Bandmaster (Warrant Officer), Royal Marines (Ch (WO) BM),

---

16 Admiralty Circular Letter N. 7327/1903 of August 1903 'New Scheme for the Organisation and Training of Bands for His Majesty's Fleet'.

17 This became Channel, Atlantic, Mediterranean and China Fleets in 1905.

18 In 1905 these became string bands and only efficient bandsmen of long service and pensioners served in them.

and were to be borne in lieu of the new rating of Bandmasters, 1st Class[19] (BM 1st Cl). This letter would have left all RN Officers in no doubt about the shake-up that the Admiralty was applying to music in the Senior Service.

A General Order Royal Marines[20] (GORM) stipulated that recruits entering Royal Naval Bands were subject to the same requirements for physical fitness as other Royal Marines recruits.

HMS *Crescent*, a Second-Class cruiser, had one of the first bands from the School to be sent abroad, leaving in 1904 for a three-year commission as the Flagship on the South Africa Station. On the 25th February the RMB under Ch BM Smith led the ship's company from their barracks down to the dockyard, which they reached at 8.55am. At 9.00am the Colours were hoisted and the commissioning pennant broke at the masthead whilst the guard presented arms and the band played *God Save the King*. Stores were taken aboard on the 26th and then on the 27th, when storing was completed, the band played on the upper deck for the crew for one hour, this being a regular Saturday evening routine in the Royal Navy.[21]

Less than a year after it had opened, cracks were starting to appear in the structure that was the RNSM. The administrative and support staffing levels of the School were obviously much too low. This situation had repercussions upon the RMA since its staff had to become more involved in the work of the school.

The Admiralty approved the plan proposed by the Colonel Commandant, RMA and, after correspondence and discussion between the Admiralty and the Treasury, the DAG, RM received a letter dated 8th October 1904 from the Admiralty.[22] Comprehensive details of staffing and duties relating to the Royal Naval School of Music and its 'satellite' schools at the Divisions were provided. At this time the staff of the Central School (Eastney) comprised the Commandant (Major), the Assistant Commandant (Captain or Lieutenant), the Adjutant (Quartermaster and Honorary Lieutenant) and the Musical Director. They were supported by a Superintending Clerk (Warrant Officer) and two Chief Bandmasters, or Bandmasters First and Second Class. Additional NCOs were a Gymnastic Instructor (Sergeant), a Sergeant Major and a Senior Clerk (Sergeant) with three NCO or Gunner Clerks. At the 'Divisional Schools' the Adjutant, with two Sergeants, was to act as Captain commanding the Band Company with responsibility for discipline whilst the Divisional Bandmaster[23], who would be assisted by a Bandmaster from the RNSM at Eastney, was responsible for the training of the Band ranks attached to his Division, as directed by the Commandant of the School of Music. He would also, subject to the approval of the Commandant at Eastney, arrange for visiting instructors. The Commandant would periodically visit the Band ranks under training, and check on the progress of the training, at the Divisions. All Band ranks would return to Eastney to complete their training and for forming into bands for embarkation. Eastney was to be the 'Musicians Depot' where all higher training was to take place to fit men for soloists and the higher ranks of the Band Service. Band ratings would return to the Divisional schools from Service afloat in the same manner as Marines return to their Divisions, and would assist with instructional duties as required. Maximum number under training at each Division other than Eastney at any one time would be about one hundred.[24]

---

19 *Examinations were begun by Mr Stretton on the 20/8/1903 when he examined a BM2 and a BdCpl. From Report Book covering 1903-1904 in RMM Archive.*

20 *General Orders, Royal Marines 1904GO04.*

21 *BM Hammond letter to A C Green and "The Log of HMS Crescent 1904-1907" by M E Donoghue.*

22 *Original letter in RMM Archive.*

23 *At this time the Divisional Bandmasters were: Chatham, WO Bandmaster C J Hoby; Portsmouth, 2nd Lt G Miller; Plymouth, WO Bandmaster F Winterbottom.*

24 *These arrangements were confirmed in 'Instructions for the Royal Marine Divisions, 1908'.*

Following this, instructions were given for the numbering of men and boys to show that they had joined the Royal Marine Bands by the use of the RMB prefix to the number. Rates were set out for civilian musical instructors and for allowances to be paid to NCOs and men of the Royal Marines Divisional or Depot Bands.

The first report received from a ship's band to be published by the Corps journal 'Globe & Laurel' appeared at the end of 1904 when HMS *Euryalus* arrived at Suva, Fiji, and a Guard and Band paraded. Next day the band played at a ball given at Government House.

On the 18th February 1905 Captain F A Nelson RMLI, Plymouth, was appointed Assistant Commandant.[25] The following year the period of appointment of Major Herbert Slessor, RMA, as Commandant of the Royal Naval School of Music, was extended for two years until the 20th May 1908. He was also made Brevet Lieutenant Colonel.[26]

On the 8th June 1905 the Admiralty issued another circular letter[27] to all Commanders-in-Chief, Captains, Commanders and Commanding Officers of HM Ships and Vessels at Home and Abroad, detailing the revised structure and operation of the RNSM. As well as confirming the description given in the previous paragraphs it added that the introduction of the new system of enlistment and training would render it impracticable to supply at once fully equipped Bands to all ships requiring them. Further details were added. Recruiting would be carried out by the Commandant RNSM of candidates between the age of 15 (in exceptional cases 14) and 22; care was to be taken to ensure that recruits are drawn "from a suitable class". Musical standards for entry and for advancement to higher rating had been set. Training would begin with a four-month disciplinary course comprising physical and other general training, including elementary infantry and rifle drill and swimming. As initially anticipated, on return to Britain Naval Band ratings wishing to transfer would be discharged to the SoM and enlisted in the RM. Men volunteering for transfer were not to be rejected on medical grounds unless they should be invalided out of the service. A limited number of CPOs holding the Naval rating of Ch BM would be selected for promotion to the new rank of Chief Bandmaster (WO), Royal Marines. Musicians serving either afloat or in Depots could still be employed as personal servants to Junior Officers but they would have to be paid set rates.

Qualifications for promotion to BdCpl were: service afloat of not less than six months; a Third Class Certificate of Education; Very Good character and having passed the examination in "First Aid" and "Stretcher Drill". Examinations for the rank of Cpl were to be introduced, subjects being Music (practical), Music (theory), First Aid and Infantry Drill (practical and detail). Promotion to BM would depend on an examination following a course of instruction at the Central School of Music. The other requirements for promotion to BM, 1st and 2nd Class, were service afloat of not less than six months as a confirmed NCO and also a Second Class Certificate of Education. Special arrangements could be put in place to allow those afloat to take the course and the examination.

Band Instruments and Music were to be supplied by the Admiralty to ships and shore establishments that were allowed bands. If a ship required a String Band, the necessary instruments were supplied, on loan, from the SoM and an annual charge levied on the Officers, the Captain being responsible for the use of the instruments and the collection of the money.

Some alterations to King's Regulations and Admiralty Instructions (KR&AI) were made, including the defining of Musicians' equivalent ranks as Bandmaster 1st Class

25 *General Orders, Royal Marines 1905, GO25.*

26 *General Orders, Royal Marines 1906, GO2527 and GO3074.*

27 *RMM Archive.*

(Colour Sergeant); Bandmaster 2nd Class (Sergeant); Band Corporal (Corporal); Musician (Private); Band Boy.

At Eastney in 1905 the Band Boy's early morning routine was to rise at 6.15am, make beds for inspection, clean their area and then wash. Breakfast was at 07.00 - toast supplied but butter or margarine had to be purchased by the individual. 8.15 Parade and infantry drill until 09.00. Educational training of Boys and Recruits was carried out by RM Schoolmasters who also assisted in the schools for the children of the ranks serving at the RMA Barracks.[28]

Also In 1905, the RNSM assembled a band of over forty for HMS *Renown*, which was preparing for a Royal Tour to India and Burma. *Renown's* band was under the direction of the RNSM Musical Director E C Stretton who was made a Temporary Lieutenant (Temp Lt) for the duration of the tour. He wrote a march called *The Royal Tour* to mark the occasion. Amongst the band of forty-one were future notables such as Lt E W Faithfull and Musical Directors S Fairfield and A C Green. On their return Major H S Neville White (OCRM) commented in his report[29] that, "They [the band] have reached a high pitch of excellence and, as a string band, certainly they need not fear comparison with some of our finest military bands. It has been an education to listen to them, and the only regret expressed on all sides is that so fine a band should now be scattered to the four winds".

Throughout the history of the RNSM many fine bands must have suffered a similar fate. When a ship returned home and went out of commission its band returned to the School and its members were granted leave according to their service afloat. When they returned from leave they were drafted to other ships as they were commissioned. The opportunity was taken to mix the older, experienced men with the younger men when a band was being formed for service in a ship.

By January 1906, the strength of the Royal Marines Bands had grown from the inception of the School less than three years earlier to 946 with 34 bands embarked. HMS *King Alfred* was typical of a ship's band complement, having ten men trained at Chatham, five from Plymouth, four from Forton and five from Eastney.

Ships' bands normally served afloat for a period of two to three years before returning to the School. However, drastic changes were needed to ensure that standards of not only ships' bands, but also those of the shore establishments, would be raised. In 1907 the C-in-C Plymouth's Band was severely shaken when a Bandmaster from the RNSM took over. Set in their ways for many years the ex-Army and Navy Musicians suddenly found that they had to arrive much earlier for practice and, on completion, had to clean their practice area.

The Band of the Boys' Training Establishment, HMS *Ganges* at Shotley, located ten miles from Ipswich, became a Royal Marine Band in 1906. Classed as a ship's band its strength was normally between eighteen and twenty. Its function was to assist the instruction of young entrants of fifteen or sixteen years of age through their basic training period. Apart from these duties the band provided concerts throughout the East Anglian region.

Bandmaster Stretton transferred to the Royal Artillery in 1907 and was replaced by Charles Franklin as the Musical Director of the RNSM. Second Lieutenant Franklin had been serving as Director of Music, Egyptian Army[30] and was given the King's permission to wear the Insignia of the fourth class of the Imperial Ottoman Order of the Osmanieh. This had been conferred upon him by the Khedive of Egypt and authorised by the Sultan of Turkey in recognition of valuable services.[31] Franklin was granted the rank of

28 *Educational notes by Instructor Lt Cdr F J Wilkins (Rtd) - Blue Band Editor 1951-1954.*
29 *Globe & Laurel 1906 Jan.*
30 *General Orders, Royal Marines 1907, GO842.*
31 *General Orders, Royal Marines 1907, GO5642.*

Quartermaster and Honorary Lieutenant from the 13th July 1907.[32] The role of the Musical Director included full responsibility for the musical training of all Band ranks at the Central School at Eastney although he was also expected to visit the Divisional schools to carry out practical examinations of those under training. He was also responsible for engaging Visiting Instructors[33] for the Central School. The Assistant Commandant was responsible for auditing the RNSM accounts and for assisting the Commandant with the administration of the School as well as for deputising for him in his absence. The RNSM Quartermaster was responsible for all musical instruments, music and equipment in use at the School and by bands on board ships throughout the world.[34] He had to prepare annual estimates for instruments and maintain an accurate ledger of their distribution.[35]

Band Boys of 17 years and above who were being trained at the Divisions were to undertake a Musketry Instruction Course. This course allowed twenty rounds firing with the Morris Tube in the shooting gallery and forty-five rounds on the rifle ranges.[36]

In 1908 the first class of BdCpls took the examination of the Royal Academy of Music. During the same year, the Lords Commissioners of the Admiralty directed that all RN Band ranks undergoing training at Chatham and Plymouth should be transferred to Eastney for completion of training.[37] A further announcement[38] ended musical training at Forton Barracks on 30th November 1908 and, finally, a GORM[39] of 1909 confirmed that all RM Band ranks (WOs, NCOs, Men and Boys) still allocated to RMLI and RMA Divisions for training should return to the Central School of Music at Eastney.

The first RM Band to serve on the Mediterranean Station was that of HMS *Queen*, the Flagship of the Mediterranean Fleet during 1907/1908. The second was HMS *Bacchante*, all the other ships of the Fleet still having Maltese or Italian Bands.[40]

In 1907 the King inspected the Mediterranean Fleet, which could muster a Naval Brigade of three thousand Seaman and one thousand Royal Marines. Following his passage through the ships of the Fleet the King disembarked from the Royal Yacht and his procession drove through the Malta streets lined by the men of the Naval Brigade. All Buglers and Drum and Fife Bands had been disembarked from the ships of the Fleet. Five battleship bands under the Fleet Bandmaster were at the Custom House with the Guard of Honour and a further six battleship bands and the Drum and Fife Band were with the Battalions along the route. On the day of the inspection the Naval Brigade took position on the Marsa. The King then inspected the Brigade, which marched past, reformed, Advanced in Review Order, halted and gave three cheers.[41]

On the 12th February 1908 it was announced that Brevet Lieutenant Colonel Herbert Slessor RMA would be retained as Commandant, Royal Naval School of Music, until the 20th May 1909.[42] At the end of the year Captain F A Nelson, Assistant Commandant RNSM, exchanged with Captain John Bush RMLI of the Portsmouth Division.[43] The School Quartermaster's job was made even more complex when the Admiralty decided to allow music to be exchanged between ship's bands. Exchanges had to be on the basis that

---

32 *General Orders, Royal Marines 1912, GO2 January.*

33 *NCOs or men of RM Divisional or Depot Bands could be employed instead of civilians. They were paid an allowance of one shilling per day for a five day week and they had to provide at least ten hours of instruction per week. Civilian instructors, not being paid Servicemen, were paid a maximum of 2shillings per hour.*

34 *Tables of 'Estimated Duration of Band Instruments etc, RN School of Music' were published to assist this process.*

35 *Instructions for Royal Marine Divisions 1908.*

36 *General Orders, Royal Marines 1907, Errata.*

37 *General Orders, Royal Marines 1909 GO90.*

38 *General Orders, Royal Marines 1908GO78.*

39 *General Orders, Royal Marines 1909GO90.*

40 *RMB729 M Booth recollection to A C Green.*

41 *In 1908 The Prince of Wales went to Canada in HMS Indomitable with Mr H Reeby and an RM.Band.*

42 *General Orders, Royal Marines, 1908 GO443.*

43 *General Orders, Royal Marines, 1908 GO86.*

music exchanged was of a similar value; that the receiving band must accept responsibility for the music's condition and also that vouchers should be sent to the RNSM by each band giving details of ships and music exchanged so that accurate records could be maintained.[44]

It was in 1910 that military duties, which would have far-reaching consequences for Royal Marine Bands, were formulated.

"Fire Control Duties. - Instruction in the Fire Control duties will take place prior to the men being drafted to sea, on expiration of training at the Royal Naval School of Music, and will be of one week's duration. On completion of the course a qualification of 'VG1', 'VG', 'G', 'F' or 'Indifferent' is to be awarded according to ability, and the result is to be noted on the Drill and Musical History Sheet by the Gunnery Officer carrying out the Instruction".[45] Further detail was added in 1911:

"Syllabus of instruction in the Working of Fire Control Instruments:

1. To set a Dumaresq instrument[46] from the data supplied. To read off the rate and deflection:
2. To set the rate on a Range Clock, to understand its mechanism sufficiently for it to be worked with intelligence:
3. To work the Vickers and Barr and Stroud Transmitters:
4. To be able to set a Gun Range Indicator, and to read off from it the ranges to be set on the Transmitters:
5. To transmit Ranges, Deflection and Bearings by Navy-phone, using the authorised nomenclature; and to work a fire gong".[47]

At the same time "VG in working of Fire Control Instruments" was added to the requirements for Band Corporal and Bandmaster 1st and 2nd Class promotions. The 1922 General Standing Orders stated that: "Instruction in the use of Fire Control Instruments is to be carried out at Eastney, and for formed bands in HMS *Excellent*, in accordance with the syllabus laid down in the Gunnery Training Manual".[48]

Why were the men of the bands initially chosen for this particularly dangerous task? One theory[49] is that the Musicians at this time were designated as Lower Quarter Ratings and this meant that, along with Chefs, Writers and others, they were part of the gunnery system of the ship. The logical use for these 'spare hands' would be ammunition handling but since this could have put hands and fingers in danger they were given the task of working in the Transmitting Stations.

The result of the introduction of these military duties will be seen as this story develops; at this point it is sufficient to say that, in a war-time situation the Musicians of the Royal Marine Bands would be placed in a very dangerous environment indeed.

Herbert Wright described his first experience of joining HMS *Temeraire* at Plymouth. "The ship was alongside and directly we got there we had to change into working rig and help to take in stores. This went on for several days. Finally, when ready for sea, the band got the usual job in the depths of the ship working the fire control instruments. In addition to this we had our stations for 'in' and 'out' torpedo nets. When taking in ammunition we were kept busy. Our worst job was when taking in coal. Two thousand tons at a time was nothing unusual, our job being running the sacks of coal as they were hoisted on board on to barrows and cast them onto bunker chutes halfway along the ship". When Musn John

44 *General Orders, Royal Marines, 1908 GO72.*
45 *General Standing Orders, Royal Marines 1910, para 1163, page 227.*
46 *One of the types of Transmitting table in service at the time.*
47 *General Orders, Royal Marines 1911, December, page 148.*
48 *Para 1362, page 224.*
49 *Lt Cdr B Witts, HMS Excellent Museum Curator.*

Allen joined his first ship, HMS *Russell*, a 13,000ton battleship en route to Malta for a major refit, he kept a diary. One day in May 1909 at Dover he noted, "Coaled 1,466 tons from 6.00 am until 01.00 am next morning. The Band started at 05.45 am and finished at 10.30 pm. Had to play four pieces an hour. During the intervals played on the quarterdeck. Band had 7 days' leave stopped for being two minutes adrift from playing a double for coal ship morning when the call sounded *Fall In Hands for Coaling*". Unlike the Captain of HMS *Russell* who was happy for his band to entertain the crew whilst they coaled ship the Captain of HMS *Temeraire* obviously believed in using all hands for the purpose of coaling.

By 1910 all foreign Musicians had been eliminated from the system and band ranks stood at 1,300 with 900 in the Fleet's fifty-three bands. The remainder, aged fifteen to twenty-three years, were at the School - which was producing about 120 Musicians and boys each year. By this time the School was operating smoothly with a well-defined curriculum for recruits, for Band Corporals and for Bandmasters. Twenty-three Professors were responsible for ensuring that all pupils received the training necessary to enable them to play an orchestral and a wind instrument to a high standard. In addition pupils were taught music theory, first aid, infantry drill, physical training, swimming, musketry and English education in classrooms within two huge buildings. The Corporals' Course took each of these topics further and culminated in examinations. Bandmasters' Classes included elements of music, harmony, practical knowledge of all wind and string instruments used in bands and orchestras, scoring for military band and for small orchestra and being able to show proof of intelligence as a conductor. A minimum of 75% in all subjects had to be achieved to pass the RAM examination. It was also in 1910 that the award for the Best Student of the Year presented by the Worshipful Company of Musicians (WCM) was instituted.[50]

Henry Lidiard, the Bandmaster who brought the first Royal Navy Band, HMS *Impregnable*, into the RNSM and now a Chief Bandmaster (Warrant Officer), was promoted to Quartermaster with the honorary rank of Lieutenant for duty at the RNSM.[51] He was posted to the Royal Marine Light Infantry and wore that unit's uniform. Captain R F C Foster, RMA, was appointed Second Assistant Superintendent at the RNSM on the 9th January 1911.[52] By 1911 the RNSM had retrieved all of its Musicians and staff from the Divisional training facilities and, as a result, had made adjustments to its own staff, which now consisted of Superintendent, 1st Assistant Superintendent, 2nd Assistant Superintendent, Quartermaster, Musical Director, Superintending Clerk, two Bandmasters, Bandmaster in charge of stores, seven clerks and Band Corporals and Musicians as required for instruction and other duties.[53]

In 1912 the members of the band of the RNSM suggested a concert on South Parade Pier, Southsea, in aid of the *Titanic* Disaster Fund and as a tribute to the heroic conduct of the liner's Musicians. An orchestra of a hundred under Lt Franklin was used for this. A Naval and Marine Tournament was held at the United Services Ground, Portsmouth in late August and an RNSM band of eighty augmented by the bands of HMS *Victory* and HMS *Excellent* performed under Lt Franklin. Admiral Lord Charles Beresford was given the Freedom of Weymouth and the massed bands of the ships that happened to be in Portland Harbour took part in the ceremony. HMS *Hercules* was the Flagship and her Bandmaster was therefore in charge of the event. Whilst each Divisional Band had a Bugle Major and a Drum Major (CSgt or Sgt) no RM Band had either of these appointments. Drum Majors would be found from within either the band or the RM Detachment. A Drum Major was necessary for such a massed bands display so BM T H W Read prevailed upon BdCpl G C Weinrich to assume the responsibility and he made a magnificent job of it.

50 *From the notes of J Trendell.*
51 *General Orders, Royal Marines 1910, GO3588.*
52 *General Orders, Royal Marines 1910, GO5951a.*
53 *General Orders, Royal Marines, 1911 Errata 1666.*

Total strength had reached 1,450 by 1913 and embarkation and disembarkation were now very frequent. HMS *Highflyer* was commissioned for the East Indies putting a British band on that station - previous bands being Goanese.

An International Peacekeeping Force consisting of British, German, Austrian, French and Italian forces with the British in command was sent to occupy Scutari (Albania) in 1913 to protect the Muslim inhabitants from ethnic cleansing by the Montenegrins. This area would soon become Yugoslavia. The band of HMS *King Edward VII* went ashore with the marines and sailors. The entire force was billeted together and the only other band was with the Austrian contingent. The two bands could not be massed since the pitch of the instruments was different. The band played every other evening throughout the stay and impressed all, especially the Mallisori tribal chiefs who attended a reception given by Vice-Admiral Burney, who commanded the International Force. The King's Birthday was celebrated by a parade that all Forces attended. The Band with the RM and Seaman Detachments returned to HMS *King Edward VII* when the West Yorkshire Regt (The Prince of Wales's Own) relieved them.[54]

The lighter side of the life of a RM Musician at sea was apparent through the Concert Party. Open to all, this provided the opportunity for talent and, in particular, imagination to shine. The band of HMS *Minotaur* on the China Station at Wei-Hai-Wei opened the ship's concert party on the 12th September with an overture. Whilst the Glee party was very popular the band claimed the honour of providing the chief feature - a gymnastics display by members of the band! Proceeds from the concert party went to the Seamens' and Marines' Orphans' Home.[55] The part played by RM Bands afloat cannot be over-emphasised. As a Military and Ceremonial Band it was constantly used for moving men about their duties in an orderly manner; the ship's daily routine which included the Morning Colours Ceremony, Divisions, Prayers, physical training and Evening Colours was much more impressive to a ship's company when a band was aboard. There was also the frequent need for parades ashore and since many ships were 'flying the flag' appearance was most important not only to those watching but also for the morale of the ships' crews. The Band was also used to give an impressive welcome when foreign royalty or foreign officials visited the ship. At all sporting occasions the Military Band was employed and frequent variety programmes were played on board to help relieve the monotony of long voyages and routine.

The Musicians were used to providing orchestral music for luncheon and dinner parties when visitors were aboard. Orchestral and variety concerts for the ship's company were often held and the band also played each Sunday at Church Service. During a ship's commission scarcely a week would go by without a performance by the ship's dance band, or without its support of the Ship's Concert Party. Thus it was generally accepted that a band helped increase the efficiency of the ship, raised the morale of its crew and was very important to the daily business of showing the might of the British Navy to friend and potential foe alike.

Back in Portsmouth the Divisional Band of the RMA and the Band of the RNSM both played at the funeral of Captain G V Wildman-Lushington, one of the first Royal Marines to qualify as a pilot and serve in the Naval Wing of the Royal Flying Corps.[56] The pilot was buried with full military honours in Christ Church Cemetery on Portsdown Hill, overlooking Portsmouth.

---

54 *Reports sent back to UK. (Originals in RMM Archive).*

55 *Globe & Laurel and A C Green notes.*

56 *'Flying Marines' by Major A E Marsh.*

As the year came to an end BM C T Leeder, who had been a bass player in the band of HMS *Impregnable* in 1903, was given an unusual posting. He was sent to the Gold Coast in West Africa as the bandmaster of the Gold Coast Regiment, part of the West African Frontier Force. His band was formed from native Musicians.

Two of the larger and more important RN establishments had their own bands at this time. One was the Band of Nore Command and the other was that of HMS *Excellent*. Nore Command itself was formed in 1547 and covered the Thames Estuary and River Medway area. This was an area that might bear the brunt of any attacks and invasions upon the country or, conversely, would be one of the launching points for raids or invasions against our enemies. The first recorded Bandmaster of the Band of the C-in-C The Nore was BM G Welsh in 1912. HMS *Excellent* was the RN's School of Gunnery Training on Whale Island, a man-made island in Portsmouth Harbour. This establishment also dealt with the ceremonial training of officers and men in the Royal Navy. For these reasons, and because of the importance of its very large officers' mess, HMS *Excellent* was given its own band in 1895. In 1904 the Bandmaster, W C Windram, and the active service members of his band were absorbed into the RNSM organisation and they became an RM Band. The band was seldom drafted to sea and it retained its permanent nature until World War I.

1913 saw the Tenth Anniversary of the RNSM. During that ten year period, the numbers who had passed through the School were 11 Warrant Officers, 26 Bandmasters 1st Class, 38 Bandmasters 2nd Class, 112 Corporals, 966 Musicians and 246 Band Boys.

Brevet Lieutenant Colonel Gerald R Poole RMA was appointed Superintendent at the Royal Naval School of Music, vice Phillips who was promoted, effective from the 1st March 1914.[57] A few months later Major A P Liston Foulis, RMA, vacated the appointment of First Assistant Superintendent having served only a year of his appointment.

The war years 1914-1918 brought forth many tales of hardship, valour, and humour about Musicians. Band ranks were particularly at risk on board ship because of their 'secondary role'. Trained in gunfire control since about 1910 they were responsible for manning the Transmitting Station, or Stations, located in the very bowels of the ship. When closed-up and at Action Stations they knew that there was little chance of escape.

Bandmaster 1st Class Henry Lodge c1918. Mentioned in Despatches and awarded Meritorious Service Medal for service at Jutland on board HMS Marlborough

On the 18th July the Reserve Fleet had assembled for a Spithead review as an exercise in mobilisation. Prince Louis of Battenberg, the First Sea Lord, countermanded the order for the dispersal of the Fleet on completion of the Review. As a result the Reserve was well prepared for the mobilisation which came on the 1st August 1914. Buglers sounded the recall all over Portsmouth and Gosport. In addition, and within a matter of hours, all ships from the Reserve Fleet had bands detailed to them by the staff of the RNSM.

Those who had not been allocated to ships were called the 'Ready-men'. A few days later a band of twenty-four, including BM Faithfull, was formed from the ready-men. There were five BdCpls, twelve Musicians and six Band Boys.[58] This band was needed for the Royal Naval

57 General Orders, Royal Marines 1914, GO 17, March.
58 Diary of J Allen and Blue Band articles 2000/2001.

Division on the orders of the First Lord of the Admiralty, the Rt Hon Winston S Churchill who, whilst issuing instructions for the complement of the Brigade noted: 'A band must be provided. The quality is not important. There must be sufficient pupils at the Naval School of Music to provide for this. The Band is to join on Saturday next'.[59] It is ironic that the first bands from the RNSM to see action were involved not at sea but on land in Belgium when BM Faithfull's band acted as a Red Cross Party at the siege of Antwerp.

Following their return, and further training, they embarked in the SS *Franconia* as part of Drake Battalion of the Royal Naval Division. It would appear that instruments were not taken on board - they were certainly not taken ashore, unlike at Antwerp.

On the 24th April the *Franconia* was ordered at full speed to Cape Helles, Gallipoli, where the Division, including the band as first aid party and stretcher-bearers, went ashore at about 0800hrs on the 26th. Between then and the 24th December 1915, when it was recalled for Sea Service, the band members were part of the Mediterranean Expeditionary Force in the Dardanelles. Drake Battalion formed up on the beach and then, in silence, marched in single file to a place on the cliffs about a mile away. It was very cold and little sleep was had. Next morning they were bombed by two Turkish planes but this was ineffective. The Turkish artillery was also shelling the position. There was no shelter from either shell or shrapnel since orders had been given not to dig-in for fear of digging up dead men. Bodies were strewn all over the cliffs.

On the 31st July 1915 BM Faithfull and his Band Corporal, John Allen, were Mentioned in Despatches - "Behaved in a gallant and courageous manner in action at Cape Helles 17th May to 31st July". Three Musicians from Drake Battalion (Billings, Kensey and Harper) died of wounds or disease at Gallipoli. The Royal Naval Division was to remain at Helles until the very end, the last of its units leaving on the night of the 8th/9th January 1916; only two weeks after the Musicians had been withdrawn.[60]

1st November 1914 had brought the first heavy loss to the Band Service when the entire band of twenty-four (BM 2nd Cl Barber) died when HMS *Monmouth* was sunk at the Battle of Coronel off the coast of Chile. HMS *Good Hope*, the Flagship of Admiral Cradock, was also sunk but she was not carrying her band because she had left the Reserve Fleet Review on August 2nd before the band had gone aboard. In the same month another complete band was lost when HMS *Bulwark*, an ancient battleship moored off Sheerness, blew up. This band, led by the School's Senior Bandmaster WO E Scofield, had been the band of HMS *Excellent* at Whale Island for many years and all its members were well known in Portsmouth.[61]

Sgt John Allen. Photograph taken in February 1916, shortly after his return from Gallipoli

The Home Fleet spent a great deal of time under steam, but moored, in the great natural port of Scapa during the early part of the war. Poised to respond to any threat from the German Navy this represented a stand off that meant both sides had thousands of servicemen effectively removed from other theatres of war.

Each Wednesday afternoon the band of the flagship, HMS *Iron Duke*, would play on the deck of the

59 *The Royal Naval Division. D Jerrold 1923.*
60 *'Marcher' article - Blue Band journal.*
61 *Marines from the Medway' Lt Col B Edwards RM, RMHS Special Publication Number 20.*

Musician G C Weinrich who changed his name during 1915 or 1916 to G C Keen. This photograph was taken before 1914 when he was promoted BdCpl. He served until 1946, ending his career as Major GC Keen, Assistant Musical Director of the Royal Naval School of Music – as shown in this caricature.

Hospital Ship *Maine*. On Wednesday the 30th December 1915, whilst *Iron Duke*'s band was carrying out this duty, BM 2nd Cl Parker was conducting the band of HMS *Natal*, moored about three hundred yards away, in a programme for her Officers and guests. A huge underwater explosion was heard and HMS *Natal's* 9.2" turret was hurled into the air. All fifteen members of the band were killed.

The official establishment (1915) of the School and its bands was 1,500 men and boys made up as follows: one Quartermaster; one Musical Director; one Sergeant-Major: one Superintending Clerk; eleven Bandmasters (WO); two Company Sergeants-Major; thirty-two Bandmasters 1st Class; forty-seven Bandmasters 2nd Class; one hundred and four Band Corporals; one thousand two hundred and seven Musicians and ninety-three Band Boys.

The seventeen members of the band of HMS *Russell* were saved when that ship was sunk after hitting a mine off Malta. In May 1916, the Battle of Jutland took place. The mightiest Fleet that the world had ever seen left Scapa, Cromarty and the Forth Bridge area. By midnight on May 30th it was sailing across the North Sea.[62] The Fleet carried forty-seven bands - a total of almost seven hundred Musicians - almost half of the RNSM strength and about twice the total strength of the current Royal Marines Band Service. The British and German Fleets made contact in the afternoon and HMS *Lion* (Admiral Beatty's Flagship) and HMS *Princess Royal* immediately engaged the German battleship SMS *Lutzow*. Within an hour *Lion* had received two direct hits from *Lutzow* and, a little later, she received another, much more serious blow when 'Q' turret, manned by the RM Detachment, received a direct hit.[63] Musn J H Hoad was the only member of the band of HMS *Lion* to be killed.

Meanwhile SMS *Von der Tann* scored three devastating hits on HMS *Indefatigable* in one salvo causing one of her magazines to explode. Seconds later she was hit by another salvo from the German battleship that caused her to blow up and sink.[64] All but two of her crew perished, including BM 1st Cl Barham, BdCpl Schummacher and thirteen Musicians.

HMS *Queen Mary* had been firing at the SMS *Seydlitz* and inflicting a good deal of damage when she came under fire from not just *Seydlitz* but *Derfflinger* as well. Renowned for her accurate gunnery The *Queen Mary* was making little impact upon the *Seydlitz* because of the effective German armour. Like *Indefatigable* The *Queen Mary* was unable to withstand the heavy and accurate bombardment. Five hits prefaced a massive explosion that split the ship in two. Further explosions tore her apart and she sank, taking 1,266 of her crew to their deaths. Amongst the dead were all of the men of the RM Band - BM 1st Cl J Taylor, BdCpls T Smith and A Wood and twelve Musicians. The battle continued during the afternoon. HM Ships *Invincible*, *Inflexible* and *Indomitable* were hitting the German battle cruisers but, once the range closed sufficiently, the Germans replied and *Derfflinger* and *Lutzow* concentrated their fire on Admiral Hood's Flagship, the *Invincible*. She was hit by a full salvo and the Royal Marines' 'Q' turret received a direct hit that caused the turret magazines to explode. Unlike the *Lion*, nobody was able to take action to prevent the flash from reaching the main magazines

---

62 *The British Fleet consisted of 28 Dreadnoughts, 9 battle cruisers, 8 armoured cruisers, 26 light cruisers, and 75 destroyers 'The Royal Navy Day by Day' A B Sainsbury.*

63 *"Many of the gun crew were killed. Major Harvey, despite serious wounds, was able to order the crew of the cordite magazine to flood it, thereby preventing an explosion in the main magazine. He was awarded a posthumous VC" 'The Royal Marines and the Victoria Cross' by Matthew Little.*

64 *'British Battle Cruisers' - P Smith.*

and with a shattering explosion the ship split into three and sank immediately. Only two officers and three ratings survived the sinking that took the lives of BM 1st Cl G Deacon, BdCpls Chance and Jamieson and fourteen Musicians. Musician A G S Flippence received the Distinguished Service Medal for his service at the Battle of Jutland.

Ships of the 1st & 2nd Battle Cruiser Squadrons, 1st, 2nd & 3rd Light Cruiser Squadrons and attached ships engage the German Fleet during the Battle of Jutland. Most of these ships carried Royal Marine Detachments, Buglers and Bands

The bands played a large part in maintaining and raising morale, overcoming boredom and monotony as well as reducing the effects of fear and concern, during the war years. They not only provided the orchestra for ships' concerts but the bandmaster usually produced the whole show. This included pantomimes at Christmas, occasional musical comedies and frequent concerts. BM A C Green achieved such fame with a series of shows that word reached the RNSM Director of Music who wrote to congratulate him, stating, "Such performances do credit to this Institution and do a great deal of good. Given the same numbers our bands can compare favourably with the Divisional Marines Bands, a fact that wants to be known and this is the way to do it".

On the 9th January 1917 the battleship HMS *Cornwallis* was torpedoed and sunk by U32 sixty-two miles southeast of Malta. BM Weedon and his band, with the exception of Musn A E Gray who was killed, were all rescued. HMS *Queen*, a veteran of the attempted forcing of the Dardanelles had been sent to Taranto with a Battle Squadron. All were on loan to the Italian Government but gradually all, except *Queen*, withdrew to England. The ship's company, including the band, were ordered to make their way back to England overland. The band left *Queen* on the 17th February, did not get a good meal until five days later in France, made contact with the British Army at Boulogne and marched into Eastney Barracks eight days after leaving *Queen* in Taranto.[65]

Bandmaster Leeder of the Gold Coast Regiment died of heart failure on January 21st. He had returned home to England in 1915 following his tour of service, only to be reappointed to the same position.[66] Effective from the 17th April 1917, Bandmaster (WO I) A E Whiting was promoted to Quartermaster, honorary rank of Lieutenant, vice H E Lidiard. For the purpose of this promotion to Quartermaster Whiting was transferred to the RMLI. In June 1917 Captain Franklin, the Musical Director of the RNSM, was granted the honorary rank of Major.[67]

Recruitment continued throughout the war years with many promising Musicians joining as 'Hostilities Only' - although it was hoped that they would adopt the Band Service as a profession. Retired BM T Porteous was one of those who came out of retirement to be a civilian Instructor at the School of Music 1914-1918. The band of HMS *Queen Elizabeth* would frequently land for orchestral practice at the YMCA, Rosyth under the direction of the well-known composer and conductor, Hamilton Harty, who was on the Admiral's Staff

65 *Naval Operations Vol IV (Official History of the War) Newbolt.*

66 *It is not known if his death was related to any particular incident, neither is it known if he and the Band were involved in the action against the Germans in Togoland. The Regiment were certainly involved in the campaign that culminated in the destruction of the German radio station at Kamina.*

67 *General Orders, Royal Marines 1917. June & July.*

at the time. Walking around the orchestra Hamilton Harty made the observation that "I never knew you had such individual talent in the band". Eleven well-known orchestral Musicians had found their way to it.

July 1917 brought another tragedy when HMS *Vanguard* sank following a massive internal explosion. Oil burned on the sea and hot debris falling on the island of Flotta set vegetation alight. The sea was strewn with wreckage, oil and bodies. Over eight hundred men died in this explosion including BM 1st Cl J T Vitou and the entire band.

September 1918 saw the arrival of HMS *Achilles* in New York. The ship's band and detachment took part in a "Britain's Day" Parade that was led by Lt John Philip Sousa and his US Marine Corps Band. Sousa's band was 150 strong and had more trombones in the front rank than the *Achilles* band had Musicians! Despite that the RM Band, at the rear of the parade, included Sousa marches and were warmly congratulated on their performance.

HMS *Kent* featured in one of the very last actions of the war. Musn R H Stoner joined this ship straight from the RNSM aged 16 years and 6 months. Upon arrival in Devonport the entire crew, including the band, loaded 2,000 tons of coal and 200 tons of upper deck cargo. Within a few hours of completion the ship had been completely washed down and the band was playing for a party. With the slightest sea running the 6" gun casemates on the lower deck allowed the sea in causing the Mess Decks to be perpetually flooded. There were no bathrooms, washing was carried out in tubs and buckets and, when they reached the tropics, there was severe rationing of drinking and washing water as well as of food. It was impossible to keep music stands upright, which made practice a serious problem - especially since much time was spent in the Transmitting Station or with Fire Control duties. The *Kent* arrived in Hong Kong in time for the Armistice celebrations but she then sailed for Vladivostock. Escorted by an icebreaker she made her way further along the coast to bombard the advancing Bolsheviks. Hong Kong was then reached in time for the Peace Celebrations in May 1919 before the band and the crew were sent back to England - the *Kent* remaining in Hong Kong to be broken up.[68]

By the end of 1918 the band of HMS *Glory* had been at Murmansk for two years. The crew were relieved after twelve months but the band had to remain on board. The ship was frozen in for about six months and rations, at the height of the U-boat offensive, became very short. Coaling ship took place in temperatures of -20ºC, the Russian Revolution began and there was an epidemic of 'Black Flu'. Early on Christmas Day 1917 BM Woodman vanished from his bed in the sick-bay. This was during the period when the ship was iced-in. He was never seen again and no trace of him was ever found.[69]

Musn J Skuse, a very talented violinist who had been in the Band of HMS *Renown* for the Royal Tour to India in 1905, died following the torpedoing and sinking of HMS *Britannia* by a German submarine off Cape Trafalgar on the 9th November. He succumbed to his wounds in the Royal Naval Hospital, Gibraltar on the 11th November 1918 - Armistice Day.

The Prince of Wales received the Royal Naval Division, which by then comprised one Royal Marine Battalion with four Royal Naval Battalions, on Horse Guards Parade on the 6th June 1919. The men of the Division felt that having music provided by a band of the Brigade of Guards instead of a band of the RNSM was an insult to the Senior Service. However, Royal Marine Bands from the Royal Naval School of Music were given the privilege of leading British troops through Paris on the 14th July 1919 when they were led by Drum Major Hamilton.[70]

---

68 *Captain Stoner's recollections written for A C Green.*

69 *Footnote added to A C Green's Roll of Honour.*

70 *'Britain's Sea Soldiers 1914-1919' by General Sir H E Blumberg RM.*

The Lords Commissioners of the Admiralty had approved the establishment of the rank of Warrant Officer Class II in February 1916. At the same time those who had been serving as Warrant Officers on the 27th August 1915 were made Warrant Officers Class I. Bandmasters were amongst those who qualified for the WOI rank.[71] Four Warrant Officer Bandmasters were promoted to Chief Bandmaster RM (Commissioned Warrant Officers) in 1919. They were, on the 1st February, J G Welsh MBE, A Moffatt and H Reely. T H W Read was promoted on the 5th June.[72]

From December 1920 Bandmasters were shown in the Navy List as Warrant Officers.[73] Warrant rank had been introduced in the Royal Marines in 1881 when the four Royal Marine Divisional Bandmasters were amongst those given the rank. In 1904 Warrants were given to the Musical Director and the Bandmaster of the RNSM (Stretton and Lidiard). The Royal Navy had Warrant Officers since the seventeenth century and because of the close link between the RN and the RNSM it was necessary to ensure parity between Bandmasters at sea and their equivalent Royal Navy ranks. In 1920 it was decided that Warrant Officers could be promoted to Commissioned Officers from Warrant Rank under conditions applicable to Naval Warrant Officers except that the condition relating to sea-time would be waived in the case of Sergeants-Major, Superintending Clerks, and Bandmasters. The latter would be called Commissioned Bandmasters[74] and to indicate the rank they wore a single star on their lower arm. After becoming 'a Commissioned Officer from Warrant Rank' - the title Commissioned Warrant Officer having been abolished - their next promotion would be to Lieutenant (Director of Music) or Lieutenant (Quartermaster) depending upon the appointment that they were given. If made Lt (QM) they would remain in the Band Service but in a non-musical capacity - usually as a Company Commander.[75]

On the 24th August 1920 BM E W Faithfull, veteran of Antwerp and Gallipoli, became the first Band Boy to reach Commissioned rank. He qualified for promotion in Military Law and RM Subjects, becoming Lieutenant and Quartermaster RM for duty as a Company Officer at the RNSM. Bandmaster H L Smith, whilst retaining his seniority, became the Sergeant Major of the RNSM. Band Colour Sergeant S Fairfield was promoted Bandmaster (Warrant Officer) vice Smith. At the same time Band Colour Sergeant C Marks became Acting Bandmaster (Warrant Officer).[76] In December 1920, Lt C E Maton, Quartermaster RMA, became a Company Officer at the School. It was also in 1920 that the School was given an appointment for a regular Drum Major. His rank could not exceed Band Sergeant and the appointment would be for three years.

With the RMLI Plymouth Divisional Band accompanying the Prince of Wales to Australia in HMS *Renown* in 1920, the ship's band, supplemented by Musicians from the RNSM to become a band of thirty-two, was sent as duty band to Plymouth Division in their stead.

Qualifications for attaining the rank of Corporal in the RNSM were laid down. The successful candidate would need to have a minimum of six months' sea service; 2nd Class education certificate; "Very Good" character on his reports; "Very Good" in working of ships fire control instruments[77] and a certificate for passing the prescribed examination of Band Corporal. At the same time the requirements for Bandmaster 1st and 2nd Class were

---

71 *General Orders, Royal Marines 1916, GO 20 February.*

72 *General Orders, Royal Marines 1918.*

73 *General Orders, Royal Marines 1920 GO184.*

74 *General Orders, Royal Marines 1920 GO184.*

75 *In 1949 WOs would be re-titled Branch Officers. The junior grades were all titled 'Commissioned...' and wore a small star on their shoulder. The senior grades were titled 'Senior Commissioned...' and wore a large star on their shoulder.*

76 *General Orders, Royal Marines 1920, GO146 September, GO 156, October and GO183 December.*

77 *'Fire Control Instruments' was the standard term for all equipment and systems, ranging from telephone systems to the Transmitting Station equipment, used by the Royal Marine Musicians as part of their gunnery role.*

six months' minimum sea service as confirmed NCO; 2nd Class education certificate; 1st Class Certificate in First Aid; "Very Good" in working of ship's fire control instruments and a certificate having passed the prescribed examination for Bandmaster.

Every member of the RNSM donated one day's pay towards a Memorial to comrades who had died in the 1914-1918 War. The Memorial to the men of the Royal Marine Band Service who lost their lives during World War I comprised a set of five silver side drums and a silver-finished wooden bass drum. These drums were dedicated and presented at a parade held on the 5th March 1921 when some four hundred men of the School of Music were present.

During 1920 a number of appointments in the Corps were abolished. The only effect upon the RNSM was that nobody would be employed specifically to superintend the boys at the School. Instead, this duty would become part of the duties of Musicians and NCOs.[78] Another reduction was made by replacing four civilian Instructors with an additional NCO Instructor. This was quickly followed by an announcement that the employment of Civilian Professors at the RNSM would be discontinued and that an Instructional allowance would be paid to 1st and 2nd Class Bandmasters and Band Corporals who undertook this work.[79] Two more (WO) Bandmasters, W C Windram and G K Clarke, were promoted to Commissioned Bandmasters as of 17th May 1920. Shortly afterwards Commissioned Bandmaster T H W Read retired at his own request and Bandmaster 1st Class T W Trimmer and CSM H L Smith were both promoted to Bandmasters (WO). In 1920 the ranks of Bandmaster 1st Class and Bandmaster 2nd Class were abolished and the ranks of Band Colour Sergeant (BdCSgt) and Band Sergeant (BdSgt) were to be used in their place.[80] During 1921 this was rescinded and the old ranks of Bandmaster 1st Class and Bandmaster 2nd Class were reinstated.[81] Band Sergeant L P Donne was promoted to Warrant Officer on his appointment, effective 25th March 1921, as Superintending Clerk at the School, whilst J G Welsh MBE was confirmed as Lieutenant for duty as Musical Director RNSM and, as a result, Acting Bandmaster C Marks was confirmed as Bandmaster (WO) vice Welsh. These changes were effective on the 3rd November 1921. Three more men passed in Military Law and RM Subjects on the 28th June 1921 to qualify for Commissioned Rank. They were Bandmasters (WO) A Pragnell and F M Radcliffe and Sergeant-Major (WO) H L Smith.

The Band for HMS Renown, wearing the Garter Blue uniform, rehearse on the Eastney playing fields. Lt Fairfield is on the left of the band and the Drum Major is Bandmaster Hamilton

During 1921 the practice of having Section Leaders for Band Boys was introduced. They were selected by the Commandant and had to have twelve months' service; a 2nd Class Certificate of Education; 'Very Good' at Infantry Drill, Physical Training and Fire Control as well as having passed their swimming test.

At an RNSM Welfare Committee meeting in 1919 members had been unanimous in their desire to sever RNSM connections with the Royal Marines. A new uniform was seen as a good way of announcing this and, as the Royal Marines were quite indifferent, the Clothing

78 *General Orders, Royal Marines 1920, April GO64.*
79 *General Orders, Royal Marines 1920, GO121 July.*
80 *General Orders, Royal Marines 1920GO168, 169 and174.*
81 *General Orders, Royal Marines 1921GO127.*

Committee recommended the change.[82] As a result the RNSM band formed for HMS *Renown* for the Royal Tour in 1921 was the first to wear the new uniform known as the 'Garter Blue Band Service Ceremonial Uniform'. This had a light blue band replacing the scarlet band around the cap; a pale blue collar on the tunic; a girdle with pale blue edging and trousers with a pale blue welt. An AGRM's report stated that, by mid July 1922, "Feeling had quite changed and the Band Service is anxious to retain its connection with the Corps and fears that the new uniform may be regarded as a mark of severance". Within a couple of days the First Sea Lord and the First Lord of the Admiralty had agreed that the 'Naval Band' should revert to red facings and that the King had given his approval. An RMO was issued on the 21st August 1922[83] stating that uniform facings would be scarlet and that all pale blue faced uniforms should be returned at the earliest opportunity. Part two of the RMRO stated that a return would be made to the use of buff leather waist-belts for ceremonial purposes.[84] For the 1921 Royal Tour, Bandmaster (WO) S Fairfield was made a temporary Director of Music, with the rank of Lieutenant.[85]

It was on the 20th June 1922 that BM 2nd Class FG Stagg was appointed as the first official Drum Major of the RNSM, an appointment that he held until 26th June 1924 when he was promoted to BM 1st Class and embarked on HMS Barham. Drum Major Stagg and the RNSM Band led the Portsmouth Division of the Royal Marines Light Infantry through the city when they amalgamated with the Royal Marine Artillery at Eastney (Blue Band March 1971)

By 1922 changes to the staffing levels of the Royal Naval School of Music had occurred.[86] The Commandant was now called the Superintendent but was still a RMA, or RMLI, officer. He was now assisted by two Company Commanders, one of whom had to be an RMA or RMLI officer and would be in charge of Musicians and NCOs, maintain confidential records and have responsibility for legal work and any Courts Martial duties. He also retained responsibility as Auditor of accounts. The junior Company Commander was in charge of Band Boys and performed Adjutant's duties in respect of parades, drill, military efficiency etc. He was also responsible for recreational training and games, and gave lectures on hygiene, sports and other subjects. He was also Treasurer for local funds. The Musical Director was responsible for the musical training of all Band ranks and also for assessing NCOs and Musicians disembarking and embarking. He was also responsible for assessing all candidates for promotion and for entry into the School. He would arrange the instrumentalists in bands for HM Ships prior to embarkation and also visit and inspect the bands at UK establishments. An Assistant Director of Music was responsible for the musical training of Band Boys and the instruction of candidates for promotion, and theory work for Band Boys. These men, plus the two Company Commanders and the Quartermaster, were supported by a Parade Sergeant-Major, a Superintending Clerk, two Bandmasters as instructors and two Company Sergeants-Major. The Superintendent would be in post for three years and the Bandmasters for two. The remainder would be permanent until retirement or promotion.

Cpl Frank Bonner, 1923-1927. Joined RNSM prior to WW1 and served as bandmaster on HM Ships including Renown, Barham, Queen Elizabeth and Emperor of India until 1935. He returned as a Pensioner during WW11 and led the Band of HMS Royal Arthur – Butlin's Holiday Camp at Skegness which had been taken over by the Admiralty

During 1922 the Geddes reductions caused some members of the Band Service to leave. Over five hundred Lieutenants left the Royal Navy and the Captains' list was cut by a third. Many others, including men of the Band Service, decided to leave rather than face the threat of further cuts - which did occur in 1926 and 1929.

In 1924 the Band from the RNSM under BMs A C Green and Drum Major F G Stagg appeared at the Royal Tournament. The same RNSM Band, suitably

82 'Proposed Alterations to RM Band Clothing' ADM1/8629/131-PRO, Kew.
83 RM Band. Band Ranks Uniform. PRO.
84 'Proposed Alterations to RMBand Clothing' ADM1/8629/131-PRO, Kew.
85 General Orders, Royal Marines 1921GO147.
86 Instructions for the Royal Marine Divisions 1922.

augmented, also played at the British Empire Exhibition, Wembley, as a result of which it received further praise and thanks. Also in 1924, the march *Braganza*[87] was presented to HMS *Excellent*, the Royal Navy School of Gunnery on Whale Island. This was the Regimental March of The Queen's Royal Regiment (West Surrey).[88] The RNSM Band featured with the Divisional Bands from Chatham, Portsmouth, Plymouth and the Depot RM at the Wembley Tattoo in 1924. They were under the direction of Lt J C J Hoby, the Senior Director of Music, RM. This appearance was repeated the following year although on that occasion they were massed with the Chatham Division Band only.[89] At home in Portsmouth the RNSM had opportunities to demonstrate their high standards. They were massed with the Portsmouth Divisional Band and the bands of HMS Excellent and the RN Barracks under Lt R P O'Donnell for the King's Birthday Review. They returned to Southsea Common to play for the unveiling of the War Memorial by HRH the Duke of York on October 15th. An innovation was the performance by the RNSM Band Boys' Choir. 1924 ended with the School having 63 Band Corporals and 673 Musicians.

Courses for Bandmasters (1st and 2nd Class) and Corporals were being run on a regular basis with full details being published in 'General Standing Orders' and 'General Orders'. The Syllabus for the examination of Instructors was published in a similar manner, as and when required. Typically, two courses were run for each of the three examinations each year.[90]

By now the Royal Naval School of Music had been in existence for a little over twenty years. It had surmounted its problems of insufficient space during its embryonic years and, in so doing, had laid solid foundations for the future. Since then it had not just endured the First World War but, despite crippling losses, had earned the plaudits, and the sympathy, of its many admirers. It had then reviewed and strengthened its own leadership and organisation, passed through the Corps amalgamation with little effect upon its structure and could now point to many years of having provided more than what the Royal Navy had required - a Band Service of skilled and disciplined Musicians, but with a military role as well.

1925 saw the achievement, albeit inadvertent, of a milestone in military music. Whilst in Montreal BM J Allen received an invitation to broadcast on CNRM (Canadian National Railways Montreal) broadcasting station on the 3rd September 1925. Whilst announced as the Royal Marine Band of HMS *Calcutta* it was to perform as an orchestra. Two or three days after the broadcast a messenger arrived on board HMS *Calcutta* with a package addressed to "Bandmaster Allen, HMS *Calcutta*, Montreal Harbour". The covering letter said: "In the course of some experimental work the other night, we happened to make some recordings of two of the numbers broadcasted by you from Station CNRM, and thinking that you would like copies of them, we have pleasure in handing you herewith, with our compliments, a copy of each selection. Signed H Berliner". The notepaper was headed "The Compo Company Limited. Canada's Largest Record Manufacturer." Inside the package was a recording of *Cavalleria Rusticana* and of *Bacchus*.[91]

Discussions took place between the RNSM and the Royal Academy of Music in 1925 that appear to have culminated in the adoption of the examination for the Royal Academy

87 *Played in Excellent's Wardroom when passing the port.*

88 *A regiment that served with the Marines and now regarded as being associated with the Royal Marines.*

89 *Official programmes.*

90 *General Orders, Royal Marines 1924, GO74.*

91 *Recordings are in the RMM archive. H Berliner and the Cedo Company, whose trademark was "APEX", were experimenting in electrical recording from radio broadcasts - as opposed to placing a microphone in front of the radio loudspeaker. If these recordings are electrically produced they could be one of the first recordings, if not the first, made by this method in the world.*

Certificate and the Service award that has developed into the LRAM diploma and the Director of Music qualification.[92]

Whilst the Depot Band was on board HMS *Repulse* for the 1925 Royal Tour of South Africa a duty band, under BM H J T Taylor, was sent from the RNSM to the Depot, Deal.

During the 1920s new silver instruments were being procured and the bass drum was emblazoned. All made the RNSM Band sound and look much better, although the quality of the Admiralty supplied instruments was always poorer than those used by the Divisional bands. The band of the RNSM was being mentioned with increasing frequency in England whilst all over the world ships' bands were giving concerts and broadcasts. The Concert Band of the RNSM was made up from Musicians waiting for ships plus a few of the older boys. To earn such a reputation with a band that had little stability or continuity was testament to the system, to the staff and to the quality of the Musicians. During 1926 they were asked to entertain the Lords Commissioners of the Admiralty aboard the Admiralty Yacht *Enchantress*. Such was the reputation of the School that the Editor of the 'Globe and Laurel' requested that the RNSM "should blow its own trumpets a little louder within the pages of the journal".[93] 1926 also saw the introduction of the RNSM Annual Prize-giving. It was reported that provision had been made for an increase of about three hundred on the establishment of the School that year.[94]

Standardisation of musical salutes was being considered at this time and the RNSM was asked to make suggestions. The march of the same name from Bellini's opera *Norma* had been used as the Salute for Flag Officers (other than Cs-in-C) and for Governors but it was felt necessary to change this for something British in origin and more stirring in character. The RNSM was asked to play all suggestions for a combined RN and RM Committee to judge on the 9th June 1926. The unanimous decision, later confirmed in an AFO, was for *Iolanthe* to be adopted as the General Salute for Flag Officers not entitled to *Rule Britannia*, and for *Garb of Auld Gaul* to be adopted as the General Salute for Governors, High Commissioners, British General Officers and Air Officers; Foreign Officers and Officials. The musical arrangement of *Iolanthe* was made by Lt Fairfield.

In 1927 the 12th Bn Royal Marines, a composite Battalion with elements of all three Divisions, departed from Portsmouth in support of the threatened International Legation in Shanghai. They were marched from Eastney to the Dockyard by the Portsmouth Divisional Band and a band from the RNSM, under BM J W Relph, which was placed in the centre of the Battalion. They were met at the top of the High Street by the Blue Jacket (Royal Navy Volunteer) Band of C-in-C HMS *Victory*, BM WO T Hawkins, and embarked to the sounds of the massed bands. They sailed to the sounds of the Band of the Portsmouth Division , the Drums and Fifes of the Division and the Band of C-in-C HMS *Victory* all under the direction of Capt. R P O'Donnell. Upon arrival in Shanghai the band of HMS *Hawkins* playing *A Life on the Ocean Wave* greeted them and, later, the 12th Bn took part in the King's Birthday Parade in Hong Kong being led by the massed bands of HMS *Frobisher* and HMS *Hermes* under BM I H Hoyte.

Another major event of 1927 occurred when HMS *Renown* took the Duke and Duchess of York to Australia. A band of thirty-five with BM Martyr as Drum Major, plus sixteen Buglers from Plymouth Division with Sgt Douglas as Bugle Major were aboard. Temp Lt A Pragnell was in command of band and bugles. Eight Silver Bugles, two from each Division and two from the Depot were taken. This was the first time that they had been used afloat and they were kept in a glass cabinet on the aft deck when not required for

92 *Correspondence in RMM Archive.*
93 *A C Green unpublished papers and Globe & Laurel.*
94 *Globe & Laurel 1926 p102.*

Bandmaster Percy Barnacle, Bandmaster HMS Royal Oak, Malta, 1928. As a result of the Bandmaster being insulted by Admiral Collard whilst conducting his band, and other similar incidents, the Officer Commanding Royal Marines complained about the "insult to the Corps". The Admiral was court-martialled

duties in conjunction with the Guard of Honour. Four Buglers would be on watch at all times and bugle calls were played to great effect. One Bugler was forward, two amidships and the fourth was on the Quarter Deck. The twelve Buglers not on watch sounded *Divisions*, *Evening Quarters*, *Sunset* and some other calls from a platform halfway up the aft funnel. This enabled them to be heard not only throughout the ship but also over the surrounding area when in port. The Drum and Fife Band had to Beat Retreat on the Quarter Deck when in harbour; the band played from Sunset minus ten minutes to Sunset minus two minutes when the massed Buglers sounded the *Alert*. A relief of sentries (six men) fired a salvo on the forebridge before the Massed Buglers sounded *Sunset* accompanied by ruffles of drums followed by the *Carry On*. The Drum and Fife band quickly became very popular with the ship's company and would often perform on the forecastle in the early part of the First Watch. Whilst in New Zealand the Officers gave an 'At Home' to five hundred of Auckland's citizens. The Orchestra played from 3.30pm to 4.15pm when the Drum and Fife Band gave a display on the jetty. Following this the Pipers[95] played from 4.45pm until 5pm. The Jazz band then entertained until the end of the 'At Home'. The Drum and Fife Band attracted a great deal of attention since they were rarely seen on a Foreign Station. This band of sixteen was drawn from the ranks of the Detachment having been especially selected for this purpose. The entry to Sydney was a very complex operation, especially for the Guard and Band. On the day of entering harbour lower deck was cleared at 08.50 am by which time the band had fallen in on the Quarter Deck. The band commenced the musical programme, arrangements having been made so that the band and the Pipers who were on 'B' turret did not play simultaneously. The programme included band and bugles combined for the two bugle marches *Marching Through Georgia* and *Sambre et Meuse*. These two pieces impressed both the crowd and the crew since they were rarely heard on board a man-of-war. One of the Band's principal duties was, with fourteen Buglers, to lead a parade of 25,000 ex-servicemen through Melbourne on Anzac Day. The band was followed by part of the Ship's Company and the RM Detachment. Forty-two other bands were in this parade and His Royal Highness took the Salute. It was estimated that 800,000 people watched this parade. Whilst in Melbourne the full military band made five broadcasts. From Australia the Royal Tour progressed via the East Coast of Africa to Mauritius, Suez, Gibraltar and Portsmouth.[96]

The band from the RN Barracks Portsmouth was sent, with a CplBug and three Buglers from Portsmouth Division, to join HMS *Champion* a 3,750 ton Portsmouth based cruiser for passage to Russia during August 1928. The ship's task was to recover the bodies of thirty-eight British crewmen of the submarine L55 lost in 1919 and recently recovered by the Bolsheviks. The Guard, Band and Buglers paraded as the coffins were hoisted on board. At 4.30pm HMS *Champion* sailed with the band playing Chopin's *Funeral March* after which the Buglers sounded *Last Post*. Four H Class submarines met her as she reached the Nab Tower off Portsmouth and they escorted her into Portsmouth Harbour. Band and Buglers were on the aft superstructure. Sentries remained by the coffins until after sunset when the Buglers again sounded *Last Post*.

95 *Three sailors were especially embarked as Pipers. They brought two sets of pipes with them, a third set was purchased by the Wardroom and a fourth set was brought on board by the Drum-Major of the Portsmouth Division the night before Renown sailed. The fourth set was for a Scotsman in the RM Detachment. The Drummers were trained to accompany the Pipers.*

96 *Notes relating to the tour of HMS Renown were, mainly, taken from the Report of the OCRM, Maj T L Hunton.*

A similar duty befell the band of HMS *Cumberland* when the 'hero of Zeebrugge', Major Edward Bamford VC DSO RM, died as the ship approached Shanghai. Six men of the RM Detachment carried his body, draped in the Union flag, on their shoulders from HMS *Cumberland* to a tug alongside. The ship's band, under BM H Kerslake, played Chopin's *Funeral March* and the Guard of Honour remained at the present arms until the tug passed out of sight on its way to Shanghai.

In 1928 two ships, HMAS *Australia* and HMAS *Canberra*, were launched. These were to be the pride of the Royal Australian Navy (RAN) and the RNSM was given the task of training the two bands, each of one Bandmaster and fourteen Musicians. This situation had also occurred in 1913. The RNSM can be credited with helping to set up the Royal Australian Band Service, especially since a retired Bandmaster, E P Snook, helped to set up the shore-based Musicians at Flinders Naval Depot (now HMAS *Cerberus*). This position was filled by a succession of Royal Marines Band personnel, some retired, and others on loan.

On a warship 'X' turret, which is one of the after turrets, contains the guns that are normally manned by the Royal Marine Detachment. In March of 1929 HMS *Devonshire* re-commissioned and, after working up exercises, the ship sailed to join the Mediterranean Fleet at Malta, arriving there in July. With the rest of the 1st Cruiser Squadron the *Devonshire* reached the Aegean where the Squadron was to take part in gunnery exercises. Her first salvo was fired at about 10 o'clock. This was accompanied by a violent explosion and a sheet of flame from 'X' turret. The OCRM and two of his detachment were killed outright and a further twelve died either on board *Devonshire* or the hospital ship *Maine*. Sergeant Snell was missing, presumably blown overboard. All members of the Band (BMII P D Evans) were in the transmitting station. Immediately following the explosion the band was involved in removing the bodies in blankets from the turret to be prepared for burial. The bands of HMS *London* and HMS *Royal Oak* together with the Buglers of the Squadron were massed to lead the cortege, which included two hundred men from the Squadron, on the two and a half mile journey to the cemetery at Volo. A Memorial Service was held at sea at the scene of the accident.

Portsmouth Guildhall on the 16th November 1929 was the scene of the last of a series of RNSM concerts. There was a symphony orchestra of 80 performers and a full military band of 60 performers. All were drawn from the RNSM, the C-in-C's Band, the RN Barracks Band and from HM Ships *Excellent* and *St Vincent*. In addition the RNSM supplied a choir of two hundred Band Boys! Lt S Fairfield and Lt A Pragnell were the conductors.

The British base at Wei-Hai-Wei was returned to the Chinese with all due ceremony on the 1st October 1930. At the pier a Seaman's Guard of twenty-five and a guard of the same size found from the Argyll and Sutherland Highlanders (Princess Louises') were paraded with the band from HMS *Cumberland* under BM C R M Robinson. Meanwhile, for the Ceremony of Rendition at Government House, twenty seamen, twenty Royal Marines and twenty men from the Argyll

Bandmaster F P Harrison with a group of his Musicians from the cruiser HMS Suffolk. This was the Flagship of the 5th Cruiser Squadron, part of the China Fleet, and she was visiting Tokyo. Her Captain, centre and on the Bandmaster's right, is Commodore G P Bowen OBE. On the Bandmaster's left is Captain E J Woodington RM, Officer Commanding Royal Marines

Major H Lidiard on board HMS Duke of York on the 17th April 1947

and Sutherland Highlanders were on parade with the band of HMS *Kent* under BM (WO) Papworth.

It was announced in early 1930 that the Royal Naval School of Music would move from Eastney to Deal where there would be more room and better facilities.

On the 1st October 1930 at 9am the men of the RNSM paraded at Eastney Barracks. Following an inspection the Royal Marines, Portsmouth Division, Band and Bugles marched the parade out of the Barracks. Royal Marines lined the drive and the guard turned out. As the parade made its way towards Fratton Station the Divisional Band played *Old Comrades*. At the head of the parade, alongside Capt Faithfull, marched Maj H E Lidiard. Twenty-seven years earlier he led the first band into the new RNSM and now he led the last band out of it. The Royal Naval School of Music at Eastney had closed, having achieved what it had been established to do. The standard of music in the Royal Navy had been raised to that of the Royal Marines; it had provided bands to the ships of the Royal Navy that enhanced the reputation of the service and the country all over the world, and it also provided men who had earned the respect of their comrades in both peace and war. The loss of the School from the Portsmouth area undoubtedly left a musical void and it was very fortunate for the local population that the young Lt Dunn and the Portsmouth Divisional Band were able to increase their local engagements to compensate.

Upon arrival at Deal the men of the RNSM were met by the Drum and Fife Band of the Depot, Deal, under Drum Major W J Small. (The Depot Band, under Lt Ricketts, had been disbanded a few months earlier). The transfer of the RNSM meant that the Chief Schoolmaster and his staff at the Depot RM had to take on the training of Boy Buglers and Boy Musicians in addition to Royal Marine Recruits.[97]

In 1932 the number of RN ships that were allowed bands was over forty. Other ships that were entitled to bands but were not carrying them because they were undergoing refit or being placed in Reserve included the battleships *Barham*, *Ramillies* and *Repulse* (all in Reserve) and *Argus* (aircraft-carrier), *Effingham* and *Emerald* (both cruisers).

Another milestone in Royal Marine Band history occurred on the 20th March 1934 when massed bands of the Mediterranean Fleet under Fleet Bandmaster A C Green played, for the first time, Green's arrangement of *Sunset for Band and Bugles*. This took place in the Alameda Gardens, Gibraltar, as the flag was lowered. This has become the acknowledged manner in which the *Sunset* call is presented by the Royal Marines during the ceremony of Beating Retreat.

Ship's massed bands play during a Review of the Royal Navy's Mediterranean Fleet, Malta 1933

At the 4th Balkan Olympic Games in Athens the massed bands of HM Ships *Queen Elizabeth*, *Royal Sovereign* and *Glorious* entertained a crowd of 90,000. They stepped off and

97 Educational notes by Instructor Lt Cdr F J Wilkins.

performed a comprehensive marching display that was much appreciated by the massive crowd. At this time the Royal Navy still maintained its position as the most powerful navy afloat. This was due not merely to the number of vessels that were distributed throughout the world but also to the amount of time spent exercising and training. Whilst the bands of the Mediterranean Fleet were performing so nobly at venues such as Naples and Malta they were also spending much time at sea practising their skills in the Transmitting Stations. Technology was gradually developing to match the progress in gunnery techniques and the band commissioning system demanded that the teamwork necessary to achieve efficiency should be constantly practised.

Back at Deal the RNSM continued with the daily toil of clothing parades, coaling fatigues, bed filling, gym at 5.30 on a winter's morning, lighting the fires in the stone gymnasium in South Barracks and what seemed like a never-ending stream of kit and marching order parades. All this was in addition to the musical training. Despite having to endure all of this there was an occasional feeling of loss when the time came to move on to a band. There was a fierce pride in the standards attained and in being an 'RMB'.

1935 was Silver Jubilee Year and RM Bands were involved in celebrations throughout the world. HMS *Sussex* was in Japan with the Duke of Gloucester whilst HMS *Neptune's* band, augmented with six Musicians from the RNSM and with two Buglers from HMS *Hood*, was with the Prince of Wales in Cardiff. They led the column from the station to the City Hall where a Royal Guard formed up with the Band to receive His Royal Highness. On the 5th July the Prince of Wales visited the Depot and toured the RNSM. He took the salute at the march past led by the Boys' Band. HMS *Devonshire* was in Port Said and, on the 6th October, the King of Egypt's son, Prince Farouk, came on board. As the *Devonshire* left harbour all ships were dressed overall and paraded Guards and Bands in the Prince's honour. The band of HMS *Kent* (BM WO G L Read) massed with the band of the Royal Inniskilling Fusiliers in Shanghai. The band was much appreciated - especially as they marched back through Shanghai at one o'clock in the morning! HMS *Suffolk* was in Kobe, Japan. HMS *Norfolk* was at Mauritius and HMS *Carlisle* at Capetown. The Massed Bands of the Mediterranean Fleet were joined by the bands of the Royal Artillery (Malta), the 1st Bn The Duke of Wellington's Regiment and the 2nd Bn The Rifle Brigade (Prince Consort's Own) to perform on Palace Square, Malta. Under the leadership of Commissioned Bandmaster (Cd BM)[98] A C Green each of the Bandmasters had the opportunity to conduct a part of the programme.

In Portsmouth, for the King's Birthday Parade, the various bands of Portsmouth Port and Garrison massed with the Portsmouth Divisional Band. The C-in-C's band and the bands of HMS *Victory*, HMS *Excellent*, the Royal Artillery (Portsmouth) Band, the 1st Bn The York and Lancaster Regiment and the 1st Bn The Rifle Brigade (Prince Consort's Own) were under Lt F V Dunn, Director of Music of the Portsmouth Divisional Band.

The First Lord of the Admiralty visited the RNSM in 1935, the number of Band Boys at the School being three hundred and forty at this time.

1936 had a particular, and peaceful, landmark. The combined bands of Portsmouth Command under BM G C Keen made two commercial recordings on the Columbia label. The first recording was *Nautical Moments*, arranged by Winter, and because of its length had to be split across both sides of the record. The second recording had *Sea Songs Medley Number 3* arranged by Vaughan Williams on one side and *Ship Ahoy March* by Mackenzie on the other.

Very few records relating to the training of RNSM ranks for their duties in Fire Control and Transmitting Stations exist; however, in the '*Gunnery Training Manual 1937*' are found

98 *From 1920 Warrant Officers could be promoted to Commissioned Officer and, in the Royal Marine Bands, were called Commissioned Bandmasters and identified by a single star on the lower arm. Their next promotion would be to Lieutenant.*

details of the courses that they had to pass as part of their training. The 'Other Ranks (RN School of Music) Qualifying in Fire Control' course lasted eighteen days and comprised 'Elementary Principles of Fire Control - Definitions' (one day); 'Control Position of a Battleship, Main and Secondary Armaments, and a Cruiser' (one day); 'Clocks, Dumaresque.[99] Usbourne's Fall of Shot Indicator, Change Over Switches and Telephones' (four days); All other Fire Control Instruments, Rangefinders, Inclinometers and Bearing Measuring Instruments. Method of Plotting Time and Range, and Time and Bearing' (one day); 'Use of Fire Control Table supplied to a Modern Ship. Communications. Standard Method of Passing Orders. Communication Drill. Control Procedures. Standard sequence of orders' (four days); 'Use of Director. Personnel stationed in the more important control positions and their duties' (one day); 'General Outline of Concentration procedure. Recording parties. Use of records. Use of Stop Watches' (one day); 'High Angle Control' (two days); 'Lifebuoys, Hammocks, Knotting and Splicing' (two days), all followed by a one day examination. At the end of the course each man had to be capable of carrying out the duties of any person in the control position or transmitting station of a battleship or cruiser. There was also a course (Number 63) for those needing to requalify in Fire Control. It was carried out at RN Gunnery School, Chatham. The subject was Fire Control and lasted eight days (forenoons only) and there was no examination. However, candidates for promotion to Band Corporal or Bandmaster 2nd Class had to have a short practical examination. If they re-qualified successfully the following annotation was made on their individual History Sheet: "VG in working of fire control instruments." There was also a course for formed bands re-qualifying before embarkation. (Course 64). The course, 'Fire Control', lasted four days and would be one of three courses depending upon the ship being drafted to.

At the time of the Munich Crisis (1938) the Reserve Fleet was mobilised and all of the Musicians in the School went to join them. This meant that the Boys' Band took over the duties of the Depot Band - which they did with very satisfactory results. The School had been very successful in reducing the number of Band Boys being sent to sea before they had been advanced to Musician by recruiting and training more of them to satisfy the demands of the Royal Navy. Unfortunately the trend had not continued into 1938-1939 and hindsight tells us that this is the very time when a surplus would have been invaluable.

Educational qualifications obtained by study ashore and afloat also illustrate the size and scale of the RNSM, which had to apply itself to the concept of 'distance-learning'.

The average wastage for the years 1938/1939 was 5% and it was deemed necessary to arrive at a datum figure for the establishment size by either estimating the size of the band requirement four years hence or by fixing an arbitrary figure and doing the best with it. The modern RMBS is now able to do the former but in 1939 with about fifty bands all over the world and war on the horizon it would have been utterly impossible. In both 1938 and in 1939 the Reserve Fleet was manned by denuding shore establishments.[100]

The School was run according to 'Superintendents' Instructions' which covered Officers' Leave, Musical Instruments, Drill, Discipline, Requests, Drafting, Company Administration, Private Engagements, Promotion, Equipment, Band Boys and Vocational Training. Maj Leech-Porter's Instructions reveal a well-ordered existence, as did his preparations for the forthcoming war contained in the confidential document 'Orders for Mobilisation - RN School of Music'. These preparations, on receipt of the order 'Prepare to Mobilise' or 'Mobilise', would be initiated by Buglers sounding *RN School of Music* followed by *Assembly* in East Barracks and North Barracks as well as five Buglers sounding the same

99 *The plotting table in the Transmitting Room.*

100 *Superintendent Lt Col McCausland's Report on the Band Service 1938 - 1941. RM Museum.*

calls in Deal. It was anticipated that twelve bands would be formed and sent to embark immediately on receipt of the order to mobilise.

A RNSM Band was chosen to accompany Their Majesties the King and Queen to Canada and the United States in HMS *Repulse* during 1939. Whilst the School had provided bands for Royal Tours previously this was the first occasion that it had been with the King. Lt A C Green was appointed to the *Repulse* as Director of Music. The ship's band (BM A J Bennett) was retained with the addition of BM I A T Russell and BM G C McLean as Drum Major, plus four Musicians embarked whilst the ship was at Portsmouth. Preparations were intensive. Ex-Buglers in the RM Detachment joined the heavily rehearsed marching band. Two concerts were to be presented to Their Majesties by the ship's company and, as usual, the band was heavily committed to these. Lt Green wrote a ship's march called HMS *Repulse* that included in the trio the West Country tune *To Be A Farmer's Boy* since *Repulse* was a Plymouth ship. Sadly, thanks to a campaign by the Daily Express the tour of HMS *Repulse* was cancelled just at the last minute. The newspaper campaign was based upon the fact that the *Repulse* was the only ship in commission that would be able to deal with the German pocket battleships. Questions were asked in Parliament and the Prime Minister, Neville Chamberlain, gave in to pressure. Whilst the tour went ahead it was on the especially chartered SS *Empress of Britain*. Disappointment at the cancellation of the participation of HMS *Repulse* in the tour was keenly felt through the Band Service since it was seen as the ultimate recognition of the quality of the bands produced by the Royal Naval School of Music.

There was now talk of mobilisation. Re-enlistment of Pensioners was open to all Band ranks. Those already discharged could return provided that they had not been out of the Band Service for more than 5 years. What would be the impact of this second great conflict of the century upon the country, its services and, in particular, the Royal Marines Band Service?

Upon the outbreak of war the Fleet was mobilised and Pensioners were recalled for duty. Five bands were mobilised in one morning! At this time the disposition of all ranks was 612 at the RNSM, 487 embarked in thirty-one ships of the Home Fleet and 367 embarked in twenty-three ships on foreign service. HMS *Royal Arthur*, the reception camp for naval personnel at Skegness (Butlin's Holiday Camp) had the first Pensioner Band. Their musical comeback was splendid in spite of dental and other difficulties. Soon they were playing orchestral programmes twice a week in the Officers' Mess and twice weekly in the various Dining Halls for the new entries and the ship's company.

In July the Admiralty issued its 'Mobilisation Return - No 1' that detailed the complements for all RN Ships. At this time each of the three Cs-in-C at The Nore (Chatham), Portsmouth and Plymouth (HMS *Pembroke*, *Victory*, and *Drake* respectively) had bands consisting of a Cd BM or BM(WO), a BdCpl and eleven Musicians. This was a peace time complement and these bands could be removed in the event of mobilisation, a situation that would also apply to the bands at HMS *Ganges* (Shotley Barracks), HMS *St Vincent* (Boys' Training Establishment) and HMS *Caledonia* although in this particular case a reserves, or Pensioner, band was to be sent as soon as possible. Mobilisation would also affect the complements of Flagship Bands. In such cases a Cd BM or BM(WO) would serve in all Fleet Flagships of the Home, Mediterranean and China Fleets and a BMI would serve in other Flagships replacing, where necessary, any BMII. The complement of Musicians would be increased to twenty-one in Fleet Flagships of the Home, Mediterranean and China Fleets; to fifteen in other Flagships over 8,000 tons and in cruisers below 8,000 tons which were Flagships of Cs-in-C on Foreign Stations and to thirteen in cruisers below 8,000 tons which were Flagships other than Cs-in-C on Foreign Stations. These figures reflect not only the need to retain the ability of a band to provide musical support according to the seniority of the ship's commanding officer but also, since any shortfall had to be made good by an equivalent increase in the size of the RM Detachment, the necessity of the Musicians to the fighting capability of the ship through their Fire Control duties and abilities. All cruisers on Foreign Stations that were not allowed an RM Band were entitled to a Ship's Musician. These were usually recruited locally but, if not obtainable in wartime, any additional Able Bodied or Ordinary Seaman would be allowed.

At the RNSM, mobilisation would have the effect of the School losing six of its eleven BMI, five of its eleven BMII, fourteen of its eighteen BdCpls and thirty-five of its forty strong band. By comparison the Divisional Bands at Chatham, Portsmouth and Plymouth would not lose any of their strength because of mobilisation.[101]

Only two weeks after Great Britain declared war on Germany the RM Band Service sustained its first casualties when two members of the band of HMS *Courageous*, Musns Etridge and Humble perished when the aircraft carrier was torpedoed and sank.

On the 14th October the inadequacies of the defences of Scapa Flow were demonstrated when the German submarine *U-47* managed to penetrate them and sink the veteran battleship HMS *Royal Oak* with the loss of 786 men including BM F C Golding, BdCpl W C Bonner and Musns Treleaven, Webb and Green.

After two and a half years in command of the RNSM Maj Leech-Porter was relieved by Lt Col McCausland who had been recalled from the Retired List. He assumed command on the 8th January 1940. The Musical Director, Capt A Pragnell, and his Assistant Musical Director, Lt A C Green, decided to introduce additional training in order to ensure that Musicians being drafted to ships were of the highest possible standard. Warrant Officers were allocated a number of classes to supervise with musical instruction in the evening following the morning's musical instruction or drill and an afternoon's Radio Telephony.[102] This enabled a very comprehensive and easily accessible record of progress of each Band Boy to be maintained.

All Home shore establishments were supplied with Pensioner Bands during 1940 since a military band for training purposes was considered a necessity. Pensioners arrived at the Depot on a Sunday, were kitted out on Monday, drew their instruments on Tuesday and went off to their band as if they had only been on leave.

Permanent Pensioner Bands were allocated to the following establishments between 1939 and 1942: HMS *Royal Arthur*, HMS *Raleigh*, HMS *Drake*, HMS *Collingwood*, HMS *Excellent*, HMS *Ganges*, HMS *Pembroke*, HMS *Victory*, HMS *St George*, HMS *Osprey*, HMS *St Vincent*, HMS *Glendower* and HMS *Europa*.

Another permanent band was formed from Hostilities Only (HO) recruits and sent to HMS *Proserpine*, a Shore Establishment at Scapa in November 1940.[103]

In February the Band of HMS *Exeter* returned to Deal in triumph following the action off the River Plate. A large band from the School under BM Holt and led by Drum Major Frost was at the head of the procession that marched through cheering crowds along High Street and the Strand to East Barracks. *Exeter* together with *Ajax* and HMNZS *Achilles*, all carrying RM Bands, were damaged as they attacked the German pocket battleship the *Admiral Graf Spee,* which fled into Montevideo harbour where she was scuttled. A high price was paid for the victory. Boy Bugler R B Hill was killed on the bridge of *Exeter* when it sustained serious damage and the Captain of Marines, a Corporal and five Marines were

101 *Admiralty Mobilisation Return No 1 - Complements of HM Ships. RM Museum.*

102 *Telephones used for communication in gunnery control.*

103 *Superintendent Lt Col McCausland's Report on the Band Service 1938 - 1941. RM Museum.*

The shell of the drum removed from HMS Swift. Notice the emblazonment, the tack pattern and remnants of the rope
Courtesy: Programa de Arqueologia Subacuatica, Instituto Nacional de Antropologia, Argentina

'Napoleon inspecting the Royal Marines on HMS Bellerophon' (1815) by Capt J S Hicks RM. Note the young Drummer

One of a series of Royal Marine uniform illustrations drawn by E Hull in 1829

'Old Clarence Barracks, 1847' by A C Snape. This was the barracks for the Portsmouth Division until 1848. Note the Drummer

'Woolwich Barracks, 1835' by Arman (above) probably showing the band playing after Church service, and by Melton (below), showing the ceremony of Trooping the Colour.

'The Royal Marine Artillery at field gun drill on Southsea Common' by Daniel Cunliffe c.1845.

ontemporary painting, dated 1851, of Bandmaster W Rogers by Lt Col W G Masters RM. The sword was a gift from the Tsar of Russia and is now in the Royal Marines Museum (see inset)

'Drummers of 1854', a water-colour by Lt Col Masters. Note the swords, and the drum badge on the back of the helmet

'Musicians', another painting of 1854 by Masters. The Drummer's uniform still resembles the Mameluke design of the 1820

/usician David Barnes of the Band of the Royal Marine Artillery. Barnes enlisted in 1865 and was discharged in 1892. It is likely that he is a member of the RMA Band pictured in Chapter 7

The Depot, Deal Drum Major, c.1902-10. Used with permission of Mr J Rawlinson

killed. The Bandmaster of the *Exeter*, L C Bagley, was Mentioned in Despatches for bravery in the action.

At Deal HO Musicians, aged between eighteen and forty-six, began arriving in great numbers and by the spring of 1940 there were one hundred and fifty at the School, some of them being outstanding instrumentalists. Unfortunately about half of the applicants were cornet players. The first squad completed preliminary military training and was passed out in a similar manner to RM recruit squads.

In February/March 1940 some of the large houses on the Walmer sea front were requisitioned by the Admiralty, bands of eleven were formed from the Musicians and each band was allocated to a certain house to practise. On the 3rd June about twelve bands from the sea front houses paraded in embarkation order at East Barracks before being sent to various destinations.

During the spring of 1940 the Battle of France was raging and the children and people of Deal were being evacuated. The Admiralty decided that the Band Boys would go to the RM Reserve Camp at Exton, Lympstone, which they did, with the staff and the Senior Assistant Musical Director Lt A C Green, on the 30th May. Two weeks later, with tons of stores and records, the remainder of the School left East Barracks for Plymouth. All musical practice was carried out in the dungeons of a fort. In September both wings of the School moved again, this time becoming a single unit once more in a camp at St Andrew's Road, Malvern in Worcestershire. This had been built as an alternative location for the Admiralty, should it be forced to leave London. There were many large underground rooms that could be used for practice. Facilities at Malvern were very good with four blocks A, B, C and G, which were named Auber, Beethoven, Chopin and Gounod, being available to them. Beethoven Block was used for musical practice with a practice room for each class. Gounod Block was the administration building and housed the Quartermaster and his assistants and the Paymaster. The School also had its own Naval Sick Quarters with a Principal Medical Officer, a Surgeon Lieutenant RNVR and also a Dental Surgeon.

In early June 1941 the aircraft carrier HMS *Glorious*, having evacuated a number of Hurricane squadrons from Norway, was steaming southwards when she was seen by the German ships *Scharnhorst* and *Gneisnau* on patrol. *Scharnhorst* opened fire at a range of 14 miles and hit the *Glorious*, starting a major fire. *Scharnhorst* continued to hit the carrier and she eventually sank. 1,515 men were lost in this action including Musns Cook, Wybrow and Jones who were killed whilst BM F Woodcock and the rest of the band of HMS *Glorious* were 'Missing, Presumed Dead'.

The 'Globe and Laurel' correspondent on board HMS *King George V* wrote, in 1941, "Whilst the gunnery requirements take a great deal of the bandsmen's time and energy in these days, yet they still have the moral obligation to provide entertainment of all kinds for the ships company - an important psychological consideration just now. And I must say the bands are doing it right well".

Dance bands were a particularly popular form of entertainment and the band on board HMS *King George V* were fortunate in having Tony Moore from Henry Hall's Band, who made his own orchestrations of popular music, and Norman Parker from the Birmingham Hippodrome orchestra amongst their number. One watch of the band was completely HO. HMS *Nelson* also had a very good dance band, BdCpl Seymour's "*Swing Four*", and when weather permitted dances were held on the upper deck when in harbour. HMS *Hermione* had a seven-piece dance band whose popularity was largely due to the efforts of HO Musn L Young who rehearsed and arranged programmes and also organised the "*Hermione Three*", a vocal trio. HMS *Newcastle* staged a weekly show featuring "*Mascagini and his Ambassadors of Rhythm*" with a few novelty numbers thrown in. In between the dance numbers "*Mascagini and his Choir*" were featured! Also, on Sunday evenings, "Music Lovers' Half-Hour" was very popular with the ship's company. The band of HMS *Duke of York* under BM W B Willmot gave some lunch-hour concerts whilst in harbour but the work of the 'dockyard mateys' slowed down as they too watched the concerts - which were subsequently stopped. The band then made occasional broadcasts over the ship's radio instead. HMS *Victorious* band included eleven HOs, most of whom were well-known Musicians in civilian life. The band provided the ship's company with up-to-date dance programmes and were also the backbone of all the impromptu concerts.

1941 was the worst year yet for the Band Service. The peak in numbers serving afloat in all theatres of war was reached with 949 at the RNSM and UK shore establishments plus 1,045 embarked in 64 ships. The light cruiser HMS *Bonaventure* was sunk in the Mediterranean with the loss of BM Brain, BdCpl Packer and Musn Goymer. Musn A Howden of HMS *Fiji* went to visit BM Rogers of HMS *Gloucester* when the *Fiji* docked in Alexandria harbour. *Gloucester* and *Fiji* sailed for Crete and were together during most of the attacks that followed. German bombers attacked all ships in the area and HMS *Gloucester* was badly hit and sank. Only two of the band survived. They were Musns Brisley and Macdonald. The latter was taken prisoner and formed a band in the New Marlag prisoner-of-war camp. The remainder were posted 'Missing, Presumed Dead'. HMS *Fiji* steamed around the *Gloucester* and dropped most of her own Carley floats to the survivors. Eventually HMS *Fiji* herself ran out of ammunition and was reduced to firing practice and smoke shells in a desperate attempt to keep the bombers away. She received several direct hits after which she sank with the loss of BM Wenham and seven members of the band, all 'Missing, Presumed Dead'.

The day before the *Fiji* and the *Gloucester* were sunk HMS *Suffolk* sent a fateful radio signal. She was patrolling the Denmark Strait searching for the German battleship *Bismarck* which was known to be on the loose in the North Sea. *Suffolk's* signal told HMS *Hood* that she had found, and was shadowing, the *Bismarck* and the *Prinz Eugen*. At 0535 on the 24th May the *Hood* spotted the *Bismarck* and commenced firing at 0553. With only her fifth salvo the *Bismarck's* gunners scored a hit on *Hood's* weakest area - the after deck above the ammunition storage - and at 0600 the *Hood* blew up and sank taking 1,419 men, including BM Herod, a Band Corporal, thirteen Musicians and a Band Boy, with her.

A few days later HMS *Orion* was severely damaged by enemy aircraft south of Crete. Six hundred soldiers rescued from Crete were killed and BdCpl Cole and three Musicians were killed in the TS. The ship went to America for repairs after removal of most of the dead at Alexandria. The Musicians' bodies were not recovered until the ship reached America as, during the attacks on the ship, damage had caused the TS to be flooded with fuel oil.[104] In a seven-day period the RM Band Service had lost forty-four men, including two complete bands.

On the 24th November HMS *Dunedin* was torpedoed by *U-124* in mid-Atlantic. BM Sargeant, BdCpls West and Jones, seven Musicians and a Band Boy were lost. Next day, off Libya, *U-331* torpedoed the battleship HMS *Barham*. BM Chard and twelve Musicians were lost - 'Missing, Presumed Killed'.

On the 10th December Japanese torpedo aircraft attacked and sank HMS *Prince of Wales* and HMS *Repulse* off Malaya. Five members of the Band Service were lost. In the Mediterranean, less than three weeks after the loss of the *Barham*, the entire band of HMS *Galatea* was lost when, on the 15th December, the cruiser was torpedoed and sunk by a German submarine thirty miles from Alexandria. In December 1941 HMS *Neptune* was with the ships of Force K searching for an enemy convoy. Twenty miles east of Tripoli the *Neptune*

104 *Notes to A C Green by T Bridle.*

hit two mines, one of which wrecked her propellers and steering gear. The following ships sheered off immediately but the *Aurora* and *Penelope* also hit mines. *Neptune* drifted onto a third mine and developed a heavy list. The destroyer *Kandahar* went to her rescue but a mine blew her stern off. The *Neptune* then hit a fourth mine and capsized. All but one of her company, including eleven men from the Band Service, were lost. Other individuals were lost as a result of enemy action during the year. Total losses in 1941 were ninety-nine.

In some ships the band managed to get away unscathed, the band of HMS *Ark Royal* being an example of this. On the 13th November 1941 *Ark Royal* was on her way towards Malta once more when, at 1541hrs, the German submarine *U-81* fired three torpedoes. Only one hit but it was a crucial blow since it detonated near the starboard boiler room. Half of the band had been closed-up in the TS, the other half being due to take over at 1600hrs. Those who were preparing to go to the TS followed orders and made for the flight-deck. Even tilted as she was nobody thought the *Ark Royal* would sink but, at 0613 next morning, she did. The crew were taken the thirty miles to Gibraltar for passage back to the RNSM. Only one man, a seaman, lost his life in the "*Ark*".[105]

At Malvern the School's volunteer orchestra had grown to fifty-five performers with CSM McLean and LCpl Annereau as vocalists and Musn W Ivory, a former member of the BBC Scottish Orchestra who had joined as an HO, as solo violinist. The Dance Band, led by BM S C Low, was also making a name for itself. Lt Kenward took a large band on tour to the Clydeside area for "*Music While You Work*" concerts whilst a band of fifty-five under BM W T Lang was touring London for War Savings Weeks. The School contributed a great deal to War Savings, Warships, Wings for Victory and Salute the Soldier weeks. Any bands awaiting draft were sent around the country in support of these. School bands also gave many concerts in factories and in shipyards as well as performances for the Red Cross and other Charities.

One barrack room at the School contained twenty-five NCOs and men with a combined age of 1,197 years; a combined service of 615 years and eighty-eight medals and seventy-one Good Conduct badges between them! They were not all Pensioners since they included a "youngster" with only eleven years' service! (The 'average person' was forty-eight years old with twenty-five years man's service.)

By the summer of 1941 the Admiralty had decided that the RNSM must vacate Malvern and, once again, the only option was to split the School. The Band Boys, with Capt Smith as CO and Lt Green as Musical Director, went to a holiday camp called Howstrake Camp, near Douglas, on the Isle of Man. This was known as Junior Wing and Howstrake would remain its home for the next five years. The Senior Wing moved to Scarborough with the Superintendent, Lt Col H L M McCausland, Capt A Pragnell, Musical Director, and Staff. They were housed in two hotels, the 'Clifton' and the 'Norbreck'. The Malvern Camp became HMS *Duke*, a RN training establishment and in time had a RM Band of its own.

A shortage of musical instruments was beginning to cause difficulties for the School. They were not easy to obtain at a time when the demand was increasing and there was a danger that some instruments would disappear for the duration of the war. Cellos and string basses were withdrawn from bands in small ships where suitable storage was not available.

1942 brought even greater demands upon the RM Bands of the RNSM. To promote the war effort, further extensive tours of industrial areas and the provinces were made by bands from Scarborough under Lt Kenward, Lt Keen, Lt Papworth and BM(WO) Davis. Several BBC recordings were made whilst touring. From Scarborough, the bands of fifty from Senior Wing became known as Touring Bands. The Boys Band ran Talent Spotting

105 Notes to A C Green by T Parnell.

Competitions on the Isle of Man for the troops of all three services with Sub Lt Jon Pertwee RN of HMS *Valkyrie*, a radar-training establishment, as the compere.

Members of the Band Service were involved in some of the heaviest fighting at sea of 1942. They were in HMS *Penelope* (nicknamed the "Pepperpot" because of the amount of holes in her) undergoing repairs in the most bombed place on earth - Malta. Under almost constant bombing raids from German Stukas and JU 88s that were intended to destroy all the shipping in the harbour, she could not move until her damage repairs were completed. The ship's artificers and shipwrights worked alongside the men of the dockyard in between the air-raids.[106] Musn Jemmett died in a Malta hospital of natural causes during this period and BM S C Cooper was Mentioned in Despatches.[107]

HMS *Naiad* was sunk by *U-565* north of Mersa Matruh on the 11th March 1942 with the loss of Musn Page, 'Missing, Presumed Killed'.

On the 29th of the same month German forces attacked Russian Convoy PQ13 on route to Murmansk. HMS *Trinidad* and HMS *Eclipse* engaged three German heavy destroyers that were threatening the convoy. One of the most bizarre incidents of the war then took place. *Trinidad* engaged the German destroyer Z26 and inflicted serious damage with her opening salvoes. *Trinidad* pursued Z26, manoeuvring into a position where she could fire her own torpedoes. At 0922hrs the Torpedo Officer fired one torpedo. A few seconds later he fired the other two but they were frozen into the tubes and remained there. A few minutes later a torpedo was seen running towards *Trinidad*. Evasive action was taken but it was too late. The torpedo struck the port side just forward of the bridge and exploded. This torpedo was the one that *Trinidad* herself had fired. As a result of either a malfunction in the gyro-mechanism, possibly freezing, or water turbulence caused by exploding shells the torpedo had run wild. Incredibly it ran in a semi-circle and, within the entire space of the Arctic Ocean, had collided with the *Trinidad* steaming at full speed. The torpedo exploded in the RM Barracks[108], causing the flooding of one of the boiler-rooms and destroying the Damage Control HQ. Many ratings and Officers in these areas were killed. The TS, where the band was closed-up at Action Stations, was two decks below. It was plunged into darkness, the ventilation system pulled fumes in from the explosion and the bulkheads between the men and the oil fuel were seriously weakened. The emergency lighting came on and the Musicians, regaining their places around the two tables, one large the other small, attempted to re-establish contact with the bridge. The small table had been seriously damaged so its operators moved into the main area. The RN Officer ordered the only seaman in the party to report to Damage Control and seek assistance. When the heavy hatch was opened a mixture of oil fuel and seawater poured into the room. Despite the difficulties caused by the oil the seaman managed to climb the steel ladder and get through the hatch. The Officer then gave the order 'Abandon TS' and ushered the men past him. Three men had escaped through the hatch when, due mainly to the increasing list of the ship, the heavy counterbalanced hatch cover slammed down on the man climbing through it, breaking his back and trapping him there. The hatch could not be opened by either those below or above and, by that time, the fuel oil and sea-water mixture was up to waist-height in the compartment. At that point the weakened TS bulkhead gave way to the pressure of fuel oil behind it and tons of oil burst into the compartment drowning those who were trapped there. Those who had escaped from the TS made their way up oily ladders and through damaged mess decks and the RM Barracks with its huge hole in the side. Eventually they found their way up to the deck, the only three survivors from the

---

106 *HMS Penelope was the model for HMS Artemis in C S Forester's book 'The Ship'.*

107 *'Our Penelope' (HMS Penelope) by her Company 1943.*

108 *RM Messdeck was always known as the RM Barracks.*

RM Band of twelve that had worked together for more than a year. *Trinidad* managed to reach Murmansk where the bodies were recovered from the TS and buried at sea.[109]

The war in the Far East was at its height with the Japanese still on the offensive. HMS *Cornwall* was one of several ships sunk in the Indian Ocean by Japanese carrier-borne aircraft on the 5th April 1942. Nine of *Cornwall's* Musicians were 'Missing, Presumed Dead'. One of the ships accompanying *Cornwall* was the *Dorsetshire*. BM Upstell was in the TS with an RN Sub-Lieutenant and a Petty Officer. All hatches were battened down as an estimated fifty aircraft attacked. Hit by four bombs, all lighting and communication was lost and she began to list heavily. Realising the situation the Bandmaster ordered one of his men to open the hatch. The ladder above the hatch had fallen across the hatch cover and it could only be moved a small amount. In desperation the Musician forced his way through the small gap and moved the obstruction. All of the band managed to escape and made their way up to the deck where they were told to leave the ship by the Commander. Approximately half the crew went down with the ship and the remainder were left either in the sea or in boats, awaiting rescue. The sea was covered in fuel oil and heavily infested with sharks. After spending twenty-seven hours in the water they were rescued by British destroyers.[110]

The British aircraft carrier HMS *Hermes*, with two other vessels, was sunk in action off Trincomalee, Ceylon. *Hermes* had little anti-aircraft armament and her aircraft were operating from a shore base so she was virtually defenceless. BM Roe and nine Musicians were killed.[111]

Efforts to relieve the beleaguered island fortress of Malta were stepped up during the summer of 1942. Operation *Vigorous*, an attempt to force supplies through from the East, was mounted. German aircraft attacked and bombed the convoy and amongst many other casualties was HMS *Hermione*, the victim of a torpedo attack by *U-205* that claimed the life of BdCpl Vincent. Operation *Pedestal* proved to be a story of epic proportions as the convoy battled through to the relief of the island. The Axis forces knew about the convoy as soon as it passed through the Straits of Gibraltar and German submarines were positioned to intercept them. The first casualty was HMS *Eagle*, falling prey to *U-73* which fired four torpedoes into her. The *Eagle* sank with the loss of more than two hundred of her crew, including nine members of her band. Amongst the escorts was HMS *Manchester* which, whilst passing the Island of Pantelleria, was hit by torpedoes fired from an Italian E-boat. The Captain decided to scuttle the ship rather than let her be captured. When all arrangements were made for scuttling, the Starboard Watch left the ship and made for the North African shore by either swimming or using Carley floats. On reaching Tunisia they were taken to Algiers by train and thence across the Sahara Desert to an old French Foreign Legion outpost called Laghouat where over a thousand prisoners were held in a compound about 100 yards square with barrack rooms that held forty men each. They remained there until, just prior to the Allied landings in North Africa, they were all transferred to occupied France. Four Musicians were amongst the group repatriated in 1943.[112] Five other members of the band were interned but released to return to the UK, reporting to the RNSM on 25th November 1942.[113]

A band was in HMS *Nigeria* escorting Russian convoys and, later, convoys to Malta. *Nigeria's* BM Ridout was a prime example of the calibre of men that the School was producing. During 1940 he had organised many concerts ashore and afloat in the

109 *Information to A C Green by R Palmer, a band member, and from "The Ship That Torpedoed Itself".*
110 *Information supplied by BM Upstell to A C Green.*
111 *Information from Musn A H G Kidd to A C Green.*
112 *Musn P Herring to A C Green.*
113 *Official War Logbook of RNSM - RMM Archive.*

Newcastle and Scapa Flow areas. The ship then spent many months at sea on patrols to Murmansk, went to Spitzbergen and covered Commando raids in Norway. They entertained Russian Army Musicians aboard the ship whilst in Murmansk. The Bandmaster was highly regarded by Admiral Burroughs and everyone else on board because of his constant efforts organising concerts and keeping morale high. During 1942 the *Nigeria* was transferred to the Mediterranean to escort the Malta convoys. The band was responsible for manning the High Angle Control Positions (HACP) and the Transmitting Station (TS). On August 12th a torpedo from the Italian submarine *Axum* struck the ship killing all members of the band in the forward HACPs and TS. All were married men, all the single men being in the after HACP. The ship returned to Gibraltar with her fo'c'sle almost awash. The surviving members of the band then had the task of opening the hatches, removing the remains of their Bandmaster and eight members of the band and burying them at sea off Europa Point.[114]

BM Erridge was killed on board HMS *Phoebe* on 23rd October and the final casualties for 1942 took place on board HMS *Arethusa*. Engaged upon Operation *Stoneage*, another attempt to re-supply beleagured Malta, HMS *Arethusa* and the rest of the convoy had to fight off continuous air attacks from 0600 on 18th November. Then, at 1800 on the same day, she was torpedoed. She was towed stern-first back to Alexandria with her crew fighting raging fires and a rising gale and, when she eventually arrived, she carried 155 dead including BM Walker and eight members of the band.

HMS *Exeter*, of the Battle of the River Plate, was part of an Allied strike force that encountered a larger Japanese force. *Exeter* received a direct hit that put six of her eight boilers out of action. She slowed down and fell behind and had to decide whether to scuttle or make a run for it. Her Captain decided upon the latter. Restricted to a maximum speed of 23 - 26 knots she found herself boxed-in by vastly superior Japanese forces. For two hours she managed to manoeuvre and score hits on the Japanese forces before she received a direct hit that broke her main steam supply pipe and stopped her dead in the water. The order was given to scuttle and then to abandon ship. All members of the band were reported missing but some were later found to be prisoners in Japanese hands. Amongst these was BM Vidler. 'Bandy' Vidler was put to work in the prison camp hospital at Macassar where he met, and worked closely with, a Dutch Medical Officer, Dr Adrian Borstlap, in the Camp Hospital and in the Sick Bay. Eventually 'Bandy' himself contracted beri-beri and hunger odema. His own experience told him that he would not survive very long. Dr Borstlap wrote that, "We agreed that when the moment came [to transfer Bandy Vidler to the hospital close to the morgue - the usual practice for those close to death] I would not linger at his side when doing my rounds, telling him the dirty story of the day etc but would pass on without stopping. When that dreaded day came, I could see him staring at me from afar as I entered the ward. He followed my every step. He already knew too, and when I passed him, I did not stop. We just looked each other in the eye, as I said softly 'goodbye Bandy'. Then I had to run out of the ward so that the boys would not see me crying. Later that day, April 24th 1945, in complete peace 'Bandy' Vidler passed away. A Truly Great Man".[115] Four other members of the band of HMS *Exeter* also died in captivity.

The Captain of a Royal Navy warship drew alongside a troopship that he was escorting across the Indian Ocean and kept his ship in perfect position for forty minutes whilst his RM Band gave a concert to the hundreds of soldiers lining the troopship's rails. At the end of the concert the warship's Captain flashed "Hope you enjoyed it" and resumed his former station in the convoy.

---

114 *Musn G Lillford information to A C Green.*

115 *Blue Band Winter 1984.*

The Boys of Junior Wing were invited to take part in the annual Manx Music Festival 1943 and they played a very prominent part in it. A band of twelve Instructors took part in a BBC programme of Manx music whilst the Junior Wing gave an orchestral concert in the Manx Museum. Orchestral concerts were held on a regular basis at the Villa Marina where the programmes were very testing and provided excellent experience for the young Musicians. A 1943 Christmas Concert was put on at Howstrake Camp. This was produced by CSM K McLean and featured not only the orchestra but also the Boys providing comedy sketches, gymnastic displays, tap dancing and a sketch entitled 'A Band Boy's Dream of Howstrake'. The Schoolmaster and the Chaplain shared the compering of the show.

At Scarborough, during 1941 and 1942, the large Touring Bands were also giving concerts and Albert Marland, a pianist of great renown who, prior to joining the Royal Navy and transferring to the RNSM, was a member of Henry Hall's Band, played many of his own arrangements. Marland was also a member of the "*Celeste Octet*" a new ensemble from the RNSM that gave concerts in Scarborough. Capt Donne conducted these concerts and they were a great success. A joint RNSM and RAF Concert was given to an audience of over a thousand.[116] Marland and his arrangements were included in many RNSM concerts before Captain Dunn arranged for him to be drafted to the Portsmouth Divisional Band.

BM Pattinson and an eighteen-piece combination made recordings in London for Forces Overseas, being announced as the '*Royal Seafarers Dance Orchestra*'.

In August 1942 Maj-Gen T L Hunton submitted his report[117] on the Royal Marine Band Service. On the questions of the developing RN Volunteer Bands at the Home Ports and also the desire on the part of several senior RN Officers to have a band of their own, Hunton recommended that if the RN wanted bands then the RNSM and its RM Bands should be transferred to it. He made a strong case for such a transfer but with the caveat that the RNSM was functioning very well as a Royal Marines Department. He did highlight the fact that RM Bandsmen generally felt that whilst they were in the Royal Marines, they were not of them. His major recommendation was that consideration should be given to whether the RNSM should come under the RN or the RM and, if the answer was the latter, then the RM Home Port Bands should be increased in size so that there would be no requirement for the large RN Volunteer Bands. He also recommended a number of detailed improvements to the Band Service many of which, such as an equivalent to the Army psm[118] qualification, were gradually taken up.

Changes at the RNSM in 1943 included the retirement of Capt A C Green after thirty-nine years in the Band Service. Capt L P Donne was also placed on the Retired List. Capt G C Keen was appointed Director of Music, Junior Wing Howstrake Camp, Isle of Man. Lt Col H L M McCausland, who had been Superintendent of the RNSM since January 1940, was relieved by Col H D Weir.

Band Boys in the Isle of Man were issued with forage caps but these were only worn for a short time before being replaced by the beret.

A subtle change in the role of the RNSM took place in 1944 when it had to supply a band for the RM Infantry Training Centre at Lympstone (later the Commando Training Centre RM). The band found it strange to be living on shore again and marching with morning parades. They were issued with battledress. Later this band was drafted to Wales and replaced by a band of twenty-four Divisional Band Pensioners.[119] A band was also supplied for the Royal Marines Depot at Deal. The latter comprised Pensioners with an

---

116 *Scarborough newspaper cuttings.*
117 *Hunton Report. PRO ADM1/1191.*
118 *"Passed School of Music".*
119 *Globe & Laurel 1940 p429.*

average age of 49, an average service of 26 years and 79 medals between them. Their main work was on the parade ground.

In order to maximise the numbers available for RM Bands, Musicians were to be employed on general duties at the Royal Marine Divisions when they reached pensionable age. An alternative was to serve with the band at Lympstone. Band pensioners previously under the 'call-up' age were now to be recalled for service provided that they were medically fit. This meant that every potential source of manpower available to the RNSM, apart from the continuing enlistment of young men, had been committed to the war effort.

Musn Lovick was killed on board HMS *Cleopatra* on 11th July 1943 and six members of the Band, including BMII G C McLean, were wounded. "At the time of the ship being damaged the ship was at Defence Stations, or Cruising Watches, so that only about six of the band were actually closed-up at the time and I was in fact dozing beside the HA Table with my lifebelt for a pillow and my spectacles beside me. Out went the lights and such was my haste that I left both behind. The main lower TS was quite undamaged and dry while we all made the upper deck without difficulty. The remainder of the band were lying down for a rest after a sleepless night using the after HACP one deck below the upper deck. One of our members, Musn R H Lovick, was preparing to use the bathroom and was almost at the point of impact and was severely injured. He passed away about eight hours later and was buried at sea. Only five of us were uninjured and we made a strange sounding combination on the quarter-deck for entering harbour".[120]

Four Musicians were killed in HMS *Uganda* on 13th September and there was only one survivor from the band of HMS *Charybdis* when she was sunk near the Channel Islands on 23rd October. She had left Plymouth with five or six destroyers to engage a German convoy. When the ship had gone to Action Stations, the Gunnery Office piped the plan of attack to the guns and to the fore and aft TS "We will attack the convoy line-ahead and will go through it, guns blazing, sink what we can then turn through 180° come back and sink the rest". The ship and its crew had been together for two years in the Mediterranean and on the Russian convoys; their confidence was such that this seemed perfectly feasible. The guns began firing and almost immediately a large explosion caused the ship to shudder, the lights to go out and communication between the TS and the guns was lost. The ship had been torpedoed. A few seconds later another explosion rocked the ship which began to heel over. The Petty Officer gave the order to evacuate the TS and the Musicians were relieved to find that their hatch cover had been opened from the outside (a standing procedure for the Helmsman in the event of the ship being abandoned). Despite this, only one Musician survived.[121]

Musn K R Macdonald, a survivor of HMS *Gloucester*, and the only RM Bandsman prisoner of war in German hands, wrote to the Musical Director to say that he was now the Bandmaster of the Prison Camp band, that he had eighteen in the orchestra and also had small combinations and a dance orchestra. They had been able to produce comic operas that he had orchestrated for ten performers from the vocal score. They also played for stage shows, accompanied Church Services and organised weekly music classes.

Three days after a band arrived at HMS *Kestrel*, the Royal Naval Air Station (RNAS) on Worthy Down near Winchester, the orchestra made its debut at a ship's concert. They were co-opted into the BBC ITMA show and also played in the pit for ENSA and other shows.

Life at sea was not without its moments of humour and incongruity. Musn Nicholls wrote from HMS *Diomede* that the Band whalers crew were away from the ship when they heard *Band Call* across the water. They pulled quickly to the ship's boom, leapt out of the

120 *R H Plowman - letter to the author.*
121 *Letter from Musn Penfold to A C Green.*

boat, grabbed their instruments and, still clad in their rowing attire, the quintet played for hoisting the cutter - conducted by the coxswain.

It was during 1943 that the Italians surrendered although the Germans still fought in their country. The landings at Anzio (Operation *Shingle*) took place in January 1944 but the Allies found it very difficult to move out of the beachhead towards Rome to the north. On the 17th February HMS *Penelope*, having left Naples, was off Nettuno - which was part of the beachhead. As dawn broke the order "Heavy Armament Fall Out" was given and the men of the RM Band Starboard Watch left the TS and made their way to the Band Mess. Just as they arrived there a torpedo fired by *U-410* struck the ship, which stopped dead in the water with a pronounced list to starboard. This was the third hit that *Penelope* had sustained during this commission and the crew reacted to this latest incident in a calm, resolute manner, making their way to the deck to abandon ship. Within one minute and twenty seconds of the torpedo strike the ship had sunk taking well over half of her crew with her. BM Langford and Musns Blandford, Nicholson and Pickett were amongst those who lost their lives when the ship sank.[122]

HMS *Asphodel*, a corvette of 1015 tons, was torpedoed and sunk whilst on convoy escort duty off Cape Finisterre on 9th March 1944. The German submarine *U-575* scored what was, by this stage in the war, a rare success for the German submarine service. Musn B W K Denness was listed as "Missing in action, presumably killed".[123]

Things were progressing well with newly promoted Maj G C Keen as the Director of Music of the Junior Wing on the Isle of Man. He had inaugurated three boys' orchestras - each graded to suit its members' abilities - plus a Junior Dance Orchestra. The Boys' Ceremonial Band was 70 strong. Maj Keen continued the season of weekly concerts at the Villa Marina and these were very often preceded by a Military Band garden concert in the afternoon. There were also several BBC broadcasts in conjunction with the Manx choirs.

As D-Day approached ships, crews and bands began, unknowingly, to prepare for the task ahead. The band for HMS *Arethusa* joined her at Chatham in early January 1944 and the ship immediately left to join the Home Fleet at Scapa Flow. Once there the ship's routine became a series of exercises of all types. The band would be called on at any time of the night or day to close up in the TS for what was called 'Low Angle firing'.[124] They also practised closing up in the 'CP', which was the control position for the 4" anti-aircraft guns, and for close range LA firing. Damage control routines were also practised over and over again. The band's sleeping accommodation was not the best; some slept in the mess deck whilst others were on the upper deck in the area of the torpedo tubes. Whilst *Arethusa* was at Scapa the King came to inspect the Fleet. He stayed on board the Flagship, HMS *King George V*, and every night throughout his stay he gave a dinner party for various officers from the ships of the Fleet. This meant a lot of work for the Flagship band and, following the King's departure, the C-in-C Home Fleet, Admiral Sir Bruce Fraser handed the Bandmaster, W T Lang, a personal message from the King. It said, "His Majesty wishes to thank the band for their perseverance. As a sailor he fully realises the inconvenience to which they have been put". A few weeks later HMS *Arethusa* left Scapa and called at Greenock to provision and load ammunition. As the ship cleared the Firth of Clyde the crew was told that they were going to support the Normandy landings. Two days before D-Day the ship arrived off the Lizard and received a signal to say that the operation was cancelled for 24 hours because of the weather. Next morning, in company with other units of the Home Fleet they joined the US Fleet off the Isle of Wight and proceeded to their positions for the

122 *Account given to A C Green by Musn J Clark.*
123 *No explanation has been found for Musician Denness being on board a corvette - a ship too small to carry a band.*
124 *Main armament is known as LA.*

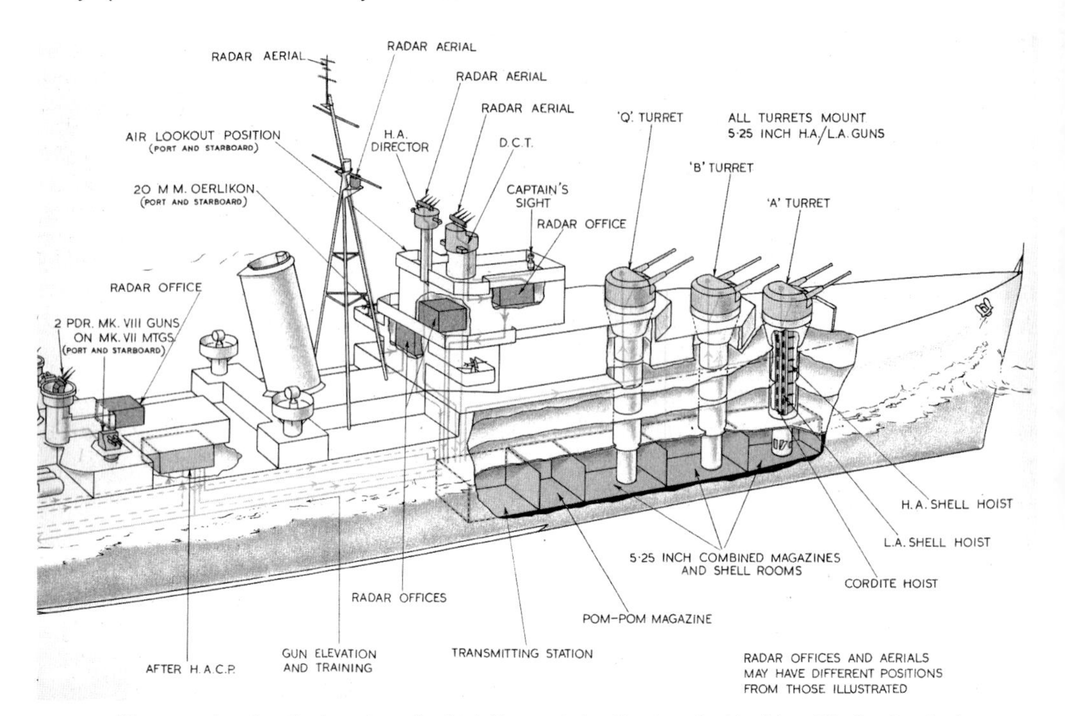

Diagram showing the location of a ship's Transmitting Station, the Musicians' 'Action Station'

landing. All were to support the 6th Airborne Division and, if required, the landing of two infantry divisions. The nearest large town would be Caen. On the day of the landing HMS *Arethusa* was the first cruiser to move into position and also the first cruiser to open fire. The band were employed in the TS and also as relief telephone operators on the 20mm Oerlikon close-range anti-aircraft guns.

The band of HMS *Frobisher* claimed to be the first military band to land in France since Dunkirk. They were certainly the first RM Band ashore.

Meanwhile HMS *Arethusa's* TS broke down. Unable to calculate the ranges and bearings for the ship's main armament the band had to use a range clock and a Dumeresque table - both of which were mechanical as opposed to electrical instruments. Each time an air raid materialised guiding of the bombardment stopped as the band went to action stations on the 4" anti-aircraft guns. By the end of D-Day the ship was almost out of all ammunition and so she returned to Portsmouth to re-ammunition, provision and refuel. The ship returned to Normandy on June 10th and, that night, they put to sea in company with HMS *Mauritius* to intercept enemy destroyers. The ships were travelling at 30 knots in line astern with *Mauritius* leading when she detonated a magnetic mine. Because of the speed the *Arethusa* took the brunt of the explosion. The after CP[125] was temporarily put out of action by the explosion. The following day the ship went to its normal two-watch sea routine with main armament bombardment during the day and anti-aircraft duties at night. Musicians were now working twenty-four hours without sleep and then grabbing rest jammed against the TS table and cramped in spare corners. So much firing had taken place since D-Day that the forecastle and upper deck had split in two places. The food was awful as the cooks were also constantly at action stations and the chemical smoke that was put up as a screen made life very uncomfortable. On the 14th the ship went to Portsmouth to replenish stores and the Musicians resumed band duties to play as the ship entered harbour and then to entertain the crew as stores were taken aboard. By 0730hrs on the 15th the ship was ready to return to Normandy again. Cars drew up on

125 Control Position.

the jetty and Air Chief Marshal Sir Charles Portal, Chief of the General Staff General Sir Alan F Brooke, Admirals Ramsey and Cunningham, Generals Ismay and Laycock and then Lord Lascelles (the King's Private Secretary) came aboard. At 0800 the King came aboard and HMS *Arethusa* put to sea heading for her usual spot. On arrival the VIPs went ashore to dine with General Montgomery. Returning in the evening the guests were conveyed back to Spithead where the King and the VIPs disembarked. The crew had to wear No 2 uniform (best blues) all the time that the VIPs were aboard.

Next morning the ship left harbour with band playing and sailed to its Normandy anchorage. The constant firing of *Arethusa's* guns was causing more vibration damage. Nearly all the lavatory pipe-work had parted company and there were queues to use the few that were still serviceable. The 24th June brought continuous shelling and air attacks from the Germans. Two acoustic mines exploded close by the ship. On the 24th the two radar sets were out of action, the after water storage tank was put out of action and the after gyro-compass, the only one working at the time, was broken. One of the propellers was damaged and out of line; Y turret was out of action; one of the turbines and an oil fuel tank were also damaged. The ship was ordered to Portsmouth and left the Normandy area at two knots to avoid setting off more mines. Once into the open sea speed was increased to 20 knots but the vibration was awful. The ship then received orders to make for Glasgow. As they arrived in the Firth of Clyde the band of a very battered HMS *Arethusa* was playing marches on the after gun deck. Cheering crowds lined the jetties as the ship moored.[126]

At about this time Maj F J Ricketts (Kenneth Alford) retired for medical reasons. The position of Director of Music Plymouth Division was given to Mr R H Stoner, Commissioned Bandmaster. This was the first time that a Director of Music of a Divisional Band was appointed from within the Corps. Eighty-one applications had been received for this position. Ten were short-listed for interview and whilst Mr C Nalden, Bandmaster of the Royal Artillery (Portsmouth) Band, was found to be most suitable and best qualified the Board recognised that Mr Stoner would also make a suitable choice. In 1944 the GOC Royal Marines issued instructions that, in future, preference would be given to RNSM ranks when vacancies occurred in the Divisional bands provided that such ranks had completed nine years' service.

The Manx Music Festival included winning solos by future Directors of Music, P Neville and P Sumner. When VE Day was announced a scratch band had to be put together at Scarborough for local celebrations as the two bands were on duty away from the town. A big parade was held in Douglas, Isle of Man, with the Boys' Band leading and wearing white helmets - the first time that white helmets had been worn on the Island.[127] Liberation Parades were taking place throughout Europe as the Allies achieved 'Victory in Europe' and RM Bands featured in many of them.

Whilst the war was still being fought in the Far East it was decided that a band should be formed to tour RN and RM establishments in India. BM C H Brown was in charge of a band of fifteen that crossed from Ceylon to India by ferry and then, following a two-hour train journey to Manadapan, they re-loaded into lorries for a hot, dusty journey to their accommodation which turned out to be a hut with three broken camp beds! More bedding was eventually found and the band prepared for their first concert. The piano supplied was totally out of tune and was substituted by the Padre's portable organ. The band then put on a show in the welldeck of an LCT (Landing Craft Tank) that was moored in the middle of the stream. BM Brown later reflected that "the delight of the LCT crews and other personnel repaid the bother entailed". During their stay the band also played for

126 *From a diary kept by Musns Webster and Baker who passed the diary from one to the other as watches changed.*
127 *Lt Col Neville recalls BM 'Doc' Compton making them march to football practice wearing the helmets!*

Divisions, Church, Wardroom, and two variety stage shows. Following this the band moved by train to Madras and then Visagapatam. The journey was appalling with temperatures as high as 125°F, with smells to match and water that was almost hot enough for tea. Entertainment was provided in a variety of locations including Calcutta, Bombay, Poona and various Landing Craft, and other, Bases before returning to Colombo at the end of an arduous seven-week tour.

Two amenity ships had been commissioned to provide floating entertainment for the men of the Far East Fleet, the SS *Menestheseus* and the SS *Agamemnon*. RNSM bands were sent to each. Members were selected who could show evidence of versatility as they had to be able to play as a first class dance orchestra, a salon orchestra or a grand concert orchestra. Some of the best Musicians in the Band Service found themselves on these ships. The London theatrical tailors, Morris Angel Ltd, fitted them with white Tuxedo jackets and dress trousers and this was undoubtedly one of the best engagements for men from the RNSM. A theatre, a cinema and a brewery capable of brewing 1,800 gallons of beer a day were amongst the facilities in these ships. Other duties that fell to the bands included patrolling Hong Kong and Singapore when they were reoccupied, helping at Prisoner of War and Internment Camps and, as always, providing entertainment wherever they could.

The Musicians of HMS *Exeter* were liberated from a Japanese prison camp but five of their number had died in captivity. They were BM Vidler, BdCpl Buckle and Musns Bance, Harris and Wilkin.

With the war over, stock could be taken of the effort given by the Royal Marine Bands from the Royal Naval School of Music. At a peak during the war the total number serving was 1,900 including 280 Pensioners and 300 Hostilities Only. Casualties totalled 225, representing 25% of those serving afloat. Awards totalled two MBEs; three BEMs; nine DSMs and thirty Mentions in Despatches.

In 1945 ships of the Royal Navy continued to be on station all over the world and many of them had to remain on duty for some time following the cessation of hostilities. At Rosyth King Haakon of Norway and the entire Norwegian Royal Family embarked, with all due ceremony of Guard and Band, on HMS *Norfolk* and were returned to Oslo where they arrived on the 7th June.

HMS *Leander* arrived in the United States shortly after VE-Day and the band under BM W H Cotton played at the Mulberry Exhibition at Philadelphia on ten consecutive days. The band also had several engagements in New York where they were attached to the shore establishment HMS *Saker*. The ship then called at Montreal where thirty-five British schoolchildren who had been evacuated from the United Kingdom early in the war were taken aboard. During the passage home the band spent a great deal of time entertaining these children.

HMS *Swiftsure* was one of the first ships to return to Hong Kong following the occupation. The Royal Marine Detachment patrolled the town, rounding up looters and helping to bring a return to law and order. The band also took part in this work although "Bandy" with a Tommy gun did cause some misgivings! At Batavia and at Singapore the band of HMS *Sussex* (BM Jackson) worked hard at various Prisoner of War Camps and at Internment Camps.

In December HMS *Sirius* made a goodwill trip to King Ibn Saud of Saudi Arabia and provided a Guard and Band for the Crown Prince at Jeddah. Returning to Malta the band were paid off, some returning to the United Kingdom whilst the rest joined the Band of C-in-C Malta. This band was also known as the RM Central Band, Malta. Under BM WO E H Weller it mainly consisted of men from three ships *Liverpool*, *Sirius* and *Ajax* supplemented with men from the UK. Its temporary headquarters were at RM Training Centre, Mediterranean, which was at Ghain Tuffieha, Malta.

As the Second World War came to a close it became apparent to many that radical changes were needed to the musical service that the Royal Marines provided to the Royal Navy and to the Corps itself.

Band complements for the Home Fleet were reduced. The majority of the battleships and cruisers were to be used for training young seamen and therefore only a reduced RM Detachment was required and, usually, no band. HMS *King George V's* band had transferred directly from HMS *Nelson* thus ensuring a smooth continuation of its proven musical and ceremonial efficiency. Massed bands from HM Ships *King George V*, *Implacable* and *Superb* gave a performance aboard the *King George V* and the BBC recorded most of the band's musical duties.

In 1945 the Superintendent of the RNSM had submitted his draft 'Instructions for the RN School of Music' to the CGRM. This document not only described the organisational, administrative and educational systems that were in place but also clearly demonstrated that everything was prepared for the RNSM of the future. The wind of change was blowing and the School was clearly ready. The Instruction included, "The functions of the RM Band Service as part of the Corps of Royal Marines, is the provision of bands for the Fleet, Royal Naval and certain Royal Marines Shore Establishments. Personnel are trained at the Royal Naval School of Music for this Service and at Royal Naval Gunnery Schools for Fire Control duties in the gunnery organisation of HM Ships".

The staffing of the School was described in detail and showed that it was run on the lines of a RM Division with the Superintendent, who was responsible for discipline, training and administration, reporting directly to the CGRM on all matters relating to the School whilst communicating directly with Naval Authorities on all matters relating to the RM Band Service. The School was organised into Headquarters, Senior Wing (Trained Soldiers) and a Junior Wing (Band Boys under training). The Superintendent had a Second-in-Command who, as well as commanding the RNSM in the absence of the Superintendent, was Field Officer General Duties; Examiner of Accounts; President of the Officers' Mess and of the Institute Fund; Supervisor of the SNCOs' Mess and also responsible for welfare. A Company Commander was appointed for each of the Companies. Other staff were the Adjutant, Superintending Clerk, Drafting Officer, Paymaster, Quartermaster (V), Quartermaster (M)[128] and the Musical Director and Assistant Musical Director.

In Melbourne the massed bands of the First Aircraft Carrier Squadron of the British Pacific Fleet Beat Retreat at the Shrine of Remembrance on 27th January 1946. The aircraft carriers were HMS *Indefatigable*, HMS *Implacable* and HMS *Glory*. The seventy-two Musicians were massed under the baton of BM (WO) S C Cooper and the Drum Major was BM 2nd Cl A S Pinniger. The massed Buglers were led by SgtBug Griffin RM of HMS *Indefatigable*. The whole ceremony was broadcast by the Australian Broadcasting Company and short-waved to the BBC in London.

Capt Herbert Kenward MBE RM. Musical Director RNSM 1946 - 1950

At the RNSM Headquarters at Scarborough the drafting situation was becoming increasingly difficult as the demobilisation continued. Some of the HO ranks had gone and all of the Pensioners except four Bandmasters and ten Musicians who had volunteered to stay on. When the final three hundred HOs were demobbed maintaining the appropriate instrumentation became a problem that lasted until recruitment levels rose. Changes in the hierarchy of

128 V = Victualling; M = Music.

the School included Maj A Pragnell's retirement and replacement as Musical Director by Capt H Kenward.

BM R H Willmot arrived at HMS *St Vincent* with a new band only to find that he had inherited a Corps of Drums and a Drum Major. They were all Wrens and were from all walks of life - including the acting profession. Since they were very popular with the Captain the Bandmaster had to "adopt" them. However he quickly found that they were very efficient and very popular at local functions.

A band from the RNSM under Cd BM K A McLean completed a successful tour of Combined Operations bases in the Largs[129] area and a party of RMB ranks augmented the Chatham Divisional Band when it went to Germany.

The January 1946 Accommodation Return for the RNSM indicated that the Senior School, Scarborough, was accommodating one Officer, forty-three SNCOs and two hundred and ninety-nine other ranks in the Norbreck and Clifton Hotels whilst the Junior School at Howstrake Camp on the Isle of Man was accommodating ten Officers, twenty-five SNCOs and two hundred and eighty-eight other ranks. This total included five Wrens and two hundred and thirty-one Band Boys. The need to relocate the two Wings of the School to a common site was paramount and in August 1946 the move was made to a former American Army Camp at Broadwell Grove, Burford in Oxfordshire. A letter of appreciation from the Lieutenant Governor of the Isle of Man to the Officer Commanding RNSM was sent on their departure. On September 10th the Commandant General visited Burford. He stressed the need for recruitment to build up and maintain the "Royal Naval Band Service" and promised that improved conditions for band ranks were on the way.

Changes to uniforms were made at this time. The famous lyre over globe and laurel cap badge was to be replaced by the globe and laurel with lion and crown cap badge worn by all Royal Marine ranks and the 'RMB' shoulder title was to be replaced by the 'RM'. Musicians would continue to wear the lyre collar badges. Bandmasters 1st Class would wear a lyre encircled by a laurel wreath surmounted by a crown as a badge of rank. They would also wear a leather sword belt and carry a sword. The Senior NCOs held "a night of gloom" in the Mess to mourn the loss of the two items that had been worn with great pride and marked them as men of the RNSM and the Royal Marine Band Service - the lyre cap-badge and the "RMB" shoulder-title.

Lt G C McLean DSM, MBE RM (brother of K. McLean) as bandmaster at HMS Urley, the RN Air Station at Ronaldsway, Isle of Man with Wren officers in 1945/1946

In the 1946 Victory March the RN and the RM led the military section of the parade. Dr Thomas Wood MA MusD(Oxon) Hon ARCM wrote an evocative description of the Parade for the 'Globe and Laurel' which included the following passage: "And there were the Royal Marines. They marched as they alone can march, twelve abreast, in two columns of six that that divided at the Cenotaph; a detachment drawn from all units, under the command of Lt Col F B Pym. Ahead of them were the Massed Bands of the Chatham, Portsmouth and Plymouth Divisions and the Royal Naval School of Music; and if ever a man had a right to be proud it must have been Drum Major Louis Beer, in front. Up swelled a roar of cheering; the men marched by and were gone".[130]

129 *Scotland.*

130 *It is not known what contribution Woods made to this parade. The bands may have played Wood's march 'St George's Day'.*

In 1946 the RM adopted RN conditions and rates of pay. This gave the RM Warrant Officer the same conditions of service as Warrant Officers in the Royal Navy. Other effects were that the maximum age of service for Directors of Music was reduced from sixty to fifty with an option of serving, at Admiralty discretion, to the age of 55; the qualifying period for promotion from Lieutenant to Captain was increased from three to eight years.

A number of Committees were formed, and reports written, regarding the post-war and future development of the Corps in general, or the specific organisation of the RNSM and the Divisional Bands in particular. The 1946 Lamplough Committee and the subsequent Newman Committee addressed the reorganisation of the Corps whilst the Leech-Porter Committee focused upon the Corps' musical constituent.

The bands of the Home Fleet began to return to their peacetime status during 1947. The Fleet visited the Clyde during 1947 and Royal Guards and Bands paraded for Their Majesties. The Fleet Bandmaster conducted the orchestra of the Fleet Flagship at all of the concert performances. At a display ashore the Fleet Massed Bands were joined by the Royal Marine Bands of HMS *Daedalus*, Flag Officer Scotland and Northern Ireland (FOSNI) and RNB Chatham. These bands together with eighty-five Band Boys, three more Drum Majors and twenty Buglers provided a very impressive performance.

Burford was a good location from which the Band Boys went on trips to Cheltenham and Oxford where they were able to attend performances by well-known orchestras. Dr Malcolm Sargent visited the School in January and officiated at the pass-out parade of HMS *Triumph's* Band. He inspected the School, including the Boys' Instruction classes, conducted the Symphony Orchestra and, at the end of the day, was presented with a miniature timpani made by BdCpl McGain-Harding. It was also in 1946 that Sir Felix Cassel began the annual presentation of the Silver and Bronze Medal to Band Boys of the RNSM.[131] Later in the year Sir John Barbirolli, the conductor of the Hallé Orchestra, also visited the School as did Noel Coward.

Col R A R Neville wrote to the Commandant General in June to propose that his 1947 inspection should include witnessing a display with four bands, the basis of the proposed display for the 1948 Royal Tournament at Olympia. The Commandant General was given a complete view of the training and the abilities within the School, whilst also ensuring that he was aware of the concerns of the Staff. He was met by a Guard of Honour and Band; passed out the band for HMS *Newcastle*; saw the auditions for the Oceanaires Dance Band, watched the display by four bands and attended a symphony orchestra concert. His main impressions were of the efficiency of the training, the atmosphere of enthusiasm and pride and the hard work that had gone into making Burford as comfortable as possible.

A band of one hundred and twenty Musicians under Capt H Kenward, plus the Oceanaires Dance Band under BM Hotham, appeared at the Royal Albert Hall on Trafalgar Day 1947 for the RN Old Comrades Association. As Musical Director of the RNSM, Capt Kenward now had forty bands and approximately twelve hundred Musicians under his direction. The Boys' Company had a Senior, and a Junior, Orchestra, a Dance Orchestra and a Military Band.

HM the King approved the change of BM1st Cl and BM 2nd Cl to Bandmaster and Band Sergeant. This enhanced the status of Bandmasters by bringing their title into line with their duties and provided bands with Senior NCOs as an instrumentalist and second-in-command. Prospects in the Band Service were now better than ever, their fine work during the war years was bearing fruit and, through their own actions, the bands were much more widely known in both Service and civilian circles. Whilst the Portsmouth Divisional Band was on Royal Duty in HMS *Vanguard* a band from the RNSM, under Lt B C

131 J Trendell's notes.

Barnes, covered the musical requirements of the Division. This included a hasty visit, with a Royal Guard, to Denmark for the funeral of King Christian X.

During 1947 a proposal to amalgamate the Group Bands, the RNSM and their RM Bands was made. At this time there was a definite need for cutbacks and amalgamations and anything that had a hint of reduction and savings had a very good chance of gaining an interested audience. However, in this case the other Group Bands and the RNSM opposed the proposal.[132] At the same time the RNSM issued their own Conference Report which advocated an expansion of the RNSM to make good recent loss, improve quality by increasing band sizes and eliminate the need for Volunteer Bands. A similar report the following year proposed two classes of band and a fundamental change to Watchkeeping Duties whilst on board ship. Many recommendations were followed but the drive for expansion was not.

November 1947 saw the Royal Wedding of Princess Elizabeth and Prince Philip and a band of sixty from the RNSM under the Musical Director was prominently positioned outside Westminster Abbey. Also in 1947 the RNSM was instructed to provide a band for 3 Cdo Bde, Royal Marines, and there was an increasing demand for bands for Naval shore establishments.

In 1948 Dr T Wood, the President of the Royal Philharmonic Society, nominated the Musical Director, Capt H Kenward to be a Member of the Society. His subsequent election represented an honour to the Band Service.

Meanwhile 3 Cdo Bde, complete with its own band, was in Malta having completed training in early 1948. The band, under BM Dixon,[133] became commandos at least in dress since they wore the khaki battledress and green beret of the Brigade. They also wore white belts and anklets. Although part of Brigade HQ the band was responsible for the entertainment of all units. They were sent to Tripoli to entertain 42 Cdo. They also spent time at Castel Benito with the RAF giving concerts and playing at cocktail parties and guest nights. St George's Day was celebrated by Beating Retreat in Malta where the band used the unusual 'lane'[134] formation during the troop. The band returned to Tripoli in June and, as well as playing for Commando units, they entertained the various Army Regiments stationed there with military band programmes, orchestral concerts and dance bands. In July the band took part in the Changing of the Guard at the Palace, Valletta, on Saturday mornings, with units of the Royal Malta Artillery, and then with 40 and 45 Commando who took over the Guard duties for some weeks. They were also involved in the ceremonies for the Shah of Persia during his visit to Malta.

An article published in 'Musical Progress and Mail' in June 1948 painted a detailed picture of the RNSM's training. "As far as education was concerned the School recruited youngsters of 14 and 15 because it was recognised by the Board of Education as providing full-time education. A recruit would be given a general education for two years beyond the school leaving age, would receive full board and lodging and uniform and would be paid each week. In addition he would be musically trained in the three musical disciplines of orchestral, military band and dance band work. During the three to four years of training the proportion of musical training would be gradually increased. A mixture of civilian professors and Non-Commissioned Officers were used for musical training whilst RN Instructor Officers were used for other subjects. As they progressed boys took their place in the Junior Orchestra, the Senior Orchestra, the Military Band of the Junior Wing

132 'The Royal Marines' (Revised edn) Maj Gen J L Moulton.

133 According to Brig Wills, Dixon's version of "Sarie Marais" was officially adopted by 3 Cdo Bde.

134 Band forms two files based upon the outer files of the band, leaving a large space, or lane, between.

and perhaps the Boys' Dance Orchestra. Each year the Worshipful Company of Musicians awarded two Cassel Prizes for the best students on a string and a wind instrument.

Once a qualified Musician, preparation would commence for promotion. The Fleet Bandmasters had an important part to play since it was their responsibility to train and prepare those individuals serving on ships so that they could make maximum use of their time when they returned to the Senior Wing at the School.

Following promotion to Bandmaster he would serve a period at sea in charge of a band and would then serve further commissions afloat, alternating with being a Bandmaster at a Royal Navy or Royal Marine Shore Establishment or with Instructional Duties at the School.

Bandmasters selected for the Warrant Bandmasters' course were given a further twelve months' advanced instruction during which time they would be expected to pass the examination for Licentiate of the Royal Academy of Music (LRAM) in Military Bandmastership. They also had hold a First Class Certificate of Education. Warrant Bandmasters were employed as Senior Instructors or as Fleet or Port Bandmasters where they would have about six bands under their command.

At any one time at the School there would be two or three Corporals' courses, one or two Band Sergeants' courses, one Bandmasters' course and one Warrant Bandmasters' course being run. Officers' Courses were run as required.

In addition to the individual training courses there would be the training of draft bands. This usually covered about two months during which time the Musicians detailed for the band of a newly commissioning or recommissioning ship were welded into an efficient combination. These bands had to practise in dance, military and orchestral work as well as a parade Band. Before embarkation they had to be passed by the Musical Director as proficient and a full report written on them.

In support of all this training and commitment the School's Drafting Officer had a very complex task to manage the drafting of individuals to suit the commissioning and re-commissioning of ships; the training of individuals as well as the men who were passing out of the School or retiring from the Band Service. The Quartermaster (Musical) had a music store and workshops which, at that time, were probably unique for a musical establishment. The store carried enough stocks of instruments and parts to maintain all of the RM Bands in commission plus those about to be commissioned and the instruments for two hundred and fifty Boy Musicians under training. Big reserves had to be kept to meet such things as the fluctuations in the number of Boys under training, which could rise to four hundred, and the damage to stringed instruments caused by tropical climates. The workshops were started during the War when it was extremely difficult to maintain the numbers of instruments necessary for all of the ships' bands. All repairs to instruments could be carried out other than major re-conditioning.

The Library was required to supply music for the students at the School and for all of the bands at sea and in Naval Establishments all over the world. Dance Band music was bought by the individual bands themselves since the popularity of such music was deemed to be very short-lived. Forty compositions for symphony orchestra were despatched in 1948 to the Commando Brigade Band touring North Africa. Over six thousand compositions were held in the library and some dated back to the formation of the RNSM in 1903. The School also had a reference library of eight hundred books of musical reference.

A band from the RNSM under Capt H Kenward was involved at the unveiling of the Roosevelt Memorial, being positioned close to the American Embassy in Grosvenor Square, London.[135]

135 *'Marcher' article Blue Band Spring 1998.*

At this time the RNSM was probably at its peak. It was certainly an exciting place to be as Maj A H R Buckley discovered: "As a mere sojourner in their midst, the writer has been struck by two points in connection with this branch of the Corps. First, its outstanding esprit de corps, which yields to none and is an object lesson to many; second, the quite unjustified lack of knowledge and appreciation of its merits and services, not only by our own Corps, but also by many of the Royal Navy which it serves so well, and the general public".

Another 'first' for RM Bands occurred when the Musical Director and a military band of fifty-four Musicians from the RNSM played at a Royal Garden Party on 8th July. As the RNSM was not allowed a Staff Band, the many commitments for which the School was asked to provide bands or orchestras had therefore to be met by forming combinations for each engagement from the drafting margin available. That these bands compared favourably with other Service bands, which were virtually permanent in composition, was a measure of not only the instrumentalists' ability but also the ability of those directing them, since they only had very short periods for rehearsal. Time and again the School put on a fine show at short notice under these difficult circumstances.

Capt A C Green wrote, "Recognition had at last come to the Band Service after forty-five years of existence and great service in two World Wars, the great ceremonial occasions in London throughout the year and hundreds of other public engagements at home and abroad and BBC broadcasts. Recruiting was soaring, and an astonishing return to pre-war efficiency in musical standard fostered by an esprit-de-corps second to none in a Corps so justly famed for this quality. 1948 would be regarded as a milestone in progress".

Prospects for promotion within the Service were greater than ever before and arrangements were being made for examinations to be taken abroad so that sea-going Musicians were not penalised. The Military Band made a number of recordings of marches to be used as records for instructional purposes on board ships that were not entitled to bands.

Bandmaster Dunham with HMS Raleigh Band c.1948/1949. Most of the band, including the Drum Major, are Wrens

As far as the RNSM and its Band Service was concerned the major event of 1948 occurred on the 1st June. It had been decided to follow the example of the Memorial Silver Drums for those of the Band Service who had died in the First World War and that a Memorial was needed to commemorate the dead of World War Two. A Memorial Committee was appointed to arrange the collection of the money and to select what should be purchased as the Memorial itself. A representative of every rank in the Band Service would sit on the Committee. This included two Band Boys, one of whom was a section leader. There was a suggestion that the Silver Memorial Drums should be replaced as they were very worn and rarely used but there was a keenness to have trumpets and they were duly chosen. The fourteen fanfare trumpets were purchased and 1st June was the date set for their dedication and their presentation. The rules relating to these trumpets were set down in 'The War Memorial Charter' and the Book of Remembrance became the third part of the Memorial.

Firstly, the School Chapel of St Cecilia, the Patron Saint of Musicians, was dedicated by the Chaplain of the Fleet. The orchestra and the choir of forty-five Band Boys were in the Chapel. The Second Sea Lord, CGRM, Chief of Staff Royal Marines and all three Group Commanders were present (by this time the three RM Divisions had become Groups). Following the Dedication of the Chapel everyone moved outside to the arena. Here the Massed Bands were drawn up before a dais that carried the Book of Remembrance and the stands carrying the Memorial Trumpets. During the Dedication Service the Commandant General read the lessons and the Book of Remembrance was blessed. All ranks were called to attention and, in the silence, the School Chaplain handed one of the trumpets to the Chaplain of the Fleet for Dedication "*In memory of those who gave their lives in the service of their country*". The Commandant received the trumpets and, with the Musical Director, handed each of the fourteen to those who had the honour of receiving them on behalf of the Royal Marines Bands. On the command a moving fanfare was sounded: *The Spirit of Joy and Thanksgiving for Victory, and Meditation for those who gave their lives in its cause,* known simply as *To Comrades Sleeping*, and composed by Leon Young, a wartime survivor of HMS *Hermione*. After an address the service concluded with the inspiring words of Sir Francis Drake's prayer and the singing of the Naval Hymn, *Eternal Father*. Responsibility for the 'Act of Memorial' by the Massed Bands of the RNSM passed to Lt Lang. A fanfare by Curzon was played and then the four bands marched on to *Nancy Lee* before performing a complex marching display to Alford's *By Land and Sea* and *HM Jollies* at the end of which they had formed two bands. The drums Beat Retreat and the bands stepped off again to Safroni's *Imperial Echoes,* finally halting in front of the dais as one band of two hundred. Led by four Drum Majors and the large Corps of Drums the band played Dr Thomas Wood's *St George's Day* followed by another fanfare by Leon Young, then *Rule Britannia* and the Evening Hymn. Capt A C Green's arrangement of *Sunset* was played as the Ensign was lowered, followed by the National Anthem. The Second Sea Lord took the salute and the bands marched off to the Regimental March.

Having provided Musicians to augment the Group Bands at the 1947 Royal Tournament it was the turn of the Massed Bands of the RNSM themselves in 1948. Musicians drawn from the Fleet and from RN and RM establishments augmented the School Band to produce a band one hundred strong. Maj Dunn of the Portsmouth Group was asked to rehearse the music for the event. The massed bands under Lt Lang, who had devised the intricate marching display, were called 'The Staff Band of the Royal Naval School of Music' in the programme. The bands, playing almost the same programme as that performed at the Act of Memorial at Burford a few days earlier and using the Memorial Trumpets for the first time in public, gave a very good musical and marching display in slow and quick time, based upon Lang's original display at Burford. This was the template for the Beat Retreat performances on Horse Guards Parade. Army and RAF bands later adopted this type of display.[136]

During 1948 Sir Malcolm Sargent was appointed Honorary Advisor in Music to the Royal Marines. It was hoped that Sir Malcolm would visit the School annually to witness the musical instruction given to the Boy Musicians and to other instrumentalists.

Meanwhile the Band Service maintained its work at sea. By 1949 there were thirty-nine bands spread all over the world. BM Harwood was serving in HMS *London* on the Yangtse River when HMS *Amethyst* was trapped by the Chinese. HMS *London* was also fired upon and the bandmaster was later awarded the DSM for his services in dealing with the wounded men, with damage control parties and in the very overcrowded Sick Bay.[137]

136 *Globe & Laurel and Official Tournament Programme.*
137 *Article in 'Warship World' Vol 8 No 3.*

3 Cdo Bde Band toured Cyprus for six weeks entertaining troops, Beating Retreat at Nicosia, Larnaca and Limassol and providing orchestral programmes. The Brigade Band took part in 'A Ceremonial Parade to Celebrate St George's Day' at St Patrick's Barracks Malta. The massed bands of the Mediterranean Fleet (HMS *Vanguard*, *Forth*, *Liverpool*, *Ocean* and *Euryalus*) and the Brigade were under the direction of CdBM Fitzgerald. The parade itself was an interesting hybrid. It was based upon the ceremony of Trooping the Colour but a *Feu de Joie* was substituted for the Trooping. After that the ceremony became a Beat Retreat. The musical programme had some intriguing items in it. The opening march, *Lilliburlero*, was credited to Thomas Wood because he had arranged it for use as the main theme to his march *St George's Day*. This was followed by *Soldier's Chorus* from *Faust* (Gounod),[138] *British Grenadiers* and Beating of the *Assembly* by the Corps of Drums, then *Scipio* (Handel), a Royal Salute, *the Duke of York* (arr Balfour), two Alford marches *HM Jollies* and *By Land and Sea*, *Sarie Marais* arranged by Dixon,[139] *A Life on the Ocean Wave*, *Early One Morning*, *Heart of Oak* (Boyce), *British Grenadiers* and the *RAF March* (Walford). Following another Royal Salute the Bugles and massed bands played Green's *Sunset*. After the *Hymn of Malta* and the *National Anthem* the bands marched off to *Sarie Marais* and *Eagle Squadron*.

It was during 1949 that the winds of change began to blow. Consideration was being given to moving the School back to the Depot, Deal and, in August 1949, arrangements began to be made for the move. The important Leech-Porter Report was circulated in 1949 recommending that all bands should be placed under the same terms as the RNSM bands; the Royal Naval School of Music should be renamed the School of Music, Royal Marines (which was later amended to its current title); civilian instructors should be appointed and the School moved closer to London.

An Admiralty Order-in-Council (28th October 1949) abolished the 'Warrant List' and substituted it with a 'Branch List'. All officers on the Branch List were to be appointed by Commission. This meant that Bandmaster Warrant Officers became Commissioned Bandmasters and Commissioned Bandmasters became Senior Commissioned Bandmasters. This became effective for all generic titles within the Royal Navy and the Royal Marines. 'Commissioned…' wore a small star on their shoulder; 'Senior Commissioned…' wore a large star on their shoulder.

At the end of 1949 the first issue of the "Blue Band" appeared. This magazine was for the benefit of the men of the RNSM and the RM Bands. It was to appear three times a year and its first editor was Instructor Lieutenant D McLeish. The Commandant of the Royal Naval School of Music, Col P R Smith-Hill, wrote a foreword. It also contained an open letter from Sir Malcolm Sargent, the Honorary Musical Advisor.

In his report issued just prior to Christmas 1949 Maj R G S Lang, the Commandant at Burford, gave the following indication of what life for the recruit at Deal[140] would be like: "With the forthcoming move to Deal, a new system of training was to be adopted which would produce more satisfactory results. There was to be a period of concentrated parade work for newly joined recruits on their arrival. A Draft Squad would be formed each term, with Boy Musicians of seventeen and a half to eighteen years, who were to do revisionary work in all subjects prior to being passed out. Members of the Draft Squad would receive leave privileges, and wear caps and a distinguishing white lanyard. They would still be able to gain accelerated advancement, with the accompanying extra pay, on attaining the age

---

138 This was the march past of the RM Artillery until 1883.

139 Although not officially adopted until 1952 the march 'Sarie Marais' had been used by the Commandos for a very long time. It had been arranged by Lt FV Dunn of the Portsmouth Division in 1937.

140 Details of the move to Deal covered later.

of eighteen. In the educational field, the new scheme of training would enable boys to qualify educationally for promotion before leaving the Boys Wing".[141]

The Admiralty had taken the decision in 1949 to scrap the RM Commando role. Although he was able to reverse this decision CGRM had to make cuts elsewhere to compensate. Amongst these cuts was the closure of the Chatham Group, including its fine band. The distinctive badge, the White Rose of York, was lost with the band's demise. At that time (April 1950) it had to be assumed that the recommendations of the Leech-Porter Group would be approved and it was therefore proposed to plan for the disbandment of the Chatham Band.

A special train took the Boys to Deal on the 6th June 1950 and so the RNSM marched back into what used to be the Depot, Deal, but was now Royal Marines, Deal. The senior officer was now "Commanding Officer, Royal Marines Deal" and also "Commandant, Royal Naval School of Music".

Boy Musicians were housed in East Barracks, renamed the Royal Naval School of Music, whilst trained Musicians and NCOs were accommodated in North Barracks. RM Deal had four Companies. 'M' Company consisted of Musicians; 'B' Company of Boys and 'R' Company of Recruits whilst staff of the establishment were HQ Company. HQ Company was responsible for the whole establishment. Group Buglers were now sent to the RNSM for all of their training. The Depot Band became the 'Staff Band of the Royal Naval School of Music'. In addition to its parade duties this band was to enable the Bandmasters and other classes to gain experience in conducting. The School continued to deal with the drafting, promotion and records of other ranks of the Band Service.

Capt H Kenward, the Musical Director of the RNSM, retired on the 19th March 1950. The new Musical Director was Lt K A MacLean who had enlisted at Deal as a Royal Marine recruit and was awarded the King's Badge (93rd Squad). He was the only Musical Director ever to wear this badge.[142] Col P R Smith-Hill was appointed "In Continuation" as Commanding Officer, and Commandant, RNSM at Deal. In 1950 the Staff Band at Deal was twenty-five strong; eleven bands were in commission in shore establishments in this country; one band was ashore with 3 Cdo Bde in Hong Kong; eight bands were afloat in Home Waters; thirteen bands were afloat elsewhere including the band attached to the RNZN in HMNZS *Bellona*. The total number of RM Bands was thirty-four, each having a strength of between fifteen and twenty-eight. There were well over 1,000 members of the RM Band Service of whom more than 200 were Boy Musicians.

Following the return to Deal from Burford, and on account of the raising of the school leaving age, it became necessary to completely revise the syllabus of educational training of Boy Musicians in order to ensure that they would receive an education comparable to that given in a civilian secondary modern or technical school. Inspectors from the Ministry of Education inspected the School and the new syllabus and approval was given, thus enabling boys below the normal school leaving age to continue to be recruited. This revision meant the introduction of a much wider range of subjects and the fitting up of science laboratories and metal and wood handicraft workshops and this led to a much wider interest in education generally.

Boy Musicians and Boy Buglers were reorganised into Houses. Those for Boy Musicians were named after ships in which RM Band ranks suffered heavy casualties during World War II: *Gloucester*, *Neptune*, *Barham*, and *Eagle*. The first Squad to bear the title 'The Commandant General's Squad' was passed out by him in March. The Squad consisted

141 From 'Commandant's Report' (Papers of A C Green).

142 The King's Badge is awarded to the best recruit in the senior squad (known as the King's Squad). Recipients are known as King's Badgemen and wear the badge on their upper left arm throughout their service.

of Senior Boy Musicians who trained together before being rated Musician 2nd Class. A Commandant General Royal Marines (CGRM) Certificate was introduced and awarded to the best all-round Boy Musician in the Squad. This has since been replaced by the 'The Prince's Badge'.

The first Royal Marines Beat Retreat on Horse Guards Parade took place in June 1950. This had not been attempted before and Maj FV Dunn was asked to take responsibility for the musical programme whilst Lt Lang of the RNSM was responsible for devising the display and for all parade work. The Group Bands from Chatham, Portsmouth and Plymouth together with the bands of RNB Chatham, RNB Portsmouth and RNB Plymouth, as well as bands from five shore establishments, HMS *Daedalus*, *Excellent*, *Gamecock*, *Ganges* and *Raleigh*, totalling 260 Musicians, assembled and rehearsed at Eastney. It was for this display that Lt Lang introduced what was at that time a fairly adventurous and unusual marching display. This display, based upon his original concept for the presentation of the Memorial Fanfare Trumpets at Burford and later used at the Royal Tournament, was to set the precedent for all future Beat Retreat performances on Horse Guards Parade. When the bands arrived in London very bad weather prevented any rehearsal on the Parade itself. The programme started with a fanfare played upon the fourteen Memorial Fanfare Trumpets of the Royal Naval School of Music and directed by Lt W Lang.

The massed bands were led by three Drum Majors from Chatham, Portsmouth and Plymouth Group Bands and two from the RNSM.[143] The Corps of Drums moved into position to Beat Retreat which was preceded by a fanfare played on the thirty-two Silver Bugles. It was the first occasion since the presentation that all thirty-two had been sounded together. Drummers from the RNSM were using the World War I Silver Memorial Drums so all three Memorials from the two world wars were on parade.

The Royal Marines had in 1903, as the Admiralty had wished, instituted a structure and a discipline that encouraged the Naval or recruit Musician to meet new and consistent standards. The bands produced were of a much higher standard than previously - although not as well equipped instrumentally as the Royal Marine Divisional Bands. In their own eyes, and in the eyes of many others, the Royal Marine Bands were every bit as good as the Divisional Bands and they cited the fact that they were, at this time, being invited to play at events that were previously the preserve of the Brigade of Guards or Royal Marine Divisional Bands. War service had raised their profile whilst the efficiency with which the provision of bands was carried out endeared them to the Admiralty and to the Royal Navy. 'The British Survey' for April 1950, printed the following: "The diplomatic and ambassadorial consequences of routine cruises engaged in 'Showing the Flag' are obviously of the highest importance. A first class band of the Royal Marines is probably the best exponent of the art of public relations yet devised by man". So, at the close of the half-century the music of the Royal Navy was in a much-improved state.

However, the war was four years in the past and, as ever when a war begins to fade in the memory, cuts in manning loomed over the armed forces and the scene was set for not only cuts but also amalgamation. Who would bear the reductions and who would gain the upper hand? Would it be the flexible, adaptable Royal Naval School of Music with its Royal Marine Bands or, by comparison, the insular Group Bands who did their own recruiting and training on an individual basis and whose terms of enlistment prevented them from being drafted to other bands?

Direct entry into the Group Bands ceased and all recruits had to enter the Band Service via the School of Music. The Musical Director of the School of Music became the

143 *It is believed that Spencer of the RNSM led the parade as Senior Drum Major.*

first "Director of Music, Royal Marines" and the Directors of Music of the Group Bands at Portsmouth and Plymouth became "Director of Music, Portsmouth" and "Director of Music, Plymouth" respectively. Both of these bands retained their special cap badges and the Portsmouth Band also retained its Royal Yacht shoulder flash.

As a result of the amalgamation further changes were approved. All other ranks in the Royal Marines Band Service, except for Boy Musicians, would wear the Globe and Laurel on the collar and not the Lyre of the RNSM. Also, all trained personnel would wear the broad red stripe on the trousers, not just the Group Bands, whilst boys under training would continue to wear the lyre collar badge and the narrow trouser welt in order to distinguish them from Royal Marine recruits under training. The King approved these changes on the 2nd of November 1950.

It is important to note how much the RNSM and its RM Bands brought to both the amalgamation and the current Royal Marines Band Service: the Massed Bands Beating Retreat display; marching routines; predecessor of the Prince's Badge; the Memorial Silver Trumpets; the War Memorial Silver Drums; the setting of *Sunset*; the Medal of the Worshipful Company of Musicians (begun in 1910) and therefore the relationship between the two organisations; the Cassel prize; Band Conferences that were started in 1948: the framework of instruction and training with civilian professors and Service instructors that is still relevant in, and applicable to, the current Royal Marines School of Music. The idea of the Winter Concert season, so important to the Bandmasters' Course, was created for that very purpose by the RNSM. The philosophy of promotion through the ranks to Officer level came from the Royal Naval School of Music. The Group Bands brought their distinctive headdress badges and the Silver Bugles that had been paid for by the Officers of the Corps but, probably most significantly, the changes they had to make in order to become fully integrated resulted in them becoming as flexible as the Royal Marine Bands.

Cap badge worn by Musicians of the Royal Naval School of Music

PART 2 - THE STORY FROM 1950 TO THE DECADE OF CHANGE - THE 1980s

Chapter 10: The Royal Marines Band Service - The Formative Period 1950-1953

'The Lost Division'. The Colours, Drums and Memorial Silver Bugles of the 1st (Chatham) Grand Division

Capt K McLean had the distinction of being the only Director of Music to wear the King's Badge on his sleeve. Having enlisted in the Royal Marines in 1924 he was made a King's Badgeman when his Squad, 93 King's Squad, passed for duty in 1926. He then transferred to the RNSM and only a year later passed out as a Musician (Flute and Piano) and went to the band of the C-in-C Portsmouth. In 1949 he was appointed Deputy Director of Music and then, upon the retirement of Capt H Kenward in 1950, he was promoted Captain and appointed Musical Director of the RNSM at Deal.

In September 1950 he was placed at the focal point of the new Royal Marines Band Service. From being the last Musical Director of the RNSM he became the first Director of Music of the RMSM with, alongside him, Maj F V Dunn, Director of Music of the Portsmouth Group and Capt R Stoner, Director of Music of the Plymouth Group. Two of them were products of the RNSM whilst Maj Dunn was the last serving Director of Music to have been appointed as a civilian.

As has already been noted, the Leech-Porter Committee had discovered that only Maj Dunn was in favour of amalgamation. Dunn's counterpart, Capt Stoner, was very much against it. Various options had been studied and discussed with, it can be assumed, the RNSM and the Group Bands each trying to ensure that their own organisation remained as intact as possible. Options had included the possibility of the Groups losing all of their bands in favour of a single, large, staff band.

This situation was obviously very difficult for McLean. In September 1950 he found himself carrying the responsibility for the School, for all bands in commission at Shore Establishments and the band ashore with 3 Cdo Bde in Hong Kong. He had approximately eight bands afloat in Home Waters and thirteen afloat elsewhere including the RM Band attached to the Royal New Zealand Navy in HMNZS *Bellona*. He also had the new Royal Marines School of Music Staff Band. There were well over one thousand members of the RMBS, including more than two hundred Boy Musicians. By comparison, Dunn and Stoner each had only one band and, whilst Dunn was a Major and therefore outranked both McLean and Stoner, none was more senior than the others.

Capt McLean had inherited a very large, and a very tough, job and the retirement of the Commandant, Col P R Smith-Hill, who could have given McLean the benefit of his experience and maintained continuity, would not have helped. It also has to be remembered that the Staff Band of the RMSM had only been formed in February of the same year and that the School had also taken on the training of Boy Buglers of each of the Divisional Headquarters in 1948. All of these would have had to be integrated into the already complex training schedules of the school. As if this difficult situation was not enough, McLean had four bands at sea in a war situation.

Princess Elizabeth visits HMS Glory in 1950. It is likely that two Ship's Bands are drawn up on the deck of the Light Fleet Aircraft-carrier

In the Far East, just prior to the outbreak of the Korean War, the combined bands of HMS *Triumph*, *Kenya* and *Jamaica* Beat Retreat following exercises with the US Navy. Instead of returning to the UK *Triumph* was ordered to Korea. Ships' bands from these three ships, plus those of HMS *Ceylon*, *Belfast*, *Glory*, *Theseus*, *Birmingham*, *Ocean*, *Newcastle*, *Newfoundland* and *Unicorn* would be continuously involved in the cycle of active service, refits and rest in Hong Kong or Japan for the next three years as the Korean War, sometimes called, by those who were there, 'The Forgotten War' took place. All Musicians had military, as well as musical, roles to fulfill. Some, on cruisers, were part of the Fire Control systems - much employed during the bombardments of enemy positions, whilst those on the Light Fleet Carriers learnt the intricacies of re-arming aircraft with rockets, bombs and cannon-shells.

All bands continued to entertain and to maintain morale, both on board and ashore. One notable example were the members of *Belfast*'s Dance Band who "sallied forth in a landing craft, dressed in jungle green, did the equivalent of a Bickleigh assault course in scaling a cliff with string bass and drum kit and gave forth for an hour. The troops, mainly American, were astonished and extremely enthusiastic". Since the Army left their bands in Hong Kong the RM Bands in Japan and the Korean War Zone were in great demand. One Bandmaster was Mentioned in Despatches for distinguished service whilst on board HMS *Theseus*. Once again ships' bands earned the respect of the Royal Navy, the Royal Marine detachments and many others for their ability to take on any task whilst maintaining their own skills and the morale of those with whom they came in contact.[1]

The Ship's Band of HMS Glory takes position for Divisions whilst the ship is at Kure, Japan, for rest and recuperation in 1952. She had been operational in the Yellow Sea against North Korean targets

The Band of 3 Cdo Bde, consisting of twenty-three Musicians plus Buglers, was formed in 1948.[2] The Brigade[3] had served in the Middle East and in Hong Kong but, in June 1950, it moved to Malaya to meet a growing threat from terrorists and bandits. Upon arrival in Malaya each member of the band was issued with a rifle and fifty rounds of ammunition before an uncomfortable twenty-five hour train journey, during which time all had to take turn as sentries and there was little to eat. A sixty-five mile journey in lorries, through darkness and torrential rain, brought the band to Brigade HQ at Ipoh. The experience of the

1 *Unless stated otherwise all information regarding the Korean War period is from G & L and Blue Band.*
2 *Unless stated otherwise, all information about service in Malaya has been taken from G & L and Blue Band.*
3 *3 Cdo Bde comprised 40, 42 and 45 Cdo.*

journey plus their own training equipped the band to move around the country without escort. They immediately set out to tour all Commando and Troop locations, staying one night in each location and carrying their own bedding as well as dance and military band instruments and music. The band provided their own defence when making journeys, a Bren gun being manned on each vehicle with every member of the band armed.

A symphony orchestra was formed from amateur Musicians supported by men from the Brigade band. They were titled 'The Perak State Philharmonic Orchestra'. Three months after the band's arrival, August 1950, a tour around 40 Cdo positions was undertaken. As there was a high risk of ambush armoured vehicles of the 4th Hussars led the band, still armed with Bren-guns and personal weapons, in their transport. This type of work continued through 1951 and into 1952. During that year the band, augmented by with woodwind and brass players from the 12th Royal Lancers (Prince of Wales's) Band,[4] performed '*Messiah*' with a choir of sixty drawn from the local European, Chinese and Tamil communities. In March 1952 the band played for a series of Memorial Services, Parades and March Pasts as the various Commando Units left for Singapore, until they themselves packed instruments and left. After living in tents in a transit camp for fourteen days they travelled with Bde HQ and 42 Cdo to Malta, playing for troops, officers and cabin passengers every night.

One of the last events to take place at the RNSM was a music festival. This was such a success that the public hoped that it would become an annual event. Two Symphony Concerts by the 75-piece orchestra attracted full houses but the two military band concerts and the concert with the Deal and Walmer Handelian Society were not as successful. The local press said, "Quite apart from the standard of playing, this is the largest festival ever staged by the School, and it is the biggest and most momentous musical event in the history of Deal". The playing received great critical acclaim and Capt McLean must have felt well satisfied.

It was in this year, at the same time as the other changes, that the rank of Staff Sergeant in the Band Service was changed to Staff Bandmaster to avoid misunderstanding of their status in relation to Bandmasters and Band Sergeants.[5]

The Band of the Flag Officer Scotland and Northern Ireland (FOSNI) at HMS *Cochrane* (BM 1st Cl Margetts[6]) was withdrawn after ten years. Another loss was to be the very busy band at the Infantry Training Centre RM. One of their last tasks was to travel to France to take part in the D-Day celebrations. They left Portsmouth in HMS *Suvla*, a Landing Ship Tank, and arrived off Arromanches at 0930hrs. Having waded ashore they quickly began a very full programme being joined by the Drums of the 5th Bn The Bedfordshire and Hertfordshire Regiment. Their programme included Beating Retreat and playing for luncheons and dances. They re-embarked at 0200hrs on the 7th June, three days after their arrival.

At the end of 1950 the CGRM requested Board of Admiralty approval for the re-issue of Full Dress uniform to RMBS other ranks. At that time there were about 8,000 in store in the UK, about 87% of them being part worn and handed in at the beginning of the war. Although deterioration was occurring there were enough to clothe the entire RMBS indefinitely at the rate of one per man. It was intended that Band Sergeants would wear the same as other Musicians.[7] He made the point that the improved appearance would match the Foot Guards - who were wearing full dress. This request was granted and yellow braided tunics were issued in accordance with an AFO.[8]

4 *The Lancers having relieved the Hussars.*
5 *AFO 7588/1950.*
6 *Mentioned in Despatches in 1945.*
7 *This was later changed.*
8 *AFO3422/51. File in PRO, Kew.*

Despite the reductions that had taken place since the end of the Second World War Britain was still able to maintain, albeit reduced, Fleets around the world. Whilst the Far East Fleet was engaged in support of operations in Korea and Malaya the Home Fleet, the Mediterranean Fleet and others tried to maintain the prestige and repute of Great Britain. Inevitably, as the Empire began to decrease in size so did the need to maintain such a presence throughout the world. The Mediterranean Fleet had ended the year of 1949 with a visit by HRH Princess Elizabeth to the Fleet in Malta. The massed bands of HMS *Glory*, *Liverpool* and *Kenya* were on the flight deck of *Glory* when the Princess came aboard to inspect the Royal Guard and the Officers and men of the Fleet. During the visit the bands of the Mediterranean Fleet (*Liverpool*, *Gambia*, *Ceylon*, *Euryalus*, *Glory* and *Forth*) combined with the band based at St Angelo, Malta, to Beat Retreat. On conclusion the band played *Hymn of Malta* and the National Anthem before marching off. The Maltese Parliament adjourned for one hour to allow its members to watch the ceremony.

Ships of the West Indies Fleet also carried out exercises and cruises. Whilst at Bermuda, the band of HMS *Glasgow* went ashore to carry out military training. Then, in Hamilton, the band continued, albeit on its own, the ceremony begun the year before by the band of *Jamaica*. A military parade such as Beating Retreat was a rarity for the inhabitants, and the American tourists, of Hamilton.

Beating Retreat was not the only ceremony performed by bands in the various Fleets. Guards and Bands, Divisions and Colours were frequently carried out. As well as ceremonial the bands played for receptions and concerts as well as the entertainment of officers and crew. Ships completed their commissions and returned to Great Britain for refit with their bands returning to the RMSM as previously happened with the RNSM. This cycle continued through the early nineteen fifties.

The Staff Band played for the WRNS Association reunion at the Royal Albert Hall, the Memorial Silver Trumpets appeared with the Band of C-in-C The Nore at the opening ceremony of the Sailor's Chapel in Lincoln Cathedral and the band, under Capt W Lang, took part in the 1951 Royal Tournament with the RM Drill Squad. The Staff Symphony Orchestra, under Capt McLean, gave a Matinee Musicale on two consecutive nights to a large and appreciative audience. The Boys' Military Band took the place of the Staff Band for the King's Birthday Parade at Deal. In June the Boys' Symphony Orchestra gave a Festival Concert. Maj F V Dunn conducted the final rehearsal and acknowledged the high standard of their performance.

The first Colours for 3 Commando Brigade were presented on Floriana Parade, Valetta, Malta GC on the 29th November 1952. The Massed Bands and Drums of the Brigade were formed by the Bands of HMS Glasgow, HMS Ocean and HMS Tyne and were under the Direction of Maj F V Dunn and Drum Major R G Knox, both from Portsmouth Division

Maj Martin Pound RM wrote the following about the way the Boys were organised. "It has at last been possible to introduce a 'House' system which would appear to have some chance of being satisfactory and permanent. Several methods have been tried, but the restlessness of the School of Music during the war years and immediately after made it particularly difficult for a really sound method of grouping the boys for competitive purposes to be more than temporarily established, as the accommodation differed so much in each new station. With a prospect of a life-time at Deal, however, the Boys Wing can look ahead and plan on a firm basis, and with this in mind four Houses have been formed. These have been named '*Gloucester*' '*Eagle*' '*Barham*' and '*Neptune*' after ships which suffered heavy Band casualties during the war. Boys have been able to choose their own Houses and the friends they wish to have with them. New entries, after the lapse of a month or two from joining, will be allowed, as far as possible, to select the house to which they would like to be attached. Blocks of accommodation have been allotted to each of the Houses, which are at present about 42 strong. Each House has an Instructor Officer as Housemaster, and there are also NCO Musical Instructors attached."[9]

Many of the events of the next sixteen months were subsumed by the preparations for the Coronation of HM Queen Elizabeth II. However, during that period a number of other important events occurred.

November 1952 saw the Presentation of Colours to 40, 42 and 45 Commando, RM, at Floriana, Malta GC. This triple presentation would not occur again for forty-nine years.

In the Editorial of the April 1953 issue of 'Globe and Laurel' appeared the following: "Major F Vivian Dunn MVO ARAM, Director of Music at Eastney since September 1931 has left the Barracks to take up his appointment as Director of Music at Deal. He will be remembered for his musical contribution, both by members of the Corps and the city music lovers. We wish Major Dunn all good fortune and welcome in his stead, Captain K A McLean LRAM" In the same journal, the Corps Gazette records: 'Major F Vivian Dunn MVO ARAM to Deal as Corps Director of Music. 1.3.53: Captain K A McLean LRAM to Portsmouth as Director of Music, vice Major F V Dunn 1.3.53.'

On Coronation Day, June 2nd 1953, HM The Queen appointed HRH The Duke of Edinburgh to be Captain General Royal Marines. The appointment, originally known as Honorary Colonel, had first been given to Queen Victoria's second son, Alfred who was also Duke of Edinburgh, on the 9th December 1882.[10] The RMSM was the venue for the 50th Anniversary Celebrations of the Band Service in September 1953. The programme of events included an Orchestral and Military Band concert by the Boys' Wing, a Symphony Concert by the Combined Orchestras and a Jubilee Massed Bands Concert, both with the Portsmouth and Plymouth Group bands joining the band of the RMSM. During the reunion that preceded the Golden Jubilee Dinner the Band Boys gave a ceremonial display that was, once again, prepared by Capt W Lang. The band used the Silver Memorial Drums and the Memorial Silver Trumpets. On the 27th October 1953 Maj F V Dunn was promoted Local Lieutenant-Colonel. The arrival of the new Royal Yacht HMY *Britannia* in London on the 15th May 1954 with The Queen and her family on board marked the end of a year of ceremonial on a scale that could never be repeated again.

---

9 'Blue Band' Winter 1951.

10 When he died the title was changed to Colonel-in-Chief and given to the Duke of Cornwall and York, who subsequently became The Prince of Wales and then King George V, on the 1st Jan 1901. The title then passed to Edward as Colonel-in-Chief then, after the abdication, to King George VI who changed it to Captain General.

Chapter 11: Reductions and Rationalisation

The new Royal Marines Band Service was not only involved in fighting by sea and by land but was also entering a period when, at times, it was fighting for its very existence. This applied to the other Services as politicians sought to make cuts or endeavoured to create Tri-Service organisations without any regard to the traditions and history that led to the esprit de corps and pride that was, and still is, a huge factor in the training and performance of any military unit. Cutbacks, Defence Reviews and changes always seemed to be in the background.

In 1953 a scheme for coping with the shortage of manpower together with improvements to the conditions of the RMBS was approved by CGRM.[1] The Home, Mediterranean and Far East Fleets would each have one large Fleet Band of forty-five under the control of the C-in-C. Each of the Fleet Bands would be under a Staff Bandmaster. It was anticipated that by September 1957 natural wastage would reduce the size of these bands to about thirty-seven all ranks and then, as a result of high recruitment during 1951/1952, the numbers in each band would increase. The Fleet Bands were expected to be able to produce a military band, a dance band and a small orchestra all at the same time and it was also expected that the need for other combinations could be satisfied.

It was during 1956 that the titles 'Junior Bugler' and 'Junior Musician' replaced those of 'Boy Bugler' and 'Boy Musician'. This was necessary because the Royal Navy had removed all reference to 'Boy' ratings. It was also during 1956 that The Queen Mother visited Deal to open the new accommodation blocks. The major military event of 1956 was the landing at Port Said, Suez, by 3 Cdo Bde. During this operation two Officers and nine other ranks were killed. Their bodies were brought back to England and some were reinterred at the RN Cemetery, Gosport on 17th December 1956. The Bands of C-in-C Portsmouth, the Home Fleet and the Portsmouth Group Band under the direction of Captain K A McLean, led the cortege on its journey from the RN Hospital to the cemetery. HMS *Newfoundland* had been at the southern end of the Canal and engaged the Egyptian frigate *Domiat*. After a short battle the Egyptian ship was sunk by *Newfoundland's* gunfire. The only Band Service casualty, BSgt Evans, had been wounded by shrapnel and was sent home.

In 1956 the Band of HMS *Triumph*, the ship that for several years had been engaged upon RN Officer Cadet training, marched into Dartmouth, to become the College band with a new title, the Band of HM RM Britannia Royal Naval College.

January 1st 1957 heralded changes to Officer rank structures based upon the new Special Duties List. Commissioned Bandmasters became Second Lieutenants SD(B) and Senior Commissioned Bandmasters became Lieutenants SD(B). In addition Lieutenants became Captains but there were no changes to the ranks of Captain and Major.

On 26th January 1957 the 50th Anniversary of the Garrison Church at Deal (St Michael's and All Angels') was celebrated. Lt Col F V Dunn conducted the orchestra and after the service the CGRM presented the British Empire Medal to Senior Drum Major C H Bowden.[2]

On 17th May 1957 Capt J E Talling took a Band and Corps of Drums of fifty-one onto HMS *Ark Royal* which was moored at Rosyth in preparation for a visit to the United States. The band was a composite one made up of the band of HMS *Eagle*[3] and Home Fleet as

1 *From 'Blue Band' Winter 1993 and report in RMM.*
2 *The title 'Corps Drum Major' was not used until some time in the 1970s.*
3 *HMS Eagle was in dry dock and did not require the band.*

well as ranks from the School of Music. Staff BM Martin was Drum Major. Next day the Guard and Band practised a drill display in readiness for the visit and then, on the 21st HMS *Ark Royal* and the other ships of the Home Fleet assembled at Cromarty to rehearse for meeting The Queen returning from Copenhagen in the Royal Yacht. The Fleet's capital ships, the three aircraft carriers HMS *Ark Royal*, *Albion* and *Ocean* steamed out to meet the Royal Yacht and her escort of three destroyers. During the steam past the crew manned ship and the Guard and Band were paraded. As soon as Royal Duties were completed HMS *Ark Royal* sailed for the United States. The ship spent fifteen days at various cities on the eastern seaboard during which time the Guard and Band paraded on twenty-six occasions (four of them being Royal) and gave one drill display, Beat Retreat six times and gave five other public performances.

1957 was not only a particularly busy year but it was also the year when the Band Service was expected to have recovered from the cutbacks of 1949 and the changes of 1953. It was also the year in which the first major Defence Review, intended to reduce the size of the Services, was promulgated. As a result of the changes to the RMBS military role, brought about by developments to ships' gunnery systems, it was proposed by CGRM's staff, in 1958, that the Band ranks should have training in Nuclear, Biological and Chemical Warfare with a view to this becoming their operational commitment.

CGRM's proposal for band reductions, issued in 1958, was to be the first of many reviews of the Band Service that would litter the next fifteen years with huge amounts of paperwork requiring much staff work and causing much concern for those who were part of the Service.

The Commandant RMSM wrote to the CGRM to suggest that the nomenclature concerning bands be altered. Apparently officers from other services were of the opinion that a Class B band was of a lower standard than a Class A Band. His suggestion was that a Group Band of thirty-eight ranks should retain its name but Class A Bands with twenty-four ranks should be called 'Command Bands'. The Class B Bands of eighteen ranks including the Bandmaster or Band Officer should be called a 'Ship's Band'. This was approved and issued as AFO 676/62.[4]

By 1962, the Band Service consisted of eight Command Bands in the UK, four bands on foreign service, eight bands on ships and four bands on Home Service including the two RM Group Bands.

Future officer requirements for the Band Service had been calculated as one Major, four Captains, two Captain/Lieutenants and eight Lieutenant/2nd Lieutenants. It had already been agreed that all Captains within the RMBS would be styled Director of Music and would be appointed to both administrative and band appointments with this title. Direct promotion from Lieutenant to Captain would cease; it was unwise to promote young and outstanding Musicians to Director of Music too early and exceptional circumstances would be necessary to retain a Director of Music beyond the age of fifty.

An AFO was issued in 1961 stating that promotion from 2nd Lt to Lt would be by selection from 2nd Lts having four to eight years' seniority. Promotion to Captain would also be by selection from Lts and, for a short time, 2nd Lts who had passed the examination for Director of Music. The appointment of Principal Director of Music and promotion to Major would be made from Royal Marines Band Service Captains, provided that a suitable candidate was available. The Admiralty reserved the right to appoint the PDM from outside the RMBS if a suitable candidate could not be found from within.[5]

4 RMM Archive.
5 AFO1585/60(U)276.

In 1962 an attempt was made to introduce a Regimental Bandmaster as a Regimental Sergeant Major of the RMBS but, following discussion, this proposal was not accepted by the CGRM. In 1964 the matter was resurrected but, once again, it was turned down.[6]

Band Service instrumental categories were reviewed in 1963/4 and as a result, the Flute and Piano category was changed to Flute/Tenor Saxophone and Piano/Cornet; Solo Cornet and Solo Clarinet were to be taught the violin; Bassoon and Oboe were also to be taught the guitar or piano-accordion.

During 1968/69 the RN was due to centralise their Pay, Records and Drafting functions and the CGRM directed that RMBS drafting, promotion and records be transferred from the Band Service[7] to the new organisation. After a number of meetings it was agreed that because of the specialist knowledge required for the drafting of RMBS other ranks to the various types of bands a Band Officer would be appointed as Assistant Drafting Officer (Band). It was deemed necessary to confirm the remaining responsibilities of the Commandant of the RMSM. These responsibilities were the musical training of all Band ranks; the musical instruction of all classes of candidates for promotion and the musical training and initial administration prior to embarkation of all RM Bands newly formed for service. In addition he had responsibility for the correct accounting and returns relating to the receipt, custody and issue of musical instruments on charge to the School and those obtained for the use of RN[8] and RM Bands as well as maintaining liaison with RN and RM formations, units, establishments or ships to which a RM Band was allocated. He also needed to liaise with the appropriate schools of the Army and RAF on training or technical music matters. Queen's Regulations and Admiralty Instructions were altered accordingly. By implication it can be seen that, at this time, the duties of the Principal Director of Music were almost totally concentrated upon the musical performance of the RM Bands and not their administration.

During the late 1960s and the 1970s a series of reviews relating to Joint Service Training, the future of the RMSM at either Deal or Eastney and the costs of, and income from, military bands took place. Some of these were Tri-Service whilst others only involved the Royal Marines. Some emanated from questions in parliament whilst others were local matters. The result was that vested interests and overlapping of topics under discussion prevented progress and prompted the Royal Marines to take the initiative and following the reports of the Corps' Way-Ahead Committee and some covert financial investigations it was announced that the RMSM would move to Eastney in 1981. A year before this the Corps had responded to an MoD initiative to re-open the discussions into Tri-Service Training of Musicians by supporting the suggestion that the Army should undertake a study of the work of its bands. However the proviso was that any Royal Marines involvement in joint training would require the inclusion of all Army Staff Bands including the Household Division. Shortly after this the decision was taken by the MoD not to pursue the joint training concept. To underline this excellent conclusion the Royal Marines filed a Position Paper on their views of the enquiry. Their conclusion was that the line to be taken should be that '...forming a joint musical establishment would be an extravagant sop to the protagonists of rationalisation for its own sake, which the Navy cannot afford". The 1977 Walden Report was commissioned to define the organisation, deployment and conditions of service of the Royal Marines Band Service and the bugle section of the technical branch. This comprehensive report contained many detailed recommendations, many of which were put into practice, and concluded that generally the status quo should be maintained,

6 *RMM Archive.*

7 *This duty had been carried out by a General List officer with Band Service staff.*

8 *The RMBS is responsible for Volunteer Bands, providing an Instructor, usually a BdCSgt, who trains, rehearses and administers the band. This provides good experience and training for the VBI.*

whilst acknowledging that the RMSM would relocate to Eastney by 1981. A little later the Under Secretary of State (Royal Navy) confirmed that the move of the RMSM from Deal to Eastney could take place in 1981.

As part of the general restructuring of the Services several of the 'parent' organisations had their titles changed on 31st October 1969. Portsmouth Group RM and Plymouth Group RM ceased to exist and were replaced by Training Group Royal Marines and Commando Forces, Royal Marines respectively; as seen earlier C-in-C Portsmouth became C-in-C Naval Home Command and, due to cuts to the Royal Navy as well as rationalisations, C-in-C Plymouth became Flag Officer, Plymouth. The C-in-C Home Fleet became C-in-C Western Fleet with the band, under Capt P Sumner, increasing in size from eighteen to forty-three. In July 1968, and following discussions regarding reductions to the RMBS, the Naval Personnel Division (NPD) informed the Royal Navy of the provisional plan for the reduction of the RMBS[9] By 1973 the remaining bands were to be the Royal Marines School of Music (RMB Deal), Portsmouth Group (RMB Eastney), Plymouth Group (ITCRM), C-in-C Western Fleet (HMS *Pembroke*), C-in-C Portsmouth (HMS *Excellent*), C-in-C Plymouth (HMS *Drake*/HMS *Raleigh*), Flag Officer Scotland and Northern Ireland (HMS *Condor*), HMS *Ganges*, Britannia Royal Naval College, Dartmouth and HQ 3 Cdo Bde.

On 24th August 1970 the Infantry Training Centre became the Commando Training Centre RM with a consequent name change for the band. The band of 3 Cdo Bde returned to England and was disbanded. Members of the band joined with the part of the Plymouth Group band that returned to Stonehouse Barracks in 1972 as the RM Commando Forces Band and which retained the Prince of Wales Plumes in the cap badge. The other part of the band remained at CTC being augmented by Musicians from the bands at HMS *Drake*, HMS *Raleigh* and the RMSM. BM Rawson from HMS *Drake* took charge of this band that was also renamed as the Band of HMRM Commando Training Centre.[10]

The bands of Portsmouth Group and C-in-C Western Fleet would have bands of forty-three to enable them to provide a sea-going band as well as a standard band. This would enable the Portsmouth Group to fulfil its Royal Yacht commitment and Western Fleet Band to send a small band to sea when required. C-in-C Plymouth's Band would be accommodated in HMS *Raleigh* after 1971 to provide a band for that establishment and BRNC would have to be prepared to make its band available for other tasks.

The decision not to provide Volunteer Band Instructors was reversed and requests for VBIs were sought. The Admiralty Board made the CGRM responsible for the co-ordination of band engagements for all RM Bands, including those in RN ships and establishments. Following the various discussions and negotiations the general situation at this time was that by 1973, the Band Service would lose Deal and Portsmouth Group Band and three other bands plus all ships' bands; this would leave only the RMSM at Eastney with eight other bands.

All of the reductions were linked to the closures of Shore Establishments and withdrawals of the Royal Navy. It was also decided that, after 1973, there would only be two types of band: Staff Bands commanded by a Band Officer with forty-three Musicians and twelve Buglers; and a Standard Band commanded by either an officer or a Staff Bandmaster with twenty-four Musicians and seven Buglers. The C-in-C Naval Home Command was consulted about the plan to transfer responsibility for providing a Royal Yacht Band to his own band - a prospect to which he readily agreed. The Flag Officer Royal Yachts (FORY) was also consulted and he confirmed that it would be appropriate for the C-in-C Naval Home Command Band to wear the Royal Yacht shoulder flash and the special headdress badges.

9 *RMM Archive.*
10 *Blue Band.*

The Admiralty wrote to Buckingham Palace to explain that the Portsmouth Band would be merged with the RMSM Band and how it was proposed to supply a band for the Royal Yacht. It was then pointed out that the demise of the Portsmouth Band raised the question of insignia and asked for the agreement of HM The Queen and the Duke of Edinburgh to transfer them to the Band of C-in-C Naval Home Command. Both proposals were approved on 9th November 1970. With everything apparently in place, detailed complements for the redeployed bands were constructed and published. Indecision continued until late 1972 when it was decided to retain both the RMSM and the Portsmouth Band but to disband the band at Whale Island and transfer its name to the Portsmouth Band. So, the Portsmouth Band lost its famous name and became the Band of the Commander-in-Chief Naval Home Command which allowed the band to keep its Royal Yacht flash and special headdress badge.[11]

HMS *Ark Royal* had her life extended so adjustments were made that allowed her to retain a band until she was decommissioned in 1978.

Side drum emblazonment

11 *Blue Band Vol 23 No1 p3.*

Chapter 12: Buglers & Corps of Drums 1950-1982

The Royal Marines School of Music had assumed responsibility for the training of Boy Buglers from the Divisional Headquarters in 1948. In the same year the Band of 3 Cdo Bde, with its own Corps of Drums, was formed. Two years later seven of the Chatham Division Silver Bugles were presented to 3 Cdo Bde. Brigadier C R Hardy wrote, from Brigade HQ in Malaya, 'It is intended that the bugles shall be called "The Chatham Division Bugles" in memory of the old Division, and two will be allocated to each Unit and one to Brigade HQ. The Bugles will be used on Corps and Unit memorable dates and ceremonial parades'[1] The first Massed Bands Beat Retreat on Horse Guards Parade provided the first opportunity for all thirty-two Silver Memorial Bugles to be sounded together. Purchased soon after the First World War, they were immediately distributed throughout the Divisions.

Following the Second World War the practice of sounding bugle fanfares to mark anniversaries was reviewed. Between the wars it was customary for them to be sounded on morning parade when the Buglers would be in full dress, drawn up in front of the flagstaff, and under the direction of the Bugle Major. Following the reading of an account of the anniversary by the Adjutant, the Bugle Major sounded the fanfare. These fanfares were not laid down in Regulations. Prior to the Second World War fanfares were sounded on: 14th February (Battle of St Vincent 1797), 3rd April (Battle of Copenhagen 1801), 23rd April (Zeebrugge, 1918), 25th April (Gallipoli Landings, 1915), 29th April (award of the title 'Royal'), 31st May (Battle of Jutland 1916), 1st June (Battle of the Glorious First of June, 1794), 7th June (Battle of Belleisle, 1761), 17th June (Battle of Bunkers Hill, 1775), 24th July (Capture of Gibraltar, 1704), 1st August (Battle of the Nile, 1798), 26th September (Granted the Globe and use of the Royal monogram, 1827), 11th October (Battle of Camperdown, 1797), 21st October (Battle of Trafalgar, 1805), 28th October (Birth of the Corps,1664) and 11th November (Armistice Day, 1918). The review resulted in the drastic reduction of the number of fanfares being sounded to only those of Zeebrugge, Belleisle, Gibraltar, Trafalgar and the Birth of the Corps. However, to these was added 1st November (Battle of Walcheren, 1944). The fanfares were to be sounded at 1200hrs on the appropriate dates.

On the 20th February 1950 Plymouth Group gave a farewell dinner to the retiring C-in-C Plymouth. Before the meal the drums and pipes provided an impressive "Mess Beatings" under floodlights. The official C-in-C handover took place on the 16th March when the Group Band, with the Bands of HMS *Drake* and HMS *Raleigh* massed to Beat Retreat. A couple of weeks prior to this, the final of the USMC Cup, also known as the Tunney Cup, took place on the Plymouth Argyll football ground. The band Beat Retreat during the interval and, no doubt, enjoyed watching Plymouth Group team win the cup.

The Buglers of Royal Marine Barracks, Plymouth, with Captain P L Mackay and Drum Major R Woodruff, c.1949

Also in 1950, reference to a particular ceremony appeared in a letter from the High Sheriff of Cornwall. He wrote, 'Sir, I feel I should bring the following matter to your

1 *Globe & Laurel 1950, p296.*

notice. On conclusion of the Autumn Assize here [Bodmin] yesterday His Majesty's Judge asked me if I would bring the three Royal Marine Buglers over to his lodgings (where the procession stops and the Assize comes to an end) so that he could thank them personally for what he described as the best bugling he had ever been "given" on any circuit. Talking with him later showed that this was no facon de parler and that he had been as impressed with their general turn-out and drill as the way in which they blew the fanfares'.[2] For St George's Day 1951 Plymouth Group's Bugle Major Bailey composed a commemorative bugle fanfare 'Remembrance' based on the three Divisional calls and sounded on the Silver Bugles.[3]

During 1953 a Combined Services parade was held at Floriana, Malta, in the presence of The Queen and the Duke of Edinburgh. Amongst the bugles on parade were the seven Silver Bugles held by the Commando Brigade, including one that was sounded when HRH the Duke of York opened the new Parliament House, Australia in 1927 and one that was sounded in St Paul's Cathedral in 1945 at the Memorial Service for President Roosevelt.[4]

On Saturday 7th May 1955 the City of Plymouth presented the Freedom of the City to the Royal Marines. The Hoe was used for the ceremony and the Buglers who beat *Markers* and *Fall In* were dressed as Drummers of 1755 - the date when fifty companies of Marines were raised for service in Plymouth.

'1755 Drummer' waits, with Ceremonial Battalion, to step off during Freedom of Plymouth ceremony

At the Infantry Training Centre in 1955 a number of ex-Buglers in the Squads volunteered to play drum and bugle on Corps Memorable Dates.

During 1956 the title 'Junior Bugler' replaced 'Boy Bugler' in line with the Royal Navy's policy of removing all reference to 'Boy' ratings. Another change in this year was the General Order that Drum Majors were not to throw the staff. This practice had been restricted since 1946 but had not been forbidden until now.

It was about the 1954-1956 period that a School of Music bugle call was introduced for use in East Barracks, Deal. The Depot, Deal continued to use the old Chatham Division call.[5]

Eugen Harrison, a Barnardo's boy and a pupil and a member of the school band at Parkstone Sea Training School, joined the RMBS in 1956 as a bass player. He could not master the string bass and transferred to the Buglers' Branch where he earned notoriety for pranks, including trying to float C-in-C Plymouth's launch into the swimming pool in a gale which resulted in serious damage to the launch and 28 days in Detention Quarters. Service in the Mediterranean included a period of acting Drum Major. On return he, a Plymouth Bugler, was sent to Eastney. After ten attempts at gaining a transfer to Plymouth, he transferred himself to Plymouth where he was arrested. It was discovered that there was an error on his attestation form which meant that he was offered a discharge, which he accepted. He took a job as a driver-tentman with a circus and worked his way up to becoming an international circus ringmaster - such is the flexibility of the Bugler![6]

---

2 *Globe & Laurel 1950 p329.*
3 *Globe & Laurel 1951 p176.*
4 *See Chapter 13 for full details of this Parade.*
5 *By Corps Historian 16 Nov 1972. (RMM Archive).*
6 *Blue Band winter 1999, p106.*

Drum Major Knox of the Portsmouth Group Band at Eastney where he served from 1950 to 1959 before transferring to Plymouth Group. The picture was taken at Eastney in 1956 and he is wearing Dress No 1, Ceremonial Blue (Drum Major). This comprises White helmet; Tunic, cloth Drum Major; Blue tweed trousers with scarlet stripe; Sash, worsted; Sash, Drum Major; Gloves, gauntlet white; Sword and steel scabbard

In 1958 Maj-Gen I H Riches (MGRM Portsmouth) wrote to the CGRM suggesting that Cavalry Trumpets should be purchased for the Buglers' Branch to allow them to satisfy increasing requests to provide trumpeters for the old custom of sounding a fanfare and carrying the banners of the High Sheriffs when attending Assizes or other functions. The CGRM agreed to provide four such instruments to each Group for this purpose and asked for clarification with regard to whether the trumpets should carry the Sheriff's Arms. It was decided that the banners should be similar to those of the Memorial Silver Trumpets and should be used at all times. It was also decided to purchase a set of four for the Depot since they also received similar requests and the strict Rules contained in the Charter[7] would not allow the use of the Memorial Silver Trumpets. The type known as a "Herald Trumpet with chased ball and ferrule" was the best option. It was decided that the banners should be scarlet with the full RM insignia in the centre, as supplied in 1956 for the Memorial Silver Trumpets. Herald Trumpets and banners were ordered for the two Groups only. Special mouthpieces based upon the Bugler's mouthpiece were provided. These were accepted into service in 1959 but were only to be used when bugles would be inappropriate or inadvisable and it was decided that they should not be used with bugles. Four years later four more were purchased for the Depot. Since then the playing of Herald Trumpets has been part of the Buglers' duties.[8]

On occasion band ranks were wearing Dress Cords Royal, a practice that appears to have started in 1948 when those receiving the RNSM Silver Memorial Trumpets wore them. A General Order of 1958 stated that their use was restricted to the Buglers' Branch. Overall trousers were introduced for wear by Drum Majors in 1957/1958 and, initially, were not very popular. In 1958 each of the permanent bands had a Corps of Drums of twelve Buglers and, by the end of 1959, there were ninety Junior Buglers under training.

Bugler McQuigg, Portsmouth Corps of Drums, was drafted to HM Submarine *Trump* when she sailed to take part in the 50th Anniversary celebration of the Royal Norwegian Navy's Submarine Service. He was employed on various duties, including lookout, as well as being on the bridge to return salutes and play for military ceremonies. He remained on board for an additional two days as the submarine carried out torpedo trials.

Herald Trumpets are presented to Plymouth Group at Bickleigh. The Bugle Major is 'Tex' Rickard

7 See Appendix 1.
8 Account taken from official file in RM Museum.

Upon their return the submarine sent a signal to Eastney: "Very many thanks for the service of Bugler McQuigg who was a credit to the Corps in every way and a keen and useful submariner".[9]

In 1960 an Admiralty Fleet Order decreed that the Green Beret should be worn by all trained ranks throughout the Corps. Previously this had only been worn by ranks serving at Commando Units or the Commando School. This was further clarified in 1972 when CGRM's Advisory Dress Committee said that Band ranks could wear the Green Beret on limited occasions such as service in Northern Ireland, during military training and when caps were impractical, such as on board ship.

1960 also saw the introduction of rod-tension military drums. Ropes, braces, buffs and brass shells were replaced by chromed steel fittings, a plastic covered wooden shell and plastic heads. Tenor and bass drums retained the calfskin heads.[10] The following year the Captain General commented upon the imitation wood veneer that formed the rear part of the drum shell and suggested that the blue background to the emblazonment might be continued all the way around the drum. At the time there were about 350 drums within the Corps so this presented quite a problem. Trials took place on two of the recently introduced rod-tensioned drums and the Commandant General, after seeking advice from Band Officers, decided that the wood veneer should be replaced or covered with a scarlet paint finish.

Also in 1960, new Dress Belts were required for the Drum Majors who would lead the massed bands Beating Retreat on Horse Guards Parade and the Corps decided to seek advice from the Royal College of Heralds with regard to the correct arrangement of the Royal and Corps insignia. As a result the order became, from the shoulder, "Gibraltar" in a scroll; the crown, Royal Cypher and Foul Anchor (as on the Sovereign Colour); the Globe and Laurel wreath; the words "Per Mare Per Terram"; the Royal Academy pattern lyre and the drum at the lowest point. Sufficient space had to be left for miniature medals to be worn above the upper scroll and the two ebonised miniature drumsticks having gold plated crowns, caps and bands enclosed the Royal Cypher and Foul Anchor as was customary.[11] The Drum Majors taking part in the 1960 Royal Tournament were K Booth, C E Bowden, E Haybittle, G Higham and J Dillon.

On the 1st January 1961 a new pay structure, revised advancement and promotion regulations as well as specialist qualifications came into force for the Bugler Section of the Technical Branch, Royal Marines. The Specialist Qualifications were intended to improve the standard of performance on drum and bugle and to bring Buglers in line with other Sections of the Technical Branch.

Bugle Major Rickard and the Plymouth Group Buglers sound Last Post at Bickleigh Church on Salerno Day

On the 23rd April 1961, during the Corps Remembrance Day Church Parade, a Memorial tablet believed to have once hung in the Adjutant's Office (but which had been in his store) was unveiled in its new position in the Eastney Barracks Church. This Memorial took the form of a silver shield mounted in a glass fronted black case. It is a Memorial to the Buglers of the Royal Marine

9 Globe & Laurel 1960 p25.
10 BB Aug 1961 pp13-14.
11 File in RMM Archive.

Artillery who fell during the First World War. When the Corps left Eastney, this was not amongst the Memorials removed and placed for safekeeping in the Corps Museum.

In 1962 it was decided that RM Detachments would no longer be provided for fixed wing aircraft carriers; however, Buglers and bands continued to be embarked on this type of ship.

During the period of reduction and rationalisation the question of allocation and training of Drum Majors often arose and the opportunity was taken to develop a policy regarding their standards and their use. The two Group Bands and the RMSM Band had a General Duties (GD) SNCO as Drum Major whilst other bands used a Musician, a member of the RM Detachment or another Bandmaster. They would wear Drum Major's badges and would be issued with the appropriate accoutrements.

Requests, particularly from Fleet Bands, for Drum Majors of the calibre of those of the Group Bands were frequently being received by CGRM's Office. Two Drum Majors, a QMS and a Drill Leader, were trained. One went to the Mediterranean Fleet and served for three years until he returned to General Duties. He was not replaced. The second was trained and qualified as Drum Major and as a Provost Sergeant. The intention was for him to replace CSgt Charles Bowden at the RMSM who would then take over as Mediterranean Fleet Drum Major. More requests for Drum Majors were received and CGRM decided that a training and examination regime to produce quality Drum Majors was required. Portsmouth Group Commander and Commandant, RMSM, were instructed to produce a blueprint for this training. Their recommendation was that candidates should be NCO volunteers from the General and Buglers' Branches who had at least five years to serve. Training and examination would include Band Drill, use of the Staff, Band ceremonial and Band administration. This was accepted by CGRM who was then able to stop the practice of locally appointed Drum Majors. The first Bugler appointed as a Drum Major was CplBug (acting Sgt) Colin Bowden who was appointed to Eastney. [12] [13]

Details of the course were finalised and, in 1962, an RMRO was issued that detailed the length of tenure of Drum Majors' appointments.[14] A year later an RM Instruction gave details of the selection procedure and the course detail.[15] 1964 saw the inauguration of Instructional Classes for Drum-Majors. Four out of five candidates passed. In 1967, an RMRO was issued allowing Band SNCOs to apply.[16]

At the School's Junior Wing, Bugle Major Wagstaffe was replaced by Bugle Major Flook - the man responsible for maintaining 42 Cdo Pipe Band in the recent past. Thirty-five Junior Buglers were under training in Junior Wing during 1964.

Buglers also played a substantial part in the 1964 Tercentenary celebrations. As well as taking part, with the bands, in all of the ceremonial, the Portsmouth Corps of Drums performed Mess Beatings for The Queen, the Captain General and all guests attending the Corps Dinner at the Royal Naval College, Greenwich, on the 23rd July. On the following afternoon they paraded on the steps of St Paul's Cathedral and, at ten past two as the Captain General arrived for the Thanksgiving Service, they sounded a fanfare on the Memorial Silver Bugles.

In 1965 the Freedom of the City of Portsmouth was given to Portsmouth Command, Royal Navy. Drum Major J E Dillon was given, probably for the first time, the honour of drawing the Colours from the Royal Naval Barracks Wardroom.

---

12 *Official file in RM Museum.*

13 *Not to be confused with Drum Major Charles Bowden who, at this time was with the RMSM.*

14 *RMRO152/1962.*

15 *BR 1283.*

16 *RMRO 228/1967.*

Eight Buglers, with a SgtBugler were flown to Laos by the RAF in 1966. They were to support the Drums and Pipes of the 1st Bn The Gordon Highlanders and the Military Band of the 1st Bn The Argyll & Sutherland Highlanders at a Trade Fair in the Laotian city of Vientiane. The Royal Marines opened the British pageant with a ceremonial ruffle, a bugle fanfare and a ten minute display of drumming and bugling; then, after a display by each of the two Scots bands, they formed the front rank of each of the two bands and led them on for the finale. A similar display was given next day.[17]

Whilst obtaining transfers to re-emblazon a bass drum, it was realised that the current design did not include the "GIBRALTAR" scroll. As a result all tenor and side drums were checked for standardisation and correctness during 1965. It was discovered that, historically, there were large variations, and there had been little official guidance, in the painting of badges and emblems on drums. The design and purchase of new drums, and their emblazonment, had been the responsibility of the Divisional Drum Majors. The Royal Cypher 'GRIV' had often been included as well as that of the reigning monarch - a practice used on the Regimental Colours. Following the 1950 amalgamation, the Royal Naval School of Music practice of using the Royal Cypher was adopted but with additional adornment in the form of the Corps crest, or parts of it.[18] The investigations proved inconclusive and the matter was forgotten until 1967.

Further stocks of the drum emblazonment transfer were required in 1967 and the omission of "Gibraltar" was again raised. Having decided to remedy this fault further criticisms were raised with the result that a local study team, led by Major G Manuel, was given an Instruction to produce the correct emblazonment by 1971. The College of Heralds ruled that the practice of omitting the Royal lion and crown from the Corps crest because there was one in the Royal crest was incorrect. The lion and the crown were placed above "Gibraltar", EIIR was to be in the correct style and the layout on the bass drum was arranged so that the foul anchor was not obscured. These designs were then sent to the Royal College of Heralds for approval before being sent to the Department of the Commandant-General. The Lancaster Herald (Deputy Inspector of Regimental Colours) was most approving of the efforts made and gave access to the sealed pattern of the Royal Arms for the emblazonment. By this time The Queen had authorised Garter King of Arms to be responsible for not only Colours but all forms of military heraldry which included Colour Belts, drum emblazonment etc. From this it is apparent that all future changes in heraldry in the Corps would have to be approved and recorded by the College of Heralds when the Royal Arms are included.[19]

In 1971 Clarenceux King of Arms, in discussion with Chester Herald, the Advisor on Naval Heraldry, and Garter King of Arms agreed the designs for the drums of the Royal Marines and also for the drums of the Royal Navy Volunteer Bands. Paintings of the designs were laid before Her Majesty and approval for their use was given in November 1972.[20]

The Tri-Service 1968 Royal Tournament was used to demonstrate the skills and the versatility of the Royal Marines Band Service. Following an introductory fanfare, eighty Buglers marched on to give a three-minute display comprising two drum and bugle marches, *Bugles and Drums* and *Bugle Bells* and the drum beatings *Ceremonial Tattoo*. This type of display, once a very common sight since it allowed a Bugle Band to lead marching troops in the same way as the Divisional, and other, bands, ceased to be used in the

---

17 Globe & Laurel 1966 p4.

18 The Corps crest, as laid down in The Navy List, consists of the Globe surrounded by a Laurel Wreath and surmounted by the crowned lion and crown with 'Gibraltar' on a scroll. The foul anchor is placed on the wreath below the Globe with, below, the motto "Per Mare, Per Terram". This crest was devised shortly after the Corps amalgamation of 1923.

19 Corps Historians report to HQ Portsmouth Group. RMM Archive file.

20 File in RMM Archive (RM07/218).

intervening years. Whilst this is partly as a result of a much reduced need, it is also a fact that Corps of Drums were reduced to a size that made this impractical.

Between 1943 and the late 1970s, Buglers were heavily involved in running, and were responsible for the longevity of, a very individual addition to the Corps - 42 Commando Pipe Band. Although never part of the Royal Marines Band Service the pipes of 42 Cdo feature in Corps history and are well remembered by many veterans.

42 Cdo Pipe Band, first formed in 1943, being inspected by the Commandant General, General Sir Norman Tailyour, Singapore 1968

These were not the first, nor the last, pipes that appear in the musical history of the Band Service, the Corps or the Royal Navy. In 1899 HMS *Caledonia*, the Boys' Training Ship at Queensferry in the Firth of Forth had its own pipe band of five pipers, a bass Drummer and a side Drummer. A bagpipe band in one of the Royal Naval Division Battalions was referred to as the 'bagpipe marines'.[21] During a Torchlight Tattoo by the Plymouth Division Band and Bugles "'Scotch' marines marched from end to end of the square with skirling of the pipes". When a band from the Royal Naval School of Music went on board HMS *Renown* for the 1927 Royal Tour they were joined by three sailors especially embarked as Pipers. A Scotsman in the RM Detachment became the fourth piper and the Buglers were then trained in pipe band drumming. Plymouth Division had Pipes and Drums but, in 1941, during the blitz on Plymouth, the pipes were destroyed. In 1944, not only were they replaced but the Argyll and Sutherland Highlanders (Princess Louise's) conferred the honour of wearing their tartan on the pipes, marking the close association between the two regiments, which was particularly apparent during the Second World War. By 1948 these pipes were certainly in use since a photograph exists of Drum Major R Woodruff with the Pipes and Drums of the Plymouth Division at the RMA Ball at Bristol. The three pipers appear to be Musicians, despite wearing Dress Cords Royal, and they are supported by five Buglers and a bass Drummer. On the 16th March 1950 the C-in-C Plymouth was given a retirement dinner in the Officers' Mess, before which the drums and pipes gave 'Mess Beatings' under floodlights. In 1951, following a Stonehouse Barracks Dinner to the Commander-in-Chief, the Bugle Major, possibly Bugle Major Bailey, circled the table with his Pipes and, although unable to trace Sir Roderick McGrigor's clan march, received acclaim for his playing of the *Gathering of the Clans*.[22] It would also appear that the Bugle Major took advantage of the Divisional Band's absence at Festival of Britain activities, to fill the breach with Pipes and Drums wherever possible. This situation appears to have lasted for a number of months. It should not be forgotten that the RMBS had its own piper during the late 1990s when Musician Bean was featured on a great many occasions, but particularly the 1997 decommissioning of HMY *Britannia*, when the final piece of music prior to *Sunset* was *Highland Cathedral*.[23]

In 1968 the Silver Memorial Bugles, having been in service for almost fifty years, were withdrawn and issued to various Officers' Messes, the Royal Marines Band Service and the Royal Marines Museum.

21 Globe & Laurel 1917.
22 Globe & Laurel 1951 p111.
23 The full story of 42 Cdo Pipe Band is told as an appendix.

In 1969, as part of the discussions relating to joint-service training of Musicians, Lt Col Jaeger, Director of Music at Kneller Hall, visited the RMSM at Deal. He was most impressed by the Bugle and Drum Section and commented that, if rationalisation went ahead, he would be keen to adopt the RM method for the proposed Army Corps of Drums.

When the US Marine Corps Naples Detachment celebrated their Corps' 194th Birthday they invited Bugle Major Close and eight Buglers from ITCRM to take part. On the 10th November 1970 the parade included the Bugle Major and four Herald Trumpeters. Further such fanfares were played as well as drum displays at both the enlisted men's ball and the Officers' Club. Having opened proceedings at the Club the Bugle Major was asked if the Buglers could 'encore' the entire display to close the proceedings – which they did! Earlier in the same year CSgtBug Castle was ordered to use ex-Buglers to sound the Battle of Belleisle fanfare since the Eastney Buglers were away rehearsing for the Horse Guards Beat Retreat. Two CplBuglers, Angove and Mansbridge, were available and CSgt Sandy Powell, and Sgts 'Speedy' Mendoza, 'Sticks' Riches and Peter Quill were drafted in – having transferred to the ranks between nine and twenty-three years earlier. They practised the fanfare, then paraded to find that the Adjutant unexpectedly gave the order 'Colour Sergeant Bugler – sound NCO and *Markers Call'*. This was safely negotiated and so was the fanfare itself!

In 1970 it had been decided that, after 1973, there would only be two types of band, Staff Bands which would have a Corps of Drums of twelve Buglers and Standard Band with a Corps of Drums of seven. The actual strength in 1973 appears to have been fifteen Buglers with each of the four Staff Bands and five Buglers with each of the seven standard bands, a total of ninety-five Buglers. The strength in 1976 was stated as 131, presumably including those still under training.

In 1971 the 'Cambridge Arms' public house, located opposite the Jubilee Gates at Deal Barracks was renamed 'Drum Major'. Senior Drum Major Charlie Bowden performed the opening ceremony and unveiled the new pub sign, an impressive portrait of himself. The public house retained this name until shortly after Deal Barracks was closed.[24]

In the early 1960s it had been recognised that a need existed for a Bugler's Handbook. The man credited with initiating this project is Bugle Major J Wagstaffe BEM who, with the aid of his Instructional Staff led the project until his retirement in the mid-1960s. The only instructional aids available to the Buglers' Branch at this time were a limited number of internally produced publications, known as 'Crotchet Factory' publications, the laboriously and individually produced Manuscript Books of bugle calls - and also the chalk-board!

Following Wagstaffe's retirement work was continued, on a part-time basis, by a Bugler NCO until Captain Peter Sumner, Junior Wing Director of Music, realised the significance of the work and gave the Bugler NCO a year to complete the task. At the same time, and since supplies of Drum and Bugle Parts were becoming virtually extinct, the opportunity was taken to rewrite and reproduce them not only for the publication but also for distribution to the Bugle Majors of the Corps and the major RM Bands throughout the world. By about 1967 the publication was ready

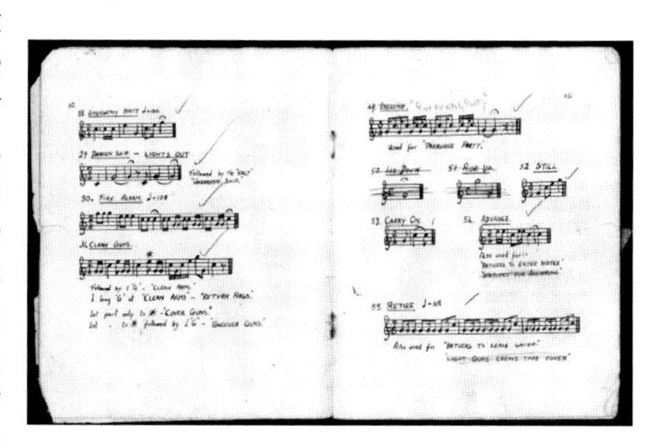

Two pages from the 'Bugle Calls of the Royal Navy and Royal Marines' which were individually handwritten

24 Globe & Laurel June 1971 p161.

A page from the BR13,' Bugler's Handbook' which not only contained bugle calls but also bugle marches and fanfares plus drum salutes, beatings and marches

for publication except that all matters regarding the legality of the contents had to be checked. Once again Captain Sumner, with the Bugle NCO, believed to be PG 'Tex' Ricards, later Bugle Major, took responsibility for this work which lasted a further four years. In 1972 'BR13 - The Buglers' Handbook' was distributed throughout the Buglers' Branch - and is still in use at the time of writing.

The Corps Memorial Date for the battle of Belle Isle occurred during the Deal rehearsals for the 1973 Beat Retreat ceremony on Horse Guards Parade. Since Corps Memorable Dates merited a bugle fanfare the Corps Bugle Major, John Satchwell, took the opportunity to use the entire forty-strong Corps of Drums to sound the fanfare *Concord*.[25]

A report by Cpl Bugler D Challis on the 1975 Drum Majors' Course appeared in 'Globe & Laurel'. He admitted that he had thought that a Drum Major's job was easy but, by the end of the course he had to acknowledge that the marching in front of the band accounted for only about 5% of the time and that the rest of the time was taken up by the duties of a Company Sergeant Major. Lectures on Beat Retreat, Battalion Ceremonial, Trooping the Colour, the role, organisation and history of the Buglers' Branch and the Royal Marines Band Service as well routines for drawing and returning musical stores and the duties of a CSM quickly filled the three and a half week course. Apart from Challis the only other Royal Marine was Cpl Bugler C Archer. The other four came from Sierra Leone, Guyana and two from the Regular Army, one from The Duke of Edinburgh's Royal Regiment and the other from The Royal Regiment of Fusiliers. Needless to say this caused some confusion with drill but the Royal Marine way was soon learnt! The course was run by the Corps Drum Major, WO2 Porter. All students passed the course.

Bugle Major John Satchwell and the Depot Corps of Drums took part in the television show 'The Generation Game' on the 17th September 1977. Following a demonstration, competitors, and host Bruce Forsyth, had to march and play the drum within the Corps of Drums.

On the morning of the 5th September 1979, at 1040hrs, muffled drums of the RM Massed Bands led a funeral procession through London.[26] Unlike Churchill's funeral where the various bands were able to alternate, the funeral of Admiral of the Fleet, The Earl Mountbatten of Burma, required the Massed Bands and Drums of the Royal Marines to play continuously for the full fifty-minute journey to Westminster Abbey. Inside the Abbey, and following the Prayers, ten Buglers from the RMSM under the Corps Bugle Major sounded the *Last Post* and *Reveille*. Following the funeral service at Romsey Abbey, a

25 *Globe & Laurel Aug 1973 p243.*

26 *It is traditional that the unit that 'leads' a military funeral is closest to the gun-carriage and not leading the procession.*

twelve-man detachment from 45 Cdo formed the firing party whilst two Buglers from the RMSM sounded the final *Last Post* and *Reveille*.

The 1977 Walden Report had pointed out that the Bugler no longer spent a high proportion of time away from the bands. Buglers valued their independence and their close links with the Corps and the Royal Navy. Many continued to enter the Branch from orphanages and sea schools as a result of tough or unpleasant childhoods. These men were institutionalised, independent and used to an ordered life of discipline and duty.[27] An Order[28] stated that whilst the Buglers would become part of the RMBS they would remain as a separate section of the technical branch of the Corps and would retain their own rank structure, promotion rosters and uniform. The Buglers' Branch was not fully integrated into the RMBS until 1979.[29]

At the beginning of the 1980s the RMBS had ten bands. They consisted of C-in-Cs Naval Home Command and Fleet; Flag Officers Scotland and Northern Ireland, Naval Home Command, Plymouth and Third Flotilla (FOF3); Britannia Royal Naval College, Commando Forces, Commando Training Centre RM and the RMSM. Five hundred and fourteen Musicians and Buglers made up these bands and, in addition, there were one hundred and twenty-four under training. Junior Musicians and Junior Buglers were being increasingly used in support of the trained bands; this gave them valuable experience, but also indicated the demands upon the Royal Marines Band Service.

Drum Major

Bugle Major

27 Conversations with ex Corps Bugle Major D Dawson who joined as a Boy Bugler in 1960.
28 RMRO105/1979.
29 General Orders, Royal Marines 1979 GO105.

Chapter 13: The Work of the Bands 1950-1982

In July 1953 the Combined Orchestras of the Mediterranean Fleet, which included those of the C-in-C and Flag Officer Flotillas, and 3 Cdo Bde gave two Coronation Concerts on successive evenings under the baton of Sir Malcolm Sargent, the Honorary Musical Advisor. Amongst the invited audience on the first night were Lord and Lady Mountbatten. The total number of men in the orchestras and the male voice choir was about one hundred and forty. The choir, whose members all had singing experience, was drawn from the three services.

The Queen and the Duke of Edinburgh visited Malta in the Royal Yacht HMY *Britannia* and, on the second day of the visit, a Combined Services parade was held at Floriana. The Royal Marines of the Fleet and of 3 Cdo Bde were formed up around the three stands of Colours (40, 42 and 45 Commandos). The music was provided by the bands of the Mediterranean Fleet and 3 Cdo Bde massed under the command of Cd BM Pottle. During the parade they trooped, quick marched, slow marched and then played a bugle march. The parade consisted of an Inspection, a March Past, a Feu-de-Joie and Three Cheers. When 40 Cdo returned to El Ballah they took with them "*that happy band of brothers, the Brigade Band*".

HMS *Bulwark* sailed to Oslo with the combined bands of HMS *Theseus* and HMS *Daedalus* and twenty Musicians from the RMSM under BM E Ough. They Beat Retreat, played in the bandstand and took part in all ceremonial ashore and aboard. In Stockholm the massed bands of the Fleet and the Highland Light Infantry (City of Glasgow Regiment) Beat Retreat and then, when the RM Bands departed, the band of the HLI went aboard HMS *Bulwark* to provide musical support.

Having slipped from South Railway Jetty, Portsmouth, in the middle of January 1955 HMS *Tyne* made her way to Gibraltar where her Guard and Band undertook the Ceremony of the Keys.[1] The parade was carried out each month by the various Regiments of Gibraltar Garrison and about once a year by Royal Marines of the Home Fleet. The next ceremony was Beating Retreat carried out by the combined bands of the Home Fleet and the Duke of Wellington's Regiment.

Lt E Ough, the Director of Music Boys' Wing at Deal took the band and orchestra to HMS *St Vincent* where their sixty-piece orchestra gave a magnificent performance in the Drill Shed to an audience of over a thousand. A few days later the Boys' Band with the Volunteer Band of HMS *St Vincent* and the RM Volunteer Cadet Corps under Bugle Major Weight Beat Retreat on the Parade Ground. The Ceremony concluded with *Sunset* by the massed bands and bugles (one hundred and eighty strong) whilst the Boys of HMS *St Vincent* manned the mast.

HMS *Superb* was at Hamilton, Bermuda, at the time of The Queen's Birthday Parade. Her RM Band was the only band in the parade and, during the march past, had to play ten marches including a "*gallop at 140 to the minute*" for the Duke of Cornwall's Light Infantry.

During 1955 the Admiralty approved the new development of sending two Bandmasters to study at the Royal Academy of Music each year for the Conductors' Course. Mr Maurice Miles was to supervise the course that included conducting, choir training, harmony, counterpoint, musical composition and individual lessons on orchestral instruments and pianoforte. Many opportunities were provided for playing in the senior

1 *Detachment and Band transferred from Vanguard to Tyne when Vanguard went to refit.*

orchestra as well as attending opera and chamber music classes. The objectives of this arrangement were to raise the standard of the selected Bandmasters and to enable them to gain knowledge that could be distributed throughout the Band Service when they returned. The first Bandmasters to be selected were Staff BM D Guthrie and BM A D Haigh. Another development that occurred at about the same time was the institution of the Band Corporals' Course. Commonwealth Students from Canada and Burma were at the School and BM Reynolds was sent to Ceylon to form a band for the Royal Ceylon Navy. This continued a tradition of RM Bandmasters forming and teaching Commonwealth bands, particularly in Australia and New Zealand.

The Home Fleet visited Leningrad in 1955 and its band was strengthened by the band of the accompanying HMS *Triumph*. HMS *Albion* was also part of the Fleet for the purpose of this visit. Two days before reaching Leningrad the Bandmaster and seven Musicians were transferred from *Apollo* to *Triumph* at sea by jackstay[2] to augment *Triumph's* band. The ships arrived with Guard and Band paraded as thousands lined the banks of the River Neva. Next evening a small orchestra was left in HMS *Triumph* for the C-in-C's dinner party and the remainder of both bands, forty Musicians, gave a concert in Tavritchesky Park that was attended by a crowd of 7,000, press and radio, and the whole concert was broadcast throughout Russia.

The Band of the Mediterranean Fleet was under the command of the Fleet BM, Cd BM Pottle who had a Bandmaster, two Band Sergeants and approximately thirty-six Musicians as the C-in-C's band. It was centralised at HMS *Phoenicia*, Manoel Island Malta. Its role was to supply music for the entire Fleet including shore establishments and embarked programmes for the C-in-C and his Second-in-Command. For these the band was split in two but was massed at various ports of call to Beat Retreat and for other ceremonies. The band was also called upon to supply music for other ships of the Fleet and had done so for HM Ships *Eagle*, *Forth*, *Gambia*, *Jamaica*, *Cumberland*, *Glasgow*, *Sheffield*, *Birmingham*, *Surprise*, *Roebuck*, *Peacock*, *Duchess*, *Wakeful* and *Diana*. On average each member of the band did five months at sea each year.

At sea in the Mediterranean the band and crew of HMS *Eagle* paid tribute at the retirement of BM K Macdonald who was completing twenty-five years of service. He left to take up a post as BM to the Rhodesian Forces.

During 1958 BM Reynolds returned to England having established a Band and Corps of Drums for the Royal Ceylon Navy. He had been loaned to them in 1955 and on arrival had to advertise, interview, audition and select the men; indent for instruments and frame Band Regulations and Examinations for Advancement and Specialist Pay. He received over five hundred written applications, mostly in Tamil or Sinhalese, and unfortunately none of them were from experienced Musicians; indeed, only two of the applicants could even play an instrument. Despite this, Reynolds was able to establish a musical training school at HMCyS *Rangalla* at Diyatalawa, Colombo. A Chief Petty Officer was sent to the RMSM and, after a year's work, he returned to Ceylon with a 'distinguished' Certificate. Bugle Major Close also went to Ceylon with the responsibility for band training as well as his usual duties. After eight months' tuition they were able to parade a ceremonial band of forty when the Royal Ceylon Navy provided a Guard and Band for the opening of the Ceylon Parliament. By 1958 Reynolds was able to leave the band in the charge of the Chief Petty Officer.

The first Eastney Exhibition took place and over 10,000 people attended during the seven-day event. Massed Bands were one of the major attractions. Thirty years after the "*Devonshire* explosion", HMS *Gambia* visited Volos and a commemorative ceremony was

2 *Rope or cable rigged between two ships under way along which a traveller block with suspended load can be hauled.*

held in the cemetery. Headed by the Pipes and Drums of the Black Watch, the Royal Marines Guard of Honour together with three Royal Navy Platoons marched to the cemetery where, in 1929, the bands of HMS *London* and *Royal Oak* had led the way.

During 1960 one of the major events was the Beating Retreat by the Massed Bands on Horse Guards Parade. The previous year Prince Philip had told the First Sea Lord (Admiral Mountbatten) that he would welcome the ceremony on his birthday (10th June) about three or four years out of seven - the years when his birthday fell on a weekend should be avoided.[3] The bands taking part were C-in-C The Nore; Flag Officer Air (Home); HMS *Raleigh*; HMS *St Vincent*; Portsmouth Group; Plymouth Group; RMSM and BRNC. Before moving to London the Massed Bands carried out the customary rehearsal on the South Field at Deal. The date was the 30th May and a special event was added to the rehearsal. Each year on the 1st June a simple act of remembrance takes place but, because the bands would be preparing to move to London, it was brought forward one day. In 1948 the Memorial Silver Trumpets had been dedicated at Burford and the *Dedication Fanfare* was sounded. The conductor had been Senior Cd BM W Lang and, in 1960, as a Captain and in his retirement year, Capt Lang once again conducted Leon Young's fanfare.

During the same year, at sunset on the 23rd February the last RM Band on the South Africa Station, based on Simon's Town, marched on to the Grand Parade at Capetown to end a tradition of a hundred and fifty years of imperial regimental music being played there. The organisers of the special event to say farewell to British military music, the 'Young South Africa League', would be the providers of the music in the future. Meanwhile in New Zealand Lt G C McLean was preparing to end what was, at the time, the longest commission in the Royal Navy. Three years for an Officer, a Band Sergeant, three Band Corporals and thirteen Musicians as the RM Band of the Royal New Zealand Navy would come to an end in March 1960 when they would leave HMNZS *Philomel*, the home of the Royal New Zealand Navy at Auckland. Finally, with all due dignity and ceremony, the last RM Band was withdrawn.[4]

2Lt Reynolds, who had been responsible for organising the Band of the Royal Ceylon Navy, found himself drafted, in 1951, to Australia on loan to the Royal Australian Naval Band Service.

3 Cdo Bde Band continued to be employed in support of the Brigade and its individual Commando units as needed. In 1963 the band found itself committed to adapting to the problems of guerilla warfare in Borneo. Prior to this the band had been with the Brigade in Aden, where they combined with the bands of the 9/12th Royal Lancers (Prince of Wales's) and the King's Own Scottish Borderers on The Queen's Birthday Parade and other occasions. In Borneo the band went on a tour of the troubled areas and, as always, the transportation of the instruments became a major headache. One of the trips was to a Royal Artillery position very close to the Indonesian border. The position could only be approached on foot. The RA had organised a party for the local tribesmen's children and it was all a great

Lt Don Guthrie conducts the Band of 3 Commando Brigade, Royal Marines, playing for the 'locals' in West Sarawak, 1963

3 *Beat Retreat file in RMM Archive.*

4 *Lt C G McLean and nine members of the band elected to remain in New Zealand upon their retirement in 1960.*

success. Radio Sarawak later asked the band to broadcast, which it did, both as a dance band and as a military band. By the time that it left the region the band had travelled further than all the other emergency troops put together.

The Royal Marines Tercentenary Year of 1964 was a year of celebration that began with the Beat Retreat on Horse Guards Parade on the 10th June. At a planning meeting Capt Neville produced a routine for the Ceremonial Parade that was accepted by the Committee but with the proviso that three further ideas be investigated. These were a bomb-burst formation, a Union Flag formation and thirdly, a 'Spin Wheel', but none of them were introduced. After the Captain General had left the parade the Massed Bands marched off to the Regimental March and instead of turning left towards Wellington Barracks they re-formed with a frontage of fourteen file and marched down the Mall towards Buckingham Palace before dismissing in the Barracks. On the 22nd July a Review Unit together with the Band of the RM Portsmouth Group and the Colours of the RM Barracks Eastney, 41 Cdo and 45 Cdo were paraded on the Artillery Ground for an inspection by, and an address from, the Lord Mayor of London. After giving the Lord Mayor three cheers the Unit left the Artillery Ground and marched through the City of London with bayonets fixed, drums beating and Colours flying led by the Band of Portsmouth Group. A luncheon at Armourers Hall, at which official guests from the United States Marine Corps and the Royal Netherlands Marine Corps were present, followed the Parade. In the early evening members of the Corps were the guests at a Lord Mayor's Reception in the Guildhall at which an orchestra from the RMSM, under Capt Guthrie, provided background music. The following day a Royal Review was held in the garden of Buckingham Palace.

On completion of the inspection the Royal Guard and Band stood fast whilst the rest of the Parade marched past. As the Royal Marines Association and the Old Comrades, who were bringing up the rear, disappeared from sight the Royal Guard gave The Queen a final salute and, followed by the Band, marched past. That evening the Corps held a dinner at the Royal Naval College, Greenwich, at which the Captain General presided and The Queen was the guest of honour. After the presentations The Queen, followed by the other guests, made her way to the top of the steps to watch the Corps of Drums of Portsmouth Group perform the Mess Beating.[5] Following the Dinner, during which The Queen, at Earl Mountbatten's suggestion, granted the Corps the privilege of drinking the Loyal Toast seated when in their own messes, a group of Musicians moved into the Painted Hall to play the 'Extras'. At 1130 The Queen and the Captain General made their way to the steps facing the Grand Square for a fireworks display to Handel's *Music for the Royal Fireworks*.

The afternoon of July 24th was devoted to Thanksgiving Services at St Paul's Cathedral and at the Roman Catholic Church of St Etheldreda. At ten past two the Memorial Silver Bugles of the Royal Marines sounded a fanfare from the steps of the Cathedral to herald the arrival of the Captain General. During the Service the Orchestra of the RMSM combined with the organ and choir for the hymns and also played voluntaries before and after the service. As the Captain General left the Cathedral the Memorial Silver Trumpets sounded a fanfare. That evening was Corps Night at the Royal Tournament and although it was not an official event it certainly dovetailed in well with all the other events. Because of the significance of the occasion it was decided that the Captain General should take the salute instead of the Commandant General and that The Queen would also attend. As a double honour for the Corps Her Majesty invited four senior Royal Marines Officers and their wives to join her in the Royal Box. The Captain General dined with the Senior Non-Commissioned

5 *The 'official' drums of Portsmouth Group were kept in the Officers' Mess. Buglers used a set of brass shell drums for practice and day-to-day use. When the official drums were required the Buglers were marched into the Officers' Mess through a rear door to collect them. Conversation with Colin Bowden.*

Officers at the Banquet held at the Guildhall, London on the 30th July. Before the top table was the orchestra of the Portsmouth Group under the direction of Capt P J Neville. Many other events involving the bands took place around the country to mark the Tercentenary Year.[6]

In December 1963 Lt Col (local) Dunn was placed on the retired list, promoted Lt Col and then re-employed whilst on the Retired List to continue as Principal Director of Music.

At the end of 1964 the CGRM was asked to authorise the purchase of a set of fanfare trumpets to replace the original Memorial Silver Fanfare Trumpets.[7] This request was sanctioned and new fanfare trumpets were duly purchased.

1965 was marked by the death of one of Britain's greatest leaders, Sir Winston Churchill. Documents[8] indicate that, although not mentioned by name but as 'a personage', preparations for Churchill's funeral began in 1959. At that time it was decided that the Royal Marines would be required to supply two bands of sixty to march in the procession plus the band of the RMSM to parade with the RN Guard of Honour. A minimum of forty Buglers, excluding those with the aforementioned bands, would be required for the ceremony. Salutes and related music were carefully considered and the expected First General Salute would be *Dover Castle*.[9] The Second General Salute was to be *Rule Britannia* (for a First Lord of the Admiralty) which would be followed by *Sunset* and *Tom Bowling*. June 1964 brought forth the Draft Orders for a State Funeral naming Sir Winston Churchill but stressed that the orders could not be transmitted since The Queen still had to sanction a State Funeral. Band requirements had been changed to fifty ranks for the RN Guard of Honour and a massed band of two Officers and sixty ranks. When he died, on the 23rd January 1965, orders for the rehearsal and for accommodation arrangements were swiftly issued. The final requirement for RM Bands was set at four Officers and one hundred and twenty ranks as part of the Armed Escort plus an augmented Group Band with the Guard of Honour. This was all based upon the assumption that The Queen would wish a State Funeral to be accorded to Churchill. On the 25th January this wish was announced, the Government endorsed it, and the funeral went ahead as planned on the 30th January.

The 1960s saw a radical change in the way that the Royal Marines could be deployed. The Commando Carriers, HMS *Bulwark* and HMS *Albion* were commissioned in 1960 and 1962 respectively[10], followed by the Amphibious/Assault Ships HMS *Fearless* in 1965 and HMS *Intrepid* in 1967. In 1962 it was decided that RM Detachments would no longer be provided for fixed wing aircraft carriers; however, Buglers and bands would continue to be embarked on this type of ship. As has already been described the period 1967-1973 saw drastic cuts and changes to the Band Service.[11]

In 1967, as a result of changes to the Mediterranean Fleet and the move of HQ to the NATO base at Naples, the C-in-C, Mediterranean became Flag Officer, Malta. Then, with all other military units based in Malta, the band of the Flag Officer, Malta, under Lt Shillito, returned to the United Kingdom. On the 5th February 1968 the Plymouth Group Band moved to the Infantry Training Centre at Lympstone.

Lt Col F V Dunn retired shortly after what could be described as his swan-song - the 1968 Royal Tournament. The display began with a fanfare, *The Royal Tournament*, played on the Fanfare Trumpets of the RMSM. Then, eighty Buglers marched in to give a three-minute display comprising two drum and bugle marches and drum beatings. The

6 *File in RMM Archive and "1664-1964 An Account of the Royal Marines Tercentenary Celebrations".*

7 *See Appendix.*

8 *File in RMM Archive.*

9 *Played when RM Guard of Honour received Churchill with a General Salute when he was installed as Lord Warden of the Cinque Ports in 1941.*

10 *HMS Hermes was not converted until 1973.*

11 *File in RMM Archive.*

ninety-piece RM Symphony Orchestra played for five minutes before handing over to the Oceanaires Dance Orchestra for a selection of music prior to the Massed Bands marching on to present a traditional display based upon *Sunset*. A week after his official retirement date, his 60th birthday, Lt Col F V Dunn was honoured in the 1969 New Years' Honours List with a Knighthood in the Royal Victorian Order - the only military Musician to be rewarded in this way.

The man who had been chosen as his successor was Maj P Neville and he found himself inheriting a prize jewel in terms of the worldwide respect that the Royal Marines Band Service had earned. However, he was inheriting it at a time when radical change was being discussed and implemented and a time when cuts were necessary. He must also have felt that he had a 'hard act to follow'. He would not have the benefit of his predecessor's hard won connections and neither could he expect to be able to shake off the mantle left by Sir Vivian Dunn very easily. Maj Neville, who had enjoyed the benefit of a year's sabbatical with Sir Malcolm Sargent and Gordon Jacob prior to becoming Principal Director of Music, immediately became involved with the work of the bands as well as continuing his involvement at various meetings and committees involved with rationalisation. It was at this time that the Band Service had to be cut from seven hundred and fifty to five hundred by 1973.

One of Maj Neville's first innovations as Principal Director of Music was to improve the setting in which the RMSM Winter Concerts took place. By extending the concert hall stage he was able to increase the size of the orchestra. Removal of unnecessary soft furnishings improved the acoustics and ordering that the dress for orchestral concerts should be No 2 blues with cloth belt gave the string players much better arm movement due to the looser sleeves.[12] Maj Neville was a great supporter of the orchestra and throughout his career he believed that extensive experience of the orchestral repertoire produced a more mature and capable Musician in the band. The recordings of this period are felt to reflect this belief and the performances by the orchestra of the RMSM both at Deal and in London during his period as PDM were of an exceptionally high standard.

Lt Col C H 'Jiggs' Jaeger, Chief Instructor and Director of Music at The Royal Military School of Music Kneller Hall, died in 1970 and his widow duly presented his large and very comprehensive library of music scores and textbooks to the RMSM at Deal for use by its students. The School was proud to accept it as a tribute to his memory.

During 1970 the Band of the C-in-C Far East Fleet, at HMS *Terror*, Singapore was withdrawn. The very last ship-borne band was commissioned to join HMS *Eagle* in June of the same year and embarked on the 2nd September 1970. Although other bands would embark for specific tours of duty they would be permanently borne by shore establishments. In 1971 the Navy vacated the RNAS at HMS *Condor* and 45 Cdo took it over. A couple of months later FOSNI Band moved to HMS *Cochrane* at Rosyth.

Maj P Neville was elected a Fellow of the Royal Academy of Music in 1972. The high regard in which the Academy held the Corps was very apparent. It was therefore appropriate that the RAM turned to the RMBS to help them celebrate their 150th Anniversary.

During 1975 and 1976 correspondence took place between the CGRM's office and the RMSM regarding the use of the word 'orchestra' in the title of a Royal Marines 'Band'. Whilst CGRM's representatives wanted strict adherence to the official titles set down as a DCI(RN) in September 1974, the RMSM found that promoters, and no doubt audiences, were confused when they went to a concert "by the Band of HM Royal Marines" only to discover that it was an orchestra. Lt Col P Neville wrote a paper explaining the situation in detail and arguing that he did not anticipate any problems over the use of the word

12 *Correspondence with Lt Col P Neville (Feb 2003).*

orchestra either from the Musicians' Union or the public. He highlighted the fact that the Orchestras of the Royal Artillery and Royal Engineers advertised themselves as such and went on to recommend that the word 'Band' should, when appropriate, be substituted by 'Orchestra'. This was accepted by the CGRM's office although it was decided not to make a formal alteration to the DCI at that time.[13]

Lt Col Neville took the Massed Bands of the Royal Marines to the Canadian National Exhibition, Toronto in August 1976. This was the first occasion that Massed Bands of any British military service had carried out such a commitment. Two years later it was repeated.

The year of 1977 was particularly notable for a number of major events that affected the Corps. The Queen's Silver Jubilee was celebrated with a series of events that featured RM Bands. On Silver Jubilee Day, June 7th, the Massed Bands of FONAC and the BRNC (Lt J M Ware) led 40 Cdo at the Silver Jubilee Thanksgiving Service where they also exercised their right to march through the City of London with Colours flying, bayonets fixed and bands playing. The Massed Bands of Commando Forces and Commando Training Centre RM paraded with a Tri-Service Guard of Honour at Buckingham Palace. The same two bands supported a pageant on the Thames that featured RM Rigid Raiding Craft and Landing Craft whilst the Band of BRNC provided music ashore.

The next major Silver Jubilee event was the Fleet Review. The aircraft carrier HMS *Ark Royal* was the flagship and this meant that the ship's band played a major musical role in the ceremonial. During the Review itself HMS *Ark Royal's* Guard and Band paraded for the 21-gun Royal Salute. As the sound of gunfire died away the Royal Yacht approached the Fleet. *Ark Royal's* crew was manning ship and the ship herself was dressed overall. Guard and Band were drawn up on the after end of the flight deck. As the Royal Yacht came abeam, prior to making a turn to starboard to cross the bows of *Ark Royal* and enter the Review Lanes, the *Alert* was sounded and the Guard and Band stepped off and marched forward to arrive with customary precision. They ceased playing after the *National Anthem*, in time for the ship's company to respond to the orders 'Off Caps' and 'Three cheers for HM The Queen' as the Royal Yacht crossed ahead of the *Ark Royal*. On the evening of the 28th The Queen dined on board HMS *Ark Royal* and the RM Band performed as a small orchestra.

FONAC's band (Lt J M Ware) was on board HMS *Hermes* and shared the ceremonial duties including two transfers to HMS *Ark Royal* when other ships of the Fleet arrived. *Ark Royal*'s band paraded on the quarter-deck with the Guard mounted to greet senior officers arriving to call on C-in-C Fleet whilst FONAC's band was on the Flight deck for the salutes to foreign ships as they took up their positions in the Review Lanes. During the weekend before the Fleet Review FONAC's dance band played for a ball in *Hermes* hangar. This was followed by Beating Retreat on the Flight Deck when, as ordered by the C-in-C, the ships of the Fleet took their time from the bugle call as Lt Ware conducted A C Green's *Sunset* and lowered their ensigns together.

On the occasions that the Royal Yacht left and re-entered Portsmouth Harbour, Royal Salutes were provided by a Guard and Band on both sides of the harbour. The C-in-C Fleet Band, and The Queen's Colour of Naval Home Command, were at HMS *Vernon* the Torpedo School, whilst the Band of the RMSM, and The Queen's Colour of Submarine Command, were at HMS *Dolphin*. An RM Band was on board HMS *Fearless*. The bands of the RMSM and C-in-C Fleet also took part in the Tattoo on Southsea Common.[14]

The Military Musical Pageant at Wembley Stadium, begun in 1969 and occurring on alternate years up to their cessation in 1985, was attended by The Queen in 1977

13 *File in RMM Archive.*

14 *Account taken from author's contribution to 'Sound the Trumpets, Beat the Drum'.*

when it was re-titled 'The Silver Jubilee Musical Pageant'. The Massed Bands of the Royal Marines took a leading role in the event with Captain W W Shillito RM being the pageant's Senior Director of Music. During the same year Captain Shillito directed the Royal Marine Bands at the Corps' main Silver Jubilee event, the Inspection of the Corps by HM The Queen in Plymouth on 5th August. In January 1978 Captain Shillito took up an 18 month appointment as Director of Music of the Royal Australian Navy's East Australia Band based in Sydney, on loan from the Royal Marines Band Service.

1978 was the 75th Anniversary of the Band Service and the 25th Anniversary of the appointment of the Duke of Edinburgh as Captain General Royal Marines. To celebrate that appointment Prince Philip directed that 'The Prince's Badge' would be given each year to the best Musician or Bugler at the RMSM provided that the candidate had attained the necessary standard. It was the Band Service equivalent of the Corps King's Badge and would be worn by the recipient throughout his career in the Royal Marines, no matter what rank he attained. It replaced the Commandant General's Certificate of Merit. The Prince's Badge was first awarded in 1978.[15]

The two Anniversaries made Beating Retreat on Horse Guards Parade even more important than usual but Lt Col Neville resisted the temptation to make radical changes for the celebrations and concentrated on a high quality performance of a traditional ceremony. The Royal Albert Hall Concert, attended by HM The Queen, the Captain General and the Earl Mountbatten of Burma was also an opportunity to celebrate and included in the programme were the joint winners of a competition for a march to celebrate the 25th Anniversary of the Captain General. The joint winners were *Virgo 57* by Musn S Reid and *Royal Salute* by BdSgt R Waterer.

On the 1st October Lt Col P Neville retired as PDM and Commandant. His career had spanned thirty-five years and he had experienced life in all areas of the Band Service. His pride in the men of the RNSM who served in ships throughout the world was immense and he felt that the work they did was never fully understood nor appreciated. His successor was Maj J R Mason who, like Lt Col Neville, was a product of the RNSM.

41 Cdo[16] supported by the Staff Band of the RMSM carried out Ceremonial Duties in London 4th - 30th November, mounting guards on Buckingham Palace, St James's Palace and the Tower of London. In 1978 duties were again shared with the 2nd Bn Coldstream Guards. Unlike the London Duties of 1935 when Their Majesties were not in residence during the Royal Marines tour of duty, Her Majesty The Queen was in London and witnessed the Guard Mounting from the Palace windows. 1979, the final year of a decade of great change for the RMBS, was overshadowed by one event. The 'Globe & Laurel'[17] carried the following announcement:

"Admiral of the Fleet, The Earl Mountbatten of Burma KG PC GCB OM GCSI GCIE GCVO DSO FRS

It was with deep shock that the Corps heard of the death of Lord Mountbatten on 27th August 1979. Lord Mountbatten was appointed by Her Majesty The Queen to the unique appointment of Life Colonel Commandant of the Royal Marines on 3rd August 1965. Not only during his period as Life Colonel Commandant, but throughout the whole of his Naval career Lord Mountbatten took a keen interest in the Corps and his wise counsels were greatly appreciated. We have lost not only a great man but a true friend. We offer our sincere condolences to his family on his death and also on the tragic deaths of the Dowager Lady Brabourne and his grandson Nicholas".

---

15 *See Appendix.*

16 *41Cdo RM were at Deal having been re-formed following the Government's decision not to disband them.*

17 *Sept/Oct 1979 issue.*

For his funeral the RM Massed Bands were under the direction of Capt G A C Hoskins whilst the band of Commando Training Centre RM was positioned on the route.

At 1040hrs on the morning of the 5th September the muffled drums of the RM Massed Bands led the procession at a dignified pace.[18] Unlike Churchill's funeral where the various bands were able to alternate, Mountbatten's funeral required the Massed Bands of the Royal Marines to play continuously for the full fifty-minute journey to Westminster Abbey.

As the coffin was borne into the Abbey the fanfare *Supreme Command*, played on the Fanfare Trumpets of the RMSM was conducted by Lt Col J R Mason. Following the Naval Prayer, the Royal Marines Prayer, the Life Guards Prayer and the Prayer of Sir Francis Drake, ten Buglers from the RMSM, under the Corps Bugle Major sounded the *Last Post* and *Reveille*. Following the funeral service at Romsey Abbey, a twelve-man detachment from 45 Cdo formed the firing party whilst two Buglers from the RMSM sounded the final *Last Post* and *Reveille*.

Helmet plate (King's crown)

18 *It is traditional that the unit that 'leads' a military funeral is closest to the gun-carriage and not leading the procession.*

Chapter 14: The Portsmouth Band 1950 -1982

Life had returned to normal in Eastney Barracks by the early 1950s. A Detachment from HMS *Belfast* arrived at Portsmouth and were met by Portsmouth Group Band and marched from the station to Eastney Barracks. HMS *Belfast* had returned from action in Korea and had berthed at Chatham from where the 'Pompey Marines' had travelled by train. A few days later a new detachment made the same journey in the opposite direction. Described as 'the highlights of the past month in Portsmouth' were two Miniature Tattoos produced during September 1950 at Eastney Barracks. In spite of rain both were well attended by families, friends and the general public.

1951 was Festival of Britain Year and one of the most popular events was the South Bank Exhibition. Many bands played there with the Portsmouth Band having four weekly engagements and, on two occasions, Beating Retreat ceremonies. On the 6th October a Musicale Matinee was given in the Officers' Mess by the Portsmouth Group Band. According to Globe & Laurel's Eastney correspondent the most notable event of November was the weekend when Eastney provided a Guard and Band for the Lord Mayor's Show (during which the Guard marched the whole way at the slope without changing shoulders and endured the verbal abuse of a bunch of students). They also took part in the Festival of Remembrance at the Royal Albert Hall and the Service of Remembrance at the Cenotaph next morning. Portsmouth Band also played at the Royal Naval Association's Annual Reunion at the Royal Festival Hall and the International Horse Show at the White City. Somehow they also managed to include a three-week tour of Scotland and all of the usual engagements fulfilled by a busy Royal Marine Band.

The Portsmouth Divisional Book of Remembrance, containing the names of 1350 officers and men, was dedicated in St Andrew's Church, Eastney, on Remembrance Day, 11th November 1951. The Church was packed and, after the Two Minutes' Silence the band played a setting of the *Last Post*, arranged by John Wright, followed by the *Reveille* played by Buglers effectively paraded outside the Church. After the Service the Band led a strong contingent of the RM Association and four companies from the Church back to the Parade. The Salute was taken outside the Officers' Mess by General Sir Leslie Hollis.

January 1952 saw preparations for, and the departure of, the SS *Gothic* on a Royal Tour to Australia and New Zealand. The Royal Yacht component of the Portsmouth Band was on board but, upon the death of King George VI, was recalled. Most of the units taking part in the Funeral concentrated at Eastney on the 12th February for rehearsal.

The Presentation of Colours to 40, 42 and 45 Cdo took place on the 29 November 1952 in Malta. The Massed Bands of 3 Cdo Bde, and HM Ships *Glasgow*, *Kenya* and *Tyne* were under Maj F V Dunn and Drum Major Knox. The Portsmouth Band had the responsibility of providing the music for the event. The GPO made the mistake of sending the music by sea. Fortunately the mistake was discovered and, since the music would not arrive in time, all of it had to be, very hastily, re-copied and sent by air.

It was in 1952 that Major F Vivian Dunn MVO ARAM, Director of Music at Eastney since September 1931 left to take up his appointment as Director of Music at Deal and Captain K A McLean LRAM came to Eastney, although Major Dunn did not immediately relinquish the Royal Yacht responsibility. The Royal Marines Band Service representation at the Coronation was to consist of the Royal Marines Portsmouth Group Band under their new Director of Music, Captain K A McLean, with the Royal Guard of Honour and The

Captain K A McLean, Director of Music Portsmouth

Queen's Colour of the Royal Marines Barracks[1], Eastney, at Westminster Abbey. With the Naval Processional Contingent were to be the bands of the Plymouth Group and the RMSM. With one of the two street lining battalions would be a RM Band formed from the bands of the C-in-C Portsmouth and HMS *Excellent*, under the direction of a Commissioned Bandmaster.[2]

Two weeks after her Coronation HM The Queen reviewed the Fleet at Spithead. HMS *Surprise* (frigate) acted as Royal Yacht and had a detachment of Royal Marines from 45 Cdo embarked as well as Maj F V Dunn and the Royal Yacht Band drawn from the Portsmouth Group Band. Despite having been appointed Principal Director of Music at the RMSM on the 1st October 1953 he did not relinquish the Directorship of the Royal Yacht Band to the Director of Music Portsmouth until after the Royal Commonwealth Tour of 1953/4.[3]

The responsibility for all RM participation in the 1953 Remembrance Ceremony at Whitehall, the Festival of Remembrance at the Royal Albert Hall and the Lord Mayor's Parade fell to the Band and Drums of Portsmouth Group under Capt K A McLean.

During November 1953 Queen Elizabeth II and the Duke of Edinburgh commenced a Commonwealth Tour in SS *Gothic*. The Royal Yacht Band accompanied them for the complete tour which included visits to the West Indies, Australia, New Zealand, Ceylon, Malta and Gibraltar. Returning through the Mediterranean the *Gothic* made an additional stop at Tobruk where the new Royal Yacht, HMY *Britannia*, was waiting for them. All transferred to the new Royal Yacht which then completed the journey home, bringing the Royal family back into London on the 14th May 1954. The band was thirty strong and under the direction of Lt Col F V Dunn who, on return, was made CVO. BM R H Horsley received the RVM (silver). The amount of music required for tours such as this was enormous, especially since the band had to perform as an orchestra and a military band as well as a number of diverse small groups, combinations and soloists. For this particular tour for approximately fifteen hundred different pieces of music were taken. This included one hundred and eighty suites, three hundred and thirty 'selections' and one hundred and thirty-four marches and grand marches.

Trooping the Colour at Eastney, 7th May 1954. Director of Music Captain K McLean marches on the right flank alongside the first rank of Musicians and the band is led by Drum Major C 'Charlie' Bowden

In 1954 Capt McLean was appointed Director of Music, Royal Yacht, and the Royal Yacht Band was twice on Royal Duties during the second half of the year. On the first occasion it provided music for the Duke of Edinburgh's visit to Cowes Week and to Britannia Royal Naval College,

1 *This was the only Colour that had also been on parade at the 1937 Coronation.*
2 *Globe & Laurel and Brigade Orders for the RN and RM.*
3 *'Fiddler on the March' by D Oakley.*

Dartmouth, (BRNC). The second occasion was to bring the Duke of Edinburgh back from Canada after his tour. During the visits to Canadian ports the band was kept very busy with the ceremony of Colours and Beating Retreat as well as providing concerts ashore and entertainment aboard the Royal Yacht. In 1955 the Royal Yacht Band accompanied The Queen and the Duke of Edinburgh to Oslo.

At Eastney the ceremony of Trooping the Colour took place at the Barracks on St George's Day 1955. This celebrated two events, the Corps Day of Reunion and Remembrance and the two hundredth anniversary of the Corps becoming established under the Admiralty as a permanent part of the Royal Navy.

To honour the band's participation in the 1953/1954 Royal Tour new designs of cap badge and helmet plate were awarded to the band in 1955. 'Royal Cypher of Her Majesty and his Royal Highness The Duke of Edinburgh, surmounted by St Edward's Crown above the Cap Badge and in the helmet plate the Royal Cypher only above the Globe and below the Crown, the device in each case to be of silver' was the official description.

The headlines of the second half of 1956 related to the threatened closure of the Suez Canal and Britain's decision to protect free trade and the passage through the Canal by invading Port Said. As a result of the fighting, casualties were taken. Some of the Royal Marines who were killed were interred at the RN Cemetery, Gosport on 17th December 1956. The Bands of C-in-C Portsmouth, the Home Fleet and the Portsmouth Group Band itself under the direction of Captain K A McLean, led the cortege on its journey from the RN Hospital to the cemetery.

In September 1956 HMY *Britannia* sailed from Portsmouth on a world tour carrying Princess Margaret as far as Kenya. The Duke of Edinburgh then joined the ship at Mombasa. Usual custom was followed with the band of fourteen being under the direction of the Yacht Bandmaster until, on the return leg, the Director of Music, Capt McLean, went aboard. This was just prior to The Queen joining the ship for a State visit to Portugal.

23rd April 1956, St George's Day and at that time the Corps Remembrance Day, was also the Anniversary of the Raid on Zeebrugge in 1918. It therefore made a very suitable date for the presentation of new Colours to the Royal Marine Barracks, Eastney. An interesting aside is that when the officers who were to carry the Colours began rehearsing a week before the event they discovered that the manufacturer of the new Colours belts had produced them to the design of a Drum Major's belt. This meant that the bucket for the pike was on the hip! Fortunately they were replaced, just in time. On the 29th April the old Colours, those of Portsmouth Division, which were presented in 1931, were laid up in St Andrew's Church, Eastney. Portsmouth Band was present on both occasions.

Three years later, on the 29th April 1959, the Royal Marines received the Freedom of the City of Portsmouth. The Duke of Edinburgh, as Captain-General, arrived and inspected the Parade, including both the Royal Marines Association and the Royal Marines Old Comrades Association. Two Victoria Cross winners, General Halliday and Lt Finch, were present in their ranks. The combined bands of Eastney and the RMSM provided the music for the ceremony. They then led the march through the streets of Portsmouth to the Guildhall, exercising the

The Band of HM RM Portsmouth Group march onto the Parade for a full rehearsal of the Freedom of Portsmouth Ceremony

new 'right and privilege of marching through the City with Colours flying, bayonets fixed and drums beating' for the first time.

During 1960 the Royal Yacht Band spent more than five months at sea before the ship went for major refit. Sea-time included two Royal visits to the West Indies and the traditional Western Isles summer cruise. The 1960s and early 1970s were a time of relative stability as far as the workload of the band was concerned - local concerts, national events and massed bands Beating Retreat on Horse Guards Parade every three years. The exception to this was the Royal Yacht Band whose members continued to provide the high standard of work required of them. Despite the comments and accusations of their non-Royal Yacht colleagues, life on board the Yacht was not one of ease and relaxation. The accommodation was adequate but small, rehearsal space left much to be desired and, as can be seen from the following data, duty was demanding and usually very high-profile. Between January and May 1963 the Royal Yacht sailed from Portsmouth to Australia and New Zealand for a Royal Tour, and back. This was a one hundred and fifty day cruise with ninety-seven full days at sea. It included forty Royal Orchestra dinner programmes, forty Royal Orchestra lunch programmes, three Royal Dinner Dance programmes and two Military Band Receptions on board, all of which required five hundred different pieces of music. The band also provided fifty military band and eight dance band concerts for the ship's company all of which required another five hundred and fifty different pieces of music. Eighty marches were used for entering and leaving harbour. Seven military band programmes were given ashore as well as two Beat Retreats.[4] Total sea-miles covered during the year were almost 45,000 - the highest to date and not to be exceeded until 1985.[5]

1963 was also the year when the Royal Yacht began her highly successful trade and business days, which often required the attendance of the Royal Yacht Band. Non-musical duties such as helping to move furniture for dinners and balls were extended to helping to host tours of the Yacht.

The Portsmouth Group Band contribution to 1964, the Tercentenary Year, began on the 2nd May 1964 when they provided band and orchestra for a Thanksgiving Service and Parade at Poole. The Orchestra played in Poole Parish Church for the Service whilst the Group Band marched the men from Amphibious Trials Unit, Royal Marines plus two Junior Squads from the Depot through Poole. On the 10th June, as part of the Massed Band of 380 Musicians and Buglers, they formed up to Beat Retreat on Horse Guards Parade. After the ceremony the bands, with a frontage of fourteen file, marched along the Mall before dismissing in Wellington Barracks. On the 22nd July the band paraded with a review unit on Artillery Ground for inspection by the Lord Mayor of London. Following a march past the Band led the Parade through the City. Next day, augmented with Buglers and Musicians from C-in-C Portsmouth and HMS *St Vincent* and under the direction of Captain P J Neville, they provided musical support for the Royal Review in Buckingham Palace Gardens. After the inspection and the speeches the Band played for the march past and, following a final salute from the Royal Guard, marched off. Following the necessary re-formation the band marched the entire parade across Buckingham Palace forecourt and back to Wellington Barracks. On the 18th September a representative unit of the Royal Marines, led by the Portsmouth Group Band, marched through the City of Portsmouth. The unit fell in at the War Memorial on Southsea Common before being marched around the city - which took about one and a half hours.[6]

4 *Globe & Laurel.*
5 *HM Yacht Britannia 1954-1997 (Privately published).*
6 *'1664-1964 Tercentenary of the Royal Marines'.*

In 1968, the Admiralty announced that, as part of the planned reductions to the RMBS, Portsmouth Group would, by 1973, have a band of forty-three to enable them to provide a sea-going band as well as a standard band. This would enable the Portsmouth Group to fulfill its Royal Yacht commitment. Indecision regarding cuts continued until late 1972 when it was decided to disband the band at Whale Island and transfer its name to the Portsmouth Band. So, the Portsmouth Band lost its famous name and became the Band of the Commander-in-Chief Naval Home Command which allowed the band to keep its Royal Yacht flash and special headdress badge.[7] On the 31st October 1969, Portsmouth Group RM ceased to exist, being replaced by Training Group, Royal Marines.

The RMB Eastney Colours presented in 1956 were, on Sunday the 6th May 1973, drawn from the Officers' Mess for the last time and taken to St Andrew's Church where they were laid on the Altar. The occasion was the forthcoming closure of Eastney Barracks and after the Service the Parade marched around the local streets with bayonets fixed, Colours flying and the Drums beating, for the last time. Lord Mountbatten took the salute when the Parade returned to barracks. The Colours were then laid up in the Officers' Mess.

The Royal Yacht Band had a particularly busy year in 1977 - the year of The Queen's Silver Jubilee. They accompanied I he Queen as she travelled over 10,000 miles around the UK and the Commonwealth, as well as the Naval Review off Spithead.

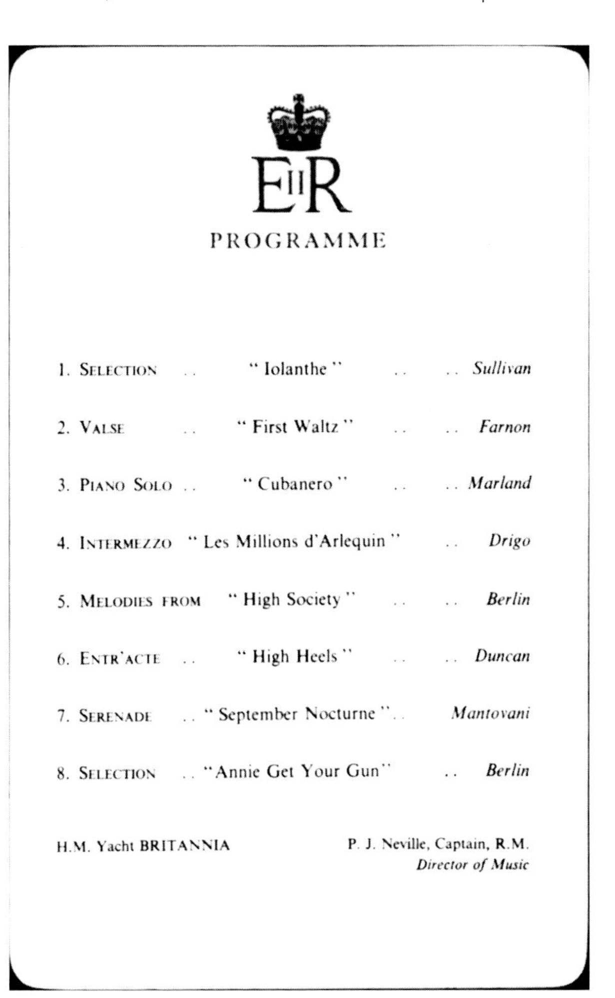

EIIR

PROGRAMME

1. SELECTION ..	"Iolanthe" ..	.. *Sullivan*
2. VALSE ..	"First Waltz" ..	.. *Farnon*
3. PIANO SOLO ..	"Cubanero" ..	.. *Marland*
4. INTERMEZZO	"Les Millions d'Arlequin"	.. *Drigo*
5. MELODIES FROM	"High Society" ..	.. *Berlin*
6. ENTR'ACTE ..	"High Heels" ..	.. *Duncan*
7. SERENADE ..	"September Nocturne" ..	*Mantovani*
8. SELECTION ..	"Annie Get Your Gun"	.. *Berlin*

H.M. Yacht BRITANNIA

P. J. Neville, Captain, R.M.
Director of Music

7 *Blue Band Vol 23 No1 p3.*

Chapter 15: The Plymouth Band 1950 - 1972 and then RM Commando Forces Band 1972-1982

New Colours were prepared for presentation to the Plymouth Division in 1938 but, before the ceremony could take place, the Second World War commenced and the Colours, originally presented towards the end of Queen Victoria's reign, were pressed into further service. The Colours suffered extensive damage during the bombing of Stonehouse Barracks in 1940. They continued in use until1951 when, on the 1st August, new Colours were presented by HRH Prince Philip, Duke of Edinburgh, the first time that he had carried out this duty. The Band of Plymouth Group, Royal Marines, and the Drums of Royal Marines Barracks, Plymouth were led by Captain R H Stoner, Director of Music and Drum Major R Woodruff.

Captain R H Stoner, Director of Music, Plymouth, from 1944 to 1953 when he left the Royal Marines to join the Sierra Leone Police as their Director of Music. One of the events of his final year in the Corps was his band's participation in the film 'Innocents in Paris'. He is shown on the set of the film that starred Alastair Sim, Claire Bloom and Margaret Rutherford

1952 saw the death of the Captain General Royal Marines, HM King George VI, with the funeral taking place on the 15th February. The Plymouth Group Band augmented by twenty-three Musicians from the RMSM, Deal, and under the command of Capt R H Stoner was in the procession, leading representative detachments of the RN and RM.

The Royal Marines Band Service representation at the Coronation consisted of the Royal Marines Portsmouth Group Band under their new Director of Music, Captain K A McLean, with the Royal Guard of Honour and The Queen's Colour of the Royal Marines Barracks Eastney,[1] at Westminster Abbey. With the Naval Processional Contingent were the bands of the Plymouth Group (Drum Major L Keefe), and the RMSM. With one of the two street lining battalions would be a RM Band formed from the bands of the C-in-C Portsmouth and HMS *Excellent* under the direction of a Commissioned Bandmaster.[2] The annual Royal Marines Tattoo was even more successful in Coronation Year and, as always, concluded with a ceremonial marching display by the Band of the Plymouth Group Royal Marines who then marched in all of the participants to the tune of the rousing *Marching Through Georgia*.

At the 1954 Alamein Reunion at Wembley the combined Bands of Portsmouth and Plymouth gave a stirring display under the direction of Capt W Lang, Plymouth Band's new Director of Music who, a few months earlier, had once again directed the Massed Bands at the Royal Tournament.

On Saturday 7th May 1955 the City of Plymouth presented the Freedom of the City to the Royal Marines. Although only the City of London has the authority to question the right of a military unit to enter its precincts with *'Drums beating, bayonets fixed and Colours flying'* many cities, towns and even villages make this symbolic gesture of respect and honour. The Hoe was used for the ceremony and the Buglers who beat *Markers* and *Fall In*

1 *This was the only Colour that had also been on parade at the 1937 Coronation.*
2 *Globe & Laurel and Brigade Orders for the RN and RM.*

were dressed as Drummers of 1755 - the date when fifty companies of Marines were raised for service in Plymouth. As the Casket containing the Certificate of Freedom was passed to the Corps representative the fanfare *Gibraltar* was sounded on fourteen silver bugles. Following the speeches the Battalion presented arms and, led by the Band and Drums of the Plymouth Group, they marched through the city.

Captain William Lang reached retiring age in 1960. He had joined the RNSM, aged 16, in 1921. During the Second World War he was WO Bandmaster on four different battleships and a cruiser. In 1947 he was appointed Assistant Musical Director at the RNSM where he gained fame as the architect of the Beating Retreat ceremony. Lang was succeeded by Captain Paul Neville, another product of the RNSM, who took the Plymouth Group Band to Liverpool for the St George's Day ceremony where they played on board the ferry-boat *Royal Iris*. A year later Neville transferred to the Portsmouth Band and was replaced by Captain Leo Arnold who led the Plymouth Band until 1966 when he returned to the RMSM as Director of Music, Boys Wing.

Drum Major Woodruff and Bugle Major Rickard with the Plymouth Band - 'Salerno Day' 1960 at Bickleigh

One of Captain Arnold's first duties at Plymouth was on the occasion of the Presentation of Colours to 41 Commando, Royal Marines, by HRH Prince Philip, Duke of Edinburgh, the Captain General Royal Marines. This took place at Stonehouse Barracks on the 7th April 1961; the Band and Drums of Royal Marines Plymouth Group were under the command of Captain Arnold, Drum Major R G Knox and Bandmaster L A W Negus.

Presentation of Colours to 41 Cdo at Stonehouse Barracks, 7th April 1961. With the unit in hollow square the Captain General, having presented The Queen's and Regimental Colours, prepares to speak

The Plymouth Group Band contribution to 1964, the Tercentenary Year, began on the 10th June as part of the Massed Band of 380 Musicians and Buglers formed to Beat Retreat on Horse Guards Parade. After the ceremony the bands, with a frontage of fourteen file marched along the Mall before dismissing in Wellington Barracks. On the 24th April the Band was at Liverpool, supporting the RM Forces Volunteer Reserve, Merseyside with their celebrations. These included a dinner, an 'at home' for the public and, in the evening, a Beat Retreat. During the period 1st to 3rd May similar support was provided to RMFVR, Bristol. In this instance the support included a dance band, a military band playing at an outdoor concert, a Beat Retreat and the orchestra for the Thanksgiving Service. Two dates were selected for celebrations in the Plymouth Group area. On the 2nd September the Group Band Beat Retreat in Stonehouse Barracks whilst, on the 28th October, officers and men from 41 Cdo and 43 Cdo plus other units paraded at the Barbican and then marched through the city with bayonets fixed, Colours flying and drums beating, as Honourable Freemen of the City.[3]

Another important ceremony took place at Stonehouse Barracks on the 22nd July 1965 when the Captain General presented Colours to 43 Cdo, Royal Marines. Once again Band and Drums were under the command of Captain Arnold and Drum Major Knox. During June 1966 the Plymouth Group Band journeyed to France partly for the birthday celebrations for HM The Queen but also to mark the last official function of this type at 'SHAPE', Supreme Headquarters Allied Powers in Europe The Plymouth Group Band thus became not only the last British military band to appear in Paris before the Second World War (and the first to march through after the liberation) but also the last to appear at SHAPE in that location. The Band, with a Company from 43 Cdo, again went to France in 1967, this time to mark the 25th Anniversary of the Dieppe raid. A number of ceremonies were undertaken at various locations in the area during the three-day visit.

The Band of HM Royal Marines Plymouth Group and Corps of Drums, with Director of Music, Captain Paul Neville

In 1968, the Admiralty announced that from 1971, as part of the planned reductions to the RMBS, C-in-C Plymouth's Band would be accommodated in HMS *Raleigh* to provide a band for that establishment. The C-in-C Plymouth became Flag Officer, Plymouth in 1969 and his band also changed its name. In February 1968, following a farewell concert in the Stonehouse Barracks' Globe Theatre, the Plymouth Group Band left Stonehouse and moved into a brand new band complex at the Infantry Training Centre at Lympstone. At the end of March the band accompanied the Commandant General to Gibraltar for the Ceremony of the Keys and a number of other engagements, including an orchestral concert. On the 12th May the Plymouth Band joined with the Military Band, Pipes and Drums of the 1st Bn Argyll and Sutherland Highlanders to give a massed bands display at the Citadel. This event, in aid of SSAFA, Soldiers, Sailors, and Air Force Association, recalled the many links between the Royal Marines and the Highlanders. These links included Maj F J Ricketts RM who had previously been Bandmaster of the 'A&S', and the fighting together, as the 'Plymouth Argylls', during the Singapore campaign in 1942. On 31st October 1969 Plymouth Group RM ceased to exist, becoming Commando Forces, Royal Marines.

3 '1664-1964 Tercentenary of the Royal Marines'.

During their stay at Lympstone the band, now with Captain A E Pottle as Director of Music, took part in the 25th Anniversary of D-Day at Ouistreham. The Parade lasted six hours and during the evening the Plymouth Band massed with the Royal Hampshire Regiment Band, the Southern Band of the Royal Air Force and the Pipes and Drums of the 51st Highland Division (Volunteer Reserve) to Beat Retreat at Bayeux.

Just before he retired Captain Pottle led the Plymouth Band throughout the 350th Anniversary Celebration of the sailing of the Pilgrim Fathers from Plymouth in the *Mayflower*. Captain WW Shillito was the new Director of Music, joining in September 1970.

In 1972 part of the Commando Forces Band returned to Stonehouse Barracks, amalgamated with Musicians from the disbanded 3 Cdo Bde Band and retained the name of Commando Forces Band, as well as the Prince of Wales Plumes as part of their badge. The Band was, from January 1972, part of the Commando Logistic Regiment, which was also based in Stonehouse Barracks. The other part of the band remained at CTC[4] being augmented by Musicians from the bands at HMS *Drake*, HMS *Raleigh* and the RMSM. BM Rawson from HMS *Drake* took charge of this band which was also renamed as the Band of HMRM Commando Training Centre.

Norway was the destination for the band in June 1972. Captain Brian Carter (later Colonel) was the first resident Royal Marine Liaison Officer with the Northern Norwegian Army, based in Harstad, and recalls the band giving concerts and, on one occasion, marching through the streets: "The Police had forgotten to stop the traffic but the Drum Major remained undaunted and continued to march straight towards the oncoming traffic forcing it to reverse!"

In October 1973 the band became the first RM Band to play in Berlin since World War 2 and also undertook three trips to Northern Ireland to entertain members of the Corps on deployment and also the general public. For the third successive year the "Commando Forces Festival of Military Music" took place in Plymouth. The Staff Band of the Royal Artillery, Woolwich, together with elements from 29 Commando Light Regiment RA also took part.

"The British are Coming!" was the name given to the 1976 tour by the Band of Commando Forces (band of 60) and the Band, Pipes and Drums of the 1st Battalion The Black Watch (band of 69 including dancers) to mark the USA bicentennial anniversary. The Tour Director of Music was Capt W W Shillito and Lt J Roberts RM was the Tour Administrative Officer. The Black Watch furnished a Bandmaster, Pipe Major and the Tour Commander. Advance publicity had been carried out by Bugle Major Woods and a representative from the Black Watch, both of whom spent a great deal of time in old style uniforms. On completion both were congratulated for conducting themselves in an exemplary manner during this period. The pace of the tour was intense with sixty-three performances being given in ten weeks. This required travelling sixteen thousand miles of which fourteen thousand were by Greyhound type coaches. The Director of Music felt that the tour was a great success but strongly recommended that for any future tours command should be in the hands of Royal Marines.

The 1st July 1976 was the date when 40 Cdo received new Colours from the Captain General on Plymouth Hoe. The Band of Commando Forces provided musical support for the ceremony, the march through the city and other events. In Malta during 1977, 41 Cdo were Trooping the Colour to mark their disbandment and the start of the British withdrawal from its famous island base. March 16th saw the Band of Commando Forces (Capt W W Shillito) providing musical support for the last parade to be held there after one hundred and seventy-five years of close military links. The Life Colonel Commandant of the

4 *Infantry Training Centre became Commando Training Centre in 1970.*

Royal Marines, Admiral of the Fleet The Earl Mountbatten of Burma, took the salute as 41 Cdo, which had been re-formed in 1960, once again passed into history.[5]

Following this, and as part of the celebrations of The Queens Silver Jubilee, the Massed Bands of Commando Forces and Commando Training Centre RM paraded with a Tri-Service Guard of Honour at Buckingham Palace. The same two bands supported a pageant on the Thames that featured RM Rigid Raiding Craft and Landing Craft whilst the Band of BRNC provided music ashore.

The Commando Forces Band troops at the same time as the Colour of 41 Cdo is trooped through the ranks for the last time. St Andrew's Barracks, Malta, 1977

"The main Corps event to mark the HM The Queen's Silver Jubilee will be an Inspection of the Royal Marines by Her Majesty in Plymouth on August 5, 1977. The Inspection should be a colourful and memorable occasion." - so instructed the CGRM, exactly one year before the date of the inspection. The ceremony had to last for one hour and ten minutes and comprised a Royal Guard of Honour provided by 42 Cdo with their Queen's Colour; a march, drive and fly-past of detachments of Commando Forces to demonstrate the Corps roles world wide and its equipment; a band display; and a series of 'tableaux' designed to illustrate as many abilities and skills as possible and to enable The Queen to meet as many men as possible. Once again Capt W W Shillito directed the bands of Commando Forces and Flag Officer Plymouth. Further visits to Northern Ireland took place in the late 1970s.

5 *A few months later the Government reversed its decision and 41Cdo RM was re-formed at Deal.*

Chapter 16: The Royal Marines School of Music 1953 - 1982

In 1951 the rate of recruiting to the Band Service was increasing. It was hoped that one hundred and fifty boys a year could be persuaded to join so that, by 1954 or 1955, there would be between five and six hundred boys at the School. Since the number of recruits was increasing, alterations were made to the structure of the Boys' Wing during 1952. RM subalterns became housemasters and the Boy NCO system replaced the Section Leaders.

Important events of 1954 included the recruitment of two more stringed instrument professors and the reinstatement of the orchestral concerts, previously run by the RNSM, to raise the standard of the orchestral performance. During the year the number of boys under training had increased from three hundred and thirty the previous year to three hundred and seventy, although this was still thirty below the Admiralty anticipation. New music practice huts were brought into use at this time.

At the end of 1957 Prince Philip, the Captain General, visited the Depot Deal where he saw all the various stages of the training of recruits and Musicians. He was particularly interested in the range of handicrafts that the Junior Musicians undertook. In the same year it was announced that the RMSM Band would be making a recording for the HMV record company in the New Year. It was considered to be an honour to be selected to record with this company.

As a direct result of the Defence Review and the proposed change in the Musician's military role Commandant RMSM agreed that Junior Musicians could have an 'acquaint' with NBCW training during their final term as Commandant General's Squad and that two days of a band's pre-embarkation training should be spent on NBCW training. The

B/Cpls. P. J. Gay   F. W. Stagg   R. S. J. Sharp   J. C. T. Stone   C. V. Tottle   D. Pullan   M. J. Whelan   R. N. S. Rose
B/Cpl. Green   A. Towse   P. I. Williams   P. C. Waddington   J. W. Carruthers   B. Anderson   J. Hargreaves   F. Matthias   J. A. Yates
B/Sgts. J. E. C. Bearman   C. P. G. Bull   H. C. Farlow   G. E. Wallace   D. C. W. Saunders   Sgt./Bug. F. J. Bowles   B/Sgt. R. D. Jewell   A. O'Donnell
B/Mds. A. C. Lihou   R. Spencer   J. W. West   S/Bmdr. R. A. Winchester   W. J. Machon   L. R. Jennings   B/Mdrs. J. E. White   J. Coleman   Bug./Maj. J. W. Wagstaffe   S/Bmdr. G. G. Ship
Mr Becker   Mr. Beat   Mr. Collins   Mr. Royston   Mr. Stride   Mr. Whitford   Mr. Dudley
Mr. Thatcher   Mr. Mettyear   Mr. Jocelyn   Lt. (B.M.) E. Barnes (Director of Music (J))   Capt. E. S. Ough   Col. B. J. D. Lumsden, O.B.E. (Commandant)   Major A. D. Macpherson (Officer Commanding)   Mr. Hargreaves   Mr. Freer   Mr. Caru

Instructional Staff of the Junior Wing, Royal Marines School of Music, Deal 1957

The Band of the Royal Marines School of Music parade in front of the new North Barracks accommodation block, 1960

Juniors' acquaint consisted of six lectures on alternate Saturday mornings with the subjects being respirator drill and gas chambers; war gases; radiac instruments; effects of radiation and defence against radiation.

During 1964 and 1965 the training of Junior Musicians had to be re-considered since the raising of the school-leaving age to sixteen in 1970 would have a direct impact upon recruitment. The Corps enjoyed a special dispensation that allowed them to recruit and enlist from schools at any time after the age of fourteen. The School of Music possessed the facilities and staff to ensure completion of the boy's education as if they had remained at school. However, to maintain the status quo would require expanded and upgraded facilities. The Commandant of the Depot recommended that the recruitment age should be raised to fifteen, the same as the recruitment age of Junior Buglers, and that no Junior should be enlisted below the statutory school-leaving age in the future. On the 1st October 1965 a RMRO was published stating that the minimum age of recruitment of Junior Musicians would be raised to fifteen on the 1st April 1966. The intention was then to fall in line with the raising of the school-leaving age when it occurred in 1970.[1]

A repercussion of the 1968 cuts was that the training of Junior Musicians had to be assessed in the light of a smaller throughput and a required reduction in the length of training from three to two years. The School of Music examined the problem and looked for reductions in the non-musical subjects taught at the school. The recommendations were that Handicraft Training should be removed and Parade Work and House Disposal be reduced. An increase in the tempo of musical training was also advocated. A warning that these reductions would result in the major loss of the Junior Wing Band and Orchestra was reluctantly accepted by the CGRM, as were the recommendations.

In October 1970 the Commandant of the RMSM informed HQ Training Group that, after five terms of the new syllabus, it was the professional opinion of the Directors of Music and the Music Professors that the two-year training period would not produce adult Musicians of a sufficiently high calibre to maintain present standards. Neither would the syllabus allow sufficient time for the teaching of general citizenship responsibilities. It was then decided that manning levels could allow the reinstatement of the eight-term programme from 1972 so CGRM sought, and received, the approval of the Admiralty in April 1971 to reinstate the eight-term syllabus from 1972.

By 1980 the one hundred and twenty-four Junior Musicians and Buglers under training were being increasingly used in support of the trained bands - which provided them with valuable experience. This included, for some, a trip to Canada with the RMSM Staff Band for the National Exhibition at Toronto.

During this thirty year period the 'Staff Band', as the Band of the Royal Marines School of Music was known, was extremely busy and earned a reputation as one of the finest military bands in the country. In many ways it was structured in the same way as the old Divisional, later Group, bands. Following the post-war amalgamation the Group Bands had to relinquish the conditions and duties that had previously allowed them to

1 *RMM Archive.*

concentrate solely on their musical abilities. They now had to recruit and train for a military as well as a musical role, they had to maintain certain levels of fitness and were drafted to suit the requirements of the service rather than the individual band - or Director of Music. However, the Staff Band at Deal, particularly during the period when Lt Col Dunn was the Principal Director of Music, was, to a large degree, exempt from non-musical demands and as a result was able to build and maintain a reputation for excellence. This was also one of the reasons that Lt Col Dunn prevented Royal Marine Bands, apart from the Staff Band of the Royal Marines School of Music, from making recordings.

The Prince's Badge

PART 3 - THE MUSICAL ROLE FROM 1982

Chapter 17: Developments into the 21st Century

At the beginning of the 1980s the RMBS had ten bands: C-in-C Naval Home Command, C-in-C Fleet, Flag Officer Scotland and Northern Ireland, Flag Officer Naval Home Command, Flag Officer Plymouth, Flag Officer Third Flotilla (FOF3), Britannia Royal Naval College, Commando Forces and Commando Training Centre RM plus the RMSM and twelve Volunteer Band Instructors. This totalled five hundred and fourteen Musicians and Buglers with one hundred and twenty-four Juniors under training.

The Britannia Royal Naval College Band went to Canada where they paraded with bands from the United States, New Zealand, Canada and also the Gurkhas. Commando Training Centre, RM Band visited the United States and the Band of Flag Officer Third Flotilla, following a deployment with HMS *Intrepid* and summer leave, embarked in HMS *Invincible*.

Whilst, on the surface, all seemed normal for the Band Service at this time, further changes were being planned. The recommendations of the Walden Report began to take effect and this, combined with cuts to the 1981 Defence Budget, meant that a reduction in strength of three bands over a period of five years was necessary. The overall reduction in numbers would be approximately 100 all ranks. Concern about the ability to meet the demands of major ceremonial, and events such as the Royal Tournament, in future years was expressed. It was decided that the RMSM would be retained in Deal but then all plans for changes to the Band Service were postponed as, during early 1982, the situation in the South Atlantic began to deteriorate.

The Falklands War slowed the pace of defence cutbacks and, for a while after the campaign, the Government found it difficult to reinstitute the proposed cutbacks because of the strength of feeling that the country had for the Armed Services. This 'embarrassment factor' did not hinder the Government for too long and, in April 1983, the Band of Flag Officer Naval Air Command was stood down.

The last of the cuts initiated in the early 1980s took place in 1987 when the Band of the Flag Officer 3rd Flotilla was disbanded. This was a sad day for the Band Service since it represented the demise of the sea-going band. This band had travelled the world in support of almost all of the RN's major ships, and had been used in a military role in the Falklands.

Senior Non-Commissioned Officers selected for commission attended an eight-week Special Duties Officers' Course and, upon successful completion, attended a post commissioning course followed by, in the case of Band Officers, an acquaint with the various specialist duties of the Band Service. This changed in 1988 when successful candidates from the SD Officers Selection Board attended a sixteen-week course in Officer Training at the Commando Training Centre RM. The second course of this type included, for the first time, a Band Officer, Lt J Hillier, who went on to win the coveted Sword of Honour at the end of his course.

During 1989 Sir Vivian Dunn KCVO, OBE, FRAM was 'clothed' as the Master of the Worshipful Company of Musicians. During his year in office he oversaw the admittance of HRH The Duke of Edinburgh as an Honorary Freeman of the Worshipful Company. For the occasion Sir Vivian arranged a number of English tunes as *A Selection of English Songs*. Comprising *Fine Old English Gentleman*, *Early One Morning*, *The Lincolnshire Poacher*, *Drink To Me Only*, *Drinking*, *John Peel*, *Here's a Health Unto Her Majesty* and *Rule Britannia* the selection was played by a Baroque Quintet from the RMSM.[1]

Shortly after the Deal bombing in 1989 it was decided that RMB Eastney would close and the Band of C-in-C Naval Home Command would move into the RN Barracks, HMS *Nelson*. However, Defence cuts included a moratorium on spending which delayed the closure of Eastney and the relocation of C-in-C Naval Home Command's band. This led to a postponement of the decision regarding the new location of the RMSM, which meant that Deal was expected to retain the School for perhaps a further five years.

During 1990 a study into the size, terms and conditions of service, promotion, deployments and the military role of the RMBS was begun. This, the Hunt Report, was completed by the autumn of 1990 and resulted in a number of important changes. The Band Service was to undertake a modified Basic Fitness Test (BFT) and a new Military Training package was to be designed for implementation in April 1991. More musical tuition was introduced earlier into the initial training curriculum and Command Courses were graded instead of being pass or fail. Overall terms and conditions of service and the recruitment of women into the Band Service were to be the subjects of further studies.

The 1991 Beating Retreat on Horse Guards Parade took place against a background of manpower cuts amounting to a reduction of twenty-four Musicians and Buglers over the next six months. Under 'Options for Change', a strategy brought about by the upheaval in Eastern Europe and a resultant need to change Defence Policy, the Band Service would number, by April 1992, four hundred and thirty-two serving in seven bands, the RMSM and other appointments such as Volunteer Band Instructors. This compared very favourably to the cuts taken by other services.

On the 1st June 1991, the Band Service ceased to wear the green beret. The wearing of this had been seen by many as an anomaly since the Royal Marine commando has to fulfil certain training requirements to earn this badge of achievement whilst the Musician and Bugler did not.

On 31st October 1991 the last Royal Marine units still based at Eastney, led by the Band of C-in-C Naval Home Command, without its Royal Yacht complement, marched out of the RM Barracks. The band were relocated a few miles to the west in Eastney Block, HMS *Nelson*. Discussions regarding the recruitment of women continued with the acceptance that this would require a number of fundamental changes to be made. The official announcement was made in the House of Commons just before Christmas - women would be accepted into the Royal Marines Band Service from September 1992.

Repercussions from the 'Options for Change' Government Strategy continued to permeate their way through all Armed Services. Another policy, mainly driven by Treasury, was for things to be 'resource driven' rather than 'demand led', a policy that would have serious repercussions since military music is an expensive provision, difficult to define in terms of value for money and therefore a 'soft target' for Defence cuts. Volunteers for redundancy were called for, this being coupled with a desire to reorganise the Band Service into fewer, but larger, bands that were geographically located to areas of RN and RM concentration; a key factor in this being the future of Deal. The redundancy programme called for about ninety volunteers for redundancy, however in order to meet this target about twenty-six compulsory redundancies were necessary.

Just before Christmas it was announced that the Band of C-in-C Fleet would be disestablished at the end of March 1994. This amounted to a cutback of about 20% and

1 *'Fiddler on the March' Derek Oakley.*

was the greatest change to the Band Service since the Leech-Porter Report. The future of the School of Music remained uncertain but it was a decision that remained fundamental to the future of the Band Service. As the Royal Navy was concentrated at Portsmouth and Plymouth and the Royal Marines were nearly all in the West Country it was becoming obvious that Deal was increasingly more and more isolated. In addition, the cost of maintaining three aging and under-utilised barracks was extremely high. On 14th July 1994 the Secretary of State announced that Deal Barracks would close in March/April 1996. It was later confirmed that the RMSM would transfer to Portsmouth Naval Base in April 1996. The Navy Board approved the reorganisation of the RMBS with a complement of three hundred and fifty-eight officers, men and women with a total of five bands located at Portsmouth, Plymouth, Scotland, Commando Training Centre RM, and Britannia Royal Naval College.

Every two years in Plymouth a concert 'Music of the Night' takes place at the Royal Citadel. It also involves 29 Cdo Regiment, Royal Artillery and the Staff Band of the Royal Artillery as well as civilian choirs and dancers. Six performances attract capacity audiences of 5000 each night. In 1994, to mark the close and long-standing association with the 29 Commando Regiment, the Royal Marines presented the Royal Regiment of Artillery with the old march of the Royal Marine Artillery, *Soldiers' Chorus* from *Faust* by Gounod, to be used as the official quick march of the 'Commando Gunners' of the Royal Artillery. With half of the Plymouth Band committed to 'Music of the Night' the other half took part in the 'Armed Service Week' - a week-long recruitment show on Plymouth Hoe featuring all aspects of the work of the armed services and culminating with a Beating Retreat ceremony each evening. The band then played at the opening of the Imperial War Museum, North, by HRH Prince Philip. Following this the band was split into two bands (Port Band and Starboard Band) in order to cover the summer engagements and the leave period. Port Band covered the four day Plymouth Navy Days event which required two marching displays and a Tattoo on each of the four days.

On 29th July Lt Col J Ware retired from the position of Principal Director of Music, Royal Marines. His period of office had covered times of threat and great change. He was to be succeeded by Lt Col R Waterer who inherited the responsibility for the operation of a smaller Band Service that was still expected to meet the same commitments, as well as the task of relocating the School of Music to Portsmouth and investigating the training of Musicians at civilian colleges.

On the 18th September 1994 the Plymouth Band played at the Cenotaph for the 40th Anniversary of the Royal Naval Association. As they returned to Plymouth their coach left the M5 near Bristol and crashed. Musn Barry Holland was killed and ten members of the band were seriously injured. Forty-eight hours after the accident the band honoured a commitment to play at Plymouth Pavilions and donated their performance fee to begin a trust fund for Barry's family.

On the 1st January 1995 a signal was sent to all Royal Navy and Royal Marine establishments stating that the Royal Naval White Ensign would, as part of the integration of the Corps into the Royal Navy, be flown in all Royal Marine units. In the same year it was announced that a three-year trial of a Musician Bursary Scheme would commence in September. The objective was to see whether, as an alternative to the military Schools of Music, it would be possible to obtain the military Musicians necessary to sustain all of the three Services, from civilian colleges. The Services had already registered concerns regarding the civilian sector's ability to meet the required standards and to develop and foster the necessary ethos. It had been decided, partly because of these reservations, to continue the Service Schools of Music, in their current form, until the results of the RMBS-led trial were fully known.[2]

The main events of 1995 were the anniversaries of events linked to the end of World War 2. The first of these was in Malta where the Band of Britannia Royal Naval College gave concerts, marching displays, played for Colours and unveiling ceremonies, Beat Retreat on a number of occasions and even featured their clarinet choir at a reception. Victory in Europe was celebrated in the United Kingdom at Hyde Park where the RMBS led the bands of all three services in a Drumhead Service and then bandstand and variety concerts. The following day again featured the massed bands but this time in a Ceremony of Peace and Reconciliation attended by The Queen, the Royal family and many Heads of State. The final event, on the evening of the Monday, was a party that culminated in a beacon lighting ceremony with, once again, the RMBS leading the Massed Bands of all services. Two months later the final events to mark the end of World War 2 took place with a Service of Remembrance and Commitment at Buckingham Palace and, next day, a massed bands display on Horse Guards Parade which included orchestra and choir. Following this, the final act was the Massed Bands' march along the Mall to parade in front of The Queen for the Sunset ceremony which featured the Royal Marines Buglers and A C Green's arrangement of *Sunset for band and bugles*.

An RMRO[3] was issued to confirm the closure of Deal under the " Front Line First" series of initiatives. The final Pass-Out Parade took place on the 21st March 1996 with a public ceremony on the 22nd. The Barracks at Deal would close on the 29th. By the 1st April, rationalisation of the Band Service would be complete and training at the RMSoM[4], Portsmouth, would recommence on 15th April. Upon arrival at Portsmouth the PDM was to assume the additional title of Commandant, RMSoM.

Tri-Service Beat Retreat, Horse Guards Parade 1995. The massed bands of RM Commando Training Centre, the Light Division, the Brigade of Gurkhas and the RAF march along the Approach Road led by RM Corps Drum Major J O'Connell. © Colin Dean

The move of the Royal Marines School of Music and Headquarters, Royal Marines Band Service, to Portsmouth in March 1996 provided great opportunity for facility re-design, rationalisation and coordination of effort. From within one building SOM's Department could offer a complete musical service to all of the Royal Marine Bands. Instrument supply and repair, Central Music Library, publishing of the RMBS journal 'Blue Band Magazine', band recording, editing, production and marketing facilities were further enhanced by locating the Staff Arranger and Recording Engineer within the building thereby allowing the whole musical process to be administered through one tightly-knit organisation located within HQ RMBS. The new facilities were subjected to a constant stream of visitors from other military services and civilian organisations keen to view them.

In 1997 Musicians were once again at sea. The Plymouth Band joined HMS *Illustrious*'s commission to Hong Kong via Gibraltar, the United Arab Emirates, Singapore, Pakistan, India, the Philippines, Japan and Australia.

2 *It was decided that the trial was not a success and, by this time, the RMBS had alternative arrangements in place.*
3 *RMRO 010/96.*
4 *From about this time the abbreviation RMSM was changed to RMSoM to avoid confusion with the Royal Military School of Music.*

A number of unrelated but important incidents occurred in 1999. On 1st July the ranks of RM Officers were aligned with those of Army Officers. Captain Directors of Music became Majors and Lieutenants became Captains. On completion of the Special Duties Officers' Course and the Director of Music Course, Lt P Weston was appointed Director of Music to the CTC Band making him the first holder of the Prince's Badge to become a Director of Music. A new Memorial to those who died in Service this century was placed in the Garden of Remembrance at the Royal Marines Museum and The Blue Band Magazine celebrated its fiftieth year of publication.

The 1999 Royal Tournament was the last, and its final performance was on the 2nd August. This was a Tri-Service event led by the Massed Bands of the Royal Marines. During the same year the Royal Marines Beating Retreat on Horse Guards was, at the time, unique in that it only required one word of command - which was the order to step off. Apart from that, all movements were carefully synchronised to the music and the result was a particularly high-quality performance of music and drill.

2000 continued as 1999 had ended with the Royal Marines Band Service leading every major Tri-Service event. The Royal Military Tattoo 2000 (RMT2000) was another unique event that provided an opportunity for military bands in general, and the RMBS in particular, to show how they can adapt and use technology whilst maintaining the standards of drill and music for which they are famous. The Band Service Recording Engineer created a recording of all the music to be played complete with voice-overs, special effects and a computer click-track. This became the key to everything that occurred, especially the conducting of the military bands. Lt Col Waterer used two earpieces as he conducted; one was for the computer click-track, the other for cues. It was a magnificent tattoo that provided a fine example of how the Royal Marines Band Service led not only musically but also in many other ways. They could field a team of professionals capable of writing and arranging music for special events; planning and co-ordinating all aspects of display from parade work to concert work and, using their own technical ability, provide lighting, stage management and recording skills.

During 2000 the Edinburgh Tattoo was taken, as a complete show, to New Zealand. The Plymouth Band represented the Royal Marines and the Principal Director of Music (Lt Col R Waterer) was the show's Musical Director.

On Thursday 12th July 2001 the Captain General presented new Colours to 40, 42 and 45 Commandos on Plymouth Hoe. The ceremony began with the Corps Bugle Major and the Corps of Drums marching the Old Colours, Majors in Waiting and hassock bearers from the Citadel and onto the Hoe. The Massed Bands, formed from Plymouth, CTC and BRNC bands, then led the Parade onto the Hoe, countermarched and halted with the Corps Bugle Major and the Corps of Drums. Following the Captain General's inspection the Band trooped in slow and quick time before taking position in rear of 42 Cdo. With the hollow square formed the three Bugle Majors led three groups of Buglers forward to pile drums. Instead of taking place to a series of commands the piling of drums was achieved by taking cues from the march, *Great Little Army*, being played by the massed bands. As the Buglers marched off the Corps Bugle Major gave the signal for the Colours Officers to step off, setting the next phase of the display in motion. Two Buglers were positioned at each of the sets of piled drums to hold the new Colours during the Service of Consecration. The drums were retrieved using the music *Army and Marine* to cue the various movements. On completion the band stepped off and assumed a position at the rear of the parade as it marched off the Hoe. The band then led the parade on a march through Plymouth.[5]

5 *When Gen Sir Peter Whiteley took the salute at the rehearsal "Garb of Old Gaul" was not played as the General Salute because, when serving, he had adopted a 'personal' Musical Salute - the first six bars of Grieg's "Homage March Sigurd Jorsalfar".*

In the same year the 32 members of the same band deployed, as part of Medical Squadron on board HMS *Fearless*, with 3 Cdo Bde on Exercise *Saif Sareea 2* in Oman. This provided the opportunity for the band to practise their secondary role and perform their primary role in a variety of instrumental combinations. The other members of the band carried the burden of the usual programme of events including the International Maritime and Air Show in Malaysia.

The Massed Bands of all three Services were again on parade on Horse Guards, together with civilian Musicians, choirs and other organisations, for the 100th Birthday celebrations for HM Queen Elizabeth, The Queen Mother, on the 19th July 2000. Once more they were under the baton of Lt Col R Waterer and the musical arrangement for the complex musical march past was the responsibility of WO2 Bandmaster M Dowrick.

During early 2001 Plymouth Band was busy with the series of Roebuck Concerts, which included the Bandmasters' Class rehearsing the chamber music for woodwind by Strauss, Dvorak and Jacob; long rehearsals of the difficult works was followed by the conducting at the concert under the scrutiny of the Course Assessors. Following this the band was heavily committed to the preparatory work, rehearsing and recording the music to be played at the Mountbatten Festival of Music. The concert series and the MFM was followed by events related to The Queen's Golden Jubilee, and a journey to the Falklands to mark the 20th Anniversary of Op *Corporate*. Snow had fallen all night but stopped long enough for the band to parade, albeit in six inches of snow, and for two Tornados to fly past. Following the inspection, prayers and speeches the Band and Guard marched through Stanley where they later gave a concert. Amongst this busy schedule in such poor conditions they still took the opportunity to give an impromptu performance at the local nursing home.

As a result of reductions and reorganisations, the Army introduced a policy of having both a Director of Music and a Warrant Officer 1 Bandmaster for each band. Parity was established when the RMBS Warrant Officer ranks were adjusted so that all RM Bands could also have a WO1 as Bandmaster. It was also announced that, due to a shortage of General List Officers the position of Staff Officer to the Band Service (SO3) would, from 2003, be filled from the Band Service itself. Another milestone was reached with the graduation of the first twelve members of the RMBS to gain BMus Degrees, during 2001.

By January 2002 changes at both Corps and Band Service levels had altered the Royal Marines Band Service into something almost unrecognisable to those who had served between 1950 and 2000. The initial change that led to a chain reaction throughout the Corps was the reorganisation of its highest echelons and full integration into the Royal Navy and Fleet Headquarters. Commandant General Royal Marines assumed the additional title, and responsibilities of, Commander of UK Amphibious Forces with a newly formed battle staff. Remaining elements of Headquarters Royal Marines, under the newly established Director, Royal Marines, were also integrated into Fleet Headquarters. The five Royal Marine Bands were located at Portsmouth, Plymouth, Scotland, Commando Training Centre RM and Britannia Royal Naval College, Dartmouth, with a total complement of 347 men and women, plus a further fifty-three ranks under training. The Royal Marines School of Music within HM Naval Base, Portsmouth, continued to provide training for all instrumentalists plus academic training for potential Bandmasters and Directors of Music. All of the music courses were fully accredited through the University of Portsmouth, giving all ranks the opportunity to gain degrees at BMus(Hons) and Master of Music levels. The Royal Navy's Flag Officer Training and Recruitment was, through the Commandant of the Royal Marines School of Music, responsible for the administration of this training. Commandant General

Royal Marines, still exercised full command over the RMBS and its deployed bands. Band engagements were coordinated by HQRM through an annual engagements conference; at that time approximately 1000 requests were received each year, plus other short-notice requests that were allocated according to availability and priority.

By this time the secondary role of the RMBS had been clearly defined to suit the requirements of the Corps. 60% of the RMBS were assigned to specific roles related to medical duties with the Primary Casualty Receiving Ships, such as RFA *Argus*, and with Medical Squadron of the Commando Logistic Regiment. The other 40% were assigned roles relating to security duties at Commando Training Centre, RM Poole, RM Stonehouse and Royal Marine Barracks Chivenor or as part of the Corps casualty reporting cells. Men and women of the Royal Marines Band Service had, as a result of their primary and secondary roles, to not only reach and maintain higher standards of musical and ceremonial ability than their predecessors but also had to maintain levels of fitness plus military and secondary role training that were much higher than anything that had gone before, the possible exception to this being the Royal Marine Bands that served on ships of the Royal Navy during the two World Wars. 'New Entry Recruits', immediately on joining the RMSoM, undertook a twelve-week course in military training that is similar to the first fifteen weeks' Commando recruit training syllabus. After successfully completing a number of exercises run by the RM Military Training Team the recruits pass-out and progress to their musical training which is two years for Buglers and two years and eight months for Musicians.

Op *Tay Bridge* took effect on the 30th March 2002 when HM Queen Elizabeth, The Queen Mother, died. The Corps provided a marching detachment of four hundred, the same size as the Royal Navy, the Army and the Royal Air Force, as well as three bands.

The Queen's Golden Anniversary celebrations took place in 2002, the final event being the Review of the Armed Forces at HMS *Excellent*. Lt Col R Waterer once again directed the music as Tri-Service Senior Director of Music and it was most appropriate that almost his final act as PDM was to conduct the RM Band as The Queen left Southsea Common. Lt Col C J Davis became Commandant RMSoM and Principal Director of Music and was able to announce that The Queen had honoured his predecessor by making him a Member of the Royal Victorian Order and, to recognise his achievements in music, he had also been awarded an Honorary Doctorate in Music from the University of Portsmouth.

The new PDM's first engagement was the Edinburgh Military Tattoo, at which the RM Scotland Band performed. On completion he was confronted with Op *Fresco*, the operation that required the military services to cover strikes called by the Fire Brigade Union . Almost immediately two hundred members of the Band Service, out of a total Corps commitment of five hundred and fifty, began training as Breathing Apparatus Rescue Teams, and drivers and crew for the Green Goddess fire appliances that were, once again, returned to service. Directors of Music, Bandmasters and Senior NCOs were given responsibility for Temporary Fire Stations which included co-ordinating call-outs and deploying units to emergencies. This level of involvement meant that about 75% of musical engagements had to be cancelled and, in order to maintain the training programmes, a composite band, known as the Rear Party Band, was formed at Portsmouth from those not operational with Op *Fresco*. Due to the rank ratios required in the fire-fighting teams, the Rear Party Band contained a very high proportion of SNCOs. Despite this commitment the annual Mountbatten Festival of Music went ahead in 2003 but the Massed Bands Beat Retreat on Horse Guards Parade had to be replaced with a smaller ceremony in the grounds of Buckingham Palace. Since 2003 marked the 50th anniversary of the appointment of The Duke of Edinburgh as Captain General Royal Marines, the occasion could not be allowed to pass without the traditional ceremony taking place in some form. By the summer of 2003 the Fire Service dispute had been settled and members of the RMBS returned to their normal, musical, duties.

The demands of Op *Fresco*, the Fire-fighters Union strike, disrupted the work of the Plymouth Band at the end of 2002 and during the early months of 2003, as did the need for all bands to contribute personnel to deploy on RFA *Argus* during Op *Telic*. During the autumn the band performed at Holland's World Harbour Days, which also provided the opportunity to celebrate the close association between the Royal Marines and the Royal Netherlands Marine Corps.

One of the casualties of the combined effects of Op *Fresco* and Op *Telic* was the Band of Britannia Royal Naval College. All members of this band, apart from the Band Secretary, were deployed or reassigned until both commitments were completed in full. The band was reinstated during the summer of 2003, this time under the command of a Director of Music instead of a WO1 Bandmaster. The Band's engagement list included the usual visit to the British Embassy in Washington DC for Corps Birthday and Trafalgar Night celebrations.

A further advancement to the RMBS technical capability was made when its Stage Manager, Musn Karl Westlake, received a 1st Class BA (Honours) Degree in Stage Management and Technical Theatre. This course of management level study, coupled with many years of practical experience, gave the Band Service the ability to contribute well-informed input to the production planning of major events.

2003 marked the 100th Anniversary of the forming of the Royal Naval School of Music at the Royal Marine Artillery Barracks at Eastney. The anniversary was celebrated in a number of ways but the principal event was the Special Exhibition at the Royal Marines Museum which was opened by The Duke of Edinburgh, Captain General Royal Marines. The exhibition was a joint effort, pooling the resources of the Museum staff and its Collections with the skills of serving members of the RMBS, particularly the Supply Officer (Music), Capt Henderson, and his team. The anniversary celebrations were dampened by the news that, during the redevelopment of the Deal Royal Marines School of Music site, a mysterious fire destroyed the Concert Hall. In the early 1900s the building had been a chapel and a school but it had been used as a concert hall for many years. The IRA bomb that killed eleven members of the RMBS in 1989 was detonated behind this building. The Memorial Garden placed at the site was also destroyed in the fire although the Memorial Stone itself was saved. The following year the developers renovated the area and incorporated not only the Memorial Stone but also the railings and gates designed and made by a former Royal Marine Musician.

One of the first engagements of 2004 was the naming of the world's largest liner, The *Queen Mary 2*, by Her Majesty The Queen. A marching band plus fanfare team were on board, as was the Royal Philharmonic Orchestra, for the celebrations and the ceremony. After the struggle to find enough Musicians to form a band for the 2003 Mountbatten Festival of Music, the 2004 series of concerts brought a welcome return to normality with the full resources of the RMBS available. A new presenter, BBC newsreader Darren Jordan, and Bugler Helen Petty sounding the solo *Sunset* provided two 'firsts'.

Britannia Royal Naval College Band embarked on HMS *Invincible* for a ten-week deployment to Florida and Norfolk, USA. Apart from taking part in two military exercises they were scheduled to take part in the Independence Day celebrations. The ship's company appreciated the entertainment which included a joint rock band concert with the ship's own band. They also performed a number of Beat Retreat and entering/leaving harbour ('Procedure Alpha') ceremonies. Another notable event for BRNC Band was the award of the Freedom of Entry to Dartmouth by the Dartmouth Town Council - the first award of this type to a military band.[6] The occasion was also marked by the release of a new recording - '*Hosts of Freedom*'.

A recording released at a similar time was '*Harrison's Dream*', the first in a series of three recordings of symphonic wind band music, the brainchild of the Principal Director of Music, Lt Col Chris Davis. The recordings were made by a carefully selected composite band. The première performance of the title music took place in November 2007 when Professor David King conducted the Portsmouth Band in front of an audience of 600, including the composer, Peter Graham.

At the end of July 2004 the RM Scotland Band went to Gibraltar for two weeks to support the Royal Navy being given the Freedom of Gibraltar to mark three hundred years of allegiance and friendship. In addition the band took part in Changing the Guard ceremonies, and a number of concerts including one in Casemates Square and a joint concert with the Volunteer Band.

Since 2002 the RMBS has had the opportunity to send two Musicians to spend twelve months with the NATO Band which is based in the Regional Headquarters of Allied Forces Southern Europe (HQ AF South) at Bagnoli, in Napoli. The band, formed in 1951, was originally a US Navy band and most of its forty members are still from the United States, the remainder being from Greece, Turkey and Italy. RMBS Musicians are particularly welcome since they are the only double-handed Musicians. Having them allows the band to accept invitations to play at dinner parties and to increase the number of musical combinations that the band can provide. Another example of 'international opportunity' is the 'Long Look' exchange. Originally begun in about 1984, this has developed into an exchange visit for all ranks of any service. Occasionally Musicians are selected; in 2000 WO Tony Smallwood (RMBS) exchanged with a WO from the Royal Australian Navy. In 2004 the RMBS was unable to send a representative but the Director of Music of the RAN Band, Sydney, Lt Michelle Coleman, visited the RMSoM for the four-month duration of *Long-Look*.

After the major changes to the hierarchy of the Corps in 2002, a Royal Marines Strategic Study was published in 2004. Those two intervening years had given greater exposure to the Corps expertise and abilities across the full maritime theatre, to the extent that complete integration with the Royal Navy had been achieved without detriment to Royal Marine regimental issues. The 2004 Defence Review White Paper put great emphasis onto the need for the Royal Navy to remain an armed service with the capability to quickly respond by land, sea and in the air to threats in any part of the world using the latest technology and other resources. Embedded at the heart of this was 3 Commando Brigade with the additional amphibious capability provided to them through HM Ships *Argus*, *Albion*, *Bulwark* and *Ocean* and also the Bay class landing ships, as well as other elements of the Royal Marines. Whilst the future of the Royal Marines appeared promising there was no room for complacency, especially for those traditional targets for cuts - military bands. It was also in 2004 that Merit Based Promotion was introduced throughout the RMBS.

One of the features of the 2005 Mountbatten Festival of Music was the Largo from Vivaldi's Concerto in D for Lute and Strings. This was transcribed by Major Nick Grace for guitar and strings and played by Musician Adrian Breen and string players from Portsmouth and Britannia Royal Naval College Bands. (Image courtesy of Les Scriver)

6 1st September 2003.

Britannia Royal Naval College celebrated its centenary in 2005. Whilst committed to many official engagements at locations such as NATO HQ in Naples, Washington DC and Antwerp (to celebrate the start of the British Presidency of Europe) the BRNC Band also celebrated the centenary. A recording of the music played during Dartmouth's Passing Out Parades, *Sound Off Divisions*, was produced and an outdoor concert complete with fireworks was performed on the College parade ground.

A trend in the increasing number of requests for voluntary redundancy was investigated in 2004/2005. The main cause was found to be the slow promotion from Musician or Bugler to the rank of Corporal. At this time 60% of those promoted to BdCpl or CplBug had waited at least ten years for their promotion. In order to try to reduce the rate of leaving, the new ranks of Brevet Band Corporal and Brevet Corporal Bugler were introduced, effective from the 1st February 2005.

During 2005 the Plymouth Band took the opportunity to play an orchestral concert with the Plymouth Philharmonic Choir at the Plymouth Pavilions. The music included Vaughan Williams' *Sea Songs*, Stanford's *Song of the Sea* and Elgar's *Sea Pictures*. Shortly after this the band took part in another joint concert, this time with the Polperro Fishermen's Choir, before setting off to Jersey for the Liberation celebrations which were led by HM The Queen. The autumn of 2005 was fully occupied with the Edinburgh Tattoo, events related to Trafalgar 200 and events in Saudi and Basra. The Clarinet Quintet travelled to Riyadh, Saudi Arabia, to provide a variety show for the International School, a Sunset ceremony for the RAF's Battle of Britain celebrations and entertainment for a Trafalgar 200 Dinner. The school variety show included the Quintet and Corps of Drums performing as a jazz combo and a folk group as well as providing a 'Generation Game' and, not unnaturally, a Clarinet Quartet and Corps of Drums. The Guest of Honour at the T200 Dinner was CGRM and the Corps of Drums' contribution was crowned by them leading the singing of sea shanties.

On the 28th October twenty-seven members of the band left England for Basra, Iraq. The journey included a transfer from a Boeing 747 to a Hercules at Qatar and trip to Basra wearing full body armour, helmets and with the lights off. The six days included three Beat Retreats, one for CGRM and the Corps RSM; two performances by the Big Band, the jazz quartet, rock band and Plymouth's folk ensemble 'The Rumbling Gussets'. Because of the situation the band had to carry helmets and body armour everywhere and experienced 'the odd mortar being fired into the base'.

Life in the RMBS is not just about music and performance. Behind the scenes a great deal of work, much of it seemingly mundane and uninteresting, is very necessary and essential to maintaining the RMBS as an efficient organisation. Value for money, whilst maintaining the standards required of an organisation that, because of its role, is always under close scrutiny, is essential. Supply Officer Music initiated further attempts to improve procurement contracts for uniforms, accoutrements and instruments. Balancing the need to maintain standards whilst trying to reduce costs is not an easy task - particularly when a prospective supplier might have no knowledge or experience of military use, custom or tradition is awarded a Ministry of Defence contract. This type of situation demands that members of the RMBS, usually experienced SNCOs, spend a great deal of time on quality control of such contracts. Another example of work behind the scenes is that whilst the supply of music is probably recognised as a major task for SOM's Department, the responsibility extends beyond the purchase, and provision, of music to areas related to copyright issues and arranging commissions and contracts.

All of these 'behind the scenes' matters assume even greater significance in a year such as 2005. With bands distributed on various ships during the International Fleet Review off Spithead, an International Drum-Head Service at Southsea, the International Festival of the Sea - a four-day event in Portsmouth Dockyard - plus Trafalgar 200, the Edinburgh Military Tattoo, Victory in Europe and Victory in Japan commemorations in London and elsewhere, a heavy load was placed upon not only the men and women of the RMBS but also upon their instruments, uniforms and accoutrements. Much of the high-profile work of the bands in a year such as 2005 is in addition to their regular work. King's Squad pass-outs at CTCRM, Divisions and pass-outs at Britannia Royal Naval College and a host of other regular tasks still had to be covered. During 2005 the five bands of the Royal Marines Band Service covered more than 1200 engagements which equates to twenty per band per month. In addition to the performance schedule is the time required for practice, for rehearsal and for travelling.

2006 began badly for the entire Royal Marines Band Service with the news of the death of their highly respected, recently retired, Principal Director of Music, Lt Col Richard Waterer. He died aged fifty-six, on the night of the 10/11 January, at the Valley Forge Military Academy, Pennsylvania, where he was Commandant of Cadets. He was Principal Director of Music, Royal Marines, from 1994 to 2002. His successor, Lt Col Chris Davis, wrote, 'Nobody can question his integrity or loyalty and we who still serve have much to thank this outstanding 'Officer and a Gentleman' for; long may we live up to his high standards and expectations'. The Funeral Service and Celebration of Richard's life took place on the 26th January at Portsmouth Cathedral. The bands of Commando Training Centre, Royal Marines, and Portsmouth (Royal Band) provided the Processional Band and the Orchestra respectively. HRH The Duke of Edinburgh, Captain General Royal Marines, was represented by Lt Gen Sir Robert Fulton, the Representative Colonel Commandant, Royal Marines.

Following the ceremony of Beating Retreat on Horse Guards Parade in front of the Captain General in 2006, the Massed Bands of the Royal Marines marched up the Mall. (Image courtesy of Les Scriver)

In April 2006 Captain Jon Ridley took part in the exchange visit to Australia, Exercise Long-Look, as part of his Officer Training. He assumed the appointment of Officer-in-Charge and Musical Director of the Australian Navy Band, Melbourne, at HMAS *Cerberus*, the Royal Australian Navy's Recruit Training Base. The exchange included opportunities for concerts, massed band concerts and, being a training establishment, pass-out parades. Captain Ridley returned to England to become Director of Music, RM Band of Britannia Royal Naval College.

Following the summer break the band returned to duty in time for the Plymouth Navy Days in Devonport Dockyard. During October a String Quartet performed in Cyprus, Washington and Oman at events marking the Corps Birthday and Trafalgar Day. At the same time twenty-four members of the band plus the Director of Music and Drum Major visited Estonia in support of The Queen and Prince Philip's first State Visit to the Baltic States. The band played in Vilnius, Lithuania, then visited Latvia and Tallin, Estonia, where the Jazz Band entertained The Queen at the Baltic State's largest Art Museum, called KUMU. Next day the band mustered alongside HMS *Liverpool*. The visit concluded with a televised Trafalgar Day Concert on 21st October in the Estonia Concert Hall, home of the Estonian National Symphony Orchestra.

The eighteen-month programme of making improvements to uniform and accoutrement procurement was showing signs of success by 2006. Many of the projects initiated by the two very experienced Bugle Majors were completed in time to achieve the high standard of appearance required of the Massed Bands on Horse Guards Parade in 2006. This included the issue of stay bright metal-wear which, although scheduled for 2007, was obtained earlier.

The 2006 Beating Retreat was fully rehearsed on Whale Island, Portsmouth. The need for practically the entire Band Service to be available for this event created a situation that even the Firefighter's strike could not achieve - an Army band had to be used to provide musical support to a King's Squad pass-out parade at CTCRM. The Band of the Prince of Wales' Division marched on to the CTC Parade; a situation that no-one could recall happening before.

Following the 'Britannia Proms 2006', the Band of Britannia Royal Naval College departed, at the behest of Lt Gen Sir Rob Fry, the Senior British Representative in Iraq, for a ten-day trip to Baghdad. The flight involved a Boeing 747 and a Hercules C130 and the need to wear helmets and body armour on the approach to Basra airport. Security was tight and force protection was heavy; 2000 killings and kidnappings had occurred in the past month. All engagements were carried out in full ceremonial whites including a formal band photograph with General Fry on the parade ground in front of Saddam's huge archway formed from crossed swords. The General remarked that 'This is the first time since Saddam's regime that such formal attire had been worn on this parade'. Engagements included a shared concert in the US Embassy on the 4th July; Mess Beatings, Beat Retreat and Orchestra for the General's dinner party; Brass Quintet Soiree at the local hospital and a less formal gathering at the General's house. The band correspondent wrote the following summary: 'We played music at the highest level using almost every musical combination available to us. More importantly we did it dressed as Royal Marines, in our ceremonial uniforms with helmets, in some of the most bizarre of locations'.

A composite band formed from Portsmouth, Plymouth and CTC band ranks joined forces with the Band of the Grenadier Guards for the ANZAC Tattoo in Sydney. Other participants included bands of the New Zealand Army, pipers, Zulus, Tongans and a couple of girl marching bands. All bands participated in the Sydney Parade on ANZAC Day.

Changes to Supply Officer Music's Department in 2006 included the appointment of BdCSgt Bromley as the new Chief Librarian and BdCpl Deacon as the full-time Band Service Recording NCO, his first task being to establish the new Editing Suite.

Following the partial loss of the Deal Concert Hall through fire in 2003 and the subsequent remedial works, and improvements to the site, the annual Service of Remembrance for those killed in the Deal bombing of 1989 had expanded over the intervening years. By 2006 it was felt that, despite the genuine efforts by those involved in the annual event, the original small gathering of Royal Marine Band Service family and friends had grown into what resembled a November Remembrance Parade. As a result, and by common consent, a less formal service was reintroduced.

Three days after the Deal Memorial Service, on the 25th September, a Memorial Service for Don Lusher, the Royal Marines School of Music's Trombone Professor and Director of the RMSoM Big Band, took place at the Salvation Army's Regent Hall, London. With representation from the International Salvation Army Staff Band, the Don Lusher Big Band and some of the country's finest jazz Musicians, plus a RMBS Brass Quintet, it was a fittingly memorable event for such a modest and sincere gentleman and professional Musician of unquestionable ability.

Less than a fortnight later, on the 8th October, the annual Memorial Service for Musn Bob Simmonds, one of the men killed in the Deal bombing, was held at All Saints' Church, Alton in Hampshire. This particular year also marked the occasion of the Blessing of the six, especially commissioned, All Saints' Church bells. Each bears an inscription, the largest having the words 'The Royal Marines School of Music - Per Mare Per Terram'.

2007 marked the 25th Anniversary of Op *Corporate* - the recapture of the Falkland Islands. Portsmouth and Plymouth Bands were on Horse Guards Parade for the national event whilst, with one exception, all other bands were engaged in similar events across the country. The exception was the band from BRNC which was flown to the islands themselves. Mount Pleasant Camp, usually home to twenty people, had contingents from the Royal Marines, the Royal Navy, the Rifles and the RAF. The first job was a concert in Christchurch Cathedral which was attended by Prince Edward, Earl of Wessex, at which Falkland's veteran BdCSgt Halsey, still serving, played a trombone solo. Rehearsals for next day's Liberation Parade took place at night to the sound of drum beatings only, since it was too dark to read music. Following the Parade the BRNC Dixieland Band entertained at a Reception. The next two days saw the band split into smaller units and ensembles in order to provide maximum coverage of the requested events. A television link-up allowed the Memorial Service at San Carlos Cemetery to be shown at the Horse Guards event. In driving rain and horizontal sleet the BRNC Buglers piled drums before making their way to a position high on the hill for the sounding of *Last Post* and *Reveille*. A total of thirteen official musical engagements took place and the success of the complex logistical arrangements was acknowledged as being due to the meticulous planning of the BRNC Band Secretary, CSgtBug M Williams.

On the 1st September 2007 the Order of Precedence for the Army was changed. This had an important effect upon the Royal Marines Band Service since the Royal Marines were removed from this order of precedence as, by now, they were completely part of the Royal Naval Service. This, in turn, meant that the Royal Marines, and its Band Service, would no longer take precedence only when the Royal Navy was on parade, but at all times.

During 2007 the Royal Navy adopted a strategy known as Lean Transformation. This was developed originally by the Toyota Car company as a process to improve the organisation's output. The RMBS was subject to a 'Lean Event' in October 2007 and, initially, the intent was towards removing a number of military positions from the RMBS. Through a process of self-analysis, information relating to the number of RMBS commitments, their locations and the number of man-hours spent in rehearsal and performance was captured. Other major factors included the periods of time spent travelling to and from commitments and the methods used to prioritise the engagements and task them to the bands. The results provided hard, compelling, evidence of the amount of work undertaken by each band and the need to re-assess their size, locations and the process by which commitments were prioritised and tasked. The RMBS aim was to make recommendations that would enable the RMBS to optimise efficiency in terms of providing bands that could better, and more fairly, cover a workload which varied from region to region.

The ability to relocate bands to assist this process would have provided the best option but practical and financial constraints prohibited this. With three bands located within a 50-mile radius in the West Country and the BRNC Band being based in Dartmouth, a less than ideal location for an organisation required to travel around the UK, a significant recommendation was to relocate the band from BRNC. The primary aim of this was to improve the regional balance of demand and thus output of the RMBS; the BRNC Band contribution being subject to its proximity to other bands and the travel time from

Dartmouth. An additional factor was the impending cost implication of refurbishing the BRNC rehearsal facility to meet Health & Safety requirements.

At the time three of the five RM Bands were complemented to forty-four (including their Corps of Drums) plus the Director of Music. Given that a RM Marching Band should comprise thirty-five plus DoM and Drum Major, and that each commitment required at least four security ranks, managing this requirement with forty-five personnel, when an element would be on various training and promotional courses or unavailable for other reasons, had proven impossible. Subsequent discussion determined that each band should be no less than fifty-four (including the DoM) and that bands of equal size and capability were the best option for future structure.

The method by which RM Bands were tasked to commitments came under intense scrutiny. The current system of holding an RMBS Engagements Conference to determine the programme of commitments for the forthcoming financial year in the preceding November 'silted-up' the programme. Recommendations to dispense with the Engagements Conference and to adopt a more flexible, four-month rolling planner; a system similar to the principle used by Navy Command Headquarters for all Fleet assets, was formulated.

These recommendations, made to the Deputy Commandant General Royal Marines and the Chief of Staff Capability, were subsequently accepted with the implementation process scheduled to begin in 2008.

The end of an era also occurred in 2007 when Lt Col Paul Neville retired as Director of Music of the 'All Stars Band'. On the 18th March 1990, 130 retired Musicians of the RMBS gave a concert, on behalf of the Deal Bombing Relief Fund. The idea came from David 'Joe' Forbes and, with the help and support of Steve Misson, Pete Rose and Terry Williams the concept was brought to fruition. Lt Col Paul Neville was asked to conduct and the concert raised £7,000 for the Fund. Over the years the concerts continued until 'Colonel Paul' retired after eighteen years of concerts which raised more than £140,000 for the Deal Fund. A year later, on Sunday the 8th March 2008, the 'All Stars Band' annual concerts continued under their new Director of Music, Captain David Cole.

In a previous chapter the story was told of the Second World War experiences of men of the RNSM serving with Royal Marine Bands on board warships. HMS *Gloucester* was sunk by German aircraft during the Battle of Crete in May 1941. Over seven hundred men of the Royal Navy, Royal Marines and the Royal Marine Band perished. Musician Ken Macdonald survived and spent the rest of the war in German prison camps. Following repatriation he rose to the rank of Bandmaster and then transferred, in 1958, to the Rhodesian Army Band from which he later retired as a Major. It was his wish that his ashes would be committed to the deep to rest with the men who lost their lives on board HMS *Gloucester*. Following his death in 2007 the current HMS *Gloucester* carried his ashes to Crete and, over the wreck of its predecessor, the Ship's Company gathered for the service as Ken Macdonald's wish was granted.

Katherine Jenkins joined the Band of the Royal Marines for part of their performance for the 2007 Festival of Remembrance at the Royal Albert Hall. (Image courtesy of Les Scriver)

Yet another 2007 anniversary was marked on the 20th December when BdCpl Louise Simpson, Saxophone and

Violin Instructor at the RMSoM, became the first female to receive the Long Service and Good Conduct Medal. She joined the first New Entry Troop in September 1992 at Deal.

The first stage in the implementation of the Lean Transformation recommendations was to relocate the BRNC Band to a more effective location. The aspiration was to return a band to the London area but this proved cost prohibitive. HMS *Collingwood*, a Royal Naval technical training centre first opened in 1940, eventually offered two possible solutions. Meanwhile, to compensate for the loss of a band lodging at BRNC their workload would be managed by the other two West Country bands based at Commando Training Centre Royal Marines and HMS *Raleigh*. With each of the bands restructuring to a strength of fifty-four, including Corps of Drums and admin staff, the associated work related to branch development, complement and career management, instrumental balance and rank structure could be accommodated.[7] In parallel with these developments was the increasing momentum behind the need to deploy RMBS ranks with the United Kingdom Joint Force Medical Group for Operation *Herrick 9*.

Throughout August 2008 the bands of Portsmouth, Plymouth and Scotland formed the Massed Bands of Her Majesty's Royal Marines at the Edinburgh Tattoo performing to over 250,000 people. The musical programme included an opening fanfare by Major Dowrick, *Marchambra* (Richards), *Time Off* (Watson), *The Gael* and the most popular item - *Children of Sanchez* (Magione arr McGain-Harding).

The Band Service was heavily committed to supporting the Corps in Basra at Christmas (Portsmouth Band) and then again in March/April for the Transfer of Authority of the Multi-National Division (South East) from British to United States forces (Plymouth Band).

The beginning of the withdrawal of British troops from Iraq was signalled by a ceremony held at Basra International Airport on the 31st March 2009 at which Maj Gen Salmon RM, the General Officer Commanding the Multi-National Division handed over command to an American headquarters force. Musical support for the ceremony was provided by the Plymouth Band which had arrived on the 26th. The band met Maj Gen Salmon and his staff next morning and were asked to give an impromptu performance - which they did. As a result, staff from the Foreign and Commonwealth Office persuaded the band to play at their own function the next evening but, before that, the band had to provide background jazz for General Salmon and his guests at the Headquarters soiree. In addition, members of the band needed to reconnoitre in preparation for future tasks. The next day, intended for rehearsals for all of the forthcoming events and performances, was lost to lectures related to life in Basra. At General Salmon's farewell function the band performed a small concert that included the post horn gallop, *Rule Britannia* and *Land of Hope and Glory*. To everyone's surprise the concert ended with General Salmon playing Acker Bilk's *Stranger on the Shore* on Musn Charlotte Stuss's clarinet! Next morning at 0530 the band was airlifted by two Merlin helicopters with Apache helicopter gunship escorts to the Basra Operations Centre next to the Shatt al Arab waterway for a marching display rehearsal at 0830. The ceremony, hosted by Maj Gen Mohammed Huweidi of the Iraqi Army, consisted of a feast for 250 people. Before the feast the band gave a twenty minute marching display and, during the feast, the jazz band provided background music. On arrival at the airport for a rehearsal of the Handover Ceremony the Bandmaster and Drum Major were asked to provide a thirteen minute display. Time was spent carefully constructing this with the result that a display of twelve minutes and forty-seven seconds was prepared. It was at this point that they were asked to cut it down to eight minutes! The

7 By comparison, in 1899 the RMA had a band of thirty-one under Band Master Green, plus twleve supernumaries. In addition the RMA had a Corps of Drums of seventy-four under its Bugle Major and Drum Major.

Transfer of Authority Ceremony commenced at midday on the 31st March. Media coverage was high including live transmission to BBC News. The band started the ceremony with a marching display, this being followed by prayers, *National Anthems*, speeches, the raising and lowering of the Colours, a Blessing and then a march past in front of a great many senior officers, including the Chief of the UK Defence Staff. On completion the band made preparations for the return journey having, in the tradition of the Royal Marines Band Service, exhibited resourcefulness, adaptability and professionalism.

On Saturday 28th February 2009 the Scotland Band together with a marching detachment from 40 Commando conducted a ceremonial parade exercising the rights of the Corps, which had been granted the privilege of the Freedom of the City of Gibraltar in 1996. Torrential rain did not prevent locals and visitors from lining the route and applauding. The salute was taken by, amongst others, the Governor of Gibraltar, Lt Gen Sir Robert Fulton KBE, RM. In addition, a monument marking the association between the Corps and the Rock of Gibraltar, sited near the point where the Marines first came ashore in 1704, was dedicated. Before they left, the Scotland Band, conducted by the Principal Director of Music Lt Col Chris Davis, gave a concert in St Michael's Cave. This was Col Davis's last appearance as conductor before he retired.

Hansard, 30th April 2009, reported the Armed Forces Debate in the House of Lords. Media attention was appropriately diverted towards the cause of the Gurkhas at this time with the result that the debate did not receive the coverage that perhaps it deserved. Lord Judd made reference to the commitment and esprit de corps of the Royal Marines; Earl Atlee put the Corps into context by stating that 'It is worth remembering that, by the standards of many countries, our Royal Marines Commandos *are* Special Forces', and Lord Burnett felt it important that the task-force formation be recorded in detail. He stated, 'There were the following Royal Marine formations, other than 3 Commando Brigade Headquarters to which I have already referred: 42 Commando, 45 Commando, the Armoured Support Group, the UK Landing Force Command Support Group with the Commando Brigade Reconnaissance Force, 539 Assault Squadron Royal Marines and eighteen members of the Royal Marines Band Service'. He continued, 'In the seven month deployment, the Commando Brigade and its attached ranks have seen combat of a ferocity that has not been witnessed since World War 2. Our Armed Forces now have greater battle experience than at any time since the war'. The part that the Royal Marines Band Service could play, and had played within, and in support of, the Corps had been noted.

Following the tragic deaths of two serving members of the Royal Marines Band Service, Major John Kelly and BdCpl Andy Thompson, a cycle ride for charity was organised. This event, '*Bandies on Bikes*', began on the 18th May 2009 and involved fifteen members of the Band Service cycling from the Deal Memorial Bandstand along the coast to HMS *Raleigh* in Cornwall. A further nineteen riders joined for parts of the ride. Sponsorship was needed to fund the event which raised more than £30,000 for the RM Benevolent Fund, St Luke's Hospice and the Deal Memorial Bandstand Trust.

Plymouth Band, with Musicians from Portsmouth and CTC Bands, recorded the music of the 2009 Massed Bands Beating Retreat ceremony on Horse Guards Parade. Whilst this was happening four members of the band were playing, as a jazz quartet, at the London Boat Show. They played for an hour each day and included the feature, begun the previous year, of composing a new blues number - every day!

The 2009 Beating Retreat ceremony on Horse Guards Parade marked the 88th birthday of The Prince Philip, Duke of Edinburgh, Captain General Royal Marines, and took place on the 9th-11th June and, whilst maintaining all of the characteristics of the

Rehearsals for Beating Retreat on Horse Guards Parade are carried out at HMS Excellent, Portsmouth, and then on Horse Guards itself. This image shows the bands, under the baton of Lt Col N Grace and the watchful eye of the Corps Bandmaster, rehearsing the finale sequence on Horse Guards Parade

traditional display, was also innovative and imaginative.

On the 9th July Plymouth Band played at a Buckingham Palace garden party celebrating 100 years of Royal Navy flying. Whilst they played by the lake the Portsmouth Band were playing next to the Palace itself.

The outcomes of the accepted Lean Transformation recommendation came into effect on 16th June 2009. The BRNC Band, having been closed for some fourteen months in order to enable a band's strength of personnel to be deployed to Afghanistan, relocated to HMS *Collingwood* in Fareham. The search for a new location was restricted due to a lack of suitable or available premises resulting from the run-down of the military estate. Corps Bugle Major Lee Cullen was given the responsibility of Project Manager and oversaw the plan to establish the Band in HMS *Collingwood* in adequate and effective facilities. The newly styled Band of Her Majesty's Royal Marines, Collingwood (not HMS Collingwood) was formed on Tuesday 16 June 2009 under Major Jason Burcham. Whilst refurbishment awaited completion the band shared Portsmouth Band's facilities until early September when the band marched into HMS *Collingwood* to take up residence. Their band complex, 'Waterer Hall' named after the late Principal Director of Music, Lt Col Richard Waterer, was opened by Mrs Sue Waterer and the Second Sea Lord, Vice Admiral Sir Alan Massey on 25 September 2009 with 'Colonel Richard''s mother, Eileen, in attendance. Whilst the remaining outcomes of Lean Transformation were expected to be completed other measures, such as Strategic Defence and Security Review, have seen the recommendations take slightly different directions.

Once it was agreed that a Royal Marines Band would not be returning to Britannia Royal Naval College arrangements had to be made to close the band facilities. Having been given the unique 'Freedom of Entry' to Dartmouth it now became necessary for the Freedom Scroll to be returned to the Mayor and Town Council. On the 20th May 2009 the band was temporarily re-formed in order to say farewell to Dartmouth, a much loved location for those serving with the 'College Band'. The band marched from the College to Coronation Park where they Beat Retreat to a very large audience. On completion and with the Bandmaster carrying the framed scroll, the band marched into the town where the Freedom Scroll was officially handed back to the town. By prior agreement it was then presented to the Royal Marines Museum for retention as part of Corps history. The final act was to march through the town. Less than four months later the pre-1950s situation was recalled when a new BRNC Royal Naval Volunteer Band was formed by Major Phil Watson and undertook its first rehearsal in the College's Caspar John Hall. The remit of the band is to provide a musical presence within the College and also to provide the supportive people of Dartmouth with a band for events and concerts throughout the year.

For personnel of the RMBS some of the most memorable events of this period were associated with the return of 3 Commando Brigade from operations in Afghanistan. Collingwood Band marched a detachment to the Palace of Westminster on the 30th June whilst, a day later, Plymouth Band led the Brigade in a Freedom Parade through Plymouth to the Hoe.

On the 12th July 2009 the bands from Portsmouth and Collingwood joined forces for the annual Deal Memorial Bandstand Concert and Dedication Service shortly before the 20th Anniversary of the Deal bombing. Over 10,000 people attended the concert which could also be viewed on large screens erected for the purpose. The Fleet Air Arm celebrated its 100th anniversary and 'Fly Navy 100' celebrations were held on board HMS Illustrious in Liverpool with Prince Andrew attending and taking the salute during Scotland Band's Beat Retreat on the deck of the aircraft carrier. Earlier in the year Michael McDermott wrote a competition winning composition to accompany a short film intended to mark the anniversary. Given the title *Daedalus*, it was premiered at the 2009 Mountbatten Festival of Music.

The 2009 November Remembrance period included all of the traditional events and duties. This year retired members of the Band Service were invited to be part of the RMA contingent. At the insistence of the RMA Chief Executive, Brig Charlie Hobson, they were placed at the head of the marching column. This position particularly suited them as, when the beat of the bass drum was lost and the step began to falter, they began to sing *A Life on the Ocean Wave*. The singing was picked up by the RMA marching column, and the watching crowd, as they made their way to Horse Guards Parade - in step.

Collingwood Band covered the Remembrance Service at Portsmouth Guildhall. One of the band's first overseas appearances was at the 65th Anniversary celebrations of Walcheren, a major event in the Corps calendar. They also visited the Falklands where they had many engagements. For one of these, fifteen members of the band were deposited by helicopter in a field near Hill Cove. They were to play in a local community hall (a barn) to a capacity audience of 70% of the local community - eight people! By the end of the concert Major Burcham could address all members of the audience by their first names and, when offered an encore, the audience invited the band to have a drink with them first!

An annual RMBS undertaking is the Reunion. Traditionally held in September or October this includes a Saturday evening social event and a Sunday morning Memorial Service in Portsmouth Cathedral. A record number of serving and retired members of the RMBS attended the 2009 event. The marching display takes place in the gymnasium and features the Band of Training Company of the Royal Marines School of Music - a daunting task for the Students, considering the calibre and background of the audience. The RMBS production team, BdSgt Deacon and Musn Westlake, provided lighting, PA system and special effects but the stage belonged to the School of Music, this year supported by the fanfare team from the Collingwood band. Under the direction of Bandmaster, Training, WO1 Dean Waller the band's excellent display opened with the fanfare *Eastney* and culminated in *Parade of the Charioteers* and the classic *Sunset* ending. After the Principal Director of Music's address, all returned to the Mess for food, drink and further musical entertainment. Like the RMSoM Band's performance, the preparations for the Memorial Service began months in advance. Usually selected names of those who died during the Second World War are read out by the Corps Drum Major but as 2009 was the twentieth anniversary of the Deal bombing the names of those murdered at the barracks were heard. The orchestra was provided by the Portsmouth Band with the Fanfare Team from Collingwood Band on hand to play the RMBS Memorial Fanfare *To Comrades Sleeping*. Academic Professor Dr Liz Le Grove played the organ and, in pride of place, were the Silver Memorial Drums and the Memorial Trumpets of the Royal Naval School of Music. Portsmouth Cathedral was full to capacity. The pre-Service music was from British composers Holst, Purcell and Elgar.

In December 2009 the annual march competition was re-instigated as 'The Richard Waterer March Competition' with prize-money coming from 'The Waterer Fund' which was initiated to enhance individual standards throughout the Band Service. Eleven entries were whittled down to six finalists with the winner being WO2 Bandmaster Russ Young whose march, *Spirit of Youth*, was played at the 2010 MFM concert.

Each year one of the Royal Marine Bands performs an outdoor concert at the Royal Marines Museum. In 2010 the Royal Marines Collingwood Band played to a capacity audience in this very attractive setting

The 21st annual 'All Stars' Band concert took place on the 14th March 2010. Captain David Cole conducted the band with guest conductor Kenji Kawashima from Japan. Profits from this concert brought the overall donations for the series to over £170,000.

Since the beginning of 2010 Plymouth Band's tasks have included a recording of concert band music, the Roebuck concerts, the Supersession of the Commandant General Royal Marines at CTC where they performed as both orchestra and parade band; also a Big Band concert in Stonehouse Barracks, Plymouth which featured jazz, swing and vocals with even the Corps of Drums making an appearance in Handy's *St Louis' Blues* march. This period also included the band's annual military training package and assisting with the trials of the new Marine Evacuation System on board RFA *Argus*. This latter task involved casualty evacuation from the ship via an inflatable slide into a 100-man life raft which, in rough weather, was then set adrift to a point where a helicopter airlifted a weighted stretcher from the raft - an exercise never carried out before. This exercise was essential training for the band which could, in their deployed role, be required to use this equipment in a real situation. These performances, tasks and duties, carried out during the early months of 2010, illustrate the variety of skills and performance levels as well as the flexibility and adaptability inherent in a modern Royal Marines Band.

After a short break the RM Collingwood Band marched onto the lawns of the Royal Marines Museum to Beat Retreat. The salute was taken by Brig P R Denning, the Deputy Commandant General Royal Marines

Chapter 18: Buglers & Corps of Drums from 1982

This most important period of the development of the RMBS was drawing to a close. The reports, the planning, the discussions and the changes that had so characterised the last ten years were necessary to ensure the future of the RMBS at a sensible and practical size and with the necessary resources.

On the 21st January 1982 the Junior Buglers' training was expanded when the first one-week course on the General Purpose Machine Gun was introduced. This took place at Hythe Ranges and the course included drills, stripping the weapon, stoppage drills, camouflage, concealment and moving with the weapon. Range-work was followed by the AP Weapons Test with all members of the test passing. As an 'extra' the Junior Buglers were introduced to the new Iron Weapon Sight for the SLR.

As a result of the full integration of the Buglers' Branch into the Royal Marines Band Service the re-taking of the Falkland Islands became the first operation in which Buglers officially had a closer working relationship with Musicians than they did with the Commando units. However, there was still one duty that perpetuated the traditional bond between Bugler and marine. On Friday, the 21st May 1982 four Royal Marines were buried at sea and, as this took place, Buglers Naylor and Smith sounded *Last Post*. Another example of the need for a Buglers' Branch with a degree of independence from the Band Service was at establishments such as the Commando Training Centre where Duty Buglers were required. In addition to the regular work of the band the Buglers had also to support and provide for morning parades, daily routine calls and visiting VIPs. At this time, early 1982, the Branch had thirteen ranks under training, seven of whom were expected to pass for duty in April. The Junior Bugler intake for 1982/83 had been reduced yet again, resulting in only two candidates commencing training in April. The Corps Bugler Major, WO1 Crofts, observed that there were still men in the Branch who could recall the time when there were more than eighty in 'Buglers' House' at the RM School of Music.[1] As a result of this low intake the Training Band, for a period of time, had to practise marching and parading without a Corps of Drums. The planned intake for 1984 was eight.

On the 25th February 1983 the Band of Flag Officer Naval Air Command was disestablished and its Corps of Drums dispersed to other bands. FONAC's final 'Blue Band' report made a point of how diverse the work of a small band and Corps of Drums can be. Recent work had included a drums display in front of 10,000 people at Birmingham Exhibition Centre, a concert at the Strode Theatre in Street and one of many appearances on the television magazine programme 'Pebble Mill at One'. This final appearance provided the opportunity to introduce a composition for band and drums called *Time Off* written by Musician (later Major) Phil Watson. An exciting piece that marked a departure in style, it was used in the following year's Royal Albert Hall concert.[2] Planning the display programme for the annual Buglers' Reunion was always a matter for attention to detail and careful rehearsal since the audience comprised the performers' peers and also the branch's very knowing 'old soldiers'. The 1983 programme comprised a balance of the old and the new and opened with the Herald Trumpet fanfare *Ferneham* (Angove) which was composed in 1981 for the opening of Fareham's new concert hall. Traditional beatings were *First Mess Beatings*, *Emblazoned Drums* (Dunn), *Hilton* (Piner), *Pompey No 1's* (anon) and *Salute to Wagstaff* (Piner). The 'new' items were the antiphonal bugle fanfare *Echoes*

1 *Blue Band Vol 33, No 1, p21.*
2 *Blue Band Vol 34, No 1, p15.*

(Piner) and *Drum Scherzo* (Piner), a complex piece of drumming featuring strathspeys, reels, quicks, slows and hornpipes. The finale was the bugle fanfare *Merioneth* (Hayward). As a mark of appreciation for his work on this display Bugler Piner, not the senior NCO, received the glass of port from the saluting officer[3].

Corps Bugle Major A C Crofts retired from the Royal Marines in 1983. He was the first member of the Buglers' Branch to be appointed Warrant Officer 1st Class, Colin Bowden being the first to have been appointed Warrant Officer 2nd Class.

An amusing interlude occurred in November 1984 when SgtBug Gibbs and a group of Musicians and Buglers went to Aviemore for the skiing. They woke up on the first morning to find a total 'white-out'; no ski-ing, all roads impassable. Having assisted the snow-bound villagers they offered their services to the Highland Roads Department who had 300 motorists stranded in Drumochter Pass. With ropes, shovels and their two land-rovers they spent the next, sub-zero, day freeing motorists. Amongst those dug out and 'freed' were 'three land-rovers full of Pongos', a mountain rescue team, various AA vehicles and two snow-ploughs. As well as receiving thanks from the Police and the Roads Department they were pleased to learn that the local radio had announced that 'The Royal Marines were in Drumochter Pass'!

To mark the twenty-fifth anniversary of the issue of the first Herald Trumpets on the 24th March 1959, the original eight trumpets, which were issued to Portsmouth and Plymouth Corps of Drums, were reunited on Plymouth Hoe where a celebratory fanfare was sounded.

In 1987 two Buglers were invited by the Royal British Legion in Rio de Janeiro to take part in their Remembrance Service. This proved very successful and so the invitation was repeated in 1988, CSgtBug Tommy Lawton and Bugler Alan Piner being detailed for the task. A faulty aircraft engine followed by an air traffic controller's dispute meant that they landed at Rio a couple of hours after they should have been playing at the British Legion dinner. The Remembrance Day Service was held in the Anglican Church in Rio and was attended by the British Ambassador and the Naval Attaché to Brazil. *Last Post* and *Reveille* were sounded. That evening they attended a service in an Anglican Church forty miles outside Rio. The Church's normal congregation was about ten people but the attraction of two Royal Marine Buglers boosted this to 54. The wreath was laid by the Consul General. Whilst this was the end of the official duties they were asked if they could stay and play at the cocktail party to mark HMS *Endurance*'s arrival in Rio. Principal Director of Music RM was contacted and gave approval and the two Buglers then prepared for the ship's arrival. They prepared maps for the crew and RM Detachment showing the best 'runs ashore', where to eat and what sights to see. They arranged a party with the US Marines serving at the US Consulate for the RM Detachment. When *Endurance* berthed the two Buglers went on board and joined with the RM Detachment for the Sunset Ceremony.

Two years later Bugler Piner was awarded the British Empire Medal for his contributions to the Buglers' Branch. It was presented to him on board the Royal Yacht by Prince Philip.

The theme of the 1990 Royal Tournament was 'The Sea Soldier' and featured a display from the King's Squad, Royal Marines. The Squad was supported by a large Corps of Drums, the Buglers having arranged suitable music for the display and then rehearsed the intricate display with the Squad.

40 Cdo deployed on exercise in April 1990 taking Bugler McGowan with them. PT every day, SA80 weapon training, acquaints with anti-tank weapons and lectures on electronic warfare, helicopter marshalling and much more filled the Bugler's time as he

3 *Blue Band Vol 34, No 2 p40.*

was integrated into the Unit. During one of his solitary bugle practice sessions he was asked by the CO to play 'The Charge' - meaning the call used by the US Cavalry in the movies. When Exercise *Dragon Hammer* began the Bugler was with Commando HQ. Alpha Company moved forward to attack the 'enemy' positions, held by the USMC and the French Foreign Legion, and the Bugler was ordered to go with them. As they advanced to contact enemy fire broke out and the Bugler heard the immortal words shouted by the Sergeant Major, 'Bugler, sound the Charge'!

The exercise was followed by a period of cross-training with the NATO forces, and as part of this training the Bugler was included in the SPIE-rigging (Special Patrols Insertion Extraction). Ten men wearing special harnesses clip onto ropes hanging from a Chinook helicopter which then lifts them for a twenty minute flight over the mountains. After this he was put with Bravo Company and took part in live firing exercises.

The following year Bugler Bolton served as ship's Bugler on board HMS *Edinburgh* when she deployed to the United States. On board he was trained as Bosun's Mate which enabled him to steer the ship during a six hour watch. Exercises were interspersed with a great many individual Ceremonial Sunsets. The ship represented Great Britain and the Royal Navy during Operation *Desert Storm* ceremonies. Bugler Bolton opened the New York ticker-tape parade by sounding 'Colours' and was featured on New York television. This Bugler must have a strong claim to being the last member of the Royal Marines Band Service to wear the Green Beret.

The Royal Navy Volunteer Band movement is ably supported by the Royal Marines Band Service through a variety of ways but principally through Volunteer Band Instructors. These are Bandmaster qualified Musicians who provide instruction, training and administration in return for the opportunity to gain experience in preparation for becoming a Bandmaster with a Royal Marines band. During the period 1992-1994 Corps Drum Major John Griffiths decided that Volunteer Band Corps of Drums should also benefit from the experience and skills of the Royal Marines Band Service. He sent Bugler Lee Cullen, with the rank of Acting CplBug as a Bugler Volunteer Band Instructor to all of the Volunteer Bands at home, abroad and on board ship.

Periodically Buglers are detached to accompany major ship deployments. Two Buglers were part of HMS *Invincible*'s company when she sailed for the Adriatic in support of United Nations' efforts in Yugoslavia/Bosnia. The Buglers' role, apart from working with the band and training its Corps of Drums, was as 'Posties' in the Mail Office. Having Buglers on board allowed the ship's band to broaden its repertoire to include, amongst other things, the ceremony of Sunset.

In 1993 new ground was broken when Bugler Alan Piner, whose belief in a new project was strong enough to convince the Principal Director of Music amongst others of its importance, sounded all of the bugle calls used by the Royal Marines and Royal Navy. These were recorded, as was a Colours ceremony, a number of marches and salutes and then the story of a day in the life of a Royal Marines Barracks through the duties of a Bugler was narrated by Richard Baker. This was almost a curtain-call for Bugler Piner, since later in the same year he retired after a career spanning forty years. He served in eleven ships and with five Commando Units including 42 Cdo Pipe Band, which he joined in 1967 as Lead Drummer. Bugler Piner's contribution to the Royal Marines Band Service generally and the Buglers' Branch in particular was significant, it being generally acknowledged that he was the man who pushed forward the boundaries of what was composed for, and played by, Buglers and who, by example, imbued those who followed him with a similar desire to continually raise the standards.

Four Buglers from Deal flew to Kiev to provide Mess Beatings for the British Ambassador, also taking the opportunity to visit the Ukrainian Ministry of Defence Band, during 1994. Two other Buglers served on board HMS *Ark Royal* during her 1994 deployment. Whilst on board they recruited, taught and choreographed three of the ship's company into a Corps of Drums. 1994 and 1995 were particularly busy years for the RMBS and especially the Buglers' Branch with requests for support for the Second World War Anniversaries coming from all over the world.

The transfer of the Royal Marines School of Music from Deal to Portsmouth in 1996 occurred when, for several years, no Royal Marines Buglers had been trained. Reductions in the number of bands had resulted in the status quo being maintained and the instructional staff had concentrated on teaching cadets, and also students from abroad. On completion of the Massed Bands Beating Retreat on Horse Guards Parade in 1996 the Corps Bugle Major was able to report that the Branch consisted of sixty-eight all ranks serving in five bands, the School of Music and with himself, as Branch Advisor, based at HQ RMBS. Rank structure consisted of one Warrant Officer (1st Class) - the Corps Bugle Major, two WO2s, five CSgts, ten Sgts, eleven Cpls and thirty-nine Buglers. It was intended that at least six New Entry Buglers would be selected for training as part of the School's 1996 intake. He also reported that new styles of drumming and stickwork were being introduced and incorporated into routines. In addition new and important compositions were being produced by the Branch.

In 1994 the International Military Music Society was invited to visit the RM Portsmouth Band. The talented Corps of Drums, seen here, produced three Corps Bugle Majors, one Bugle Major and three Drum Majors. © John Ambler

Early in 1997 the Band Service had two bands deployed, one on the Royal Yacht and the other on HMS *Illustrious* (Ex *Ocean Wave*), each with a Drum Major and four Buglers. In addition a Bugler was deployed on board HMS *Fearless* which was also taking part in Ex *Ocean Wave*. It was anticipated that a proposed reduction from sixty-seven all ranks to sixty-two would be achieved through retirement and early leavers. It was also hoped that ten New Entry Buglers would be accepted in the forthcoming auditions. A training course for Drum Majors took place, for the first time, at HMS *Raleigh* which was felt to be a much better location than the School. This training base could provide good parade-ground facilities and access to the educational facilities and experts in subjects such as Military Law. All four candidates were successful, each achieving good passes.

In 1997 changes to the position of Branch Advisor took place. It had been traditional for the Corps Bugle Major to be the Branch Advisor, usually at WO1 level. However, in 1997 it was decided that either the Corps Drum Major or the Corps Bugle Major could be the Branch Advisor and that being WO1 was not a pre-requisite for that appointment. As a result the Corps Bugle Major, WO1 J F O'Connell, reverted to Corps Drum Major and WO2 C Lawton became Corps Bugle Major, combining this with his previous position as Portsmouth Band Bugle Major, and also Branch Advisor. A new Bugle Major, Training was appointed with the task of upgrading all of the Buglers training. This particularly applied to the musical qualifications which needed to reflect the higher professional musical standard now required of a Senior Non-Commissioned Officer, Bugler. Much more emphasis on composition, aural and harmony was to be included and musical studies were to be performed on bugle, drum and E*b* herald trumpet in front of an examining board. Following the 1997 auditions, eleven New Entry Buglers were under training, including the first female.

Due to heavy commitments and unexpected illness the Corps of Drums due to parade at the Cenotaph on Remembrance Sunday 1997 found themselves short of one Bugler. BdSgt Davies quickly exchanged his trumpet for bugle and stepped into the breach, although the sharp-eyed might have spotted the one pair of trousers with a wide red stripe.

The 1998 Mountbatten Festival of Music featured *The Gael,* a piece of music from the soundtrack of the film 'The Last of the Mohicans'. In order to give it authenticity some of the Buglers appeared in period uniforms - which were 'run up' by Bugler Jackson who, not long before, had built a series of sound baffles for the Portsmouth Band Concert Hall. To continue these examples of handicraft talents provided by members of the Buglers' Branch, Bugler Scollick hand-painted all of the period drums used during *The Gael.* 1999 was to be a year of, by current standards, substantial sea-time for the Buglers. Four were deployed to HMS *Ocean* and one rank to each of HM Ships *Fearless* and *Glasgow,* with three ranks on board HMS *Marlborough.* Some aspects of the commands given during Beat Retreat on Horse Guards were to be altered to the extent that the Buglers were enjoying telling the bands that the Musician's old adage of 'just switch off and follow Stix' would no longer apply once rehearsals began!

The years of 1998 and 1999 were particularly notable for the endeavours of Bugle Major Platts, the School's Bugle Major and his team of Instructors. The standards of the Specialist Qualification courses for military side drum, B*b* bugle and E*b* herald trumpet were raised with the resultant success rate being very good. In addition, and for the first time, all the Buglers at the RM School of Music were examined on the military side drum by the Guildhall School of Music. The results speak for themselves: two High Honours, seven Honours and one Merit. All four New Entries were given High Honours. In the winter of 1999 the Bugle Major, the Drum Professor and an Instructor from the School visited the Percussive Arts Society International Conference in Ohio and were able not only to watch, listen and take part with some of the greatest Drummers and Corps of Drums in the world, but also to discuss the latest equipment and techniques.

The first Drum Majors' Course of the 21st century included a slight change to the traditional format. The two-week drill phase was followed by three weeks spent learning the duties of a Company Sergeant Major. All four students passed the course. The Buglers' Reunion, which followed a few weeks later, featured a display that covered the history of the Buglers' Branch from the raising of the Marine Companies (with Drummers) in 1664. This series of displays, which were linked by narrative, proved enormously successful and well received by the audience of more than a hundred serving and retired Buglers. During the summer two members of the Branch were deployed as Ship's Buglers: Bugler Needham to HMS *Manchester* bound for the West Indies, and Bugler Sumner to HMS *Newcastle* sailing to Singapore. The Royal Military Tattoo 2000 on Horse Guards Parade was far from being an outdoor Royal Tournament. One hundred and eighty three pieces of music from the massed corps of drums and the massed bands of all services required the Drum Majors to work to fine tolerances as they moved their bands to suit the scenes that were being enacted in front, to the sides and in rear of them, often involving fast moving vehicles or galloping horses. The Corps Drum Major, WO1 Bugler A D Bridges RM, led the team of Tri-Service

Drum Majors. One of his first problems was that he could not brief his team until all of the scenes had been decided, the music selected, displays rehearsed and timings checked. By the time these had been decided only two weeks were left for the Drum Majors to plan, prepare, rehearse and become proficient in a ninety minute marching display involving seven major bands from different services. Planning and rehearsal techniques developed by Royal Marine Buglers and Drum Majors, plus the relationship built up between Drum Majors, band sergeants major and senior non-commissioned officers at recent Tri-Service events, were of major importance. To the Drum Majors and the drums were added the front rank of the Guards and the RAF bands for the important march through to taped music and then, when familiar with the music, they marched and sang. The Royal Marines' practice of then adding the bands, without their instruments, further developed the display by highlighting and then overcoming any problems that occurred as well as allowing the familiarising of all individuals with their part in the display. Knowing that communication would be difficult because of the distances and sound levels involved, the Drum Majors planned most of the movements to suit the music so that Musicians could mark their march-cards. Communication within the ranks was also encouraged. The event was an outstanding success, much of it due to the work of the Drum Majors of all three services led by those of the Royal Marines.

A few days later Horse Guards Parade was the venue for the massed bands of all three services as the Nation paid homage to HM The Queen Mother on the occasion of her 100th birthday. A great number of civilian organisations took part and, in this instance, the planning needed to suit the size of each group and the time required for each of them to march past (or walk, trot, run etc). Whilst adaptability and flexibility were required on the day, the performance still required careful planning.

Plymouth Band were due to fly to Malaysia for a twelve day tour when, shortly before rehearsals, Plymouth's Drum Major broke his ankle. The Corps Drum Major packed, travelled to Plymouth for rehearsals and then, with a band SNCO, travelled ahead of the band as the advance party.

Following the announcement that, under the new 'Pay 2000' arrangements, the Buglers' Branch would be paid less than Musicians, nine representative members of the branch were selected from all ranks to be assessed by the Joint Services Evaluation Team. Questionnaires and individual interviews were followed by a visit from the Evaluation Team. As a result of the strength of the cases made the announcement was reversed; Buglers would continue to receive the same pay as Musicians.

The CTC Corps of Drums with members of the current King's Squad gave an immaculate display of drill on Jim Davidson's 'Generation Game' television show in February 2001. In the summer of 2001 the Portsmouth Corps of Drums gave a display of drum beatings in the television show 'Star Lives' which featured Russ Abbott. Following a tour of Russia, Plymouth Band returned to England leaving a four man Corps of Drums to join HMS *Illustrious* in Oslo for The Queen's Birthday celebrations.

Four Buglers passed out of basic training in November 2000 and began the newly designed and extended musical stage of training in January 2001, scheduled to Pass Out and join their bands in January 2003.

High profile events in 2001 included the Mountbatten Festival of Music, the International Festival of the Sea and the Presentation of Colours to the three Commando Units that comprise 3 Commando Brigade on Plymouth Hoe. This latter event featured the traditional, but not often used, sight of the Corps Bugle Major leading the Corps of Drums as they marched the old Colours onto the Parade.

Many of those who had played and marched on Horse Guards Parade to celebrate The Queen Mother's 100th birthday in 2000 found themselves on parade at her funeral in 2002. With draped drums, staff and Drum Major's belt the solemn ceremonial was immaculately carried out.

Later in 2002 four members of Scotland Band's Corps of Drums were flown out to Dubai for a high profile engagement on board HMS *Ocean* in the presence of CGRM. At the other end of the spectrum, back in the UK, CplBug Andy Finn got so fed-up playing with the band for the Brickwood's Field Gun Run competition and getting really wet that he joined the field gun crew and got even wetter!

As 2002 ended preparations were put in place to cover the anticipated fire-fighter's strike. Both the preparations and the strike cover, Op *Telic*, are described elsewhere in this publication; needless to say that all members of the Buglers' Branch were involved. During 2003 a small orchestra and the Corps of Drums from the RM Band of Britannia Royal Naval College travelled to Washington DC for the annual Trafalgar Night celebrations at the British Embassy. The 2003 Massed Bands Beating Retreat on Horse Guards Parade was severely curtailed by the Firefighter's strike. It was also the final event for Corps Drum Major Bridges before his retirement. Instead of Masses Bands, a band of ninety plus the Fanfare Trumpet team performed for the Captain General, HM The Queen and 550 invited guests in the gardens of Buckingham Palace. Just a few weeks before the event the Corps Drum Major and the Corps Bugle Major designed and planned the event. A week later, and with a sound recording of the programme music, they took the Portsmouth Corps of Drums to Whale Island to test the planned display against the music. When the Musicians arrived in Portsmouth they were incorporated into the rehearsals, which took just two and a half days to complete. The event itself was a complete success, albeit a disappointment for those who could not get to see it live, and for those who would normally watch the television coverage.

2004 began with a Drum Majors' Course, the first to be organised by the new Corps Drum Major WO2 J Whitwham at HMS *Raleigh*. All four candidates were successful, each gaining superior passes. The following month was February and traditionally that means the Mountbatten Festival of Music which, once again, was an outstanding success and, as always, managed to showcase the breadth of skills and the variety of music that the RMBS can provide. A few months later the same men and women were doing what they are renowned for, impeccable marching displays and leading important parades as the 60th Anniversary events related to the Second World War were remembered.

An unusual task was given to two Plymouth Band Buglers. Having been flown to Alexandria, Egypt, they played at a ceremony for the reburial of some of Nelson's sailors who had been killed at the Battle of the Nile. Originally buried on Nelson's Island they had been exhumed and were to be re-buried in the Chatby Military Cemetery. Coffin parties were provided by HMS *Chatham* and the ceremony went very well despite a sand-storm. The two Buglers also went on board the ship, at the 'invitation' of her Captain, to perform the Sunset ceremony that evening.

During the summer of 2005 the Buglers' Branch was very busy with the International Fleet Review off Spithead, the International Drum-Head Service on Southsea Common and then the four-day International Festival of the Sea in Portsmouth Dockyard. These events were followed by the VE and VJ-Day celebrations and then, lasting into the autumn came the series of events that became known as 'T200' - the 200th Anniversary of the British Fleet's victory at Trafalgar and of the death of Admiral Lord Nelson. As well as all of these events two of the bands, Plymouth and BRNC, also covered the Edinburgh Military

Tattoo. During the same period four Portsmouth Buglers went, with the band, to Dubai for the annual St George's Association Ball, a concert and a Beat Retreat. Five Buglers from the same band went to Russia. This included a visit to the British Embassy in Moscow and then to Murmansk for the anniversary of the Russian convoys, which was attended by HRH the Duke of York and thousands of veterans.

It was at this time that the Corps Bugle Major, WO1 Platts, took the opportunity to review, in the RMBS journal, the recent developments in the training of Buglers. He wrote: "Just over six years ago we began to push the boundaries regarding our performance standards at both Grade Eight and Certificate level with the Guildhall School of Music. Over the past three or four years, this latter level has been fully embraced and accepted across the Corps of Drums and the high marks attained by our individuals have been noted by the Guildhall. Unfortunately we have recently found ourselves in a situation whereby the Guildhall was not able to offer a higher level of performance for the foreseeable future; neither did they have a clear directive when it would become available - if at all. It was during this interim period that the Guildhall School of Music and Trinity [College] amalgamated and became known as Trinity/Guildhall. I was introduced to the Director of Music and the Chief Examiner of Trinity who were both aware of our recent successes with the Guildhall and [were interested] in developing a further level of examination based upon Trinity's ideals. In view of our performance achievements, innovative training and forward-thinking principles, I am now delighted to announce Trinity's acceptance of Associate level (ATCL) for the snare drum. Without doubt, I believe the Trinity/Guildhall partnership has thrown the gauntlet to the Associated Board's international domination in the examining world and they have subsequently mapped-out a unique and challenging opportunity within the music industry. Furthermore, this venture in conjunction with the Associated Board's diploma project (exclusive to Buglers within the Royal Marines Band Service) has provided me with a great sense of optimism for our future identity, both within the Band Service and the wider music world. At last, the beginning of widespread recognition and common acceptance of our unique profession."

This summary includes a reference to the serving Buglers who, over the past few years, had succeeded in learning, practising and then passing the examinations necessary to meet these new standards, and this in the face of the level of work required of them.

The Corps Bugle Major also gave his views on a subject whose beginnings have never been satisfactorily explained, stick drill. Questions about why this is done, does it relate to signalling, and why the Buglers changed from wooden to white painted sticks are frequently asked. Some attempt to find a plausible explanation but none have yet succeeded. Stick drill, now more commonly known as stick work, is not written down. The only references to stick positions or movements in BR13, 'The Bugler's Handbook', relate to 'attention' - arms lowered and hands holding sticks together over the drum; and also 'The Ready' - arms raised, sticks held horizontally in line with mouth, right stick above left, tips overlapping by about an inch. BR2118 'Royal Marines Drill' also refers to the above plus the positions of the sticks whilst standing at ease, and the positions after cease playing, on the march not playing, marching at ease and the resumption of playing after marching at ease. Neither stick drill nor stick work whilst marching, or performing beatings on the move or at the halt, is mentioned. It was the belief of the Corps Bugle Major that stick drill should develop and new stick movements should be used if they complemented the composition.[4] However, he qualified this by insisting that such developments should be used sparingly for fear of their effect being diluted through over-exposure. He used the example of the 'ripple' which, it is believed, was first used at the 1996 Mountbatten

4 *In relation to Drum or Mess Beatings, drum statics or as part of a performance featuring band and drums eg 'Riverdance'.*

Festival of Music as part of the Corps of Drums' contribution to *Riverdance*: "It is worth pointing out that approximately ten years ago we introduced slow stick work, not as a training or operational requirement but something that could add diversity to our repertoire. There were concerns at the time; however, over a relatively short period, these initial apprehensions slowly diminished and it is now a regular feature in many pieces we perform". He then went on to make the point that the design of the stick work, or rudiments, was an integral part of the Drummer's trade, as much as scales are for other instrumentalists, and that Buglers compositions should "incorporate fluency, control and Musicianship". All of these comments were of course based upon the fact that the Buglers' Branch is totally reliant upon self-generated compositions and fully dependent upon individual initiative and motivation.

In March 2005 the Corps Bugle Major and Portsmouth Corps of Drums were involved in a major recruitment presentation at the Royal Opera House as part of 'National Percussion Day'.

Later in the year, 2005, the Plymouth Corps of Drums, with a Clarinet Quintet, went to Riyadh in Saudi Arabia where they were both involved in a variety show with drum beatings, the clarinet quartet, jazz group, folk group and a 'Generation Game', at the International School. Beat Retreat and *Sunset* was provided for the RAF's Battle of Britain celebrations and also a Trafalgar Night Dinner at which the guests included the British Ambassador and the Commandant General Royal Marines. At this dinner the Corps of Drums' contribution was crowned by them leading the singing of the sea shanties.

2006 was a year when, unexpectedly, opportunities arose for promotions within the Branch - situation that had not been anticipated prior to 2007. As a result a promotion was made to each of the CSgt, Sgt and Cpl ranks. It was also noted that although promotion within the Branch had been very slow for a number of years, a number of senior personnel would be leaving in the next three years which would open up promotional opportunities. As ever promotion was based upon the availability of 'dead men's shoes' and not just ability.

Planning and preparations for the 2006 Beating Retreat on Horse Guards Parade once again highlighted the restrictions imposed by such small numbers. Forty Buglers were available with a manning margin of 10% as spares. In the event this margin was barely enough. Like the Corps Drum Major, this was the Corps Bugle Majors' first 'Horse Guards', as it is known, and each was determined to make their mark on the occasion. Items were introduced to enhance the exposure of the Buglers' Branch. An additional, and new, bugle fanfare within the customary preliminaries; the Corps Bugle Major conducted the Band and Bugle Fanfare. The usual 'Minstrels' Turn' by the Buglers was omitted and the Advanced in Review Order to the tune of *British Grenadiers* took place but without the drums playing. The *pièce de resistance* for the Buglers was their marching display to the emotive and exciting *Gladiator*. The impact and success of this piece of music was dependent upon two lines of Buglers, each twenty strong, advancing towards each other and, at precisely the right time, beginning to turn so that they formed one straight line of Buglers on the penultimate

The Corps of Drums lead the Massed Bands along the Mall and around the Victoria Memorial on completion of the Ceremony of Beat Retreat on Horse Guards Parade 2006. (Image courtesy of Les Scriver)

The Rehearsal on Horse Guards Parade for the 2009 Massed Bands Beat Retreat. Two views of the Corps of Drums' Beating Retreat display, and an image showing the five Drum Majors leading the split Massed Bands during the bugle march. The Fanfare Team stand at ease in front of the Guards Memorial

The future: Corps Bugle Major A J Piner leads forward the Corps of Drums of the Royal Marines School of Music during the 2010 RMSoM Pass-out Parade in the Portsmouth Guildhall Square.

beat and halted on the final beat of the music. During rehearsals this had been difficult to achieve but by sheer professionalism, by the key positioning of the most experienced Buglers and by communicating and respecting each others' ability they reached the point where they were able to continually repeat this manoeuvre successfully. On Horse Guards Parade this was stunning.

Whilst the BBC broadcast, as usual, the 2006 Ceremony of Beating Retreat on Horse Guards Parade they chose not to support the same event in 2009.

However, in 2009, the Mountbatten Festival of Music was recorded on DVD. The musical programme was carefully devised to include items that had a strong visual content and also some favourites from previous years, such as *Riverdance*.

During the 2010 Mountbatten Festival of Music the Corps of Drums produced a performance that showed, to great effect, their skills, diversity and entertainment value. Following typical Corps of Drums support to the 'Glenn Miller Band', drum beatings using brooms, dustbins, water barrels, tins and anything else that could be beaten held the audience enthralled and earned the loudest and longest ovation of the show. This set of images from the rehearsal shows them fronting the Glenn Miller Band: the percussive 'sweepers'; the 'Stomp' style drums and the Stompers in 'competition' with a highly disciplined Royal Marines Corps of Drums. (Images courtesy of Les Scriver)

Chapter 19: The Portsmouth Band from 1982

A few months after the death of Earl Mountbatten of Burma, BBC Radio Solent, in conjunction with Southampton City Council, presented a tribute to Mountbatten which took the form of a concert and simultaneous radio broadcast. This was followed by the release of a recording. HRH The Prince of Wales was the guest of honour and the musical programme was played by the Band of Naval Home Command directed by Capt G A C Hoskins.

1986 opened with HMY *Britannia* en route to New Zealand where the Royal Family would join her. Having just passed through the Suez Canal news was received of civil war breaking out in Aden. The Queen agreed that the Yacht should assist in Operation *Balzac*, the evacuation of British nationals from Aden. The crew transformed the Royal Yacht into an evacuation ship, including a large sick-bay, and the members of the band were all assigned tasks for helping the evacuees when they came aboard. The Bandmaster (R C Grainger) and the Drum Major (J K Griffiths) were to be immigration officers with the remainder of the band divided into beach, stores and stretcher parties. HMS *Jupiter* and HMS *Newcastle* joined the Yacht and, when the situation ashore was felt to be at crisis point, the Yacht was ordered to move towards Khormaksar Beach, close to the British Embassy. The boats were unable to beach so the men from the Yacht had to carry the children and the injured from the beach to the boats. The fighting was getting heavier with tanks and artillery now engaged. Damage was widespread. The ship sailed for Djibouti to land the evacuees and, on the way, the band 'rigged up' and gave a concert on the Veranda deck. The Yacht returned to Zinjibar and then Little Aden and, after taking more refugees aboard, returned to Djibouti. By the end of the emergency 1,068 men, women and children of 55 different nationalities had been brought aboard and, as always, the band had thrown itself into assisting in any way it could - from musical concerts and entertainment to carrying bags of rice and warming baby bottles.[1]

On 31st October 1991 the last Royal Marine units still based at Eastney, led by the band of C-in-C Naval Home Command, marched out of the RM Barracks, the band being relocated a few miles to the west in Eastney Block, HMS *Nelson*. A display was given in the Portsmouth Guildhall Square as part of the closure ceremonies and the Corps flag at RM Eastney was hauled down for the last time, on this occasion by two members of the Band Service.

On the 1st April 1994 the cumbersome, and by now almost meaningless, title of the 'Band of Her Majesty's Royal Marines Commander-in-Chief Naval Home Command' was dispensed with, and replaced by the traditional 'Band of HM RM Portsmouth' albeit without the 'Division' or 'Group' to link it directly to the Corps. In 1996 the RMSM band was disestablished giving further responsibilities to the Portsmouth Band who, as well as meeting their usual

During the 1994 IMMS visit Captain D Cole conducted his Portsmouth Band and Corps of Drums in Lt Col Sir Vivian Dunn's 'Prelude to the Morning'. © *John Ambler*

1 *It is believed that this is the only time that the Royal Yacht was used in her originally anticipated 'dual role'.*

The Corps of Drums feature in 'Prelude to the Morning'.
© John Ambler

commitments, would have to support the training programmes, particularly the Bandmasters' Course.

During 1997 the Portsmouth Band attended the Nova Scotia Tattoo whilst the Royal Yacht contingent were on board for the world cruise that included a visit to Hong Kong where they massed with Plymouth Band for the hand-over ceremony.

In the UK one of the largest engagements for the Band Service was the International Festival of the Sea held in Portsmouth Naval Base. The Portsmouth and CTC Bands gave concerts and marching displays over the three-day period with 11,500 people attending the massed band concert on the Sunday evening.

The Royal Yacht Band was aboard when Britannia left Portsmouth for the last time on 20th October 1997. They visited eight major ports around the UK including the Pool of London where the ship was used for a dinner for Senior Naval Officers and also accommodation for European Royal Families who had come to London for the Golden Wedding celebrations of The Queen and The Duke of Edinburgh. On 22nd November she entered Portsmouth flying her paying-off pennant and came alongside South Railway Jetty. On 11th December the Service of Thanksgiving and Decommissioning Ceremony took place. The finale was provided by the Royal Yacht Band and took the form of a traditional Beat Retreat. The Band had the final, unspoken, word. At the end of an emotional ceremony they stepped off, marched along the jetty playing *Heart of Oak*, countermarched towards The Queen playing *A Life on the Ocean Wave* and, as they approached her, the Director of Music and the Drum Major saluted The Queen before again countermarching. The band broke into *Auld Lang Syne* and for probably the first, and only, time the Drum Major and the Director of Music, together at the front of the band, saluted the great ship as they marched her full length before the band turned and left the jetty.

RM Portsmouth Band plays on board HMY Britannia on one of the many occasions that she sailed from Portsmouth. © John Ambler

Following the ceremony The Queen and Duke of Edinburgh expressed a desire that the Portsmouth Band should retain its Royal Duty status by continuing to accompany Her Majesty on Royal tours. A few weeks later The Queen conferred the title 'Royal Band' upon the Portsmouth Band.

As 1997 ended so did the routine that 'the Portsmouth Band' had developed, and become accustomed to, during almost fifty years. No more Eastney Barracks - home of the Royal Marine Artillery Band since 1868 and then Portsmouth Divisional Band; no longer the honour and prestige of serving on board the Royal Yacht. In addition, messes were now to be shared with the Royal Navy. In the place of this way of life had come new responsibilities, duties and links to its near-neighbour within the Portsmouth Naval Base - the Higher Training Department of the Royal Marines School of Music. Also, regular annual commitments, once shared by the bands of C-in-C Naval Home Command, C-in-C Fleet and the Staff Band of the Royal Marines School of Music, became the responsibility of the Portsmouth Band.

In 1998 it was announced that Captain David Cole had been awarded the MVO and Musn John 'Shiner' Wright the RVM for their services on board the Royal Yacht. 'Shiner' was only the second Musician ever to receive this award, the first being Musician Huw 'Taff' Morris in 1997. Prior to 'Taff''s award only Colour Sergeants and Warrant Officers were awarded the RVM.

1998 also saw the band take part in one of the annual series of concerts held at Kneller Hall, the Army's School of Music. Student Bandmasters conducted the concert with the exception of *Trafalgar* which was conducted by Principal Director of Music, Lt Col Richard Waterer. In May a band of twenty-four left from Heathrow Airport for a visit to St Petersburg. They landed at Helsinki, transferred to HMS *Somerset* and sailed into St Petersburg. After the first marching display the Bandmaster, WO1 John Kelly, was presented with a bouquet, as was the Drum Major, Mark Snell. Having a staff in one hand and a bouquet in the other proved too much of a challenge for him as his first signal after the step-off would be to 'wheel' - so he 'presented' his bouquet to the Bandmaster! A joint outdoor concert with the Russian Navy Band of St Petersburg proved to be fraught with disaster as the electrical power supply blew up; this was fixed just before it poured with rain and then, just as John Kelly stepped up to make his speech, the church bell-ringers commenced their weekly practice! Next day's march around the Peterhof Palace resulted in another soaking from a cloudburst. This ended the march without a note of music being played. This was quite fortunate since the band had left its music in the hotel. The final day saw a successful 'play-off' for HMS *Somerset* and then the band flew home. A week later a section of Portsmouth band left for an eleven day trip to Poland in HMS *Invincible*. The dance band, the jazz quintet and string quartet entertained the various messes whilst the Buglers provided mess beatings and drum routines. Band personnel assisted in a ship's exercise by acting as bloodied and burnt victims of a hangar fire. The first performance once Poland was reached was a Beat Retreat in the ship's hangar for six hundred guests. The band played at a Memorial Service at the Westerplatte monument, the band wheeling into position next to the Polish Navy Band. This was followed by a Beat Retreat in Gdansk, then back to the ship where the Jazz Quintet entertained the Polish Defence Minister and many other guests. The following day consisted of sailing to Sopot for a concert and Beat Retreat on the jetty and a String Quartet at the Ambassador's Reception in Gdansk. The band then returned to Portsmouth on *Invincible*. The rest of the year continued with the usual heavy programme of concerts and parades plus an 'International Festival of the Sea' in Portsmouth and a trip to the Brisbane International Tattoo.

2001 saw the Portsmouth Band combining with BRNC Band for the second International Festival of the Sea in Portsmouth Naval Base. About 9,000 people watched the Gala Concert, the festival's final event and the culmination of several days of parades, Beating Retreat and Big Band concerts. Following this hectic event the band de-stressed with a week of adventure training. Other musical events included a welcoming ceremony for two visiting Chinese warships and the Submarine Association's 100th Anniversary which included a Service in Westminster Abbey attended by HM The Queen and Prince Philip. Another annual engagement was the St George's Society Ball at the Grosvenor House Hotel which required orchestra, dance band and a parade band for Beating Retreat.

The first training concert of 2002 took place in January and included Captain Nick Grace joining the Bandmasters' course to take his Director of Music examination. The concert also featured a piano concerto composed by Major Phil Watson. This concert was followed by military training, a package that covered weapon handling and Nuclear, Biological and Chemical warfare. This was completed a week before the Mountbatten Festival of Music. On completion of this important and successful series of concerts the band completed concerts in Buxton, Leeds and Leamington Spa, returning briefly to Portsmouth before a concert in Chatham for the Chatham Cadets. Four members of the band were sent to help Medical Squadron, Commando Logistic Regiment on exercise in Sennybridge.

The Band then went on leave but was urgently recalled upon the death of Her Majesty Queen Elizabeth, The Queen Mother. Like all State funerals the organisation was already in place, enabling musical rehearsals and band drill to commence immediately. This initially took place in HMS *Nelson* but soon moved to London. On completion the band returned to Portsmouth to support the Bandmasters' course in the final, orchestral, Spring Concert. The summer was full of engagements related to The Queen's Jubilee celebrations. On Jubilee Day itself the Portsmouth Band, supplemented with ranks from BRNC Band, were the only band to form up within the gates of Buckingham Palace for The Queen's procession to St Paul's Cathedral. This, usually regarded as the preserve of the Bands of the Brigade of Guards, was regarded as a great honour by the Portsmouth Band (the 'Royal Band'). Later, as part of the massed bands, they provided music for the performers taking part in the procession for the Royal Family.

The Queen then visited Portsmouth as part of her Jubilee Tour and Portsmouth Band provided a parade band as part of the Tri-Service display, and also a major part of the Tri-Service orchestra that played during the Royal lunch.

June 2002 also saw the 20th anniversary of Op *Corporate*. Portsmouth Band was involved in the remembrance parade and march past in Gosport and the Falklands Memorial Service in Pangbourne College, attended by HRH The Duke of York and Major General Julian Thompson. This period also saw the band's participation in the annual Graspan Parade in London, King George's Fund for Sailors concerts in Portsmouth and Worthing, Portsmouth Lord Mayor's Parade, displays in Blenheim Palace, at Greenwich and the Corps Museum and then a concert at Margate before adventure training in Wales. Rehearsals and preparations for a trip to the USA followed, the main event being a Beating Retreat Ceremony at the British Embassy in Washington. Heavy rain just before the ceremony necessitated the band being reduced in size and an indoor routine rehearsed. Then the weather changed again and the original, outdoor, routine was carried out. On return to Portsmouth the band were on hand to play the march compositions of Lt Col Richard Waterer as he left HMS *Nelson* for retirement. Summer leave was curtailed for the unlucky members of the band required for a Tri-Service Searchlight Tattoo at Fort Nelson, Portsmouth. Queen Alexandra's Royal Naval Nursing Service centenary was marked by a concert by the Portsmouth Band in Portsmouth Cathedral. This was followed by rehearsals and concerts in Bexhill and Monmouth before deployment on board HMS *Ark Royal*. The three-week deployment included crew entertainment on the journey to Gibraltar where the procedure for entering and leaving harbour took place. Entertainment by various combinations continued during the trip to Malta where the band Beat Retreat on deck and played ashore. On return to Portsmouth the first event was the first Training Concert of the autumn. Whilst the band rehearsed in St Mary's Church a WW2 500lb bomb was discovered, causing the dockyard area to be evacuated. Fortunately a quick-witted Band Sergeant managed to gather up most of the band uniforms as he went - leaving only two members of the band 'looking like work experience applicants in their civilian attire'. About this time a Brass Quintet travelled to Japan for the regular English Festival. Work continued through the autumn, accompanied by increasing threats of the Fire-fighters Union calling a strike. As the threat increased so did the work rate of the Band Secretary and a carefully selected team. Lists of fire fighting personnel, drivers and ranks required for Breathing Apparatus and Recovery Teams were published. Training and reorganisation took place at the same time as musical engagements were selectively cancelled and personnel were redistributed to suit the developing situation.

In 2003, on completion of Op *Fresco* and a deployment to Iraq as part of Op *Telic*, both described elsewhere, Portsmouth Band had the opportunity to travel to St Petersburg to celebrate the 300th Anniversary of the naming of that city. They took part in a parade along Nevsky Prospect, gave two concerts at Peter and Paul's Fortress and a tattoo featuring bands from all over Europe. The band also travelled to Moscow to Beat Retreat at the British Embassy. Some members of the band went to Italy for a birthday party in Florence where, amongst other things, they Beat Retreat for the guests. Whilst this was going on the remainder of the band were performing a number of concerts in the Huddersfield area - a regular tour for this band. These diverse events were followed by a trip to France where the band Beat Retreat alongside HMS *Cardiff* at Angouleme. Next day they Beat Retreat in the barracks of the same town and gave a joint concert with a French band in the evening before returning to Portsmouth and the familiar programme of training concerts, military training, adventure training, KGFS concerts and other events.

The busy routine continues year on year with occasional special events or anniversaries giving the opportunity for the band, or parts of the band, to experience new places, music and events. The other factors that have impacted upon the life of Portsmouth Band since the turn of the century, apart from becoming the band responsible for training duties, include the increased need to improve physical fitness, broaden the ability to perform as part of the regular Corps and be able to fit quickly and seamlessly into the Commando Logistic Regiment or the teams on board RFA *Argus* as required.

'Trafalgar 200' was the major event of 2005, involving all of the bands at various times but with Portsmouth Band, not surprisingly, usually taking the lead. The first event, the International Fleet Review off Spithead in June saw Royal Marines Bands strategically deployed around the Fleet. This was followed by an International Drum-Head Service at the Royal Naval War Memorial, Southsea, at which the Band of the Commando Training Centre joined with the Portsmouth Band, the Portsmouth Cathedral Choir and local school children. Some 10,000 people attended the event. The finale was another International Festival of the Sea, a four-day event within the Portsmouth Naval Base.

The 200th Anniversary events continued into and through October and included musical support for the Trafalgar Despatch Parade in London and beacon lighting in the Victory Arena which The Queen attended and which was shown live on BBC television. Celebrations ended with the large parade band in Trafalgar Square and many quartets and small orchestras playing at various dinners. 2006 saw the band split to provide parade bands simultaneously in Dubai and Sydney, Australia. Dubai included a St George's Society Ball, school visits and every ensemble that the RMBS can provide. In Sydney the band, supported by ranks from Plymouth and Lympstone bands, paraded through the city, took part in a three-day Tattoo and were involved in the annual ANZAC celebrations. It was then time to return for Beating Retreat on Horse Guards Parade.

The 2006 November Remembrance Ceremonies again featured a superb display by the Portsmouth Band in the Royal Albert Hall as part of the Royal British Legion Festival of

Drum Major Boorah leads the Portsmouth Band past HMS Victory during the 2005 International Festival of the Sea. (Image courtesy of Les Scriver)

Remembrance. Each year the RMBS has to provide a seven minute display that, whilst maintaining its traditions of military music and precise parade work also features something new and exciting. The full effect of this tends to be lost to those who watch the festival on television due to the cutting and editing that creates a disjointed recording that shows neither aspect at its best. The music selected as 'new and exciting' was certainly that: *Children of Sanchez;* a Latin American piece written by Chuck Mangione was arranged by the RMSoM Warrant Officer Training, Dean McGain-Harding. It featured Musn Mark Upton on flugel horn and Musn Adrian Breen on classical guitar as well as the entire band and Corps of Drums.

Uppermost in the minds of all personnel during 2007 was the developing situation in Afghanistan, including the RMBS's own build-up to deployment and the developments inspired by the Lean Transformation, as well as concerts and fund-raising events. Portsmouth Band were heavily featured in the City of London initiative 'City Salute' which, in a twelve week period, raised £850,000 from City donors for facilities for the wounded at Headley Court and Selly Oak Hospital. The major event was held on the steps of St Paul's Cathedral hosted by Jeremy Clarkson with Royal patrons Prince William and Prince Harry in attendance.

At the end of 2008 the band was flown to Basra to provide musical support to the coalition forces.

The Brass Quintet, Jazz Group and Concert Band entertained and performed a number of carol concerts. Basra had been quiet for a number of weeks but, part way through *Hark the Herald Angels Sing*, the alarms sounded and band and audience immediately took cover.

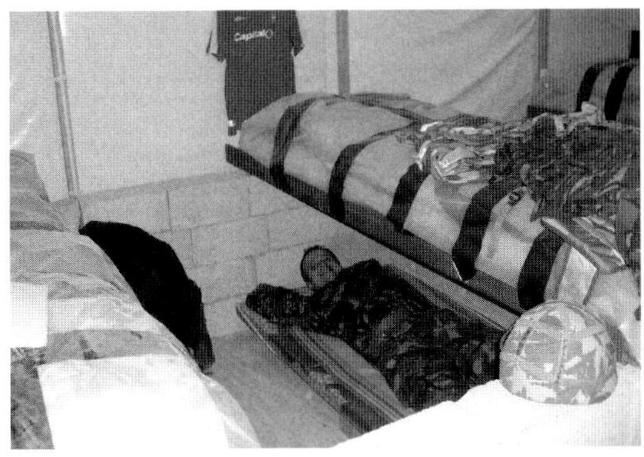

Accommodation - Iraq 2008. Sleeping within, and beneath, the blast protection

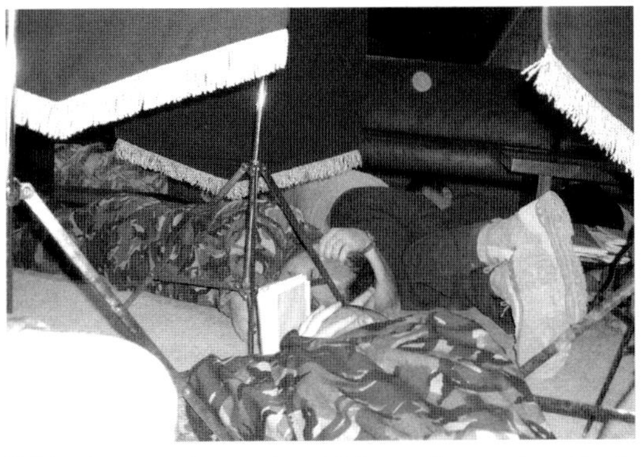

With alarms going and amid fears of a mortar attack, Maj Grace, his band and audience all take cover

Beat Retreats were performed at the Divisional Training Centre at Shaibha and at the Multi-National Division Headquarters. The Brass Quintet also took part in an emotive carol service at the only Christian church in Basra, performing with the choir who sang in English and Arabic.

Maj Grace sings an English Carol to the accompaniment of a Brass Quintet in Basra's only Christian Church

The annual trip to Dubai took place in spring 2009 and included several performances at the Ambassador's Residence plus a number of small concerts and Beat Retreats at local schools. The Woodwind Quartet diverted to Doha in Qatar for an additional performance. The main event of the week was the St George's Society Charity Ball where the orchestra, the parade band and the dance band performed. Whilst one part of Portsmouth Band were in Dubai the other part finished Easter leave and then completed a number of engagements, including the annual Navy versus Army match at Twickenham, the Principal Director of Music's 'Dining Out' and the Windsor Castle Royal Tattoo. The Royal Tattoo required a large band and they were accommodated in the transit blocks at Pirbright. All of these engagements were sandwiched between rehearsals and performance of the Mountbatten Festival of Music and the Massed Bands Beating Retreat on Horse Guards Parade.

Later in the year one of the highlights for this band was the annual St George's Club Ball at the Grosvenor House Hotel, London. The versatility of the Royal Marines Band Service is particularly on display at this event with parade band, orchestra, function band and a team of Herald Fanfare Trumpeters. The band enjoys playing for such a supportive audience who are not ashamed to celebrate this country's long and proud heritage. This was followed by the November ceremonies and a range of Christmas concerts. A few members of the Portsmouth Band were held back from Christmas leave for one final performance which was to 'play in' HMS *Gloucester* as she arrived back from a deployment in the South Atlantic.

Grenade and Cypher Cap Badge with the additional 1954 Cypher

Chapter 20: The Band of HM RM Commando Forces 1982 through to the Band of HM RM, Commando Training Centre, RM

In 1982 the band was called upon to support once again 3 Cdo Bde during a military operation; what was to become known informally as the Falklands War and militarily as Op *Corporate* was about to commence. The military role of the band will be told in detail elsewhere in this book. Maj Gen J J Moore, commanding Commando Forces, Royal Marines and Brig J H A Thompson, who commanded 3 Cdo Bde, wanted the band to function as Musicians as well as in a military role. To this end the band instruments had to be smuggled aboard in one of the large 'chacon' containers since, officially, the band had been ordered to board without them. The Commando Forces Band began by establishing themselves aboard the *Canberra* and removing their instruments from the chacon to the band's new quarters. Next evening a concert was given in the Stadium Bar. The band felt rather uncomfortable that the men watching their concert might be the same men who needed this room when it assumed its emergency role of operating theatre. The band was cross decked to both *Sir Percivale* and HMS *Fearless* to give concerts.

SS *Canberra* paused at Ascension Island for a busy period of stores rationalisation and training at the end of which the band gave a concert for 40 Cdo who were joined by their former CO, Brig Thompson. The first item on the programme was the *William Tell Overture*, which began to a stunned silence. However the 'Lone Ranger' passage at the end broke the ice and a mighty roar went up. The troops were invited to join in, using various percussion instruments, as the band played Latin American music. Audience participation increased until the concert became a huge sing-song. The concert ended with the band's special finale number - *Hootenanny*, a foot-tapping, hand-clapping selection of country and western tunes. This ended with the whole Commando on its feet and Lt Col M P J Hunt, 40 Cdo CO, told Capt Ware that "If he could have given his men rifles and put them ashore at that moment they would have walked right across and nothing would have stopped them."

The band was equally as impressed with the Commandos as the Commandos were with the band. BdSgt R Ireland wrote: "We played for 40 Cdo and what a concert! The men of the Commando were entertaining the band with sing-songs, 'Zulu Warriors' and anything else they could think of... the cheering and singing must have been heard at home. The men were so enthusiastic and the spirit they have is incredible. Brig Thompson could lead these men on a route march right through Argentina. Heaven help the Argies if this lot go ashore".

Whilst at Ascension the band disembarked and marched to Georgetown to rehearse for Beating Retreat, the real thing taking place next day on the old garrison parade ground.

After the Argentinian surrender their prisoners of war were taken back to Argentina on the *Canberra* which then returned to the Falklands. There the band gave two concerts in Stanley Cathedral before leaving for the United Kingdom. The Commando Forces Band played every night during the journey back. This was an important phase for the returning troops since it allowed them to relax. On the last night at sea Capt Ware's new march *San Carlos* was played during a Beat Retreat that ended, by popular demand, with *Hootenanny*. As *Canberra* sailed up the Channel, Buglers sounded appropriate bugle calls from the ship's bridge. The band was playing as the ship neared the jetty then, after a final *Hootenanny*, the instruments were put aside and the band joined the others at the ship's rail as the Band of C-in-C Naval Home Command played *Canberra* alongside.[1]

1 *'Our Falklands War' G Underwood.*

On 12th October representatives of the Task Force, with FOF3 Band leading the RN contingent and the Band of Commando Forces leading the RM contingent, marched through the City of London to the Guildhall. The bands proudly wore their Lovat uniforms and their green berets. It is believed that this, and a similar parade in Plymouth, was the only occasion when the Commando Forces Band wore the Prince of Wales Plumes as part of the cap badge in their berets.

On 20th May 1983 SS *Canberra*, having been completely refitted, sailed from Southampton for a cruise to Spain and back. It was appropriate that the Band of Commando Forces played for an hour on the quay as the passengers boarded and then the band went aboard themselves. The next day was San Carlos Day and the skipper, Capt D Scott-Masson, followed Royal Navy custom of parading a Baron of Beef to mark the anniversary of a successful engagement. In order to satisfy demand the band gave two consecutive concerts in the Stadium. They ensured that the music was patriotic and they received tremendous ovations. The Big Band played in the evening and, although it was intended that they would only give two or three shows during the two-week trip, they actually played almost every night - which meant that they missed a lot of evening dinners! Other combinations that played to entertain the passengers were the jazz quartet, the eight-piece dance band, a string quartet, the rock group, a full orchestra and a military band. It was intended that the band should Beat Retreat in Uigo, Spain, but the British authorities decided that the locals might not appreciate a British military band standing on Spanish soil on the anniversary of the Falklands War playing *Rule Britannia,* so it was cancelled. A few months later the Commando Forces Band supported the visit of HM The Queen and the Captain General to Royal Marines, Poole.

The plans for further reductions to the Band Service continued when, in 1985, the bands of Commando Forces and Commando Training Centre RM, formed in the early 1970s, were reconstructed. The Commando Forces band was a direct descendant of the Plymouth Group band and, as such, its members wore the Prince of Wales Plumes as part of their cap-badge and helmet plate. Transfer of the Plumes to what had been the other half of the split Plymouth Group Band at Commando Training Centre was approved by HM The Queen on 12th March 1985.[2] On 1st April 1985 the Commando Forces band ceased to exist and the band of Commando Training Centre became the Band of the Royal Marines Commandos, based at Lympstone with Capt J M Ware as the Director of Music. Because of this arrangement the band had full authority to wear the Prince of Wales Plumes as it was a direct and continuous descendant of the Plymouth Group Band.

The frequent Commando tours of duty in Northern Ireland were supported by their own Cdo Forces Band and also FOSNI's Band would visit not only to entertain but also to recruit. 1986 found their visit to West Belfast coinciding with that of a 45 Cdo tour of duty. Apart from entertaining 'Royal' the band also carried out two public engagements. An extract from an article[3] describes how they worked together: "The band did a couple of displays, one at Musgrave Park Hospital which was the base of 45 Cdo 'B' Echelon. For this gig we had most of the Company on the ground and our own clearance/close protection patrol while we worked. We fell in behind the main gate and the patrol went out doing the whole bit... taking good cover... ducking and weaving... total observation... 'Royal' at his best. One minute later the band went out doing the whole bit... regimental march... immaculate dressing... marks of expression... 'Bandy' at his best. Both sides of the Corps on the ground together doing what they do best and doing it well".

The band of the RM Commandos undertook a trip to Norway, not to entertain but to undergo Arctic Survival Training. Skiing, lectures, carrying Bergens and learning to survive

2 *RMRO 52/85.*
3 *Blue Band Vol 37 No 3 page 76.*

in tents at night in the Arctic as well as survival in snow holes, and under snow sheets were all included in their training. The band finally took part in a Medical Squadron Exercise that involved acting as a decontamination unit at the hospital complex.[4]

A major deployment occurred in 1992 when the band was transported to Singapore to relieve C-in-C Fleet Band continuing the deployment in *Invincible* and RFA[5] *Olwen* through Malaya and back through the Persian Gulf to the UK. In true ship's band style they performed as a military band, concert band, orchestra, jazz band, dance band and other small groups.

In the first half of 1994, almost without a murmur, the Band of HM Royal Marines Commandos became the Band of HM Royal Marines Commando Training Centre, Royal Marines. One of the first tasks for the newly-named band was in France marking, with other bands and military units, the 50th Anniversary of the Normandy landings. The veterans' parade took place on Gold Beach and the band played at other services and acts of remembrance during the weekend. At the end of 1994 the band carried out a five-day deployment to the Falklands to mark the 150th anniversary of the British colony and the Royal Navy's success at the Battle of the Falklands in 1914. This was followed by a deployment to Northern Ireland in support of 42 Commando. Concerts were also given for the Royal Ulster Constabulary and the Army at Bessbrook. The 'locals' were also entertained at Bessbrook Mill and the band completed six concerts in four days in four different venues.

Whilst the massed bands were at the Royal Albert Hall they received a message: "Sincere good wishes for a successful MFM. Sorry we can't be with you but busy here flying the flag. Best regards. Lt Andy Henderson and the Band of HM Royal Marines CTCRM, Warwick Long Beach, Bermuda." The band was marking the closure of HMS *Malabar* and two hundred years of RN presence on the islands.

The band traditionally performs at the CTC Officers' Mess Summer Ball. The Ball always has a theme and in 1995 the theme was 'Tropicana'. Bandmaster Clive Close had the job of selecting suitable music from the Music Library and, on this occasion, BdSgt Dowrick was responsible for musical arrangements. The slow, languorous, music used for the Cadbury's Flake advertisement became the opening fanfare, and his 'Summer Slow' included *Bali Hai* with the band swaying from side to side, by numbers, like palm trees. After *Hawaii Five-O* and the *Peanut Vendor* a drum roll and the distinctive first three notes of the *National Anthem* had everyone at attention and the Commandant saluting, only to find that the band smoothly went into an upbeat version of *The Bare Necessities*! This was followed by a swift escape as the band marched off to *I Wanna Be Like You*!

Recruiting was very strong in 1997 and the band found themselves kept busy with the demands of King's Squads and related tasks. In the autumn of 1997 the band played at Twickenham before the England rugby international against South Africa immediately before flying out to Malaysia for a ten-day visit, principally for the Langkawi International Maritime and Aerospace Exhibition. The band was to support the Defence Export Services Organisation which was responsible for the British trade delegations at the exhibition. Quintet work, a fanfare team, cocktail trio and a full concert band were all required in addition to supporting the exhibition. There was also a dance band concert at the Awana International Hotel to a crowd estimated to be in excess of a thousand strong.

After the usual parades and concerts during early 1998 the band was heavily committed when HM The Queen visited the Commando Training Centre. Beginning with a parade band and fanfare team the band reappeared in various forms and sizes as the tone of the visit became more relaxed. This was followed by a host of Regimental dinners, King's Squad Pass-outs and similar events. When the Captain General visited the Commando

4 *Blue Band Autumn 1988 p 45.*
5 *Royal Fleet Auxiliary.*

Logistic Regiment at RMB Chivenor for the Ajax Day Memorial Parade the CTC Band provided musical support. To complete the first half of the year the band went to HMS *Chatham* which was in Lisbon, Portugal for EXPO'98 which was visited by Prince Philip. A trip to Modena, Italy for an International Band Festival was the next major event. Military bands from Spain, Poland, Austria, France and Italy were also taking part and, after a Beat Retreat, all bands paraded through the streets of Modena covering a distance of about four miles in darkness. Problems were caused by the Polish band marching behind the Royal Marines at about 160 paces per minute and, inevitably, catching up. After this the Festival really started with all of the bands giving concerts.

The 1998 International Festival of the Sea in Portsmouth was the next major job for Commando Training Centre's Band. Then came a visit to Belgium to play at the NATO headquarters for 'British Day'. The jazz quartet played for the reception where more than forty different countries were represented. This was followed by a display by the full parade band and then a return home to the King's Squads and even Divisions at Britannia Royal Naval College.

In October the band played at St Paul's Cathedral for the Seamen's Mission and then the Commandant General's supersession. This involved the band playing as an orchestra, a dance band and parade band all in the space of twelve hours.

During 1999 the CTC Band visited Singapore in support of IMDEX Asia '99, which began at the High Commissioner's residence. In the same year the band was flown to Naples to join HMS *Ocean* for the Exercise *Argonaut* deployment and, on the 22nd September 1999 an Act of Remembrance for the tenth Anniversary of the Deal Bombing was held in St Christopher's Church, HMS *Ocean*. A gun was fired to mark the two minutes' silence throughout the Task Group.

Local concerts and King's Squads through 2000 and early 2001were punctuated by occasional concerts in other parts of the United Kingdom. During 2001 the band journeyed to Copenhagen in support of HMS *Cardiff* which was visiting the city. A Beat Retreat was performed alongside and, the following day, the band marched through the city to perform another Beat Retreat in the Town Hall Square. The following day the band provided the pre-match and half-time entertainment at the Brondby v Copenhagen football match and then travelled outside the city to perform another Beat Retreat, this time for local VIPs and businessmen. The purpose of this visit was to help celebrate the Battle of Copenhagen which, ironically, the British won partly as a result of Nelson ignoring the signal to withdraw by placing his telescope to his blind eye. A joint service of remembrance was held and the band gave a final concert before returning home.

Lord 'Paddy' Ashdown provided the narration for an ambitious recording project. 'The King's Squad' was the title and it followed the routine of the parade, using music typical of the parade, including the new march *The King's Badge*. It was released in 2002. In the same year the band played at the Cup Final between Arsenal and Chelsea which took place at the Millennium Stadium. Later in the year the band went to Dieppe to help mark the 60th Anniversary of Op *Jubilee* when 6,000 allied troops carried out an amphibious attack on the Dieppe beaches. At the time it was the biggest raid against Nazi Europe and about 4,000 of the attacking force became casualties. A parade on the sea front, in front of veterans from Britain, Canada, United States and France was followed by the *Sunset* ceremony. On the way back to Lympstone the band stopped at Harwich to play at the naming ceremony of a new cruise liner.

Following 2004 Easter leave the CTC Band went to Norfolk, USA, for the Virginia International Tattoo. Other participating military bands included the US Atlantic Fleet Band

and the USMC Quantico Band. CTC Band also performed a Beat Retreat ceremony at the NATO Headquarters.

In October of 2004 the RMBS was invited to share the stage at the concert given at the end of the annual National Brass Band Championships at the Royal Albert Hall. This was the first occasion that a military band had been given this honour. The combined bands of CTCRM and BRNC, under the baton of Lt Col Chris Davis, joined the Black Dyke Mills Band, conductor Dr Nicholas Childs. The Royal Marines opened proceedings with the Fanfare Trumpets, Corps of Drums and Band. The first half of the concert was shared by the individual bands whilst the second half became a massed bands concert, the programme of music being *Deep Space Nine*, Monti's *Czardas* and, as the finale, *Windows of the World*. As an encore the massed bands played *Cry of the Celts*. The RMBS, through their Stage Manager, took responsibility for providing the special lighting effects.

Malta was visited in 2005 when the band provided musical support as The Queen opened and hosted the Commonwealth Summit Conference. A busy schedule of parade, concert and ceremonial programmes supplemented the work of the string quartet and other combinations directly involved with the summit itself.

With the Plymouth Band being deployed on board RFA *Argus* during early 2006 the CTC Band was called upon to cover some of that band's regular work. Included amongst their own commitments was an important event which, in their own words, was described as follows: "Arguably one of the proudest days for anyone in the Royal Marines, where chests are puffed out more than usual, arm swings more exact and necks are as far back in the collar as possible, was leading hundreds of former Bootnecks for the Graspan Parade. There is something quite special about a Royal Marines parade, marching through London, from Horse Guards, past Buckingham Palace and the Guards Barracks... and back again".[6]

Not long after this, the band was back in London, via rehearsals in Portsmouth, for the Massed Bands Beating Retreat on Horse Guards Parade. After this the annual round of concerts, military training and Pass-Out Parades continued throughout 2006 and into 2007 when, as one of the first events marking the 25th Anniversary of the Falklands campaign, the band went to Liverpool. Included amongst the band's contribution to these events was a concert for Falklands' veterans in the Painted Hall at Greenwich where they were joined by a number of well-known artists including Edward Woodward, Kate Adie, Engelbert Humperdinck and Rolf Harris who, according to the members of the band, stole the show.

During early 2009 the band played at Silverstone for the British Grand Prix and at the National Memorial Arboretum, Alrewas, for the Armed Forces and Veterans Day. A Royal Marines Memorial Wall, sited next to the parade ground at Commando Training Centre, was unveiled and dedicated on the 27th September 2009 with the CTC Band providing musical support. The Memorial Wall was built to celebrate the lives of those who had made the ultimate sacrifice since the year 2000 when the increased level of operational commitment led to a higher level of fatalities within the Corps.

A month later the band went to the United States to fulfil engagements previously covered by BRNC Band. The venues included the British Embassy, the US Navy Memorial and the new United States Marine Corps Museum. Earlier in September, the CTC band played for a King's Squad Pass-Out Parade at which a former member of the RMBS, Musician James Woodland, completed Commando training having transferred a year earlier. The tradition of 'changing over to the ranks' appears to linger on.

6 *Globe & Laurel June 2006 p193.*

Chapter 21: The Royal Marines School of Music from 1982

On the 1st November 1982 Lt Col J R Mason retired and Lt Col G A C Hoskins, although originally gazetted to assume the dual responsibilities of Principal Director of Music, Royal Marines and Commandant RM Deal, became PDM whilst Lt Col D Watson RM became Commandant.[1] The reason for the Commandant General's decision to revert to the old system was the forthcoming changes of use, including a possible expansion into a Tri-Service Defence School of Music, at Deal.[2]

The intended relocation of the RMSM to Eastney still had not taken place. Pressure from the Deal local community and its representatives for the maintenance of the status quo was extremely strong and the costs of moving to Eastney were rising. During the period, September to November 1985, the band of the RMSM toured the United States with the Pipes and Drums of the Argyll and Sutherland Highlanders. The tour, which commenced with a press call on board the aircraft carrier USS *Intrepid*, covered 16,000 miles and seventy-three performances in sixty-eight major cities with only four free days during the three months' period. The USMC fully supported the tour by providing Colour Guards and uniformed attendance at most venues.

Once again the Royal Marines undertook London Duties in 1986. This was the first time since 1978 and only the third occasion that this had occurred. This time 42 Cdo had the responsibility for mounting guard on Buckingham Palace, St James's Palace and the Tower of London. For the first time a guard was required at Windsor Castle so an extra band had to be provided. The RMSM supported L Company and Support Company in London whilst the Fleet Band from Northolt supported K Company at Windsor.

From the 26th October 1987 the Depot, Deal, became the RMSM, Deal, giving it a new autonomy within the Corps.

During 1988 it was announced that Capt J M Ware would assume the mantle of Principal Director of Music upon the retirement of Lt Col G A C Hoskins in 1989.

Six months later, Lt Col Ware found himself having to cope with possibly the largest tragedy that the Band Service had ever suffered. At 0825 on the morning of the 22nd September 1989, as members of the RMSM Band were in the Recreation Room preparing to assemble on the Parade for rehearsals, a massive blast occurred within the room. The walls were blown out allowing the solid concrete roof to fall in. Marines were obviously the first to the scene but were quickly followed by the emergency services. The Irish Republican Army later admitted responsibility for the atrocity. Two days after the explosion Countess Mountbatten of Burma, Vice Lord Lieutenant of Kent, accompanying Prince Philip, as Captain General, visited Deal and the hospitals where the injured lay. The Captain General reminded everyone that the British had a long and proud history of not giving in to those who imagined that they could bomb us into submission. Next day Mrs Thatcher, the Prime Minister, visited the Barracks making it abundantly clear that she knew where the fault lay. Later, the Archbishop of Canterbury also paid his respects.

From the attitude of his men Lt Col Ware knew that it was necessary to get back onto the road and "do what we do best". From that came the decision to march through Deal, as an act of therapy for the band. It was also an indication of the intent to tell the world that the RMBS was going to continue in its usual manner and it was an act of defiance to show

---

1 *Lt Col G A C Hoskins correspondence.*

2 *Tri-Service Training of Musicians was raised throughout this decade, and was the subject of a detailed Parliamentary debate, but these files are not yet open to the public.*

that the bombing was a failure because the Band Service, the country and the world were determined that the bombers would not succeed.

On 29th September, the Junior Musicians and Junior Buglers marched along Canada Road, halted, laid a wreath and then returned to Barracks. A short while later, out of the prying sight of the media, Corps Drum Major J Griffiths called the Band of the RMSM to attention and then the band stepped off to *A Life on the Ocean Wave*. They marched out of the gates and, where the flowers had been laid, halted in respect. After a minute's silence the band led the parade through the town of Deal proudly bearing their scars. Gaps were left in the ranks of the band to show where they had lost their comrades. The Commandant General took the salute. As they marched they remembered the men who had been killed:

BdCpl John (Andy) Cleatheroe
BdCpl Trevor Davis
BdCpl Dave McMillan
BdCpl Dean Pavey
Musn Mick Ball
Musn Richard Fice
Musn Richard (Taff) Jones
Musn Chris Nolan
Musn Mark Petch
Musn Tim Reeves
Musn Bob Simmonds

A Relief Fund administered by a Board of Trustees was set up to account for, and disburse, the assets of the Fund. By the third week in November three-quarters of a million pounds had been donated and a substantial amount had been paid out. The Band Service rigorously pursued a 'business as usual' policy and not one engagement was missed. A Memorial Service for those killed was held in Canterbury Cathedral on the 22nd October, an event of national significance that was attended by the Captain General and Margaret Thatcher. The appearance of the RMSM Band and the Junior Choir at the Festival of Remembrance was particularly poignant as was the following Mountbatten Festival of Music when HM The Queen and Prince Philip attended.

One of the many Deal bombing fund-raising events was the 'All Stars Concert' that featured one hundred and twenty-six ex-members of the RMBS under the leadership of Lt Col Paul Neville. Over £7,000 was raised from their concert at the Winter Gardens, Margate, which subsequently became an annual event. As a result of the Deal bombing it was decided that the RMBS Memorial Day would, in future, be the Sunday closest to the 22nd September.

Several changes occurred which had an effect upon life at the RMSM from 1992 onwards. The co-operation with the Royal Academy of Music changed when the Academy took the decision not to offer diplomas to outside students. The RMSM had to look elsewhere for its professional Military Band Conducting qualification. A partnership with the Associated Board of the Royal Schools of Music resulted in a very suitable curriculum and format being developed for the new diploma. A number of changes were made to the relevance of the Bandmasters' course syllabus in 1990/91 to make it appropriate to current educational thought and practice. The Band Musicianship course at University College Salford, taken as a Director of Music qualification, was upgraded from a two-year General to a three-year Honours Degree. Sixteen males and the first females (ten) joined New Entry

Squad 2/92 for training at Deal on the 31 August 1992 and, in an attempt to encourage recruitment and retention, the Second Open Engagement (2OE) was introduced. This meant that service until the age of fifty could be approved for outstanding NCOs and instrumentalists.

The RMSM band spent four weeks on tour in Canada. This included two weeks at the Nova Scotia Tattoo, the first time that Royal Marines had appeared at this event. During the autumn the Royal Yacht Band accompanied HM The Queen to St Petersburg, the first visit of a British Monarch to Russia. President and Mrs Yeltsin and senior Russian officials were entertained to dinner on board and witnessed Beating Retreat. A particularly important event for the Band Service occurred when the RMSM Band was invited to give the Gala Concert at the British Association of Symphonic Bands and Wind Ensembles (BASBWE) conference. The only professional symphonic wind bands in the UK are those of the Armed Services. As a result of the success of the concert the RMSM was invited back as guest band to give the concert the following year. In between these two occasions Lt Col Waterer had been invited to attend the largest band conference in the world, the 1994 International Band and Orchestra Clinic in Chicago, where over eleven thousand Band Directors, musicologists and senior Directors of Music of US and European Armed forces met. At the Conference Lt Col Waterer was elected to the Board of Directors of the Sousa Foundation, the only British Director of Music ever to hold this appointment.

On 3rd April 1995 Lt Col Sir Vivian Dunn died. His contribution to military music was enormous, a fact that was reflected not only by the attendance at his funeral on the 10th April and his Memorial Service at St Martin's-in-the-Fields on the 7th July but also in the wealth of correspondence and obituaries that followed the announcement.

Friday, 22nd March 1996 was the day that the RMSM, Deal, officially closed. The Closure Ceremony, including Beating Retreat, took place in heavy rain but the crowds of about 6,000 people were massed on both sides of the road as the band marched through the town and back into the Barracks for the last time.

The prison cells, now practice rooms, line the corridors of the Royal Marines School of Music

The RMSM band was disestablished which meant that further responsibility would fall to the Portsmouth Band who, as well as meeting their usual commitments, would have to support the training programmes, particularly the Bandmasters' Course. The Students and Instructional Staff moved into what had been the Royal Navy Detention Quarters (DQ) inside Portsmouth Naval Base.

Adjacent buildings housed a large rehearsal room, classrooms, offices and messing facilities and were clustered around an open area used as a parade ground.

The cells of the DQ provided excellent individual training rooms for the students. HQ Band Service Royal Marines, including Supply Officer Music's Department, was located in Eastney Block with the Portsmouth Band.

The very important Instrument Repair Workshop was located close by. A strong case for retaining this facility, based on the fact that all repairs and overhauls to woodwind, brass, stringed and percussion instruments could be carried out, had been made. The point was made that both the Army and the RAF were envious of the system and that the Army had expressed an interest in copying the RM design as part of their future restructuring.

Significant steps were taken with regard to all levels of training during 1997. The RMSoM was transferred to the Flag Officer Training and Recruiting (FOTR)[3] making it part of RN Training. This covered the Initial Training of Musician and Buglers as well as the Bandmasters, Drum Majors and Director of Music courses. The RMBS Military Training Team, part of the HQRMBS team, retained responsibility for New Entry Basic Military Training, RM Bands and RMSoM Annual Military Training, RMBS Advanced Command Training and support to wider RM Command. The other significant change was the formalising of professional links with the University of Portsmouth. From September 1997 all courses run by the RMSoM would be accredited by the University thus allowing RMBS Musicians to gain professional civilian qualifications at each stage of Specialist Training throughout their careers. Following a validation process the School was accredited as a centre for degree study. The RMSoM was compared very favourably with some of the most learned musical institutions in Britain.

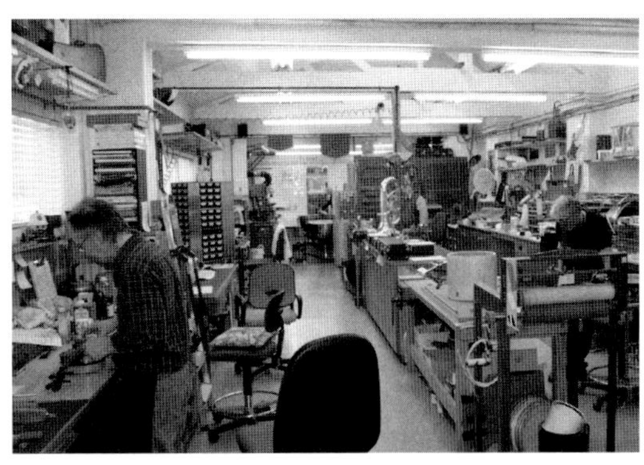

The RMBS Instrument Workshop, a much-admired facility

Other important facilities are the Instrument Store, seen here, the Central Music Library and the Recording Suite

The Principal Director of Music also took the opportunity to ensure that the Director of Music examinations were applicable to the new regime. This examination was laid down in Royal Marines Instructions and consisted of two parts; part 1 being a written examination whilst part 2 was practical. Since 1997 the syllabus has been developed further to include an extended wind band rehearsal and a substantial orchestral work, each of which requires a detailed analysis. Candidates also have to arrange a piece of wind band music and provide an orchestral composition. These subjects, plus the practical examinations, provide the opportunity to gain the Fellowship Diploma of the Royal School of Music (FRSM) and the Masters Level Award in Conducting. The Examining Board consists of the PDM, the Director of Music (Training), the Academic Professor (Higher Training) and two external examiners representing the Associated Board.

During the autumn term 2001 the School had forty students on the M3 and B3 courses, studying for Musician and Bugler initial qualifications, as well as twenty-one New Entry Recruits on their twelve week initial military training package. Of the twenty-one, seventeen successfully negotiated the four military exercises and passed out in front of the Commandant General Royal Marines in November. As well as carrying-out engagements in the British Isles the Training Band travelled to Italy for a Wind Band Festival and Iceland for the annual USMC Ball. They also took part in the Mountbatten Festival of Music. In 2002 the School was invited to play a joint concert with the London College of Music and, later

3 *RMRO 064/97.*

in the term, a concert with Trinity College of Music. They also carried out a number of engagements in local Wardrooms and Messes which were much appreciated.

A typical week in training, at this time, can be illustrated by using extracts from a student Musician's diary:[4]

"Monday: After a week of Adventure Training in the French Alps, going back to work on Monday was a bit of a shock to the system. However, we were all delighted when instead of the usual circuits we set up the gym for the Inter-Services Boxing Championships. The rest of my day was spent practising long notes, scales and studies to get my instrumental stamina back after taking a week out from practice. In the afternoon I had a wind quintet rehearsal."

"Tuesday: My morning was spent preparing my piece and study for my professorial lesson. In my lesson we discussed a possible piece that I could play for the Cassel Prize, a competition involving playing a chosen piece in front of judges. I settled on Elgar's *Romance* which is also one of the pieces I will be playing for my grade eight exam. Tuesday evening's orchestral practice involved strings only, so being a reed player I spent the evening making reeds".

"Wednesday: Parade band in the morning practised basic drill movements whilst playing instruments. In the afternoon for Recreational Training, we went ice-skating in Gosport. After a week of skiing I expected to find it easier than I did: however, I wasn't as bad as others who spent most time sitting down rather than standing up. 10/10 for effort though."

"Thursday: The morning started with a Fitness Test at HMS *Temeraire*. I spent the rest of the morning going through scales and concert band pieces for the evening's rehearsal. In the afternoon an aural lesson was followed by a history lesson. The evening's band rehearsal involved those of us on an engagement the following week".

Parade Band drill led by the Drum Major, Royal Marines School of Music, on the school's own Parade

4 Globe & Laurel.

"Friday: We had parade band in the morning in which I played the cymbals, after which I had a scales test and then spent the rest of the morning practising my studies and pieces. After lunch I had a harmony exam, which consisted of four-part harmony writing. I then spent the rest of the afternoon practising the Elgar *Romance*."

"Saturday and Sunday: My weekend was spent mostly on board the base and in the accommodation due to the dreadful weather and the fact that it is the end of the month and nobody has any money".

For the M3 students the summer term brought the qualification exams, the passing of which meant the completion of training and joining a trained band. Summer term also meant an increase in the number of engagements. During June 2002 Training Company performed twelve public engagements ranging from a fanfare team at Winchester Cathedral for Princess Alexandra to Beating Retreat on board HMS *Fearless*. The term also included an adventure training week and, in 2002, the majority went to Sennybridge for outward-bound activities including pony trekking and rock-climbing. The remainder sailed from Portsmouth to Cherbourg and back.

In October 2002 the School provided a Corps of Drums and Jazz Group to fly to Cyprus to entertain British forces as part of the Trafalgar 200 celebrations.

The 2003 Mountbatten Festival of Music was under severe threat as a result of Op *Fresco*, the Royal Marines deployment to cover the Firefighter's strike. The Principal Director of Music, determined that the strikers would not cause the loss of this event, mobilised the majority of Training Company to take part - an experience that many were not anticipating for a number of years.

It was about this time that the old 'Nissen' rehearsal hut was demolished and a new replacement built. The intention was to name it after Captain E W Faithfull who led his band, as medical orderlies and stretcher bearers, throughout the Gallipoli campaign. However it was decided, by the Royal Navy sponsors, that as it was a training facility for other ranks it would be inappropriate to name the facility after an officer. For that reason it became 'Parker VC Hall'.

Facilities at the Royal Marines School of Music were particularly stretched during 2004. New Entry Troop 1/04 was followed by a second intake, 2/04, in September. The intakes were of such a size that student numbers increased to over one hundred for the first time in ten years, and were

Adventure training is an important part of the School programme as it helps to raise fitness, confidence and team-spirit

Students at orchestral practice in the new rehearsal room of the School of Music. The portrait of Parker VC can be seen on the back wall

certainly the highest ever at HMS *Nelson*. Although this meant that the training facilities needed reconfiguring and that the training regime of one student per cell (or training room) would be stretched to the limit, it also meant that the high numbers allowed the forming of a greater variety of ensembles, a 'seven across' parade band for Open Day and also reinvigorated the traditional House system. Double practice rooms were converted into two singles, the Elements classroom became practice rooms and the students' 'coffee-boat' was used to replace the classroom. It was calculated that these modifications would allow student numbers to peak at one hundred and fifteen in 2006-2007. So what was the trigger for this sudden recruitment, bearing in mind that the Royal Marines Band Service recruiting philosophy is to recruit today to replace those due to leave in two or three years time? In 2002 and 2003 the fire-fighter's strike and the military response to it (Op *Fresco*) meant that a great deal of time normally spent on music practice, rehearsal and performance was lost to the bands. This period of time was a great deal longer than might be apparent. The bands had to prepare and train prior to receiving confirmation that the strike would take place and, when the strike was called off, further time was lost to the necessary cleaning and return of kit and equipment, outstanding leave and return to unit or band. In addition, the long lay-off from concentrated playing required a long period of time to regain the instrumental stamina and normal levels of performance. Many found this a deeply frustrating situation and, whilst they had signed up for military as well as musical duty, being asked to respond to a civilian dispute was not acceptable to them and, as a result, many left. Others resigned because they had enjoyed the experience of being a fire-fighter and, being fit, young, and now trained and experienced to a certain level, they left to join the Fire Service. As a result the Royal Marines Band Service found itself having to recruit and train an exceptional number of replacements.

Although the peak of one hundred and fifteen students never materialised the school did reach a point where every practice room was in use and numbers were high enough to enable two parade bands and/or two concert bands to be in existence at the same time.

In 2005 Pre-Joining Training was introduced for all those moving from Training Company to the Trained Bands. This was a two-week course designed to refresh the military skills learnt during New Entry military training. The two weeks included weapons training, NBC (Nuclear, Biological and Chemical) training and first aid. Also in 2005 the School of Music visited Norway and took part in the Dagen Maloy Festival, a first for a Royal Marines Band - although not for want of trying on the part of the organisers. This festival is indicative of the Norwegian enthusiasm for music-making at every level. Despite the population of Norway being only 4.5million people the School Band found that they were band number seventy-one out of one hundred and eighty-six local bands!

The 2005 Mountbatten Festival of Music was a landmark for the students at the Royal Marines School of Music. The School was closed as every member of Training Company took part in the concert, either as programme sellers, stage crew, spotlight operators, security or as members of the massed bands.

Master-classes are a fairly regular feature of life at the School of Music and in 2005 one was given by percussionist Craig Blundell, an outstanding clinician who has worked with many famous Musicians in the world of current popular music. He laid particular emphasis on the importance of rudiments and dedicated practice of basic techniques. Craig had trained as a Bugler at the Royal Marines School of Music.

Christmas 2005 was marked in the usual manner with a concert at St Mary's Church in Portsmouth; always an opportunity for the various ensembles to be seen and heard and, on this occasion, it featured performances from the concert band, the choir and the orchestra. Those on the Bandmasters' course provided their own arrangements of some of the carols. The showstopper was the choir and a performance of *Bohemian Rhapsody* which brought the house down. A new venture was begun in February 2006 when a concert featuring the Students of the School and the Student Bandmasters in Higher Training was performed at Southampton's Turner Sims Concert Hall.[5] Students from every level of the School, from Phase 2 trainees up to a Director of Music under training, performed a programme of wind ensemble music. This concert has since become a regular part of the training programme for Students and for Bandmasters.

A major change took place when the Royal Marines School of Music ceased to be the administrative responsibility of the Maritime Warfare School at HMS *Collingwood* and moved under the wing of the Commando Training Centre, Royal Marines. The 2007 School of Music Open Day reinforced this change when, instead of a Royal Naval officer being the Guest of Honour, Brigadier A Salmon OBE ADC, Commandant of the Commando Training Centre, Royal Marines, officiated. Prior to the Open Day the School enjoyed further master-classes from Martin Roscoe (piano), the Royal Academy of Music Trombone Section and Herbie Flowers (bass trombone).

In preparation for the beginning of the 2007-2008 year slight adjustments were made to Training Company's 'House' system in order to better align it with the training system. Unlike the post-Second World War system, the current organisation only involved two houses, *Gloucester* and *Neptune*. *Eagle* House was reintroduced and each of the three houses would now represent a year of training, the Students moving from one house to another.

Neptune House was designated for Phase One, New Entry Training, consisting of a ten-week[6] basic training package to be followed by the two and a half terms of musical training plus military continuation training, all leading to the Term Three exam.

Gloucester was the House name for those undertaking Phase Two, Terms Four to Six training, ending with the Term Six exam.

Eagle House was reintroduced for Phase Three, Terms Seven to Nine, ending

Early morning inspection at the Royal Marines School of Music, 1st June 2010. The Students are paraded by a Corporal, Drill Instructor, attached to the RMBS Military Training Team and then inspected by the Director of Music (Training) and three Warrant Officers or SNCOs

5 Now held at the New Theatre Royal, Portsmouth.

6 This was the only year that a ten-week military training package was used. Prior to this it had been fifteen weeks and, following this ten week trial, the package reverted to fifteen weeks.

with the Term Nine final exam. With their shorter training period Buglers would move into *Eagle* for their final term only.

These arrangements allowed suitable Students to be 'fast-tracked' as those who merited it could move directly from *Neptune* House to *Eagle* House.

Under the Director of Music (Training), Major M P Dowrick, the Training Band recorded a compact disc in time for the 2008 Open Day. Produced entirely within the RMBS and recorded under the RMBS 'Chevron' label the recording had many purposes. It was a 'shop window' for recruitment, for the School and for the Band Service and also raised funds for the charity 'Help for Heroes'. At least £5 from the sale of each disc was donated to this charity. The musical content of the recording reflected both the Open Day concert and the Beat Retreat programmes, making it a keepsake and a reminder for all those who took part or attended.

As the rehearsals for the Beating Retreat on Horse Guards Parade required all Bands, including that of the Commando Training Centre, RM, to be in London, the School parade band was despatched to Lympstone to rehearse and play for the June 2009 King's Squad Pass-out Parade. A full rehearsal took place on arrival, part of which (according to one young participant) served to clarify "which orders were for the Band and which were not"! Next morning they and the King's Squad rehearsed in a final preparation for the afternoon's Inspection and Pass-Out Parade.

During 2010 the House arrangement was further modified in order to blend experience with inexperience. Each House now has a number of students at each phase of training, plus supervisory staff. This creates an environment where the new, inexperienced, recruit is living and working alongside members of the two Troops who are one and two years ahead of themselves. This allows natural mentoring to take place which, in turn, imparts confidence, learning and experience.

The well-equipped Higher Training Department where Student Bandmasters and those on the M1/B1 courses study

The second part of the Royal Marines School of Music is the Higher Training Department where potential Bandmasters of the Royal Marines Band Service are trained, and the musical component of the M1/B1 courses are taught. This department is located on the upper floor of the building that houses Portsmouth Band and Supply Officer Music's Department.

Strong links with Portsmouth University are still maintained and, at the time of writing approximately seventy members of the Band Service are undertaking music degree courses. There are two routes towards this degree. Men and women who pass the Bandmasters' course can use that qualification, and the qualifications that led to it, as accredited prior learning which they can 'top-up' with other modules for their degree. The alternative route is to begin whilst a student at the School of Music. Passing the taught course during the two years of training at the School qualifies them to Level 1. Distance learning over the next four/five years will take them through Levels 2 and 3 to their degree. Each level equates with a year of a 3-year full-time music degree. The distance learning course utilises the support of Higher Training staff and the Academic Instructor at each band. Support is also provided by Internet resources, especially the Visual Learning Environment link to the University. One of the big advantages of the RMSoM musical training to degree level is that students are accommodated, looked after, paid a salary and, when they achieve their degree qualification, they do not have a massive debt to repay.

Strong links with the Royal Marines Museum also exist. Each year the new intake of recruits spend a day at the Museum getting a general overview of Corps history. During Term 3 the Students again visit the Museum but this time to gain a detailed knowledge, which is later tested, of the history and development of the Royal Marines Band Service and its important role within the Corps. To facilitate this, the author, as a member of the Museum staff, gives them a complete tour, drawing out the Band Service involvement in times of peace and war in both their musical and military role.

Like any other educational establishment, standards have to be met and inspections have to be passed. The School of Music is subjected to three levels of inspection. There is an annual inspection, known as a 'First Party Audit' which is carried out by a team from the Commando Training Centre, RM, who check that all documentation is in order and that the training is being delivered to required standards. Every two years the 'Second Party Audit', carried out by the MOD Fleet Targeted Assurance Team check that the MOD approach to training is being met. Finally the 'Third Party Audit' can take place at any time with only 24hrs' notice, this being carried out by OFSTED. This inspection is particularly aimed at quality of training, Instructor qualifications, diversity and Duty of Care. It is the Duty of Care that examines the organisation that is the Royal Marines School of Music most stringently. Unlike a school, where this responsibility starts when school opens and ends when school closes, members of the School of Music staff are responsible for care, particularly with regard to those under the age of eighteen, for twenty-four hours a day, seven days a week. It is also necessary to ensure that any student can be given access to a Chaplain, or the equivalent in other religions, at any time; and that any reasonable form of support can be accessed when needed.

The School also has an 'Internal Feedback System' which allows all students, including those on the Bandmasters' course, to air their views on any matter, directly to the Director of Music (Training). This facility is also available to the Instructors and Professors.

The University of Portsmouth also applies its rigorous Quality Assurance procedures to all accredited RMSoM programmes of study. The School is reliant upon having suitable students to train to the calibre required by the RMBS. Recruitment is of paramount importance; it is also an activity on which large amounts of time, effort and money can be expended if not carried out thoughtfully, carefully and imaginatively.

At the turn of the 21st century indications were that future recruitment would come not only from schools and colleges but also from music colleges and universities and many high calibre, mature recruits were obtained from those sources. Since then the situation has changed. University education has become ever more expensive and statistics show that only a very low percentage of those obtaining degrees in music actually go into performing; the vast majority either go into teaching or an entirely different occupation, thus making attempts to recruit from that source of limited appeal. Advantage was taken of the fact that the Royal Marines School of Music can offer training to Bachelor of Music status and so the weight of the recruiting effort was put into enabling young people in schools and colleges, who were thinking of a university musical education, to consider the Royal Marines as an alternative. Part of this 'enabling' process was to make those in a position to guide young people fully aware of the opportunities that the Royal Marines School of Music could provide, and especially the fact that the conventional route to a musical degree was not actually producing many 'performers'. The phrase "we need to influence the influencers" is almost a mantra for recruitment.

The RMBS Recruiter WO2 Ian Davies at the Festival of Remembrance in 2007. Amongst his medals and decorations can be seen the MBE, awarded for his work raising the standards and methods of recruiting and selection. (Image courtesy of Les Scriver)

Surprisingly, this recruitment is carried out by one man, WO2 Ian Davies MBE who initially operated, in isolation, as the 'recruiting arm' of the Royal Marines School of Music. Recruitment consisted of visits to schools - taking bands or ensembles to teach, entertain and encourage interest in the Band Service.

This extended to workshops and demonstrations in such venues as the Royal Marines Museum; or these could be organised on a regional basis. In 2009 the Band Service Recruiter became a Special Recruiter under the Captain, Naval Recruiting. One of the advantages of this arrangement is access to, and working alongside, others with specialist knowledge and experience. Another is access to the Royal Navy's Careers Acquaint Facility at HMS *Collingwood*. This facility has accommodation, training rooms and many other features that allow five-day pre-audition residential courses to be run for up to twenty potential recruits. The facility has its own staff plus, when being utilised by the Royal Marines Band Service for one of their three courses a year, a Royal Marine SNCO. These three courses, the first of which commenced in 2010, provide the potential of gaining sixty recruits.

Candidates arrive at the facility, are provided with a uniform and accommodated in six-person rooms. They experience the life-style of a recruit from 0630 until 2200 for each of the five days. They spend one day at the Royal Marines School of Music, one day with one of the Royal Marine Bands, visit one of the Royal Navy Type 45 destroyers and use the SA80 weapons simulator. Probably most importantly they carry out all of the physical tests, including the swimming test that they will undergo at the actual audition. It has always been known that, despite the information that is given to potential candidates, the majority of them underestimate the level of physical fitness that is expected of them. Very often this results in the loss of potentially good Musicians or Buglers, or candidates having to return for a second audition. By undertaking these tests during the acquaint week, potential audition candidates not only realise what is expected of them but are also shown how to best prepare themselves to attain it. This has already resulted in remarkable improvements to the fitness levels of candidates at audition. Feedback from the most recent course has indicated that of the twenty candidates, eighteen have confirmed that they wish to audition.

Recruitment has now become a matter of bringing the young people to the Royal Marines Band Service rather than taking the Royal Marines Band Service to the schools. However, visits to schools and to specialist events are still essential. The current instrumental shortfall is oboe, bassoon and flute. The first two are not surprising since the instruments are expensive for a family to afford and they are not 'fashionable' since they (the bassoon in particular) are not regarded as solo instruments. The problem of the unusual shortfall in flautists was solved through a schools recruiting visit to Ireland where the instrument is a popular and traditional one. This was a great success.

The next step in recruiting is to take technology into the schools, rather than a band. Young people are not only familiar with technology but they expect inter-activity to be part of everything they do. To this end a high-tech, educational, 'inter-active' package has been developed. Being easily transportable this new equipment will allow the Recruiter to interest the young people, to get a large amount of information across to them in a form that they understand and enjoy, and to make assessments of individual suitability.

In having a single Specialist Recruiter the Royal Marines Band Service is different from the Army which has a recruiting team of one officer and several NCOs and other ranks. Whilst maximising the flow of quality potential recruits into auditions he also has to work efficiently in order to minimise costs. The Royal Marines Band Service, through its recruitment policy has developed, and is continuing to develop, inventive, imaginative and effective ways of obtaining the raw material necessary to ensure that its standards are protected for the future.

The Royal Marines School of Music is an organisation based upon a structured educational system but it also has the ability to adapt to the needs of its parent Band Service and, because of the increasing requirement for a military role capability, the needs of the Corps itself. Surrounding the core training structure is the need for flexibility, and the need to develop the ability to seize opportunities to gain experience as well as to adapt to circumstance. Unlike most educational establishments there is also the need to instil within its students an understanding of the need for fitness, for team-spirit and mutual support, and for high personal standards - all of which must become automatic and unquestioned. This can all be illustrated by examining the Royal Marines School of Music through the academic year 2009-2010.

Chapter 22: Year at the Royal Marines School of Music, 2009 - 2010

Part of the School's Corps of Drums

Inspection by the Principal Director of Music and the Corps Drum Major

Marching Display in Gunwarf Quays, Portsmouth

A Year in Training (1) - the Training of Musicians and Buglers, September 2009 - 2010.

Every member of the Royal Marines Band Service, no matter what rank or appointment be attained, started from this point.

The most obvious end result of the RMSoM training is the passing-out of trained Musicians and Buglers to join one of the Royal Marines Bands. This is showcased by a concert and Beating Retreat ceremony in Portsmouth where those passing out receive their certificates and awards. This took place in August 2010 and, in particular, the eighty-strong military band Beating Retreat was extremely impressive - so impressive that members of the audience were heard to ask, "How can the Royal Marines School of Music pass out this many Musicians and Buglers each year, and why do they need this many?" The truth of the matter is that the eighty strong band consists of all those due to pass out over a three year span. The impressive band was made up of twenty-four students who were passing out, or who had passed out in recent months, plus the students who hope to pass out in 2011 and 2012. The numbers involved at various stages of training during the 2009-2010 academic year are as follows:

Phase 1 Training. (Troop Number 1/09 - students who joined in 2009)

- September 2009. 26 Recruits joined.
- New Entry Military Training.
- 19 Musicians started Terms 1 - 3.
- 5 Buglers started Terms 1 - 3.
- July 2010. All 24 passed into Phase 2A training

Phase 2A Training. (Troop Number 1/08 - students who joined in 2008)

- September 2009. 30 students joined from Phase 1.
- 24 Musicians started Terms 4 - 6, but 4 passed out early.
- 6 Buglers started Terms 4 - 6.
- July 2010. 4 Passed out early and remaining 26 passed into Phase 2B training.

Phase 2B Training. (Troop number 1/07 - students who joined in 2007)

- September 2009. 30 originally joined the Troop.
- 19 Musicians started Terms 7 - 9.
- No Buglers started Term 7 since all four in this Troop passed out early.
- July 2010. 2 Musicians passed out early at Christmas 2009, 3 more passed out at Easter 2010 and remaining 14 passed out in August 2010. The 4 Buglers passed out the previous year.

14th April 2010. The Royal Marines Young Musician of the Year Competition: The Cassel Prize.

The Cassel Prize is the traditional competition for Students of the Royal Marines School of Music to enter as accompanied soloists. This year it was held in the New Theatre Royal, Portsmouth, allowing the public the opportunity to watch for the first time. The judging panel consisted of the Principal Director of Music, Royal Marines; the Academic Professor of Higher Training for the Royal Marines Band Service and this year's guest judge, Chi Chi Nwanuko MBE who is currently the Principal Double Bassist and founder member of the Orchestra of the Age of Enlightenment as well as the Endymion Ensemble. The contenders were:

Sonata for Clarinet (Saint-Saëns)	Musician Annie Richardson, clarinet
Scottish Fantasy (Bruch)	Musician Alice Hudson, violin
Fantasie Pastorale (Eugène Bozza)	Musician David Hedley, oboe
The Great Train Race (Ian Clarke)	Musician Natalie Wade, flute
Cantabile et Presto (George Enesco)	Musician Natalie Wade, flute
Concertino in Eb Major for Trombone (Ferdinand David)	Musician John Walker, trombone
Restless (Rich O'Meara)	Musician Russell Baker, percussion
The Love of L'Histoire (Charles DeLancey)	Musician Russell Baker, percussion

Cassel Prize Winner: Musician John Walker. (Silver award)
Cassel Prize Runner-up: Musician Russell Baker (Bronze award)
Most Highly Commended Musician: Musician Alice Hudson (Mark Petch Memorial Cup)

The 2010 Pass Out.

6th August 2010 - the Royal Marines School of Music Concert, Prize-giving Ceremony and Beating Retreat took place in the Portsmouth Guildhall and the Guildhall Square respectively. A total of twenty-four Buglers and Musicians passed out from the School or, having passed out early, returned from their bands to take part in the ceremony and performances. Sixty-four Musicians, including the usual small number of Instructors, were on stage performing as a concert wind band and as an orchestra. Increased to an eighty-strong Parade Band they then Beat Retreat on the Guildhall Square, drawing the ceremonies and performances to a close. The twenty-four Musicians and Buglers who passed out will now make their way to their Bands, in some cases returning to their new bands, whilst the remainder return to the School in order to continue the training that will see them pass out over the next two years.

Trophies were presented for a number of achievements: Lord Northbourne Cup for the Best New Entrant; Musical Efficiency Award for the Best All Round Musician; Bugle Major's Trophy for the Best All Round Bugler; the Ken Mettyear Memorial Cup for the best final examination mark in either the Musician 3 or Bugler 3 courses and the Lady Dunn Award for an outstanding contribution to the Royal Marines School of Music. The Lady Dunn award this year went to the two civilian tailoresses whose knowledge, experience and sheer hard work ensures that uniforms are of the highest standard - including making good manufacturers' errors when required. The premier award, the 'The Prince's Badge' for the best Student leaving Training, was not awarded this year. This is not a reflection upon the standard of the Troop but an indication of the strict criteria against which the award is made.[1]

---

1 *See separate Appendix for full list of Prince's Badge winners.*

The Guildhall Pass Out Concert: Conducted by Major A Thornhill RM, unless stated.

The Concert Band of Her Majesty's Royal Marines School of Music.
- *The Flag Parade* (Williams arr Waller)
- *Light Cavalry* (Suppé)

The Orchestra. Conducted by WO2 Bandmaster I Hutchinson
- *Fantasy on Handel's Largo* (Handel arr Naughton)
- *Star Wars* (Williams)

The Big Band. Directed by Mr Gordon Campbell.
- *A String of Pearls* (Miller)
- *American Patrol* (Miller)
- *It Must be Jelly Cause Jam Don't Shake Like That* (Miller)

The Concert Band of Her Majesty's Royal Marines School of Music.
- *Toccata in D Minor* (Bach)
- *Fantasy for Violin* (Hess arr Waller)
- *Les Clochettes* (de Grau arr Cole)
- *Silverado* (Broughton arr Waller)

Following the concert finale the Director of Music (Training) Major A Thornhill, the two featured violinists and the RMSoM Concert Band enjoy the applause. © John Ambler

The Guildhall Square Pass Out Beating Retreat: Under the Direction of WO1 D V Waller, Bandmaster (Training) Ceremony led by Corps Bugle Major A J Piner RM and Drum Major S Blair RM.

Preliminaries by the Buglers of the Royal Marines School of Music.
- *Drummer's Call*
- *The Band Call*
- *The Fall-In*

Parade Music
- *Sarie Marais* (Toonsetting arr Dunn)
- *Heroic Fanfare* (Murtha arr Waller)
- *Soldier an' Sailor Too* (Piner/McDermott)
- *March and Air* (Dunn)
- *Ark Royal* (Waller)

Beating Retreat Ceremony
- *Drum Beatings: Portsmouth No 1's* (Trad)
- *Bugle Fanfare: Dynamo* (Lee)
- *Slow Beatings: Glyn Eric Green* (Lee)
- *Drum Static: Farewell to the Depot* (Jones/Green/Macefield)

Parade Music and Finale
- *Shrewsbury Fair* (Neville)
- *Jurassic Park* (Williams)
- *1812 Overture* (Tchaikovsky)
- *Dear Lord and Father of Mankind* (Parry arr MacDermott)
- *Sunset* and *Rule Britannia* from *'The Battle of Trafalgar'* by Elms.
- *National Anthem* (arr Jacob)
- *Heart of Oak* (Boyce)
- *A Life on the Ocean Wave* (Russell arr Dunn)

A Year in Training (2) - RMSoM Musicians and Buglers Courses, September 2009 - 2010.

WO1 Dean Waller, Bandmaster (Training), conducts the finale of the RMSoM Pass-Out Beating Retreat ceremony. © John Ambler

The Musicians and Buglers M2 and B2 qualifications may be taken after a minimum of twelve months' service. Passing this assessment based course gives musical qualification for the rank of Corporal. A further military training package, the Junior Command Course, has to be passed before the rank of Corporal can be awarded. The M2/B2 course is a task-book based course, covering the history of music and also harmony, which is taught whilst carrying out normal duties with a band and then assessed over a two-week period, which includes a recital, at the RM School of Music.

The M1 Course lasts twelve-weeks and, on completion, the SNCO students may be appointed Volunteer Band Instructors, or be expected to deputize for the Director of Music and Bandmaster within an RM Band. When working with any band, rehearsal time is always at a premium, so students should know how to prepare their scores for effective rehearsal. Course students have the opportunity to conduct a work of moderate difficulty in public and also gain experience of parade band conducting. Students learn to compose and arrange proficiently, so harmony, music theory, scoring and compositional technique are taught and assessed with each student producing a substantial composition or arrangement; then rehearsing and recording a performance. In viva voce lessons, considerable emphasis is placed on repertoire knowledge and an understanding of each instrument's characteristics. Aural training develops the ability to rehearse perceptively, while a study of music history and analysis gives students an insight into a wide range of compositional techniques; these are crucial for the interpretation and rehearsal of music as well as for crafting the students own compositions and arrangements. Following the M1 Course, students are encouraged to take a diploma in Wind Band Directing.

The B1 Course includes projects, written assignments and music theory plus the development of leadership and Corps of Drums administration skills.

A Year in Training (3) - RMSoM Drum Majors' Course, May 2009 - 2010.

Frequency of this four week course is every two years but for practical reasons it is run on an 'as required' basis. The purpose of the course is to train Bugler NCOs to lead a military band on parade. This includes the ability to command a playing band in executing ceremonial and marching manoeuvres whilst also developing an exact knowledge of the Drum Major's signals and timing. It is also the opportunity to gain knowledge of, and familiarity with, those areas of band administration and discipline for which a Drum Major is responsible. Candidates must have a good musical knowledge and high standards of deportment and bearing. They must also hold the rank of Corporal Bugler or above. These courses are currently held at Plymouth since the Course can use the very large Parade ground and the good classroom facilities.

A Year in Training (4) - RMSoM Bandmasters' course, April 2009 - April 2010.

Students who have achieved a high standard in all areas of the M1 Course and receive a recommendation are offered a place on the Bandmasters'Course. This qualifies the student musically for the rank of Warrant Officer Bandmaster; it is also the most advanced music course run by the RMSoM. The Course lasts for fifty-two weeks, including seven weeks' leave during which work is set. The Bandmasters' Course is focused on conducting, composing and arranging. The Course is extremely comprehensive, as successful students will eventually need to show a high degree of musical leadership, a command of sophisticated techniques and understanding of artistic considerations, whether in conducting, rehearsing, arranging or composing. Therefore, it is crucial that students should possess a thorough knowledge of music history and analysis, compositional techniques, musical forms and structures, etc.

'Bandmastership' assessments test all subjects taught on the Course. A recording is supplied but no written music. Students transcribe the music from the recording, using their aural skills, and then arrange it for wind band or orchestra, as directed. They may need to add an introduction, interludes or postludes and to vary the harmony or add countermelodies. Finally they have to rehearse and record a performance of their arrangement. Students develop advanced skills in conducting and rehearsing wind bands, orchestras and small ensembles. They conduct in at least eight concerts during the Course and parade band conducting is also developed to a high standard.

The Course benefits from considerable input from external specialists: Professor Paul Patterson gives regular composition tutorials and Malcolm Binney is the Conducting Professor. Master classes and other sessions with leading musicians are arranged as appropriate; Conductor Marin Alsop and composers Nigel Clarke and Martin Ellerby have recently taught. Students also attend the renowned Canford Summer School in wind band conducting. During the Course students take two external professional diplomas: a music theory diploma offered by Trinity Guildhall and the Licentiate diploma of the Royal Schools of Music.

Both the Mi and the Bandmasters' Courses are accredited by the University of Portsmouth at the highest level of undergraduate study, successful students in both courses being able to complete their honours degree after completion of a small "top-up" package which is typically completed within one year.

During the 2009/2010 academic year the following music was directed by, unless otherwise stated, the Student Bandmasters.

17th Sept 2009. Winter Concert 1: The Band of Her Majesty's Royal Marines, Portsmouth (Royal Band).

- *Suite of Old American Dances* (Robert Russell Bennett)
  - *- Cakewalk - Schottische - Western One Step - Wallflower Waltz - Rag*
- *Best of the West End* (arr. McDermott) - Conductor: Capt Richard Long
- *My Fair Lady* (Loewe arr. Cacavas) - Conductor: Lt Col Nick Grace
- *Symphonic Songs for Band* (Robert Bennett)
  - - Serenade - Spiritual - Celebration
- *Bui Doi* - Trombone Solo[2] - from 'Miss Saigon' (Schönberg arr. Curtis)
- *West Side Story* (Bernstein arr. Liston) - Conductor: Lt Col Nick Grace

2 *Soloist: BdCSgt Gary Halsey.*

8th October 2009. Winter Concert 2: The Orchestra from the Band of Her Majesty's Royal Marines, Portsmouth (Royal Band).

- *Pulcinella Suite* (Stravinsky)
- *Romance in F* - Violin Solo[3] - (Beethoven)
- Excerpts from '*Swan Lake*' (Tchaikovsky) - Conductor: WO1 (Bdmr) Tom Hodge
- *Serenade for Strings* (Elgar) - Conductor: Lt Col Nick Grace
- *Marche Joyeuse* (Chabrier)
- *Pavane* (Fauré)
- *Praeludium* (Jarnefelt)
- *Pavane pour une Infante dé Funt* (Ravel)
- *Farandole from L'Arlésienne Suite No 2* (Bizet)
- *St Paul's Suite* (Holst) - Conductor: Lt Col Nick Grace

12th November 2009. Winter Concert 3: The Band of Her Majesty's Royal Marines Collingwood.

- *Saturnalia* (Malcolm Binney)
- *Bermuda Triangle* (Adam Gorb)
- *Tranquility* (Adam Gorb)
- *Gallimaufry* (Guy Woolfenden)
- *Passacaglia* (Tim Jackson)
- *Sun Paints Rainbows on the Vast Waves* (Bedford) - Conductor: Tim Reynish
- *Sea Songs* (Thomas Knox) - Conductor: Maj Jason Burcham

17th December 2009. Winter Concert 4: The Band of Her Majesty's Royal Marines School of Music with the Choir of St Mary's Parish Church.

- *Sleigh Ride* (Anderson) - Conductor: WO2 Dean McGain-Harding
- *Unto us a Boy is Born* (arr Prentice)
- *It Came Upon the Midnight Clear* (arr Prentice)
- *Away in a Manger* (arr Dednum)
- *Hark the Herald Angels Sing* (arr Dednum)
- *Troika* (Prokofieff) - Conductor: WO2 Dean McGain-Harding
- *The Holly and the Ivy* (arr Miller)
- *God Rest You Merry* (arr Miller)
- *In the Bleak Mid-Winter* (arr Carter)
- *Angels from the Realms of Glory* (arr Carter)
- *Hook* (arr Custer) - Conductor: WO2 Dean McGain-Harding
- *In Dulci Jubilo* (arr Robinson)
- *O Little Town of Bethlehem* (arr Robinson)
- *Silent Night* (arr Weites)
- *O Come All Ye Faithful* (arr Weites)
- *Stop the Cavalry* (Lewie) - Conductor: Bd Sgt H Clay
- *Laurel and Hardy* - Conductor: Maj Andy Thornhill
- *Chrimbledance* (Wiffen) - Conductor: Maj Andy Thornhill
- *Highland Cathedral* (Korb) - Conductor: Maj Andy Thornhill
- *Silent Night, Sunset, Rule Britannia* (arr Curtis) - Conductor: Maj Andy Thornhill

---

3 *Soloist: Musn Justin Wilman.*

14th January 2010. Spring Concert 1: The Orchestra from the Bands of Her Majesty's Royal Marines, Portsmouth (Royal Band) and Collingwood.

- *Die Fledermaus* (Strauss)
- *Symphony No 8 in G Major Op.88* (Dvořák)
- *Thunder & Lightning Polka* (Strauss) - Conductor: Capt Ian Davis
- *O Mio Babbino Caro*[4] (Puccini) - Conductor: Capt Ian Davis
- *Rusalka's Song to the Moon*[5] (Dvořák) - Conductor: Capt Ian Davis
- *Vltava* (Smetana)
- *Laughing Song from Die Fledermaus*[6] - Conductor: Capt Ian Davis
- *Radetzky March* (Strauss) - Conductor: Maj Andy Thornhill, Director of Music RMSoM

5th February 2010. Spring Concert 2: Wind Ensembles from the Band of Her Majesty's Royal Marines, Portsmouth (Royal Band).

- *Serenade in E flat major for 8 winds K.375* (Mozart)
- *Serenade in C minor for 8 winds K.388* (Mozart)
- *Serenade in B flat major for 13 winds K.361 Gran Partita* (Mozart)

(This concert was given at the Turner Sims Hall at Southampton University)

25th February 2010. Spring Concert 3: The Band of Her Majesty's Royal Marines Collingwood.

- *Aces High* (Ron Goodwin) - Conductor: Lt Col Nick Grace
- *Spiel* (Ernst Toch)
- *Lincolnshire Posy* (Percy Grainger)
- *Festivo* (Edward Gregson)
- *John Gay Suite* (Buxton Orr)
- *In League with Extraordinary Gentlemen* (Peter Graham)
- *Spitfire Prelude and Fugue* (William Walton)

25th March 2010. Spring Concert 4: The Orchestra from the Bands of Her Majesty's Royal Marines, Portsmouth (Royal Band) and Collingwood.

- *Russlan and Ludmilla* (Glinka)
- *Variations on a Theme by Joseph Haydn* (Brahms)
- *Egmont* (Beethoven)
- *The Wasps* (Vaughan Williams)
- *Concerto for Alto Saxophone and Orchestra*[7] - 2nd Mvt (Binge)
- *Finlandia* (Sibelius)
- *Symphony No 4 in F Minor, Op 36 - 4th Mvt* (Tchaikovsky)

The students are also examined through mid-course examinations, periodic progress tests and Viva Voce examinations. Final examinations in all subjects are set by the RMSoM. Passing the Bandmasters' course qualifies the student for the responsibilities of Warrant Officer Bandmaster. During this period all six students, including the first female student, successfully passed the Bandmasters' course.

---

4 *Vocalist: Lisa Moffat.*
5 *Vocalist: Lisa Moffat.*
6 *Vocalist: Lisa Moffat.*
7 *Soloist Bd Sgt Ian McGleish.*

A Year in Training (5) - RMSoM Training for Director of Music Qualification, 2009 - 2010.

This very important course builds on the foundation of the RMSoM Bandmasters' course. It is a two-part musical qualification designed to give the candidate an advanced, comprehensive and thorough training of relevance to the work of a Director of Music. The course will also provide at least one civilian qualification in order to confirm that the candidates' standards equate to their civilian counterparts in higher education and the music profession.

Part A is taken at a conservatoire or university and will have duration of up to two years, usually leading to a post-graduate qualification. Whilst this course is managed, administered and assessed by the conservatoire or university, both the course and the candidates progress are monitored by the RMSoM. To be approved by the RMSoM the course must be able to provide extensive and rigorous tuition in advanced conducting techniques; must be able to draw upon a variety of ensembles of relevance to the RMBS for conducting practice and must also provide opportunities for regular concert performances by the candidates. Whilst the level and diversity of musical study should ensure a broadening of the candidate's musical experience, a very large amount of practical work, underpinned by theoretical learning and understanding, is of paramount importance. During the course the Principal Director of Music, RM, or the Director of Music of the RMSoM will visit the candidate at least twice during the course and will also maintain contact with a member of staff from the institution who can comment in detail upon the candidate's progress.

Part B is managed, administered and assessed by the RMSoM. It consists of a period of preparation followed by the Director of Music examination. The preparation builds on and develops the musical training of Part A towards the candidate having the ability to take overall musical responsibility for a Royal Marines Band, giving it purpose and fostering a professionally stimulating environment for all band members. In addition, the candidate must be competent to set innovative musical programmes of a standard and content expected from a Royal Marines Band, rehearse the band in an efficient manner, engage and communicate with the public, concert promoters and others and to possess a high level of professional credibility in terms of technical accomplishment and interpretational/ artistic decisions. A successful candidate will have also demonstrated a good knowledge and understanding of strategic planning, policy and practice concerning the RMBS, the Royal Marines, the Royal Navy and, where relevant, the Ministry of Defence.

A Year in Training (6) - Military Training for RMSoM Students and the RMBS, including forthcoming changes.

A revised format for New Entry Military Training commenced in September 2010. This began with five weeks' training at RMSoM, followed by six weeks at the Commando Training Centre, Royal Marines, returning to the RMSoM for the final four weeks, managed by the Military Training Team based at RMSoM. This training period is virtually the first fifteen weeks of the Royal Marines Commando Course but with some of the tactical element omitted. It will cover basic tactics, navigation, husbandry, signals, physical training and field-craft. The Military Training Team consists of a CSgt Troop Commander, four Corporals (Drill Leaders and Physical Training Instructors) and one female Instructor.

Annual Military Training Package.

Two weeks prior to Easter 2011 all students will undertake this training. Phase One and Two Students will undertake a one week Military Field Exercise. Phase Three Students (those due to pass out) will also undertake a 1 week Military Field Exercise plus the ACMT

Advanced Combat Marksmanship Test (ACMT) formerly the Annual Personal Weapons Test (APWT).

Band Military Training.

This is for all members of the trained bands, and other serving RMBS personnel. This training, again organised by the Military Training Team, currently takes place annually and consists of the ACMT, Chemical, Biological, Radiological and Nuclear Training (formerly NBC Training) and a navigation exercise on the ranges.

Command Course Military Training.

During 2006, HQ Band Service initiated an intensive three-week course for those about to take the Junior and Senior Command Courses. As usual this was designed and delivered by the Band Service Military Training Team and focused on the military skills of navigation, map reading, patrolling and the orders process. With the growing need for all members of the RMBS to take their place within any deployed military force, it was necessary for Command Courses to be approached with even greater commitment and confidence. Such was the success of this additional training that it resulted in, with the exception of four personnel who were injured and had to be 'Returned to Unit' (RTU), a 100% pass rate in both of the subsequent courses.

The Junior and Senior Command Courses have been further developed to suit the military command role that is required of the modern Bugler and Musician. The courses are now run simultaneously but with a higher assessment level for those taking the Senior Command Course. It is a six-week course with Week 1 being a non-assessed refresher course run by the Band Service's Military Training Team. Weeks 2 - 6 are at the Commando Training Centre, RM, undertaking training that has been jointly designed and delivered by the Band Service Military Training Team and the CTC Senior Command Course Training Team. In order to be promoted to Corporal the Musicians and Buglers have to show that they can command and lead at Section level[8] whilst promotion to Sergeant requires good performance at Troop level.[9] These revised Command Courses incorporate the lessons identified during Op *Telic* (Iraq) and Op *Herrick* (Afghanistan) with one of the most important additions being assessment of the individual ability as a Vehicle Commander, an ability essential to the Band Service role within Commando Logistic Regiment, Royal Marines, as ambulance, and other vehicle, drivers.

The training regimes described above are designed to ensure that all members of the RMBS maintain the required levels of fitness; are up to date with current military practice and are also familiar with the latest equipment, kit, weapons and combat techniques such as patrolling and day/night navigation. Additional, specialist, training is given when a band, or part of a band, is deployed in its military role.[10] One of the latest developments is that, with much of the training, at all levels, being concentrated at the Commando Training Centre the need for a female Military Training Instructor has been recognised and acted upon. This female Military Training Instructor has now completed a five-week module within the Skill at Arms course and is now qualified to conduct weapons training within the Royal Marines Band Service. A Band Service aspiration is to have not only a qualified Academic Instructor within each of the bands but also to have a qualified First Aid Instructor and a qualified Weapons Instructor similarly embedded.

---

8 *(Section = 8 men).*

9 *(Troop = Three eight-man Sections plus HQ totalling about thirty men.*

10 *Described in detail in Part 4.*

'HMY Victoria & Albert II, 1864' by W F Mitchell. HMY Alberta is astern. Bandmaster Earle and the Band of the Portsmouth Division probably played on both ships

'he P&O liner Medina taking King George V and Queen Mary to India in 1911; Lt B S Green and the Band of the Royal Marine Artillery accompanied them and, as a result of their service, the King awarded the special cap badge

'Armistice Day 1924' by W Tim Macdonald. The Cenotaph was unveiled at 11.00am on the 11th November 1920, a Tuesday, by King George V. Only the Guards Bands were present. In 1921 and 1922 the Buglers from the Royal Marines, Chatham Division sounded Reveille, whilst in 1923 there was a reduced Service. In 1924, the date of this painting, Royal Marines Buglers sounded Reveille and trumpeters of the Royal Air Force, involved for the first time, played Last Post. The sixteen Buglers were from Chatham Division and it is interesting to note that, despite the amalgamation of the Royal Marine Artillery and the Royal Marine Light Infantry the year before, the Chatham Buglers still wear their scarlet tunics. It is known that the Band did not change their tunics until 1927 but this the first suggestion that the Buglers also retained theirs. It is also interesting to note that this is the first year that the Ceremony took the form we now know so well

Divisional tunic belonging to a Musician of the Portsmouth Division, RMLI, and dated 1918. At that time tunics would be made by the Barracks tailor possibly using local outworkers.

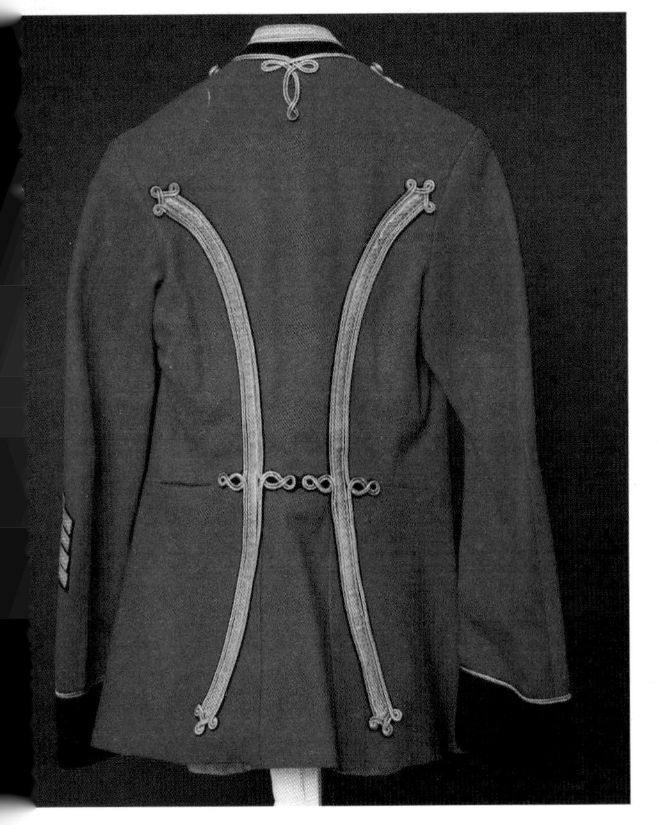

It is believed that the tunic was produced in 1918 and remained in service until about 1920 when the design changed, mainly through the amount of braiding being reduced. The buttons carry the wording 'Royal Marines Light Infantry' which is incorrect, the name being 'Royal Marine Light Infantry'. It was this pattern button that led to confusion over the name in recent years

Mozart: Clarinet Concerto K.V.622(2nd Movt)

Corps of Drums

Hess arr. Waller: Fantasy for Violin

Webb arr. Naughton: MacArthur Park

Lemon: Helter Skelter

Harty arr. Johnson: In Ireland

Graham: Windows of the World - Rainforest

Beethoven: Marche Militaire

Berger: D'Ysebahn

Trad arr. Johnson: Home on the Range

Whelan arr. Cole: Riverdance

Whelan arr. Cole: Riverdance

Damare arr. Johnson: Pandora

Coulter arr. Hancock: Home Away from Home

Richards: Demelza

Leyland/Graham arr. Tripp: You Raise Me Up

Following the Ceremony of Beating Retreat on Horse Guards Parade in 2009 the Massed Bands of the Royal Marines led by the Corps of Drums march along The Mall and past Buckingham Palace. The Fanfare Team brings up the rear. © Les Scriver

The Massed Bands of the Royal Marines at the 2008 Edinburgh Tattoo. © *Colin Dean*

'The Royal Marines at the Mansion House in their Tercentenary Year – 1964. From the painting by Charles Stadden, Commissioned to Celebrate the 25th Anniversary of the Royal Marines Historical Society -28th October 1989' Reproduced by kind permission of the Society

PART 4 - THE DEVELOPING MILITARY ROLE.

Chapter 23: Introduction - Through two World Wars

It was in 1910 that the military duties that would have such far-reaching consequences for Royal Marine Bands were formulated. This was only seven years after the 'Band Service' was formed - the Divisional Bands, at that time a total of two hundred all ranks representing about 11% of the total musical support to RN and RM, were not given true military roles until after 1950, and that was only as a direct result of their amalgamation with the Royal Naval School of Music and its bands.

"Fire Control Duties. - Instruction in the Fire Control duties will take place prior to the men being drafted to sea, on expiration of training at the Royal Naval School of Music, and will be of one week's duration. On completion of the course a qualification of 'VG[1]', 'VG', 'G', 'F' or 'Indifferent' is to be awarded according to ability, and the result is to be noted on the Drill".[1] Further detail was added in 1911:

"Syllabus of instruction in the Working of Fire Control Instruments:

a) To set a Dumaresq C of R Instrument from the data supplied. To read off the rate and deflection;
b) To set the rate on a Range Clock, to understand its mechanism sufficiently for it to be worked with intelligence;
c) To work the Vickers and Barr and Stroud Transmitters;
d) To be able to set a Gun Range Indicator, and to read off from it the ranges to be set on the Transmitters;
e) To transmit Ranges, Deflection and Bearings by Navy-phone, using the authorised nomenclature; and to work a fire gong".[2] At the same time "VG in working of Fire Control Instruments" was added to the requirements for Band Corporal and Bandmaster 1st and 2nd Class promotion. The 1922 General Standing Orders stated that: "Instruction in the use of Fire Control Instruments is to be carried out at Eastney and for formed bands in HMS *Excellent* in accordance with the syllabus laid down in the Gunnery Training Manual".[3]

The result of the introduction of these military duties will be seen as this story develops; at this point it is sufficient to say that, in a war-time situation the Musicians of the Royal Marine Bands would be placed in a very dangerous environment indeed.

World War II.

A Musician in a ship's band wrote an excellent first-hand account of life at sea during a Malta convoy. "A ship such as *Cleopatra* had a band of fifteen members, including a Bandmaster and a Corporal and on said ships were two compartments known as transmitting stations or TS for short. The main one was situated as far below decks as possible, hopefully to keep it safe from damage and the other one just below the upper deck. The said TSs were the heart of the gunnery system and I say this with 'tongue in cheek', although I heard it said many times that we bandsmen were supposed to be

1 *General Standing Orders, Royal Marines 1910, para 1163, page 227.*
2 *General Orders, Royal Marines 1911, December, page 148.*
3 *Para 1362, page 224.*

intelligent, having had the brains to learn music. Hence the TS was our domain and action station, which at times turned out to be a rather dangerous one to say the least. Each TS comprised a plotting table, full of dials, handles etc to be manipulated. Complete with red firing button, set off by one of us when all guns had been loaded and ready by sailors and marines. After receiving an estimated range from the spotting officer way up above, the rest was up to us, as to whether or not we hit an enemy ship or aircraft! Not a pleasant job down there in that tiny compartment during the heat of a Mediterranean summer, hearing bombs and shells around us and not knowing whether we would ever see daylight again. Any damage directly above could of course make it difficult to say the least, or impossible for us to get out. All hatches battened down of course all through any action. There were many who heard the terrible sound of a torpedo hitting your ship, only feet away from your position! An unearthly silence, no lights and ship listing at 45degrees! Yes, I was below at that time and remember so clearly our PO [Petty Officer] in charge saying 'Right lads, up top as fast as you can go'. I doubt anyone who has not had a similar experience can ever contemplate our relief and prayers at reaching the upper deck and blue skies almost in a matter of seconds, such was our haste to see daylight. At least 23 stokers and seamen plus one bandsman were killed on that occasion. Fortunately we didn't sink and after a slow return to Malta, the wounded and dead were taken ashore. I volunteered with others to remove bodies from the engine room and then, as Bugler, was there at the Malta Naval Cemetery playing the *Last Post* and *Reveille* at their burial service. I have lost count of the number of times that duty fell to me during those years. Well comrades, I could obviously write so much more, but time and space will not allow. Sufficient to say that Royal Marines Bandsmen at sea were not medical orderlies or stretcher bearers as is so often quoted, but played an active part in the fighting of each ship in which we served".[4]

The Bass Drum of the Hood Battalion of the Royal Naval Division. Used on the Western Front during World War 1

4 *Written by A L Fry RMBX1240 and published in Blue Band, Winter 1995 p77. With reference to the comment about playing bugle it should be noted that Mr Fry makes the point that, as a Musician, he played cornet, violin and bugle.*

Chapter 24: 1945 to 1989 - the year of the Deal Bombing

Post World War II.

The 'traditional' military role of the two world wars began to change and develop almost as soon as the Second World War ended. In 1945 the Superintendent of the RNSM was able to state that "Personnel are trained at the Royal Naval School of Music for this Service and at Royal Naval Gunnery Schools for Fire Control duties in the gunnery organisation of HM Ships" but a few years later he was recording that Musicians should no longer undertake Fire Control Duties because it entailed harbour Watch-keeping which prevented the band from practising and performing. He suggested Damage Control duties, since this involved standing watches at sea only, and this was accepted by the Admiralty and the traditional role gradually ceased. However, this was certainly not universally adopted since, during the Korean War, the Musicians' military role on cruisers remained as part of the Fire Control systems whilst those on the Light Fleet Carriers were taught to re-arm aircraft with rockets, bombs and cannon-shells. The reputation of the Musician to adapt to whatever task was required was further enhanced by the Band of 3rd Commando Brigade when they accompanied the Brigade to Malaya. On arrival they were each issued with a rifle and fifty rounds of ammunition for a twenty-five hour train journey, during which they all had to take turn as sentries. This was followed by a sixty-five mile journey in lorries, through darkness and torrential rain, which brought the band to Brigade HQ at Ipoh. This 'training' equipped the band to move around the country without escort, and to provide their own defence when making journeys, a Bren gun being manned on each vehicle.

The cuts and changes resulting from the 1957 Defence Review coincided with changes to ships' gunnery systems. The following year CGRM's staff proposed that Band ranks should have training in Nuclear, Biological and Chemical Warfare with a view to this becoming their operational commitment. This was accepted and Junior Musicians received an 'acquaint' during their final term and all Band ranks had two days of their pre-embarkation training on NBCW work.

3rd Commando Brigade - Aden and Borneo.

3rd Cdo Bde Band continued in support of the Brigade and its individual Commando units as needed. In 1963, after working together in Aden, Brigade and Band deployed to Borneo which was in the grip of guerrilla warfare. The band toured the country giving concerts to the Commando Units, any other British unit serving there and also the civilian population. It was calculated that by the time they left the region, the band had travelled further than all the other emergency troops put together.

Northern Ireland.

It was ironic that, despite all of the discussions about changes to military roles, individual Royal Marine Bands could find themselves in potentially dangerous situations whilst carrying out their musical role. Commando Forces Band went to Northern Ireland in September 1972 in support of 40 Cdo. The band played at all of 40 Cdo's tactical locations and their HQ. They also supported community relations by playing for the Belfast community in areas deemed by their hosts to be safe. Probably as a result of this cooperation it was agreed that the bands could wear green berets on limited occasions such as performing in N Ireland, during military training and when caps are impractical eg when serving on ships[1]. In September 1977, and at other times when the Commandos were deployed there, the band of the Commando Forces moved to Ireland to entertain the Units. Flakjackets and berets were the order of the day on those occasions.

Civil Aid - Fire-fighters strike 1 (Op *Burberry*).

As well as the musical and military roles the RMBS have, in recent times, been amongst the first to be called upon when aid to our civil authorities is needed. Two thousand men of the Corps were deployed on fire fighting duties (Operation *Burberry*) in December 1977 as men of the Fire Service went on strike. This force included Musicians from the bands of the RMSM Staff Band, Commando Forces and the Commando Training Centre, RM, who were sent to the Midlands and to the Glasgow area. Since the engines and equipment of the Fire Service could not be used, old fire engines were pulled from military stores and made ready. Painted green they soon became known as 'Green Goddesses'. A Glasgow school was burnt down by its pupils and the Band Service had to do the best that it could with its 1½" canvas hoses that burst all too frequently.[2] The fire-fighters's strike lasted thirteen continuous weeks taking them well into 1978.

Falklands War (Op *Corporate*).

The real watershed with regard to post-World War 2 military service for the RMBS came in 1982. Argentine military forces invaded the Falkland Islands and South Georgia. The Government, after a period of diplomatic negotiation, sent a Task Force to the South Atlantic. The Band of Commando Forces was added to 3rd Commando Brigade. Trained in casualty-handling and in First Aid, the intention was for the band to be based in SS *Canberra* initially and possibly come ashore later.[3] In the early hours of the morning of the 4th April Capt J Ware, D of M of the Commando Forces Band, was told to recall his band from leave. First priority was to draw the necessary equipment and to begin training as part of Commando Logistic Regiment's Medical Squadron. The band left the barracks on the 8th April and joined the *Canberra* at Southampton. As the ship sailed it was played out by the Band of FOF3 (WO II T Attwood), also recalled from Easter leave. FOF3 band then returned to Easter leave only to be again recalled, this time to fly to Gibraltar to join SS *Uganda*. This educational cruise ship was being hurriedly converted to a hospital ship and the band was soon thrown into the hard work of making the ship ready for its new role. They became part of Naval Party 1830, Surgical Support Team No. 4, and underwent training for their stretcher-bearer role. The average age of this band was twenty-one. The ship's complement numbered one hundred and twenty plus the band and it was evident that, when organised into watches, the medical skills were spread very thinly. Medical training for the band was initiated and as the ship sailed towards Sierra Leone they became involved with exercises for the launching and recovery of ships' boats, flying stations and Replenishment at Sea. They designed and constructed CASEVAC (casualty evacuation) routes to help them in their role of quickly unloading casualties from helicopters on the landing pad and getting them down to the wards and the clearing station below. Periods of training and refresher courses in radio and signals procedure, the preparation of casualty control lists, Nuclear, Biological and Chemical Warfare (NBCW) updates and physical training on deck were all taken in the stride of the band. Rehearsals were fitted in

1 *CGRMs Advisory Dress Committee files.*
2 *Account taken from author's contribution to 'Sound the Trumpets, Beat the Drum'.*
3 *'No Picnic' Maj-Gen J Thompson.*

and after a few days at sea they attended a Medical Squadron briefing about what would be done if things went badly.

Meanwhile full-scale exercises for air-disembarkation of *Canberra* took place with 3rd Parachute Regiment (3 Para) as guinea pigs and the Musicians as marshals. The whole of 3 Para were flown off the ship during this exercise. The band also helped with the handling of loads being distributed, or redistributed, around the Fleet by helicopter.

The training and refresher courses continued whilst at Ascension and included weapon training, use of Arctic ration packs, watching films of battle injuries in Vietnam to give an indication of what the band might have to deal with, lectures on distress and bereavement and other subjects. In the evenings they entertained the troops with pop groups and concerts of various types.[4]

By the time that the Task Force had sailed 8,000 miles the Commando Forces Band on board *Canberra* had changed from a purely musical role to a fully-fledged medical one prepared for an operational situation. The climate had changed from hot at Ascension to very cold with rough seas as they approached the Falklands. As *Uganda* sailed south she made for the Red Cross safe area, arriving there at 1700hrs on 11th May. The band stowed their instruments, and waited.

As the *Canberra* sailed south so the lectures and training continued: 'Aircraft Recognition', 'Falklands Weapons' and 'Eye Injuries'. On 15th May the ship came within striking distance of Argentine aircraft. Next day Surgeon Commander R Jolly[5] briefed the band and the rest of Medical Squadron about the proposed invasion plans. Later, because of the fear of not being able to maintain sterile conditions, the band spent several hours taking up floor tiles from a room designated as an operating theatre.

In order for the landings to take place *Canberra's* Royal Marines had to be cross-decked to the Assault Ship HMS *Fearless*. The Musicians acted as guides by leading the various sub-units, fully equipped and armed, through the passageways of the ship and out to the boat-decks. This had to be managed carefully in the correct order to get the men to the right place at the right time. The band were then mainly occupied with ammunition sentry duties until, at 1120hrs the emergency stretcher party closed-up on deck and four members of the band carried down the first fatality to be brought on board the ship, one of the crew of a Sea-King helicopter that had crashed.

Friday the 21st was the most action packed day as far as the *Canberra* was concerned. The ship was under continual cannon and missile attack but the band continued to unload casualties from the helicopters and move them down to the reception area. The method that had been developed for this was to carry the stretcher from the helicopter to the head of a ramp. A Musician on deck then lowered an injured man down the ramp using a rope pulley system. On the deck below would be two men ready to guide the stretcher down and to carry it to the ward or the theatre. Musn G Latham was lowering a wounded man down the ramp when the *Canberra* came under attack from what appears to have been three Argentine aircraft. Despite being in a very exposed position he coolly continued to lower the wounded man and only took cover when he knew that his colleagues below had taken responsibility for the situation. The ship was at maximum alert all day as the Argentine air attacks were almost continuous. The men continued these duties throughout the next day, working from 0100hrs, having being woken after only two hours sleep to work through the night. They were told that, now that the landings were established, the ship would sail from Falkland Sound and would return each day at dusk to evacuate casualties. Before this occurred the band were involved with the burial at sea of four Royal Marines.

4 *'Canberra: The Great White Whale Goes to War.' (Diary kept by BdSgt Ireland).*
5 *Surgeon Cdr R Jolly who commanded Medical Squadron of 3 Cdo Bde.*

A member of the band prepared the bodies and then the small Church band played the *Naval Hymn*. Two Buglers sounded *Last Post*. Shortly after this the pop group rigged up to entertain the survivors of HMS *Ardent* who had been brought aboard.[6] On 2nd June twenty-seven Argentine casualties were brought on board. They were Special Forces and were considered dangerous so the Musicians were issued with SMGs and live ammunition.

The band continued to move and unload casualties, help in the wards and provide stores moving parties. As the operation ashore progressed so the number of Argentine prisoners increased. Four thousand had to be documented, de-loused, fed and guarded. Following the surrender on 14th June *Canberra* took on many more prisoners and the band was now armed at all times. The prisoners were then taken to Puerto Madryn in Argentina. During the passage the band threw all Argentine military equipment over the side of the ship. Whilst *Canberra* had seen action in Falklands Sound the FOF3 band in SS *Uganda* had also been heavily committed. The casualties started as a trickle but the flow soon increased; sailors with burns and flash burns and marines with gunshot and other wounds. The band carried them below, to the operating theatres and back to the wards, they took them to X-ray, they dressed their wounds and changed their beds. Each member of the band fought his own battle against exhaustion. On several occasions BM Attwood had to order his men to rest or get a meal. Then the Argentine prisoners came. Amongst them were boys of thirteen, who had all been living in the field for weeks; some had dysentery. They were bathed, reassured and guarded. The medical teams were fully stretched and the band removed stitches and, on one occasion, even hand ventilated a marine with breathing difficulties. The red crosses painted on the ship did not prevent the Argentine Air Force from 'buzzing' the ship. A total of seven hundred British and Argentine casualties received treatment aboard *Uganda* during the operation.

Two Buglers sounded *Last Post* as a burial took place on a wet hillside overlooking Ajax Bay. The band played for the return of the Governor to the island and also led an Airborne Forces parade through Stanley. *Uganda*, with the band on board, returned to Southampton on 9th August. The two bands undoubtedly upheld the reputation of their predecessors who, during the two world wars, performed so well in action. Major Ewen

The Band of Commando Forces with its Director of Music Captain John Ware, leads the Royal Marines contingent through London on the 12th October 1982 as part of the Falklands Parade. The Band wears the unique cap badge in their green berets. (© Colin Dean)

6 HMS Ardent was hit by four Argentine bombs. Fire and explosion damage was so great that the order to abandon ship was given and the crew transferred to Canberra.

Southby-Tailyour[7] wrote, "Let no one take them [the bands] away from us for their presence in action is an integral part of the morale (including their medical support duties) of the Royal Marines, and morale has an irreplaceable role in achieving, and celebrating, victory".

Northern Ireland (2).

Not only was the Falklands operation a watershed, it was also an interlude to the frequent tours of duty in Northern Ireland supporting various Commando Units. The Band of Flag Officer Scotland and Northern Ireland regularly deployed to the province to entertain and to recruit. Apart from entertaining 'Royal' the band also carried out public engagements. An extract from an article[8] written by a Musician describes how the band and the Commando unit worked together, "The band did a couple of displays, one at Musgrave Park Hospital which was the base of 45 Cdo 'B' Echelon. For this gig we had most of the Company on the ground and our own clearance/close protection patrol while we worked. We fell in behind the main gate and the Commando patrol went out doing the whole bit… taking good cover… ducking and weaving… total observation… 'Royal' at his best. One minute later the band went out doing the whole bit… regimental march… immaculate dressing… marks of expression… 'Bandy' at his best. Both sides of the Corps on the ground together; doing what they do best, and doing it well".

Civil Aid - Aden.

Band involvement in military or civil aid roles is not always planned. In 1986 HMY *Britannia* had just exited the southern end of the Suez Canal when news that civil war had broken out in Aden came through. The ship's complement transformed the Royal Yacht into an evacuation ship, including a large sick-bay, and the members of the band were all assigned tasks such as beach, store and stretcher parties, for helping the evacuees when they came aboard. The men carried and rowed the children and the injured from the beach to the Royal Yacht whilst the fighting ashore became heavier. The Yacht made several journeys to different parts of Aden giving aid and evacuating refugees. By the end of the emergency 1,068 men, women and children of 55 different nationalities had been brought aboard and, as always, the band had thrown itself into assisting in any way it could - from musical concerts and entertainment to carrying bags of rice and warming babies bottles.[9]

Deal Bombing.

Whatever the perceived value of the Royal Marines Band Service as a military force fighting alongside the Commando Units, there can be no doubt that it is recognised as one of the icons of the Corps. This makes them a target; and the Royal Marines Band Service carries the scars - not just from the two World Wars but also from 0825 on the morning of the 22nd September 1989. At that time an explosion rocked the town of Deal in general and the Royal Marines Barracks in particular. When the dust cleared it could be seen that a concrete-roofed recreation room had been destroyed. Eleven men of the Band of the Royal Marines School of Music lay dead or dying. Many more lay injured, some of them seriously. The Irish Republican Army admitted responsibility for the atrocity. The full story is told elsewhere in this book but mention of it in this section, in the chronology of events that illustrate the military role of the Royal Marines Band Service, is essential.

---

7 *'Reasons in Writing - A Commando's View of the Falklands War' Maj Southby-Tailyour.*

8 *Blue Band Vol 37 No 3 page 76.*

9 *It is believed that this is the only time that the Royal Yacht was used in her originally anticipated 'dual role'.*

Chapter 25: Iraq, Kosovo and Iraq again

Iraq 1 - 1990 (OP *Granby*).

On the 2nd October 1990 an advance party from C-in-C Fleet Band joined RFA *Argus*, the Primary Casualty Receiving Unit, at Plymouth in preparation for deployment to the Persian Gulf. They were soon involved with the ship's routine and loaded stores, equipment and medical supplies.[1] Two days later the rest of the band under Capt M Goss joined - the largest formed body of Royal Marines to be deployed to the Gulf. Lt Col J Ware, veteran of the Falklands War, wrote, "Engaged primarily as medical orderlies they will also be active in a musical capacity, providing the invaluable moral and psychological support which only a band can. Once again, as in the Falklands Campaign in 1982, the Band Service has the opportunity to prove that, even in modern times, there remains a need for a group of able Musicians who are also intelligent and flexible enough to adapt quickly and efficiently to any task which may present itself".

Included amongst the pre-embarkation training was fire fighting at sea and, once at sea, training included first aid, Nuclear Biological and Chemical Decontamination (NBCD) and stretcher handling. Training and exercises continued on arrival in the Gulf and the band volunteered themselves as First Aid teams. Rehearsals and concerts were part of the ongoing routine of duties, as was ship protection, and training. By mid-December the ship was frequently at Action Stations although the Fleet Band's war did not start until January 17th when four potential air threats occurred. As the allies gained supremacy the ship sailed north and the band became involved in watching for mines. Shortly after this, Iraqi bodies began to be recovered from the sea and the band were involved in preparing them for burial at sea - a most unpleasant duty that moved the ship's Chaplain, the Reverend S Pickering to write, "I know I am quite biased, but it is just an example of their fortitude, professionalism and dedication, all exemplified with their usual courtesy and good humour. A joy to work amongst, and with. Thank you. Every Blessing".[2] Following the cease-fire, and after Beating Retreat at the British Embassy at Abu Dhabi - possibly the last occasion when an RM Band wore green berets - they flew home to RAF Brize Norton. All were later presented with the 1991 Gulf Medal by Admiral Sir Jock Slater.

Exercise *Bright Star* - 1999.

In 1999 the Band of Commando Training Centre, RM, was flown to Naples to join HMS *Ocean* for an exercise deployment. When Egypt was reached Exercise *Bright Star* involving 85,000 troops from eighteen countries over a three-week period began. The band took part in a series of musical and military engagements ranging from playing for an Officers' dinner in the middle of the desert to acting as casualties to test the medical evacuation systems. In some cases they were exercise casualties for medics from Britannia Royal Naval College Band who had been flown to Egypt as part of Medical Squadron, Cdo Log Regt. The BRNC Band was split into two Troops and operated two Forward Dressing Stations (FDS) throughout the exercise. With the band running these two FDS it was shown that Medical Squadron could provide ample medical cover for 3rd Cdo Bde, and by moving a FDS forward by road and air the optimum time for medical cover could be achieved.

1 *Diary of Bug M Williams.*
2 *Blue Band Autumn 1991 p40.*

The Band Service was crucial to this achievement. During 'Distinguished Visitors Day' the Secretary of State for Defence made a point of telling CTC Band how much everyone was talking about the band's performances over the past few weeks. The band later assisted in preparing for an emergency landing on *Ocean* by a damaged Chinook helicopter.

Kosovo - 2000. (Operations *Agricola*, *Trojan* and *Sexton*).

During the 2001 Festival of Remembrance men and women representing the Kosovo Band formed part of the Royal Marines Band Service display. (Image courtesy of Les Scriver)

At the end of the year some of those who had led the way during RMT2000[3] found themselves leading the way in a different theatre: Operation *Agricola* - Kosovo, as part of the Medical Squadron near Pristina. A specially formed band of thirty volunteers, known as K Band, underwent arduous training for this deployment. First Aid refresher courses were given at CTC and, for the SNCOs, training in Combat Stress Trauma Management. The RMSoM's Military Training Team took them to Longmoor for a week's field training followed by a week's field exercises on Copehill Down. Lectures and exercises included field-craft, weapon training, map-reading and medical exercises using recruits from the School of Music as casualties. Lectures at the United Nations Training Advisory Team establishment on Salisbury Plain were followed by two and a half days' training in the FIBUA[4] village and an exercise to test the knowledge and experience that had been accumulated. They were flown into Kosovo in an RAF C130 Hercules and received an hour's lecture on the area and, in particular, minefields. Med Sqn then moved to Harden Lines[5] for the handover from 5 Medical Support Regiment RAMC. Working with the undermanned Medical Staff they were split into two Troops, each under a Troop (Band) Sergeant, and their duties included driving, manning the Battlefield Ambulances and the Medical Stores. Ambulance Troop provided three-man teams consisting of a Vehicle Commander and a First Aider, both of whom were Musicians, and a fully trained Medic. The Musicians were also rotated through other tasks including Operation *Trojan* (escorting Serbian casualties who required medical treatment but were living in Albanian areas); Operation *Sexton* (assisting United Nations Forensic Teams investigating war crimes through the exhumation of bodies); guard duties and armed escorts, manning vehicle check-points and emergency ambulance crews. They also went on patrol with Commando units in Pristina, Obilic and Kosovo Polje and, as part of KFOR, took convoys from Pristina to the Greek border and elsewhere - with Musicians as Convoy Commanders.

They also entertained not only the troops but the local population, particularly the children. Eighty-six musical engagements were carried out in the six-month period. A campaign of hearts and minds has no finer assets than music and humour and the Musicians and Buglers proved that they have both in abundance.[6]

---

3 *'Royal Military Tattoo 2000', the tri-Service display on Horse-Guards Parade.*
4 *Fighting In a Built-Up Area.*
5 *LCpl H E Harden VC RAMC was awarded a posthumous VC whilst serving with 45 Cdo in WWII.*
6 *Conversation with BdSgt I Davies, Troop Sergeant.*

Iraq 2 - 2003 (Operations *Telic 2* and *James*).

On the 6th January 2003 the Royal Fleet Auxiliary (RFA) *Argus* slipped her moorings and left England for Exercise *Endeavour*. The ship carried, in addition to its normal complement, a composite group of Musicians and Buglers from all five Royal Marine Bands. This band was formed shortly before Christmas 2002 and included a number of men and women who had spent much of the previous few months on Op *Fresco* covering the fire-fighters strike. The selected men and women had, on completion of Christmas leave, gathered in the large band-room at Portsmouth to check kit and equipment before boarding the *Argus*. For the Royal Marines Band Service this was not a new experience. Since the men of C in C Fleet Band had served on board in a medical capacity during the first Gulf War in 1990-1991, strong links had been forged between the ship and the Band Service. However, with such a diverse range of operational roles to cover, this was the band that would write the textbook for future deployments.

One of the ship's many, and diverse, roles was to carry sufficient facilities and trained personnel to enable it to provide the Primary Casualty Receiving Facility (PCRF) for any Royal Navy Task Group, or Royal Navy Task Group acting in support of land-based operations overseas – particularly those spearheaded by the Royal Marines. The PCRF was a small, but high-tech, hospital consisting of an Emergency Department and Operating Theatres, Intensive Care and High Dependency units and General Wards. The facility could provide one hundred beds, at which time it would be known as PCRF100 but, in non-operational situations, had twenty-five beds available as standard and was known as PCRF 25.

Since the First Gulf War the Band Service had regularly carried out exercises on board the ship. Through careful planning and rotation of personnel the Band Service could provide trained and skilled men and women capable of joining *Argus* with only the minimum of refresher training. Their role would be to support the skilled medical staff of the Royal Navy and the Commando Logistic Regiment, Royal Marines, by taking responsibility for transferring casualties, usually brought on board by helicopter, from the flight-deck down to the Medical Facility.

Within this task was the additional requirement of providing a chemical monitoring team within the PCRF. This team had to check, monitor and, when necessary, decontaminate casualties upon flight-deck arrival.[7] The ship, originally a roll-on, roll-off ferry which was taken up from trade (TUFT) for the Falklands and purchased two years later, was converted to the PCRF role in 1990-91 and, as a result of her age, was not well-suited either to combating a chemical attack or to receiving chemically contaminated casualties.

Casualty transfer of a number of Iraqi casualties from helicopter to the hospital via the helicopter lift on board RFA Argus. RMBS personnel wear the Red Cross vests

In addition to fulfilling their medical duties at training, practice and action station levels, the band would have to provide musical support to RFA *Argus* and to major ships of any Task Force that the *Argus* accompanied.

7 *This was in addition to a weapons search.*

Such was the background to the ship's departure from Southampton Docks on the 6th January 2003. Forty-seven band ranks were selected for the exercise but, as details of the deployment to the Gulf became clearer, five were stood down. The ship returned to Southampton on the 9th January and the band was given a weekend pre-deployment leave. Departure for the Gulf would take place on the 14th January. During the course of the exercise the final band complements and duties had been discussed between RN and Cdo Logs medical staff and the Director of Music (DOM).

Upon sailing on the 14th the ship reverted to PCRF25 since the additional bed-space was required for transporting five 820 Naval Air Squadron (NAS) helicopters to the Gulf. This level of medical support required a band of twenty but Captain N Grace, the Officer Commanding Royal Marines and Director Music (also the PCRF Operations Officer), raised this to twenty-four, plus himself and the Drum Major (who was also Company Sergeant-Major), in order to provide the necessary level of musical support. This situation would continue until about the 7th February when PCRF25 would convert to PCRF100, as a result of the helicopters leaving. At this point a further sixteen band ranks, required due to the increase in facility capacity, would fly out to join the *Argus*. In the meantime these ranks would undertake additional training or, in some cases, specialist training in Post Trauma Stress Management at Birmingham's Selly Oak Hospital and Haslar Hospital, Gosport. The selected band comprised a Bandmaster, who doubled as PT Instructor, two BdSgts with responsibilities for stowage as well as Band Service public address systems and electrical installations, three Cpls one of whom was the Music Librarian, and fourteen Musicians. The Corps of Drums comprised three Buglers under the command of a CplBug. Such a deployment requires back-up and this would be coordinated from Headquarters by Maj Thornhill, Staff Officer, Band Service; Capt Weston, SO3 (Drafting Officer) and Captain Henderson, Supply Officer (Music). All were Band Service Officers.

Two days after sailing Capt Grace was able to signal Commodore Miller, HMS *Ark Royal*, to the effect that the Band was established on board *Argus* and would be capable of providing the majority of musical combinations for Beating Retreat, ship's concerts, string quartet, dance and Dixie bands, jazz trios and quintets in support of the deployment. Due to imposed kit limitations the band, named 'The Band of HM Royal Marines, RFA *Argus* Deployment 03', would parade in either Combat 95 or half-lovat with beret uniform; ceremonial uniforms were not available. Most of the band spent most of the day moving medical stores from one part of the ship to another (and sometimes back again!)

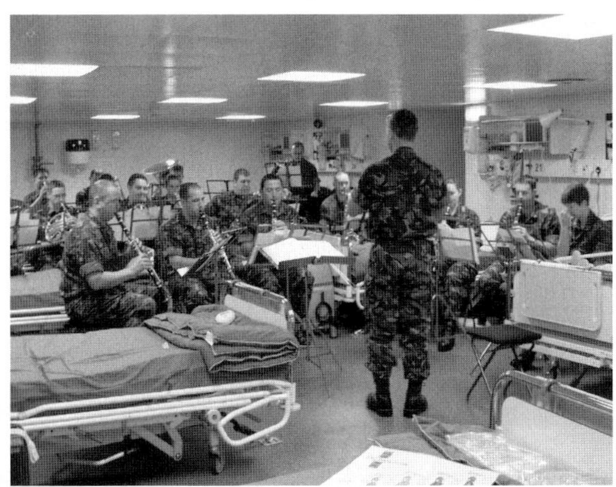

The Military Band provides music for a Church Service in the High Dependency Unit, RFA Argus

On the 19th, the full military band provided musical support, consisting of two hymns, plus *All Through the Night* and *Fantasy on British Sea Songs* as the opening and closing music for the Church Service.

For some, this was the first opportunity to perform since the beginning of October because of the Op *Fresco* commitment. On the same day the ship passed through the Straits of Gibraltar and Supply Officer Music was provided with the information necessary to keep the families of the band ranks advised of the developing situation via a Family Link letter – a role that he would maintain throughout the deployment. By this time training programmes for casualty handling, physical training and musical support were in place and being supplemented by exercises. Lectures on a range of subjects such as NBC, damage control and Fire-fighting (the latter not being appreciated by those who had recently returned from Op *Fresco*) were presented by Flag Officer Sea Training (FOST) staff. The damage control lecture was followed, next day, by an exercise. Of particular importance this week was the need to ensure that everyone was properly trained in the procedures necessary for flight-deck work. This was followed by three days hands-on training with 820 NAS, and then a night exercise with helicopters landing on board, and the Casualty Handling teams practising the drills. Casualty Handling duties are physically demanding and, as a result of these exercises, the DOM implemented compulsory daily Physical Training which was enthusiastically led by the Bandmaster, BdCSgt D Sharp. Band rehearsals were initially held in the ship's large, and very noisy, hangar and so the High Dependency Ward was used when not required for patients. The FOST report, following their three-day visit, gave the ship a 'Just Satisfactory' rating but specifically praised the RMBS personnel's attitude and professionalism.

There was also a steady stream of real casualties which allowed a valuable element of realism to be experienced. Band ranks also had the opportunity to work with, and learn from, the RAF Aeromedical Team. Musician Hairsine later described the role of the RAF team for The Blue Band web-page: 'On board we have an aeromed team whose job is to liaise with their colleagues… they have also been instructing us in different types of helicopters and working alongside us when practising for casevacs… they supervise the casualty's safe transit onto whichever sort of helicopter they have brought. It is quite a long process as we all have to make sure that the patient is secure and stable for what may turn out to be a long and not necessarily smooth flight ashore. Today's casevac saw the release of five people back to their respective countries'. Musician Hairsine passed out of training in August 2002 and was drafted to the RM Band of Britannia Royal Naval College. He enjoyed playing in a few concerts before he became involved in Op *Fresco,* being stationed in Bristol at Avon's busiest temporary fire station. At the end of the year he joined the RFA *Argus* - all this in less than six months.

A week later, as preparations to move to PCRF100 level began, the lack of on board accommodation became a serious problem with all units having to shed personnel. Capt Grace was able to overcome this by de-selecting three of the ranks due to join as part of the PCRF100 complement.

The Ceilidh Band play for the Burns Night celebrations on board the Argus. The vocalist is BdCpl Shuggie McGleish, veteran of most of the RMBS military and civilian aid deployments from Op Telic 2 up to, and including, Op Herrick 9

The Church Service on the 26th January again featured opening and closing music, this time *Irish Tune from County Derry* and *Broadway Showstoppers* respectively, with three hymns - plus the opportunity to rehearse *Jubilate* fanfare as an introductory piece. By this time the band was playing, in various forms, around the ship as much as the training regime permitted. During the previous evening the Ceilidh

Band played in the Wardroom for Burns Night and then repeated the programme for the Junior Rates' bar on the Sunday evening.

A few days later the Task Force could see the coastline of Cyprus and, during this period, an opportunity for further training presented itself in the form of Exercise *Wader*. During the exercise seven 'casualties' were received on board and successfully dealt with. This exercise also provided the opportunity for the Casualty Handlers to become familiar with more of the various helicopters being used by the coalition forces and to develop different routines for the different types.

Casualty handling techniques for the removal of stretchers from a wide range of helicopters, including the US Pave Hawk, had to be learnt and practised

On completion of the transit of the Suez Canal by the Task Group, Captain Grace began planning to entertain crews and troops on board HM Ships *Ocean* and *Ark Royal*, as well as RFA *Argus* herself. The musical content would be a mixture of Military Band, Big Band, Dance Band and a display by the Corps of Drums, culminating in a traditional Naval Finale. Logistically this presented great difficulties since the movement of a band of twenty-six ranks with instruments, lighting and amplification requires not only careful planning but also the allocation of special resources. The equipment has to be transported in large flight-cases and everything has to be on the deck by 1300hrs in order that everything can be rigged up prior to the evening concert. Afterwards everything has to be de-rigged which means that, usually, camp beds have to be borrowed so that the band can stay overnight. There is also the small matter of distance between ships which can alter significantly during an overnight stay on board. Under the circumstances helicopter support, ideally a Chinook since the total weight of equipment was about 4,000lbs or 1.75 tons, would have to be requested. The Sea Kings of 820 NAS Squadron could do it but it would take several lifts to accomplish it.

On Tuesday the 4th February, with temperatures rising above 27ºC, a chemical attack exercise took place. This required the donning of full NBC kit including respirators. The following morning was spent attending lectures which meant that the PT had to take place at the hottest time of the day. The following day required the use of NBC kit again as the band rehearsed casualty decontamination; this being a task for four people, each carefully monitoring each other's condition. The afternoon provided relief as the band rehearsed for the next evening's 'Showcase' concert. Friday morning began with physical training and circuits, quickly followed by more casualty decontamination drills in full NBC kit and a temperature of 27ºC. After lunch, preparations were made for the evening's concert which began with *Jubilate* Fanfare. This was followed by *Symphonic Marches* by Williams, *Time Off* by Watson and *Stars and Stripes Forever* by Sousa, all featuring the Corps of Drums. *Boogie Woogie Bugle Boy* led the way for the Big Band and then the Dance Band. Bandmaster D Sharp gave his monologue *Memories from the Coalmine* to the tune of Dvořák's *From the New World* Suite. The Corps of Drums then introduced audience participation with their own version of The Generation Game. Following this came the finale, beginning with the exciting *Riverdance* and progressing through the *Evening Hymn* and *Sunset*, *Britannic Salute*,

Heart of Oak and *A Life on the Ocean Wave*. Anyone who had served in the Falklands would have recalled the journey South when the Band of Commando Forces gave concerts on board SS *Canberra* that raised the morale and patriotism. This time it was the Band of RFA *Argus* that evoked patriotism and pride within their audience, resulting in the lusty singing of the great anthems and marches. As in the Falklands the dual purposes served by Royal Marine Bands, both of them worthwhile and essential, were apparent. To add to the entertainment men of 820 NAS made a guest appearance as the Village People and sang their version of *YMCA* re-titled as 'PCRF'.

A Brass Quintet played the programme of music for the 9th February Church Service. At this time the Task Group was heading into the port of Salalah in the Red Sea so the opportunity for flight-deck entertainment, including a barbeque and music provided by the Big Band, was taken. The ship docked in Salalah to receive stores and for the thirteen additional members of RM Band RFA *Argus* to come aboard. Also joining was the remainder of the PCRF staff, mainly drawn from Haslar Hospital, Portsmouth and Derriford Hospital, Plymouth. 820 NAS had flown from *Argus* the previous day, thus releasing the necessary space.

These new arrivals had departed Brize Norton on the 7th February following a twelve hour delay to their flight time. They landed at a joint RAF/USAF base in Oman eight hours later and were accommodated in chalets with air conditioning and fridges. Next day they visited the USAF base and purchased Camelbacks[8] before relaxing for the rest of the day. On the 9th February, they made the two-hour drive to Salalah Port and joined the *Argus*. Their next few days were spent on lectures and training designed to enable them to be fully integrated into the PCRF organisation.

During the period between the sixteen band personnel being separated from the main body and when they rejoined it they had gained valuable experience that would complement that collected by their colleagues on the *Argus*. On the 20th January they had joined Birmingham Selly Oak's Accident and Emergency Department. A large variety of casualties passed through the Department during the two watch system that they operated. They also experienced the process of dealing with a corpse, later described as morbid but useful. Following this a number of them embarked upon a Stress Management Course, known as Trauma Risk Management, at Haslar Hospital, Gosport.

On the 13th February SgtBug A J Piner with two Buglers and four band ranks transferred to HMS *Ark Royal*. These ranks were to provide a Corps of Drums and a string quartet during the evening of the visit of Rear Admiral Snelson. These personnel were transferred by ship's boat.

A similar concert programme was to be performed in the main hangar on board HMS *Ocean* on the 16th February. Because of the location and security situation seven members of the RMBS, under the command of the Drum Major CSgtBug Taylor, were left on *Argus* to provide an emergency casualty handling capability. On the Sunday this group provided music at the Church service by forming a sextet of five clarinets and one trumpet! Boat transfer of the band to *Ocean*, which was alongside in Salalah, proved interesting and, at one point, five members of the band were hanging onto a rope ladder on the side of the ship when the Landing Craft coxswain was unable to hold his vessel against the hull of *Argus*. The planned Saturday concert in *Ocean's* hangar was cancelled when it was discovered that most of the Royal Marines would be ashore on exercise. As a result everyone watched a football match and then the England v France Rugby international, in between which the Big Band played for the ship's company. On the Sunday the band on board HMS *Ocean* enjoyed a lazy ships routine whilst, following the Church service,

8 *A drinking system carried in the same way as a backpack.*

the Drum Major put his small team through a marathon session of physical exercise. The planned 'Showcase' concert took place. The audience was swollen by the ship's company from HMS *York* and the crews of the embarked NAS. A screen was positioned above the band so that the words of all of the patriotic songs could be projected onto it. The screen was also used to show images of the deployment. Three encores were demanded and the band felt that this was one of the most unforgettable concerts they had ever given. The band was able to spend the weekend on board *Ocean* and took advantage of the additional facilities that this ship could provide.

On the Monday the *Ocean* was unable to sail because of the high winds and the band had to remain on board. This coincided with a major exercise on *Argus* when the scenario was a mass casualty intake as a result of a ship hitting a mine. The Drum Major's team of seven took everything in their stride and managed to get all of the casualties to the PCRF in the prescribed manner. Next day the band was transferred from *Ocean* to a secure compound in the desert. The band finally managed to get back to *Argus* on the Wednesday and was immediately thrown into lectures. This was interrupted by a fire in one of the engine rooms which left the ship stationary whilst the fire-crews, not the RMBS, extinguished the blaze. The next day saw a return to NBC drills. Friday the 21st February saw the introduction of defence watches for the PCRF.

Commodore Miller visited the *Argus* on the 22nd February and saw the band at practise. At the same time SgtBug Piner and BdCpl Lomas were flying to *Ark Royal* with a string quartet and a Corps of Drums to provide Mess Beatings and music for the Commodore's dinner that evening. Church Service the following day took place with the ship at anchor off Kuwait. As well as the three hymns the band played *Nimrod* and *West Side Story*.

On the Monday two American rescue helicopters, Pave Hawks, arrived to see the facility and also to brief the RMBS casualty handlers on their stretcher drills. Two days later mail arrived from home – which was great for everyone's morale. In between these highlights were opportunities for the dance band to rehearse and for personal practice. Standing defence watches were still required and this meant that exercises, such as the fire practice which occurred this week, had to be practised twice. Canulation, the insertion of a needle into a vein for the passing of fluids, was also practised this week. The two Pave Hawk rescue helicopters returned with two 'casualties' for a casualty simulation exercise. During the debriefing the Americans said that they were very impressed with the speed and efficiency of the band and the medical staff. Towards the end of the week the physical training was stepped up and so were the Beat Retreat rehearsals.

Left: Officers & crew had an unexpected treat when the band's trip ashore to entertain troops was cancelled and the band gave their 'Showcase' concert on board RFA Rosalie instead
Right: The Buglers take part in the Rosalie concert

The 'Showcase' concert was brought to HMS *Ark Royal* on the 28th February. The ship's Volunteer Band, under BdCSgt Neighbour, performed as a Rock Band in advance of the concert itself. The concert on *Ark Royal* generated the same strong feelings as did the earlier concerts on *Argus* and *Ocean*.

Everyone returned to *Argus* and then boarded Sea King helicopters for the journey to RFA *Rosalie*, previously known to many as *Fort Grange*. The expected trip ashore to entertain troops with the 'Showcase' concert was cancelled so the band put on a show for the crew and guests on board the *Rosalie*.

This turned out to be the best audience yet and so more musical entertainment, in the form of the Ceilidh Band and Dance Band was provided the following night. To complete the musical support the band formed up as a parade band to Beat Retreat during an Arabian sunset on the 7th March.

The Blue Ensign is lowered as Sunset is sounded on board RFA Rosalie off Saudi Arabia during the ceremony of Beating Retreat

Trad Jazz and Big Band was provided on the Saturday and through donations and the raffle of one of the band's specially designed t-shirts the band contributed £550 to the ship's charity, the Great Ormond Street Children's Hospital. On Sunday the 9th March all ranks returned from *Rosalie* to *Argus*. Two days later the Under Secretary of State for Defence paid a visit to the PCRF.

The following week, whilst not relaxed, was like the lull before the storm. 'Phys' continued, band practice continued, mail arrived and the week ended with another concert. On the 16th March, with the *Argus* at anchor, the band provided Church Service music comprising four hymns including the *Naval Hymn* and, in addition, *Schindler's List* and The *Gael*. Next day, following the regular 'phys' and a 'man's game' of netball, a brief was given on the Chinook and Merlin helicopters and how to approach them when receiving casualties. Next, a lecture on body handling reinforced how near the ship, and the band, was to the conflict and the task for which all had been training. To focus the collective mind further an exercise was carried out with the ship's aircraft lift out of action. This required casualties to be lowered to the PCRF by crane – a slow procedure.

On the 18th March hostilities began and the music had to stop. The band was issued with Nerve Agent Pre-Treatment Systems (known as NAPS tablets), Atropine injectors and spare respirator canisters. A much appreciated letter arrived from previous Principal Director of Music, Lt Col Graham Hoskins. Next day began with personal preparations; letters and phone calls giving reassurance to family and friends, stowage of unnecessary equipment and the order to commence taking the NAPS tablets. Defence Watches began that evening with the band being split into Port and Starboard watches. Next morning Captain Grace gave the band their final brief; mine watch duties were begun and 'Action Stations' was due to be sounded in the evening. Captain Grace cancelled this as the ship itself was not in any danger. However, the ship moved into a forward position that night as UK and US forces launched preliminary attacks ashore.

At 1000hrs next morning, the 21st March, the ship received its first casualties when Iraqi POWs, requiring expert medical treatment, were brought on board. The band disembarked them from the helicopter and searched them before taking them for treatment. One Musician recollected that the first casualty that he saw 'had a wound like you see in an American war film - a neat round hole either side of his leg with little blood or mess. The next casualty provided a reality check with the same Musician having to apply resuscitation and the rest of the team using a range of casualty handling skills on the way down to the hospital where they assisted the medical staff in rolling, checking, removing clothing and preparing the casualty. Members of the band, together with nurses, were on mine-watching duties. Other casualties were received and operated upon, and at the end of the day the band was praised for the professionalism exhibited whilst carrying out the handling duties.

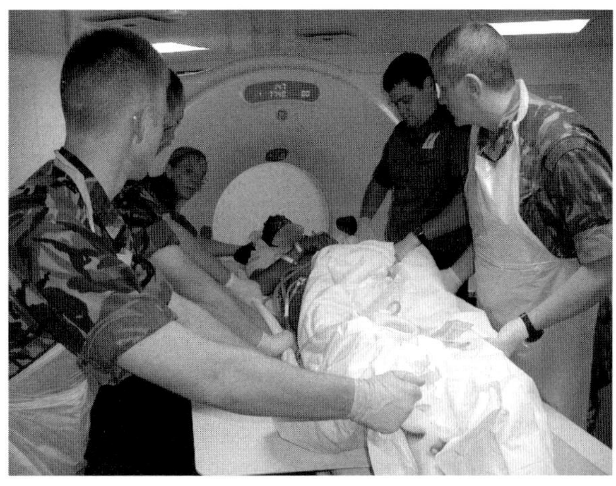

Members of the RMBS (flash visible on Musician on right) assist with scanning a patient in the ship's High Dependency Unit

Next day's Church Service was conducted in the Junior Rates' Galley since the usual location, the High Dependency Unit, was being used by patients. On the 24th the casualties continued, one requiring specialist psychiatric nursing. During the afternoon of the 26th both Watches were required when two Chinooks brought in nineteen stretcher cases, the situation not being helped by a heavy thunderstorm, high winds and lightning. They were required to assist on the wards because of the number of casualties and the severity of their injuries. One of the band commented, "Some of the things seen were quite horrific. The sights, sounds and smells were really difficult to take in and at some points many of the staff had lumps in the throats, such an emotional evening." Another attempted to move an Iraqi patient only to find there were no legs to lift. That night a very ill American patient was in the Intensive Care Unit and needed two nurses to look after him. They took him off his ventilator in the morning as he was breathing on his own and making good progress. Operations, including an amputation, were taking place on a regular basis.

The ship's Captain visited the facility on the Thursday and a group of Musicians and Buglers found some fruit which they distributed to the patients. Whilst the food was planned to suit the Iraqi diet and religious requirements there was still a difference that made the fruit very welcome. The American patient, although badly injured, was recovering to the extent that he was transferred to the High Dependency Unit. News came that nineteen casualties, British, American and Iraqi were being flown in but only four British casualties arrived.

The Buglers were also given the task of operating the clinical waste incinerator as well as mine-watching and casualty handling. By Mother's Day the American was recovered enough to be taken up to the deck to enjoy some sunshine; however, by this time there were five patients in the Intensive Care Unit. Later that day the Casualty Handlers went up to the deck to transfer a four year old girl, hurt in a road traffic accident to Intensive Care.

By the 29th March over fifty casualties had been taken from helicopters down to the PCRF. As a result of the work they were doing the members of the band were continually receiving praise from the doctors and nursing staff.

As a result of the rapidity of the advance the status of the *Argus* medical facility was soon downgraded from Role 2 to Role 3. On Sunday the 6th the last casualty was operated upon and later recovered enough to leave Intensive Care, allowing both departments to be cleaned and closed down. Monday the 7th saw the final casevac of enemy prisoners of war back to Kuwait and also the first rehearsal for the Beat Retreat planned for the 13th April. The last remaining casualties were loaded onto helicopters for the flight ashore on the 8th.

On the 10th April Captain Grace again wrote to all of the families and friends: "Since the outbreak of the war the ship has received sixty-seven casualties with a wide range of injuries from minor to major injuries. The level of care received is of the highest standard and all members of the band have played their part in this. The training carried out during our passage out to the Gulf has proved invaluable both physically and mentally, coping with heavily laden stretchers and injuries of varying degrees of severity'. The intention was for the PCRF to stand down in the next few days and for the band to fly back to UK on the 16th April. He continued, 'Homecomings are very happy and emotional occasions. However, this is a side of many deployments that tends to get forgotten. There will be a period of readjustment for both those returning and those of you who have coped extremely well at home without us. This period of adjustment is different for everyone, but talking to each other about your experiences both at home and on *Argus* will help. There will be plenty to talk about... As I have said previously, I am very proud to have served with them during this deployment."

Also on the 10th, Musician Ross Hunt, whose plans to run his 5th successive London Marathon were disrupted by this deployment, ran the marathon on one of the ship's running machine and raised a further £1200 for charity. He was assisted by various members of the ship's complement taking turns to run alongside him on the second running machine. All members of the band accompanied him at some point - including Musn Mike Hearman who ran the penultimate mile wearing his full chemical and biological protective gear including his respirator.

On the 13th April the Band of RFA *Argus* Beat Retreat on the ship's flight deck in front of all those who had served with them for the past three months. The music began with *Thunderbirds*, ended with the Naval finale and, in between, was a programme of well-known and much-loved music. To quote Captain Grace, 'The performance was spectacular, the setting mystical and the appreciation wholehearted. It has been a privilege to work with professional medical staff from the Royal Navy, Army and the Royal Air Force where we have forged new friendships'.

Taken from the massive bulk of RFA Argus' superstructure, a perfect vantage point from which the ship's company watched Beating Retreat on the 13th April 2003

Not only did the band provide Casualty Handlers; they also manned the Medical Communications

Network with the coalition forces on a twenty-four a day basis, operated the clinical waste incinerator, carried out mine watch and provided musical entertainment that, as always, showed the value of a military band in lifting spirits and raising morale - particularly when playing to, and entertaining, men and women of their own Service. One of the Doctors said, 'I wish we had a Royal Marines Band in every one of our British hospitals, you Bandies get things done'. One of the things that the 'bandies' got done was to install a pulley system. Two of them, Drum Major Dave Taylor and Bandmaster Dave Sharp, asked what the procedure was in the event of a power failure to the lifts – how would casualties be taken up and down. They then built a pulley system – just in case. When, some time later, members of the band returned to *Argus* for training – the pulley system was still there!

The Band of Her Majesty's Royal Marines RFA Argus 2003

On completion of the deployment the Director of Music's recommendations confirmed that the process used through exercise and deployment was broadly the right one. He reinforced the need for musical instruments to be taken on deployments and emphasised that a band complemented at thirty-nine should be deployed with the PCRF when on Medical Exercises or Operational Duty. He also stressed that the Director of Music should deploy at all times with the band, including exercises, because of his duties as the Operations Officer.

Whilst Captain Grace and his band had been on board RFA *Argus* another group from the Royal Marines Band Service had been serving in Iraq itself. Following a period of refresher training in the UK, a Decontamination Troop of thirteen Musicians was sent to Camp Gibraltar just outside Kuwait City as part of 3 Cdo Bde. They arrived there on the 7th February and remained for about four weeks before moving, with the Brigade, to Camp Viking on the Iraqi border where they remained for a further three weeks living in shell scrapes.[9]

9 *Two-person dug-outs with sandbag walls and a tent-like cover over the top. Very low and offering good protection.*

Scud missiles were fired at the camp, the closest landing within a kilometre of them. Three days after the Allied bombardment started they moved into Iraq. Half of the Troop, 'Decontamination Two', went to the port of Umm Qsar and were responsible to the Commando Forces Surgical Group (CFSG) for the total chemical protection of the port. The other half, 'Decontamination One', was deployed in support of 40 Cdo and, when the assault on Basra began (Op *James*), they followed the attack and were given the tasks of general protection and convoy escort duties and were provided with three Land Rovers, each equipped with a General Purpose Machine Gun, and a quad bike.

The role of the Troop gradually became one of a protection force for the battlefield ambulances that were escorted by a team of three from the decontamination team, each armed with an SA80 as a personal weapon, in one of the Land Rovers. What began as an eight-hour operation lasted six days as they remained on call and moved forward to collect casualties from the point of wounding. When Basra fell the Troop was with J Company, 40 Cdo, and was amongst the first into one of Saddam's Royal palaces. They later moved back to Al Zabia and then to Kuwait for recovery to UK.

Noble and manly music invigorates the spirit, strengthens the wavering man, and incites him to great and worthy deeds.

Homer: The Iliad, c.1000BC

Chapter 26: Cyprus and Afghanistan

The Cyprus Reinforcement Unit - 2007.

During rehearsals for the 2007 Mountbatten Festival of Music it was announced that it was very likely that members of the RMBS would need to undertake the necessary training and be ready to deploy to Cyprus. This deployment would be at Company strength, approximately one hundred all ranks, and its purpose was to relieve Army units of part of the guarding duties necessary to maintain the security of British interests on the island. These are largely based upon the Western Sovereign Base Area (WSBA) centred upon Akrotiri and the Eastern Sovereign Base Area (ESBA) at Dhekelia. 1st Bn the Royal Welch Fusiliers, the Resident Infantry Battalion, were required to serve in Afghanistan and Iraq in support of Op *Herrick* and Op *Telic* and this had caused the Army to ask the Royal Navy for support, which was provided by tasking the RMBS. The RMBS would take responsibility for WSBA whilst the Royal Regiment of Fusiliers (RRF) would continue with responsibility for ESBA.

The Warning Order for the deployment was received on the 16th February 2007 and, on the 26th, a Royal Marine GD officer (Lt Col) with Capt Jon Ridley of the RMBS and a Platoon Weapons Instructor flew to Cyprus for a reconnaissance visit. This enabled the extent of the task, and the amount and type of pre-deployment training required, to be assessed.

This was a milestone deployment for the RMBS since it would be the first time that they had operationally deployed in this strength and as an independent force. They would also be taking musical instruments in order to maintain musical skills and to provide operational musical support. In order to provide this number the Royal Marines Band of Britannia Royal Naval College, supplemented by personnel from Portsmouth, Plymouth and Scotland Bands, would deploy. These arrangements caused a ripple effect which meant that RM Plymouth Band were recalled early from Easter leave to support the Lord High Admiral's Parade at BRNC, non-priority engagements were cancelled and those tasked for the Cyprus Reinforcement Unit (CRU) would not get Easter leave until they returned.

Pre-Deployment Training included of a week's training at Longmoor Ranges where everyone had to pass the Combat Infantry Test Shoot using the Susat sight on their SA80 personal weapons.

A training package covering unarmed combat, four-man patrolling techniques, section battle drills and Vehicle Check Point manning was also undertaken. Lectures on Improvised Explosive Devices (IEDs) and Rules of Engagement (RoE) were given. Time was not available for Public Order Training. Prior to the training

Elements of the RMBS Military Training Team and the RM CRU Band at the Longmoor training facility

package the eighty-three members of the RMBS were integrated with twelve Royal Marine Commandos. These men included the Operations Officer, two Platoon Weapons Instructors, one Stores Accountant, Motor Transport Corporal, a Signaller and six ranks who would be spread amongst the various RMBS teams. The Advance Party, Capt Ridley plus nine Headquarters staff, deployed on the 26th March, the main body arriving four days later. Prior to taking over as Cyprus Reinforcement Unit all weapons were zeroed on the Akrotiri ranges and the 'Old Cookhouse' at Episkopi was turned into a storage and band rehearsal room. On the 1st April the official handover from The Royal Welsh (The Royal Welsh Fusiliers) to the Royal Marines Band Service took place. Part of the handover was to raise the White Ensign, despite the protests of the Infantry Battalion's RSM.

As soon as the Advance Party had arrived they had received a request from the Army to provide further support, but to the ESBA at Dhekelia. It was agreed that the RMBS would provide two teams from the 2nd to the 16th of April. This was in addition to their main military tasks of guarding duties at Episkopi, Salt Lake and Troodos.

The operations/control room at Troodos Camp

The camp on Mount Olympus

Headquarters Staff, under Company Commander Maj Grace, RMBS, were established in the Espiscopi Operations Room. This HQ would control and monitor operations at all RMBS locations. The remainder of the personnel were split into an Operations Troop and a Camp/Training Troop. These two Troops alternated every seven days. The purpose of the Camp/Training Troop was broadly two-fold. Firstly it provided the opportunity for Buglers and Musicians to maintain their core musical skills, and secondly it enabled further, and continuous, military training. Each morning physical training, usually cross-country running, circuits and sprints, would be followed by band or military training. The latter consisting of a mixture of zeroing weapons, range-firing at static and moving targets, driver training, testing knowledge of the Rules of Engagement as well as revision of patrolling and other drills and riot control. This troop would have weekends free for adventure training and personal pursuits.

Operations Troop had to maintain 24 hour guarding of the Main Entry Points of Episkopi, Troodos, Salt Lake Site and, in addition but for the first two weeks only, the agreed duties at Dhekelia. The teams at each of these locations also had to maintain patrols and provide Quick Reaction Forces capable of deploying in 5 and 30 minutes (QRF5 and QRF30).

High in the Olympus Mountains were the twin sites of Troodos Camp and Mount Olympus.

Two commanders (RMBS), a WO1 and a BdCSgt, had four teams covering the guarding and patrolling duties. This was an ideal area for training exercises, particularly patrolling, location and arrest, general infantry skills and off-road driving skills.

The small, prison-like establishment at Salt Lake Site had a proportionally small but effective establishment, usually commanded by an SNCO.

A White Ensign flies over the Salt Lake Site guarded by a blue-bereted Musician of the Royal Marines Band Service

It was in this area during the second week that a prominent local dissident was arrested by the Base Area Police. He was taken to Episkopi where, in anticipation of a protest by his supporters, the Episkopi QRF5 and QRF30 teams were both stood up and, although prepared for Public Order work, successfully adopted a non-confrontational posture. It later transpired that support for this trouble-maker was on the wane and, as a result, only a handful of supporters arrived. Although their Public Order skills were not tested and only QRF5 was deployed this was a useful, and unplanned, test of the QRF role. Throughout the deployment, especially the early part, surprise callout exercises, requiring both foot and vehicle response, were conducted on a daily basis.

Fresh pairs of eyes inevitably spot things normally taken for granted, or accepted as the norm. As a result improvements were made to Standard Operating Procedures (SOPs) and enhancements were suggested. Unused or faulty equipment was reinstated or repaired and the general standard of some operational procedures was raised by the combined knowledge and general standards of the RMBS and the Marines. This is not necessarily a criticism since any new unit will lack familiarity and will test, ask and probe in order to be sure. One simple example of this type of situation was the civilian contractor who was still using a pass that had expired four years earlier. Another example would be the condition of some of the accommodation which, in some areas, could be and was, improved by hard work, higher standards and minimal expenditure.

The shoulder-flash is the only indication that this Royal Marine on patrol in the Troodos Mountains is in the Royal Marines Band Service

Organisation was based on the 1-9 operational system configured as G1-9 for Ground forces; N1-9 for Naval Forces; J1-9 for Joint Forces, of which the Band Service personnel were a part. This is broken down into component parts:

1 = Personnel, Welfare and Administration

2 = Intelligence and Security
3 = Operations
4 = Logistics and Operational Support
5 = Planning
6 = Communications and Signals
7 = Training
8 = Finance
9 = Civil & Military collaboration.

In this particular deployment the RMBS was operating principally in the areas of J2 and J3. Later, in Afghanistan, their main areas of influence or impact would be J3 and J4 and, to a lesser degree, many of the other areas.

From the RMBS point of view lessons were identified and resulted in changes to RMBS training. An example of this was the unexpected need, associated with the dissident incident described earlier, for the QRF5 force to secure a helicopter landing spot. The need to upgrade this type of drill and thereby reduce unnecessary radio communication was recognised and noted for future RMBS training doctrines. Public Order Training was also identified as a means of boosting the confidence in handling local labour disputes, which did occur.

Recovery was made difficult by an Army request to extend the deployment beyond the agreed date of the 14th May 2007, at one point a recovery date of 6th June being suggested. It was only after the OC Royal Marines, Cyprus Reinforcement Unit, had issued a strongly worded statement detailing the impact this would have on RMBS commitments that agreement was reached and a flight home on the 16th May was secured. The White Ensign was taken down on the 14th May when the operational role of CRU was handed back to 1Bn, the Royal Welch Fusiliers.

Musical Support had commenced on the 13th April, slightly less than two weeks after the CRU deployment began, the opportunity occurring when a Corps of Drums gave a display of Mess Beatings for the Ladies' Guest Night at the SNCOs' Mess at Dkehelia. A String Quartet then played throughout dinner. Both were repeated at the Officers' Mess on the 20th, the day after the Jazz Group had played for an hour and a half in support of a fund raising event at the Barracks. On the 21st, Episkopi Barracks School Hall was the venue for a Farewell Concert for the 1st Bn The Royal Welch featuring the Corps of Drums, Big Band, Jazz Band and the Ynysybwl Male Voice Choir.

Wednesday the 25th April was Anzac Day and at Waynes Keep Cemetery a Brass Quintet played incidental music plus, during the Dawn Service, *The Lord is My Shepherd*. Buglers sounded *Last Post* and *Reveille*. The Brass quintet then played background music for a breakfast reception at the International Cafeteria, Nicosia. The television coverage included an interview with Major Grace.

The Royal Marines Band in concert at the Episkopi Barracks School Hall

On the following Saturday an RAF versus the Army rugby match at Akrotiri provided an opportunity for the Marching Band to perform before the match, and at half-time.

The Commander, British Forces, attended this event as he did the 10th Anniversary of the Cyprus Joint Police Unit a few days later. This was held at Episkopi WO & Sgts' Mess and featured Mess Beatings by the Corps of Drums and then a String Quartet playing throughout dinner.

Build-up to the start of the rugby match at Akrotiri

Undoubtedly the musical highlight of the deployment was the concert in aid of Service Charities at the Pissouri Amphitheatre, which was built in 2000 and is a superb outdoor venue. Major Grace and Captain Ridley shared the conducting in a programme that produced standing ovations and many calls for encores from the capacity audience of over a thousand. The concert raised £6,000 for Service charities.

The Corps of Drums display during the concert in the Pissouri Amphitheatre

Major Grace conducts the Band in the unique setting of the amphitheatre

Afghanistan - 2007 (Op *Herrick 5*).

Not long after 3rd Commando Brigade deployed to Afghanistan, they took casualties and, almost inevitably, a fatality. Two Buglers were hurriedly sent from England to Camp Bastion for the Repatriation Ceremony. They remained there whilst CplBugler Jon Lee and Bugler Dan Johnson prepared to travel to Afghanistan and to remain with the Brigade during its deployment. They were to join Medical Squadron, part of Commando Logistic Regiment, Royal Marines. The 'Loggies' were part of 3rd Commando Brigade, as were 42 and 45 Commando and other supporting units. Whilst the main duty for Buglers was to be the sounding of *Last Post* and *Reveille* at Repatriation ceremonies, a task which everyone hoped would only be needed infrequently, if ever, they were trained to carry out many other tasks within Commando Logs, the Band Service's military deployment unit.

Preparations for the deployment consisted of two weeks at HMS *Nelson* for Operational Tactical Training including lectures on mines, gas attacks and medical treatment. These were followed by exercises in patrolling and weapons handling. CplBug Lee had served as part of the Medical Squadron on board RFA *Argus* during the second Gulf War and had, at that time, received training and gained experience in casualty handling and medical work.

Wearing CS95 desert camouflage and carrying hat box, suit cover with ceremonial uniform, a grip and a bugle (no drums to be taken), webbing, Bergen and weapon they, with Commandos laden with huge quantities of kit and equipment, boarded a Tri-Star at RAF Brize Norton. The flight took them to Kabul where they all transferred to a Hercules C130 for the onward flight to Kandahar, which was under mortar attack as they arrived. Next morning they flew into Helmand Province and Camp Bastion. On reporting to the Sgt Major, Medical Squadron, and then the Commanding Officer, they realised that nobody really knew what to do with them; they also learnt that some of their new colleagues even thought that members of the Band Service were 'civvies' who were used to being accommodated in hotels! Eventually it was decided that both would work in the stores as part of Close Support Squadron, a unit of Royal Navy and Royal Marine Ambulance Drivers and Medics. Initially the work mainly comprised sorting, preparing and packing medical packs for the forward units. A little later in the deployment CplBug Lee served as an Ambulance Driver.

Ambulance driving was a link in the fast-moving chain of recovery from point of wounding to Camp Bastion Hospital and then to the United Kingdom. Most of Jon Lee's work involved transporting casualties from the flight lines where their aircraft or, more likely, helicopter had landed, to the hospital at Camp Bastion.

Casualties treated and prepared for evacuation to Britain would be collected from the hospital by ambulance and taken to the flight lines where the ambulance would reverse up to the ramp of a C130 Hercules which would have engines running for a quick turn-around. The medical crew would effect the transfer and, upon seeing a 'thumbs–up' in his rear-view mirror, the driver took his ambulance to the side of the runway until the aircraft had taken off. His earlier experience on RFA *Argus* proved useful on a couple of occasions when mass casualties were encountered. These were mainly civilians who had been caught in mortar attacks and, often children were amongst the casualties. On at least one occasion the Corporal Bugler found himself in theatre removing burnt clothing and 'rolling' the casualties to check for unseen injuries or wounds. One such incident involved casualties from an Afghan Army road accident.

The deployment lasted five months and, whilst being arduous and difficult, it took place during the winter which reduced the scale of conflict and, as a result, the number of casualties. However, the ambulances had to be available twenty-four hours a day, seven days a week.

Op *Minimise* was the arrangement whereby all personal and media communication was automatically blocked. This meant only one thing – a man, or men, had been killed or had died. The purpose of this complete communications black-out was to ensure that the man's family received the news in the proper manner, from the appropriate people and with all available support

Land Rover battlefield ambulances collecting civilian casualties from a Chinook helicopter at Camp Bastion

in place. It is a simple means of protecting families from hearing such news in any other way.

Repatriations usually consisted of two ceremonies in two places. When the body of a Royal Marine was to be flown out of Camp Bastion, the entire camp then paraded at the flight lines. The ambulance would arrive and a party of the marine's comrades then carried his coffin into the hollow square for the Church Service. The Buglers sound *Last Post* and *Reveille* and the coffin is carried onto the Hercules aircraft. The Parade remains at attention until the aircraft takes off, bound for Kandahar. The Bugler, or Buglers, board another aircraft for the same destination. A second service, following the pattern of that held at Camp Bastion, takes place in Kandahar with men and women representing the countries that make up the Multi-National Force paraded and the Buglers wearing full ceremonial uniform, not combats. This is the dead man's final flight home.

At the end of the deployment the two Buglers flew back separately to RAF Brize Norton where weapons were handed in, and leave was taken.

The last words in this part of the story are those of the recently promoted SgtBug Jon Lee: "The repatriation ceremonies were so important to the lads, they were so grateful to us for just being there to sound the calls and enable them to properly say goodbye to their 'oppos'".

Afghanistan - 2008-2009 (Op *Herrick 9*).

On the 12th December 2007 the names of those volunteers selected for the Op *Herrick* deployment were announced.[1] The structure of the deploying force would be two bands of eighteen ranks, each under the command of a BdCSgt. Group One, which would deploy from October 2008 until January 2009 would be under the command of BdCSgt Steve Bacon as Bandmaster. Group Two would be under BdCSgt Jos Tiley, also as Bandmaster. The primary role of the band would be within the Medical Squadron of Commando Logistic Regiment, Royal Marines, (CLR, RM) as drivers of ambulances and support vehicles. All ranks would need to be suitably driver-qualified.[2] Medical Squadron, Commando Logistic Regiment, is the backbone of the UK Joint Force Medical Group's Close Support Squadron.[3]

Prior to Easter leave the thirty-six ranks reported to Portsmouth for a two-week training package, organised and run by the RMBS Military Training Team, prior to joining CLR. Band instruments were sent ahead by sea to Pakistan then by lorry over the North-West Frontier into Helmand and then Camp Bastion. The first two days consisted of presentations and weapons tests at HMS *Nelson*, followed by a day at Tipnor Range and a pistol shoot before departing for Longmoor for various weapons training and exercises including GPMG shoots. Training at Portsmouth also covered target indication, judging distances, vehicle drills and the NATO sequence of orders. After passing the Advanced Personal Weapons Training course the band went on leave prior to joining CLR's Medical Squadron, at Chivenor on the 14th April. They would remain with them for training until the 12th September.[4] A week long joining routine and endurance course was followed by all ranks driver training on the Battlefield Ambulance (BFA), which was a Land Rover variant, and on the four ton DAF vehicles plus live firing qualification for those requiring it. This was followed by Exercise *Rosedale Walk* at Queen Elizabeth Barracks, York, for those joining Ambulance Troop.

1 *Blue Band.*
2 *Blue Band.*
3 *Globe & Laurel. Commanding Officer, CLR,RM.*
4 *Blue Band.*

The remainder of the period until summer leave was filled with driver training and qualification on the Mastiff, Vector, Saxon and six and nine ton MAN Support Vehicles entering service as a replacement for the 4 ton DAF vehicles; providing medical cover for 3Cdo Bde exercises at Folkstone and at Lulworth Cove, plus a Mission Rehearsal Exercise in July.[5] This occurred at the time when plans were being made for convoys to carry spare parts for the Kajaki Dam turbines from Bastion far into the north of the country. Convoy training began, complete with Apache helicopters, and the Musicians were included since they would be driving the convoy ambulances. They also provided real-time medical cover. However, the M5 could not prepare the drivers for conditions in Afghanistan. In the event the Parachute Regiment got the spares through before the Royal Marines arrived in the country.

In early September the Op Herrick 9 UK Joint Force Medical Group formed up in its entirety at the Army Medical Services Training Centre, near York, for a validation exercise, Exercise *Hospex*, designed to test the entire casualty evacuation chain.[6] Final administration, including next of kin forms and issue of NATO Red Cross identification cards to all in the casualty chain, was completed. Lt Cdr M P Smith RN, was the Officer Commanding Medical Squadron and Second in Command of the JFMG. Major J Burcham of the Royal Marines Band Service served as the Adjutant, JFMG. During the six-month training period an innovative plan to identify and train medical trauma teams to work at the FOBs had been developed and introduced by RN personnel.[7]

Musical instruments, loaned by Supply Officer (Music) Dept in lieu of their own which were somewhere in Pakistan, had been taken to Chivenor for an Officers' Mess Beat Retreat. The Big Band played for the SNCOs' Mess and as much rehearsal as possible was fitted in.[8] BdCSgt Bacon, the Bandmaster, was forced to hold the Beat Retreat indoors because of the poor weather. On completion he asked the OC Commando Logistic Regiment, Col Maynard, for permission to march off. The Colonel asked which band this was; they were wearing desert camouflage uniform so had no identifying features. The Bandmaster replied 'Sir, this is the Royal Marines Band, Chivenor'. The Colonel was delighted to have his own band, albeit only for a short while![9]

In its operational capacity Medical Squadron would have over one hundred and fifty medical and dental personnel providing 'Role 1 level' health and trauma care to all personnel deployed as part of Task Force Helmand. Whilst operational, Medical Squadron also has to be able to mount and sustain two 'Commando Forward Surgical Groups' (CFSG). Each comprises four Medical Sections, which are identical to a Regimental Aid Post, plus two Field Surgical Teams and two Evacuation Sections capable of providing a limited holding facility until rearward evacuation by helicopter or battlefield ambulance takes place. Each CFSG is used to support any of 3 Cdo Bde's missions. The Royal Marines played a football match against Exeter City FC in aid of 'Help for Heroes' and the band, wearing desert uniform again, provided pre-match entertainment and a mini - Beat Retreat during the half-time interval.[10]

Normally the Squadron, whilst at RM Barracks, Chivenor, comprises RN Medical Assistants and General Duties Marines in approximately equal numbers. The latter group provided the majority of drivers required to move the Commando Forward Surgical Group, or they served as Ambulance Drivers. For *Herrick 9*, the thirty-six RMBS personnel would

5 *Blue Band, also Globe & Laurel 2009 p116-118.*
6 *Globe & Laurel 2008 p376.*
7 *Globe & Laurel 2009 p116-118.*
8 *Blue Band.*
9 *BdCSgt Bacon*
10 *Globe & Laurel. Commanding Officer, CLR,RM.*

take over this role allowing the GD Marines to form a Close Support Troop within Landing Force Support Party to provide close support to the Combat Logistic Patrols, (CLPs).[11]

When deployed, CLR Medical Group, including the hospital facility at Camp Bastion, would have more than four hundred clinical staff drawn from the Defence Medical Services, and would have responsibility for providing medical care from point of wounding to the UK via the 'Role 3' hospital at Bastion. To do this the Med Squadron would have to place RN Medics in every major FOB location with at least one professional medic on almost every foot patrol and CLP – hence the need to develop the plan already mentioned and why the RMBS personnel would need to slip into their new role without further training.[12]

The Firing Ranges outside Camp Bastion. As well as using them for weapon zeroing, Med Troop also provided real-time medical cover when the ranges were in use

During mid-September, the advance party arrived in theatre and worked with 15 Close Support Squadron from 13 Air Assault Support Regiment during the planning and execution stages of a forty vehicle Combat Logistics Patrol. This entailed a journey from Camp Bastion to FOB Delhi, and return, all carried out as part of the handover process.[13] BdCSgt Bacon was the only RMBS representative in the advance party, travelling well ahead of his band in order to maximise the benefits of a long, comprehensive, handover.

Seventeen RMBS ranks left RAF Brize Norton by civilian flights to the United Arab Emirates where they transferred to a C17 aircraft for the flight into Camp Bastion. On arrival they were processed through the Bastion routine of one night in Transit Accommodation followed by two days of lectures and weapon zeroing on the ranges.[14]

Task Force Helmand was commanded by Brig Gordon Messenger RM. The Joint Force Medical Group and other 'echelon' units were part of Joint Force Support. Five hundred and forty-seven ranks from UK Armed Forces formed the Joint Forces Medical Group which was under the command of 3 Cdo Bde's Senior Medical Officer. Medical Squadron, CLR, formed the core of this Group and provided its Second-in-Command as well as the Command and Control elements and the Regimental Medical Group HQ.[15]

Medical Group had its own camp within Bastion with work locations close by. Accommodation

Medical Group accommodation pods within Camp Bastion

11 (G&L 2008, p377).
12 Globe & Laurel 2008, p463.
13 Globe &Laurel 2008, p461.
14 Blue Band.
15 Globe & Laurel 2009, p116-118.

consisting of four large Pod complexes of six smaller pods each capable of housing eight people.

In addition there were two Ablution Pods with showers, washbasins and toilets. Each person had a camp-cot, with thin mattress and a hanging wardrobe. Other facilities included two well-equipped fitness tents, volleyball and basketball courts and several outside areas for weight training etc. Nearby was a church and a welfare tent with television, games and books. Catering facilities were of a high standard. Phone cards were issued for thirty minutes' free communication each week. There was also a laundry run by locally employed civilians where everyone could have one bag of washing per day laundered free of charge.[16] At this time the expectations were still that all RMBS ranks would be either ambulance or vehicle drivers for the duration of the deployment. Ambulance Troop's duties were to transfer patients, provide medical cover for the weapons ranges and the delivery of casualties from the Helicopter Landing Site to the hospital. At night, provide an ambulance service for AEROMED evacuation of casualties and patients, usually bound for Selly Oak Hospital, Birmingham. Keeping the ambulance clean in an effort to maintain a sterile environment was also their responsibility. Each Ambulance carried two RN Medical Assistants, in addition to the Driver.[17] Ambulance Troop was therefore responsible for the transfer and movement of all casualties, including the dead, in and out of Bastion, including those on the AEROMED flight. This troop was also responsible for transporting local national casualties, including the deceased, from and to the Camp Bastion Main Entry Point where they would be collected by relatives. Duties of the Motor Transport Troop were the upkeep and maintenance of the fleet of fourteen vehicles, including the six ambulances which were permanently used in Camp Bastion, when not manned. Two long wheelbase Land Rovers were kept in the Motor Transport section and used for a variety of tasks which included delivering people, equipment and signals around Camp Bastion. Also included were the mail run, distribution of water and taking people to, and collecting medical supplies from, the Flight Lines. Three other Land Rovers were held and maintained by the MT Section for the hospital and were allocated to the hospital QMS and to the MERT and ALEO teams.[18] The MT Section also had two Bedford 4-ton trucks and a Vector for ambulance duty on CLPs.

The Vector ambulance proved to have poor crew protection compared to other vehicles

The role of the Duty Watch-keeper was primarily to monitor and record all medical missions that occured within Regional Command (South) and to provide and maintain situational awareness, such that instant reports could be provided to the Commanding Officer, JF Med Gp, at any time. The Medical Rules of Eligibility determine who could be treated at Bastion Hospital and the list includes ISAF casualties, local nationals and Afghan National Security Forces. The Watch-keeper was also responsible for ensuring that transportation for patients and casualties was coordinated and managed, including the repatriation of local nationals.[19] SgtBug Jim Butler was one of three Watch-keepers, the

16 *Blue Band.*
17 *Blue Band.*
18 *The work of the MERT and ALEO teams will be explained later.*
19 *Globe & Laurel 2009, p116-118.*

other two being an RM and an RN Officer, and their task was, put simply, to coordinate all non-medical aspects of casualty recovery. Alongside him was a Signaller (Musician) who maintained communications with ambulance crew operating in and around Camp Bastion. The team, part of Joint Forces Medical Group, was located in the Command Centre at Camp Bastion. Their Officer Commanding was the Commander, Close Support Squadron. The Signaller monitored transmissions from the Chinook helicopter and, as experience was accumulated, so the Watch-keeper/Signaller team understood more about the condition of the casualty. This enabled them to provide additional information to the hospital allowing a higher level of preparedness to be achieved.

Watch-keepers used a '9 Liner Medevac Request' to relay data between the helicopter and the hospital command about the incoming casualty transfer. By completing the 'nine-liner' the Watch-keeper is passing the maximum information between hospital and helicopter.

The Med Group's Operations Room where a Watch-keeper and a Signaller monitored and controlled the movement of casualties into the Hospital

The casualty chain from point of wounding began with either a helicopter being called directly into the area of the casualty, or the casualty being carried to the nearest Commando Forward Surgical Group (CFSG) or Regimental Aid Posts in either a Forward Operating Base or one of the smaller bases. Everything was time-based, Surgeon-Commander Rick Jolly's Falklands maxim of getting casualty's into a hospital situation within one hour still applies. The CFSGs were designated Role 1 or Role 2 based upon a system of concentric rings around Bastion, Role 2 being the closest, the hospital itself being Role 3.

Communications into the Camp Bastion Watch-keeper was via the on-line chat system. Dialogue needed to be crisp, snappy and without drama. The first indicator that a casualty needed assistance would be the on-screen message "Contact [followed by the contact's call sign] - wait out", followed by the casualty alert "1x casualty, 9-liner to follow" and then "9-liner follows: 1 - xxx, 2 - xxx, 3 - A , 4 - B, etc., up to Line 9" Lines 3 to 8 used a single letter from a multiple choice to give information, whilst lines 1,2 and 9 required short text to give location of casualty, call-sign and conditions at helicopter collection point.

A Helicopter Landing Spot, known as 'Nightingale' was dedicated to the hospital and only used for receiving casualties. Casualties were usually brought in by a Chinook helicopter, call-sign 'Tricky', with a trauma team on board.

This team was known as a MERT (Medical Emergency Response Team) and consisted of a Paramedic, an anaesthetist and two specialist Medics. The MERT Chinook was alerted by the same signals that reached the Watch-keeper. Also on board the helicopter was an eight-man force protection team whose job was to react to enemy action against the helicopter, especially if the helicopter had to make an emergency landing. At this particular time the Bastion Force Protection Regiment was The Rifles. The MERT team was different from the RAF AEROMED teams which served on aircraft bringing casualties back to UK with an Air Evacuation Liaison Officer (AELO), in command. Casualty Evacuation to the

A Chinook helicopter, call-sign 'Tricky', landing on the 'Nightingale' helicopter spot and being met by Land Rover ambulances

UK was by C17 aircraft from Bastion Flight Lines and these were usually routine military flights with a team of nurses to provide continuity of care between Bastion and Selly Oak - unless a CCAST team was required in which case a special flight would be arranged.

Fire tenders were tasked by their own Watch-keepers and were usually deployed with the ambulance to the Helicopter Landing Spot. RMBS personnel drove the ambulance with a Medic in the back. Sometimes one of the RMBS accompanied and assisted the Medic on the return trip. On one occasion a Musician was told to hold a clamp placed on a wounded man's main leg artery to make sure that it did not spring off during the bumpy ambulance journey. As the man was rushed into the hospital, was prepared and taken into theatre so that Musician went with him, holding onto the clamp throughout the major surgery. RMBS personnel were also responsible for 'sanitizing' the casualty, a process for ensuring that the casualty had all ammunition, weapons etc removed in the casualty reception area before being taken into the hospital. The same sanitizing procedure was also necessary for those who had been killed. Usually webbing was removed before the casualty was put onto the helicopter but it was still necessary for the check to be carried out.

Ambulance Troop was also responsible for the transfer of casualties from an adjacent pad used by the American helicopters, call-sign 'Shocker'. The Americans used a number of helicopter types, always working in pairs. By activating the 'Shocker' call-sign Ambulance Troop could ascertain the type, number and condition of casualties that the Americans were bringing in. Lapses in discipline and the occasional absence of recognised procedures by non-UK helicopters could slow the transfer process. Occasionally a foreign helicopter carrying casualties would land virtually unannounced.[20]

In mid-January it was decided to place a Musician in a Watch-keeper role at Kandahar. Musician John Park was the first person responsible for this 'singleton' post, later being relieved by Musician Michelle Andrews.

Transfer of bodies to 'Rose Cottage', the name given to the building used to hold the bodies, and later to the Repatriation Ceremony, was also an RMBS responsibility. Musician Mike Smith, less than impressed by the ambulance to hearse 'conversion kit' used previously, found suitable materials to fashion weighted and draped black curtains that could be easily fitted and removed and which gave suitable dignity to the vehicle. He then manufactured five more sets for use when a number of coffins were flown out. Only one set of coffin rollers existed[21] so, from the RAF helicopter maintenance facility, having explained what he needed and why, he obtained enough for all of the ambulances. Of the six practice coffins only one was found to be properly weighted so, from workshop scrap heaps, he built up five more sets of weights. The five coffins were in poor condition so they had to be repaired and reinforced before weighting. In conjunction with the Padre and the

20 *On one occasion a Bell Huey helicopter of the Poppy Eradication Force landed and the doors were slid back to reveal four badly injured Afghans just lying on the cabin floor.*

21 *These had been part of an aircraft or helicopters ramp assembly.*

Hospital RSM he did what he could to make the room, used by friends of the dead man to pay their last respects, as suitable and as private, as he could make it.[22] In advance of the repatriation the coffin and the hearse were dressed and prepared by Musician Smith. When the hollow square was formed he then drove the hearse out and reversed it into position ready for the bearer parties to carry the fallen into the waiting aircraft. As well as carrying out his normal duties Musician Smith, assisted by other members of Ambulance Troop, undertook nineteen out of the twenty-three repatriations that took place during 3rd Cdo Bde's *Herrick 9* deployment in Afghanistan.[23] A full handover was given to the incoming Army unit.

Vigil Services took place in the late afternoon or the early evening, whilst the body lay in Rose Cottage. The Camp Bastion personnel formed up in the traditional hollow square inside which a Service of Remembrance took place; after this a number of the man's friends offered their own eulogies. The two Buglers sounded *Last Post* and *Reveille* and, if possible, this would be followed by a gun salute.

SgtBug Butler and Bug Vyse sound the calls at a Memorial Service

The Parade was then dismissed. The Repatriation Service was also known as the Ramp Service. Held in the early morning, usually between 0200 and 0300, so that the flight out took place before it became fully light, this Service was for the dead man's Unit only. It was usually attended by the Unit CO and RSM although the Adjutant stood in when the situation demanded. The Unit formed up, two or three deep either side of the route along which the coffin would be carried to the aircraft. Buglers positioned themselves at either side of the bottom of the ramp. The Chaplain then led the bearer party towards the aircraft, his voice barely audible above the roar of the aircraft engines. The Buglers sounded *Last Post* and *Reveille* as the coffin reached them and was taken into the aircraft and secured. The aircraft then took off. Watch-keeper SgtBug Jim Butler, who also sounded the bugle calls on many such occasions, described what happened next: 'The aircraft would usually take off and fly a large circle out of Bastion, then make a low fly past directly above the, still formed up, parade's heads. Sometimes the aircraft would deploy 'chaff' flares as it pulled up and disappeared into the night sky, very poignant and moving'. The Service, much more intimate than the Vigil, was over. On return to the UK CplBug Stu Vyse, speaking of sounding the bugle calls at the Vigil and Repatriation Services said, "It was pressure, real pressure. Memorials and Remembrance are part of our job. We do them all of the time, up and down the country. Out there, it is different, it is pressure - but I will do it again if asked, it is important and it is what we do".

Cpl Hairsine and Musician Smith added that everyone in the Medical chain from point of wounding to the hospital and beyond that maintained an interest in all of the casualties who passed through their hands. A 'watching brief' was kept on the men who were brought in; if anyone from Ambulance Troop went to the hospital he would ask about the man he brought in earlier and word would flow back along the chain to all of the team. When a man passed away, all in the chain felt as if they had lost a battle; shoulders

22 *As a result of this work Musician Mike Smith was asked to remain in Afghanistan rather than return as planned. He agreed and stayed for the full term of the RMBS deployment.*

23 *The other four occurred whilst he had a short period of rest and recuperation and these were covered by Cpl Hairsine and others.*

slumped, heads dropped and silence was sought. Everyone involved had to find their own closure to these situations.

Logistics Support comprised two Close Support Squadrons. The Land Force Support Party, (LFSP) was a Royal Marine responsibility, commanded by a Royal Marine Major. The second Close Support Squadron, for the Logistic Support Squadron, (LS Sqd) was provided by the Gurkhas. LS Squadron had deployed in mid-September 2008 and was commanded by a Major of the Royal Logistics Corps (RLC).

The Commanding Officer of the CLR, RM, described the logistics operation as being on the scale of a Logistics Battlegroup. Added to this was the need for Battlespace Management across the entire province of Helmand, this needing careful and comprehensive co-ordination of the communication assets as the Combat Logistic Patrols moved from one Battlegroup's Area of Operation to another.[24]

Although not part of the original job description, Combat Logistics Patrols (CLPs) became part of RMBS duties. It was essential that an ambulance accompanied each CLP; therefore each CLP deployed with two members of RMBS as crew and with Naval Medics. Drivers received training in night driving using night-vision goggles. These convoys, with Camp Bastion as their hub, travelled out to the various Forward Operating Bases and other locations. They principally moved ammunition, medical supplies, clothing and food but sometimes people as well. The convoy size varied, as did the routes, and the convoys could comprise up to two hundred vehicles. Sometimes the whole convoy went to one destination whilst, at other times, the convoy took a route that enabled several locations to be supplied. The original ambulances, Vectors, were not mine-proof and efforts to improve crew protection were unsuccessful. The crew positions were directly over the wheels and therefore exposed to the full blast from an exploding mine. Four US Tempest vehicles were being used by the Explosive Ordnance Disposal (EOD) units and were frequently parked up in Camp Bastion. In typical 'Bandie' style negotiations took place and a Tempest was made available for use as the CLP ambulance. The only problem now was that the currently deployed H9a Band only had a few men trained to drive the Tempest; all the rest were trained only on the expected vehicle of use - the Vector. Drivers in H9b Band were trained on the Mastiff which was scheduled to arrive to replace the Vector in time for the handover. This put the responsibility for the CLPs onto the limited number of Tempest drivers.

The Tempest vehicle that was converted for use as a Combat Logistic Patrol ambulance

Planning a CLP took up to seven days due to the convoy size and complexity, not to mention the need for thoroughness. The process included analysis of the mission, battle procedure and orders amongst its many facets. A reconnaissance of the route would be undertaken, combat supplies ordered, mandatory training undertaken and all vehicles inspected by Drivers and Vehicle Mechanics to ensure 'Operational Fitness', a higher standard than 'Road Fit'. A recent development is the 'eye in the sky' – the Unmanned Aviation

24 Globe & Laurel 2009 p460.

Vehicle (UAV) which, as part of its 'spotting' role, can beam down images of his route to the Patrol Commander. After 'Orders' and briefing a Rehearsal of Combat Coordination drill takes place to ensure that all members of the CLP understand the tactics, techniques and procedures – no matter what nationality, Service, trade or specialisation they might be. Weapons are test-fired, communications are checked and an enforced rest time is taken prior to departure.

Each CLP requires the full range of 3 Cdo Bde assets (Information, Surveillance, Target Acquisition and Reconnaissance - known as ISTAR). These assets include fire support from the air and from artillery, armoured support and international contributions from such as Danish, Estonian and US units.[25]

On return to Bastion the operation cannot end until all vehicles are de-serviced, faults reported, radios returned, weapons cleaned and handed in, and post-operational inspections on all vehicles are carried out.[26]

A large percentage of the JF Med Gp change at the three-month point and the RMBS is no different. H9a had the first four months' deployment and H9b the second four months' deployment. This included a long handover since the RMBS were scattered in various bases and camps. During the first thirty days in Afghanistan CLR's LFSP and LSS[27] conducted four Combat Logistic Patrols and delivered approximately twelve hundred tons of combat supplies. The first CLP, re-supplying FOBs Robinson and Inkerman plus Sangin, had two hundred and nine vehicles, and required five hundred and nineteen personnel, although a 'typical' CLP would be in the order of one hundred vehicles and up to three hundred personnel.[28] Five mine-strikes, or Improvised Explosive Device (IED) contacts, one rocket propelled grenade (RPG) attack and a serious road traffic accident (RTA) were survived without loss.[29]

It was expected that the tempo of three or four CLPs per month would be attainable with CLR's RM Vehicle Mechanics and REME contingent.[30] However, CLPs are not only hard on vehicles but also on personnel. They require drivers to routinely undertake twenty hour continuous journeys over rough terrain with usually only a few hours rest before commencing the return journey to Camp Bastion. Outside air temperatures approach 40ºC but vehicle cab temperatures can be much higher, particularly in those vehicles carrying additional armour which have their windows sealed closed. Few vehicles are air-conditioned.[31] Dust is a problem since, whilst driving for many hours with visibility at a mere 20 metres is a strain because of the dust from the vehicle in front, dropping back is not an option since the tyre tracks will disappear and an IED might be struck. Return journeys are made as soon as possible since delay gives the Taliban more time to set an ambush or plant IEDs. Patrols are always multi-national and can include Afghan Army or Police, US or Danish Forces. LFSP itself is 50% Royal Marines with the other half either Royal Navy or Army. Army Drivers are from 12 Sqn, 1 LSR, RLC.[32]

With an RMBS force of only twenty Other Ranks, the need to supply ambulance drivers in support of the CLPs, as well as meet the existing commitments, meant that the three Tempest drivers, BdCSgt Bacon, BdCpl Edwards and Musn Marsh, took part in eight CLPs between mid-October and mid-December. During thirty-eight days of this period two, sometimes all three, were out on patrol. They, like others in the RMBS contingent,

25 *Globe & Laurel 2008 p376.*
26 *Globe & Laurel 2009, p20/21.*
27 *Commando Logistic Regiment's Land Force Support Party & Logistic Support Squadron.*
28 *Globe & Laurel 2008, p461/2.*
29 *Globe & Laurel 2009 p460 LFSP.*
30 *Globe & Laurel 2009 p460 LFSP.*
31 *Globe & Laurel 2009 p460 LFSP.*
32 *Globe & Laurel 2009, p20 - 21.*

were part of the forty per cent of Commando Logistic Regiment's manpower who were forward based, providing medical, engineering or replenishment support alongside the fighting units.

There is no 'typical' CLP. Each has its own incidents, its own, usually unpleasant, surprises. The preparation begins with the Bandmaster nominating the drivers who then all attend the 'Orders' Group. On one particular occasion the two drivers with their crew and medics took the two vehicles to the building where the meeting would be held. They parked some distance away on either side of the building and began walking towards it. A 'whooshing' sound was heard and, instinctively, they hunched down. A missile came into the area passing just over their stooped backs and embedded itself into the Hesco walling, but without exploding. Had it done so, lives would certainly have been lost.[33] The Musician closest to the passing missile found that his clothing and back had been burnt to the extent that he was flown back to England.[34]

Following 'Orders', preparations are made before, during the hours of darkness, the CLP leaves Bastion. Progress is very slow due to the need to use IED detectors. CLPs such as this particular one, out to FOB Gray at Now Zad, involved travelling across Highway 1 and then along a road known as 'IED Alley' before cutting across the desert towards Now Zad, once a village but then taken over by the Taliban. Fighting in the area was frequent and fierce and, until recently, FOB Gray was garrisoned by the Estonians but now US forces held it. For those in the convoy this had the advantage that the US could deploy Cobra helicopters as a protection force over the convoy for most of the journey.

On one occasion, whilst in FOB Gray and preparing to bed down for the night, a missile was fired into the base causing a loud explosion. The US troops immediately began firing 120 or 150mm mortars into the area where the missile might have been launched from, a great deal of ammunition being expended. On a different occasion the CLP was returning to Bastion when an explosion and a smoke cloud to the side made the Convoy Commander give the order to speed up to thirty miles an hour for ten minutes. It soon became a white-out with drivers unsure of where the vehicle in front, or in rear, actually was. The order to slow down resulted in the dust cloud dissipating and the Tempest crew realising that the large vehicles in front and behind had been a matter of only a few inches away from them, but out of sight.

The men and women of the RMBS who worked on the casualty recovery and care path had to endure the sights and sounds of badly hurt servicemen, and civilians - men, women and children who had been injured, even mutilated for life. Those Musicians on the CLPs rarely, thankfully, had to endure those sights and sounds. Instead they had the fear of the unknown to face. As one man put it, "It was like two different types of stress or trauma that had to be overcome". One evening he rang his wife and, after a few minutes of conversation she said, "You are going out tonight aren't you". It was not a question; it was a statement - across thousands of miles a wife recognising a husband's tension. Following the conversation the sanitisation process took place; the removal of rings and anything personal, anything that could provide a weakness for a captor to exploit. A last look at pictures of wife and family then stow them away until the return.

During the return from a CLP to FOB Robinson, and as the convoy was approaching IED Alley at about 0200hrs, soft sand was encountered and many vehicles became bogged down. The only three vehicles in the convoy with towing equipment began their long

---

33 This incident occurred on a Thursday, the third Thursday in a row that such an attack had taken place; not once did the missile explode.

34 The wounded Musician Scullion sent his own 'nine-liner' to the Duty Watch keeper. BdCpl Hairsine, one of the BCRs (Battlefield Casualty Replacements), was then deployed to Afghanistan, where he became Tempest trained and was then able to relieve the load upon the three men bearing the brunt of the convoy ambulance work.

slow work. A call came over the radio net that the ambulance, which was close to the rear of the convoy, was needed at the front. The only way to get there was to drive alongside the convoy through virgin sand and hope that they would neither hit a mine nor get bogged in. They reached the casualty who had sustained potentially serious neck and back injury during a towing operation. A 'nine-liner' had been sent and the helicopter would land at the front of the convoy. Musicians and Medics worked together to get the casualty onto a stretcher and into the Tempest, never an easy task due to the height of the Tempest's floor. The ambulance drove forward through the soft sand towards the pick-up point only to become completely bogged down 100metres short. The only course of action was to collect and then carry the patient on a four-man stretcher over the difficult terrain to the pick-up point. Panting from the exertions, they set the stretcher down. As the unmistakeable sound of an approaching Chinook increased so the men crouched down over the patient, clothing pulled tight around them, goggles on, huddled together for protection. The noise increased, the downdraft came closer and closer and the clouds of swirling sand became denser and denser. Light permeated through the dust and the darkness as the helicopter touched down just a few metres away from the Medics, Musicians and patient. The patient was quickly lifted and carried into the brightly lit body of the Chinook where the MERT team took charge of him. The four men turned, ran down the ramp into the absolute darkness of the desert night and huddled on the ground as the engine noise, the vibration and clouds of sand rose and the Chinook rose, turned and gained height. Brushing the worst of the sand from their clothing, and out of the skin cracks and crevices that were within reach, the men trudged back to their ambulance to prepare for its extraction. Next day, one of the men mentioned that, as they were walking away from the pick-up point he had seen what he was sure was a mine that had been exposed by the downdraft from the helicopter rotors. Whether they had walked past a single, stray, mine or through a minefield will never be known.

On another occasion BdCpl Hairsine was driving the Tempest with Musn Gray as Signaller. They departed Camp Bastion in the Tempest ambulance at the rear of a convoy of more than seventy vehicles bound for FOB Edinburgh, far to the north. The eight hour journey was given a twelve hour 'window' to allow for bad weather and because they were 'proving' the route.[35] With bad weather and knee-high mud the Tempest, although a fairly large vehicle, struggled to cope with the deep ruts cut by the preceding, larger, vehicles. The two man crew of the Tempest, being driver and signaller, had to remain awake at all times. This would not normally be a problem but the outbound journey took thirty-five hours to complete. The return journey was very much the same with, at one point, the whole convoy 'leagured up' in the desert with everyone detailed off for sentry duty throughout the cold night. This was 'learning the job on the ground'.

Such are the recollections, just a few of a great many, from the CLPs. The overriding recollections are of the heat, the cold, the sand clouds, the discomfort and the unknown.

The handover from H9a to H9b band consisted of two overlapping phases: recovery and deployment, which were based upon the arrival of the H9b Band at Camp Bastion on the 15th January 2009 and the departure of the H9a Band from Camp Bastion on the 19th of the same month. Unlike H9a, the H9b group flew direct from Brize Norton on an RAF Tri-Star into Kandahar where they transferred to a flight into Camp Bastion. With a few flight delays causing late arrival and the time required for the incoming band to be processed through the Bastion induction, only a day or so remained for the handover to take place. However, this was not a problem since three key members of H9a Band, Major J Burcham,

35 This means a new route was being used and extra care needed to be taken. For example, a wadi bisected their route and there were only two possible crossing points – a fact well known to the Taliban.

SgtBug J Butler and BdCpl D Edwards remained in Helmand for the whole deployment and therefore provided continuity.

The Camp Bastion 'Arrivals' building with Ambulance Troop's Bedford 4-ton lorry carrying Herrick 9B band's equipment and kit. This was the beginning of the handover

Recovery began when BdCpl Button, his task at FOB Price now complete, withdrew the ten miles from the Gereshk area to Camp Bastion on the 5th December after two months operating as an RMBS 'singleton'. On the 20th January the three Musicians furthest away from Camp Bastion, Musns Botham, Ginn and O'Malley flew the three hundred and fifty miles back from their work in the Kabul Sick Bay. On the 2nd January Musn Park had deployed to Kandahar as a Watch-keeper working with the CCAST Team there. On the 20th January he also returned to Camp Bastion in time for H9a Band's complement to fly back to Brize Norton, via a stop at Cyprus for the compulsory 'decompression' stage. A few days after her arrival with H9b band, Musn Andrews flew to Kandahar to assume the role of Watch-keeper whilst Musns Robertson, Sharp and Walton deployed to the Kabul Sick Bay. H9b Band was now fully integrated and operational.

Unlike H9a Band, members of the H9b Band were plunged straight into Combat Logistics Patrols when, on the 30th January, BdCSgt Tiley and Musn Gray were tasked as ambulance drivers on Op *Gypsum 16*, a CLP supplying FOB Dwyer and Delhi. Six further CLPs supporting the three Battle Groups, South, North-West and North were carried out prior to recovery. CplBugs Johnson and Stephenson had assumed responsibility from SgtBug Butler and Bugler Vyse for Vigil Services and Repatriation Ceremonies. By the time H9b Band's recovery took place the two teams of Buglers had been involved in the repatriation of thirty-three men who had fallen.

The role of Musicians and Buglers within an operational environment has changed remarkably since the late 1970s. The current role is more like the one held by their predecessors, trained at the Royal Naval School of Music and serving during the First and Second World Wars. The Falklands War saw a return to the team of people able to revert to the provision of music for ceremony and entertainment from within a specific military role. More recent operations such as *Telic* and *Herrick* have seen that role become even more organic. For the Royal Marines Band Service the days of a band flying into a war zone, providing very formal entertainment and then flying home again have gone. Should the occasion arise then the ability to operate in that manner is certainly there. However, that type of entertainment has its own inherent problems such as allocation of resources for transportation and accommodation. Operational personnel have to be allocated to security and so the circumstances surrounding such 'fly in, fly out' visits by military bands begs the question 'Is the entertainment worth the efforts?' This, in turn will lead to even more uncomfortable questions and even argument in respect to the worth of military bands in general. The period from *Telic* to *Herrick 9* has seen great developments in how to use Musicians and Buglers in specific military roles that are not 'invented' but enable them to use their skills and training in a way that allows more highly skilled personnel to work in a more appropriate environment – hence the phrase that, in an operational environment, the Royal Marines Band Service becomes a 'force multiplier'. From within this environment the Band Service has the ability and capacity to emerge and not only provide musical entertainment of various types but usually without the need for support from others.

During *Herrick 9*, as has already been described, the Buglers once again provided that particular element to the meaningful ceremony that nobody ever wants to occur, Repatriation. The deployment also coincided with November ceremonies and, although only two in number, the Buglers were able to sound the calls at Camp Bastion, at Lashkar Gah and at Sangin. The full military band paraded for the Remembrance Service at Camp Bastion. Musicians supported Religious Services by the provision of a regular pianist and, during the Christmas period, a pianist and a Brass Sextet for two different Midnight Mass Services. During Christmas Day a small Military Band of about fourteen Musicians played carols and marches for an hour.

Christmas Day morning and the Royal Marines Herrick 9a Band play Christmas Carols and marches

The Military Band was followed by the Dance Band

The two Buglers ensured that a suitable drum display, in full ceremonial uniform despite the temperature, was provided for the Corps Birthday

This was followed by the Dance Band which also played for about an hour. The First Sea Lord made a surprise visit on Christmas Day and found, to his great delight, the band playing Christmas carols. In addition to these specific occasions, music was provided for the Corps Birthday and for Trafalgar Night and various engagements within Camp Bastion. For the Corps Birthday the two Buglers, SgtBug Butler and Bug Vyse, gave a two-man drum display in full ceremonials at an all ranks dinner in Camp Bastion.

One hundred and thirty people sat down for dinner on Trafalgar Night and the Jazz Band, Ambulance Drivers, provided an hour's musical entertainment which was extended by a further hour and then only ended because of the shift change-over and the imminent visit of the Secretary of State for Defence. Like the deployment on board RFA *Argus* in support of Op *Telic* musical support in Afghanistan, although the

Musical entertainment for the Corps Birthday

geographic and physical situations were very different, also had to be tailored to suit the circumstances. Also like *Telic*, by being firmly embedded and 'organic', tailoring could be accomplished through the flexibility that was available. The rock band was a particular asset, catering as it did for the age group of the Service personnel and not having the musical problems associated with other instruments. The main difficulties in the provision of music during this deployment were the tempo of operations, the distances between locations and the shift/emergency cover work patterns. In addition the musical instruments had to be sent home in early-mid February – a few weeks in advance of the band leaving. Apart from this final point, the difficulties were largely overcome by using smaller groups and ensembles.

Musn Andrews in Kandahar and the team from Kabul were all recovered on the 28th March and, following decompression leave in Cyprus, the H9b Band arrived back at Brize Norton on the 3rd April 2009.

Lessons identified were all in relation to the pre-deployment stage of the deployment. Calling for volunteers for this type of operation proved unsatisfactory since it resulted in Musicians and Buglers from all bands having to be brought together with a resultant 'gap-filling' drafting problem. Not only did this cause a great deal of turbulence within the RMBS but it also risked sending the message that deployment could, if wished, be avoided by not volunteering. As a result the Band of Commando Training Centre, RM, was identified for the next Afghanistan deployment. This means that the well-practised routines that form part of any current international musical tour, such as training, transport and the provision of a rear-party for logistical and other back-up, can be utilised.

The other main concerns, including changes to pre-deployment training, could also be eradicated by allocating a specific band. Role-specific training could be carried out on a regular basis, rather than pre-deployment, with the parent unit eg Commando Logistic Regiment, RM. Another major advantage would be that the Band's own internal training and monitoring organisation could be expanded to maintain records of vehicle-specific driver training and validity of licences as well as monitoring what are known within the RMBS as 'showstoppers' – events which, if not done on schedule, can prevent someone from being deployed. Nowadays these include vaccinations for Hepatitis A and B, CRB checks, and training in, or for, Damage Control Party, Manual Handling, First Aid and other training requirements.

The RMBS provides the moral component of the 'Fighting Power' triangle. Each point of the triangle has a purpose that enables the triangle to retain its strength and operational ability. The three purposes are conceptual, physical and moral. 'Conceptual' provides the doctrine, the operational procedures, the planning and the way that the force goes about its work. It is the cerebral component. The 'Physical' part includes, to oversimplify, the 'boots on the ground', the arms, the equipment, the kit, the fighting forces and their support, including the ever important medical support, whilst the 'Moral' component covers the things that create and maintain the will to fight. These include communications with home, pastoral support and the effect of music. The RMBS brings skills and experience to not just one but two of these vital components, the 'Physical' through its permanent place within the Medical Support function; the 'Moral' through its ability to bring music to a number of situations that cover preparing to fight, relaxing from the fight and, when necessary, Remembrance.

The Tempest Ambulance in a convoy of vehicles on a Combat Logistics Patrol

Afghanistan - 2010 (Op *Herrick* 12).

On the 6th September 2009 CplBug Caleb Brown joined 40 Cdo at Norton Manor Camp having volunteered for duty as the unit Bugler during their deployment as part of 4(Mech) Brigade. The Unit had been ordered to take fifty members of the Royal Marine Reserve with them which meant that they were up to, if not over, complement. They knew they had to take a Bugler with them but resisted taking two. Three days later he was taking part in a Battle Fitness Test, but this was the 'bootneck' version. Fortunately he was a fit man who had made sure that he improved that fitness during the run-up to joining the unit. Following this, and whilst the Commandos carried out further military training, the Bugler was sent to Leconsfield for a six week heavy vehicle driving course, rejoining in time to participate in the unit's Remembrance Service. He then faced the Unit Combat Fitness Test which once again was the 'bootneck' version with a 65lb Bergen which he managed to carry for the full eight-mile 'yomp'. He then went to RAF Benson where he attended, and passed, the five-day Landing Point Commanders Course.[36] Returning to the Unit he took part in exercises on Salisbury Plain and at the realistic 'Sindh Kalay' Afghan village at the Stanford Training Area in Norfolk. The Annual Personal Weapons Test was then carried out

36 *The qualification necessary to be able to work with helicopters, to be able to pack and load rope nets, and then attach them to hovering helicopters of various types.*

in snow near Taunton, Somerset. Musicians and Buglers always use the Iron Sight on their SA80 weapons and, as a result, Caleb now using the much better 'Susat' sight', achieved 'Marksman' rating with the best score.

Following Christmas leave training at Folkstone commenced, and continued, in heavy snow and general bad weather. This, and the pre-Christmas snow at Taunton, was not providing ideal training for the heat of Afghanistan. Not needing to take part in the Commando fighting Company exercises the Bugler was sent on the Telescopic Forks Handlers Duties Course. As part of Motor Transport Troop, 40 Commando Logistics Company he was being sent on all courses necessary to provide him with the skills required by them. Prior to Easter and pre-deployment leave MT personnel prepared and moved all of 40 Cdo's vehicles to storage areas. Following leave, kit was issued and Caleb Brown and a RM clerk were sent on a three-day Unit Postal Orderly's Course at Deepcut.

C Company was first to fly to Afghanistan followed, two weeks later, by the main body who were despatched at daily intervals. The route was Brize Norton to Camp Bastion with stops at Cyprus and Kandahar. Oppressive heat and four long, and mandatory, days of training constituted their welcome. This included Caleb Brown's introduction to the Op *Barma* and *Kala* mine clearance drills using the Vallon metal detector, fingertip searching and two and four-man mine detection drills. The fighting troops did a further four days of exercises but Caleb and the clerk were detailed as Unit Postal Orderlies. The following day and because of his qualifications he was sent to the loading park on the outskirts of Camp Bastion. This was known as HUSLE Park (Helicopter Under Slung Load Equipment) and he was to work with one other man filling the large rope nets with equipment, vehicles, kit and, in the main, ammunition, water and rations.

CplBug Caleb Brown reaches to connect a static line to the Chinook hovering above the two-man Underslung Load Team

The routine was that loads were completed and waiting for the Chinook to collect. The pilot would see the load waiting and would hover over the load. Caleb and his colleague would climb to the top of the load and, as the helicopter descended with its hook dangling below it, one of the men would attach a static probe to the hook to discharge the static electricity and then the load would be hooked on. Once the men were clear the helicopter lifted the load and flew to whatever FOB it was destined for.

These two men were on call twenty-four hours a day, seven days a week for this task. Their office was an ISO container. They serviced every flight that went to Battlegroup North (40 Cdo's area), working with Chinooks, Merlins, Sea Kings and the American CH53 (Sea Stallion) and Russian civilian I-Kat helicopters.[37] As time went by the calls for buildings

37 *All other battlegroups were supplied through the Joint Helicopter Support Squadron, a combined Army/RAF unit led by the RAF.*

equipment and construction materials declined and nearly every load consisted of water, rations and ammunition.

During the first two weeks in June the Unit Postal Orderly went on Rest and Recuperation leave to the UK and Caleb Brown was detailed as his replacement. This coincided with the build-up to Father's Day and all Battlegroup North mail, a hundred sacks a day, had to be emptied sorted by FOB, OP or Camp and re-bagged. Very often this required a working day of 0730 to 2100/2200hrs. Shortly after this Caleb's own R&R became due, and on his return he rejoined the HUSLE Park. Although this duty really required two men Caleb's 'oppo' was needed elsewhere and so Caleb managed on his own. By this time, the work was reducing as the Unit made preparations for the 'Relief in Place'. At Caleb's suggestion, the 40 Cdo part of HUSLE Park was shut down and a handover to the Joint Helicopter Support Squadron was arranged. In turn, they would handover to the Parachute Regt as they replaced 40 Cdo and the rest of the Brigade. The final stage of the deployment was the compulsory 24 hours in Cyprus before flying to Brize Norton, then returning to the Unit to sign in and return body armour before going on leave.

Following the 'thumbs-up' signal from the ground team the Chinook pilot gains height with his load

All of the training, and all of the tasks described above, were part of the secondary role of the Bugler. His primary role in Afghanistan, as in other theatres, was as a Bugler at Repatriation Services.

CplBug Brown brought a unique set of experiences to what was, in many ways, a lonely task. A Commando is a close-knit group of men, steeped in their unique ethos, their capabilities and their achievements. To enter such a group is not easy, especially when you wear a blue beret. Although a Bugler, Caleb Brown had spent ten years as a Musician (Euphonium and Cello) in the Royal Marines Band Service during which time he had served as a member of a Decontamination Troop, in support of Medical Squadron, Commando Logistic Regiment, RM, during the assault on Basra during Op *Telic*. After his return he elected to return to the Royal Marines School of Music and re-train as a Bugler, which he successfully did. Following promotion to CplBug he qualified as a Drum Major and, at the time of *Herrick 12*, was serving as Assistant Drum Major for Plymouth Band. Afghanistan required all of his experience, knowledge, fitness and determination.

4(Mech) Brigade consisted of 40 Cdo, The Mercian Regiment, The Gurkhas, The Rifles and elements of many other services, regiments and smaller units. CplBug Brown's primary role was to sound bugle calls as men from the unit, known as 'the losing unit', left on their final journey. For others - like the Mercian Bugler and the Royal Logistics Corps Piper it was not their primary role; they were soldiers first. Occasionally the Royal Marine Bugler and the Mercian's Bugler played together. A similar arrangement was attempted with the Gurkha and the Royal Marine Bugler but, during practice, it was discovered that the differences in the keys of the two bugles made this impractical so the Gurkha stepped down from this task. Later in the deployment the Mercian Bugler was himself wounded and sent back to England, leaving CplBug Brown to shoulder the full responsibility. During the deployment he became 'Camp Bastion Bugler' and, as such, was involved in the Battle of Britain ceremonies on RAF Day and played at the Danish Flag Ceremony, the Danish equivalent to Remembrance Day.

As in *Herrick 5* and *9*, both a Vigil Service and a Ramp Service were held following a man, or men, being killed in action. The Vigil Service was a 'duty attend' for all at Bastion, except those on essential duties. When the Brigade suffered its first 'killed in action' losses, the thirty minute Vigil Services were held at 1700 hrs but, by June, the temperatures were such that, until August, they took place at 1900. All four of the Brigade Padres would attend and the Padre of the 'losing unit' led the Service. In the event of multiple 'losing units' the Padres would arrange who should take the lead. The Camp Bastion garrison would parade fifteen minutes before the Service. As this was a Vigil Service the coffins were not present. Senior officers and any VIPs arrived and then the Padre would lead the Service of Remembrance. On completion, the unit's Commanding Officer, followed by two of the dead man's friends, would speak. The Commanding Officer then spoke the words of the Regimental Prayer, the Garrison Sergeant Major called the Parade to attention and either the GSM or the Unit Regimental Sergeant Major would recite the Words of Remembrance. The Bugler then sounded the *Last Post* and a single artillery-piece would be fired. After the One Minute Silence the gun would be fired again and the Bugler would sound *Reveille*. Sometimes the Royal Marine Bugler carried out this duty for Army personnel and, when this was the case, he sounded the Army version of *Reveille*, the *Rouse*. Following the Blessing, the Parade was dispersed.

The structure of the Vigil Service was frequently subjected to variation due to the number of 'losing units' and the number of casualties. As a result a rehearsal, taken in slow-time, would be held earlier in the day for the main participants.

The period during which the Ramp Service took place was charged with emotion. For any Bugler in this situation, no matter what war or what conflict, the immediacy of the death of a serviceman and the closeness, and the loss, of his comrades brought not only emotion - but extreme pressure and, during this particular tour, isolation. No matter how good the training, no matter how great the experience, sounding *Last Post* at the graveside of an Old Comrade or at a Memorial Service on Remembrance Sunday cannot compare with this situation.

Out of respect for the occasion, and despite the heat of the late evening, the Royal Marine Bugler wears full ceremonial uniform. Having marched to the aircraft he would take position at the foot of the lowered ramp. Unlike the Vigil, this Service is for the 'losing units' and they then march on and line up, forming a deep avenue which ends at the ramp. On arrival, the ambulances stop at the far end of the avenue and, out of sight behind them, the coffins would be prepared and shouldered by the bearer-parties. The Parade is called to attention by the RSMs who then take position alongside their Commanding Officers. The padre leads the coffin, or coffins, along the avenue of men. A stranger might expect silence and darkness but the aircraft engines have to be kept running; the inside of the aircraft is brightly lit with the human avenue bathed in the light from floodlights. If there is only one coffin then the padre will lead the coffin into the fuselage and the CO and the RSM will follow. If there is more than one then the COs and RSMs march into the aircraft when they are all in position. With coffins in the fuselage, the bare-headed bearer parties at attention beside them and the COs and RSMs, also at attention but wearing headdress, along the side of the fuselage, the padre speaks the final words. He turns and walks down the ramp, in line with the Bugler, and turns about to face into the fuselage. The padre bows. From this point, everything is carried out by cues initiated by the Bugler. He turns out at 45 degrees and the COs and the RSMs come to the Salute. The Bugler sounds *Last Post* and counts the one-minute Silence. When this is complete, he turns to face out and this is the signal for the Salutes to be cut and the bearer parties to replace headdress. They turn and march off, followed by the COs and the RSMs. By this time the Bugler has marched away into the darkness beyond the pool of light. The padre gives a blessing, before they all turn about and step off. The aircraft ramp is raised and, when it reaches the point of closure, the floodlights are turned off and the world is plunged into darkness. Thirty minutes later the aircraft takes off for the journey to Wootton Bassett.

'We have compelled every land and every sea to open a path for our valor, and have everywhere planted eternal memorials of our friendship....'

Pericles: Funeral oration over the Athenian dead. 431 BC

Chapter 27: Looking Back

In 2002, at the point of writing the final chapter of 'The Royal Marines Band Service', I began my summary of what was then the current situation, as follows:

"The Royal Marines Band Service enters its second century as a homogeneous organisation based upon the early years of the twentieth century when the Royal Navy entrusted the Royal Marines with the provision of not only its music but also a very important secondary role. During the intervening century both have developed to the point that the Band Service is acknowledged as one of the finest, if not the finest, in the world whilst it would also be difficult to find any military Musicians who play such an integrated part when their secondary role is required. As part of a comparatively small but highly effective Corps that, by virtue of the development of modern warfare, is at the forefront of any activity that requires Great Britain's armed forces to be involved, the Band Service has to maintain the same efficient, highly-trained and streamlined profile as the Corps itself. This, like most things that are effective and successful, has not happened overnight but is the result of careful development and the recognition that, however difficult or inconceivable, adaptability and resourcefulness are essential commodities for survival.

So the current Band Service is a compact, streamlined organisation that is smaller than it has ever been during its history, a situation entirely in line with the general rationalisation of the services over the last forty or fifty years. Its role and duties have also changed. No more the need for permanent sea-going bands in support of the Royal Navy; no more tours with the Fleets or the Royal Yacht to outposts of Empire or Commonwealth. The demise of the Royal Tournament must be a warning that the days of such displays are numbered. Costs and availability of military bands and a reduced public awareness of this type of entertainment at a time when all appears to be geared to the young and to the electronic age are all contributing to a reduced demand for the military band generally. Yet all is not doom and gloom as the Mountbatten Festival of Music continues to go from strength to strength, links with professional Musicians become ever stronger and the Band Service itself becomes ever more efficient, financially viable and an attractive career for young, and mature, Musicians. As well as all that, rather like the jewels in the crown, the Royal Marines Band Service is renowned for its ceremonial role – and is instantly recognised through its distinctive uniform, its music and its élan.

The Royal Marines Band Service has, particularly in recent years, been carefully honed. Overheads have been slashed and resources have been concentrated but not at the loss of quality of Musicianship or standard of performance, product or professionalism; quite the opposite has been effected through new approaches to training and the development of attractive facilities that help to improve self-reliance and efficiency. The introduction of women into the Band Service has been accomplished smoothly and the resulting integration, and the passing years, are proof that it has worked and that, whether male or female, all are fine Musicians or Buglers - and that is what matters."

Most, possibly all, of the above is as appropriate now as it was almost a decade ago. However, two points need to be added: firstly, the Royal Marines Band Service, like all parts of the Armed Services, has now to evolve and maintain standards whilst anticipating future cuts to funding. Secondly, since the above words were written, the Royal Marines Band Service has been tested in its secondary, military, role – and not found wanting -

quite the opposite, as Chapters 25 and 26 testify. Not only have the men and women of the Royal Marines Band Service smoothly integrated into their military role but, whilst doing so, they have continued their traditional musical role in a more efficient manner.

Whilst 'in theatre' they do not represent a drain on other resources. They do not require additional accommodation, food or transportation. Most importantly of all they do not require protection; their music and entertainment value do not have to be set against the impact on, or the disruption to, front line personnel. In theatre their versatility and availability is such that they can provide many forms of musical entertainment, music for religious service, for ceremony or for celebration, and not forgetting remembrance. Perhaps most importantly of all, they are working with their peers; they are neither visitors nor guests – they are now a fully integrated part of the team.

Do these two books, added to the works of Trendell, Oakley, Miller, Field, Kreyer and others, complete the story of the Royal Marines Band Service up to 2011? No, they do not. There is still much to learn, much to research and to record. Our knowledge of history is not given to us on a plate; we have to learn by taking clues and finding links. None of the artefacts, documents or images that the Royal Marines Museum receives can be considered as separate, unique, entities; they are each a small part of the whole. Dr Chris Underwood, currently working on the wreck of HMS *Swift* in Argentina may be able to assist in our understanding of the development of drums used by Marines. Similarly, the acquisition of a Conspicuous Gallantry Medal by the museum will require research to broaden our knowledge of the involvement of a sixteen year old Drummer in the Ashanti War that caused him to receive the medal from Queen Victoria at Windsor Castle at the age of eighteen. And then there is the subject of uniform…

Some of the first drummers of 1664 would have been involved in a sea-battle against the Dutch off Lowestoft during the following year. Men of the Royal Marine Bands of the RNSM would have served during the two World Wars, as would the men of the Buglers' Branch; heavy losses being sustained by both. Korea, the Falklands, and a host of small wars and actions took place during the second half of the twentieth century. The recruiting and entertainment role in Northern Ireland caused the Royal Marines Band Service to be identified as a legitimate, military, target by the IRA. A year later musicians and buglers on board RFA *Argus*, were the Corps representatives during Op *Granby*. Operation specific training and improvements to standards of physical and military training throughout the Royal Marines Band Service, including the School of Music, have all contributed to the growing competence exhibited in the military role.

The primary role of the Royal Marines Band Service is, of course, the provision of music to the Royal Navy and to the Royal Marines. Recently a unique opportunity occurred to integrate their collective memories of recent military deployments with their musical skills. This was through an innovative concert and the related recording. Lt Colonel Grace developed his concept of a concert to raise monies for Royal Marines Charities by commissioning a challenging new piece of music dedicated to those Royal Marines who had made the ultimate sacrifice. This piece of music was to be written for wind band with choir, mezzo-soprano and boy treble. The venue would be Exeter Cathedral and many of the other items on the programme would reflect conflict, personal loss and remembrance. Composer Adam Gorb was commissioned, in association with librettist Ben Kaye, to write the thirty-minute, five-movement work to be called *Eternal Voices* and the eighty-strong Exeter Festival Choir, Musical Director Nigel Perrin, gladly accepted the opportunity to take part. The mezzo-soprano and the boy treble would express the thoughts of the wife and son of a Royal Marine killed in action, whilst an additional element was added by the appearance of Sir Trevor MacDonald who, as narrator, played the part of himself – a newsreader bringing the bulletins of the day from Afghanistan. These bulletins were spoken between each of the music's movements and included the following:

"The bodies of two Royal Marines killed while on patrol in Afghanistan five days ago have been flown home. The repatriation ceremony was held at RAF Lyneham in Wiltshire for the two Royal Marines from Somerset based 40 Commando. The pair were killed when their vehicle was caught in an explosion in Helmand Province near Kajacki. They had been on a six-month tour, with two weeks to go before they were due to return home. Both were given medical treatment at Camp Bastion but died as a result of their wounds."

This reading brings recollections of Musicians and Buglers who also served in Afghanistan; whether duty watch-keeper, signaller or ambulance drivers; entertaining on patrols, handling casualties, respectfully caring for the dead or sounding that last bugle call at the end of a ramp, the men and women of the Royal Marines Band Service had played their part.

The Band of the Commando Training Centre, Royal Marines, was under the baton of the Principal Director of Music and the concert began with a processional, the 1st Movement of Karl Jenkins' suite *The Armed Man* played and sung by band and choir. The remainder of the programme included music by Elgar, Gorecki, Stanford, Vaughan Williams and a traditional Naval finale with the insertion of Parry's *I Was Glad*. Also included was the new march *Wootton Bassett* written by Major Peter Curtis as a tribute to the people of that town who took it upon themselves to encapsulate the feelings of the nation towards those who gave the ultimate sacrifice. The Commandant General Royal Marines, Major General Buster Howes, ended the concert with an inspirational speech that included mention of the forty members of the performing band who had been training and exercising in preparation for their own deployment to Afghanistan in April 2011.

The Royal Marines Band Service remains at the very peak of military music throughout the world. Long may the circumstances exist for it to continue.

Royal Marine Artillery Blue Cloth Helmet Plate

Chapter 28: Looking Forward - Lt Col Nick Grace PDM RM

I have been invited by the author John Ambler, to write the final chapter to this most informative and enlightening book about the Royal Marines Band Service. It certainly gives me the opportunity to thank John for his considerable time and effort in collating all the information and presenting it in a clear and practical manner. He has brought the story of this incredible organisation up to date and in such detail that it will be a source of information for anyone with the slightest interest in the Royal Marines Band Service and military music.

My task is to give an insight into what the future holds for the Royal Marines Band Service. Following the Strategic Defence and Security Review (SDSR) of October 2010, there remains uncertainty as to the eventual consequence of this review. As history has demonstrated on several occasions, there is always a surprise waiting around the corner. Who would have predicted the Falklands war of 1982, the first Iraq war in 1990, Kosovo, the events of 9/11 and the subsequent 2nd war in Iraq and then Afghanistan? Short of having a crystal ball, there are far better people than me to see into the future. However, over the last 29 years of my service, the Royal Marines Band Service has adjusted, developed and maintained the relevance and value of military music to defence.

The immediate future, as this book goes to print, will be the deployment of 41 Musicians from the RM Band Commando Training Centre Royal Marines to Afghanistan during *Herrick 14*. They will work with the Joint Force Medical Group based in Camp Bastion providing the ambulance drivers, radio operators, motor transport coordination and the Adjutant for the Joint Force Medical Group. Although they will have their musical instruments with them, the opportunities to provide the essential musical support will be limited. Planning is in place to deploy a designate musical group, of up to 18 Musicians, for a short tour of the operational theatre providing specific musical support. This will include playing contemporary popular music to the troops on operations at the main base areas including the forward operating bases (FOBs). This also provides the opportunity for the military commanders to utilise the unique effect that music can deliver in the operational environment.

There will come a time in the operational tempo of war where gaining the confidence of the local population can be best achieved through the medium of music. Music can cross cultural and language barriers like nothing else and without the use of force, as demonstrated and proven in the previous chapters of this book. The security environment needs to be considered, but when the time is right, music can be deployed like a precision guided missile into key areas of influence. This is certainly an area where Royal Marines Musicians and Buglers, including those from the bands of the other two services, can and will be utilised effectively in the operational environment in the future.

As for the operational demands on the bands, this should reduce as the British Government's aspiration to withdraw from the Afghanistan area of operations in the next few years, will result in a reappraisal of priorities for the RM Bands' operational role. The pressure to justify military music and the roles played by the Royal Marines Bands will; however, remain for the foreseeable future. The justifications for the RM Bands have very much been centred and articulated around the RM Bands' military role. Although this has proved important in the past, it will not be decisive in the future, as the musical primary role and the effect music brings to defence is paramount and pivotal to the future of the

RM Band Service. The arguments for the future of the Royal Marines Band Service should focus on the excellent musical support and output that is provided. This is why Musicians train for up to 3 years and Buglers up to 2 years to achieve musical excellence and provide the capability that is admired the world over.

To remain at the forefront of military music in this country the importance of the Royal Marines School of Music (RMSoM) based in Portsmouth is fundamental. Although there are no clear plans as yet, financial pressures will have an influence and as a result the future of music training in the military will come under close scrutiny in the near future. Whatever the outcome the training at the RMSoM is the envy of the other services and much of it is recognised as best practice. If there is a move to combine music training with the Army and RAF Music Services, the Royal Marines model for music training must be used to maintain the quality of military music into the future.

The requirement for musical support from the RM Bands remains as high as ever and there will be no let up of this in future years. The current structure of the RM Band Service with 5 bands based around the country has met requirements extremely well. Any further reduction in the current numbers of personnel will have a profound effect on the future structure of the bands and their output for Defence.

The future vision for the Royal Navy and Royal Marines is looking ahead to 2025, by which time there will have been at least a further 2, if not 3, Defence Reviews. The size and shape of the naval service may well be vastly different from today and realistically with even less manpower than the 30,000 to be achieved by 2015. The RM Band Service cannot expect to be unaffected by this in the future, but it will be the decisions of the Admirals and Generals to decide what they require from military Musicians.

There will still be a place for the pageantry, spectacle and emotion that military music brings to the British way of life. It is perhaps the one thing that this great country of ours is not only renowned for, but can deliver extremely well. Military music is the glue that binds the 'fabric of the nation' and links the history and heritage of the country with its future. Once it is removed, it will not be regenerated and we must guard it for future generations to enjoy and appreciate.

Finally, with the advent of a withdrawal from Afghanistan, the financial crisis and a perceived reduction in the appetite by the British Government and the general public to enter into armed conflict, is there a future for military music? I would suggest that there will be an even greater reliance on the positive impact that military music brings to defence both at home and abroad. To influence in a positive manner without the use of force is extremely efficient and effective use of a military asset. It is not the only asset that defence can deploy, but it complements and can deliver an effect in all corners of the world. The famous Musician and violinist Yehudi Menuhin is reputed to have said: "*Perhaps the greatest strength of music is its capacity to communicate beyond the spoken or written word; it can cross barriers of language, of culture and of age*". If articulated in a manner that is clearly understood by those in power and influence, the future can be secure for an organisation that continues to deliver high quality military music as a potent weapon for good.

The Royal Marines Band Service will continue into the future, providing the Naval Service, Defence and the State with the visible manifestation of musical and ceremonial excellence that underpins the fabric of the nation. Uniquely it has, and will continue to deliver, specialist military and musical capability for the Royal Marines and the Royal Navy in the operational environment. This is provided by the dedication, commitment and quality of the Musicians and Buglers that are the heart and soul of the Royal Marines Band Service, Per Mare Per Terram.

Appendix 1: Abbreviations

Any book on a military subject is bound to include many abbreviations. Whilst traditional official abbreviations are used throughout this book the reader should be aware that some of these are in the process of alteration as a result of current changes in communication - especially emails. An example is 'Royal Marines School of Music' which is traditionally RMSM but has now become RMSoM to avoid confusion with Royal Military School of Music which had already been allocated RMSM as part of its MOD email address.

Adjt	Adjutant
AFI	Admiralty Fleet Instruction
AFO	Admiralty Fleet Order
AGRM	Adjutant General Royal Marines
Asst Cmdt.	Assistant Commandant
BB	The Blue Band Magazine
BdCpl	Band Corporal
Bdr	Bombardier
BM	Bandmaster
BSS	'Britain's Sea Soldiers' by Col C Field RMLI
Bde HQ	Brigade Head Quarters
C2	Communications
C-in-C	Commander in Chief
Capt	Captain
CBF	Commander British Forces
CBM	Corps Bandmaster
Cd BM	Commissioned Bandmaster
CDM	Corps Drum Major
Cdo	Commando
CFSG	Commando Forward Surgical Groups
CGRM	Commandant General Royal Marines
CO	Commanding Officer
COS, RM	Chief of Staff, Royal Marines
Col Cmdt	Colonel Commandant
CPO	Chief Petty Officer
DAG	Deputy Adjutant General
DCI	Defence Council Instruction.
DOM	Director of Music
DROPS	Demountable Rack Offload and Pick-up System
Fl BM	Fleet Bandmaster
G&L	The Globe & Laurel Journal
GD	General Duties
GO	General Order
HLS	Helicopter Landing Site/Spot
HUSLE	Helicopter Under Slung Load Equipment.
Hon Lt	Honorary Lieutenant
HQ	Headquarters
ICP	Incident Control Point
IED	Improvised Explosive Device
ISAF	International Security and Assistance Force
J4	Logistics and Operational Support
JF Sp	Joint Force Support
JOB	Joint Operational Base.
KR & AI	King's Regulations & Admiralty Instructions
LG	London Gazette
MEP	Main Entry Procedure, Quick Reaction Force
Musn	Musician
NCO	Non-Commissioned Officer
OCRM	Officer Commanding Royal Marines
OIC	Officer in Command
OinC	Order in Council
OOD	Officer on Duty
PCRF	Primary Casualty Reinforcement Unit
PO	Public Order
PRO	Public Record Office (Now National Archives)
PTI	Physical Training Instructor
RAM	Royal Academy of Music
RC(S)	Regional Command (South)
RM	Royal Marines
RMB	Royal Marines Band
RMBS	Royal Marines Band Service
RMHS	Royal Marines Historical Society
RMI	Royal Marines Instruction
RMLI	Royal Marine Light Infantry
RMM	Royal Marines Museum
RMRO	Royal Marines Routine Order
RN	Royal Navy
RNB	Royal Naval Barracks
RN D by D	'Royal Navy Day by Day' by A B Sainsbury
RNSM	Royal Naval School of Music
RMSM	Royal Marines School of Music (pre 1996)
RMSoM	Royal Marines School of Music (post 1996)
SOP	Standard Operating Procedure
SS of P	'Sea Soldiers of Portsmouth' - Ambler/ Little
Tempy Lt	Temporary Lieutenant
TS	Transmitting Station
WngO	Warning Order
WO RM	Warrant Officer, Royal Marines
White & Green Fleet	White = Hire cars; Green = Military Vehicles

Appendix 2: Chronology 1664 - 2010

Note (1) Items without a source reference are from 'Royal Marines Band Service' by John Ambler, or other publications listed in the Bibliography.
Note (2) Whilst the inclusion of all changes to uniform is beyond the scope of this chronology, selected changes to uniform such as special headdress badges, are shown. Selection has generally been based upon information contained in Orders and other Regulations, supported by suitable contextual entries.
Note (3) For explanation of 'Source' abbreviations see Appendix 1.
Note (4) Orders and Instructions are sometimes dated after an event has occured. This can affect the accuracy of dates given in 'year' and 'date' columns.

Year	Date	Event	Source
1664	28 Oct	The Duke of York and Albany's Maritime Regiment of Foot, later the Marines and then the Royal Marines, was raised by an Order-in-Council this day. It specified that: *"Twelve hundred men are to be put into one Regiment under one Colonel, one Lieutenant Colonel and one Sergeant Major and to be divided into six Companies, each Company to consist of two hundred soldiers; and to have one Captain, one Lieutenant, one Ensign, one Drummer, four Sergeants and four Corporals..."* These Company Drummers represent the first specialisation in the Corps and the present Buglers' Branch of the Royal Marines Band Service can trace its unbroken history from these six men.	*OinC, RMRO 144/77*
1747	28 Feb	The ten Marine Regiments were placed under Admiralty control.	*BSS Vol 1 p 86*
1767	12 Jan	Marine Band formed at Plymouth (3rd Grand Division).	
1768	11 Jun	*"The Band to wear white breeches and stockings with black buckled garters at Guard Mounting".* The first dated reference to a Marine Band at Portsmouth (The 2nd Grand Division) although it is believed that a band was formed there in 1765.	*GO - Portsmouth Div*
1775	17 Jun	Drummers were part of Major Pitcairn's force during the American War of Independence and took part in the Battle of Bunkers Hill . (From Blumberg's precis of Admiralty Letters)	*RMM Archive*
1780		Corps strength was one hundred and forty six Companies each of one hundred and eighteen Privates and four Drummers. Therefore, approximately five hundred and eighty four Drummers in the Corps. (From Blumberg's precis of Admiralty Letters)	*RMM Archive*
1781	8 Oct	First dated reference to a Marine Band at Chatham (The 1st Grand Division) although it is believed that a Fife and Drum Band was formed there in 1773.	
1783		Corps strength now one hundred and fifty seven Companies, including, approximately, six hundred and twenty-eight Drummers. (From Blumberg's precis of Admiralty Letters)	*RMM Archive*
1802	29 Apr	The Marines were granted the title Royal.	*G&L 1922 p52*
1804	18 Aug	Formation of the first three Artillery Companies.	*OinC*
1805	15 Aug	Woolwich Division formed.	
1820	Jul	First reference to a Band at Woolwich Barracks. From *Woolwich Crisis of 1820*	*RMM Archive*
1823	23 Jul	The first Band of the Royal Marine Artillery formed. At this time the Artillery Companys were at Chatham.	*SS of P*
1824	1 Jun	Royal Marine Artillery Companys first occupied Fort Cumberland.	*ARCH 15/3/2 - RMM*

Year	Date	Event	Source
1826		Chatham Divisional Band accompanied the British Ambassador to Russia for the Coronation of Tsar Nicholas 1, the first time that a British band left Britain to attend a foreign ceremony. An Imperial Russian sword, suitably engraved , was presented to the Bandmaster. This sword is now in the Royal Marines Museum Collection.	
1832	6 Feb	Band of the Royal Marine Artillery disbanded as part of the 1832 reductions.	*OinC*
1848	29 Mar	Royal Marines occupy Forton Barracks, Gosport, moving from Clarence Barracks, Portsmouth.	*G&L 1922 p40*
1859	22 Oct	Formation of a separate Royal Marine Artillery Division.	*SS of P*
1861	2 Jan	The Band of the Royal Marine Artillery, Bandmaster Thomas Smyth, was formed at Fort Cumberland, Portsmouth.	*SS of P*
1869	17 Mar	Woolwich Division disbanded.	*OinC*
1876	5 Jul	*"Headdress badge of the Portsmouth Division Royal Marine Light Infantry Band, Bandmaster Mr J F C Kreyer, to be adorned with the Prince of Wales' plumes"*. This honour was granted by Queen Victoria for their musical support during the Royal Tour to India by HRH the Prince of Wales (later King Edward VII) on board HMS Serapis.This was the first recorded instance of a Royal Marine Band going to sea for an extended period of time.	*G&L 1903. BB Spring 2000*
1882		*A Life on the Ocean Wave*, written by Henry Russell and arranged by Jacob Kappey (Chatham Div Band RM) was officially recognised by the War Office (only) as the March Past of the Royal Marines. (See 1920 for recognition by the Admiralty and 1927 for confirmation of acceptance by the Royal Navy).	*RMI 1110/1975*
1889		Regulations for enlistment of Buglers laid down.	*GO 1889/46*
1890	21 Mar	Small band, under a Sergeant, formed at the RM Depot. This band was only utilised for recruit training purposes.	*RN D by D.*
1892		Divisional Band strength set at one Bandmaster, two Sergeants, two Corporals, twentyfive Musicians and ten Supernumeraries (six Buglers and four Gunners or Privates). Supernumaries to be trained to fill vacancies due to retirement, or other causes. The Depot Band strength was to be one Sergeant for duty as Bandmaster, one Sergeant, one Corporal, seventeen Musicians and five Supernumeraries (three Buglers and two Gunners or Privates).	*GO 1892/3*
1893		Enlistment of twenty-six boys, in excess of the regular establishment of Buglers, to be enlisted with a view to training them as Buglers.	*GO 1893/1*
1894		*"In matters referring to the Portsmouth Division RMLI, the Division to be referred to by that name and not as is frequently the case at this time - as the 'Gosport Division'".*	*GO1894/52*
1895		*"Bandmasters will, invariably, be in uniform when leading their bands".* The Bandmasters of the time usually wore civilian clothing whilst conducting their bands.	*GO 1895/46*
1899		Four RMLI Buglers were amongst the force that fought its way onto the Graspan heights during the South Africa War.	
1900		RM Depot Band brought up to strength and given official recognition in 1900.	
1901	Jan	*"Band of the Chatham Division, RMLI, to embark on the SS Ophir to accompany HRH The Duke of York on the Royal Tour of the British Empire".*	*GO 1901/4*

Year	Date	Event
1901	1 Feb	Duties of RM - funeral of Queen Victoria: The Bands of the RMA and Portsmouth Division, RMLI, were massed under 2nd Lt G Miller Bandmaster, RMLI, and played during the funeral procession from Osborne House to Trinity Pier, East Cowes (1st February 1901). A Guard of Honour, with Band and King's Colour of Portsmouth Division RMLI, was mounted at Clarence Yard, Gosport, for the disembarkation of the King, the Royal Family and the remains of the late Queen on the 2nd February. The Band of the Chatham Division RMLI was the band chosen to represent the Royal Marines in the funeral procession through London on the 2nd February. ***GO 1901/34***
1901	Dec	Commodore Winsloe of the SS *Ophir* wrote to the Colonel Commandant of Chatham Division RMLI expressing his appreciation of the Band's excellent behaviour and playing throughout the tour. ***GO1901/152***
1902	1 Mar	White Rose of York granted to Chatham Divisional Band by the King. To be worn upon the Regimental cap badge and helmet plate. Granted in commemoration of the band's attendance upon The Duke of Cornwall and York during his voyage to the Colonies during 1901 and 1902. ***GORM 31/1902***
1902	9 Mar	HM the King presented the Medal of the Royal Victorian Order to Mr Frank Winterbottom, Bandmaster of the Plymouth Division, RMLI, on board the Royal Yacht *Victoria and Albert*. ***GO 1902/44***
1903	20 May	Establishment of the Royal Naval School of Music within the Royal Marine Artillery Barracks at Eastney. The Royal Marines assumed responsibility for the provision of music to the Royal Navy by training Royal Marine Bands to serve on board the ships of the Fleets. ***OinC*** and ***GO 1903/49***
1903	10 Jul	The Band of HMS *Leviathan* became the first band to transfer from the Royal Navy to the Royal Marines. The first man to sign his papers and become RMB1 was Arthur William Shepard.
1903	22 Jul	The Band of HMS *Impregnable*, which had paid off on the 25th May, marched into the Royal Marine Artillery Barracks at Eastney as RN Bandsmen, later to become the first Royal Marine Band produced from the Royal Naval School of Music.
1904	31 May	Extra pay for Bandsmen serving in Royal Yacht. The Admiralty approved an allowance of one shilling per day to a maximum of twenty Band NCOs and Musicians whilst embarked and serving in HM Yacht; to take effect from 14th January 1904. The Admiralty stressed that Musicians embarked for Royal Yacht service would not necessarily be from the RMA Band. ***GO 1904/64***
1904	Aug	*"Buglers' equipment will no longer include swords, scabbards and frogs. All items in service ashore to be withdrawn immediately; all those in service afloat to be withdrawn upon disembarkation."* ***GO 1904/75***
1905	Apr	*"Cap badge of special design to be worn by WOs, NCOs and men of RM Bands when embarked for service in HM Yacht. To be issued upon embarkation and returned to store when disembarking."* ***GO 1905/p107***
1908	Aug	Temporary musical training of band ranks at Chatham and Plymouth to cease since this training is to be returned to the Royal Naval School of Music and RMLI Forton Barracks as from 30th September 1908. ***GO 1908/55***
1908	30 Nov	Temporary musical training of band ranks at RMLI Forton Barracks to cease and this training to be concentrated, as intended, at the Royal Naval School of Music, Eastney, as from 30th November 1908. As a result of this concentration the new series of individual numbering (RMB series) would, henceforth, always be used. All clothing and equipping of band ranks now to be supervised by 1st Quartermaster, RMA. ***GO 1908/77***
1912	1 Apr	A special badge consisting of a gilt grenade on which was mounted the Royal Cypher 'GvR' and crown in silver surrounded by a gilt laurel wreath was conferred upon the Band of the Royal Marine Artillery by the King. This followed the voyage to India on board the P&O liner Medina. ***GORM 44/1912***

1914	4 Aug	War declared.	
1914	Aug	Title of Commissioned Bandmaster, Royal Marines, to be changed to Director of Music. Number of Directors of Music fixed at two, apart from the Musical Director of the Royal Naval School of Music to whom this Order would not apply. On promotion to Director of Music the honorary rank of Lieutenant will be applied. After ten years of commissioned service the honorary rank of Captain will be given and, after a total of fifteen years' commissioned service the honorary rank of Major will be awarded. Directors of Music to be compulsorily retired at the age of 65.	*GO 1914/59*
1917		Abolition of fee to Drum Major for training of Buglers.	*GO 1917210*
1918	7 Mar	Institution of King's Squad & King's Badge by King George V.	
1918	Jun	Owing to difficulties at RM Divisional HQ in training Buglers to replace those transferring to the ranks, twelve boys were enlisted at the Depot RM Deal for training as Buglers. Four would be transferred to each RMLI Division. On completion they will be transferred to their Divisional HQ and further Buglers trained in their place.	*GO1918/129*
1918	11 Nov	Armistice Day.	*BSS III p380*
1919	26 Jun	First occasion that a Royal Marine Band appeared as the resident band at the Royal Naval, Military and Air Force Tournament - later the Royal Tournament - when Mr P S G O'Donnell and the Band of the Plymouth Division, RMLI undertook this duty. This was the first Tournament since 1914.	*Story of the Royal Tournament - Binns*
1919	Aug	Award of a distinctive badge for musical efficiency. RNSM Musicians who have reached the standard required for the granting of the Musical Proficiency Allowance (KR & AI vol II, App XV, Part III, No 11) were issued with a badge, a red star, to be worn on the right arm below the elbow.	*GO1919/158*
1920	18 Jan	Memorial Silver Bugles first sounded by Portsmouth Division RMLI. The Officers of the Royal Marines purchased thirty-two Silver Memorial Bugles for Officers killed during the First World War. Issued in groups of eight to the RMLI Divisions at Chatham, Portsmouth, Plymouth and also the Depot.	*G&L 1920 pp27* & *30*
1920	24 Aug	Bandmaster W E F Faithfull, veteran of Antwerp and Gallipoli (where he was wounded and earned a Mention in Despatches), became the first Band Boy to reach Commissioned rank when he was promoted Lieutenant and QM.	
1920	Nov	Confirmation of rank 'BdCSgt' and 'BdSgt' being substituted for Bandmaster 1st Class and Bandmaster 2nd Class. Previously described in GO 1920/169. (See GO 1921/127)	*GO1920/174*
1920		Capt & Brevet Major A R Chater, the Adjutant at the Depot, Deal, presented a pair of silver and ebony drumsticks to be used by the most efficient Drummer at the Depot each year. Awarded to Bugler Crane (1920), Bugler Tyler (1921) and Bugler Astle (1922). The tradition then lapsed but the drumsticks were retained and are now part of the Royal Marines Museum Collection.	
1920	Dec	Warrant Rank was assigned to those who had been appointed as a Bandmaster or Commissioned Bandmaster provided the appropriate qualifications had been attained.	*GO 1920/184*
1920	24 Dec	Award of the The Prince of Wales' Plumes to Plymouth Division Band following the Royal Tour to Canada on HMS *Renown*. This band was selected for its Musicianship and for its dedication to duty whilst on active service during the Great War.	*GORM 206/1920*

1920 — *A Life on the Ocean Wave*, written by Henry Russell and arranged by Jacob Kappey (Chatham Div Band RM) was officially recognised as the March Past of the Royal Marines by the Lords Commissioners of the Admiralty. (Thirty-eight years after the same recognition by the War Office) ***RMI 1110/1975. MO 1524/1924; GO 1921, (errata to previous).***

1921 18 Feb — First six Band Boy Section Leaders appointed at RNSM. Selected by the Superintendent based upon 12 months' service, 2nd Class Certificate of Education, 'VG' in Infantry Drill, Physical Training and Fire Control and having passed the swimming test. Cleanliness, appearance and behaviour, musical ability and sportsmanship were also taken into account. Object was to encourage Band Boys of exceptional ability and those likely to be candidates for future promotion. ***GO1921/40***

1921 5 Mar — On this date the set of five Memorial Silver Drums and a silver finished bass drum were Dedicated as the Official Royal Naval School of Music War Memorial and presented at a parade held at the RNSM, Eastney. Over one hundred and forty men of the RNSM plus fifty-five Buglers and also two Musicians from Royal Marine Divisional Bands lost their lives during World War 1. ***G&L 1921 pp 53 & 84***

1921 2 Aug — Three O'Donnell brothers promoted Lt as Directors of Music on same day. ***BB Aug 1979 p35***

1921 11 Nov — The Service of Remembrance at the Cenotaph, unveiled the previous year, included the Royal Marine Buglers (Chatham Division) sounding Reveille immediately after the two-minutes' silence and the singing of *O God, Our Help in Ages Past*. This was repeated in 1922 but in 1923 there was a reduced Service.

1921 — Titles 'Band Colour Sergeant' and 'Band Sergeant' to be withdrawn and the old titles of 'Bandmaster 1st Class' and 'Bandmaster 2nd Class' reinstated. (See also GO 1920/174) ***GO 1921/127***

1923 28 Apr — Gosport War Memorial Hospital opened, commemorating the 68 officers and 1,703 other ranks of the Portsmouth Division Royal Marine Light Infantry from Forton Bks who died in WW1. This number includes seventeen Buglers. ***G&L 1996 p157***

1923 3 Aug — As part of the amalgamation of the Royal Marine Artillery and the Royal Marine Light Infantry the Portsmouth Division of the RMLI, based at Forton Barracks was integrated with the Royal Marine Artillery at Eastney Barracks. This resulted in the special badge of the Prince of Wales plumes, awarded 5th July 1876 to the Band of the Portsmouth Division RMLI, being transferred, along with many members of the band, to the RM Depot, Deal Band. The Colours were transferred to Eastney. ***AFO 1643/23, G&L 1923 p130, BB Spring 2000.***

1924 11 Nov — Service of Remembrance at the Cenotaph again featured sixteen Buglers from the Chatham Division. Despite the 1923 amalgamation they were still wearing red tunics. RAF trumpeters, involved for the first time, played the Last Post. This is the year that the ceremony took the form that is used today.

1925 3 Sept — The first direct recording from a radio broadcast by a military band took place when the RM Band of HMS *Calcutta* was recorded, playing as an orchestra, in Canada. ***ARCH 23/2/3 - RMM***

1925 — Design of Divisional Drum Majors' Dress Belts standardised by the Adjutant General Royal Marines, as a result of the RMA/RMLI amalgamation. ***PRO File ADM1/8808***

1926 — Standard pattern for design of Drum Majors' staffs to be used by the Royal Naval School of Music and by the Bands of Commanders in Chief at Portsmouth, Plymouth, Atlantic Fleet, Mediterranean Fleet and China Fleet introduced. ***PRO File ADM1/8808***

Year	Date	Event
1927	11 Mar	Additional music approved for use and inclusion in KR & AI: RN March Past *Hearts of Oak*; RM March Past: *A Life on the Ocean Wave*; RN/RM Advance in Review Order: *Nancy Lee*; General Salute for British Flag Officers not entitled to *Rule Britannia - Iolanthe*; General Salute for Governors etc - *Garb of Old Gaul*. ***AFO 626/27***. Also ***KR & AI Ch II, Sec XII*** (For 'Salutes' only)
1929		Standard pattern for design of Divisional Band Drum Major's staffs introduced. ***PRO File ADM1/8808***
1929		Drill for Buglers formalised for adoption at Royal Marine Establishments - includes the 'Flourish' ***GO 1929/128***
1930	1 Oct	The Royal Naval School of Music moved from Eastney Barracks to the Depot, Deal. The School had outgrown the space and the facilities that Eastney could provide. The Depot Band, under Lt Ricketts, had been disbanded a few months earlier.
1934	20 Mar	The first performance of Bandmaster A C Green's musical setting of *Sunset* took place in the Alameda Gardens, Gibraltar. This had been specially arranged in response to Admiral Fisher's request for a *"spectacular show for the visit of the First Lord and the Board of Admiralty"*. ***BB Winter 2007***
1934	23 May	First performance in Malta of Bandmaster A C Green's musical setting of the *Sunset* call. ***G&L 1934 p226***
1935	24 Aug	Royal Marines carried out London Duties for the first time - the Jubilee year of the King's Reign - during the period 17th August -19th September. The Massed Bands consisted of thirty-five from Chatham Division, nineteen from Portsmouth Division and eleven from Plymouth Division. In addition there were eleven Drummers (two tenor and nine side drums) plus thirty-three Buglers. Chatham Division Drum Major (Sgt W Day) and Bugle Major (Sgt E B Astle) were in command of Drummers and Buglers respectively whilst the massed bands were under the direction of the Senior Director of Music, Royal Marines, Captain P S G O'Donnell of Chatham Division. Buglers and Drummers wore Bugle Cords, Royal, for the first time. As well as the Royal Palaces the Corps provided the Bank of England Picquet and the Hyde Park magazine guard. ***Brigade Orders. G&L 1935 p273***
1936		Dress Cords, Royal, to be worn by Bugle Majors and Buglers (Corporals and below) in review order and when on leave. ***AFO 1539/35*** & ***GO 1936/79***
1939	3 Sept	War Declared. Corps strength 12,000.
1940	30 May	Band Boys evacuated from Depot, Deal to RM Reserve Camp, Exton, at Lympstone because of the Depot's proximity to the battle of France. Two weeks later the remainder of the RNSM followed and moved into a fort at Plymouth.
1940	Sept	Royal Naval School of Music moved from Plymouth to a camp outside Malvern, Worcs.
1941	22 Aug	The RNSM was split in two and, on this date, the Senior Wing moved to two hotels in Scarborough whilst Junior Wing moved to Howstrake Camp on the Isle of Man.
1944		Major Ricketts arrangement of *A Life on the Ocean Wave*, written by Henry Russell, became the version used by the Corps. ***GO 1921*** and ***AFO 626/27***
1945		Royal Marine Bands in Shore Establishments in the UK to revert to the wearing of white helmets with white belts and cross-belts.***GO 1945/1452***
1946	25 Apr	Senior Wing of the RNSM moved from Scarborough to Burford, Oxfordshire ***RMRO 579/46***
1946	8 Jun	Victory Parade in London. ***G&L 1946 p181 & 208***
1946	1 Aug	Junior Wing RNSM moves from Isle of Man to Burford, Oxfordshire. ***RMRO 945/46*** & ***GO 1946/1051***

1946 31 Dec Warning instruction - reorganisation of the Corps. Portsmouth, Chatham, and Plymouth Divisions will become Groups and will be given specific functions. *AFO 2727/47*, *GO 1947/540*

1946 Drill - New RM Instructions to be issued. To include marching as well as bugle and drum stick drill. *GO 1946/1065*

1946 The practice of Royal Marine Drum Majors throwing the staff in the air will only be carried out at the discretion of the Major General Royal Marines, on the parade ground of a Royal Marine Establishment. *GO 1946/1457*

1947 1 Jul Functional reorganisation - Royal Marine Divisions become Royal Marine Groups. Bands to be known as Group Bands. *GO 1947/576* & *RMRO 440/47*

1947 Oct Inauguration date of the Cassel Prize. Rt Hon Sir Felix Cassel presented money to the Worshipful Company of Musicians for medals/prizes to encourage education and training in music in the three Armed Services.

1947 Under the new Pay Code Boy Buglers will no longer be required to undertake instruction in the playing of the fife. At the discretion of Commanders, instruction in the fife may be given to Buglers who have completed their first commission at sea.

1947 RM Band Service - Changes to Bandmaster ranks. Bandmaster I to become Bandmaster and Bandmaster II to become Band Sergeant. *AFO 6101/46*. *AFO 3862/47*. *GO 1947/718*

1948 1 Jun Memorial Day for the men of the Royal Marine Bands of the Royal Naval School of Music instituted. The fanfare *To Comrades Sleeping* subtitled '*The Spirit of Joy and Thanksgiving for Victory, and Meditation for those who gave their lives in its cause*' composed by Leon Young became the *Dedication Fanfare*. It was composed for the ceremony at which the Silver Memorial Fanfare Trumpets (the Official Royal Naval Band Service War Memorial for World War II) were dedicated at Burford, then the home of the Royal Naval School of Music. This fanfare was to be sounded each year as laid down in the Charter - but not to be played for any other purpose. *G&L 1948 p200*

1948 8 Oct HM King George VI agreed that the appointment of Colonel-in-Chief of the Royal Marines should become Captain General Royal Marines. *OinC*

1948 15 Dec First Buglers under training reported to Burford for training at the RNSM. A training team had been formed and, from this date, training would be done at the School and not at the Groups. *BB Autumn 1989 p53*.

1948 As a result of the introduction of new SNCO rank titles (AFO 3862/47) badges of rank introduced for Bandmasters - a lyre encircled by laurel wreath and surmounted by a crown, and for Band Sergeants - three chevrons. *AFO 1206/48*. *GO 1948/163*

1948 Wearing of ornaments and shoulder flashes - correct positions. *GO 1948/312*

1949 28 Jan The Order in Council of 1871 introducing Band Boys into the Royal Navy and the Order in Council of 1903 introducing the rank of Band Boy into the Royal Marines were both rescinded. The rank of Band Boy to become Boy Musician. *OinC*

1949 5 Apr Throughout the Corps the 'Warrant List' and 'Warrant Officers' to be replaced by 'Branch List' and 'Branch Officers'. Bandmaster (WO), RM Band, becomes a Commissioned Bandmaster and a Commissioned Bandmaster, RM Band, becomes a Senior Commissioned Bandmaster. *OinC*

1949 6 Jul Sir Malcolm Sargent's appointment as Hon Advisor in Music announced in House of Commons. *Hansard*

1949 Brass instruments replaced by silver plated ones. *BB. Aug 1961 p13* &*14*.

1950 1 Feb Relocation of Royal Naval School of Music from Burford to Deal was completed on this date. *AFO 4227/49*, *GO 1950/50*, *RMRO 50/50*

1950 27 May Chatham Group Band heavily involved in the ceremony for the disbandment of Chatham Group, Royal Marines. *G&L 1950 p142*, *RMHS SP No 23*

1950	28 May	Chatham Division Colours laid up in Rochester Cathedral after being paraded through the streets. ***G&L 1950 p142, RMHS SP No 23***
1950	23 Jun	First Beat Retreat by the Massed Bands of the Royal Marines on Horse Guards Parade, London. Ceremony was based upon the displays by the RNSM at the 1948 Dedication Ceremony and their Royal Tournament appearance in the same year. This was the first occasion that all thirty-two Silver Memorial Bugles were sounded together.
1950	31 Aug	Chatham Group officially ceased to exist. Chatham Band was lost as a result of the closure of RM Barracks Chatham and its special badge, the White Rose of York awarded in 1902, was lost with it. ***RMRO 125/50, RMRO 312/50. G&L 1950 p223***
1950	1 Sep	Amalgamation of Group Bands with RNSM. No further direct entry to Group Bands, all recruiting through School; members of Group Bands to retain old conditions only until engagement expires; automatic promotion for Group Musicians to become merit based. RNSM becomes RMSM; Group Bands become Staff Bands. Musical Director of RMSM will be 'Director of Music, Royal Marines'; other DoMs will be 'Director of Music, Portsmouth' and 'DoM, Plymouth'. These bands to retain special cap badges & Portsmouth to retain 'Royal Yacht' flash. All RM Bands on RN ships and at RN establishments became part of the RMBS. Records of Portsmouth and Plymouth Band Ranks transferred to the RMSM from where new numbers in the RNSM 'RMB' series would be issued. This also applied to Chatham Band ranks transferred to the new RMSM Band and also to ranks of the C-in-C Nore Band. Instructions relating to uniform (Lyre collar badge and wearing of broad red stripe trousers) to be issued. ***AFO 2333/50*** and ***RMRO 312/50***
1950	9 Oct	Band rank of Staff Sergeant changed to Staff Bandmaster "*to avoid misunderstanding of his status in relation to Bandmasters and Band Sergeants*". ***OinC. AFO 2333/50*** and ***GO 1950/492***
1950	2 Nov	RNSM Collar Badge (the lyre) to be replaced by the Globe & Laurel except for Boy Musicians who would continue to wear the lyre on the collar and would also retain the thin red trouser welt, not the broad red stripe. The King approved these changes on this date.
1951	27 Jan	To mark the occasion of the return of the Royal Marines School of Music to Deal in January 1950, the Commandant General approved the title 'Commandant General's Squad' to be given to the senior squad of Boy Musicians under training. In addition, the Commandant General approved of the best all-round Boy Musician in the Commandant Generals Squad being awarded a Certificate of Merit to be called the Commandant General's Certificate. ***RMRO***
1951		Full dress for RMBS Other Ranks re-introduced. (Dress 1A: Band Order for RM Band Service. White helmet or cap, blue cloth tunic, tweed trousers, white belt, white gloves. For ceremonial use as ordered) Dress Regulations to be amended. ***AFO 3422/51 GO 1951/395***
1952	28 Aug	South African tune *Sarie Marais* adopted as the quick march of the Royal Marine Commandos. See GO 1977/171. ***BR 1958 programme***
1952		Intake of 100 National Service Musicians to the Band Service. ***GO 1952/209***
1952		The correct pace for marching in quick time in the Royal Marines is 116 paces to the minute. Rifle movements are to conform to this. ***GO 1952/340, RMRO 8/19/113***
1953	24 Apr	*"RM adopted The Globe and Laurel based on the old English air Early One Morning as their slow march. The march was first used at a Guard Mounting at St James's Palace by the London Bn RM formed especially for London ceremonial duties in 1935".* There is some doubt between authorities on such matters regarding when, even if, this slow march was adopted. The late John Trendel stated that it had not been officially adopted whilst Captain Derek Oakley wrote that it was "...*Later to be adopted as the Official Slow march*". (See also 10th June 1964, AFO 143/64) ***BR 1958 programme.***

Year	Date	Event	Reference
1953	2 June	Coronation of HM The Queen. HRH Prince Philip appointed Captain General Royal Marines.	*LG 26 May 53*
1953		Fleet Band scheme introduced.	
1955	24 Oct	Following their seven month world tour HM The Queen and Prince Philip awarded their combined cyphers (EiiR/PP) to the Portsmouth Group Band that accompanied them. This was an addition to the special badge awarded to the Royal Marine Artillery in 1912.	***RMRO 369/55*** and ***GO1955/369***
1955		Boy Buglers formed into a separate House, unnamed at this time, for sports purposes. This was intended to intensify competition for House championships.	***G&L 1955 p124***
1956	13 Apr	Change of title from Boys to Junior.	***AFO 963/56***, ***RMRO 167/56***
1956		RM Bands - Drum Majors - Drill with the Staff. *"Throwing the staff in the air is not in keeping with the position and dignity of a Drum Major. His primary duty is to control and lead the band and not to give a personal display. The practice of throwing the staff in the air by Drum Majors in public or when the public are present is to be discontinued. More effective use should be made in the movement of the Staff by Drum Majors in slow and quick time, and the necessary amendments will be made in due course to 'Drill (Royal Marines) 1953 Part V, Band Drill - Ceremonial"*	***GO 1956/246***
1958	9 Jun	Massed Bands Beat Retreat on Horse Guards Parade.	
1958		Wearing of Dress Cords Royal restricted to Buglers' Branch, not Musicians.	***GO 1958/11***
1960	2 Jun	Massed Bands Beat Retreat on Horse Guards Parade.	
1960	7 Oct	Warning order regarding wider wearing of green beret by officers and other ranks. Restriction to wearing by Commando Formations and Units to be revised.	***RMRO 324/60***
1960	25 Nov	AFO decreed universal wearing of green beret. Previously only worn by ranks serving in Commando Units or the Commando School. *"Green beret now to be issued to ORs of the RMBS and Buglers on attaining Adult 1st Class status or on first draft to an HM Ship, RN Establishment, or Commando Unit or formation - whichever is sooner. After issue green beret will be part of compulsory kit. RM and RM Band Officers are to provide themselves with the green beret when required".*	***AFO 3118/60 RMRO 324/60***
1960		Layout of Royal/Corps insignia on Drum Majors' Dress Belts checked by Royal College of Heralds and amended to suit current protocol.	***RMM Archive File***.
1960		Rope tensioned drums replaced by rod tension.	
1961	3 Feb	Revised structure of the RMBS Special Duties List. Admiralty approval of changes to promotion and structure. Ranks to remain in the cumbersome form of 'Major (SD(B))' - 'Major, Special Duties, Band'.	***AFO 1585/60 (Continuation of)***
1961	31 Mar	Closure of Nore Command & disposal of C-in-C's RM Band.	***BB Apr 1961 p33***
1961	21 Jul	Stick drill for Royal Marine Buglers. 'Attention' drill changed. No pause between coming to attention and bringing sticks across the body. Buglers to carry out these movements at the same time.	***GO 229/61*** and ***RMRO 5/20/187***
1961		Method of wearing bugle cord described. When carrying a drum, bugle to be carried on a shortened cord passing under the right epaulette - bugle to be carried in the right hand at all times.	***GO 1961/215***
1961		Last National Service Musicians left the RMBS.	
1963	29 Nov	Issue of white drill leg aprons for RMBS Drummers & Buglers. The buff leg apron to be withdrawn.	***GO 1963/296***

Year	Date	Event	Source
1963		Band of C-in-C Home Fleet to be located at HMS *Pembroke*, Chatham, from 1st March 1963.	*GO 1963/57*
1963		Metal wrist badges for Drum and Bugle Majors being manufactured in Portsmouth.	*GO 1963/151*
1963		First Drum Majors' Course.	
1963		New Rank Insignia for Staff Bandmaster - a lyre surrounded by a laurel wreath. To be worn on blue uniforms and Khaki drill. On other orders of dress the current (QMS) insignia to be worn.	*GO 1963/203*
1963		Khaki tie issued to Band ranks and Buglers in preparation for the introduction of Lovat uniform.	*GO 1963/289*
1964	1 Apr	Lovat dress introduced.	*RMRO 66/64*
1964	10 Jun	From this date the Regimental slow march of the Royal Marines will be The *Preobrajensky March*. Earl Mountbatten offered the march to the Royal Marines instead of the present Regimental Slow March The *Globe & Laurel* which is based upon the same air as the Regimental Quick March of the Women's Royal Army Corps. This march will be retained by the Royal Marines as an Inspection piece. Also phrased as: Prompted by Admiral of the Fleet Earl Mountbatten, the Royal Marines adopted the *Preobrajensky March* as their Regimental Slow March in place of The *Globe and Laurel* based on *Early One Morning*. The new march was the ceremonial slow march of the Preobrajensky Guards commanded by the Grand Duke Sergius of Russia, Mountbatten's uncle and Prince Philip's great uncle. The first public performance was on Horse Guards Parade on this day.	*AFO 143/64. RMI 1110/1975. Inscription on the score - RMM Archive*
1964	23 Jul	As part of the Corps Tercentenary Celebrations a Royal Review was held in the gardens of Buckingham Palace. Musical support was provided by the Band of Portsmouth Group augmented with Buglers and Musicians from the Bands of C-in-C Portsmouth and HMS St Vincent under the direction of Capt P J Neville.	
1967	Aug	Introduction of CG's Certificate of Merit for Buglers.	*GO 1967/241*
1967		Band Ranks to be eligible for selection as Drum Majors.	*GO 1967/228*
1967		Move of Plymouth Group Band to Infantry Training Centre RM.	*GO 1967/280*
1967		Band of C-in-C Mediterranean Fleet was disestablished.	
1968		As a result of condition and age, the Memorial Silver Bugles will no longer be sounded. (See also RMRO 43/68)	*GO 1968/43*
1968		New NCO structure in Band Service - Introduction of Band Colour Sergeant rank.	*GO 1968/251*
1968		The Commandant General's Piper' 1. During his recent visit to 42 Commando RM the Commandant General approved that the title of the Commandant General's Piper was to be held by the leading piper in 42 Commando's Pipe Band. 2. This appointment confers on the holder the entitlement, when in pipe band uniform, to wear a Skian Dhu presented by General Sir Norman Tailyour KCB DSO. 3. The first person selected to hold this appointment is RM21534 Lance Corporal I Anderson.	*RMRO 234/68*
1969	1 Jan	Band of HM RM C-in-C Western Fleet formed. With a strength of forty-three this was one of the two largest bands and was regarded as the Staff Band of the Royal Navy.	*BB*
1969	21 Jan	Malcolm Sargent Cancer Fund for Children. First concert in aid of this charity held in Portsmouth Guildhall, preceding the Royal Albert Hall concerts.	*File 6/1/505(128) RMM*
1969	23 Feb	The Silver Memorial Bugles withdrawn from service and issued, as Corps Silver, to the Officers' Messes at Plymouth and CTC as well as the RMBS and the RMM. (See GO 1968/43).	*RMRO 43/68*

1970	Jun	Band of C-in-C Far East Fleet disbanded.
1970	9 Jun	Massed Bands Beat Retreat on Horse Guards Parade.
1970	1 Aug	Daily rum issue abolished in the Royal Navy. ***G&L 1970 p3***
1970	2 Sep	Last RM Band detailed for regular service on board a Royal Navy warship embarks in HMS *Eagle*. ***G&L 1970 pp270*** and **291**
1971	29 Apr	Headdress to be worn by Fanfare Trumpeters. Instruction from Dept of the CGRM: *"Her Majesty has now expressed a wish that when parading with a band in helmets the trumpeters should conform to the dress of the band. Trials carried out at the School of Music have shown that this presents no real difficulty. Having regard to the fact therefore that the trumpets at present used for ceremonial purposes are not the original memorial trumpets the Commandant General has ruled that white helmets are to be worn when the trumpeters parade with a band in this dress".* ***File 6/6/19 RMM***
1971		Band of HM RM C-in-C Western Fleet became HM RM C-in-C Fleet.
1972	3 Jan	Plymouth Band change title to Band of HM Royal Marines, Commando Forces. ***RMRO 52/1985***
1972	11 Jun	*Army & Marine* adopted as Regimental March of the Commando Logistics Regt.
1972	1 Jul	Rank of Warrant Officer reintroduced into RN & RM. ***G&L 1972 p195***
1972	6 Dec	Bands permitted to wear green berets on limited occasions eg when performing in Northern Ireland, during military training, and when caps are impractical eg in ships. CGRM's Advisory Dress Committee File. (RM 5/20/277 Pk2) ***RMM Archive***
1972		HM The Queen approved the designs for drum emblazonments to be used by the Royal Marines and the Volunteer Bands of the Royal Navy. This followed Corps representatives' discussion with, and approval from, Clarenceux King of Arms, Chester Herald (Advisor on Naval Heraldry) and Garter, King of Arms. New design introduced in 1973.
1973	6 Feb	First Royal Marines Massed Bands concert in the Royal Albert Hall. This was in aid of the 150th Anniversary Appeal for the Royal Academy of Music. Series later became known as the Mountbatten Festival of Music. Bands of C-in-C Naval Home Command, HMS Ganges and the Royal Marines School of Music took part. ***Concert Programme***
1973	12 Jun	Massed Bands Beat Retreat on Horse Guards Parade.
1974	5 Feb	Massed Bands Concert at the Royal Albert Hall in aid of Royal Marines Museum funds. ***Concert Programme***
1975	4 Feb	Massed Bands Concert at the Royal Albert Hall in aid of the Sir Malcolm Sargent Cancer Fund for Children, and Corps Charities. ***Concert Programme***
1975		Corps marches *A Life on the Ocean Wave*, *Sarie Marais* and *Preobrajensky* in place of *Globe & Laurel* confirmed. See 1977, GO 1977/171. ***BR 1283. RMI 1110/1975***
1976	8 Jun	Massed Bands Beat Retreat on Horse Guards Parade.
1977	12 Sep	RM Band of Flag Officer Naval Air Command moved from Lee-on-Solent to Yeovilton.
1977	1 Oct	Depot RM Deal Final Pass Out Parade - 229 Troop. Next day the Depot became Royal Marines Deal, and home to 41 Cdo, RM, and the Royal Marines School of Music. ***GO 1977/86. RMRO 86/77, G&L Nov/Dec 1977***
1977	14 Nov	Op *Burberry* (Fire-fighters' Strike) commenced.

1977		RMRO issued to reinforce the RM Instruction regarding the march *Sarie Marais*. *"In addition the quick march Sarie Marais may be used to commemorate the derivation of the name Commando, given in 1940 to the newly raised raiding units and the service of a number of South African Officers seconded to the Corps during the Second World War"*. (See BR1283) ***GO 1977/171**, **RMI 1110** & **RMRO 171/77***
1978	9 Mar	To commemorate 25 years as Captain General, HRH Prince Philip instituted the annual award of the Prince's Badge for the best Musician or Bugler on completion of training, under similar conditions to the King's Badge. This replaced the Commandant General's Certificate of Merit. ***RMI 0821**. **RMRO 1978/75***
1978	30 May	Massed Bands Beat Retreat on Horse Guards Parade.
1978	4 Nov	41 Cdo, RM, assumed London Duties (4th-30th November). Musical support was provided by the Staff Band of the Royal Marines School of Music under the direction of Major J Mason and led by WO2 Drum Major D Buchanan. The Tower of London was included for the first time. ***G&L 1978 p357***
1979	6 Jul	Integration of the Buglers' Branch, as a separate Section, within the RMBS; Buglers to retain own rank structure and promotion rosters. Transfer to the General Duties branch in accordance with RMI 1747 will continue to be allowed for men at present serving in the Bugler Section. For men enlisting after 1 July 1979, such transfers will only be allowed within 3 months of attaining the age of seventeen and a half or before completion of initial training, whichever is the later. Buglers who prove to be musically unsuitable can transfer at any age. WO and SNCOs will continue to be entitled to become candidates for selection for promotion to officer on the Royal Marines SD List. ***GO 1979/105***
1979	1 Oct	Wearing of Royal Marines Band Service shoulder title instituted. Review of RMBS ceremonial dress due in May 1980. ***GO 1979/106***
1980	Feb	Massed Bands Concert at the Royal Albert Hall extended to two performances for the first time.
1981		Massed Bands Concert at the Royal Albert Hall renamed 'The Mountbatten Concerts' following his murder.
1982	8 Jun	Massed Bands Beat Retreat on Horse Guards Parade.
1982	14 Jun	The Falklands War. 3 Cdo Bde included the Band of Commando Forces, with their musical instruments. This band embarked upon the SS *Canberra* as stretcher bearers but performed a number of duties and roles throughout the campaign. The RM Band of Flag Officer 3rd Flotilla (FOF3) boarded the educational cruise liner SS *Uganda* which was converted to a hospital ship. ***RMRO 16/86***
1983	24 Jan	Amendment to BR2118 Royal Marines Drill: *"The practice of Directors of Music marching in front of their bands, when there is insufficient room for them to march on the right flank, detracts from the visual impact of the band.Accordingly the following manuscript amendment to BR2118 para 1605 is to be made: 1605. Position of Director of Music. The Director of Music will be 2 paces clear of the right flank of the band and in line with the leading rank of Musicians. When there is insufficient room for the Director of Music to march on the flank he is to take up a positionat the rear of the band. If the bandmaster is not on parade he should take the normal position of the bandmaster. If the bandmaster is on paradehe should take up a position 2 paces to the rear of the bandmaster".* ***RMRO 09/86.BR 2118***
1983	31 Mar	The Royal Marine Band of Flag Officer Naval Air Command was disbanded.
1984	Feb	Massed Bands Concert at the Royal Albert Hall renamed 'The Mountbatten Festival of Music'.
1984	12 Jun	Massed Bands Beat Retreat on Horse Guards Parade.

1985	1 Apr	On this day the RM Band of Commando Forces ceased to exist and HM The Queen approved the transfer of the badge of The Prince of Wales Plumes from this band to the RM Band at the Commando Training Centre, RM. This badge had originally been worn by the Bands of Plymouth Division and then Group but, when the latter was split into Bands for Commando Forces and CTC in 1972, it passed to the Commando Forces Band.	*RMRO 52/85*, *G&L 1985 p141*
1986	17 Jan	RM C-in-C Naval Home Command Band on board HMY *Britannia* assist as beach, stores, stretcher parties and immigration officers during evacuation of British nationals from Aden. Making several trips into various beaches the Yacht evacuated 1068 men, women and children. To 24 Jan.	*BB 1986 Spring/Summer p16*
1986	17 Jun	42 Cdo, RM, carried out London Public Duties from 17th June - 15 July (the third occasion that the Corps had received this honour). In addition to Buckingham Palace, St James's Palace and the Tower of London, guard mounting was required at Windsor Castle. Two bands were needed; the Band of the Royal Marines School of Music, directed by Lt Col G A C Hoskins and led by Drum Major D Dawson was in London with the Band of C-in-C Fleet, directed by Captain E P Whealing and led by Drum Major Archer, at Windsor Castle.	*G&L 1986 p242*
1987	31 Mar	The Royal Marine Band of Flag Officer 3rd Flotilla was disbanded.	*BB 1987*
1987	26 Oct	Change of title from RM Deal to Royal Marines School of Music.	
1988	Feb	Massed Bands Concert at the Royal Albert Hall extended to three performances for the first time. This concert was video-recorded.	
1989	22 Sep	IRA bomb exploded in the Recreation Room of North Barracks, Deal, killing 10 band ranks. A further Musician died of his injuries.	*RMRO 98/89*, *RMRO 111/89* and *BB 1989 p76*
1989	29 Sep	The Band of the Royal Marines School of Music marched through the town of Deal to honour their fallen comrades, to thank the townspeople for their support and as an act of defiance towards the bombers.	*BB*
1990	22 Sep	Sunday closest to 22nd Sept to be the RMBS Memorial Day, as a result of 1989 Deal Bombing.	*BB*
1990	29 Oct	RM Band of C-in-C Fleet, deployed on board the recently converted Casualty Handling Unit, RFA *Argus*, sail from Plymouth for military service in the Gulf. Casualty handling plus Nuclear, Biological and Chemical decontamination and protection are the main operational areas for this force - which, apart from the possibility of Special Forces activity, was the only Royal Marines commitment in the first Iraq War. To 19th March 1991. *BB 1990 p 69*	
1991	1 Jun	The Royal Marines Band Service ceased to wear the Green Beret.	
1991	31 Oct	Closure of the Royal Marine Barracks, Eastney. RM Band of C-inC Naval Home Command relocated to the re-named Eastney Block, HMS *Nelson*.	*G&L 1991 p235*
1992	1 Apr	Manpower cuts announced reducing the Royal Marines Band Service to 432 ranks, divided into seven bands.	
1992	3t Aug	First women join the Corps as part of New Entry Squad 2/92 to commence training as Musicians and Buglers.	*G&L 1993 p19*
1994	25 Mar	RM Band C-in-C Fleet disbanded as part of RMBS redundancies and restructuring.	*BB*
1994	1 Apr	Bands renamed. C-in-C, Naval Home Command became Portsmouth; Flag Officer Scotland & Northern Ireland became Scotland; Flag Officer Plymouth became Plymouth; Royal Marine Commandos became Commando Training Centre, Royal Marines. Royal Marines School of Music and Britannia Royal Naval College retained their names.	*BB Spring 1994*

Year	Date	Event	Source
1994	23 Jul	Lieutenant General Sir Robert Ross, Commandant General, RM, presented a copy of *The Soldiers' Chorus* from Gounod's opera Faust to 29 Cdo Regiment, Royal Artillery, as their official quick march. This was once the Quick March of the Royal Marine Artillery.	*RMHS Newsletter Feb 2000*
1994	2 Dec	HRH The Duke of Edinburgh, Captain General, visited the Royal Marines School of Music.	*G&L 1995 p22*
1995	1 Jan	White Ensign to be flown in all Royal Marine units.	*G&L 1995 p2 (Admiralty Signal)*
1995	15 Feb	Mountbatten Festival of Music Concerts at Royal Albert Hall directed, produced and recorded entirely by RMBS officers and other ranks for the first time. This is now recognised as the largest military band festival in the world.	
1995	3 Apr	Lt Col Sir F Vivian Dunn died at the age of eighty-six. He succeeded Captain McLean as Corps Director of Music on the 1st March 1953, the title changing to 'Principal Director of Music, Royal Marines' on the 1st October 1953, an appointment that he held until December 1968. He is the only military Musician to receive a knighthood.	*G&L 1995 p 201*
1996	2 Feb	As a result of the Government's 'Front Line First' initiative the proposal to relocate the RMSM from RM Barracks, Deal to HMS *Nelson* was confirmed in the House of Commons on 25 May 1995. Relocation to be completed by 1 April 1996, concurrent with the final stage of the rationalisation of the RMBS.	*RMRO 010/1996*
1996	22 Mar	Disestablishment of the Royal Marines School of Music at Deal. Beating Retreat Ceremony by the Massed Bands of HM Royal Marines, including the Band of HM Royal Marines School of Music, culminated in a final march through Deal. Attended by 6,000 people in pouring rain.	*Official programme and reports.*
1996	29 Mar	HQ Royal Marines Band Service and the Royal Marines School of Music at Deal closed pending relocation to Portsmouth. HQ RMBS operational at HMS *Nelson*, Portsmouth, next day.	*DCI Gen 67/96*
1996	15 Apr	Training commenced at RMSM in HMS *Nelson*. The Royal Naval Detention Quarters were specially modified for the purpose.	
1996	28 Oct	Official opening of RMSM in Portsmouth by HRH The Prince Edward.	*G&L 1996 p 348*
1997	1 Jan	Musician W H Morris awarded the Silver Medal of the Royal Victorian Order in the New Year Honours List. Traditionally only awarded to Bandmasters and Colour Sergeants, he was the first Musician to receive this, The Queen's personal award.	*RMRO 002/1997*
1997	1 Jul	Responsibility for musical training at the Royal Marines School of Music transferred from the Royal Marines Command to the Naval Recruiting and Training Agency under Flag Officer Training and Recruitment.	*DCI RN 117/97 RMRO 64/97*
1997	25 Jul	HRH The Duke of Edinburgh opens new Plymouth Band complex.	*G&L 1998 p23, BB Winter 1997 p 86/87*
1997	Sep	Links between Royal Marines School of Music and the University of Portsmouth formalised. All courses run by RMSM would be formalised by the University enabling Musicians to gain civilian qualifications. RMSM accredited as a centre for degree study.	
1997	11 Dec	HMY *Britannia* Decommissioning Ceremony. Final salute to the ship was paid by the Director of Music and the Drum Major as the Royal Yacht Band, part of the RM Portsmouth Band, marched past the ship playing *Auld Lang Syne*.	*Reports and video evidence*
1998	1 Jan	Musician J Z L Wright of HMY *Britannia* awarded the Silver Medal of the Royal Victorian Order in the New Year Honours List. Only the second, and the last, Musician to receive this award for service on board the Royal Yacht.	*RMRO 002/1998*
1998	1 Apr	HM Queen Elizabeth agreed that the RM Portsmouth Band should continue to provide a Royal Band for the Royal Family. The entire Band, including Buglers, to wear 'Royal Band' flash at all times and to wear the traditional Divisional Tunic when on Royal Duty.	*RMRO 064/1998*

1999 28 May In accordance with RM officer rank alignment (DCI Gen 39/99), changes to be made to Royal Marines dress conventions. eg Majors no longer wear overalls nor gold leaf on caps. ***DCI Gen 145/99***

1999 1 Jul RM officer ranks aligned with the Army ranks. ***DCI Gen 39/99***

1999 20 Jul Final Royal Tournament - Tri-Service event led by the Massed Bands of the Royal Marines. To 2nd August.

1999 19 Aug Exercise *Argonaut 99* including Ex *Northern Approaches* (Turkey) and *Ex Bright Star* (Egypt). Major deployment involving 3 Cdo Bde, RM, the Royal Netherlands Marine Corps and the RM Commando Training Centre Band deployed on HMS *Ocean*. Other RN ships were *Fearless*, *Edinburgh*, *Percivale*, *Bedivere* and *Galahad*. To 15 December. ***G&L 1999 p350 BB 1999 p 80***

2000 10 Jul First, and only, Royal Military Tattoo - a Tri-Service event held on Horse Guards Parade and led by the Royal Marines Band Service under Lt Col Richard Waterer. To 15 July. ***G&L, BB and official programme***

2001 12 Jul Presentation of Colours to 40, 42, 45 Cdo, RM, by HRH The Duke of Edinburgh on Plymouth Hoe. Musical support from the Massed Bands formed from the RM Bands of Plymouth, Commando Training Centre, RM, and Britannia Royal Naval College under the Direction of Lt Col R A Waterer, Principal Director of Music and led by WO1 Bugler A D Bridges, the Corps Drum Major, and WO2 Bugler C Lawton, the Corps Bugle Major.

2002 22 Oct Two hundred RMBS personnel commence training and briefings to cover fire-fighters strike which began on 13 November 2002 and lasted until late January 2003. ***BB***

2003 7 Feb Composite Royal Marines Band to serve on board RFA *Argus* as casualty handlers and in other roles including musical support. Other members of the RMBS deployed to Iraq to serve as two Decontamination Teams were involved in operations in Umm Qsar and the assault on Basra. Duties extended to armed protection force for battlefield ambulances and convoy escort. Probably the most integrated military involvement of the RMBS since the end of World War II. ***BB***

2003 12 Jun RMBS Beat Retreat in the grounds of Buckingham Palace to celebrate Prince Philip's birthday and his 50th Anniversary as Captain General Royal Marines. ***BB***

2003 Special exhibition marking the 100th Anniversary of the opening of the Royal Naval School of Music at Eastney Barracks at the Royal Marines Museum. All 32 Silver Memorial Bugles were on display, this being only the fourth time that they had been together in their eighty-three year history. Visited by HRH Prince Philip, the Captain General Royal Marines.

2004 28 Apr Band of HM Royal Marines, Britannia Royal Naval College, given the Freedom of Dartmouth. The first time that a Royal Marines Band had received such an honour. ***BB***

2006 11 Jan Death of Lt Col R A Waterer, Principal Director of Music 1994-2002, at Valley Forge Military Academy, Pennsylvania, where he was Commandant of Cadets.

2006 Sep Two Buglers are deployed to Camp Bastion for duties that include Repatriation Ceremonies. ***BB***

2007 4 Jan RMBS provided the Cyprus Reinforcement Unit of ninety-five personnel. Responsible for security at British Sovereign Base Areas at Episkopi, Troodos, Olympus and Salt Lake City. Also able to provide musical support and entertainment to military and civilian population. To 15th May. ***G&L BB***

2007 The Royal Marines School of Music no longer under the direct administrative control of the Royal Navy, now placed under the control of Commando Training Centre.

2007 *Eagle* House reintroduced to the RMSM.

2009 20 May Ceremonial Farewell to Dartmouth following the announcement of the disbandment of the Band of HM RM Britannia Royal Naval College. One of the outcomes of the Lean Review was that changes to the structure and the size of the five Royal Marines Bands were required. As a result, and commensurate with the need to deploy RMBS personnel as Medical Support to 3 Cdo Bde in Afghanistan, the decision was taken to remove the RM Band from Britannia Royal Naval College and, upon completion of the Afghanistan deployment, to form HM RM Band Collingwood at the shore establishment of HMS *Collingwood*. *BB*

2009 16 Jun The Band of HM Royal Marines, Collingwood, formed under Major J Burcham. *BB*

2009 28 Sep The specially formed RM Band of Commando Logistic Regiment arrive in Camp Bastion, Afghanistan, as an operational unit within 3 Cdo Bde, RM, during Op *Herrick 9*. Pre-deployment training commenced in March 2008. Deployed to Camp Bastion and to Forward Operating Bases. Duties include MT Troop, Ambulance Troop, Combat Logistic Patrols and musical support. *BB*

2010 Apr One Bugler deployed to Afghanistan with 40 CdoRM. Apart from the Vigil and Ramp ceremonies for 40 CdoRM, and eventually 4 Mech Bde, he was also responsible, with one other, for deploying all 40 CdoRM and Cheshire Regiment stores requirements from Camp Bastion via Chinook underslung loads. *G&L* BB

2010 1 Jun The Memorial Day Commemoration for the men of the Royal Marine Bands of the Royal Naval School of Music who were killed during the two World Wars was re-instituted. The fanfare To *Comrades Sleeping* subtitled *"The Spirit of Joy and Thanksgiving for Victory, and Meditation for those who gave their lives in its cause"*, composed by Leon Young, was played by a Fanfare Team from the Royal Marines School of Music under the direction of Corps Bandmaster WO1 T Hodge. Ceremony took place on the School Parade with all Students and Staff assembled. The Dedication was read by the Director of Music (Training) Major A Thornhill, RM. *BB*

2010 New Entry Military Training syllabus expanded to include six weeks at the Commando Training Centre. *RMSM*

2010 HM RM Band of Commando Training Centre, RM, undertake training in preparation for 2011 deployment to Afghanistan as part of Commando Logistic Regiment's Medical Support Squadron. *HQ RMBS*

2010 Dec Troop 1/10 complete the first extended military training syllabus. *RMSM*

Appendix 3: Band Service Memorials

ROYAL NAVAL SCHOOL OF MUSIC

The War Memorial Charter

1. THE BOOK OF REMEMBRANCE
   The BOOK OF REMEMBRANCE will form the permanent Roll of Honour and will be placed in the Chapel of St Cecilia at the Royal Naval School of Music.

2. THE TRUMPETS AND BANNERS
   These shall be called "The Memorial Trumpets of the Royal Naval School of Music" and this title shall on no occasion be abbreviated.

3. CUSTODY
   The War Memorials shall be in the custody of the Quartermaster (Music) at the Royal Naval School, who shall keep them in safe storage and issue orders covering their safety when in use.

4. USAGE OF THE TRUMPETS
   The Trumpets are never to be played by any but R.N. School of Music personnel and when performing in public will always be conducted by a R.N. School of Music Officer.

5. FEES
   Fees will normally be charged even if the object of the function is to raise money for charity.

6. FANFARE TRUMPETERS
   Trained Fanfare Trumpeters will be maintained continuously at the Royal Naval School of Music as far as is possible. If circumstances prevent the maintenance of a team of the highest class, no engagements will be accepted, since the trumpets reflect the reputation of all ranks, past and present.

7. DRESS
   The dress for the Fanfare Trumpeters will be Royal Marine Band Ceremonial Dress with the addition of dress cords and white gloves.
   Caps will be worn as it is not possible to play the trumpets when wearing Royal Marine uniform helmets.

8. INSURANCE
   The Memorials are to be covered by a comprehensive Insurance Policy the cost of which will be met by the R.N. School of Music Band Fund.

9. THE 1914-1918 SILVER MEMORIAL DRUMS
   It is hereby decreed that all or any charter, rules or regulations drawn up in connection with the Silver Drums shall be cancelled and the provisions of this Charter, in so far as they shall apply, shall also govern the usage of the Silver Memorial Drums 1914-1918.

10. DECIDING AUTHORITY
   Subject to the provisions of this Charter, the Commandant of the Royal Naval School of Music will be vested with final decision as to the use of the Instruments mentioned herein. In this connection, it is hereby recorded that they belong collectively to the Royal Naval School of Music, as opposed to being public property, and, as a War Memorial, they shall be used only with dignity and pride.

11. MEMORIAL DAY
   The War Memorial Committee recommend that the "Dedication Fanfare" composed by Mr Leon Young shall be sounded with due ceremony by the Fanfare Trumpets on the First of June each year.

End of the Charter.

There then followed a description of the Memorials:

THE SILVER DRUMS

These consist of a set of five silver side drums and one silver finished bass drum. They were purchased by voluntary subscription of all ranks to commemorate those Royal Naval School of Music ranks who gave their lives in the War of 1914-1918. The bass drum is emblazoned with their names, whilst the side drums carry the names of the ships in which the men died.

THE BOOK OF REMEMBRANCE

This beautiful Book, in parchment bound in blue leather tooled in gold, contains the names of the 225 ranks of the Royal Naval School of Music who lost their lives during the War of 1939-1945.

THE FANFARE TRUMPETS

The set comprises 14 silver trumpets as follows:- E flat soprano, 2; B flat treble, 7; B flat tenor, 3; G bass, 2. The names of the ships in which the men died are engraved inside the bells of the trumpets, whilst the following inscription appears on each instrument:-

"These Fanfare Trumpets were purchased by the voluntary subscription of their comrades in memory of the two hundred and twenty-five NCOs and Men of the Royal Marine Band Service who lost their lives in the World War, 1939-1945, whilst serving in His Majesty's Ships and Shore Establishments".

BANNERS[1]

The banners were of Royal blue velvet with gold lace fringes. In the centre was placed the Foul Anchor with the letters R.N.S.M. above the stock. The whole design was surmounted by a Royal crown.[2]

At some point between the writing of this Charter and the 1950 amalgamation Rule 4 was changed by the addition of the following sentence: "They will normally be played only on important occasions such as National Ceremonies, Royal Naval or Royal Marine Corps occasions". No further changes appear to have occurred until 1953.

The Silver Memorial Drums and Bass Drum, the Memorial to the men of the Royal Naval School of Music who gave their lives during World War 1

Whilst the 1953 Royal Tour was in progress the War Memorial Charter was updated to suit the new organisation and fully approved by the Commandant General. The new Charter was as follows:

1 *The only known surviving copy of this original Charter is torn at this point so no official description of the banners can be given here.*

2 *Description from inspection of original banners in the RMM.*

ROYAL MARINES SCHOOL OF MUSIC

The War Memorial Charter

THE WAR MEMORIAL

1.The Memorial to all ranks of the Royal Naval School of Music who gave their lives in the War of 1939-1945 consists of a set of 14 Silver Trumpets with Banners. The following inscription appears on each instrument:- "These Fanfare Trumpets were purchased by the voluntary subscription of their comrades in memory of the two hundred and twenty-five NCOs and Men of the Royal Marines Band Service who lost their lives in the World War 1939-1945, whilst serving in His Majesty's Ships and Shore Establishments".

THE TRUMPETS

2.These shall be styled "The Memorial Silver Trumpets of the Royal Marines School of Music" and this title shall on no occasion be abbreviated.

THE BOOK OF REMEMBRANCE

3.The Book of Remembrance containing the Roll of Honour of the 225 ranks of the Royal Naval School of Music who lost their lives during the War 1939-1945 shall be retained in the Church of St Michael's and All Angels' at the Royal Marines School of Music, The Depot Royal Marines, Deal.

THE USE OF THE TRUMPETS

4.The Trumpets shall only be played by personnel of the Royal Marines School of Music and will at all times be conducted by an Officer, or specially deputed Bandmaster, of the Royal Marines School of Music. Subject to the general direction of the Commandant General Royal Marines, the trumpets will be played on occasions appropriate to their use at the discretion of the Commandant, Royal Marines School of Music.

MEMORIAL DAY

5. On the 1st June each year the "Dedication Fanfare" composed by Leon Young shall be sounded with due ceremony to mark the dedication of the Memorial Trumpets which took place on 1st June, 1948, at the Royal Naval School of Music, Burford, Oxon.

FANFARE TRUMPETERS

6.A team of Fanfare Trumpeters will be maintained at the Royal Marines School of Music. If circumstances prevent the maintenance of a team of the highest class, no engagement will be accepted, since the Trumpets reflect the reputation of all ranks, past and present.

DRESS

7.The Dress of the Fanfare Trumpeters will be No.1 Order of Dress. Caps will be worn in order to obviate the difficulty of playing in white helmets.

THE WAR MEMORIAL SILVER DRUMS 1914-1918

The Rules and Regulations concerning the Memorial Silver Drums 1914-1918 are hereby incorporated in this Charter to establish that their use shall be similar to that of the Memorial Silver Trumpets. The Memorial Silver Drums 1914-1918 comprise a set of five silver side drums and one silver finished bass drum. This Memorial was also voluntarily subscribed by ranks of the Royal Naval School of Music to commemorate those ranks who gave their lives in the War 1914-1918. The bass drum is emblazoned with their names, the side drums bearing the names of the ships in which the men died.

Although no longer part of the Charter, the covering letter from the Commandant General's Office did confirm two points regarding the Charter. Firstly, "The Memorial Silver Trumpets of the Royal Marines School of Music comprise - E flat soprano, 2; B flat treble, 7; B flat tenor, 3; G bass, 2." Secondly, "Custody - The Trumpets shall be in the charge of the Supply Officer (Music) at the Royal Marines School of Music who will be responsible for their security, and will give directions for their safe keeping when in use. The Trumpets are to be fully insured by Comprehensive Insurance cover, the cost of insurance and maintenance being borne by the Royal Marines School of Music Band Fund.

The alterations to the Charter had taken account of the amalgamation and their new location. From now Buglers' Dress Cords (Properly known as 'Dress Cords Royal') were not to be worn.[3] Investigations were put in hand for the design of gold dress cords for the Fanfare Trumpeters but they were never produced.[4]

When the Charter was finally approved by the Commandant General it was printed on suitable paper and the details promulgated as an instruction from the Commandant General.

It would appear that in 1955 an attempt was made to again change the wording on the Memorial Charter. The Commandant RMSM met with Lt Col Dunn, and Lts Gale, Fitzgerald and Ough. The major changes proposed in the Minutes and the draft document were that decisions regarding the use of the Memorial Trumpets should become the responsibility of the Commandant and two Officers of the Royal Marines Band Service; fees would be charged even if the function was for charity and the proceeds would go to the maintenance of the instruments; it was firmly stated that "Caps will be worn as it is not possible to play the trumpets when wearing Royal Marines uniform helmets" and, most importantly, it was proposed that the restriction that only the full complement of trumpets should be used and played should be withdrawn. The changes to the Charter do not appear to have been adopted since, in 1959, the Assistant Adjutant General wrote a file minute that confirms that the Charter still invested the responsibility for their use with the Commandant of the RMSM but not with Officers of the RMBS. Then, in 1963, Major Ian Wray had a telephone conversation with Lt Col Dunn who wanted Portsmouth Group Band to use some of the Fanfare Trumpets instead of the Herald Trumpets. Major Wray reminded the Colonel that the Charter precluded the use of the Trumpets on such a relatively minor occasion and that all fourteen had to be used.[5] It would therefore appear that the 1953 version of the Charter was the final version.

A dispute broke out between the RMSM and the veterans of the RNSM when the RMSM officers designed replacement banners that were red in colour and carried the Corps crest. The matter went as high as the Admiralty from whence came the ruling that the new ones would be worn until worn out and then replaced by banners of the original design.[6]

During 1957 it was realised that the Memorial Silver Drums were not being used at Church Parades and a decision was made that they should be kept on display and only used on special memorial dates.

By 1965 the Memorial Silver Trumpets were no longer playable and were replaced. The Memorial Silver Trumpets were dressed with their original Royal Naval School of Music banners and were laid up at the Depot, Royal Marines. The replacement trumpets, since they are not War Memorials, are not subject to the Rules laid down in the Charter.[7] In 1973 the Commandant General agreed to the suggestion that both the Memorial Silver Drums and the Memorial Silver Trumpets should be transferred to, and permanently laid up in, the Royal Marines Museum at Eastney. They are now retained at the Museum in showcases in the Band Memorial Room but each year they, and the Silver Drums, are returned to the RMBS for the Service of Remembrance at Portsmouth Cathedral.

Following the 1970 Beating Retreat by the Massed Bands on Horse Guards Parade Earl Mountbatten again raised the question of helmets being worn when playing the Fanfare Trumpets.[8] Since the trumpets were not the Memorials the Rule concerning the wearing of caps no longer applied and the Commandant of the RMSM was instructed to investigate the matter. As a result, it was considered practicable for the helmet WP to be worn by ranks playing the fanfare trumpets.[9] (See the entry for 29th April 1971 in Appendix 2)

---

3 *RMRO 316/1953. "In future only Royal Marines Buglers are to wear Dress Cords Royal. The issue of Dress Cords Royal to Royal Marines School of Music ranks is to cease forthwith".*

4 *Minute sheet – RM Museum.*

5 *Maj I Wray made an official record of this telephone conversation. RMM Archive.*

6 *File in HQRMBS and also Blue Band.*

7 *File 6/6/81 (Minute from Asst Adjt Gen) in RM Museum.*

8 *File Note to Asst Adjt Gen from CGRM 16/6/1970 "For the Record – Royal Marines Trumpeters' Headgear". RMM Archive.*

9 *All correspondence is in RMM Archive (RMM 6/6/19).*

Appendix 4: To Comrades Sleeping and the Royal Marines Band Service Prayer

"The Spirit of Joy and Thanksgiving for Victory, and Meditation for those who gave their lives in its cause" is known simply as *To Comrades Sleeping* or *The Dedication Fanfare*. This fanfare was initially composed for use in the 1948 Dedication Ceremony for the World War II Silver Memorial Fanfare Trumpets and the Memorial Charter states that it should always be played on the 1st June. This took place at the Royal Naval School of Music at Burford.

Prior to the Second World War, Leon Edward Stephen Young, a shop assistant, played in the brass section of his father's Salvation Army Band. He was also the local church organist and choirmaster. In 1940 he joined the Royal Naval School of Music at Deal, just before it was relocated to Plymouth. On completion of training he was posted to HMS *Pembroke*, the Chatham Naval Barracks, with the rest of a band formed for service on a new cruiser, HMS *Hermione*. Once on board he organised a singing trio, accompanied by a Drummer with himself playing piano. *Hermione* saw a lot of action culminating, unfortunately, in the Battle of Crete where she was torpedoed and sunk. Unusually in such circumstances, only one member of the band lost his life.

Later in the war Leon Young joined Commissioned Bandmaster Charles Hotham's RM Concert Orchestra where he not only played piano but was also the orchestra's arranger. After the war he was employed by HMV and worked with many of the 'stars' and famous bands of the time. He also formed 'The Leon Young String Chorale' which featured regularly on the radio. He was invited, by the Royal Naval School of Music, to write the fanfare in memory of the men of the Royal Marine Bands who lost their lives.

The practice of playing *The Dedication Fanfare* appears to have continued until 1964 when it attracted the largest parade for many years, probably because it was Corps Tercentenary Year. Bad weather forced the ceremony to be held inside the Deal Drill Shed. In 1965 'The Memorial Silver Trumpets of the Royal Marines School of Music' were removed from service and replaced by new fanfare trumpets. The Memorials were then displayed in showcases in the RMSM Concert Hall at Deal. It is not known when this event ceased, but it could have coincided with the withdrawal of the Memorials from service.

On the 1st June 1998, shortly before 0815, the School Staff, Junior Musicians and Junior Buglers assembled on the small parade within the Royal Marines School of Music, Portsmouth. It was the 50th Anniversary of the Dedication Ceremony at Burford. The parade was brought to attention by the Corps Drum Major and Lt Col Richard Waterer, Principal Director of Music and Commandant of the Royal Marines School of Music, took position with his officers and guests. He described the ceremony, the Memorials and the losses that the bands suffered before introducing a particular guest - Trevor Ford. On the 1st June 1948 Trevor had stood, wearing the uniform of a Band Boy, at the Royal Naval School of Music and watched the ceremony. He watched and listened as, fifty years later, Lt Col Waterer gave the command 'Sound the Dedication Fanfare' and, conducted by the Corps Bandmaster, the glorious strains of *To Comrades Sleeping* rang out. On this occasion it was sounded by the Fanfare Trumpeters of the Band of Her Majesty's Royal Marines, Portsmouth.

In 2009, WO1 Hodge, the Corps Bandmaster, made enquiries about the ceremony itself, and its purpose, and decided that it ought to be re-instituted.

On the 1st June 2010, on completion of the Commanding Officer's Inspection, the Musicians and Buglers under training marched off the parade only to return a short while later, now clad in raincoats as the weather became more inclement. This was to be the ending of the parade work, but also a beginning. The Corps Bandmaster had discussed his proposal that the 1st of June ceremony should, once again, become an annual event and the suggestion had been endorsed by the Principal Director of Music. The students stood with their backs to the Concert Hall as the Staff marched on to form on their left. To their right fourteen Musicians carrying fanfare trumpets marched on to the Parade, the Corps Bandmaster taking position in front of them. The Director of Music (Training), Major Thornhill, accompanied by the School Bandmaster WO1 Waller, marched on and addressed the parade. The explanation of why they were gathered on that particular day was followed by the words 'Corps Bandmaster, Sound the *Dedication Fanfare*' and, probably for the first time ever, a Fanfare Team of the Royal Marines School of Music, comprised entirely of Musicians under training, sounded *To Comrades Sleeping*. It is the intention that this simple ceremony will now take place on, or close to, the 1st June every year.

The traditional ceremony of playing the Royal Marines Band Service Dedication Fanfare 'To Comrades Sleeping' annually on the 1st June was re-instituted by the Corps Bandmaster, WO1 T Hodge, in 2010. The awareness of the traditions, history and the losses that the RMBS has suffered is an important part of the Students education at the School of Music. For this ceremony the full complement of Staff and Students are on Parade as the School's own Fanfare Team, conducted by the Corps Bandmaster, play the emotive fanfare

The Royal Marines Band Service Prayer

The original words, as written by the Reverend F Lovell Pocock, were:

'Almighty and Everlasting Lord, in Whose sight are treasured up the memories of many generations of men who have served Thee in the Band service of the Royal Marines; we thank Thee for the rich heritage of music placed in our hands, and for the joy and inspiration which it brings to men.

Enable us, thy sons, truly and godly to serve Thee, and that by Thy help and through our music, we may continue to inspire, help and lead men. We ask these things in the Name of Him Who is our Saviour and our Leader, Jesus Christ Our Lord. Amen'.

The Reverend Pocock[1] was drafted to Deal before the Second World War when the Royal Marines Band Service was one of its occupants; he returned there in 1944 and again during the 1950s. When he wrote the words to this Prayer is not known. He also wrote the Royal Marines Prayer and the Naval Collect amongst others. At some time in the intervening period the words of the Royal Marines Band Service Prayer, but not the Royal Marines Prayer, have been altered. The wording of the current version is as follows:

Almighty and Eternal Lord God, in whose sight and love live our memories of many generations of those who have served You in the Band Service of the Royal Marines; we thank You for the rich heritage of music placed in our hands, and for the joy and inspiration which it brings to men; enable us with our whole hearts to serve You, that by Your grace and through our gift of music, we may continue to inspire, help and lead men; we ask these things in the name of Jesus Christ our Lord. Amen.

1 *'With Those In Peril – A Chaplain's Life in the Royal Navy' by Rev. Lovell Pocock, 1986.*

Appendix 5: Bandmasters' Course Silver Medal Winners

Each year the Worshipful Company of Musicians present a silver Cassel medal to the student who comes top in the year-long Bandmasters' Course at the Royal Marines School of Music's Higher Training Department.

Year	Recipient
1910	BM 1 H G Cornfoot
1911	BM 2 J T Vitou
1912	BM 2 A E Morgan
1913	BM 2 A C Green
1914	BM 2 J Watson
1915	BM 1 S Fairfield
1916	BM 2 R T Jackson
1917	BM 1 W D Walker
1918	BM 2 W J Papworth
1919	BM 1 H Lodge
1920	BM 2 A Fielder
1921	BM 2 C Mansfield
1922	BdCpl S Dennis
1923	BM 2 P Barnacle
1924	BM 2 G Holloway
1925	BM 2 E Aldridge
1926	BM 2 P F Grace
1927	BM 2 W N Davis
1928	BM2 R Mullis
1929	BdCpl G J Steel
1930	BM 2 A Collier
1931	BM 2 A Howard
1932	BM 2 K McLean
1933	BM 2 F G Harding
1934	BM 2 L R Brown
1935	BM 2 J Patterson
1936	BM 2 F Woodcock
1937	BM 2 C Hotham
1938	BM 2 G C McLean
1939	BM A G Ashton
1940	BM 2 G Fitzgerald
1941	BM 2 D Whitney
1942	BM 1 J E Talling
1943	BM 2 P Cooper
1944	BM 2 W H Cotton
1945	BM 2 N L Cox
1946	BM 2 J Jemmett
1947	BM 2 B Medcall
1948	BdSgt A K Butler
1949	BdSgt R E Davies
1950	BdSgtW Newcombe
1951	BM D R Woods
1952	BdSgt P Neville
1953	BM J J Martin
1954	BM K Macdonald
1955	BM O Williams
1956	BM O Pollard
1957	BM D G Johnson
1958	BM W Shillitto LRAM
1959	BM H C Farlow
1960	BM R Woodfield
1961	BM C J Taylor LRAM ARCM LGSM
1962	BM B Plock LRAM
1963	BM D A Drake LRAM
1964	BM K N Sharpe LRAM
1965	Staff BM J D Place LRAM
1966	BM M Hutton ARCM
1967	Bandmaster V J Harris
1968	BdSgt R O Farrell
1969	BdSgt A I Kendrick
1970	BdSgt G E Simpson
1971	BdSgt A E Baker
1972	BdSgt E P Whealing
1973	BdSgt D E Clegg
1974	BdSgt K Vickers
1975	L/BdSgt D C Cole
1976	L/BdSgt T J Attwood
1977	L/BdSgt J R Perkins
1978	BdSgt P Rutterford
1979	BdSgt R A Waterer
1980	BdSgt P W Fryer
1981	BdSgt G F Harvey
1982	BdSgt J Hillier
1983	BdSgt M McDermott
1984	BdSgt R Kaighin
1985	BdSgt G Pumford
1986	BdCpl C J Close
1987	BdCpl P F Watson
1988	BdCpl C J Davis
1989	BdSgt J M Payne
1990	BdSgt A S Wall
1991	BdSgt D J Thornber
1992	BdSgt K Price
1993	BdSgt J M Camps
1994	BdSgt G R Martin
1995	BdSgt M Dowrick
1996	BdSgt G R Holman
1997	BdSgt T P Hodge
1998	BdSgt J R Burcham
1999	BdSgt R P Long
2000	BdSgt P J Curtis
2001	BdCpl J Ridley[1]
2002	BdSgt J Ridley
2003	BdSgt A C Cox
2004	BdSgt M J Hancock
2005	BdSgt D J Powell
2006	BdSgt I P Davis
2007	BdSgt H R Williams
2008	BdSgt R A Hunt
2009	BdSgt S Green
2010	BdSgt M Weites

1 There was no Bandmasters' Course in 2001so the award was made to the best student on the M1s' Course.

Appendix 6: The Prince's Badge

On 9th March 1978, His Royal Highness The Duke of Edinburgh, to mark the occasion of the 25th anniversary of his appointment as the Captain General Royal Marines and in recognition of the service provided for him by the Royal Marines Band Service, directed that the best all-round Musician or Bugler from each annual intake should be awarded a badge consisting of his Royal Cypher surrounded by a lyre and referred to as 'The Prince's Badge', the recipient to wear the Prince's Badge throughout his service in the Royal Marines in every rank. The Captain General Royal Marines further directed that the recipient should be referred to as 'The Prince's Badgeman'.

The Commandant of the Royal Marines School of Music annually convenes and presides over a Prince's Badge Selection Board to make recommendations for the award. Members are the Director of Music of the Royal Marines School of Music and the Officer Commanding Training Company. The criteria for selection are:

a. Candidates must have achieved either the Musician M3 or Bugler B3 training objectives to a high professional standard.
b. To have above average integrity, reliability, self-discipline, determination and initiative.
c. His or her ability to work as a member of a team must be above average.
d. Smartness in turnout on and off parade must be above average.
e. His or her Esprit de Corps, including the interest taken in Corps activities and sport, must be above average.
f. No candidate must have more than one offence on his/her conduct during final year of training and then only if the offence is trivial or of a technical nature where there is no evidence of deliberate misconduct and his/her performance during training has in all respects been outstanding.

If, in the opinion of the Presiding Officer, no Musician or Bugler is worthy of the award through failure to meet the qualifications laid down, then no award will be made. No Musician or Bugler may be considered for the award more than once. The Prince's Badge will be forfeited under certain conditions of misconduct.

YEAR	AWARDED TO
1978	Musician P A Evans
1979	Musician P J Ryan
1980	Musician G H Smith
1981	Musician J MacGregor
1982	Musician P A Weston
1983	Bugler M E Stephenson
1984	Musician N J Grace
1985	No award made
1986	No award made
1987	Musician W Riley
1988	No award made
1989	No award made
1990	Musician T Holland
1991	Musician P O Thomas
1992	Musician M King
1993	Musician G A Wright
1994	No award made made
1995	Musician P F Trickett
1996	Musician H Williams
1997	Musician H A Munsey
1998	No award made
1999	Musician R A Hunt
2000	Musician A Jonassen
2001	Musician A Harvey
2002	No award made
2003	Musician M J Walker
2004	No award made
2005	Musician C Down
2006	Musician W D Lindsey
2007	Musician M J Smith
2008	Bugler J W Ritchie
2009	Bugler T A Cartwright
2010	No award made

The Prince's Badge

Appendix 7: Royal Navy Volunteer Bands and Royal Marine Instructors

In a 1980 issue of Blue Band the late John Trendell wrote an excellent summary of the early growth and development of the Volunteer Band movement. Excerpts from his summary are reproduced here.

"In 1856 the Admiralty gave approval [for the unofficial ships' bands then in existence] by laying down complements for the various classes of ship and seven years later established the senior ratings of Chief Bandmaster (CPO) and Bandmaster (1st Class PO).

The fragmented organisation of Musicians in the Navy came to an end in July 1903 when the Royal Marines Band Service was established to provide ships with bands composed of disciplined and trained Musicians. The creation of this new service coincided with the construction of the great naval barracks at Portsmouth, Chatham and Devonport so that sailors could be properly housed whilst ashore.

These two reforms initiated by Admiral 'Jackie' Fisher appear to have signalled the birth of the Volunteer Band movement. In each of the new barracks at the Home Ports, brass bands were formed in the early years of the present century. Instruments were provided by the Welfare Fund and the volunteer bandsmen were recruited from the hundreds of ratings under training or awaiting draft at the depot. The majority of these bandsmen had previous brass band experience.

With an interest in naval banding aroused whilst serving in the Blue Jackets Band at the depot, many of these ratings when sent to sea were keen to continue their hobby. Soon volunteer bands were formed in numerous ships of the Fleet, even though many already possessed a professional Royal Marines Band. In many cases the Royal Marines Bandmaster acted as the instructor of the ship's volunteer band. During the 1930s the standard of performance and drill achieved by the Blue Jackets Bands at the Home Ports was such that, either singly or collectively they were invited to perform at such events as the FA Cup Final at Wembley and Rugby Internationals staged at Twickenham".

Blue Jacket Band of Royal Naval Barracks, Portsmouth, marching through Unicorn Gate. Feb 1929

In August 1942 Maj-Gen T L Hunton submitted the report on the Royal Marine Band Service.[1] On the questions of the developing RN Volunteer Bands at the Home Ports Hunton recommended that the Royal Marine Bands at the Home Port should be increased in size so that there would be no requirement for the large RN Volunteer Bands. Whether due to war-time conditions or simply a desire to maintain the status quo it was the case that, until the late 1950s, Volunteer Bands up to fifty strong were maintained in the Naval Barracks at Portsmouth, Plymouth and, until 1950, Chatham. It was virtually an acceptable practice for individual drafts to be deferred in the interests of maintaining high standards in the Royal Navy Depot Bands.

Blue Jacket Band that performed at the 1946 FA Cup Final, Wembley (probably photographed at Chatham Barracks)

To continue with John Trendell's account:

"At the end of the Second World War practically every capital ship, cruiser and

1 *Described in full in Chapter 9.*

major shore establishment had a Royal Marines Band but this state of affairs was not to continue in the post-war Navy"

"This change of emphasis has over the past twenty years [referring to the amalgamation of the Royal Naval School of Music and the Divisional Bands] given a fresh impetus to the Volunteer Band movement thus filling a great need for musical support both at sea and in shore establishments".

"The fifteen or so Volunteer Bands operating in 1980 are better equipped than ever before with first class instruments supplied out of public funds and having highly professional tuition provided by eleven Volunteer Band Instructors from the Royal Marines School of Music."

Amongst the reports issued in the post-war years was one called the "Report of the RN School of Music Conference" chaired by the CGRM and having members from various Royal Navy and Royal Marines branches as well as the Superintendent of the RNSM. The main thrust of this Report was directed towards the rapid expansion of the RNSM and the RM Bands. One of the reasons for this was to create a Band Service that was capable of supplying the needs of the Royal Navy and the Royal Marines without the need for Volunteer Bands made up of part-time Royal Navy officers and ratings. However, the Members were aware that if such expansion was approved the need for the Volunteer Bands would remain for a while and so they offered to train them to a required standard.

Divisions in Portsmouth Royal Naval Barracks circa 1946. Combined Royal Marines and Royal Navy Blue Jacket Band

In 1967 RN planning required that the strength of the RMBS be cut to three hundred and fifty by 1975/6. However, the Admiralty approved CGRM's recommendation that the RMBS be cut to five hundred, but the cuts had to be made by 1973. CGRM was able to show that the reductions would come by removing or reducing the size of various bands; also, Volunteer Band Instructors would be removed. In July 1968 the Naval Personnel Division (NPD) informed the Royal Navy of the provisional plan for the reduction of the RMBS. The decision not to provide Volunteer Band Instructors was reversed and requests for VBIs were made.

During 1973 the 'Blue Band' launched a 'Volunteer Band News Page' on the basis that it would allow Band NCOs serving as VB Instructors to keep the Band Service informed of their activities and progress. In the first issue it was announced that confirmation of a new annual Volunteer Band competition for all Royal Navy bands was imminent. This would be run on similar lines to the Fleet Air Arm's competitionfor the 'Bambara' Trophy.

It was also at this time that the responsibility for authorising instruments and Instructors passed from the RN Personnel Division to CGRM's Department, allowing better control and assistance from Deal. Three additional bands were expected to be raised during the next financial year.

The first competition was held in HMS *Collingwood* later in 1973. As well as the 'Bambara' Trophy for the Fleet Air Arm bands, the Commander-in-Chief's Trophy, a silver drum once belonging to an RN Barracks Blue Jacket Band, was available to open competition. HMS *Collingwood* (BdCSgt J Odey), the host band, won the major trophy with HMS *Daedalus* (BdSgt S Richardson) in second place collecting the Bambara Trophy as highest placed Air Command band. In third and fourth place were Yeovilton (BdCSgt J Whelton) and Culdrose (BdSgt K Whittall). The other competing bands were *Sultan* (BdCSgt V Judd) and *Dolphin* (Mr A Cooper). The competition rules for bands to compete with a free choice of parade display and concert pieces, the winners choosing the march *BB and CF* and the Sibelius tone poem *Finlandia*. The single Adjudicator was Lt Terry Freestone RM, the Editor of 'The Blue Band'.

CGRM's Department allocated Volunteer Band instructors from the Band Service to four ships for 1974/75: *Blake*, *Devonshire*, *Fife* and *Hermes*. In addition, three RM VBIs were allocated to shore establishments although two of them each had to look after two bands; *Sultan* was paired with *Excellent* (Whale Island), and *Daedalus* with Yeovilton. *Neptune* had its own VBI.

The 1975 competition was held at HMS *Daedalus* and included a Massed Band display conducted by Lt T Freestone RM who once again judged the marching and concert programmes. Commodore J S C Lea, CO of the RN Barrack Portsmouth, presented a new trophy, the Kenneth Alford Trophy, to be awarded to the best Drum Major. Results were; in first place HMS *Collingwood* (BdCSgt J Odey), followed by HMS *Heron* (BdCSgt S Richardson), also winning the Bambara Trophy, then HMS *Daedalus*, HMS *Caledonia*, HMS *Seahawk*, RNAS *Culdrose*. REA 3 M Smyth of HMS *Collingwood* was the first winner of the Kenneth Alford trophy. These were the only competitors although many other Volunteer Bands existed on ships and at other Shore establishments.

HMS Bulwark Volunteer Band, Hong Kong 1961

In 1983 RM Band FONAC closed making the FAA totally reliant upon its own Volunteer Bands.

The Volunteer Band movement continued to develop and either expand or contract according to the expansion and contraction of the Royal Navy. The Festival and the competition has grown to the extent that each band gives a programme of music for both the Parade and Concert parts of the competition and the list of trophies numbers ten. Adjudication is now carried out by a team of judges that include senior representatives from RMSM (Higher Training), the RMBS and the Buglers' Branch. The Principal Director of Music, Royal Marines, attends the event which also forms part of the required annual inspection of the Volunteer Bands. Supply Officer Music, Captain C Burns, is the Secretary of the Royal Naval Volunteer Band Association, the President being the Second Sea Lord. One trophy, the Daedalus Trophy 'Spirit of the Festival', is not part of the judging process but is in the gift of the President who, during the course of the day, decides upon a suitable recipient who embodies the spirit of the Volunteer Band movement.

The competition and Festival is now held at the Portsmouth Guildhall with, weather permitting, the Parade competition in the Guildhall Square in the morning and the Concert competition inside the Guildhall during the afternoon. In 2010 nine bands, including the newly formed Volunteer Band of Britannia Royal Naval College, took part in the competition.

The Royal Navy Pipers Society

Often taking part in the Volunteer Band Festival, although not competing, the Royal Navy Pipers Society brings another dimension to the annual event. The Society was formed in 1951, although some of the founders, three RN officers, all pipers and serving in the East Indies Fleet, had been discussing the possibility since the late 1940s. Upon return to the UK one of the officers, along with others of a like mind, decided to form such an organisation and contacted others who they knew to be pipers.

Admiral of the Fleet, Lord Cunningham of Hyndhope KT GCB OM DSO LL.D accepted the invitation to become the Founder President and was succeeded by Commodore The Duke of Montrose RNVR and then Vice Admiral the MacKintosh of MacKintosh.

Although the Society flourished during the 1960s and the 1970s the closure of many ships and shore establishments caused many of the pipe bands to be dispersed and the Society went into decline. The closure of HMS *Caledonia* in 1980 was the final straw and the Society found that it could no longer continue.

In 1993 Cdr Campbell de Burgh revived the Society by finding new members and then asking the then First Sea Lord, Admiral Sir Jock Slater GCB LVO DL, to become the President of the Society, a role that he accepted, with Commodore Sir John Clerk of Penicuik as the Honorary Vice President.

The size of modern ships, even the size of the Royal Navy itself, now makes the forming of RN Pipe Bands an impractical proposition. However, the Society functions as a forum for the interchange of information between players, keeps all RN pipers and Drummers in touch with each other and arranges several events each year at which the Society will play. Recently the Society integrated with the Royal Navy Volunteer Band Association.

Appendix 8: Royal Marines Association Concert Band

The idea for the formation of this band was born out of a visit made by Major P M H Dunn, Chairman of the Royal Marines Association, to the Chelsea Flower Show where he watched the Guards Association Band entertaining the crowds from the bandstand. Following discussions with the RMA President and Captain E P Whealing, who was on the verge of completing fifteen years as Director of Music of the Central Band of the Royal British Legion, the concept of forming a similar Royal Marines veterans band appeared to be a possibility. The idea was put to the Commandant General Royal Marines, and to the Principal Director of Music, Royal Marines, who gave the project their approval.

In May 2006 an initial meeting was held at Whale Island and thirty former Royal Marine Musicians attended. By the end of the next month the first rehearsal, with a band of thirty-five, had been held. Uniforms were a priority and, whilst it would have been inappropriate to wear Royal Marines Band Service uniform, there was an understandable desire to wear something which reflected the Corps. Following careful consideration the retired Corps Historian Major Alastair Donald suggested aspects of the Corps and RMBS uniform that could be integrated into the design, a task made easier by the fact that this was intended to be a concert, but not a parade, band.

Initially, band practice was carried out at Whale Island but it was clear that space was inadequate and larger facilities for the storage of instruments, equipment, uniforms, music library, and of course a rehearsal room, needed to be quickly located. The problem was solved when the Trustees of the Royal Marines Museum gave permission for the RMA Concert Band to use space within the Museum itself. This included the use of the Officers Dining Room as a rehearsal room. Not only would this have brought back many memories of playing for Officer's Dinners but it also meant that the Musicians were probably using the finest rehearsal room in the land!

The first concert, at Hayling Island, took place in February 2007 and the first cd recording 'Once a Marine...' was made at the end of the same year. In May of 2007 Admiral Sir Jock Slater GCB LVO DL visited the band at rehearsal and agreed to become its President. Since it began in 2007 the band has made five recordings and given numerous concerts ranging from the Museum itself to as far away as Alicante, Spain.

During 2010 a Brass Quintet, led by Jon Yates, was formed and during its inaugural year played at several London Livery Company dinners.

Recordings made by the Royal Marines Association Concert Band are:

2007	Once a Marine...
2007	...Always a Marine
2009	Haslar Farewell
2009	That's Entertainment
2009	The Pompey Chimes (single track CD)
2010	Esprit de Corps

Admiral Sir Jock Slater became the Band President in 2007 giving him a direct link to the veteran's band, the Piping Society and the Volunteer Band Association. Interestingly, when Sir Jock was about to take command of HMS *Illustrious* for her first commission he asked the RMBS Drafting Officer if he could have a Volunteer Band Instructor who could play the pipes. At the time there was only one piper in the RMBS and he, according to the Drafting Officer, was reluctant to go to sea. He, BdCSgt Ian Gordon, was duly despatched to the *Illustrious* where Captain Slater gave him the additional task of standing at the top of the aircraft ramp playing his pipes as the ship entered and left harbour. On return he admitted that it was a fabulous draft!

Appendix 9: 42 Commando Royal Marines Pipe Band

Although never part of the Royal Marines Band Service the pipes of 42 Cdo, RM certainly feature in Corps history, and Buglers from the RMBS were very much the driving force throughout its life. These were not the first, nor the last, pipes that appear in the musical history of the Band Service, the Corps or the Royal Navy.[1] The first few pages of this book include a description of how Captain Cook resisted the Admiralty's wish that two bagpipers accompanied him on his second voyage to the Antipodes. Cook had to compromise by taking one of them, Archibald McVicar, but the Maori did not appreciate the gesture. In 1899 HMS *Caledonia*, the Boy's Training Ship at Queensferry in the Firth of Forth had its own pipe band of five pipers, a bass Drummer and a side Drummer.

The Royal Navy Pipers of HMS Caledonia, 1899

42 Royal Marine Commando, later 42 Commando, Royal Marines, was first formed in August 1943 as 1st RM Battalion. For a considerable period of time it maintained a pipe band that featured heavily in unit life. It appears to have begun life when the Commando was on board HM Troopship *Ranchi* in 1943 en route from England to India. Mr Len Headley, a Corporal with the Pipe Band, recalls, "When originally formed it was a Drum and Fife Band and continued so until our arrival in India, late 1943. I think it was a shortage of fife players that prompted the change to pipes. Our Scots MO [Medical Officer], himself a piper, had suggested the change and promised to obtain the pipes".

The Medical Officer, Captain 'Doc' Rodgers RAMC felt capable of teaching the instrument and proceeded to locate chanters and, after finding volunteers, instruction began. Six sets of pipes were ordered from the Glasgow Highland Society and were forwarded to Poona for seasoning. The Unit carried out jungle training at Castle Rock, Belgaum, with 1 (Army) Commando. By the time they acquired their pipes the volunteer band was about fifteen strong and were soon capable of marching the men to the station to travel to Cocanada Combined Training Centre where the temperatures reached as high as 45°C. Mr Headley wrote again, "On Christmas Day 1944 the officers served the meals in the open air dining area whilst the Pipe Band played a selection of marches and reels ending with the march of the US Marine Corps. My association with the band came to an abrupt end at the Battle of Kangaw". Mr Headley was wounded at Kangaw, Burma. Hill 70 was taken by 42 Cdo after two days of hand-to-hand fighting. They were subjected to heavy artillery fire and had to beat off repeated Japanese counter-attacks to hold the position. This date, January 31st, is now an official Unit Memorable Date for 42 Commando.

The keenest members of the band brought a further six sets of pipes from the Highland Bagpipe Company in Sialkot City. By now the band was allowed two afternoons a week in which to practise. The unit moved to Teknaf via Trincomalee, Calcutta and Chittagong. Whilst in Calcutta the pipe band led the Unit to the station and, at Teknaf, they played on three separate occasions whilst the band was inspected and addressed by Admiral Lord Louis Mountbatten amongst others.

Three pipers played in the stern of a landing craft as the unit sailed towards the enemy held island of Akyab. This turned out to be an unopposed landing, the Japanese having already left. For the next operation the pipes were left at Akyab, the pipers going ashore in their more usual manner. When the Unit returned to Myebon two Memorial Services, requiring the pipe band to be split into two parts, took place. Captain Rodgers, the pipe band's founder and mainstay, was drafted at this time.

When the Brigade got to Madras the band was provided with its first full dress uniform complete with leopard skins, dress cords and badges for pipers and Drummers. The Seaforth Highlanders invited them for a two week period of training and this resulted in great improvements to performance and playing.

Eventually the unit embarked for Malaya but the planned landing was cancelled and the pipe band played the ship into Trincomalee Harbour instead. Following this the band went on board the various ships in the harbour, including HMS *Phoebe*, HMS *Cumberland* and the hospital ship *Vita*, to entertain their crews. This was also the first opportunity they had to play on a ship's quarterdeck. The Brigade sailed for Hong Kong with 42 Cdo Pipe Band playing the ship past the minesweepers that had swept the channel for her, and then into

1 *Most of the information in this appendix is taken from private correspondence.*

Hong Kong Harbour. They then played the Brigade through the streets, the first time this had happened since the fall of Hong Kong, and were present at the official Surrender Ceremony. In Kowloon they supported many Guard of Honour ceremonies and also played on the quarterdecks of both HMS *Duke of York* and *Anson*. After four weeks the band instituted the practice of Beating Retreat twice a week, every week. One took place at the Cenotaph, Hong Kong, and the other outside the Peninsular Hotel, Kowloon. The first loss, through draft, to the band was their Pipe Major, Sgt Stevenson. The band went to the docks to play his ship away and, just before she sailed, Sgt Stevenson presented the band with his own set of pipes.

Cpl Wright and Cpl Dalley continued to lead the pipes and drums respectively. Beat Retreats were continued as were many other engagements, including one on board the aircraft carrier HMS *Vengeance* which began with them being raised to deck level on the aircraft lift. Further drafts and demobilisations resulted in 42 Cdo RM Pipe Band being disbanded after playing on St Patrick's Night in the Officer's Club at the Peninsular Hotel. However, two pipers and a side Drummer were still practising in the New Territories in January 1947. On leaving Hong Kong a lone piper played the unit onto the train at Fanling Station and then from Kowloon Station to the docks where they boarded *Strathnaver* for Malta. During 1949 it would appear that only solo pipers played in the unit.

In 1951, 42 Cdo was in Malaya, and an attempt was made to revive the Pipe Band. An appeal was made for equipment and volunteers and the local Planters Association responded by donating the pipes and the drums. The 'Globe & Laurel' reported, "The recruits for our band have been kept playing scales on the chanter so far, but soon they will be able to blossom forth on a proper bag. This venture to revive what was a flourishing pipe band in the Commando deserves every help from within and without the unit. If anyone can donate or lend equipment we will be most grateful, but our main problem will always be pipers. So anyone with experience, please say so and join 42 Commando, which has always had the tradition of the pipe band". Two National Service Pipers were drafted to the band in 1952.

When the Commando left Kajang for Singapore on route for Malta the pipers played at Kuala Lumpar. Later that year, the Times of Malta reported that the newly formed pipe band of 42 Cdo were on parade for the first time when it participated in the Changing of the Main Guard at the Palace Square, Valetta. The Pipe Band, under Sgt Jones who had been trained by the pipers of the 1st Bn The Gordon Highlanders in Malaya, comprised six pipers, a bass Drummer and five side Drummers.

The Pipe Band on the parade at St Andrew's Barracks, Malta, prior to Changing the Guard at Palace Square, Valetta, in 1952

At the Presentation of Colours to the three Commandos of 3rd Commando Brigade, Malta 1952, 42 Commando, led by their own pipe band wearing green berets with their blue uniform, marched on to the pipe tune *Dovecote Park*, as described in 'The Story of Colours in the Royal Marines' by Major A J Donald, RM.

In November 1955 the Major General Royal Marines Plymouth, recommended to the Commandant General that the Pipe Band of 42 Commando should be reconstituted and recognised officially. His grounds were that it had become a tradition that the Unit should have a Pipe Band and that the Group Band's workload did not allow it to visit 42 Cdo often enough to provide the required martial music. If this recognition was granted it would be necessary to draft five men over complement (four pipers and a bass Drummer) to the unit as well as arranging for any National Servicemen who were pipers to join 42 Cdo RM. The CGRM was unable to support this recommendation since official recognition required the Pipe Band to be part of the Royal Marines Band Service – very unlikely in a climate of cuts and reductions, and when priorities for Bands at RN and RM establishments had already been identified. A second option would be to make the band a Volunteer Band but this would only allow the supply of a standard set of military band instruments, not pipes. It was therefore suggested that the band would be better advised to restart as an unofficial, volunteer, pipe band.

Operational requirements prevented any further action until 1959 when, in June, the Pipe Band was formed and Sgt Bugler Reginald Flook became its instructor. Flook asked to be permitted to accompany 42 Cdo when they joined HMS *Bulwark* for an overseas posting in 1960. The Adjutant of Royal Marines Plymouth, recommended this on the basis that the shortage of one Sergeant Bugler could be borne by Plymouth for eighteen months whilst Flook carried out the duties of a 42 Cdo Bugler and Pipe Band Instructor. This arrangement was allowed on the understanding that RMB Plymouth did not request a relief or an 'acting' promotion because of his absence. The side drummers were Regimental whilst the remainder were from Rifle, Heavy Weapons, Assault Engineers and Headquarter Companies. SgtBug Flook was the Pipe Major and the Drum Major was an ex-Bugler called 'Sticks' Priddy. Two years after his appointment, Flook, by now promoted to CSgtBug, was due for repatriation but volunteered to stay with 42 Cdo for a further three months so that a replacement instructor could be found. The alternatives were for a number of NCO Buglers to be trained as pipe instructors, to arrange for an Army NCO Instructor to be attached - or to disband. It was decided to retain Flook for as long as possible whilst CGRM tried to arrange for an Army Instructor to be attached. CGRM wrote to the Argyll & Sutherland Highlanders explaining the situation and the importance of the pipe band to the unit. He asked if it would be possible to send a volunteer NCO Bugler for training by the Pipe Major or an instructor. This did not bear fruit and the CGRM had to concede that, whilst he wanted the pipe band to be retained, it was completely unofficial and that the only option was for Flook to train someone from within the band complement. Negotiations continued and Captain J J Moore of 42 Cdo interviewed Flook and reported that, provided that it did not affect any possible promotion to Bugle Major, Flook was ready to remain with the unit until December 1962. A month later the Drafting Office confirmed that CSgtBug Flook would be appointed Bugle Major at the Royal Marines School of Music from December 1962 and he would have a relief, CplBug Ormonde Dobbin who would take passage for Singapore and 42 Cdo on the 1st October.

In the centre of the picture are Piper Clay (left) and CplBugler Snook. The Piper on the right wearing a beret is believed to be Vickers (or McVicar). Photograph taken in Mombasa

During 1964 and 1965 42 Cdo again cast a wide net in an effort to secure funding for the upkeep of the pipe band and its equipment. A letter to CGRM made the point that the band was currently flourishing with 42 Cdo and HQ 3 Cdo Bde in Singapore and was proving a valuable asset in the Borneo Territories. He made the point that the band was now recognised by the RMSM and the Drafting Office was sending known pipers to 42 Cdo, RM. The unit was able to provide most of the necessary and immediate resources; however, the problems of rapid deterioration of bags, and reeds, in the humid environment was one that required additional financial assistance. As a result CGRM again supported the case for the pipe band being recognised as a Volunteer Band so that it would qualify for financial assistance. On the 6th December 1965, the Brigade received the news that the 42 Cdo Pipe Band was to be recognised as an official Volunteer Band.

After a spell of duty in Malaya the Cdo returned to Singapore where there was greater opportunity for practice and expansion. Whilst en route to Australia in 1966, HMS *Bulwark* called at Labuan and a detachment from the Commando, accompanied by the Padre and a Piper, visited the Limbang Memorial. Five men of L Company, 42 Cdo had been killed in December 1962 during the successful hostage rescue operation. The Piper played a lament at the Memorial.

Since early 1966 CSgt Bugler Aubrey Bassett, who became the Pipe Major after training in the United Kingdom, had been responsible for training the band. By this time the volunteers appear to have assembled uniforms from many sources. The spats had been donated by the Argyll & Sutherland Highlanders whilst socks and belts came from the Gurkhas. The Pipe Band at RAF Seletar also contributed. The band wore their own berets and white shirts with kilts reputedly converted from blankets.[2]

The mid and latter years of the 1960s were difficult years not only for the Royal Marines Band Service but for all military bands. Government demands for cuts and reductions plus reports, and conclusions, from a series of Committees examining everything from joint Service training to costs, size and engagements carried out by military bands, probably resulted in attention on the continuation of 42 Cdo Pipe Band being deflected into the background. In November 1966 the Drafting Officer sent a letter to CGRM informing him that CplBug Cooper would be available for draft to continue the training of 42 Cdo Pipe Band. Unfortunately the Corporal could not play the pipes so could CGRM arrange suitable training? An arrangement was made with the Argyll & Sutherland Highlanders but then Cooper's draft was cancelled.

Bugler Alan Piner was drafted to the Pipe Band as the lead Drummer in 1967. Having passed his Intermediate and Advanced Drum Technique examinations he, with other 42 Pipe Band Drummers, spent some of his time playing in the RAF Seletar Pipe Band. On his return to the United Kingdom he joined the Royal Navy Piping

2 *Careful inspection of photographs does not indicate that the kilts were made from blanlet material.*

Society and won the competition for best solo Drummer in the Royal Navy's pipe bands. In winning the competition he became not only the first Royal Marine but also the first Englishman to do so.

In 1968 RMRO 234/68 The Commandant General's Piper was issued. During his visit to 42 Commando RM, the Commandant General approved the title of the 'Commandant General's Piper' for the leading piper in 42 Commando's Pipe Band. This appointment conferred the entitlement, when in pipe band uniform, to wear a Skian Dhu presented by General Sir Norman Tailyour KCB DSO. The first person to hold this appointment was LCpl I Anderson.

General Sir Norman Tailyour presents a Ceremonial Skian Dhu to L/Cpl Iain Anderson, the first Commandant General's Piper. November 1968

Also in 1968, 42 Cdo, RM, was presented with new Colours at Dieppe Barracks, Singapore, by the Captain General. The Commando was led onto the Parade by the Massed Bands of the 3rd Cdo Bde and the Commander Far East Fleet and the 42 Cdo Pipe Band. The pipe band played part of the Inspection Music and also played the Old Colours off the Parade. At that time the pipe band complement was five side drums, one bass drum and six pipers plus the Pipe Major.

In 1969 the cuts that were affecting the Band Service began to impact upon the Pipe Band. The unit was warned that the RMBS could only appoint Buglers until 1972 but after that date reductions to the Buglers' Branch would probably prevent any further support. Efforts were made to prepare the way to bid for a Volunteer Band Instructor who, it was considered, would need to be a Bugler SNCO and have attended the Army School of Piping prior to joining 42 Cdo. No evidence has been found to show that the Royal Marines Band Service was able to provide any form of support beyond the anticipated date.

On the 16th September 1971 the new Bickleigh Barracks, the home of 42 Cdo RM, was officially opened and the Pipe Band paraded.

The last references to 42 Cdo Pipe Band, or a Piper, appear in the Globe & Laurel. In a small photograph illustrating the unit leaving for Ulster in late 1971, two pipers and a Drummer can be seen on a station platform; and a photograph of the 1977 Kangaw Parade clearly shows a Piper, wearing Lovat uniform and green beret, standing alongside four Buglers carrying Herald Trumpets.

Appendix 10: RMBS Recordings since 1990

The first commercial recordings appear to have been made by the Massed Bands of the Portsmouth Command, directed by Bandmaster G C Keen, for Columbia in 1936. It was three years later that the Divisional Bands went into the recording studio when Major Ricketts and the Plymouth Band recorded a series of Alford marches for HMV. When Major Dunn became Principal Director of Music he took control of the recording policy and, with the exception of military tattoos, allowed no band except the RMSM to make recordings. This policy remained in place until Lt Col Dunn's retirement in 1968, apart from one made by Captain McLean and the Portsmouth Band in 1961. Recording companies were beginning to understand the potential in terms of re-issues and re-releases. They held the copyrights for the recordings and were able to produce re-issues which then competed with and reduced sales of new recordings. With an increase in the number of bands recording came a broadening of the type of music being played. Lt Col Neville introduced collaboration with choirs when he combined with the Morriston Orpheus Choir.

With the introduction of the compact disc came the opportunity for the record companies to dip into their archives and release compilation after compilation of recordings that were cheap to produce and buy and gave no benefit to the RMBS except Royalties. The re-issues and compilations became prolific and each World War II anniversary produced a fresh crop. Lt Col Waterer had the foresight and imagination to support the formation of an RMBS recording capability complete with its own recording engineer. This had the effect of 'locking-up' the copyright of all new recordings thereby gradually draining the recording companies of the ability to issue compilations of more recent material. Linked to the ability of The Blue Band staff to produce the artwork for the compact disc inlays, the RMBS have a powerful in-house tool that is the envy of other Services.

On a number of occasions, bands and orchestras of the Royal Marines have been involved in making recordings that were not for commercial gain. The most obvious are the recordings made during World War II for the entertainment of Allied troops. These are far too numerous to list here. There are also reports of recordings being made in the very early days of recording technology. Although no such recordings have been found the mere fact that data in the form of written reports exists is a fair indication that such recordings were made. We are, after all, dealing with not only a rare commodity, but also a very fragile one.

In an 1893 issue of 'Globe and Laurel' appears the following report:

About ten of the most accomplished performers of the Band of the Royal Marines Chatham Division are carrying out a novel engagement. They are attending the establishment of Mr Edison in London at stated times and give forth a number of martial airs, the tunes of which are received in phonographs. These instruments, thus charged, are sent to various parts of the world. The other day two of them were transmitted to the Pope whilst others have been transmitted to the reigning Princes of India, and to the different crowned heads of Europe, who thus have the opportunity of listening to lively marches, etc., originally played by instrumentalists hundreds of miles away

The following list shows some of the early technical 'landmark' recordings made by Royal Marine Bands, Divisional Bands and Orchestras and Bands of the Royal Marines Band Service until 1990. Following that, the list shows all recordings made between 1990 and 2010. Compilations and re-issues are not included and, whilst the list is as extensive as possible, it is not claimed to be absolutely complete.

THE COMMERCIAL RECORDINGS

Date	Title of Recording	Band/DoM or BM	Type	Recorded by
1936	Sea Songs Medley/Ship Ahoy	Portsmouth Cmd/Keen	78	Columbia
1939	Thin Red Line March/Colonel Bogey	Plymouth/Ricketts	78	HMV
1940	Amparita Roca/La Belle Pense	Portsmouth Orch/Dunn	78	Columbia
1953	Music by the Band of HM Royal Marines, Portsmouth	Portsmouth/Dunn	LP	HMV
1988	Mountbatten Festival of Music 1988	Massed/Hoskins	Video	TelevideoProd
1990	Music from the 100th Royal Tournament	Massed/Ware	LP	Bandleader
1990	Celebration	FOSNI/Rutterford	LP	MusicMasters
1990	A Concert Performance	CinCNavHome/Whealing	LP	MusicMasters
1990	Navy Blue	FOP/Rogerson	Cass	MusicMasters
1990	RAH/MFM 1990	Massed/Ware	LP	RMA

1990	Fleet Review	CinC Fleet/Goss	CD	MusicMasters
1990	Great Berlin Band Show	CinCNavHome/Whealing	CD	Bandleader
1991	Beating Retreat & Tattoo	RMSM/Ware	CD	Grasmere
1991	RAH/MFM 1991	Massed/Ware	LP	RMA
1992	Anything Goes	Britannia/Hillier	CD	MusicMasters
1992	Men of Music	FOSNI/Rutterford	CD	MusicMasters
1992	Kaleidoscope	Commandos/Cole	CD	Bandleader
1992	RAH/MFM 1992	Massed/Ware	CD	RMB
1992	Sound the Alert	RMSM/CinCNavHome	CD	RMB
1992	Edinburgh Military Tattoo 1992	Massed/Ware	CD	EMT
1993	Battle of the Atlantic Suite[1]	CinCFleet/McDermott	CD	Conifer
1993	Marches of the Sea	Cdo Forces/Perkins	CD	Clovelly
1993	Battle of the Atlantic	Massed/Ware	CD	Bandleader
1993	RAH/MFM 1993	Massed/Ware	CD	RMB
1993	Christmas with the Royal Marines	RMSM/Ware	CD	Bandleader
1993	Complete Marches of Kenneth Alford	Cdo Forces/Perkins	CD	Clovelly
1993	Royal Tournament 1993	Massed/Ware	CD	Bandleader
1993	Toronto International Tattoo	FOSNI/Mills	CD	Lismor
1994	Admiral's Regiment, The	CinC Fleet/Waterer	CD	MusicMasters
1994	That's Entertainment	Britannia/Hillier	CD	MusicMasters
1994	RAH/MFM 1994	Massed/Ware	CD	RMB
1994	D-Day: 50th Anniversary	CinC Fleet/Whealing	CD	Souvenir
1994	Highland Cathedral	Scotland/Mills	CD	MusicMasters
1994	Twenty-First Mountbatten Festival of Music	Massed/Ware	CD	Grasmere
1994	For Those in Peril on the Sea	Plymouth/Perkins	CD	Clovelly
1994	Martial Music of Sir Vivian Dunn	Plymouth/Perkins	CD	Clovelly
1994	Nova Scotia International Tattoo 1994	RMSM/Ware	CD	?
1995	Mountbatten Festival of Music1995	Massed/Waterer	CD	RMB
1995	Ashokan Farewell	Plymouth/Perkins	CD	Clovelly
1996	An Outdoor Overture	RMSM/Waterer	CD	RMB
1996	Mountbatten Festival of Music 1996	Massed/Waterer	CD	Blue Band
1996	The Big Band Sound	Plymouth/Perkins	CD	Clovelly
1996	Royal Tournament 1996	Massed/Waterer	CD	Bandleader
1997	Britannia Vol 1 - In Concert	Portsmouth/Cole	CD	Foldback
1997	Britannia Vol 2 - The Marches	Portsmouth/Cole	CD	Foldback
1997	Britannia Vol 3 - Royal Blue and Gold Leaf	Portsmouth/Cole	CD	Foldback
1997	The Chosin Few	Britannia/Watson	CD	Foldback
1997	Mountbatten Festival of Music 1997	Massed/Waterer	CD	Blue Band
1998	A Musical Journey - Trains, Planes, Autos	Scotland/Davis	CD	Chevron
1998	Mountbatten Festival of Music 1998	Massed/Waterer	CD	Blue Band
1998	International Festival of the Sea	Portsmouth/Plymouth	CD	Chevron
1998	The Music of Gilbert and Sullivan	Plymouth/Rutterford	CD	Chevron
1998	A Night in Concert	Britannia/Watson	CD	Chevron
1999	Beating Retreat	Massed/Waterer	CD	Chevron
1999	The Last Run - Royal Tournament 1999	Massed/Waterer	CD	Bandleader
1999	Mountbatten Festival of Music 1999	Massed/Waterer	CD	Blue Band
1999	Music for the Millennium	Plymouth/Rutterford	CD	Chevron
1999	Songs of the Sea	Portsmouth/Perkins	CD	Clovelly
1999	A Christmas Festival	Portsmouth/Perkins	CD	Clovelly
1999	Wind Machine	Portsmouth/Perkins	CD	Clovelly
1999	The Pride and Passion	Portsmouth/Perkins	CD	First Night
1999	1999 Open Day Concert	RMSM/Davis	CD	Chevron
2000	The Final Countdown	Various/Cole	CD	Chevron
2000	Mountbatten Festival of Music 2000	Massed/Waterer	CD	Chevron
2000	Royal Military Tattoo 2000	Massed/Waterer	CD	DD Video
2000	A Night at the Movies	CTC/Weston	CD	Chevron
2000	Just Marches	Plymouth/Mills	CD	Chevron
2001	International Festival of the Sea II	Plymouth/Waterer	CD	Chevron

1 *Fanfare Team only.*

2001	Mountbatten Festival of Music 2001	Massed/Waterer	CD	Chevron
2001	Trafalgar!	Britannia/Thornhill	CD	Plantagenet
2001	Celtic Salute	Scotland/Best	CD	Plantagenet
2002	The King's Squad	CTC/Grace	CD	Plantagenet
2002	Mountbatten Festival of Music 2002	Massed/Waterer	CD	Chevron
2002	Dancing Men	Britannia/Thornhill	CD	Plantagenet
2002	Adventures for Band	Plymouth/Mills	CD	Obrasso
2002	The Founders	Various	CD	IMMS/Chevron
2003	Mountbatten Festival of Music 2003	Massed/Davis	CD	Chevron
2003	Celestial Trumpet	Paul Hart/Liz Le Grove	CD	Clovelly
2003	Scottish Royals	Scotland/Kelly	CD	Chevron
2004	Marche Militaire	Portsmouth/Watson	CD	Chevron
2004	Hosts of Freedom	Britannia/Dowrick	CD	Doyen
2004	Unreleased	Massed/Various	CD	Chevron
2004	Mountbatten Festival of Music 2004	Massed/Davis	CD	Chevron
2004	Harrison's Dream	Royal Marines/Davis	CD	Chevron
2004	Fox's Marines (With Sound the Alert)	Plymouth/Various	CD	Chevron
2004	Passing In	Plymouth/Weston	CD	Chevron
2004	A Christmas Gift	Portsmouth/Watson	CD	Chevron
2005	Sound Off Divisions	Britannia/Long	CD	Chevron
2005	Mountbatten Festival of Music 2005	Massed/Davis	CD	Chevron
2005	Victory in Europe	Scotland/Smallwood	CD	Chevron
2005	Make More Sail	RMSM	CD	Clovelly
2005	Symphonic Gallery	Royal Marines/Davis	CD	Chevron
2006	Golden Trumpet	Paul Hart/Liz Le Grove	CD	Clovelly
2006	Mountbatten Festival of Music 2006	Massed/Davis	CD	Chevron
2006	Beating Retreat	Massed/Dowrick	CD	Chevron
2006	Diversions	Royal Marines/Davis	CD	Chevron
2007	Falklands Sound	Portsmouth/Grace	CD	Chevron
2007	Mountbatten Festival of Music 2007	Massed/Davis	CD	Chevron
2008	Mountbatten Festival of Music 2008	Massed/Davis	CD	Chevron
2008	Summon the Heroes	RMSM/Dowrick	CD	Chevron
2008	A Night at the West End	Scotland/Harvey	CD	Clovelly
2008	A Night at the Opera	Britannia/Ridley	CD	Chevron
2009	Mountbatten Festival of Music 2009	Massed/Davis	CD	Chevron
2009	Mountbatten Festival of Music 2009	Massed/Davis	DVD	Chevron
2009	Beating Retreat 2009	Massed/Grace	CD	Chevron
2009	Holst in Chichester	Portsmouth/Grace	CD	Chevron
2010	Mountbatten Festival of Music 2010	Massed/Grace	CD	Chevron
2010	Wooton Bassett	Portsmouth/Grace	CD (single)	Chevron
2011	Eternal Voices	CTC/Grace	CD	Chevron
2011	Mountbatten Festival of Music 2011	Massed/Grace	CD	Chevron

Chevron Recordings

Appendix 11: Music of the Royal Marines

The Quick March of the Royal Marines - *A Life on the Ocean Wave*

Originally written as a song with words by Henry Russell to a tune composed by American, Henry Epps Sargent. Bandmaster Kappey (Chatham Division) arranged the march with a part of the Naval song 'The Sea' as the trio and this was accepted as the march of the Royal Marines by the War Office in 1882.
Marches previously used include:
British Grenadiers until 1855. Chatham Division used *Hoch Hapsburg* by J N Kral and possibly *Dashing White Sergeant* as well.
Portsmouth Division used the *Coronation March* from *Le Prophete* by Meyerbeer. Royal Marine Artillery used Gounod's *Soldiers' Chorus* from Faust from 1862 until 1882.

The Slow March of the Royal Marines - *The Preobrajensky March*

Prior to 1935 the only semi-official Slow March was believed to be *Galatea* (George Miller) which was used by the Royal Marine Artillery. Submissions were required from the Directors of Music for a Slow March for the 1935 London Duties and Lt Dunn's submission *The Globe and Laurel*, was selected. No evidence of this being officially accepted has been found. In 1964 it was replaced by the *Preobrajensky March* which was presented by the Earl Mountbatten of Burma in 1964.

The Quick March of the Royal Marines Commandos - *Sarie Marais*

Written by Toonsetting and arranged by Dunn in 1937. Officially adopted in 1952.

The Quick March of the Commando Logistic Regiment - *Army and Marine*

Written by Zehle and arranged by Hewitt; this was first played as the adopted Regimental March of the Commando Logistic Regiment at the Regiment's inaugural parade on the 11th June 1972.

The Quick March of 29 Commando Regiment Royal Artillery - *Soldiers' Chorus* from 'Faust'

The Royal Marines presented the old march of the Royal Marine Artillery to the Royal Regiment of Artillery as an official quick march on 11 July 1994. The march was to be used by 29 Commando Regiment to celebrate the long-standing relationship with the Royal Marines.

The Royal Navy

Royal Navy March Past	*Heart of Oak*	Boyce
RN Advance in Review Order	*Nancy Lee*	
Naval Hymn	*Eternal Father*	

Musical Salutes

Prior to 1927 the 'Advance in Review Order' and the musical salutes were:

Advance in Review Order	*Boys of the Old Brigade* (At the double)	
Royal Salute	*National Anthem*	
General Salute	*Rule Britannia*	
Alternative Salute	*Garb of Auld Gaul*	
General Salute for 'Other Flag Officers, Governors, etc'	*Norma*	Bellini
For Inspection	12 bars Bugle	arr. Miller
	Rule Britannia	
	12 bars Bugle	
	Scipio	

The 1927 changes to salutes resulted in the following:

Royal Salute - the Sovereign	*National Anthem* (complete)	
Royal Salute - Royal Family	*National Anthem* (first six bars)	
General Salute, Admirals and C-in-Cs	*Rule Britannia*	Arne
General Salute, Other Flag Officers	*Iolanthe*	Sullivan
General Salute, Governors etc	*Garb of Old Gaul*	
Unit Commanding Officers and VIPs - not Flag Officers.	*Alert/Drum Ruffle/Carry On*	
Royal Marines Advance in Review Order	*British Grenadiers*	Trad arr. Kappey

In 1988 another salute was added:

Royal Marine General Officers — *Preobrajensky* (first eight bars in quick time)

A life on the ocean wave,
A home on the rolling deep;
Where the scattered waters rave,
And the winds their revels keep!

Epps Sargent: A Life on the Ocean Wave, 1847 (Regimental march, Royal Marines)

Appendix 12: The Royal Marine Artillery Trumpeter

(As seen in Cunliffe's painting of the RMA on Southsea Common)

The four officers in this painting are known to be Lt Col Menzies, Lt Savage (Adjutant), 2nd Lts Hall and Barnard. The Navy List indicates that the only period that these four officers served together at Portsmouth was between February 1843 and July 1844, thus providing a very precise date for the painting.

The dress of the trumpeter to the right of the picture generally followed the Royal Artillery style of the period. A red coatee with blue facings and, on the shoulders, white padded wings with a blue line is worn with a pair of white trousers. The coatee wings are considerably smaller than those worn by the Royal Marine Infantry Drummer of the time. The trumpeter wears the bell-topped pattern shako that was introduced into the Royal Marines in 1829. The helmet plate was the universal star with a crown above; in the centre was a silver foul anchor with, above it, a scroll inscribed 'GIBRALTAR' whilst below and on either side of the anchor were two scrolls bearing the motto 'PER MARE' and 'PER TERRAM'. Unlike the officers and other ranks in the painting, all of whom have a large white ball tuft on their shako, the trumpeter has a plume.

The appointment of Trumpet Major, unique to the Artillery within the Corps, was replaced by Bugle Major in 1850. The trumpet is the field trumpet, intended for sounding military calls, as was the bugle which replaced it. It is interesting to note that, whilst the Royal Marine Light Infantry Buglers wore the drum badge on their right arm, the Royal Marine Artillery Buglers wore crossed trumpets until the amalgamation of 1923 (See illustration on page 14). This badge was worn on both arms.

The RMA was also unique in having a Regimental Bugle Call and a Regimental Trumpet Call. Note the extract from the 1909 edition of 'Trumpet and Bugle Sounds of the Army'

SECTION V.—ROYAL MARINES.

ROYAL MARINE ARTILLERY.

♩. =108 Maelzel's Metronome.

Bugle

Trumpet

Much of this appendix has, with permission, been based upon information in Part One of the excellent articles 'Daniel Cunliffe's Royal Marine Artillery Paintings' by Major Alastair Donald RM and published in 'Sheet Anchor', the journal of the Royal Marines Historical Society.

Appendix 13: The Royal Marines Museum

The Officers' Mess, Eastney Barracks, now the Royal Marines Museum

Most of the paintings and photographs within this book are from the Collections of the Royal Marines Museum. Although, as the Corps Museum, its purpose is to tell the story of Marines, later Royal Marines, there is always a strong musical thread running through. This thread begins with the 1664 Drummers and currently ends with two of the most popular manifestations of the art of the military band in the world today: the Massed Bands of the Royal Marines Beating Retreat on Horse Guards Parade and The Mountbatten Festival of Music, probably the most successful military concert series in the world.

In 1975 the Museum moved from the old Portsmouth Divisional School building which it had occupied since 1958 into its current home, the original Royal Marine Artillery Officers' Mess. The building always had strong links with the Divisional Band as well as the ships' bands trained and formed at the Royal Naval School of Music. This school was inaugurated, in 1903, in buildings which stood behind the present converted Men's Barrack Block. From this highly respected school evolved the equally highly respected Royal Marines School of Music, now located in HMS *Nelson* adjacent to the Portsmouth Dockyard and just a couple of miles away from the original home.

The Divisional Band moved to this Barracks, with the rest of the Division, from Fort Cumberland, less than a mile away to the east, as soon as Eastney Barracks was completed in 1868. At that time a bandstand stood in Eastney Village where this band would give concerts. The sounds of the Drummers, later also trumpeters and Buglers, would resonate around the barracks, and probably much further afield, as their beatings and their calls regulated the duties and tasks of everyone within, and probably many without, the Barracks.

'Officers' Mess, Eastney, Christmas Ball 1876' by Charles Stadden

The Officers' Dining Room was built to an extremely high standard and features Italian marble fireplaces and finely detailed ornamental plasterwork. Attention was also paid to musical entertainment. The Dining Room is two storeys high with an adjacent first floor room having glazed doors that open to form an expansive Minstrels' Gallery for the Dining Room. The Divisional Orchestra, or Band, soloists and vocalists could be seen and heard from below.

Alternatively, smaller dinners could, and as for the Officers' Dining Room still can, be held in this Minstrels' Gallery. Access to the ornate, picture-hung gallery is via a Grand Staircase having a half-landing large enough to accommodate a small orchestra, ensembles or other small combinations. It is important to remember that the Divisional Band, like all Royal Marine Bands, could play as an orchestra or a military band, thereby providing music for all occasions.

It is therefore very natural, and fitting, that within this particular room during Museum opening hours the recorded music of the Royal Marines can always be heard, emanating from the adjacent Band Room. The fitting-out of the Band Room and the Band Memorial Room annexe was due, in great part, to the fund-raising efforts of the Royal Marines Band Service. Each year concerts and the ceremony of Beating Retreat maintain the continuity of live music provided by the Royal Marines within the elegant building, and also in the grounds.

The Minstrels' Gallery seen from the half-landing. One of the glazed doors opening into the Dining Room can be seen behind the staircase handrails whilst, below, is one of the door that lead from the Colours Hall into the Officers' Dining Room

The Museum galleries tell the chronological story of the Corps and the visitor has, at times perhaps, to work a little harder to follow the thread of music and of military Musicians - but it is always there.

As the visitor passes through the Barrack Room display an interesting photograph shows Band Boys filling palliasse with straw, not an easy task and their comfort for the next few months would depend upon how well this was done. Reflect upon the age of the boys and, in the adjacent image, the accommodation that the men, including the Drummers and Buglers, would come home to after two/three year foreign commissions on land, or at sea. Passing through galleries dedicated to the China Wars, the wars in Africa and other parts of the world, one has to bear in mind that each of the many wars fought by the Corps required Drummers or Buglers.

The First World War gallery particularly features Gallipoli and Zeebrugge where, in the case of the former, a Royal Marine Band was especially formed to be stretcher bearers amidst the trenches, mud and disease of the shattered peninsula. Three of their number lost their lives and two others were Mentioned in Despatches. In addition, six Buglers were killed in action. At Zeebrugge, Buglers went ashore armed with cutlasses. During the withdrawal one of them was killed whilst removing ammunition from the area of a fire on one of their ships. He was Mentioned in Despatches. Bands and Buglers served on board ships and a great many were killed, particularly at Jutland. Apart from their military duties at action stations they continued to play music and bolster morale in every part of the world, in peace and at war.

The first floor galleries commence with the Second World War where, to a certain extent, the story is repeated. Service on land and at sea again resulted in great loss of life. Some men became Prisoners of War and one display shows Musician K Macdonald as a prisoner in a German camp with the band that he formed. By begging and borrowing instruments from the Red Cross, and also the Germans, he was able to raise morale within the camp. Ken Macdonald was one of the few survivors from the ship's band of HMS *Gloucester* which was sunk at Crete. His wish was that, when he died, his ashes would be scattered over the wreck of the ship where many of his friends lay. Following his death in 2009 the Royal Navy carried out his wish. Across the gallery passageway images of prisoners in Japanese camps can be seen. Amongst the Musicians and Buglers who died in them was Bandmaster Vidler who tended the men in the hospital before he too became ill and died. The post-war galleries feature campaigns and operations, some of which required the participation of men and women of the Royal Marines Band Service not only in their musical or military roles but also supporting civilian organisations. An image of a fire in a Glasgow hotel draws attention to their important and effective role during the two strikes by fire-fighters. The final display in the chronological sequence of galleries covers the current conflict in Afghanistan and highlights the military and musical part still being played by the Royal Marines Band Service.

One of the jewels in the crown of the museum is the medal room which holds an enormous collection, largely based upon the collections originally assembled by the officers of the Portsmouth and Plymouth Divisions. Amongst the current collection are the medals of well over a hundred Drummers, Buglers and Musicians who were awarded them between the late 18th century and the Korean War. In this room the thread that represents the role and the bravery of these men is very strong but, like much of the thread so far, the emphasis is on the military role. This changes when passing from the Medal Room to the Band Room. Massed Bands Beating Retreat, the work of the Royal Yacht Bands, the composers and conductors, the instruments and the uniforms provide musical sight and sound. In a small annexe next to the Band Room are the official Band Service War Memorials for the First and the Second World Wars.

Outside, in the Museum grounds is a Garden of Remembrance and within it can be found the Memorial Stone "*Dedicated by the Royal Marines Band Service to the memory of all members of the Royal Naval School of Music and Buglers of the Royal Marines who lost their lives in the Second World War*". The memorial, which also bears the Corps crest, the lyre and bugle and the foul anchor, was erected to mark the 100th Anniversary of the founding of the Royal Naval School of Music.

The Medal Room at the Museum with, through the doorway, the Bandroom

Whilst there is much to see in the Galleries, the real strength of the Museum lies within its Collections, their interpretation and the knowledge of the Collections team. The key to unlocking the knowledge within these Collections and the history of all aspects of the Corps is the Library and the Archive, in which there are many primary sources. There is a growing belief that 'the web' is now the location of knowledge but until every word of every book is copied onto the web, without mistake and with every source clearly indicated, then the web cannot compete with libraries and documents for accurate, in-depth knowledge unless a lower standard is acceptable. When properly used the web can support, but it cannot replace, a library or archive especially when primary sources are contained.

Being paper-based, strong linkage exists between the library, the document collection and the image collections. The Paintings Collection and the Photographic Image Collection include a great many images of Royal Marines Bands and Buglers. This is hardly surprising since Musicians, Drum Majors and Buglers are often the public face of the Corps and, rightly or wrongly, a Royal Marines Bugler will always be one of the Corps' iconic images.

Without the Collections and Library of the Royal Marines Museum this, and many other books and publications, could not be written. The Museum is the Corps' archive and much of what it contains does not exist elsewhere.

One of two showcases holding the official Royal Marines Band War Memorials for the two World Wars.

The Royal Marines Band Service Memorial at the Royal Marines Museum

Appendix 14: Images Relating to 'Per Mare, Per Terram' Text and Appendices

The following images have been selected because of their quality, interest or detail. Hopefully, because they are much larger than the majority of illustrations in this book, they will add further enjoyment of events and situations already described in the text.
Given the title of this book, what better place to start than with the composer of By Land and Sea, one of the greatest slow marches ever written, Major F J Ricketts also known as Kenneth Alford. As Director of Music of the Band of the Royal Marines, Plymouth Division he made a number of recordings during 1939 and 1940, many of them his own compositions, that are probably the best of their type and time.

During 1939 Major Ricketts took the Plymouth Band to Toronto for the Canadian National Exhibition. They sailed on the RMS Empress of Australia and during the journey Ricketts, a great believer in thorough rehearsal, took every opportunity to play for the benefit of both the passengers and the band performance

HMS Lion, 1896. The men and boys of the Training Ship HMS Lion are shown preparing to go ashore as a Naval Landing Party. Alongside them can be seen the ship's band wearing the standard Royal Navy band uniform. To the right is the RN Bandmaster, bearded, and, in the background, the ship's Bugle Band. Of particular interest is the Drum Major who is a Royal Marine Light Infantry NCO. With HMS Implacable and the tender 'Liberty' HMS Lion formed the Training Ship establishment for Devonport until Lion was sold in 1905

HMS Victory Band 1928. For a long period the Royal Navy had two 'ships' bearing the name of HMS Victory. Admiral Nelson's flagship of that name was afloat in Portsmouth Harbour and the Royal Naval Barracks at Portsmouth, now HMS Nelson, was then also known as HMS Victory. The Barrack's Band was under the command of Bandmaster G C Keen from1927 until 1935 and was in great demand, often playing as an orchestra, by the Officer's Wardroom located just across the road from the Barracks Main Gate. In this photograph Mr Keen is seated in the centre of his band that, by its choice of instruments appears to be 'ready for anything.' Medals indicate that many of these men are veterans of the First World War and, given the date of 1928 some of them would have served during the Second World War. Second from the right in the rear rank is BdCpl K McLean later to become the first Director of Music, Royal Marines. On his left arm the 'King's Badge' can just be seen

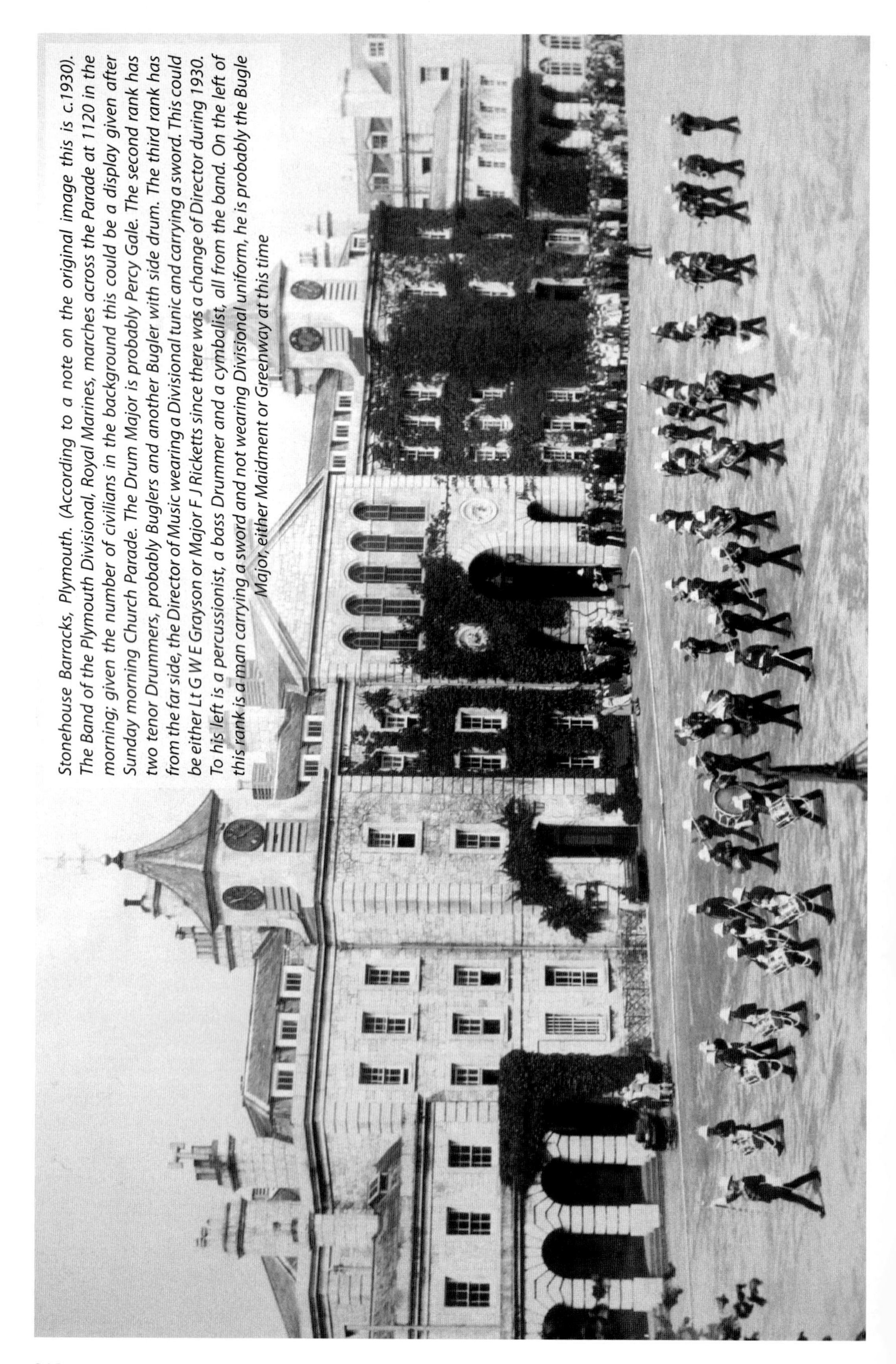

Stonehouse Barracks, Plymouth. (According to a note on the original image this is c.1930). The Band of the Plymouth Divisional, Royal Marines, marches across the Parade at 1120 in the morning; given the number of civilians in the background this could be a display given after Sunday morning Church Parade. The Drum Major is probably Percy Gale. The second rank has two tenor Drummers, probably Buglers and another Bugler with side drum. The third rank has from the far side, the Director of Music wearing a Divisional tunic and carrying a sword. This could be either Lt G W E Grayson or Major F J Ricketts since there was a change of Director during 1930. To his left is a percussionist, a bass Drummer and a cymbalist, all from the band. On the left of this rank is a man carrying a sword and not wearing Divisional uniform, he is probably the Bugle Major, either Maidment or Greenway at this time

Ships Band, Wetherby. A Royal Navy Training Establishment, HMS Cabot, was established at No 2 Hostel, Thorpe Arch, Wetherby in 1942. During 1944 the name was changed to HMS Demitrius and then, in 1946, to HMS Ceres. The main purpose of this establishment was the training of accountants. In the image many servicemen can be seen amongst the large crowd. It would appear that the parade is marching past a group of senior officers who, positioned in the doorway of the central building, are taking the salute. The band itself is a typical small band from the Royal Naval School of Music comprising a Bandmaster and fifteen Musicians

42 Commando Royal Marines

Pipe Band 1945

Back row: Mnes J Gilchrist - J H Dallay - A Lakin - T Fraser - W Hamblin - D Towell - LCpl L M Marshall
Centre row: Mnes A T Kyle - W Bain - Sgt A Stevenson - JG Wilson -WT McKenzie - Cpl P Wright
Front row: Lt J M Brassey - LtCol H H Dales - Capt J F Showell Rogers - RSM E T Bourke

This index has been constructed as a series of topics with sub-headings. The topics are:

Associations
Bands & Drums, Royal Marines & Predecessors
Bands, RM & RN Volunteer
Ceremonial, Concerts & Displays
Corps Publications
Individuals
Music, Calls & Beatings
Operations & Exercises
Places
Ships and Shore Establishments
Training & Education
Units

ROYAL MARINES BAND SERVICE & PREDECESSORS...

ROYALTY & POLITICIANS

MUSIC, CALLS & BEATINGS

HM SHIPS

MERCANTILE MARINE

Bibliography

Ambler. J & Little. M G – *Sea Soldiers of Portsmouth* – Halsgrove 2008
Ambler. J – *The Royal Marines Band Service* – Royal Marines Historical Society SP No 28 2003
Blumberg. General Sir H E – *Britain's Sea Soldiers 1914-1919*- Swiss & Co
Blumberg. General Sir H E – *Random Notes*
Blumberg. General Sir H E – *Precis of Admiralty Letters to Portsmouth Division*
Blumberg. General Sir H E & Field. Colonel C – *Random Records of the Royal Marines*
Brooks.R & Little. M G – *Tracing Your Royal Marine Ancestors* – Pen & Sword 2008
Brooks. Richard – *The Long Arm of Empire* – Constable 1999
Brooks. R L R – *Order Book*
Colledge. J J & Warlow. B – *Ships of the Royal Navy* – Chatham Publishing 2006
Donaghue. M E – *The Log of HMS Crescent 1904-1907* – Westminster Press, 1907
Donald. Maj A J – *The Story of Colours in the Royal Marines* – RMHS SP No 23 2001
Edwards RM. Lt Col Brian – *Marines from the Medway* – RMHS Special Publication No 20
Field. Colonel C – *Britain's Sea Soldiers* – Lyceum Press
Fraser & Carr-Laughton – *The Royal Marine Artillery* 1804-1923 Vols. I & II, -RUSI 1930
Furness. A W – *To India with the King and Queen 1911-1912* – Westminster Press (Gerrards Ltd)
Glenton. Robert – *The Royal Oak Affair* – Leo Cooper
Jarrett. Dudley – *British Naval Dress*
Jellicoe. Lord – *The Home Fleet 1914-1918*
Jerrold. Douglas – *Royal Naval Division* – 1923
Kappey. Jacob – *Military Music* – Musilverlag Johann Kliment (Reprint)
Ladd. James D – *The Royal Marines 1919-1980* – Jane's 1980
Little. M G – *The Royal Marines and the Victoria Cross* – RMM 2003
Lowe – *Records of the Portsmouth Division of Marines 1764-1800* (Portsmouth Record Series)
Marcher (Various articles) – *The Blue Band Magazine*
Marr. Robert A – *Music and Musicians at the Edinburgh International Exhibition 1886*
Marsh. Major A E – *Flying Marines* – Privately Published 1958
Moulton. Maj Gen J L – *The Royal Marines* (Revised edition)
Nalden. Charles – *Half and Half* – Moana Press
Newbolt – *Naval Operations Vol IV* (Official History of the War)
Oakley. Derek – *Fiddler on the March* – RMHS
Page. Christopher – *Command in the Royal Naval Division* – Spellmount 1999
Pearce. Frank – *The Ship That Torpedoed Herself* – Baron Jay Ltd
Pocock. Frank Lovell – *With Those in Peril*
Roskill. Capt – *History of the Second World War – The War at Sea Volume 1* – HMSO 1954
Sainsbury. A B – *Royal Navy Day By Day* – Ian Allan
Scott. Admiral Sir Percy – *Fifty Years in the Royal Navy* – 1919
Smith. P – *British Battle Cruisers*
Southby-Tailyour. Ewen – *Reasons in Writing* – BCA/Leo Cooper 1985
Stadden, Newark and Donald – *Uniforms of the Royal Marines* – Pompadour Gallery 1997
Swales MBE. Joffrey – *We Blew and They Were Shattered* – Singing Saw Press 1993
Thompson. Maj-Gen J – *No Picnic*
Trendell. John – *A Life on the Ocean Wave* – Blue Band Magazine 1990
Turner. Gordon & Alwyn – *History of British Military Bands Vols I, II and III* – Spellmount
Underwood. Geoffrey – *Our Falklands War*
Warlow. Lt Cdr B, RN – *Shore Establishments of the Royal Navy* – Maritime Books 2000
Wells. Capt J – *The Royal Navy, an illustrated social history 1870 –1982* – A Sutton & the RN Museum 1994
Wilson. Col L – *Bands, Drums and Music of The Queen's Royal Surrey Regiment, its Forebears and Successors*
Young. Cdr R Travers – *The House That Jack Built – The Story of Whale Island* – Gale and Polden 1955
Bid Them Rest in Peace – A Register of Royal Marine Deaths 1939-1945 (RMHS)
British Commonwealth Naval Operations. Korea 1950-53 – Naval Staff History 1957
British Forces in the Korean War – Ed Cunningham-Booth and Farrar
Canberra – The Great White Whale Goes to War

Mariners Mirror – Development of Bands in the Royal Navy W G Perrin OBE
Our Penelope (HMS Penelope) – By Her Company published by Charles Shribner's Sons
Royal Marines Records RMHS Special Publication No 2, 4 and 5
Short History of the Royal Marines, A – RMHS Special Publication No 33
With the RND on Board HMS Crystal Palace & elsewhere – a Souvenir 1915 & Issue 2
Unpublished papers of Capt A C Green, John Trendell and Tanner
Naval and *Military Record* 20/06/1917
Admiralty Circular letters; Admiralty Orders-in-Council; RM Orders and Instructions; King's Regulations and Admiralty Instructions; MoD Navy Dept Orders-in-Council, Navy List (various)
Gunnery Training Manual Vol. I 1937
The British Survey 1950
Mobilisation Return No 1 – Complements of HM Ships – Admiralty Personal Services Dept. 1939
Diaries of Musn L P Donne, W D Craig and Bugler M William
Plymouth Letterbooks 1785-1786
Portsmouth Division Punishment Book 1831-1834
Regulations & Instructions relating to the Royal Marines serving on board Her Majesty's Ships 1858
Mariners Mirror
1664-1964 Tercentenary of the Royal Marines
The Blue Band Magazine
Globe & Laurel

In addition, the material held within the Paintings Collection of the Royal Marines Museum contains a great deal of valuable research information, particularly the work of the artists who painted, or drew, what they saw for themselves. The work of the late Charles Stadden also deserves mention. Charles has been responsible for a large number of paintings, drawings and illustrations, many of which are held in the Museum's Collection. These are particularly informative with regard to uniform detail being based upon the combined research of Major Alastair Donald RM and Charles himself. A number of his drawings and paintings are included in this book.

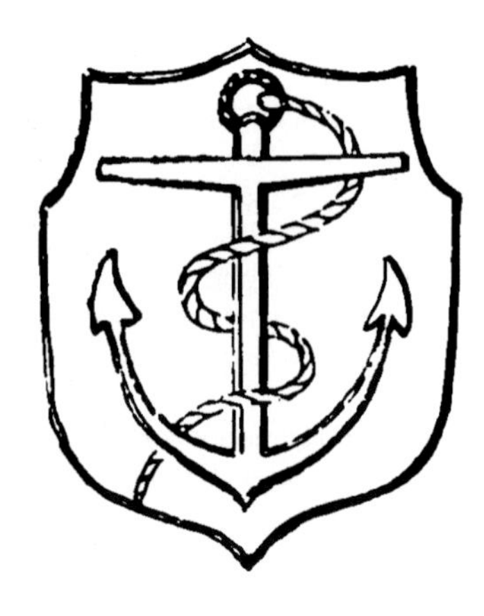

Subscribers

Ali, Tom, Charley, Drake
Ellie & Harry
Barbu Alim, IMMS
Peter Allen, Lt RM
RJ Allen, Southsea
Phil Archer Bugler
John Austin
Michael Austin
Nicholas Austin
JR Baker
Mr DG Barnett
Musn MJ Bartholomew RMB3871
RJ Bennett
A Best
Derek Beverley
Sir Henry Beverley, Lt Gen
Kenneth Booth (Worcester)
Colin Bowden
David & Fiona Bowman
Andy Boyle, Musn
The Rev D Allan Braithwaite, RN
Brattinga Peter
A Brisley
D Brown, Bandmaster WO2
G Brown
RA Browne
Garry Brownrigg Lt RNZN Rtd former WO2 Bdmr Q003776u
Ron Bubb
Capt Craig Burns RM
Ronald Fredrick Butler
Pamela Butterworth
Philip Bryett, Musician
Colin S Campbell
Phil Carrigan, Corporal
Chalky Castledine, Musn P037012N
Colin Cheesman
Kelvin Cheng Lt BBHK
V Childs
Peter Clark WO2 Bdmr
Mr & Mrs EG Cole EA2 RN Ret
Paul Collett, Musician
PJ Coomber
G Coombs
RA Cooper
Helen Cosman
WG Cox
M Crout
Colin Dean
R Derbyshire, Mne(D)
PW Derbyshire
Mr PM Doughty
D Duxbury-Williams
Mrs M Ellis
Miss VM England
Robbie Evernden
R Eyre-Tanner, Lt Cdr
Bob Farrow
J A C Fleming
Bug Paul Foley 1980-1994
Alan (Fred) Forshaw (Musn)
JR Frampton
Capt T Freestone RM
Alan Fyson
David W Gardener, RM 8724
AH Gibson, Lt RM
GR Gill, WO2 Bandmaster
Derek Gleed
D Gooch
Paul Goodlet, Capt
Lt Col N J Grace RM
JD Graham
D Greaves
Andy Gregory Capt RM
David Hadfield
Sam Hairsine, Band Corporal
W Martin Hatterlsey, Lieutenant
AJ Hercock
Roy S Hine, Musician
Terry Hissey
Maxie Horton BSN 1937-53
Peter Howse
Andrew Hudson
David Hudson
RG Hurley Lt Cdr (Ret) RNR
Frank Isaac
R Janes
J Jansen
F Jarvis
HR Johnson RM
Peter H Johnson
Mr EA Jonassen
Arthur Jones
Kenji Kawashima
I Kirby
John Kroes
Capt Tom Lambert, D of M

Subscribers

George Latham, Musician
A Le Vicount
Len Lewry
BS Libby
R Linford
Alan G Littell
John Luckhurst
John Machin
TE Mailey
S Maitland
AC Male
William Martin, Carlisle, Cumbria
Lt Col Jim Mason OBE MVO RM
Stephen Mason
Philip Mather
DR McAndrew
EA McInnes
I McLean
D Mills
Mr Wes Mills
Capt AJW Mitchell LGSM
Robert Von Motz
David A Mutter, Euph/Cello
Alec A Neville, Corporal
Albert E Nicholls
R Nicholls RN, Sub Lieutenant
Bob Niddrie
Mr Tim Norris B.Ed(Hon) LRSM
JG Odell
PE Ormerod
RAB Ouwens
CA Owen
AJ Palmer
Malcolm Perkins
Major Bob Perry RM
G Perry
Russ Perry, Musn
Donald Pimp RM4690, Marine
Mr K Poulson RMB1202
Revd. Dr. Michael Pragnell
Harry W Prescott
R Preston, BCSgt
Wilfred Price, Ex Royal Marine
Barry Radford, Band Corporal
JG Rawlinson
A Redhead
P Reeves
E Richards
Maj Jon Ridley RM
A Romney
GE Roper
Sheila Ann Scala
Derek Scott, Band Sgt
Les Scriver MBE
DJ Seed
Mike Shelvey
Mr SG Sheppard, Spalding
Ron Shooter
DF Simmonds, RMBX2996
BR Smith
Mrs Jessica Smith
Sgt Bugler Mark 'Deli' Snell RM
RA Spencer
Mr TB Spires
Morgan Sweeney, Drummer 1833-1851
PM Tate
Paul Thistlewood
Harry Thompson
D Thorne
Brian Thorogood, Musician
Mr JG Walker
D Wall
P Ward
John Ware Lt Col RM
Major EH Warren MBE
PG Watkins
Alexander George Watkinson 1942-44
B Webb
G Wells
D Westgate, Musician
Jean Wheeldon
Dave White, Ext CSgt
KG White B/Cpl RMBX3272
A Paul Whitehead , Major RM
Phillip Whitwell
JR Whitwham MBE
D Whyles
D Wilman
Ross MA Wilson
LGJ Woodhall, Sto, Petty Officer
D Woodward
Pete Yetman BdCSgt
Mr Jeffrey H Young RMB3760